55 *Victorian Prose Writers Before 1867*, edited by William B. Thesing (1987)

56 *German Fiction Writers, 1914-1945*, edited by James Hardin (1987)

57 *Victorian Prose Writers After 1867*, edited by William B. Thesing (1987)

58 *Jacobean and Caroline Dramatists*, edited by Fredson Bowers (1987)

59 *American Literary Critics and Scholars, 1800-1850*, edited by John W. Rathbun and Monica M. Grecu (1987)

60 *Canadian Writers Since 1960*, Second Series, edited by W. H. New (1987)

61 *American Writers for Children Since 1960: Poets, Illustrators, and Nonfiction Authors*, edited by Glenn E. Estes (1987)

62 *Elizabethan Dramatists*, edited by Fredson Bowers (1987)

63 *Modern American Critics, 1920-1955*, edited by Gregory S. Jay (1988)

64 *American Literary Critics and Scholars, 1850-1880*, edited by John W. Rathbun and Monica M. Grecu (1988)

65 *French Novelists, 1900-1930*, edited by Catharine Savage Brosman (1988)

66 *German Fiction Writers, 1885-1913*, 2 parts, edited by James Hardin (1988)

67 *Modern American Critics Since 1955*, edited by Gregory S. Jay (1988)

68 *Canadian Writers, 1920-1959*, First Series, edited by W. H. New (1988)

69 *Contemporary German Fiction Writers*, First Series, edited by Wolfgang D. Elfe and James Hardin (1988)

70 *British Mystery Writers, 1860-1919*, edited by Bernard Benstock and Thomas F. Staley (1988)

71 *American Literary Critics and Scholars, 1880-1900*, edited by John W. Rathbun and Monica M. Grecu (1988)

72 *French Novelists, 1930-1960*, edited by Catharine Savage Brosman (1988)

73 *American Magazine Journalists, 1741-1850*, edited by Sam G. Riley (1988)

74 *American Short-Story Writers Before 1880*, edited by Bobby Ellen Kimbel, with the assistance of William E. Grant (1988)

75 *Contemporary German Fiction Writers*, Second Series, edited by Wolfgang D. Elfe and James Hardin (1988)

76 *Afro-American Writers, 1940-1955*, edited by Trudier Harris (1988)

77 *British Mystery Writers, 1920-1939*, edited by Bernard Benstock and Thomas F. Staley (1988)

78 *American Short-Story Writers, 1880-1910*, edited by Bobby Ellen Kimbel, with the assistance of William E. Grant (1988)

79 *American Magazine Journalists, 1850-1900*, edited by Sam G. Riley (1988)

80 *Restoration and Eighteenth-Century Dramatists*, First Series, edited by Paula R. Backscheider (1989)

81 *Austrian Fiction Writers, 1875-1913*, edited by James Hardin and Donald G. Daviau (1989)

82 *Chicano Writers*, First Series, edited by Francisco A. Lomelí and Carl R. Shirley (1989)

83 *French Novelists Since 1960*, edited by Catharine Savage Brosman (1989)

84 *Restoration and Eighteenth-Century Dramatists*, Second Series, edited by Paula R. Backscheider (1989)

85 *Austrian Fiction Writers After 1914*, edited by James Hardin and Donald G. Daviau (1989)

86 *American Short-Story Writers, 1910-1945*, First Series, edited by Bobby Ellen Kimbel (1989)

87 *British Mystery and Thriller Writers Since 1940*, First Series, edited by Bernard Benstock and Thomas F. Staley (1989)

88 *Canadian Writers, 1920-1959*, Second Series, edited by W. H. New (1989)

89 *Restoration and Eighteenth-Century Dramatists*, Third Series, edited by Paula R. Backscheider (1989)

90 *German Writers in the Age of Goethe, 1789-1832*, edited by James Hardin and Christoph E. Schweitzer (1989)

91 *American Magazine Journalists, 1900-1960*, First Series, edited by Sam G. Riley (1990)

92 *Canadian Writers, 1890-1920*, edited by W. H. New (1990)

93 *British Romantic Poets, 1789-1832*, First Series, edited by John R. Greenfield (1990)

94 *German Writers in the Age of Goethe: Sturm und Drang to Classicism*, edited by James Hardin and Christoph E. Schweitzer (1990)

95 *Eighteenth-Century British Poets*, First Series, edited by John Sitter (1990)

96 *British Romantic Poets, 1789-1832*, Second Series, edited by John R. Greenfield (1990)

97 *German Writers from the Enlightenment to Sturm und Drang, 1720-1764*, edited by James Hardin and Christoph E. Schweitzer (1990)

98 *Modern British Essayists*, First Series, edited by Robert Beum (1990)

99 *Canadian Writers Before 1890*, edited by W. H. New (1990)

100 *Modern British Essayists*, Second Series, edited by Robert Beum (1990)

101 *British Prose Writers, 1660-1800*, First Series, edited by Donald T. Siebert (1991)

102 *American Short-Story Writers, 1910-1945*, Second Series, edited by Bobby Ellen Kimbel (1991

103 *American Literary Biographers*, First Series, edited by Steven Serafin (1991)

104 *British Prose Writers, 1660-1800*, Second Series, edited by Donald T. Siebert (1991)

105 *American Poets Since World War II*, Second Series, edited by R. S. Gwynn (1991)

106 *British Literary Publishing Houses, 1820-1880*, edited by Patricia J. Anderson and Jonathan Rose (1991)

107 *British Romantic Prose Writers, 1789-1832*, First Series, edited by John R. Greenfield (1991)

108 *Twentieth-Century Spanish Poets*, First Series, edited by Michael L. Perna (1991)

109 *Eighteenth-Century British Poets*, Second Series, edited by John Sitter (1991)

110 *British Romantic Prose Writers, 1789-1832*, Second Series, edited by John R. Greenfield (1991)

111 *American Literary Biographers*, Second Series, edited by Steven Serafin (1991)

112 *British Literary Publishing Houses, 1881-1965*, edited by Jonathan Rose and Patricia J. Anderson (1991)

113 *Modern Latin-American Fiction Writers*, First Series, edited by William Luis (1992)

114 *Twentieth-Century Italian Poets*, First Series, edited by Giovanna Wedel De Stasio, Glauco Cambon, and Antonio Illiano (1992)

115 *Medieval Philosophers*, edited by Jeremiah Hackett (1992)

(Continued on back endsheets)

Dictionary of Literary Biography® • Volume One Hundred Forty Two

Eighteenth-Century British
Literary Biographers

Eighteenth-Century British Literary Biographers

Edited by
Steven Serafin
Hunter College of the City University of New York

A Bruccoli Clark Layman Book
Gale Research Inc.
Detroit, Washington, D.C., London

Contents

Plan of the Series

... Almost the most prodigious asset of a country, and perhaps its most precious possession, is its native literary product — when that product is fine and noble and enduring.

Mark Twain*

The advisory board, the editors, and the publisher of the *Dictionary of Literary Biography* are joined in endorsing Mark Twain's declaration. The literature of a nation provides an inexhaustible resource of permanent worth. We intend to make literature and its creators better understood and more accessible to students and the reading public, while satisfying the standards of teachers and scholars.

To meet these requirements, *literary biography* has been construed in terms of the author's achievement. The most important thing about a writer is his writing. Accordingly, the entries in *DLB* are career biographies, tracing the development of the author's canon and the evolution of his reputation.

The purpose of *DLB* is not only to provide reliable information in a convenient format but also to place the figures in the larger perspective of literary history and to offer appraisals of their accomplishments by qualified scholars.

The publication plan for *DLB* resulted from two years of preparation. The project was proposed to Bruccoli Clark by Frederick C. Ruffner, president of the Gale Research Company, in November 1975. After specimen entries were prepared and typeset, an advisory board was formed to refine the entry format and develop the series rationale. In meetings held during 1976, the publisher, series editors, and advisory board approved the scheme for a comprehensive biographical dictionary of persons who contributed to North American literature. Editorial work on the first volume began in January 1977, and it was published in 1978. In order to make *DLB* more than a reference tool and to compile volumes that individually have claim to status as literary history, it was decided to organize volumes by topic, period, or genre. Each of these free-standing volumes provides a biographical-bibliographical guide and overview for a particular area of literature. We are convinced that this organization — as opposed to a single alphabet method — constitutes a valuable innovation in the presentation of reference material. The volume plan necessarily requires many decisions for the placement and treatment of authors who might properly be included in two or three volumes. In some instances a major figure will be included in separate volumes, but with different entries emphasizing the aspect of his career appropriate to each volume. Ernest Hemingway, for example, is represented in *American Writers in Paris, 1920–1939* by an entry focusing on his expatriate apprenticeship; he is also in *American Novelists, 1910–1945* with an entry surveying his entire career. Each volume includes a cumulative index of the subject authors and articles. Comprehensive indexes to the entire series are planned.

With volume ten in 1982 it was decided to enlarge the scope of *DLB*. By the end of 1986 twenty-one volumes treating British literature had been published, and volumes for Commonwealth and Modern European literature were in progress. The series has been further augmented by the *DLB Yearbooks* (since 1981) which update published entries and add new entries to keep the *DLB* current with contemporary activity. There have also been *DLB Documentary Series* volumes which provide biographical and critical source materials for figures whose work is judged to have particular interest for students. One of these companion volumes is entirely devoted to Tennessee Williams.

We define literature as the *intellectual commerce of a nation:* not merely as belles lettres but as that ample and complex process by which ideas are generated, shaped, and transmitted. *DLB* entries are not limited to "creative writers" but extend to other figures who in their time and in their way influenced the mind of a people. Thus the series encompasses historians, journalists, publishers, and screenwriters. By this means readers of *DLB* may be aided to perceive literature not as cult scripture in the keeping of intellectual high priests but firmly positioned at the center of a nation's life.

*From an unpublished section of Mark Twain's autobiography, copyright by the Mark Twain Company

DLB includes the major writers appropriate to each volume and those standing in the ranks immediately behind them. Scholarly and critical counsel has been sought in deciding which minor figures to include and how full their entries should be. Wherever possible, useful references are made to figures who do not warrant separate entries.

Each *DLB* volume has a volume editor responsible for planning the volume, selecting the figures for inclusion, and assigning the entries. Volume editors are also responsible for preparing, where appropriate, appendices surveying the major periodicals and literary and intellectual movements for their volumes, as well as lists of further readings. Work on the series as a whole is coordinated at the Bruccoli Clark Layman editorial center in Columbia, South Carolina, where the editorial staff is responsible for accuracy of the published volumes.

One feature that distinguishes *DLB* is the illustration policy – its concern with the iconography of literature. Just as an author is influenced by his surroundings, so is the reader's understanding of the author enhanced by a knowledge of his environment. Therefore *DLB* volumes include not only drawings, paintings, and photographs of authors, often depicting them at various stages in their careers, but also illustrations of their families and places where they lived. Title pages are regularly reproduced in facsimile along with dust jackets for modern authors. The dust jackets are a special feature of *DLB* because they often document better than anything else the way in which an author's work was perceived in its own time. Specimens of the writers' manuscripts are included when feasible.

Samuel Johnson rightly decreed that "The chief glory of every people arises from its authors." The purpose of the *Dictionary of Literary Biography* is to compile literary history in the surest way available to us – by accurate and comprehensive treatment of the lives and work of those who contributed to it.

The *DLB* Advisory Board

Introduction

In his introduction to *English Biography* (1916), Waldo H. Dunn writes, "Biography is, fundamentally, the offspring of an inherent and deep-seated desire in man to perpetuate the memory of a life. Go backward as far as we may into the history of the subject, the underlying purpose is always the same – that of memorial." Intent on capturing the spirit of the man or the value of his accomplishments, the biographical impulse toward memorial developed over time "into a narrative, a history – usually panegyric in character – of the outward great events in the life of a great man. When a writer happened not to approve of the great man's life, it was an easy matter to transform panegyric into diatribe. By one road or the other, then, the narrative came to serve an ethical purpose. It was easy, also, for the man to be almost forgotten in the course of the narrative of the events in which he participated: the memorial life-record became transformed into history."

Before the eighteenth century in England, Donald A. Stauffer claims, "the prevailing ideas of a hierarchy in Church and State had determined the main course of biography. The lives of ecclesiastical and temporal princes were worthy of record; the lives of their subjects were not" (*The Art of Biography in Eighteenth-Century England*, 1941). Intended to supplement the chronicles of history, the narrative of a man's life was delegated to a role of usefulness rather than significance. "Piety, patriotism, and family pride produced biographies; when the life of a person humbly born was set forth in print, almost invariably that person was a cleric, and the motive back of the biography was not to present an individual but to present a typical example for the edification of Christian communicants." The writing of biography was for the most part incidental; according to Dunn, "there were none who may be termed professional biographers. Either the authors turned from their usual employments to write a single memorial composition, or, in treating of historical events, they incidentally produced something that approximated biography." Variously called "lives," "characters," or "criticisms," these treatments were more appropriately biographical sketches of their subjects, attempting to provide a record of events rather than a portrayal of character. However, with the publication of William Roper's *The Life of Sir Thomas More* (1626) and George Cavendish's *The Life of Cardinal Wolsey* (1641), written circa 1557 and circa 1556 respectively, there began to appear extended biographical treatments that attempted to be informative and readable, notably Fulke Greville's *Life of Sir Philip Sidney* (1652), Thomas Sprat's *Life of Abraham Cowley* (1668), John Dryden's "Life of Plutarch" (1683), and John Evelyn's *Life of Mrs. Godolphin,* written by 1686 but unpublished until 1847.

The most important contribution to biography during this period was made by Izaak Walton, described by Dunn as "the first to take in hand the writing of deliberate biography." Beginning with his life of John Donne, prefixed to the first collection of Donne's sermons in 1640, Walton produced five biographical sketches that he described as "well-meant Sacrifices to the Memory of these Worthy men." "The five short lives which he published," writes Edmund Gosse, "though pale by the side of such work in biography as the end of the eighteenth century introduced, are yet notable as among the earliest which aim at giving us a vivid portrait of the man, instead of a discreet and conventional testimonial." Although all of Walton's subjects were writers, his *The Lives of Dr. John Donne, Sir Henry Wotton, Mr. Richard Hooker, Mr. George Herbert* (1670) belongs to the school of ecclesiastical biography "concerned with religious men and the quality of religious life." Their literary accomplishments were incidental to "the truly memorable aspect of their lives, their saintliness." According to Richard D. Altick in *Lives and Letters: A History of Literary Biography in England and America* (1965), "the emergence of literary biography had to await the emergence of the man of letters as a distinct type of social being." Although there is some discrepency as to when the term *biography* was first applied to the narration of a life, it is used by Dryden in his "The Life of Plutarch," giving evidence that the form and method of the genre were beginning to emerge. "The conception of biography had become clear in the minds of men like Dryden," writes Dunn, "even though they had not reached the point where they could consider it as related, indeed, to history, yet definitely separated from it – a literary form *sui generis*. The long process of evolution in the biographical form was, at the close of the seventeenth century, nearing culmination so far as content was concerned: a full century was still demanded to bring about that culmination."

In the eighteenth century, Altick writes, "biography was more talked about, more practiced, and more read than in the preceding hundred years." Many conditions conspired to make this a century of development and fulfillment: "Education was becoming widespread; a reading public was demanding literature which was supplied by the various forms of journalistic enterprise – newspapers, magazines, and literary reviews; men were awakening to an interest in themselves. The emphasis was fast shifting from an interest in the higher ranks of society to an interest in the common people: in the stock phrase, men were coming to a realisation, however dim as yet, of 'the brotherhood of man.' " In addition, eighteenth-century biography was greatly influenced by the rise of the novel. "The art of writing lives," Stauffer says, "helped definitely to turn fiction from the artificiality of heroic romance to the observation of life as it is lived in the world around us." The fictional impulse borrowed from biography just as the biographical impulse borrowed from fiction. Although the process was gradual, the development of English biography reached a level of maturity by the mid eighteenth century such that Samuel Johnson could write in the *Idler* number 84 for Saturday, 24 November 1759, "Biography is, of the various kinds of narrative writing, that which is most eagerly read, and most easily applied to the purpose of life."

In the early eighteenth century, biographical writing was increasingly influenced by scholarly objectivity, and this advancement is illustrated in Samuel Knight's *Life of John Colet* (1724), William Oldys's "Life of Raleigh" (1736), John Lewis's *The Life of Mayster Wyllyam Caxton* (1737), David Mallet's *Life of Francis Bacon* (1740), and Conyers Middleton's *Life of Cicero* (1741), among others. Supplementing this progression was the publication in 1740 and 1742 of Roger North's lives of his three brothers, written as early as 1715 and published posthumously in two volumes, which is notable both for his choice of subject matter as well as the subjective quality of his biographical impulse. This progression culminated in what Mark Longaker has described (in *English Biography in the Eighteenth Century,* 1931) as "the greatest contribution to the matter and method of the form in the early half of the century," Johnson's *The Life of Mr. Richard Savage* (1744). Before this time, "the life of no man, purely a man of letters, had been written and separately published." In a biography of 180 pages, Johnson essentially began "his career as a biographer of literary men with the actual beginning of literary biography." As noted by Richard Wendorf in *The Elements of Life* (1990), "In choosing to write a life of Sav-

age – and by presenting the notorious materials of his friend's life in a sympathetic but even-handed way – Johnson was in effect creating a paradigm that would influence most of the major biographical texts written in the following half-century."

According to Altick, "Samuel Johnson was the most fortunate event in English literary biography." Prior to Johnson's *The Life of Mr. Richard Savage,* "no man who devoted himself wholly to literature had been made the subject of such extended biographical treatment," and Johnson's influence is noticeable in biographies of interest to the evolution of the genre, including John Hawkesworth's life of Jonathan Swift, prefixed to his edition of Swift's works (1754–1755), Arthur Murphy's life of Henry Fielding (1762), Oliver Goldsmith's *The Life of Thomas Parnell, D.D.* (1770), and most importantly William Mason's memoirs of Thomas Gray, prefixed to his *Poems of Mr. Gray* (1775). Mason is credited with advancing the use of the letter as a biographical device, and the memoirs represents a significant step in the development of English biography. As Altick says, "The letter had been recognized as a biographical device in the early decades of the century; in fact, even as early as Walton, it had suggested itself as a method by which personality might be revealed, but it remained for William Mason to use private correspondence as the chief vehicle for the analysis of character." The methodology employed by Mason was attacked by critics, perhaps most vehemently by Johnson, but it clearly demonstrated "the utility of private correspondence in biography." In his *Life of Samuel Johnson* (1791), James Boswell writes, "Instead of melting down my material into one mass, and constantly speaking in my own person, I have resolved to adopt and enlarge upon the excellent plan of Mr. Mason, in his Memoirs of Gray." Important as Johnson was as a practitioner of biography, he was also one of the first theorists of the genre. Interestingly he would also become one of biography's most celebrated subjects. Within two weeks after his death on 13 December 1784, there appeared a biographical account of Johnson by William Cooke, followed by treatments by William Shaw, Hester Lynch [Thrale] Piozzi, Joseph Towers, and Sir John Hawkins, prior to Boswell's, described by Dunn as "that work toward which all English biography before 1791 tends, and to which all since that date looks back reminiscently." By the end of the century, additional biographical treatments of Johnson were written by Murphy (1792) and Robert Anderson (1795).

The development of biography as a distinct literary genre during the century coincided with the advancement of lexicography. Influenced by early compilations of brief lives by John Leland, John

Bale, and John Pits as well as seventeenth-century compilations – notably Thomas Fuller's *The History of the Worthies of England* (1662), Edward Phillip's *Theatrum Poetarum* (1675), William Winstanley's *Lives of the Most Famous English Poets, or the Honour of Parnassus* (1687), Gerard Langbaine's *An Account of the English Dramatick Poets* (1691), Anthony à Wood's *Athenae Oxonienses* (1691), and Charles Gildon's *The Lives and Characters of the English Dramatick Poets* (1698) – the development of the biographical dictionary during the eighteenth century is notable for the advancement in methodology of selection and accuracy of information. The publication of Giles Jacob's two-volume *Poetical Register, or the Lives and Characters of the English Dramatick Poets* (1719–1720) initiated a maturity in biographical lexicography that was continued by the ten-volume *General Dictionary, Historical and Critical* (1734–1741), compiled by John Peter Bernard, John Lockman, and Thomas Birch. The major compilation of the middle of the century was *Biographia Britannica* (1747–1766), compiled mainly by Oldys, Thomas Broughton, and John Campbell. The incomplete second edition of *Biographia Britannica,* edited by Andrew Kippis and Towers, was published in 1769, the same year James Granger produced his *Biographical History of England*. Accentuating the increasing interest in literary figures, the publication of *Lives of the Poets of Great Britain and Ireland to the time of Dean Swift* (1753), attributed to Theophilus Cibber and Robert Shiels, is notable as a forerunner to Johnson's *Prefaces, Biographical and Critical, to the Works of the English Poets* (1779–1781). Longaker refers to the magnitude of Johnson's *Prefaces:* "No work of the century in the province of biography aroused so much interest among readers and critics, and it is safe to say no series of biographical accounts has been so frequently consulted and so consistently used for quotation by students of literature."

Eighteenth-Century British Literary Biographers is designed to introduce the lives and works of those individuals who influenced the development of literary biography as a recognizable genre during the century. All were literary people, some better known than others, and yet none would have been considered primarily as a literary biographer. The professional biographer would not emerge until the following century; however, during the eighteenth century biography emerged as a literary as well as artistic endeavor. The biographer, Stauffer says, "must record the particular by the very nature of his art; but he cannot refrain from appraisals and values based upon universals. The mere decision to write the life of a certain man, the selection and combination of details, imply judgements. The biographer is a chronicler who seeks import in his chronicle. The pure historian in him makes him write of life as it is; the pure artist, shaping, ordering, emphasizing, assessing, makes him consider life as it should be, life as significant. At one pole is the encyclopedist, dispassionately collecting facts; at the other pole is the 'poet,' the creator of significant fictions. In between lives the biographer."

– *Steven Serafin*

Acknowledgments

This book was produced by Bruccoli Clark Layman, Inc. Karen L. Rood is senior editor for the *Dictionary of Literary Biography* series. Jack Turner was the staff editor. James W. Hipp and Julie E. Frick were associate editors.

Production coordinator is George F. Dodge. Photography editors are Edward Scott, Dennis Lynch, Josephine A. Bruccoli, and Joseph Matthew Bruccoli. Layout and graphics supervisor is Penney L. Haughton. Copyediting supervisor is Bill Adams. Typesetting supervisor is Kathleen M. Flanagan. The production staff includes Phyllis A. Avant, Ann M. Cheschi, Melody W. Clegg, Patricia Coate, Wilma Weant Dague, Brigitte B. de Guzman, Denise W. Edwards, Sarah A. Estes, Joyce Fowler, Laurel M. Gladden, Stephanie C. Hatchell, Rebecca Mayo, Kathy Lawler Merlette, Pamela D. Norton, Delores I. Plastow, Patricia F. Salisbury, and William L. Thomas, Jr.

Walter W. Ross and Deborah M. Chasteen did library research. They were assisted by the following librarians at the Thomas Cooper Library of the University of South Carolina: Linda Holderfield and the interlibrary-loan staff; reference librarians Gwen Baxter, Daniel Boice, Faye Chadwell, Cathy Eckman, Gary Geer, Qun "Gerry" Jiao, Jean Rhyne, Carol Tobin, Carolyn Tyler, Virginia Weathers, Elizabeth Whiznant, and Connie Widney; circulation-department head Thomas Marcil; and acquisitions-searching supervisor David Haggard.

The editor expresses his appreciation to Jason Berner and Geneviève Troussereau for their editorial assistance and acknowledges the support from the Research Foundation of the City University of New York.

Dictionary of Literary Biography® • Volume One Hundred Forty Two

Eighteenth-Century British Literary Biographers

Dictionary of Literary Biography

Robert Anderson
(17 July 1750 – 20 February 1830)

Glyn Pursglove
University College of Swansea

BOOK: *The Life of Samuel Johnson, LL.D. With Critical Observations on his Works* (London: J. & A. Arch / Edinburgh: Bell & Bradfute & J. Mundell, 1795; enlarged edition, Edinburgh: Doig & Stirling, 1815).

OTHER: *A Complete Edition of the Poets of Great Britain,* edited, with prefaces, by Anderson, 14 volumes (London: John & Arthur Arch / Edinburgh: Bell & Bradfute & J. Mundell, 1792–1795 [vols. 1–13]; 1807 [vol. 14]);

The Poetical Works of Robert Blair, edited, with a memoir, by Anderson (London: J. & A. Arch / Edinburgh: Bell & Bradfute & J. Mundell, 1794);

The Miscellaneous Works of Tobias Smollett, with memoirs of his life and works by R. Anderson, 6 volumes (Edinburgh & Glasgow: J. Mundell, 1796); Anderson's introduction published as *The Life of Tobias Smollett* (Edinburgh & Glasgow: J. Mundell, 1796; enlarged edition, Edinburgh: Mundell & Son, 1800; revised and enlarged edition, Edinburgh: Mundell & Son / London: Longman & Rees, 1803; revised and enlarged again, Edinburgh: Mundell, 1806);

Nathaniel Cotton, *Poems,* includes a memoir by Anderson (Ludlow: Printed & sold by George Nicholson, 1800);

John Potter, *Archaeologia Graeca, or the Antiquities of Greece,* 2 volumes, includes a memoir by Anderson (Edinburgh: Mundell, Doig & Stevenson, 1808); Anderson's memoir published separately as *Memoir of the Life and Writings of John Potter . . . Archbishop of Canterbury* (Edinburgh: D. Stevenson, 1824);

Wax-medallion portrait of Robert Anderson (Scottish National Portrait Gallery)

The Works of John Moore, 7 volumes, includes a memoir by Anderson (Edinburgh: Stirling & Slade, 1820);

The Works of Horace, Translated Literally into English Prose; by Christopher Smart, 2 volumes, includes a memoir of Smart by Anderson (Edinburgh: Stirling & Kenney, 1827);

The Poetical Works of James Grainger, 2 volumes, includes a memoir by Anderson (Edinburgh: Stirling, Kenney, 1836).

To the issue of the *Quarterly Review* published in July 1814, Robert Southey contributed a twenty-four-page review of the twenty-one volumes of Alexander Chalmers's edition of *The Works of the English Poets* (1810). Southey's review was severe and detailed, charging Chalmers with many sins of omission and commission. Southey naturally saw Chalmers's volumes as an attempt to succeed and replace *A Complete Edition of the Poets of Great Britain* (1792–1795; 1807), which Robert Anderson had edited. Of the relative merits of the two editors Southey had no doubts. Indeed, it is with a comparison between Anderson and Chalmers that Southey concludes his damning review: "It is scarcely possible to conceive two persons performing the same work with feelings more different than Dr. Anderson and Mr. Chalmers. The former a thorough lover of poetry, indulgent to the artist for the sake of the art: the latter a thorough-paced professional critic, so entirely ignorant of his subject as to fancy that [Richard] Glover used no trochees in his verse, and to class [Matthew] Prior, [Thomas] Gray, and [Mark] Akenside in the school of [Edmund] Spenser, and talk of their writings in the Spenserian stanza!" Southey takes the opportunity to pay a generous tribute to Anderson and to point to the important contribution Anderson's magnum opus has made to the history of English literature and to the understanding of that history:

> To good old Dr. Anderson the poets and the literature of this country are deeply beholden; it is with great pleasure that we render this tribute of justice to him while he is living to receive it. The booksellers, as their predecessors had done with Dr. [Samuel] Johnson's edition, would have begun the collection with [Abraham] Cowley. Dr. Anderson prevailed upon them to include some of the earlier and greater writers, and the four volumes which were thus appropriated, though fewer than he wished and were really required, gave the collection its chief, almost its only value. Many of the Elizabethan poets were thus, for the first time, made generally accessible, and if the good old school of poetry has been in some degree revived, Dr. Anderson has been mainly instrumental towards a reformation which was so devoutly to be wished for.

The terms of Southey's tribute are a strong indication of Anderson's importance. Nor was Southey alone in his admiration of Anderson's work. In John Nichols's *Illustrations of the Literary History of the Eighteenth Century* (volume seven, 1848) are reproduced a series of letters exchanged between Anderson and Bishop Thomas Percy. Percy had initiated the correspondence on 21 July 1798, writing to Anderson, "Your edition of the Poets of Great Britain does so much honour to their biographer and critic, that every friend to literature should assist his candid and ingenious labours; this, I hope, will serve as my apology for addressing a letter to you, without a more regular introduction." William Wordsworth was also an attentive reader of Anderson's collection. It was through Anderson that he first became familiar with the works of Geoffrey Chaucer, Michael Drayton, Samuel Daniel, and other pre-Restoration poets. The fourteen volumes of Anderson's *Complete Edition of the Poets of Great Britain,* with their 114 "Lives" of the poets (6 of them anonymously done and not of Anderson's composition) are a considerable achievement by any standards, all the more remarkable in that their editor, unlike his great predecessor Johnson, had no great reputation prior to his taking on the task.

Anderson was born on 17 July 1750; he was the son of a tenant of a small estate by copyhold in the rural village of Carnwath in Lanarkshire, Scotland. When Anderson was no more than ten his father died, and the family was left in considerable financial difficulties. Anderson received his early education in Carnwath, in the neighboring village of Libberton, and in the Grammar School at Lanark. Also born in Carnwath, one year before Anderson, was the poet James Graeme. The two were friends from their infancy. Anderson's loyalty to Graeme led to the latter's inclusion in *A Complete Edition of Poets of Great Britain,* a procedure which involved Anderson in the reprinting of a few of his own poems which had previously been published alongside those of Graeme. Anderson's biographical accounts of Graeme naturally throw light on Anderson's own early life. The two attended the parish school of Carnwath, which, Anderson recalled, "was then taught by Mr. Hugh Smith, a man of such amplitude of learning, and such copiousness of intelligence, that it would be difficult to name any branch of literature or science with which he was unacquainted." Anderson's talents received early encouragement. Like Anderson, Graeme also went on to study at Libberton with "Mr. John Brown, a teacher of classical knowledge superior to what is commonly found in remote country villages." What Anderson says of Graeme at this period, that he had "acquired a taste for general reading; was particularly solicitous to borrow books of history, poetry and divinity, and was laying in stores of information," surely holds true of himself. The two boys went on to the Grammar School at Lanark, where their teacher was Robert Thomson, brother-in-law of poet James Thomson, author of *The Seasons* (1726–1730), published in four parts. Anderson describes Thomson as one of the very best teachers to be found in Scotland. Given the high standard of much Scottish education in the eighteenth century, this is high praise and suggests that the young Anderson was very fortunate in the education he received.

Despite the financial difficulties of his family, Anderson was sent to the University of Edinburgh (again in the company of Graeme) in 1766. Anderson went to Edinburgh to study theology but later became a student of medicine. In 1778 he obtained his M.D. at the University of Stirling. He first practiced as surgeon to the dispensary at Bamborough Castle in Northumberland. He later practiced at Alnwick, also in Northumberland, where he met and married his first wife, Miss Grey. In 1784 he returned to Edinburgh; at about this time his wife died, leaving Anderson to care for his three young daughters. His marriage, however, had brought him modest financial independence, which allowed him to give up medicine and pursue his literary interests. In Edinburgh he lived, in the words of his anonymous obituarist in the *Gentleman's Magazine* (April 1830), "in a condition of life removed from affluence, but perfectly consistent with genuine independence and comfort."

Graeme died in 1773. His poems were collected and printed under Anderson's supervision in a small octavo volume published in Edinburgh the same year. The book also included a few undistinguished poems by Anderson, among them a memorial elegy on Graeme. Perhaps unsurprisingly Graeme was the subject of Anderson's first venture as a literary biographer. Anderson's memoir of his friend was published in the *Gentleman's Magazine* in September 1782, occupying some four and a half of the magazine's closely printed, double-columned pages. Anderson's name does not appear as author of this brief memoir, which closes with the declaration that the facts appearing in it are, for the most part, "from the writer's personal knowledge, and, if necessary, may be vouched by his proper signature." In one footnote Anderson refers to himself in the third person. He explains that "Dr. Anderson" was a schoolmate and university contemporary of Graeme's and notes that "Upon Mr. Graeme's death (an event the survivor deeply lamented) he added to the studies of philosophy and theology

that of medicine, in which he took the degree of Doctor, and embraced the profession of physic. . . . Amidst the severer studies of a learned and useful profession, he cherishes the love of poetry and the liberal arts, without any ambition of being distinguished as a *twofold* disciple of Apollo."

In 1793 Anderson remarried; his second wife, Margaret Dale, was the daughter of David Dale, a schoolmaster from East Lothian. Anderson became an active and respected member of Edinburgh's busy literary life. Between 1785 and 1803 he was one of the editors, along with James Sibbald and David Brewster, of the *Edinburgh Magazine; Or, Literary Miscellany,* which was later incorporated into the *Scots Magazine.* He was able to encourage young writers, the most notable example being Thomas Campbell. When Campbell first came to Edinburgh in 1798 at age twenty, Anderson befriended him and detected the promise in Campbell's early compositions. Anderson's friendship gained Campbell entry to literary circles and obtained work for him with the Mundell and Son publishing house. Anderson's support facilitated the publication of Campbell's well-known poem *The Pleasures of Hope* in 1799. Campbell, in gratitude, dedicated the poem to Anderson. Robert Chambers, in his *Biographical Dictionary of Eminent Scotsmen* (1832), paints an attractive portrait of the mature Anderson: "His character as a man was marked by perfect probity in all his dealings, and unshaken constancy in friendship. His manner was lively and bustling; and from his long-continued acquaintance with the literary world, he possessed an unrivalled fund of the species of gossip and anecdote which gives so much pleasure in [James] Boswell's *Life of Johnson.*" Anderson died of dropsy on 20 February 1830 at his house on Windmill Street in Edinburgh. By then he could look back on a long and distinguished career, the major – but by no means sole – achievement of which was his editorship of *A Complete Edition of the Poets of Great Britain.*

Anderson's general preface to *A Complete Edition of the Poets of Great Britain* is a revealing document. He traces the history of previous such collections, beginning with the forty-two duodecimo volumes edited by Robert Blair and published in 1773. Blair's collection contains the works of fewer than twenty poets, none of them earlier than John Milton. John Bell's 109 miniature volumes, published between 1776 and 1787, added the works of Chaucer, Spenser, and John Donne to the canon. The best-known predecessor for Anderson's own collection was, of course, the *Works of the English Poets,* for which Samuel Johnson provided "prefaces, biographical and critical," and which was published in 1779 and 1781. This collection contains the works and biographies of fifty-three poets, the earliest of which was Cowley. Anderson's own collection, in its general conception and in the detail of many of its biographies, can best be understood as a kind of dialogue with Johnson's. In part it expresses Anderson's dissatisfaction with the limitations of the canon as Johnson had defined it (or as his publishers had defined it; Johnson's role in the selection of those to be included was not a major one). In several of his own prefaces Anderson is also concerned with qualifying some of what he takes to be the excesses of Johnson's critical prejudices.

Anderson's preface explains the genesis of his collection. In 1792 Mundell and Son projected a reprint of Johnson's collection. Anderson recommended to them a more ambitious scheme, "which might unite the works of the ancient and modern poets in one comprehensive view, and exhibit the progress of our national poetry." The publishers agreed to Anderson's general suggestion but also wanted him "to furnish them with a *Biographical and Critical Preface* to the works of each author; an undertaking in which he engaged with more rashness than prudence, amidst cares and avocations of a far different and more important nature, and without a suitable provision of materials." Though accepting the outline of Anderson's proposal, the publishers felt unable to undertake a collection which would include all the poets he wished to include. Anderson's preface gives a list of the poets whose works he wished to reprint but was obliged to omit: William Langland and John Gower; "the best parts of" the works of John Lydgate, Alexander Barclay, Stephen Hawes, John Skelton, and William Warner; Sir Philip Sidney, Christopher Marlowe, Earl of Stirling, Francis Quarles, and Henry King; the translations of Edward Fairfax, George Sandys, and Thomas May; Andrew Marvell, Charles Cotton, Sir Charles Sedley, Charles Hopkins, John Oldman, Lawrence Eusden, Leonard Welsted, George Sewell, Moses Mendez, Charles Jenner, and James Kirkpatrick. Even with these forced omissions Anderson's is a far more comprehensive collection than any that had preceded it. Of course, to modern eyes there are also striking limitations to the collection, but these are essentially the limitations of the age rather than of the man.

In the introduction to his *New Oxford Book of Eighteenth-Century Verse* (1987), Roger Lonsdale notes that Anderson included no anonymous authors and no women. Lonsdale also adds that the collection was "calculated to appeal to a respectable readership at a precise historical moment" – the years following the French Revolution. As Lonsdale goes on to note, "moderation, decorum, restraint and propriety were the criteria controlling admission to a compilation like Anderson's." While the application, consciously or unconsciously, of the criteria Lonsdale outlines may have led to the presentation of a falsely "polite" picture of eighteenth-century verse, which modern criticism and scholarship are only now undoing, it would be historically unreasonable to imagine that Anderson could have operated any differently. His standards were those of his age, but he also played a part in creating new standards. In his choice and presentation of authors of earlier periods Anderson did much that was influential and innovative; in the choices he made among those nearer to him in time, he was more predictable and more conditioned by his own era. His collection was an influential shaper of taste and a crucial formulation of the canon for many years to come. The first thirteen volumes were published in an edition of two thousand copies and sold well. In his general preface he promises a fourteenth volume, which was published in 1807, and "a volume of Fugitive Poetry," which was never published. He also promises a separate edition of his biographical sketches, with ones of Anderson's composition replacing the six anonymous ones included in the original; however, such a volume never materialized.

Anderson was certainly diligent in his preparation of his "Lives," though he had perhaps no more than two or three years to prepare all of them. He naturally made use of the growing number of biographical collections and had read extensively in the biographical literature of English poetry. Many of his sketches begin with an acknowledgment of his major sources, and he frequently offers an assessment of the value of those sources. He begins his life of Alexander Pope, for example, by telling the reader that

> The facts stated, in the present account, are chiefly taken from the narratives of Ruffhead, and Dr. Johnson, whose copiousness and accuracy leave little to be corrected or supplied.
> Ruffhead's information was collected from original manuscripts, communicated by Warburton, and Dr. Johnson's intelligence from Spence's MS collections, communicated by the Duke of Newcastle.

The life of Jonathan Swift opens with an impressively judicious survey of previous publications:

> The life, writings, and character of SWIFT, have successively employed the researches, exercised the strictures,

and exhausted the praises of Mrs. Pilkington, the Earl of Orrerry, Deane Swift, Esq., Dr. Delaney, Dr. Hawkesworth, Dr. Johnson, and George-Monk Berkeley, Esq. Their several publications, which place his character in very different, and often opposite points of light, have occasioned great diversity in the judgments formed of them by the world, according to the different degrees of prejudice or candour in their several readers. On an attentive perusal, it will be found, that the narrations of Lord Orrerry, Dr. Hawkesworth, Dr. Johnson, and Mr. Sheridan, entitle them to the exclusive appellation of his biographers. Dr. Delaney, Mr. Swift, Mr. Berkeley, and Mrs. Pilkington come under a different description. The three former must be considered as his apologists, and the latter as a retailer of entertaining anecdotes. These are the several sources from which the facts stated in the present account are chiefly derived. Some particulars of his early life are taken from the *Anecdotes of the Family of Swift,* a fragment, written by himself, which now exists in his own hand-writing, in the University of Dublin.

Anderson was not, however, prepared to rely exclusively on such records. In his general preface he expresses his disappointment that Johnson had not by "attention and enquiry" added to the biographical information preserved about recent poets. Anderson himself was ready to make inquiry of those who had known the subjects of his "Lives." So in his life of Blair he makes extensive use of information supplied to him by the poet's son Robert Blair, Jr., then solicitor general in Scotland, and his cousin Hugh Blair, professor of rhetoric and belles lettres at the University of Edinburgh. The life of William Wilkie draws on information supplied by a variety of individuals who had known Wilkie and who are enumerated at the beginning of the sketch. Of Edward Moore, Anderson notes that "the particulars which have been recorded by his biographers are insufficient to satisfy curiosity"; he therefore seeks to supplement such accounts by "additional intelligence" obtained from the Reverend Joshua Toulmin.

The plan to which most of these brief biographies adhere is outlined in Anderson's general preface: "With a view to popular information he has endeavoured . . . to relate with clearness and simplicity what is known of the personal history and literary production of each author, whose works are associated in this collection, digested in the form of a chronicle, subjoining an estimate of his character, a critical examination of his compositions, and, by quotation, the testimonies of contemporary writers, and the judgments of the most respectable critics." The model approximates that provided by Johnson. Mark Longaker, in his *English Biography in the Eigh-*

teenth Century (1931), distinguishes the three component elements of the Johnsonian life as the narrative of biographical facts, concise character analysis, and critical survey of the works. Only rarely in Johnson's sketches, as Longaker observes, do the three elements form a coherent whole. In Anderson's "Lives" it is probably true to say that they never do. His biographical sketches fall very clearly into distinct sections. Most begin with an acknowledgment of the sources used, or a lament as to the absence of any useful sources; there follows a bare narrative of biographical facts, sometimes integrated with and sometimes followed by a bibliographical survey; a brief character sketch is then succeeded by a critical assessment. Anderson's biographical narratives are presented as a series of short paragraphs, the information presented largely without comment or judgment in readily assimilable form. Anderson's delineation of character attempts no great penetration but does, at times, achieve a genuine liveliness. He paints an attractive picture of Thomas Warton, for example: "His mind was more fraught with wit and mirth than his outward appearance promised. His person was unwieldy and ponderous, and his countenance somewhat inert; but the fascination of his converse was wonderful. He was the delight of the jovial Attic board, anniversaries, music meetings, &c. and possessed beyond most men the art of communicating variety to the dull sameness of an Oxford life."

In his critical assessments Anderson wholly lacks the dogmatic energy of his far greater predecessor. Johnson's judgments may indeed, as Anderson claims, be sometimes vitiated by "the force of prejudice"; yet most readers of Johnson will assuredly find this distraction a small price to pay for the weight and vigor that characterizes so much of his criticism. Anderson, on the other hand, pursues objectivity and tolerance with a determination that makes much of his writing merely bland. His aim, as Anderson says, was "to rise above narrow prejudices." Johnson's trenchancy is succeeded by a wholly different kind of tentativeness: "With regard to the strictures on the works of the various authors, the editor is far from being over-anxious to make others adopt his sentiments. . . . Where he has presumed to differ from the most respectable authorities, he would be rather understood to propose a doubt than to offer a contradiction."

Anderson quotes extensively from the work of others in offering his critical assessments; Johnson, Henry Headley, [Thomas] Warton, and others are certainly more forcefully present than anything one could identify as Anderson's own critical methodology or acumen. Even so, when he does trust himself to make his own judgments in his own words, he can write with purposeful clarity. His comments on Daniel, for example, have much in them that is both just and lucid:

> The style of Daniel is distinguished from that of his contemporaries, by a peculiar neatness and simplicity. The original rectitude of his judgement seems to have served him in place of examples. He uses no antiquated words and has no fantastic incongruities. He has rejected, with equal propriety, the coarse and obsolete idioms of Spenser, and the metaphysical conceits of Donne. His expression is clear and concise, and his versification correct and harmonious. He is not deficient in tenderness, and sometimes shews sublimity; but want of fire and enthusiasm is his characteristic fault.

Anderson's most recurrent note is a generous tolerance which makes him far more prone to praise than to damn. He is perhaps too readily pleased by the work of some of the minor versifiers he discusses.

In his general preface Anderson asks the reader to excuse such deficiencies of the collection as may have been caused by the inaccessibility of the libraries of Oxford and Cambridge and of the British Museum. He has had to rely, he says, "on a small private collection, and the libraries of the University, and of the Faculty of Advocates in Edinburgh, neither of which is rich in old English literature." Whatever difficulties of this sort Anderson may have labored under, he could draw on a well-stored memory and could marshal the resources of that memory to good effect. Some of his best writing comes in passages where he tracks his subject's reading as it is reflected in his writing. Anderson's brief life of James Hammond, for example, traces Hammond's indebtedness to Abius Tibullus in poem after poem, a matter on which, as Anderson notes, "Dr. Johnson is silent."

Anderson's work, then, is not especially striking for any great independence of mind. He is most often happy to quote with approval the judgments of one or more of his predecessors. Yet his diffidence is not so complete as to prevent his engaging in a kind of retrospective dialogue with some of Johnson's critical dismissals, more in a spirit of qualification than contradiction. Regarding John Gay, for example, he insists that "the estimate of his poetical character, as given by Dr. Johnson is, in some instances, too severe to be approved by readers incorrupted by literary prejudices," and Anderson proceeds to offer some cogent counterarguments. In discussing William Somerville he observes that Johnson's judgment "may be generally allowed, with some exception to his unreasonable dislike of blank verse and burlesque poetry."

In many of his sketches Anderson seems constrained both by his rather repetitive and mechanical formula and by the paucity of genuine biographical information available. However, the work could hardly have been brought to completion in the time available without some recourse to a relatively mechanical mode of operation. As to the frequent paucity of material, Anderson expresses his problem in words more eloquent than he often allows himself in his predominantly plain style:

> A poet, while living, it has been well observed, is seldom an object sufficiently great to attract much attention; his real merits are known but to few, and these are generally sparing in their praises. When his fame is increased by time, it is then too late to investigate the peculiarities of his disposition and familiar practices: "the dews of the morning are past, and we vainly try to continue the chase by the meridian splendour."

Outside the pages of this huge collection, Anderson's work as a biographer was less inhibited by such constraints or by limitations of space. Some of the sketches in *A Complete Edition of the Poets of Great Britain* are no more than two and a half pages long. Elsewhere Anderson was able to tackle the problems of biography on a considerably larger scale.

His *The Life of Samuel Johnson, LL.D. With Critical Observations On his Works* (1795) is essentially an expansion of the shorter biographical sketch in volume eleven of Anderson's *Poets,* where it was already the longest preface, occupying some fifty-seven pages. Donald A. Stauffer, in *The Art of Biography in Eighteenth Century England* (1941), says of Anderson's larger *Life of Samuel Johnson* that it is "readable, just, and derivative." This comment perhaps does not do justice to the book's virtues, as Paul J. Korshin has since argued, making the justifiable claim that Anderson's account of Johnson is "a significant step in the development of the interpretative biography of the Romantic period."

Of the more than 300 pages of the first edition, the initial 180 are essentially a chronological account of the chief events of Johnson's life. There follows an analysis of Johnson's "religious, moral, political and literary character" and of his personal characteristics. A survey of Johnson's work, under a variety of headings, is succeeded by discussion of his influence and imitators, and the book closes with extensive quotations from previous accounts of Johnson. Anderson is characteristically scholarly and judicious in the acknowledgment of his chief sources and in his clear-sighted estimation of the strengths and weaknesses of those sources. He is fully aware that "The events of the life of Johnson, 'the brightest ornament of the eighteenth century,' who has written the lives of so many eminent persons, and so much enriched our national stock of criticism and biography, have been related by friend and foe, by panegyrists and satirical defamers, by the lovers of anecdote, and the followers of party, with a diligence of research, a minuteness of detail, a variety of illustration, and a felicity of description unexampled in the records of literary biography."

Anderson makes most use of the works of Sir John Hawkins's *Life and Works of Dr. Johnson* (1787), Boswell's *Life of Johnson* (1791), and Arthur Murphy's *Essay on the Life and Genius of Samuel Johnson* (1792). He also makes extensive use, however, of the biographical accounts of Johnson by Thomas Tyers, in the *Gentleman's Magazine* (1784–1785); by Hester Lynch [Thrale] Piozzi (1786); and by Joseph Towers (1786), as well as availing himself of much of the mass of Johnsoniana which appeared in periodicals in the years following Johnson's death in 1784. He also corresponded with Bishop Percy about Johnson, as reflected in the considerably expanded scope of the 1815 edition. Hawkins's work Anderson judges to be too often less than fully relevant; Hawkins is "well-informed" but possessed of neither "expansion of intellect, nor elegance of taste," and his work is prolix. Boswell's account, on the other hand, "is written with more comprehension of mind, accuracy of intelligence, clearness of narration, and elegance of language." Anderson is equally aware of Boswell's "eccentricities," and Anderson's admiration is by no means unqualified. The discussion of his sources is given more prominence in the 1795 edition than it was later to receive in the 1815 revision. The praise of Boswell is also less pronounced.

In the pages of the narrative, Anderson is quite prepared to treat skeptically some of the claims of his predecessors, while acknowledging that they wrote from personal knowledge of Johnson. Anderson gives sensible reasons, for example, for doubting Boswell's claim that the *Rambler* essays "were written in haste, just as they were wanted for the press, without even being read over by him before they were printed." Anderson writes well of Johnson's character as he perceives it, through the accounts of others and through his obviously secure knowledge of Johnson's works. His attempt is at an early kind of "intellectual biography." He is chiefly interested in the development of Johnson's mind. He locates the key to "the history of [Johnson's] mind" in the nature of "his religious progress." Johnson's "gigantick vigour" is seen as qualified by corresponding weaknesses: "The habitual weaknesses of his mind form a striking and melancholy contrast to the vigour of his understanding. His opinions were tainted with prejudices almost too coarse and childish for the vulgar to imbibe." Johnson's literary achievement is discussed in terms of his work as "a *philologist,* a *biographer,* a *critic,* a *moralist,* a *novelist,* a *political writer,* and a *poet.*" Anderson's comments are thus presented in discrete sections. The discussion of Johnson's poems, in particular, shows some fine discrimination. As a biographer Johnson is praised for the vigor, coherence, and clarity of his narration and for the aptness of his "reflections." Anderson, however, finds him limited by his failure to make successful and sufficient use of "those minuter anecdotes of life, which oftener show the genuine man, than actions of greater importance." Anderson naturally and properly has great admiration for Johnson's powers as a critic but finds him overready to censure rather than praise, and limited by his inability to appreciate "the bold and enthusiastic, though perhaps irregular flights of imagination." Anderson's *Life of Samuel Johnson,* at the time of its first publication, was valuable as an account less partisan than most, based on a fairminded distillation of what was best in the many competing accounts that had immediately preceded it; it remains valuable as one of the earliest attempts made by a writer never under Johnson's personal spell to come to some understanding of his emotional and intellectual complexity.

Anderson's *Life of Tobias Smollett* (1796) went through several revisions and expansions after its initial appearance in *A Complete Edition of the Poets of Great Britain.* The version published as an introduction to Anderson's edition of Smollett's *Miscellaneous Works* (1796) opens with one of Anderson's most eloquent "apologies" for literary biography, on the grounds of its moral and educative usefulness, its gratification of natural curiosity, and its quality of gratitude:

In every age in which literature has been held in estimation, the lives of eminent writers have been interesting to curiosity; and persons have taken pains to collect facts respecting them, which might gratify this natural propensity, and hold out an incentive to the love of fame and the cultivation of the mind.

It has been long perceived that this is an act of gratitude; for, in every nation, they who have forfeited their time, their health, and their fortune, in composing writings, which, as they instruct by their intelligence, or please by their elegance, either facilitate the attainment of knowledge, or smooth the asperities of life, may be numbered among the benefactors of mankind, and are entitled to remembrance and applause.

A structural principle of sorts is suggested when Anderson says that in the biography of an author the works are "like the battles of a general, are the circumstances which must fix the several eras of his life." It cannot be said, though, that Anderson's account of Smollett strictly adheres to any such principle. Even if the biography is, in some sense, an act of "remembrance and applause," Anderson shows himself to be no mere dealer in the excessively panegyrical. Finding many attractive qualities in Smollett, Anderson is careful to make it clear that in both judgment and action Smollett was too often guided by "personal attachment, and hurried on by present impulse" rather than by careful and impartial examination of the relevant facts. He was guilty, at times, of "bitterness and party violence." He was "easily provoked, and vindictive when provoked"; he was too easily moved to passion, too prone to violent impulse. The moderate Anderson regrets that the strength of Smollett's emotional involvement often "distorted" his work as a historian and led him to offer critical judgments on contemporary writers which "were sometimes warped by personal prejudice, and expressed in the harsh terms of contempt." Anderson wryly observes that patience "was not [Smollett's] most shining virtue."

Anderson was strenuous in his refusal to follow the prevailing habit of reading some of Smollett's novels, notably *The Adventures of Roderick Random* (1748), as though they constitute directly autobiographical transcriptions of events of the author's life. Nor would he accept other legends without subjecting them to intelligent and skeptical analysis. Robert Graham's story (recounting an episode at which he himself was not present) of how Smollett wrote his ode "The Tears of Scotland" in a tavern while his companions played cards is treated with grave suspicion. Anderson's doubts broaden into a larger suspicion of other such accounts of "spontaneous" composition. He seems to presume that poetry is made up of works "planned at . . . leisure, fashioned with minute carefulness, and finished by gradual enlargement and progressive improvement."

Anderson is, as ever, careful to quote his sources of information when these are not to be found in standard printed sources. So, for example, one point is annotated as being based on "the infor-

mation of J. P. Kemble, manager of Covent-Garden theatre," while another passage is said to be based on "the authority of Mr. Burnet of Monboddo." Anderson's meticulousness does not entirely preclude intelligent speculation, as in his account of Smollett's failure as a physician and the possible reasons for that failure. Anderson's critical remarks on Smollett's works are intelligent and balanced. He points to both the strengths ("felicity of sentiment, description, and expression") and the limitations (inadequate research, overt prejudice) of Smollett's *Complete History of England* (1757–1758). Anderson's judgment, persuasively made and presented, is that Smollett "has not performed the duties of an historical writer with sufficient care, accuracy, and impartiality. His imagination overpowers his judgment; and he is tempted to employ his powers in the vain glow of colouring, and is more studious to dazzle the imagination with a gaudy display of splendid ornaments, than to engage the understanding by just reasoning and solid reflections."

Anderson offers some shrewd estimates of the relative merits of Smollett's novels, and he writes with particular appreciation of *The Expedition of Humphrey Clinker* (1771), to which he was attracted by its avoidance of the "extravagancies" which characterize some of Smollett's other work. While not subscribing to any attempt to read the novels as offering any simple biographical evidence, he does find in Roderick Random, Peregrine Pickle, and Matthew Bramble what he calls representations of Smollett's own character "in the different stages and situations of his own life." Anderson writes with special enthusiasm of Smollett's verse, not an area of his work to which modern criticism has paid much attention; ironically the main text of Anderson's biography closes with the claim that Smollett's verse "cannot fail to secure him a high reputation, as a poet, among posterity." Though Anderson's account surely involves an overestimation of Smollett's poetic genius, there is enough in his discussion to persuade one that Smollett's verse is by no means wholly negligible. The main body of the biography is followed by an appendix in which are printed eleven letters by Smollett and sixteen addressed to him. Some were published for the first time, including several in Anderson's possession, and others were reprinted from previous periodical appearances. All, as Anderson says, contain significant biographical information. This small collection appears to have been the first attempt to gather together Smollett's letters.

One of Smollett's other biographers was Dr. John Moore, novelist and miscellaneous writer, whose *Memoirs of the Life of Dr. Tobias Smollett* was published in 1797. Moore, who died in 1802, later became the subject of a biography by Anderson, the preface to an edition of Moore's works published in 1820. Anderson begins his biographical account of Moore with the assertion that there is little information to be had about Moore's life: "a few dates and notices, recorded in scanty memorials, scarcely more ample and satisfactory than the inscription of a common grave-stone, afford little scope for amplification and embellishment." The "scope" afforded may be "little," but Anderson seems to have little difficulty in extending his sketch to occupy some sixty pages. The first thirty-eight pages are occupied by a chronological account of Moore's life, with critical observations on his writings. This narrative is succeeded by a survey of the achievements of Moore's distinguished family and some attempt to "collect into one view [Moore's] most prominent peculiarities and distinguishing qualifications." This last involves discussion of Moore's appearance, conversation, and his character as a husband and a father. The whole is not one of Anderson's more important achievements; it displays no great penetration in the analysis of either character or writings, and it has no very compelling story to tell.

There is more of interest in Anderson's biographical sketch of Christopher Smart, the preface to an edition of Smart's translations from Horace, published in 1827. This account, however, is only a lightly revised version of that which had previously appeared in volume eleven of *A Complete Edition of the Poets of Great Britain*. The biography of Blair which introduces a 1794 edition of his *Poetical Works* is similarly based on the sketch included in volume eight of Anderson's collection. Several other of the "Lives" from his *Complete Edition of the Poets of Great Britain* were recycled as prefaces to other books, including the biographical sketches of Nathaniel Cotton and Oliver Goldsmith. Anderson's biographical memoir of John Potter is a modest piece on much the same pattern as had served for the sketches in the *Poets*. Percy's letters to Anderson provided him with much new information on James Grainger. The 1836 edition of Grainger's works, however, merely reprints the sketch from volume ten of the *Poets*.

Anderson's major achievement, *A Complete Edition of the Poets of Great Britain*, was the fruit of a genuine love of poetry and was a scholarly act of generosity akin to the acts of kindness toward living poets for which Anderson was well known. In 1806 (in Edinburgh) there was published a verse letter by the Irish poet and dramatist William Preston, under the title *To Robert Anderson, Esq. M.D. of Edinburgh, on receiving from him a Present of various Poetical Works.* Preston celebrates his friend Anderson as "the lover of the tuneful art" whose

> cares departed genius guard,
> Whose ardent friendship soothes the living bard;
> Who boasts in solid structure to combine,
> The scatter'd gems that round *Parnassus* shine.

The "solid structure" of Anderson's *Poets* is based as much on his intelligent, informed, and lucid biographical sketches as on the texts by the poets themselves. The same real, if unspectacular, virtues characterize his longer accounts of Johnson, Smollett, and Moore. Southey's tribute to "good old Dr. Anderson" was well deserved; Anderson's was a substantial contribution to the history of English poetry, insofar as he made possible a fresh understanding of the development of the poetic tradition and made available materials which had an influence on the further growth of that tradition.

Letters:

The Correspondence of Thomas Percy and Robert Anderson. The Percy Letters, Vol. IX, edited by W. E. K. Anderson, ed., (New Haven: Yale University Press, 1988).

References:

Paul J. Korshin, "Robert Anderson's 'Life of Johnson' and Early Interpretative Biography," *Huntington Library Quarterly,* 36 (1973): 239–253;

Lawrence C. McHenry, Jr., "Doctors Afield: Robert Anderson, M.D., and His Life of Samuel Johnson," *New England Journal of Medicine,* 261 (1959): 605–607.

Papers:

There are letters and papers of Anderson's in the National Library of Scotland; Edinburgh University Library; and the Bodleian Library, Oxford.

Anna Laetitia Barbauld

(20 June 1743 – 9 March 1825)

Susan Kubica Howard
Duquesne University

See also the Barbauld entries in *DLB 107: British Romantic Prose Writers, 1789–1832, First Series* and *DLB 109: Eighteenth-Century British Poets, Second Series.*

BOOKS: *Poems,* as Anna Laetitia Aikin (London: Printed for Joseph Johnson, 1773); enlarged as *Poems: A New Edition, Corrected. To Which Is Added An Epistle to William Wilberforce, Esq.* (London: Printed for Joseph Johnson, 1792; Boston: Wells & Lilly, 1820);

Miscellaneous Pieces in Prose, by Aikin and John Aikin (London: Printed for J. Johnson, 1773);

Hymns in Prose for Children (London: Printed for J. Johnson, 1781; Norwich, Conn.: Printed by John Trumbull, 1786);

Lessons for Children, from Two to Three Years Old (London: Printed for J. Johnson, 1787);

Lessons for Children of Three Years Old: Part I (London: Printed for J. Johnson, 1788);

Lessons for Children of Three Years Old: Part II (London: Printed for J. Johnson, 1788);

Lessons for Children, from Three to Four Years Old (London: Printed for J. Johnson, 1788);

An Address to the Opposers of the Appeal of the Corporation and Test Acts (London: Printed for J. Johnson, 1790);

Epistle to William Wilberforce, Esq., on the Rejection of the Bill for Abolishing the Slave Trade (London: Printed for J. Johnson, 1791);

Evenings at Home; or, The Juvenile Budget Opened, 6 volumes, by Barbauld and John Aikin (London: Printed for J. Johnson, 1792–1796; 1 volume, Philadelphia: Printed by T. Dobson, 1797);

Civic Sermons to the People Number I: Nay, Why Even of Yourselves, Judge Ye Not What Is Right (London: Printed for J. Johnson, 1792);

Civic Sermons to the People Number II: From Mutual Wants Springs Mutual Happiness (London: Printed for J. Johnson, 1792);

Remarks on Mr. Gilbert Wakefield's Enquiry into the Expediency and Propriety of Public or Social Worship (London: Printed for J. Johnson, 1792);

Sins of the Government, Sins of the Nation; or, A Discourse for the Fast, Appointed on April 19, 1793 (London: Printed for J. Johnson, 1793);

Eighteen Hundred and Eleven: A Poem (London: Johnson, 1812; Boston: Bradford & Read, 1812; Philadelphia: Finley, 1812).

Editions: *The Works of Anna Laetitia Barbauld: With a Memoir by Lucy Aikin* (2 volumes, London: Longman, Hurst, Rees, Orme, Brown & Green, 1825; 3 volumes, Boston: Reed, 1826);

A Legacy for Young Ladies, Consisting of Miscellaneous Pieces, in Prose and Verse, edited by Lucy Aikin (London: Printed for Longman, Hurst, Rees, Orme & Green, 1826; Boston: Reed, 1826);

Things by Their Right Names, and Other Stories, Fables, and Moral Pieces, in Prose and Verse, Selected and Arranged from the Writing of Mrs. Barbauld: With a Sketch of Her Life by Mrs. S. J. Hale (Boston: Marsh, Capen, Lyon & Webb, 1840);

Tales, Poems, and Essays by Anna Laetitia Barbauld, with a Biographical Sketch by Grace A. Oliver (Boston: Roberts, 1884);

Poems of Anna Barbauld, edited by William McCarthy and Elizabeth Kraft (Athens: University of Georgia Press, 1993).

OTHER: Mark Akenside, *The Pleasures of the Imagination,* edited, with a critical essay, by Barbauld (London: Cadell & Davies, 1794);

The Poetical Works of Mr. William Collins: With a Prefatory Essay, edited by Barbauld (London: Cadell & Davies, 1797);

The Correspondence of Samuel Richardson, 6 volumes, edited, with a critical and biographical essay, by Barbauld (London: Phillips, 1804);

Selections from the Spectator, Tatler, Guardian, and Freeholder, 3 volumes, edited by Barbauld (London: Johnson, 1804);

Medallion by Josiah Wedgwood; from Anna Letitia LeBreton, Memoir of
Mrs. Barbauld Including Letters and Notices of Her Family and
Friends *(1814)*

The British Novelists, 50 volumes, edited, with an essay and prefaces, by Barbauld (London:
Printed for F. C. & J. Rivington, 1810);
*The Female Speaker; or, Miscellaneous Pieces in Prose and
Verse, Selected from the Best Writers,* edited by Barbauld (London: Printed for Baldwin, Cradock & Joy, 1816; Boston: Wells & Lilly, 1824).

Anna Laetitia Barbauld gained prominence in
the last decades of the eighteenth century and the
early years of the nineteenth century as an educa-
tor, through her work as a teacher in the school she
and her husband ran for eleven years and through
her writings for children; as a poet, through her
many political, social, and religious poems in which
images and themes prepared audiences for the work

of William Blake and William Wordsworth; as a
writer of forthright, influential social and political
tracts; as a literary critic and editor, through her establishment of ethically and artistically demanding,
but reasonable, literary standards; and as a literary
biographer, through her generally objective, insightful, and knowledgeable treatment of other writers.

Anna Laetitia Aikin, born on 20 June 1743 in
the village of Kibworth Harcort, in Leicestershire,
was the only daughter of John Aikin and Jane Jen-
nings Aikin. Anna's father, a nonconformist minister and teacher, educated her and her brother John
in Greek and Latin, as well as in the modern languages. Her early enthusiasm for learning was further encouraged by the men and women she met
when her father moved the family to Lancashire to

take on the position of classics tutor at the newly formed Warrington Academy. The Warrington set, which included Dissenters Joseph Priestly, Josiah Wedgwood, and Mary Wilkinson, provided a forum for discussion of intellectual concerns, as well as appreciation and encouragement of the creative efforts of its members. Anna gained confidence as a poet through such involvement and, with her brother's further encouragement, published *Poems* in 1773. The success of this first volume prompted them to collaborate in the same year on *Miscellaneous Pieces in Prose,* which also received favorable critical reviews and was popular with readers.

In May 1774 Aikin married Rochemont Barbauld, a Dissenting minister who had studied at Warrington Academy. They moved to Palgrave, Suffolk, when the Reverend Barbauld became minister to a Dissenting congregation. There they also established a boys' school which proved a success, partially as a result of Anna's literary reputation. She continued to write, publishing *Hymns in Prose for Children* in 1781 and four volumes of *Lessons for Children* from 1787 to 1788, the latter of which she wrote for her brother's son, Charles Rochemont Aikin, whom she and her husband adopted. These works were extremely popular and used widely in the religious education of children both in England and on the Continent. *Hymns in Prose for Children,* in fact, had been reprinted thirty times by the mid nineteenth century and had been translated into several languages.

Like her predecessor Isaac Watts — whose *Divine Songs Attempted in Easy Language for the Use of Children* (1715) broke with the tradition of religious instruction for children by attempting to soften the somber tone of Calvinist doctrine with a hopeful sense of the possibility of forgiveness — Barbauld attempted to make moral instruction more attractive and accessible to young audiences. Her prose hymns, written in a simple, direct style, using a large typeface, resemble Watts's verses in the emphasis on the great reward that awaits those who recognize God's presence in their lives, though her hymns also make clear the elusive quality and difficult nature of such a realization within the modern world. Hymn 6, for example, speaks directly to the limited view of the "Child of Reason" who sees only the beauty of nature, not God's handprint on it. Barbauld's speaker implicitly calls for a greater spiritual interaction with the natural world, an imaginative empathy that will breed revelations and spiritual growth.

Critic Samuel Pickering's view that Barbauld's hymns and lessons initiated the "modern period of religious literature for children," influencing such important didactic writers as Hannah More and Sarah Trimmer, is shared by many. Indeed, Miriam Kramnick believes Barbauld's *Hymns in Prose For Children* can be seen as "a stepping-stone between Enlightenment rationalism and Romanticism." Certainly the images Barbauld used and the themes she developed were to appear again in the work of such Romantic poets as Blake and Wordsworth. Porter Williams points out that Barbauld's primary "concern, the child's capacity to feel God's 'continual presence, and lean upon his daily protection' is surely the dominant theme of *Songs of Innocence.*" Wordsworth, who disagreed with the politics in her later poetry, still thought her "the first of our literary women" and was certainly sympathetic to her rendering of the spiritual quality of the natural world, the simplicity of her poetic and prose styles, and her valuation of the common people.

Although in 1785 her husband's ill health caused them to close the school they had run for eleven years, Barbauld continued to contribute to the growing number of works written specifically for children with a collaborative effort between herself and her brother. Barbauld's few contributions to *Evenings at Home; or, The Juvenile Budget Opened* (1792–1796) are consistently didactic but imaginatively written folktales, short sketches, and dialogues that again emphasize the need for children to learn how to live morally by observing the world around them. That concern is apparent in the poetry and essays Barbauld wrote throughout the last years of the eighteenth century and into the early nineteenth century while she and her husband were living in Hampstead. *An Address to the Opposers of the Appeal of the Corporation and Test Acts* (1790), the long poem *Epistle to William Wilberforce, Esq., on the Rejection of the Bill for Abolishing the Slave Trade* (1791), and her *Civic Sermons to the People* (1792) address political and social concerns in a reasonable, forthright, powerful manner.

Residence in Hampstead also allowed Barbauld the leisure to renew friendships with the writers More, Elizabeth Montagu, Hester Mulso Chapone, and Frances Burney. In a letter to her father in 1798, Burney writes of the pleasure with which she received a visit from Barbauld, "for I think highly both of her talents and her character." And in a letter to a friend written during the same period, Burney describes Barbauld as "the authoress of the most useful books, next to Mrs. Trimmer's, that have been yet written for dear little Children, though this, with the World, is probably her very secondary merit, her many pretty poems, and par-

The Warrington Academy, where Barbauld came under the influence of dissenting intellectuals such as Joseph Priestley, Josiah Wedgwood, and Mary Wilkinson (engraving by H. F. Bellars, 1762)

ticularly songs, being generally esteemed." Though she places Barbauld's poems below her didactic prose in their moral significance, Burney goes on to praise the poems for the "piety and worth they exhibit" and the "energy that seems to spring from the real spirit of virtue" in them. She notes a change in Barbauld's presentation of herself: as she aged, she lost what Burney felt had been a "set smile, which had an air of determined complacence, and prepared acquiescence, that seemed to result from a displayed humility and sweetness which never risked being off guard."

The confidence Barbauld had developed as a writer is evident in the important editorial, critical, and biographical work she began during the last decade of the eighteenth century and carried on into the first two decades of the nineteenth century. Her apparent complacence, acquiescence, humility, and sweetness yielded to a strong show of creative and personal independence that sustained her through

periods of great personal suffering, throughout the final years of what had become an abusive marriage, and then during the years immediately following her husband's suicide in 1808. What is striking about the bulk of this work is the way in which it shows the sense of deep consideration of and respect for her purpose and subject, as well as the energy of conviction in Barbauld's poem on Wilberforce. Age seemed to have strengthened her belief in her abilities that allowed her to move with assurance into such a challenging field.

Given the fact that during the eighteenth century literary criticism by women often went unrecognized or was openly discouraged, Barbauld's efforts in this area were groundbreaking, though Charlotte Lennox's *Shakespeare Illustrated* (1753) and Clara Reeve's *The Progress of Romance* (1785), both intelligently conceived and executed works, offered her strong examples. Her own editorial, critical, and biographical work shows her to have been discriminating, candid, decisive, and just. She edited and wrote a critical introduction to Mark Akenside's *The Pleasures of the Imagination* (1794) and *The Poetical Works of Mr. William Collins: With a Prefatory Essay* (1797). Richard Wendorf, in his *William Collins and Eighteenth-Century Poetry* (1981), notes that as one of Collins's earliest editors, she was not "afraid to praise his stylistic and formal difficulties, nor . . . hesitant to begin the formidable task of elucidating the learned 'obscurity' in which he often cloaked his poems."

That same courage and ability inform her biography of Samuel Richardson, appended to her edition of *The Correspondence of Samuel Richardson*, published in 1804. While she brought a contemporary flavor to her remarks on Richardson, since she had access to materials in the possession of people who had known him, still she was not privy to letters by Richardson held in private collections; therefore, her biography is not exhaustive. Because she was dependent on the sometimes selective, sometimes failing memories of Richardson's family and, by then, aged friends and acquaintances, her biographical account of Richardson may not be "invariably correct." But it is an intellectually independent commentary, subtle, coherent, and informative. Most contemporary reviewers applauded Barbauld's work; modern critics, including T. C. Duncan Eaves and Ben Kimpel, authors of the definitive biography of Richardson (1971), generally concur that Barbauld "recounted the main facts clearly and with considerable judgment, and no evidence discovered since her time has basically changed the picture she gave."

Barbauld faced a difficult task when publisher Richard Phillips asked her to edit Richardson's letters and prepare a biographical and critical account of his life and works. Richardson had begun collecting his correspondence in 1734 and, on the advice of Erasmus Reich — who had translated *Clarissa* (1747–1749) into German and wished to do the same with Richardson's selected correspondence — prepared it during the mid 1750s with an eye to future publication. As critic Peter Sabor points out, Richardson's editorial process entailed "revising and deleting passages, and sometimes altering or obliterating names." In deference to his correspondents, many of whom wished their letters to remain private, he never published the correspondence, and neither did his daughters. When his daughter Anne died in 1803, Richardson's grandsons, the Reverend Samuel Crowther and Philip Ditcher, inherited the letters and promptly sold them to Phillips.

Barbauld began what she called the "necessary office of selection" at a disadvantage in that, as one of Richardson's biographers, Alan McKillop, contends, "the papers had been tampered with even before [she] started work, as appears from the original tables of contents prefixed to the various sections. Some of these indicate letters of such obvious value that [she] would probably have used them if they had been there in her time." As Barbauld notes, Chapone's letters, for example, were "withdrawn from the collection after Richardson's death." Thus not only had Richardson himself edited the correspondence, but apparently editing of one kind or another had been occurring over the years. As Sabor says, Barbauld "wielded her editorial powers with a license characteristic of her age." Through a process of selective abridgment and connection of letters, she reduced the original seven or eight folio volumes Phillips gave her to work with to only six; this edition, though considered the standard edition of Richardson's correspondence, contains 400 letters, only one third of which were written by Richardson. Since 560 letters by and 1,060 letters to Richardson are known to be extant today, Barbauld's edition is obviously incomplete, a criticism justly made of the work both in the early nineteenth century and recently. Additionally Barbauld's selection of letters has been faulted by Tom Keymer in his *Richardson's "Clarissa" and the Eighteenth-Century Reader* (1992), for the "undue prominence" given to letters from Richardson to young women because of the "inhibited and patronizing" aspect they give to Richardson and the "fatuous and condescending authoritarianism" they reveal in his character. Though Barbauld's edition of Richardson's correspondence — along with John Carroll's more abbreviated supplement, *Selected Letters of Samuel Richardson* (1964) — makes for an "arbitrary canon," most critics agree with Carroll that "the letters that she printed are fairly representative of the tone and contents of the correspondence."

Barbauld comments in the "Advertisement" that prefaces her edition that, while she is concerned to "gratify" the public's curiosity, "more natural perhaps than strictly justifiable, to penetrate into the domestic retirements, and to be introduced to the companionable hours of eminent characters," she does so "without impropriety," publishing no letters of living characters unless sanctioned by that person. She maintains the same standards in her "biographical account" of Richardson. In examining his life, unlike other writers of her time and those to follow her, Barbauld is not "influenced negatively by Richardson's undeniably bourgeois life and by his business success." However, she is critical of his vanity and his indulgence of that vanity at the expense of those women novelists who admired his work and were dependent on his praise and knowledge of the literary marketplace, and Barbauld's attitude perhaps accounts for her inclusion of letters that reveal this aspect of his character. But, as Elizabeth Bergen Brophy points out in her *Samuel Richardson* (1987), Barbauld "does at least take Richardson seriously and does basically approach him on his own terms."

Barbauld's biography of Richardson is accompanied by "observations on his writings," and these are yoked closely to his life, which merits consideration, she says, because he is "the father of the modern novel of the serious or pathetic kind." Thus, in her account of him, it is difficult to separate Richardson the man from Richardson the artist, and vice versa. It is also difficult to see either apart from the literary history of the novel, which Barbauld chronicles in order to show how Richardson's novels were the happy consequence of a blending of old and new, "a mode of writing . . . connect[ing] the high passion, and delicacy of sentiment of the old romance, with characters moving in the same sphere of life with ourselves, and brought into action by incidents of daily occurrence" – a far cry from the "fashionable scandal" and "licentious . . . fallen" novels of Delariviére Manley and Aphra Behn.

Such a comment reveals the specific moral stance that informs Barbauld's biographical commentary and her artistic judgments. Unlike the works and lives of Manley and Behn, Richardson's novels and his life Barbauld could, for the most part, sanction. Like her predecessor in literary biography Samuel Johnson, Barbauld – according to biographer Park Honan in his *Authors' Lives* (1990) – "establishes [her] own presence, [her] seriousness and commitment and unflappable interest in moral character" and thereby reveals as much about herself as she does about Richardson. Barbauld invokes an implicit parallel between her own criteria and Johnson's when she comments that "It was the high and just praise given by our great critic, Dr. Johnson, to the author of Clarissa, that 'he had enlarged the knowledge of human nature, and taught the passions to move at the command of virtue.'"

Barbauld relies to a certain extent on Richardson's self-portrait, the autobiographical letter he wrote to Johannes Stinstra about his early years, but she often goes beyond Richardson's words, where they obscure or conceal information, to her own illuminating conjectures – as when she

points out that "it is probable that he [Richardson's father, who had had to leave his business in London after the duke of Monmouth's rebellion] entered further into their [Monmouth's and the duke of Shaftsbury's] political views than appears from his [Richardson's] . . . account." Her aim is to illuminate her subject's life, to get to the truth of Richardson's character, but she does so respectfully: faced with another gap in Richardson's account of his life, this one relating to his place of birth, she concludes that, despite the widespread view that Richardson's avoidance was due to embarrassment over "the obscurity and narrow circumstances in which his childhood was involved, . . . in truth, the candour and openness with which he relates the circumstances of his early life, ought to clear him from this imputation." When she was faced with seeming contradictions – for example, the fact that his admirers promulgated the idea that Richardson had a classical education though he did not – she turned to his letters, to "his own assertions . . . that he possessed no language but his own," and to educated conjecture that "he might remember something of the rudiments, which he probably learnt at school," in order to smooth away the inconsistency. Barbauld then takes the fact that Richardson's lack of a classical education did not curtail his genius and uses it didactically, as an opportunity to generalize outward from Richardson's experience to encourage other self-taught youths. This generalizing tendency allows her to delve more deeply into the creative process than Richardson did and to ponder what it was that might have allowed his genius in particular to blossom. (Her analogy is a natural one, reminiscent of the biblical parable of the seed scattered to the wind, only a few of which land on fertile soil.) This method of expansion and contraction occurs frequently as she works to bring coherence and meaning to Richardson's self-portrait.

In addition to this didactic impulse, Barbauld also brings to the role of literary biographer a sense of decorum, and the two work together to inform her criticism. She finds the behavior of Pamela, Richardson's first heroine, finally too self-interested to be commendable: "In real life we should . . . consider Pamela as an interested girl; but the author says, she married Mr. B. because he had won her affection, and we are bound, it may be said, to believe an author's own account of his characters. But again, is it quite natural that a girl, who had such a genuine love for virtue, should feel her heart attracted to a man who was endeavouring to destroy that virtue?" Barbauld respectfully disagrees with her subject here, voicing an independent opinion

"The Nine Living Muses of Great Britain," circa 1775: (seated) Charlotte Lennox, Catherine Macaulay, Hannah More, and Angelica Kauffman; (standing) Elizabeth Montagu, Elizabeth Griffith, Frances Sheridan, Elizabeth Carter, and Anna Laetitia Barbauld (engraving by Page, after Richard Samuel)

formed on the basis of what is realistic and natural to character. She also faults Richardson for the "indelicate scenes" in the novel, which she finds "indefensible." Clarissa, too, is criticized for meeting Lovelace as often as she does "after the catastrophe," a situation Barbauld deems "not perfectly delicate."

Yet, with all her championing of morality and decorum, Barbauld was critical of fiction that failed as fiction, regardless of its moral. In her remarks on *Sir Charles Grandison* (1753–1754), she points out "How easily and naturally might he [Richardson] have disposed of her [Clementina] in a convent, there to complete the sacrifice she had made of her love to her religion. He probably would have done so, if a desire of making his piece instructive had not, in this instance, warped his judgment, and restrained his genius." It may come as a surprise to those who view Barbauld simply as a didactic writer that artistic coherence, being true to the fiction itself, was of equal importance to her as the message the fiction was to carry, since she viewed the former only as effective as the latter. In the following quotation, she echoes Johnson's views on the moral as-

pect of fiction but goes beyond those views: "Novels will always be different from real life, and therefore, perhaps, in some degree, dangerous to the young mind; but they must be consistent with themselves."

In her assessment of Richardson's character, Barbauld is forthright, though sympathetic to human imperfection: she attempts to balance the positive and the negative. Of Richardson's response to Henry Fielding's *Joseph Andrews* (1742), she notes that Richardson "never appears cordially to have forgiven it (perhaps it was not in human nature that he should), and he always speaks in his letters with a great deal of asperity of Tom Jones, more indeed than was quite graceful in a rival author." She is also able to view Richardson within a historical and literary context, and this stance allows her a fuller, more objective perspective on his character: "we cannot but smile on seeing the two authors placed on the same shelf, and going quietly down to posterity together."

Barbauld brings the greater literary sophistication of her age to bear on her reading of Richardson's works as well, noting with regard to the weakness of his style that "If this was considered to be the case when Richardson wrote, it is a still greater impediment to his fame at present, when we are become more fastidious with regard to style, in proportion as good writing is become more common." Catherine N. Parke, in her *Samuel Johnson and Biographical Thinking* (1991), notes that both Johnson and Virginia Woolf, literary biographers on either side of Barbauld chronologically, "believed that all biography is modern, since biographers cannot escape their points of view. Yet they also recognized their obligation responsibly to evoke the past." Such a perspective allows Barbauld the necessary distance to judge Richardson as man and artist judiciously: with respect and sympathy but also with objectivity. She applauds him for his "liberality, generosity, and charity" but notes that, while he was "benevolent and kind-hearted, . . . I do not feel sure he was a good-humored man." She found it difficult to clear him of the charge of vanity. Still she credits him with that attribute most striking in her own abilities: "he possessed the dignity of an independent mind."

Barbauld's biographical commentary on Richardson includes her caption for the illustration that serves as the frontispiece to the third volume of his correspondence: "The remarkable characters who were at Tunbridge Wells with Richardson in 1748, from a drawing in his possession with references in his own writing." The handwriting at the foot of the drawing "closely resembled that of Richardson at this stage of his career," according to critic Pat Rogers, and the parenthetical notations are by Barbauld. Rogers is convinced of the validity of the print principally because of Barbauld's inclusion of it in her edition of Richardson's correspondence. He points out that, since Barbauld "had access to so many genuine items from his hand, it seems unlikely that she should have been deceived by a forger, or prone to connive on a fabrication."

Richardson, depicted in the drawing as an isolated figure, labeled himself "Anonym." Also represented are such prominent literary figures as David Garrick, Colley Cibber, and Richard Nash, who are seen in company with members of the aristocracy. In a letter to Susanna Highmore, written on 2 August 1748 at Tunbridge, Richardson refers to himself as a "grotesque figure" in his description of life at Tunbridge, "a sly sinner, creeping along the very edges of the walks, . . . afraid of being seen, as a thief of detection." He goes on: "The people of fashion, if he happens to cross a walk . . . *unsmiling* their faces, as if they thought him in their way; and he as sensible of so being, stealing in and out of the

bookseller's shop, as if he had one of their glass-cases under his coat. Come and see this odd figure! You never *will* see him, unless *I* shew him to you." Rogers's interpretation of the subtext of the drawing, supported by Richardson's words, places the novelist in a social and artistic context. Rogers points out that Richardson's "art thus brings him social recognition but not complete social acceptance. He is permitted entrée to Tunbridge, but he is reduced to a caricatured posture of hiding in the undergrowth – marginalized not by his birth, but by his dangerous insights into hidden areas of life." Rogers concludes that while Richardson may have been isolated socially, he was not so artistically, despite the fact that he did not fully share the social stage with Cibber and Garrick; in fact, Rogers contends, "Richardson is at the centre of eighteenth-century writing."

Barbauld, too, was cognizant of the qualities of Richardson's art and mind that made social acceptance problematic, that separated him from the people he wished most to impress. This drawing, then, becomes at once a pictorial record of Richardson's essentially isolated situation in society and – through his own commentary in the key, which identifies him as a social nobody – a self-revealing artifact attesting to his knowledge of that situation. But there is an ironic current, as well, that runs under Richardson's message for public consumption, which Barbauld may also have been trading on in her depiction of Richardson, and that is the reality of his considerable contemporary artistic reputation, which must modify the ostensible reading of the drawing and point to the complexity of the biographical task she was faced with – to do justice to Richardson and to her reader. Such a biographical commentary is in keeping with Barbauld's method, to allow her subject to reveal himself through his own words and then to revise that revelation from a more objective viewpoint, going beyond what he himself was able or willing to show.

Barbauld's other critical, editorial, and biographical works share many of the same characteristics of her writing in *The Correspondence of Samuel Richardson,* in which she notes that Richardson, "like [Joseph] Addison did before him, . . . professed to take under his particular protection that sex which is supposed to be most open to good or evil impressions; whose inexperience most requires cautionary precepts, and whose sensibilities it is most important to secure against a wrong direction." She articulates her own concern for young female readers specifically in her *Selections from the Spectator, Tatler, Guardian, and Freeholder,* published in three volumes (1804), and in *The Female Speaker; or, Miscellaneous Pieces in Prose and Verse, Selected from the Best Writers* (1816). As she notes in the preface to *The Female Speaker,* she shared the concerns of Richardson and Addison as she selected the pieces to include in these volumes: she chose examples from English literature "with regard to delicacy, . . . directing her choice to subjects more particularly appropriate to the duties, the employments, and the dispositions of the softer sex."

Roger Lonsdale, the editor of *Eighteenth-Century Women Poets* (1990), points out that, given her own classical education, her productive and prestigious literary career, and her progressive political ideas, Barbauld's "views on women writers and female education are of interest." He notes that, in a 1774 letter to Montagu, Barbauld strongly opposed Montagu's suggestion that Barbauld begin her own school, since she could not sanction the production of learned women at the expense of "good wives or agreeable companions." Lonsdale also says that Barbauld resisted being identified as a "writer" and, as she makes clear in letters to Maria and Richard Edgeworth in 1804, felt "there is no bond of union among literary women." Yet, of the twenty-eight novels she included in her fifty volumes of *The British Novelists* (1810), twelve are by women.

According to her niece, Lucy Aikin, Barbauld became involved in this project as a way of managing her grief over her husband's suicide. Critic Catherine E. Moore suggests that this fact "points to something less than Mrs. Barbauld's total commitment to the project on its own merit." Yet, in critic Byron Gibson's words, as quoted by Moore, Barbauld's introductory essay, "On the Origin and Progress of Novel-Writing," and the biographical and critical prefaces to the novels offer "the most complete and the most accurate history of prose fiction to appear during the years intervening between the publication of John Moore's *A View of the Commencement and Progress of Romance* (1797) and John Colin Dunlop's *History of Fiction* (1814)."

Moore notes Barbauld's impartial inclusion of male and female novelists in the series: Barbauld makes "no divisions by gender or even by such rankings as 'major' and 'minor'" but gives men and women novelists "equal billing." In these prefaces, as in her biography of Richardson, she is literate, generous, perceptive, and objective. She is interested in showing the essential nature of both writer and work, and she does not allow prior interpretations of either to obscure her view. She admires sincerity, persistence, and genius; she applauds works that are natural, original, and good-hearted; and she

criticizes what is improbable, overly sentimental, immoral, and narrow.

Barbauld brings to her comments an appreciation for the creative efforts of the novelists whose work and lives she surveys, but she has no literary gods, as her work on Johnson illustrates. Always interested in noting where the biographical and literary intersect, her preface to Johnson's *Rasselas* (1759) declares that none of his "performances bear stronger marks of his peculiar character. It is solemn, melancholy and philosophical." She identifies Johnson with his fictional portrait of the philosopher, ascribing the power of the depiction to this autobiographical bond: "His state is strikingly and feelingly described, and no doubt with the peculiar interest arising from what the author had felt and feared in his own mind." In keeping with her attempts to reorient the reader, Barbauld suggests that "perhaps the genius of Dr. Johnson has been in some measure mistaken," for while his "remarks on life and manners are just and weighty," the world would do well to consider that "imagination had great influence over him." She points to evidence of superstition, prejudice, and melancholy in his works. While she admires Johnson's ability to face the "miseries of life," she allows for the possibility that he "perhaps exaggerates" them. The "proper moral" she deduces from the novel, that a person's choice in life needs to be informed as much by "his particular position, his honest partialities, his individual propensities, his early associations" as by his reason, reveals as much again of her own views on life as Johnson's and bespeaks the same balanced apprehension of life thematically and formally present in her own work. In keeping with her moral emphasis, Barbauld applauds the purity of Johnson's "philosophical romance," the fact that he has not "once throughout the work awakened any ideas which might be at variance with the moral truths which all his writings are meant to inculcate."

Barbauld states several times throughout her prefaces that, as a biographer, she had to maintain certain standards in handling the lives of these novelists, especially in the few cases in which the author was still living. Yet, in her preface to Burney's *Evelina* (1778), she breaks through the objective standards she has set in order to share with her readers an anecdote relating to the publication of the novel. The effect is to create a bond between biographer and subject that lends greater credibility to Barbauld's commentary, since that "pleasure . . . the young mind enjoys in the first burst of admiration which attends a successful performance" captures the sense of what Barbauld also must have ex-

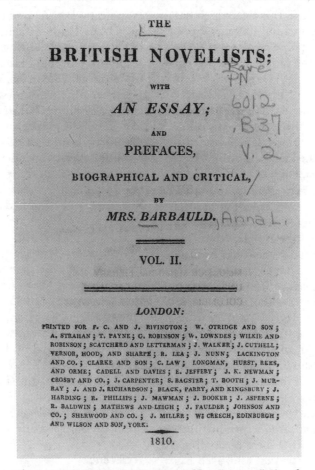

THE

BRITISH NOVELISTS;

WITH

AN ESSAY;

AND

PREFACES,

BIOGRAPHICAL AND CRITICAL,

BY

MRS. BARBAULD.

VOL. II.

LONDON:

PRINTED FOR F. C. AND J. RIVINGTON ; W. OTRIDGE AND SON ;
A. STRAHAN ; T. PAYNE ; G. ROBINSON ; W. LOWNDES ; WILKIE AND
ROBINSON ; SCATCHERD AND LETTERMAN ; J. WALKER ; J. CUTHELL ;
VERNOR, HOOD, AND SHARPE ; R. LEA ; J. NUNN ; LACKINGTON
AND CO. ; CLARKE AND SON ; C. LAW ; LONGMAN, HURST, REES,
AND ORME ; CADELL AND DAVIES ; E. JEFFERY ; J. K. NEWMAN ;
CROSBY AND CO. ; J. CARPENTER ; S. BAGSTER ; T. BOOTH ; J. MUR-
RAY ; J. AND J. RICHARDSON ; BLACK, PARRY, AND KINGSBURY ; J.
HARDING ; R. PHILLIPS ; J. MAWMAN ; J. BOOKER ; J. ASPERNE ;
R. BALDWIN ; MATHEWS AND LEIGH ; J. FAULDER ; JOHNSON AND
CO. ; SHERWOOD AND CO. ; J. MILLER ; W. CREECH, EDINBURGH ;
AND WILSON AND SON, YORK.

1810.

Title page for volume two of The British Novelists, *a collection of twenty-eight novels for which Barbauld wrote the prefatory critical biographies*

perienced as a young woman on the success of her first publication.

In sketching the events of an author's life and aspects of his or her character that would account for them, Barbauld's tone and method are sympathetic: she often couches the negative within a positive framework that softens but does not obscure it. For instance, she treats the weak plot of Oliver Goldsmith's *The Vicar of Wakefield* (1766), "full of probabilities and absurdities," only after applauding Goldsmith's strong characterization of the vicar. In her comments on Charlotte Smith, Barbauld is sympathetic to the problems faced by a poorly educated woman who married at an early age and was left to support twelve children through her literary abilities alone. Barbauld describes Smith's situation before she examines her works, not to excuse the "bitter and querulous tone of complaint which is discernible in so many of them" but to explain it. She thus manages to balance Smith's "knowledge of life, and facility of execution" with her "personal resent-

ment" and lack of moral focus, though Barbauld concludes that Smith's works "would have been more pleasing, if the author in the exertions of fancy could have forgotten herself."

Rarely harsh or blunt in her assessment of an author, Barbauld reverses her usual method of trying to frame the negative with the positive in her commentary on Tobias Smollett for her preface to *The Expedition of Humphry Clinker* (1771). Like Smith, Smollett was often querulous, yet Barbauld remains unsympathetic to his disappointments in life, partially because she deems them the result of what she views as irresponsible arrogance and partially because of the nature of his works, which she faults for "the coarseness and vicious manners which pervade them all." She says she had to include one of Smollett's novels because of their popularity with contemporary audiences, with those who could "overlook their grossness, vulgarity, and licentious morals," and she chose his last novel because it is the "least exceptionable" in terms of its moral, the "only one of his productions in this line which has not a vicious tendency." In a strong statement, preceded by sixteen pages of negative commentary, she concludes that "it is . . . to the praise of the present generation that this author's novels are much less read now than they were formerly." Clearly Barbauld's perspective is anchored in her sense of herself as a reader, her identification with other readers, and her view of her responsibility to educate readers of the novels she includes in the series. She uses biography to illuminate text.

A work's popularity, as well as its morality, determines its value, sometimes even beyond its merit as fiction. Barbauld notes that Clara Reeve's *The Old English Baron* (1778), for example, "though a novel of but a moderate degree of merit has been always a great favorite with the novel-reading public, and as such is here introduced." The work was especially popular with young audiences, "who are fond of the serious and wonderful," and "as it inspires none but noble and proper sentiments, it can do them no harm." Barbauld concludes the preface with Reeve's own words, showing Barbauld to be sympathetic to the difficult circumstances under which Reeve wrote and shrewdly willing to use that sympathy to give credibility to Reeve's words, which so closely support Barbauld's own justification for the novel's inclusion: "I have been all my life straitened in my circumstances, and used my pen to support a scanty establishment; yet, to the best of my knowledge, I have drawn it on the side of truth, virtue, and morality."

In *Eighteen Hundred and Eleven: A Poem* (1812), Barbauld risks showing her anger at England's state of near collapse, and she was criticized for her "antinationalistic doom and gloom" and presumptuous "narrowness of idea." Barbauld also continued her commitment to an equal treatment of male and female writers, and for this stance she was also criticized: Henry Crabb Robinson, her friend and, generally, supporter, found fault with the fact that she gave poet and playwright Joanna Baillie eight lines and William Shakespeare only two. After such a poor reception, Barbauld wrote little more for publication.

As a professional writer, Anna Laetitia Barbauld's career covered forty years and bridged two centuries. Throughout she almost always possessed the respect of the public and her peers. The fact that her voice is still one from which readers can learn would probably please her, since she took her responsibility as teacher seriously, whether in her poetry, her prose for children, her politically and socially motivated prose, or her critical and bio-graphical work. As one of the earliest women working in the fields of criticism and biography, Barbauld continued the work of Charlotte Lennox, Hester Lynch [Thrale] Piozzi, and Reeve, as well as that of Johnson, Goldsmith, and James Boswell, and she influenced the work of women who were to follow, such as Elizabeth Gaskell and Woolf. It is in her work as a literary biographer that her respect for the writing profession is most evident. Inherent in her informed, respectful, yet independent and direct handling of the works and lives of those engaged in that discipline is her deep belief in the importance of literature to life; this viewpoint sustained her and still gives her voice validity.

Biographies:

Jerom Murch, *Mrs. Barbauld and Her Contemporaries: Sketches of Some Eminent Literary and Scientific Englishwomen* (London: Longmans, Green, 1871);

Anna Letitia LeBreton, *Memoir of Mrs. Barbauld Including Letters and Notices of Her Family and Friends* (London: Bell, 1874);

Grace A. Oliver, *The Story of Anna Laetitia Barbauld*, second edition (Boston: Cupples, Upham, 1886);

Betsy Rodgers, *Georgian Chronicle: Mrs. Barbauld and Her Family* (London: Methuen, 1958).

References:

James Boswell, *Boswell's Life of Johnson, Together with Boswell's Journal of a Tour to the Hebrides and Johnson's Diary of a Journey into North Wales,* 6 volumes, edited by George Birkbeck Hill, revised and enlarged by L. F. Powell (Oxford: Clarendon Press, 1934–1964), II: 408–409;

Tom Keymer, *Richardson's "Clarissa" and the Eighteenth-Century Reader* (Cambridge: Cambridge University Press, 1992);

Miriam Kramnick, Preface to Barbauld's *Hymns in Prose for Children* (New York: Garland, 1977);

W. S. Lewis, ed., *The Yale Edition of Horace Walpole's Correspondence,* 48 volumes (New Haven: Yale University Press, 1937–1983);

Roger Lonsdale, ed., *Eighteenth-Century Women Poets* (New York: Oxford University Press, 1990);

Alan McKillop, *Samuel Richardson: Printer and Novelist* (Chapel Hill: University of North Carolina Press, 1936);

Catherine E. Moore, "Mrs. Barbauld's Criticism of Eighteenth-Century Women Novelists," in *Fetter'd or Free? British Women Novelists, 1670–1815,* edited by Mary Anne Schofield and Cecilia Macheski (Athens: Ohio University Press, 1982), pp. 383–397;

Samuel Pickering, "Mrs. Barbauld's Hymns in Prose: 'An Air-Blown Particle' of Romanticism?," *Southern Humanities Review,* 9 (Summer 1975): 259–268;

Katharine M. Rogers, "Anna Barbauld's Criticism of Fiction – Johnsonian Mode, Female Vision," *Studies in Eighteenth-Century Culture,* 21 (1991): 27–41;

Pat Rogers, "'A Young, a Richardson, or a Johnson': Lines of Cultural Force in the Age of Richardson," in *Samuel Richardson: Tercentenary Essays,* edited by Margaret Anne Doody and Peter Sabor (Cambridge: Cambridge University Press, 1989);

Marlon B. Ross, *The Contours of Masculine Desire: Romanticism and the Rise of Women's Poetry* (New York: Oxford University Press, 1989);

Sabor, "Publishing Richardson's Correspondence: 'The Necessary Office of Selection,'" in *Samuel Richardson: Tercentenary Essays;*

Porter Williams, "The Influence of Mrs. Barbauld's *Hymns in Prose for Children* upon Blake's *Songs of Innocence and Experience,*" in *A Fair Day for the Affections,* edited by Jack Durant and Thomas Hester (Raleigh, N.C.: Winston Press, 1980), pp. 131–146;

Paul M. Zall, "The Cool World of Samuel Taylor Coleridge: Mrs. Barbauld's Crew and the Building of a Mass Reading Class," *Wordsworth Circle,* 2 (Summer 1971): 74–79;

Zall, "Wordsworth's 'Ode' and Mrs. Barbauld's Hymns," *Wordsworth Circle,* 1 (Autumn 1970): 177–179.

Robert Bisset

(circa 1759 – 14 May 1805)

Lance Bertelsen
University of Texas at Austin

BOOKS: *A Biographical Sketch of the Authors of the Spectator,* volume 1 of *Spectator,* 8 volumes, edited by Bisset (London: Printed for George Robertson, J. Cuthell, J. Lackington & Messrs. Bell & Bradfute, 1793–1794);

Sketch of Democracy (London: Printed by J. Smeeton; Sold by J. Mathews, C. Dilly & R. White, 1796);

The Life of Edmund Burke (London: Printed & published by George Cawthorn & Messrs. Richardson, J. Hatchard & J. Wright, 1798);

Douglas; or, The Highlander, A Novel, 4 volumes (London: Printed at the Anti-Jacobin Press by T. Crowder & sold by G. Chapple, T. Hurst & J. & E. Kerby, Bond Street, 1800);

The History of the Reign of George III to the Termination of the Late War, 6 volumes (London: Printed by A. Strahan for T. N. Longman & O. Rees & W. Creech, 1803);

A Defence of the Slave Trade, on the Grounds of Humanity, Policy, and Justice (London: Printed by J. Hales & sold by J. Highley & J. Budd, 1804);

Modern Literature; A Novel, 3 volumes (London: Printed for T. N. Longman & O. Rees, 1804);

A Plain Reply to the Pamphlet calling Itself A Plain Answer, anonymous (London: Printed for the author & sold by Hatchard, Egerton & Richardson, 1804);

The History of the Negro Slave Trade in Its Connection with the Commerce and Prosperity of the West Indies and the Wealth and Power of the British Empire, 2 volumes (London: Printed by W. McDowall for S. Highley & Messrs. Richardson, J. Hatchard & J. Budd, 1805).

Robert Bisset, although best known for his *A Biographical Sketch of the Authors of the Spectator* (1793–1794) and *The Life of Edmund Burke* (1798), was also the author of two novels; a history of the early reign of George III; two proslavery tracts; and a spate of polemical, antidemocratic writing. Bisset's association with the *Anti-Jacobin Review* and its editor, John Gifford, put him at the heart of reactionary political journalism following the French Revolution. Yet "that zealous Anti-Jacobin, Dr. Bisset" (as he called himself) – however debatable his views concerning slavery and democracy – produced a surprisingly good biography of Burke and a valuable collection of short biographies of Joseph Addison, Richard Steele, and other contributors to the *Spectator*.

Robert Bisset was born to the Reverend Dr. Bisset, minister of Logierait, Perthshire, in Scotland in about 1759. The young Bisset studied at Edinburgh for the ministry but never entered the church. His reasons for this decision may be discernible in his biography of Addison (who made a similar decision), when Bisset speculates whether the clergy should be considered a "community, whose office it is to teach and stimulate men to become virtuous and religious" or "a corporate body, having views and interests peculiar to itself, and not necessarily connected with public advantage." Whatever the case, Bisset eventually earned a degree of Doctor of Laws and immigrated to England, where he was for a time master of an academy in Sloane Street, Chelsea. Eventually he became a writer of miscellaneous material for the press. His first appearance on the literary scene was as the editor of a short-lived magazine: *The Historical Magazine; or Classical Library of Public Events* (November 1788–December 1792). During this period he also completed his first significant literary work: the short biographies of Addison, Steele, Thomas Parnell, John Hughes, Eustace Budgell, Laurence Eusden, Thomas Tickell, and Alexander Pope that appear in the first volume of his eight-volume edition of the *Spectator*.

Bisset's *A Biographical Sketch of the Authors of the Spectator* comprises eight separate essays, ranging in length from five pages on Eusden to eighty-four pages on Steele. The organization of each is similar: a chronological review of the life and works takes up approximately two-thirds of each essay, followed by a summary of the author's character and an assessment of his achievement. As Bisset writes in his preface, "Criticism and discussion of moral qualities occupy a considerable share of the lives prefixed to this Edition."

"The Life of Joseph Addison," which commences the series, includes the requisite factual information and anecdotal material but is perhaps most valuable to the modern reader for Bisset's concise synopsis and critique of Addison's contributions to the *Spectator* and the lengthy review of the issues and incidents involved in the well-known dispute between Addison and Pope concerning Addison's supposed attempt to undermine Pope's translation of Homer and abuse his character. Bisset's characteristic political stance is already evident in his opinion that in "all of ADDISON's writings, the LIBERTY recommended, is that moderate, wisely regulated liberty, which experience shews to be productive of solid and permanent happiness; not that unrestrained licence which fanciful visionaries conceive or hot-headed enthusiasts desire, but which experience shews to be productive of anarchy and misery." Whether accurate or not with regard to Addison, this statement is a strong early indication of Bisset's reaction to the French Revolution, a reaction that would grow in vehemence as the years passed.

"The Life of Richard Steele" is likewise notable for the review of that author's contributions to the *Spectator* and includes a significant section on Steele's work on the *Tatler*. Bisset spends a good deal of time discussing Steele's antagonism toward the Oxford-Bolingbroke administration and its expression in *The Englishman* (1713–1715) and *The Crisis* (1714), pamphlets which eventually led to Steele's expulsion from the House of Commons. The latter part of Steele's life unfolds like a small morality play. Bisset criticizes Steele's political rehabilitation after the accession of George I (1715), during which time he used *The Englishman* to attack the fallen Oxford and Bolingbroke as "traitors and parricides." In 1717 Steele was rewarded with an appointment as "one of the Commissioners for enquiring into the estates forfeited by the late Revolution in Ireland" and later achieved temporary prosperity as joint proprietor (with Colley Cibber) of the Drury Lane Theatre. Bisset views both of these activities as leading inexorably to financial and physical disintegration due primarily to Steele's utter lack of self-discipline. From his youth onward, Bisset argues, Steele was "utterly destitute of that prudence, without which talents and benevolent disposition cannot be permanently beneficial."

The lesser lights of the *Spectator* receive more cursory treatment. Bisset admits that almost all his

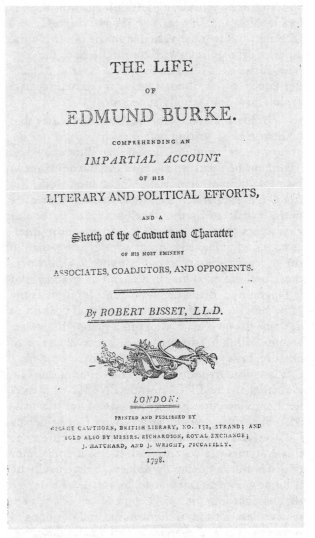

THE LIFE

OF

EDMUND BURKE.

COMPREHENDING AN

IMPARTIAL ACCOUNT

OF HIS

LITERARY AND POLITICAL EFFORTS,

AND A

Sketch of the Conduct and Character

OF HIS MOST EMINENT

ASSOCIATES, COADJUTORS, AND OPPONENTS.

By ROBERT BISSET, LL.D.

LONDON:

PRINTED AND PUBLISHED BY
GEORGE CAWTHORN, BRITISH LIBRARY, NO. 132, STRAND; AND
SOLD ALSO BY MESSRS. RICHARDSON, ROYAL EXCHANGE;
J. HATCHARD, AND J. WRIGHT, PICCADILLY.

1798.

Title page for Robert Bisset's influential biography of the British politician

information on Parnell comes from an earlier biography by Oliver Goldsmith. This fact may account for the rather discontinuous and jumbled narrative, interspersed with letters from John Gay, Pope, and others of the Scriblerus Club. Budgell is given credit for penning the "most considerable share" of the *Spectator* after Addison and Steele, and his "Essays on Education" are singled out for particular attention. Bisset's narrative of Budgell's political activity in Ireland and his eventual descent into rage, hack writing, and suicide after being ruined in the crash of inflated South Sea Company stock in 1720 is given a moralistic treatment similar to the handling of Steele's later life.

Of the three remaining authors, Hughes is discussed primarily in terms of his contributions to the *Spectator* and his innovative opera, *Calypso and Telemachus* (1712). Eusden and Tickell receive very short notices containing less information than is available in the *Dictionary of National Biography* and lacking what is most valuable in the other biographies: a detailed review of contributions to the *Spectator*. Bisset ends his *Sketch* with the "Life of Alexander Pope," which, though taking up sixty-three pages, has now been wholly superseded.

In his preface to the *Sketch,* Bisset states that "No species of writing combines in it a greater degree of interest and instruction than Biography," an argument he takes up again in the introduction to his next and most important biographical work, *The Life of Edmund Burke.* "In history," he writes, "we are more instructed by the development of particular characters than of general measures; more interested in individual enjoyment and suffering, than in the prosperity or adversity of nations. Of history, therefore, the most instructing and interesting kind is Biography." Bisset praises Samuel Johnson as the "first biographer of modern times" and goes on to describe his own method of proceeding: "If a writer set out with a predisposition either to praise or to censure, he is apt to lose sight of truth; to bend facts to a favourite hypothesis. . . . The writer of this Life is neither the FRIEND nor the ENEMY of Burke: neither *assumes* that he was consistent nor inconsistent, but will *impartially narrate* every fact he deems illustrative of his talents and character." However, this statement is patently false: Bisset sometimes criticizes Burke's actions and ideas, but generally he is his advocate and devoted admirer. To the degree that balance is achieved, it comes from Bisset's extensive descriptions of the attitudes and positions of Burke's critics and enemies in politics and the press.

Of all the praise Bisset accords Burke, the most often repeated is that (to give one version) his "writings, eloquence, and wisdom recalled Britain from the deluding errors of visionary theories to the salutary lessons of experience; from the abstraction of metaphysics and the falsities of fanciful hypothesis to the contemplation of their actual state of welfare and happiness." Conversely, Bisset's recurrent criticism focuses on the difference between Burke as "mere party man" and Burke as "philosophical politician." On the much-discussed topic of Burke's political "consistency" Bisset argues strongly for the affirmative. Indeed the anonymous critic for the *Monthly Review* (August 1798) remarked that "in no part of this volume does he forget for a moment what appears to have been his first and great object, namely, 'to prove the CONSISTENCY of Edmund Burke' . . . but that he was CONSISTENT, we think Dr. Bisset has not proved; and we doubt whether it be possible to prove it."

The *Monthly Review* critic usefully noted that although "what may properly be called the life of Burke is involved in this composition with a great variety of extraneous matter, yet that matter is frequently amusing and instructive; and, taken all together, it affords something like a general idea of our history during the period which it comprehends." Indeed, for the modern reader, perhaps the chief virtue of the biography is found in such "extraneous matter." The various lengthy analyses of the oratorical styles of the principal political figures of the time (Burke, Charles James Fox, William Pitt the Elder, Lord North, William Pitt the Younger, and Richard Brinsley Sheridan) are particularly useful in that they contain a kind of critical information not often found in modern studies. For the student of literature Bisset's recurrent denigration of James Boswell (a fellow Scot whose biography of Johnson had only recently appeared) and copious reference (both admiring and critical) to Johnson himself are potentially valuable. Bisset's critique of Johnson's politics is particularly interesting for what it tells us about Bisset himself. For while Bisset consistently abhors the French Revolution and any move toward what he sees as the anarchy inherent in "democracy," he nevertheless deplores what he calls Johnson's "high church bigotry" and engages in lengthy critiques of his political writings. Along with the criticism of Boswell as a biographer, these segments provide an interesting insight into the contemporary reputations of both Boswell and Johnson at the time of the publication of the great Johnson biography.

The *Monthly Review* critic judged *The Life of Edmund Burke* to be a distinct improvement on the highly critical *Memoirs of Burke* (1797) by Charles M'Cormick – a work Bisset attacks sharply. But Bisset's work was not without its detractors. Walker King, one of Burke's literary executors, drew up a "list of Queries relative to facts asserted by Dr. Bisset without any authority produced," and Sir Philip Francis sent King a memo critical of Bisset's biography. Francis's memo (as quoted by Joseph Parkes and Herman Merivale in their *Memoirs of Sir Philip Francis, K.C.B.,* 1867) not only points up specific errors but judges the biography to be "not much better than a catchpenny; very hastily put together, without materials beyond magazines and newspapers, and full of mistakes, but by no means without merit in point of criticism, and sound observation on some characters." Francis reports a revealing conversation with Bisset about the biography: "Bisset's principal object was to publish his book at any rate, and as speedily as possible. For all the political part, especially the panegyric of Henry Dundas, he told me I need not mind it, for, to say the truth, he was paid for it. He was in Edinburgh while the book was printing; and consequently, had no opportunity of correcting the press himself. So at least he accounted to me for the multitude of mistakes and errors in the printed copies of his work." Despite these criticisms, Bisset's strongly positive portrayal of Burke had a significant effect on later biographies. Burke's biographer F. P. Lock writes that James Prior's highly influential *Memoir of Edmund Burke* (1824) "transmitted Bisset's hagiography to the next several generations." Thus, although Burke's executors did not sponsor Bisset's biography of Burke, Lock contends that "they could have hardly written a more laudatory one. In Bisset's pages Burke the wise and farsighted statesman towers above the petty squabbles of lesser men, and leaves to posterity a storehouse of political wisdom. Not so much wrong as one-sided, most subsequent biographies have reproduced this interpretation."

During the time he was writing *The Life of Burke,* Bisset published his *Sketch of Democracy* (1796), a polemical study intent on proving "that democracy is a pernicious government." In it he reviews the democracies of antiquity, focusing on their turbulent and chaotic histories. The central subject of the book, treated in six chapters, is a history of Athenian government from the era of Draco through the defeat at Syracuse. Bisset attacks democracy as the central factor in all the troubles of Athens and draws from his examples a strongly hierarchical theory of government: "When . . . the carpenter, the shoemaker, the labourer instead of fashioning timber, leather, or earth to beneficial purposes, turn to fashioning the state, he does a double mischief, by neglecting that which he can do, and trying that which he cannot. . . . Within their own sphere, the lower orders are a just support of society; going beyond it, they bring ruin on themselves and others. So it fared with the Athenians; and similar causes will always produce similar effects." Bisset takes a similar view of democratic tendencies in Sparta, Thebes, Rome, and finally England, where he not surprisingly finds that the "more a man is conversant with the history of mankind . . . the more clearly he will see, that none in the various of constituients of HAPPINESS equal, or ever equalled the SUBJECTS of the BRITISH GOVERNMENT." An anonymous *Monthly Review* critic perhaps best sums up the overall bias and effect of Bisset's performance: "We should not . . . be warranted in saying that Dr. B. gives democracy fair play; for he dwells with pleasure on its defects, and throws its advantages into the background and the shade. He is not the judge who impartially sums up the evidence on both sides of the question, but the advocate engaged against democracy, and instructed by his brief to say nothing about it but what might persuade the jury to convict."

The antidemocratic polemic of *Sketch of Democracy* found multiple literary outlets in the following years. In 1798 Bisset began to contribute regularly to the *Anti-Jacobin Review,* a monthly successor to the famous *Anti-Jacobin; or Weekly Examiner* of William Gifford, George Canning, and John Hookham Frere. Edited by John Gifford, the *Anti-Jacobin Review* was contributed to by lesser talents but carried on the same virulent attack against Jacobinism's supposed undermining of state, church, society, and morality. Historian Emily Lorraine de Montluzin calls Bisset "one of the most fanatical Jacobin-haters in John Gifford's pay" and credits him with writing more reviews for the early volumes of the *Anti-Jacobin Review* (1798–1799) than anyone except John Gifford himself. Besides reviews, Bisset contributed a series of essays titled "The Rise, Progress, and Effects of Jacobinism," attacking such writers as Thomas Paine, Joseph Priestley, Mary Wollstonecraft Godwin, and William Godwin. But of all his dislikes, de Montluzin writes, "the greatest was democracy, a principle which he realised must prove destructive to the monarchical-aristocratic Constitution of the eighteenth century."

Bisset's opinions of Jacobinism and democracy also punctuate the first of his novels, *Douglas; or, The Highlander, A Novel* (1800), which he calls in his preface "fictitious biography." "Born myself in the Highlands of Scotland," Bisset writes, "I have written a Novel, in which I attempt to portray the sentiments, manners, and character of a Highland gentleman." Bisset undoubtedly includes some personal details, but the novel is essentially a typical bildungsroman following the rise and adventures of the hero, Charles Douglas, in school, in England, in love, and in arguments. In the preface Bisset pays homage to Henry Fielding, and it is his generalizing style that Bisset imitates. Characters such as Dr. Strongbrain, Doctor Vampus, Mr. Rhodomontade, Tim Croft, and Timothy Tattle discuss and exemplify everything from female authors to Methodist preaching to the reformist doctrines of Paine. Rounding out the adventure-love plots and the intermittent discussions of current topics are a series of journeys that allow Bisset to include extended travelogues of the Highlands, London, Margate, and so forth. *Douglas* is a pedestrian effort, interesting primarily for the way Bisset pushes his political and literary agenda at every opportunity.

Bisset's next novel, *Modern Literature; A Novel* (1804), despite its promising title, in many ways replicates *Douglas*. Again Bisset follows a young hero, William Hamilton, from his birth through eventual success in love and career. What is different is that Hamilton's career is writing. Son of a military officer, educated at Cambridge and Lincolns Inn, Hamilton opts for the literary profession, a career choice that allows Bisset to examine an even greater variety of hacks, early feminists, Jacobins, and Methodists than was possible in *Douglas*. His purpose, he writes in the preface, is to "represent the manners of the times, in various situations, but especially in literary departments." Attacks on literary, political, and religious radicalism or skullduggery appear throughout the novel but become most focused in the figures of Dick Scribble, a pompous hack who has written the "History of Jack the Giant Killer," and Jemima, a liberated protofeminist who believes that *the rights of women . . . were to act in every case according to their own pleasure; and to share in all the prerogatives of men.*" Scribble's praise of German literature and the "gigantesque," for example, functions as an extended satiric attack on the foreign corruption of British literature, and Jemima's libidinous speech before her enraptured followers, in which she attacks both female chastity and common sense, sums up Bisset's attitudes toward writers such as Wollstonecraft. During the course of the novel Hamilton publishes his magnum opus, which is reviled by Jacobins "for its political principles" and is praised by everyone else, except the jealous Scribble. Hamilton then reads Burke's just-published *Reflections on the Revolution in France* (1790) and becomes a staunch anti-Jacobin. Like *Douglas,* Bisset's *Modern Literature* includes extended travel descriptions, this time of Windsor, Blenheim, Bath, and other sites, and Bisset is again quick to use every opportunity to trumpet his ideology. In discussing the early reaction of English writers to the French Revolution, for example, he adumbrates the historical situation that eventually brought anti-Jacobin writers such as himself into the field: "Among literary men, with very few exceptions, even able and learned writers were friendly to a change of political system, and of the much more numerous class of writers that were neither able nor learned, at least three-fourths of writers became enemies to the establishment. Among these were the lowest retainers of learning. Book-makers, news-gatherers, paragraph-joiners, collectors and retailers of puns, and jokes, scrap-rakers, and other pioneers

of literature, were to a man democratic." In both *Douglas* and *Modern Literature* Bisset uses novelistic techniques to create fictional vehicles for his political message. *Modern Literature* may be one of the earliest novels to have a professional writer as its hero, but, aside from that innovation, Bisset contributes little to the development or articulation of the British novel.

During the early nineteenth century Bisset also published his six-volume *History of the Reign of George III to the Termination of the Late War* (1803) and two proslavery tracts, *A Defence of the Slave Trade, on the Grounds of Humanity, Policy, and Justice* (1804) and *The History of the Negro Slave Trade in Its Connection with the Commerce and Prosperity of the West Indies and the Wealth and Power of the British Empire* (1805). In the first work Bisset aspires to an objectivity lacked by earlier historians whom he calls "rather repeaters of party notions and reports, than original composers of authentic history." But Bisset's own bias is evident in his sympathetic handling of George III and his allies, particularly during the early part of his reign. The critic for the *Monthly Review* (October 1804) noted that "the author fairly states the acts and maxims of the early part of this reign; but he gives them a colour which all persons will not admit to be that which exactly belongs to them. Actions and measures which some have attributed to favouritism, and some have considered as indicative of high notions of power, he describes as proceeding from a laudable departure from old systems of political exclusion, and from the practice of confining administrations to a party." In other words, Bisset's is a Tory history, which, while admitting George III made grave errors in the handling of both internal politics and colonial affairs (culminating in the American Revolution), consistently throws the best possible light on the monarch's motives and actions.

The two proslavery tracts, disconcerting as they may be for the modern reader, were extreme even for their own time. Both were prompted by William Wilberforce's 1804 introduction of a bill for the abolition of the trade. Bisset's basic tactic in *A Defence* is to try to show that blacks are better off as slaves in the West than as freemen in Africa. He also argues that none of the great moralists of classical antiquity had ever written against slavery, and he challenges abolitionists to find an antislavery passage in the Bible: "In the much more perfect code of moral duty which Christianity has delivered, will the Senators point out any passages that censure such a state? This question I ask of Mr. Wilberforce, who laid a principle stress of his arguments on the contrariety of a Slave Trade to Christianity." The critic for the Edinburgh *Review* (October 1804–January 1805) savaged *A Defence,* taking particular delight in attacking the use of *Humanity* in the title. During the Parliamentary debates on slavery in 1792, the reviewer notes, "whatever doubts might be entertained concerning the policy of abolition . . . there was but one opinion concerning its injustice and inhumanity. . . . It was reserved for the writer of the work now before us to take the higher ground of justice and humanity." The critic goes on to accuse Bisset of falsifying information, plagiarizing and twisting the statements of earlier writers, and being audaciously out of step with the times: "That such a cause as the slave trade should be supported by fiction and misrepresentation, is perfectly suitable and becoming: It is a fair and natural alliance. But we must admire the courage of the writer, who, even with such an unlimited license in the weapons he was to use, ventured, at this time of day, to engage in such warfare."

In the subsequent *History of the Negro Slave Trade* Bisset attempts to defend his position by stating that, after a long investigation he discovered that no cruelty to slaves had ever existed: "I found the delinquency of traders could be no reason for discontinuing the trade, since, after a full and fair discussion, no such delinquency was found to exist. In the course of the evidence, it appeared, that by the Slave trade humanity was essentially promoted, instead of being violated." The most interesting section of the work occurs in the preface, when Bisset recounts the history of *A Defence* and responds to its critics:

> When Mr. Wilberforce introduced his bill in 1804, having in my head the general outlines of the subject, I proposed to present them in a pamphlet, which should be ready to meet the motion on its entrance into the house of peers. I was acquainted with no merchant, African or West Indian, but, on inquiry, I found Mr. King, of Brunswick-square, would be as proper a gentleman as any to whom I could apply. I accordingly wrote to

> him, had an immediate answer, and a speedy interview. He approved highly of my scheme; mentioned it to Mr. Cock, Commerce Agent for the Corporation of Liverpool, who also warmly joined in the proposition. I made my arrangements, finished the essay, and brought it out under the title of "A Defence of the Slave Trade, on the Grounds of Justice, Humanity, and Policy." Short as the time was, I received many valuable facts from friends of Mr. Cock or Mr. King. From these, and my own previous knowledge, I was enabled to execute my task, and had the satisfaction to find that it was extremely well received by all impartial readers; but, as may be expected, most warmly by gentlemen connected with the commerce. The enemies of our West India trade have shewn, by the notice they took of it, the estimation in which they held it. To about eighty pages of loose print, the Edinburgh reviewers devoted thirty-two pages of close review print, being more than three-fourths of the extent of my letter-press. In that criticism, they allow the work ability, but assert that the facts are unfairly stated. I challenged them to make good this assertion, which they have not attempted.

Although this passage focuses only on the events surrounding the production of the proslavery works, it shows Bisset busy at what was for him the typical work of the professional author: making connections, gathering information, and fighting his enemies and detractors.

The rapidity of Bisset's writing and publication in the last few years of his life was probably brought on by financial as much as ideological circumstances. He finished the preface to *The History of the Negro Slave Trade* – his fifth book in five years – on 22 March 1805; on 14 May 1805 he was dead. The *Gentleman's Magazine* obituarist surmised that "Chagrin, under embarrassed circumstances, is thought to have broken his heart."

Reference:

Emily Lorraine de Montluzin, *The Anti-Jacobins, 1798–1800: The Early Contributors to the Anti-Jacobin Review* (New York: St. Martin's Press, 1988), pp. 57–59.

James Boswell
(29 October 1740 – 19 May 1795)

John A. Vance
University of Georgia

See also the Boswell entry in *DLB 104: British Prose Writers, 1660–1800, Second Series.*

BOOKS: *A View of the Edinburgh Theatre during the Summer Season, 1759* (London: A. Morley, 1760);

Observations, Good or Bad, Stupid or Clever, Serious or Jocular, on Squire Foote's Dramatic Entertainment, Intituled, The Minor. By a Genius (Edinburgh, 1760; London: Printed for J. Wilkie, 1761);

An Elegy on the Death of an Amiable Young Lady. With an Epistle from Menalcas to Lycidas [i.e., Lycidas to Menalcas] (Edinburgh: Printed by A. Donaldson & J. Reid for Alex Donaldson, 1761);

An Ode to Tragedy. By a Gentleman of Scotland (Edinburgh: Printed by A. Donaldson & J. Reid for Alex Donaldson, 1661 [i.e., 1761]);

The Cub, at Newmarket: A Tale (London: Printed for R. & J. Dodsley, 1762);

Critical Strictures on the New Tragedy of Elvira, Written by Mr. David Malloch, by Boswell, Andrew Erskine, and George Dempster (London: Printed for W. Flexney, 1763);

Letters between the Honourable Andrew Erskine, and James Boswell, Esq. (London: Printed by Samuel Chandler for W. Flexney, 1763);

Disputatio juridica, ad Tit. X. Lib. XXIII. Pand. de supellectile Jegata quam . . . publicae disquisitioni subjicit Jacobus Boswell (Edinburgh: Apud Alexandrum Kincaid, 1766);

Dorando, A Spanish Tale (London: Printed for J. Wilkie, sold also by J. Dodsley, T. Davies, and by the booksellers of Scotland, 1767);

The Essence of the Douglas Cause (London: Printed for J. Wilkie, 1767);

An Account of Corsica, the Journal of a Tour to that Island; and Memoirs of Pascal Paoli (Glasgow: Printed by Robert & Andrew Foulis for Edward & Charles Dilly, London, 1768);

A Letter to Robert Macqueen, Lord Braxfield, on His Promotion to Be One of the Judges of the High Court of Justiciary (Edinburgh: Sold by all the booksellers, 1780);

A Letter to the People of Scotland, on the Present State of the Nation (Edinburgh: Printed & sold by all the booksellers, 1783; London: Printed for C. Dilly, 1784);

A Letter to the People of Scotland on the Alarming Attempt to Infringe the Articles of the Union, and Introduce a Most Pernicious Innovation, by Diminishing the Number of the Lords of Sessions (London: Printed for Charles Dilly, 1785);

The Journal of a Tour to the Hebrides with Samuel Johnson, LL.D. (London: Printed by Henry Baldwin for Charles Dilly, 1785);

Ode by Dr. Samuel Johnson to Mrs. Thrale, upon Their Supposed Approaching Nuptials (London: Printed for R. Faulder, 1784 [i.e., 1788]);

A Conversation between His Most Sacred Majesty George III. and Samuel Johnson, LL.D. Illustrated with observations by James Boswell, Esq. (London: Printed by Henry Baldwin for Charles Dilly, 1790);

No Abolition of Slavery; or, The Universal Empire of Love (London: Printed for R. Faulder, 1791);

The Life of Samuel Johnson, LL.D. (2 volumes, London: Printed by Henry Baldwin for Charles Dilly, 1791; revised and augmented, 3 volumes, 1793);

The Principal Corrections and Additions to the First Edition of Mr. Boswell's Life of Johnson (London: Printed for C. Dilly, 1793);

Boswelliana: The Commonplace Book of Boswell, edited by Charles Rogers (London: Grampian Club, 1874);

Private Papers of James Boswell from Malahide Castle; in the Collection of Lt.-Colonel Ralph Heyward Isham, 18 volumes: volumes 1–6 edited by Geoffrey Scott, volumes 7–18 edited by Scott and Frederick A. Pottle (Mount Vernon, N.Y.: Privately printed by W. E. Rudge, 1928–1934).

The Yale Edition of the Private Papers of James Boswell: *Boswell's London Journal, 1762–1763,* edited by Pottle (New York: McGraw-Hill, 1950; London: Heinemann, 1950);

Boswell in Holland, 1763–1764, Including His Correspondence with Belle de Zuylen (Zélide), edited by Pottle (New

James Boswell (portrait by Sir Joshua Reynolds; National Portrait Gallery, London)

York: McGraw-Hill, 1952; London: Heinemann, 1952);

Boswell on the Grand Tour: Germany and Switzerland, 1764, edited by Pottle (New York: McGraw-Hill, 1953; London: Heinemann, 1953);

Boswell on the Grand Tour: Italy, Corsica, and France, 1765–1766, edited by Frank Brady and Pottle (New York: McGraw-Hill, 1955; London: Heinemann, 1956);

Boswell in Search of a Wife, 1766–1769, edited by Brady and Pottle (New York: McGraw-Hill, 1956; London: Heinemann, 1957);

Boswell for the Defense, 1769–1774, edited by W. K. Wimsatt and Pottle (New York: McGraw-Hill, 1959; London: Heinemann, 1960);

Boswell's Journal of a Tour to the Hebrides with Samuel Johnson, LL.D., edited by Pottle and Charles H. Bennett (1936), revised by Pottle (New York: McGraw-Hill, 1961; London: Heinemann, 1963);

Boswell: The Ominous Years, 1774–1776, edited by Charles Ryskamp and Pottle (New York: McGraw-Hill, 1963; London: Heinemann, 1963);

Boswell in Extremes, 1776–1778, edited by Charles McC. Weis and Pottle (New York & London: McGraw-Hill, 1970; London: Heinemann, 1971);

Boswell: Laird of Auchinleck, 1778–1782, edited by Joseph W. Reed and Pottle (New York & London: McGraw-Hill, 1977);

Boswell: The Applause of the Jury, 1782–1785, edited by Irma S. Lustig and Pottle (New York & London: McGraw-Hill, 1981);

Boswell: The English Experiment, 1785–1789, edited by Lustig and Pottle (New York & London: McGraw-Hill, 1986);

Boswell: The Great Biographer, 1789–1795, edited by Marlies K. Danziger and Brady (New York & London: McGraw-Hill, 1989).

Editions: *Boswell's Life of Samuel Johnson, Together with Boswell's Journal of a Tour to the Hebrides and Johnson's Diary of a Journey into North Wales,* 6 volumes, edited by George Birkbeck Hill, revised by

James Boswell (engraving by E. Finden after a portrait by G. Langton)

L. F. Powell (Oxford: Clarendon Press, 1934–1964);

The Journal of a Tour to Corsica; and Memoirs of Pascal Paoli, edited by Morchard Bishop (London: Williams & Norgate, 1951).

James Boswell's impact on the development of biography as a genre and on the understanding of the requirements for good biographical writing can hardly be overstated. The discovery of Boswell's journals has not only enhanced his reputation as one of literary history's most fascinating characters but has also heightened awareness of the strengths and limitations of his biographical methods. Boswell has stimulated more vigorous personal and critical response than perhaps any other author whose major works were either biographical or historical. Boswell's writing also causes spirited reactions: it delights, charms, infuriates, and perplexes.

Some of Boswell's experiences in his youth encouraged a strong interest in the lives of "the ablest and worthiest men in the world" (from an autobiographical sketch Boswell composed for Jean-Jacques Rousseau in 1764). When Euphemia Erskine Boswell gave birth to James in Edinburgh on 29 October 1740, she intended that her son would grow up properly influenced by her rigid Calvinism, which certainly had its effect on the boy, though not as she might have hoped. But more of a factor on Boswell's formative years and his entire life was his demanding and equally rigid father, Alexander Boswell, whose direct and indirect shaping of his son's biographical perspective and literary direction has often been unappreciated. Boswell would write many years later, "I do not recollect having had any other valuable principle impressed upon me by my father except a strict regard to truth, which he impressed upon my mind by a hearty beating at an early age when I lied, and then talking of the *dishonour* of lying" – strong evidence, many Boswell supporters argue, of his trustworthiness as a biographer. While he was still a young boy, the family moved to Auchinleck, the ancestral estate with which he would remain associated until his death. Throughout his life he was forced to reconcile his ambitions and flights of fancy with the duty and responsibility expected of him as a future laird. Boswell's imagination, impatience, resentments, fears, melancholy, and various perspectives on important men in his life – primarily his father but also his tutors John Dun and Joseph Fergusson – developed in his early years.

In the fall of 1753 Boswell left for the University of Edinburgh, and, other than forging strong friendships with such people as John Johnston and William Temple, he found himself drawn to older and distinguished men, most notably Sir David Dalrymple of Hailes and Sir James Somerville, who could serve as mentors and congenial father figures. Also at this time Boswell became enamored of the Edinburgh theater world, his exposure to drama and the often-intoxicating company of actors and actresses further shaping him. But after six years his father informed him that he would be moving on to the University of Glasgow. Therefore, though Boswell completed the first stage of his formal education without the familiarity and stimulation of his early university and theater acquaintances, he at least had the comfort of coming under the tutelage of another distinguished faculty, which included Adam Smith.

Alexander Boswell's relief over his son's removal from the temptations of the Edinburgh theater world was only short-lived, for soon afterward Boswell published his first book (a fifty-page pamphlet) in early 1760, *A View of the Edinburgh Theatre during the Summer Season, 1759* – in essence a collection of theater reviews. Alexander Boswell next heard from his son that he was converting to Roman Catholicism and was considering a life as a priest or monk. Despite a stern order to come to Edinburgh, Boswell fled to London in March 1760. Even though this particular rebellion soon passed (Boswell stayed in London only about three months), Alexander Boswell was compelled to accept his son's apparent unwillingness to commit enthusiastically to an expected, sober, and self-disciplining career in the law and had to endure the young man's penchants for religious eccentricity, young women, and further publication. (Boswell wrote a considerable body of verse from 1760 to 1762.) He upset his father further by announcing his romantic intentions to pursue a military career. The ultimate result of these periodic clashes of wills was the younger Boswell's fortunate decision to seek refuge in London in the fall of 1762, but not before he took a jaunt to the border countries, which resulted in the first of his journal entries and established the practice which made possible his three major literary compositions.

The effervescent and liberating aspects of London opened Boswell's eyes not only to the literary, political, and social experience available to him but also to the possibilities of establishing friendships with some of the best-known figures of his own and the previous generation. Whereas his associations in Scotland were certainly not insignificant, now he was able (from the fall of 1762 until the following August) to meet, please, annoy, and court such men as David Garrick, Oliver Goldsmith, Thomas Sheridan, John Wilkes, and Samuel Johnson. The "Louisa" episode in *Boswell's London Journal* (as published in 1950) shows him honing his ability to present reality in dramatic form.

In August 1763 Boswell left London because of his father's insistence and headed to Utrecht, Netherlands, ostensibly to study law. Actually, this trip was the first leg on a tour of Germany, Switzerland, Italy, Corsica, and France that broadened Boswell's worldly perspective but, more important, put him in contact with yet other important men and women: Rousseau, Voltaire, and Pasquale Paoli. In his occasionally awkward and comical attempts to form bonds with and elicit information from these men, Boswell was refining the technique he would use more effectively with Johnson when next they met in London. To a curious Boswell, re-

cording his estimations and the conversations of these individuals seemed a far more fascinating and significant endeavor than contemplating a diligent and successful career in the law and a prestigious and comfortable life as the next laird of Auchinleck.

His return to Scotland in 1766 brought inevitable conflicts, disappointments, and decisions. Alexander Boswell's firm expectations resulted in both his son's admission to the Scottish bar in the summer of 1766 and James's commitment to finding a wife and raising a family. After several amours and infatuations he eventually took as his wife his first cousin Margaret Montgomerie on 25 November 1769. Although the elder Boswell agreed to the marriage, he did not fully approve; however, he lived long enough to see the birth of all five of Margaret and James's children.

The remaining years of Boswell's life were marked by his efforts to enhance his legal career (the most memorable case being that of John Reid in 1774, which Boswell lost), by his financial concerns and struggles, and by his periodic trips to London, where he continued to cultivate new and to reaffirm old friendships, especially with Johnson. Boswell published more literary work following his admission to the bar. Of the major efforts there was initially *An Account of Corsica, the Journal of a Tour to that Island; and Memoirs of Pascal Paoli* in 1768, followed by *The Journal of a Tour to the Hebrides with Samuel Johnson, LL.D.* in 1785, and finally by *The Life of Samuel Johnson, LL.D.* (1791). But these literary successes did not spare Boswell from monetary and familial crises. In 1786, four years after he became laird of Auchinleck, he moved his family to what he hoped would be a more socially congenial and financially appreciative place: London. He was admitted to the English bar that year. Unfortunately, his frequent bouts of loneliness following the death of his wife in 1789 and a cycle of illnesses and financial setbacks greatly diluted the pleasure and satisfaction he experienced after the publication of his *Life of Samuel Johnson*. Boswell died in London on 19 May 1795, five months short of his fifty-fifth birthday.

On 11 October 1765 Boswell had left Leghorn and sailed with great anticipation to the isle of Corsica. Fired by his talks with Rousseau about the Corsicans, Boswell naturally wished to ingratiate himself with one of the century's most dashing figures, Paoli, the leader of the Corsican fight for independence against the French and the Genoese. After a journey filled with anxiety, delight, some hardship, and occasional danger (including the promise of death should he debauch any of the Corsican women), Boswell at last found himself in the great man's presence. Armed with a letter of introduction from Rousseau, Boswell offered a highly suspicious Paoli the following prelude: "I am come from seeing the ruins [in Rome] of one brave and free people; I now see the rise of another." Whereas Paoli had initially examined Boswell with "a steadfast, keen, and penetrating eye," he quickly took to the young man, whose "flow of gay ideas relaxed his [Paoli's] severity and brightened up his humour." Boswell's exuberance and youthful passion for the nationalist cause led to more than his wearing of Corsican costume (including Paoli's pistols) and his reveling in Corsican custom; he was determined to influence the British government to come to Paoli's aid. Even though Great Britain failed to give the Corsicans such assistance (and the Corsican resistance was subdued in May 1769), Boswell's efforts were still strenuous. After his return to Britain, he supported the Corsican cause, printed information about his trip and the Corsican struggle in newspapers, and sought and got an interview with William Pitt. However, Boswell's most important contribution to the cause and to his burgeoning social and literary reputation was *An Account of Corsica*.

Generically *An Account of Corsica* cannot be considered a "biography, for it includes a substantial section on Corsican history and periodic accounts of the Corsicans fighting for their independence. But Boswell's depiction of Paoli and his inclusion of their conversations best reflect the talents of a biographer rather than those of a historian or political theorist. Paoli emerges from the volume as its most compelling focus. A comparison of *An Account of Corsica* and the relevant journal entries shows Boswell's strength as a biographer: the instinct to record (whether verbatim or not) what was important, memorable, and dramatic. Boswell describes various moments (even those of seemingly little importance) with the skills befitting the novelist or dramatist. The reader has difficulty visualizing for any length of time the topography of Corsica; nor is one encouraged to contemplate the potential relationship of the struggle to modern history. Rather, one visualizes vividly the personality of Paoli, and to a lesser extent, Boswell himself.

The opinions of fellow writers John Wesley and Thomas Gray testify to the book's strengths. Wesley wrote, "At intervals read Mr. Boswell's *Account of Corsica*. But what a scene is opened therein! How little did we know of that brave people! How much less were we acquainted with the character of their general, Pascal Paoli: as great a lover of his country as Epaminondas, and as great a general as

Hannibal!" Gray said, "Mr. Boswell's book . . . has pleased and moved me strangely, all (I mean) that relates to Paoli. He is a man born two thousand years after his time!" Even though Gray was not an admirer of Boswell, his and Wesley's assessments point to the talent of Boswell for the biographical portrait. Reading or hearing positive responses such as these, he could not help developing confidence in composing such biographical depictions and also appreciating more clearly the literary value of the kind of journal entry he chose to record.

Whereas critics have examined *An Account of Corsica* and found much about which to complain – the expected Scotticisms, perhaps a trivial attention to orthography, occasional inaccuracies, periodic pomposity, and general pedantry – the majority of readers have found the book valuable and reflective of the deep interest in the individual life during the eighteenth century. Boswell basked in its success; as his biographer Frederick Pottle observes, "In its sale *Corsica* was the eighteenth-century equivalent of a book-club selection," the first edition selling out within six weeks, necessitating two more printings within a year. It was generously reviewed, with excerpts appearing in the leading magazines and newspapers. The portion of the book which pleased readers most was the journal section, the part that demonstrated Boswell as most intimate with his material. As Johnson concluded, according to Boswell in *The Life of Samuel Johnson, LL.D.,* "Your History is like other histories, but your Journal is in a very high degree curious and delightful. . . . Your History was copied from books; your Journal rose out of your own experience and observation." Again, that which was biographical and especially autobiographical represented Boswell's real achievement in *An Account of Corsica*. He never failed to appreciate what his time in Corsica meant to his reputation and maturity; as he observed in 1783, "it was wonderful how much Corsica had done for me, how far I had got in the world by having been there. I had got upon a rock in Corsica and jumped into the middle of life."

In August 1773 Boswell met Johnson in Edinburgh to begin an extended tour of Scotland and its Western Isles. If he did not actually stimulate Johnson's interest in such a trip, Boswell at least made it possible by actively encouraging his older friend to come north. Johnson would not have made such a journey had not Boswell been his guide and companion. The story of the trip is well known to students of the period, and the various images are colorful and memorable: Johnson and Boswell wandering among the ruins, engaging in

Highland customs, commenting on historical and philosophical matters, meeting with local and national celebrities, and enduring the hardships of travel on land and sea. The three months spent on the journey represents the longest sustained period of time the two men were ever in each other's company.

In 1775, not long after the completion of the tour, Johnson published his *Journey to the Western Islands of Scotland,* which represents the best in eighteenth-century travel literature. Yet it would be another decade before Boswell published his account, *The Journal of a Tour to the Hebrides with Samuel Johnson, LL.D.* As expected, Boswell remained true to his habit of some ten years by noting in the journal his and Johnson's comings, goings, and conversations along the way. The delay in publication had more to do with his legal career, familial responsibilities, and his intended *Life of Samuel Johnson* than it did with any fear of immediate comparison with Johnson's more philosophical treatise. (At least seventeen months before the men met in Edinburgh, Boswell had noted in his journals the plan to write Johnson's life.) With the great fortune of cultivating Edmond Malone as friend and literary spur, Boswell began in the spring of 1785 to shape his journal notes into a comprehensive and lucid account of the tour, which reached the public in September of that year. The date is of importance, for, following Johnson's death on 13 December 1784, there began to appear biographical sketches and the prospect of fuller treatments of Johnson's life – for example, Hester Lynch [Thrale] Piozzi's *Anecdotes* in 1786 and Sir John Hawkins's *The Life of Samuel Johnson, LL.D.* in 1787, both pre-dating the completion of Boswell's own *Life of Samuel Johnson.* It was necessary, therefore, that Boswell establish his biographical rights to Johnson's legacy, and *The Journal of a Tour to the Hebrides* proved to be the best opportunity to stake that claim, given the impossibility of rushing into print a substantial biographical treatment. Even so, the need for Malone's encouragement, prodding, literary instinct, and editorial skill was paramount. That is, Boswell could not have been too confident as he and Malone sat down for their initial meeting, seeing that he had written nothing of length since *An Account of Corsica* some seventeen years earlier. Other than his journal entries, Boswell's literary work manifested itself primarily in the completion of shorter pamphlets.

As he contemplated his second major literary project, Boswell was faced with several important and difficult choices regarding his method and emphasis, the first being organization. Would he sec-

tion the work as had Johnson in his *Journey* (by locales visited), or would he choose a strict chronological arrangement (with day-by-day notations), the latter being clearly his strength? Fortunately Boswell took the advice of Malone and Sir Joshua Reynolds and decided on the diarist's method. Moreover, could he improve his style from what it was in the Corsican account, omit undesirable Scotticisms, incorporate the most pleasing phrasing, and cut or revise journal entries to illuminate most effectively the central figure of the book? And would his presentation of Johnson capture appropriately, if not always perfectly, not only the recently deceased's dignity, intellectual capacity, and philosophical brilliance but also his vigor, rough humor, and, most controversially, his various shortcomings? Yet Boswell did not have to ponder these matters alone, for always Malone was there to advise, correct, and approve.

For the second time Boswell saw his substantial literary and biographical efforts rewarded with general public enthusiasm. The initial run of fifteen hundred copies was quickly sold, and two more printings were needed in 1786. Critically, however, reviewers and some readers wondered if the work reflected what was then generally perceived as appropriate biographical writing. For example, how necessary were all the details Boswell unfurled before his readers? Was the ultimate goal of good biography – instruction – best served by so many specifics? Anticipating such an objection, Boswell, in the book itself, provided his own defense: "Let me not be censured for mentioning such minute particulars. Everything relative to so great a man is worth observing." Such advocacy was rebutted by the argument that too much which is "relative" tends both to obscure what is most important and to numb the mind, leading readers to expect little more than a minute-by-minute chronology or item-by-item descriptions, thereby forcing them to miss the potential significance of a moment from the subject's life. Still, Boswell's decision to be all-inclusive suggested his belief that the importance of persons such as Johnson was best displayed when they could be seen as men in relationship with the real world, as opposed to being perceived as mere symbols of something grand or infamous, men whose only activities worth recording were those that revealed or enhanced such a status. Besides, as Boswell realized, such particulars made the subject and the book far more attractive to readers whose interests lay less with philosophical reflection and more with unadulterated gossip.

Related to the matter of minute particulars was a more telling question: were Boswell's illustrations of Johnson's shortcomings and eccentrici-

[56.]

this morning with the illustrious
Donaldson. In the evening I went
to Temple's; he brought me acquainted with a Mr Claxton a
very good sort of a young man tho'
reserved at first. Mr Nicholls was
there too. Our conversation was
sensible & lively. I wish I could
spend my time allways in such company.

     Monday 16 May.

Temple & his Brother breakfast-
ed with me. I went to Love's
to try to recover some of the money which he owes me. But alas
a single guinea was all I could
get. He was just going to dinner,
so I stayed & eat a bit; tho' I was
angry at myself afterwards.
I drank tea at Davies's in Russel Street and about seven came
in the great Mr Samuel Johnson, whom I have so long wished
to see. Mr Davies introduced
me to him. As I knew his mortal
antipathy at the Scotch, I could
                to

Description of Boswell's first meeting with Samuel Johnson, from Boswell's journal entry for 16 May 1763 (Yale University Library)

(563)

to Davies; don't tell where I come
from. However he said From Scotland.
Mr. Johnson said I indeed I come
from Scotland, but I cannot help
it. : Sir replied he. : That I find
is what a very great many of
your countrymen cannot help. :
Mr. Johnson is a man of a most
dreadfull appearance. He is a
very big man is troubled with sore
eyes, the Palsy & the King's
evil. He is very slovenly in
his dress & speaks with a
most uncouth voice. Yet his
great knowledge, and strength
of expression command vast
respect and render him very
excellent company. He has
great humour and is a worthy
man. But his dogmatical rough:
:ness of manners is disagreable.
I

Auchinleck House, the ancestral home Boswell inherited after his father's death in 1781

ties in the spirit of established biographical practice, which often hid such blemishes under a cosmetic of lavish praise or patches of omission? Perhaps the objections were exacerbated by the fact that Johnson was not yet dead a year. As the anonymous critic for the *English Review* (1785) complained, "But allowing to Dr. Johnson all the merit which his warmest admirers ascribe to him, was it meritorious, was it right or justifiable in Mr. Boswell to record and publish his prejudices, his follies and whims, his weaknesses, his vices?" From the perspective of modern biographical theory, the answer to this question is a resounding "Yes!" Therefore whatever else may be held against the book, it did at least help to further the more detached, "warts and all" method of writing biographical portraits.

The reading public understood what many of the critics could not: that such writing was capable of being highly entertaining. The sense of anticipation the reader feels as Johnson arrives in Edinburgh results from Boswell's deft handling of his subject at the outset of a journey of which one might not expect Johnson to approve, let alone undertake in the first place: "I doubted that it would not be possible to prevail on Dr. Johnson," Boswell writes, "to relinquish for some time the felicity of a London life, which, to a man who can enjoy it with full intellectual relish, is apt to make existence in any narrower sphere seem insipid or irksome." Boswell's vivid description of a locale is quickly matched and then superseded by his memorable characterization of Johnson in that place: will the great man finally be awed by his surroundings or will he diminish the landscape through ridicule, philosophical reflection, or some physical activity like clambering among the ruins? Boswell presents the Scottish landscape through the eyes of Johnson, who becomes the real guide for the reader. The entertainment value is increased by Boswell's characterization of himself as the often naive companion, the eager Sancho Panza – at times enlarging his subject by diminishing himself, at other times subtly or more obviously revealing his power over the great man, leading him here and there, encouraging and eliciting from him pronouncements the reader is anxious to hear. Therefore, the irony of Boswell's presence adds considerably to the success and enjoyment of the book. This irony would serve him well when he turned seriously to constructing *The Life of Samuel Johnson*.

The debate over Boswell's "authentic" depiction of Johnson notwithstanding, in *The Journal of a Tour to the Hebrides* he gives most readers a Johnson they want to believe is the real thing. Most feel that what they read and envision is truly authentic, perhaps because the image of Johnson is one that the reader can not only admire but also take issue with and smile or laugh at, and thus, at times, the reader can feel superior to Johnson. Boswell seems to have understood that one appeal of biographical writing is in the shared experience: whether one agrees with Johnson's commentary (of either a grand philosophical or a mere pedestrian quality) or shares his frailties and shortsightedness, the reader often discovers a satisfying affinity with the biographical subject. In addition, Boswell's firm reliance on talk — on conversation, gossip, outburst, and observation — provides the reader with that intimacy which so much previous biographical writing lacked (and would continue to lack) due to the fact that the author generally distances himself through dry objective details, narration, and commentary, regardless of their value. Boswell's method was to involve his readers, to make them feel privy to something exciting, important, and private. With such feelings of satisfaction, why would the general reader question the accuracy of Boswell's direct quotation of Johnson?

As many then knew, *The Journal of a Tour to the Hebrides* was but a harbinger of the book Boswell had for at least thirteen years been thinking about writing. Other than *The Journal of a Tour* to the Hebrides and his substantial journal entries devoted to his meetings with Johnson over the years and those detailing conversations with others about Johnson, Boswell had the wisdom to solicit from others information about Johnson's life before the men met in the spring of 1763 and about Johnson's activities after that date, when Boswell was not in London to record Johnson's conversation. During their friendship of over twenty years Boswell saw Johnson on only 425 days — again the largest block of that time spent on the Scottish tour — and he did *not* see Johnson at all in the years 1764, 1765, 1767, 1770, 1771, 1774, 1780, and 1782. To supplement the anecdotes and conversations, Boswell had in his possession over three hundred of Johnson's letters, many of which he included or quoted from in *The Life of Samuel Johnson.*

Once more Malone became his helper: "I cannot sufficiently acknowledge my obligations to my friend Mr. Malone," Boswell writes in the "Advertisement" to the first edition of *The Life of Samuel Johnson.* On his mind as he constructed his biography was the uncomfortable reality that the public

had already read Piozzi's *Anecdotes* and Hawkins's own *Life of Johnson.* Each work would be an implied and unwelcomed presence in Boswell's book, even though Boswell had already drawn his line in the sand. In May 1787 he announced in the *Public Advertiser* that his "deliberation" regarding the progress of his biography was not only necessary but also appropriate given the importance of the man and the task: "as very few circumstances relative to the history of Dr. Johnson's private life, writings, or conversation have been told with that authentic precision which alone can render biography valuable." More specifically regarding his rivals, Boswell added, "He [Boswell] trusts that in the mean time the public will not permit unfavourable impressions to be made on their minds, whether by the light effusions of carelessness and pique, or the ponderous labours of solemn inaccuracy and dark, uncharitable conjecture."

Boswell did not work continuously on the biography in the entire period from Johnson's death in December 1784 to the publication of his *Life of Samuel Johnson* on 16 May 1791 (the anniversary of their first meeting at Thomas Davies's bookshop twenty-eight years earlier); he had his legal obligations, social diversions, and family matters to occupy much of his time. Boswell occasionally went a month or even longer without penning a word of *The Life of Samuel Johnson,* but, following a return to London in the late fall of 1788, his pace quickened and he soon anticipated the book's completion, so that by January 1789 he was already writing the introduction and dedication to Reynolds. Although over two years remained before *The Life of Samuel Johnson* reached the public, one cannot fairly accuse Boswell of literary indolence, for it was during this period that he experienced the death of his wife; he heard the devastating news upon his return to Auchinleck in early June 1789. By October and with the help of Malone, the first batch of pages was ready for the printer's attention. Boswell wrote Temple the following month, "You cannot imagine what labour, what perplexity, what vexation I have endured in arranging a prodigious multiplicity of materials, in supplying omissions, in searching for papers buried in different masses — and all this besides the exertion of composing and polishing." His depression was impossible to suppress: "I walk about upon the earth with inward discontent, though I may appear the most cheerful man you meet. I may have many *gratifications* but the *comfort* of life is at an end." Malone was in Ireland in early 1791, and a forlorn Boswell admitted to him in a letter, "Indeed I go sluggishly and comfortlessly about my work. As I

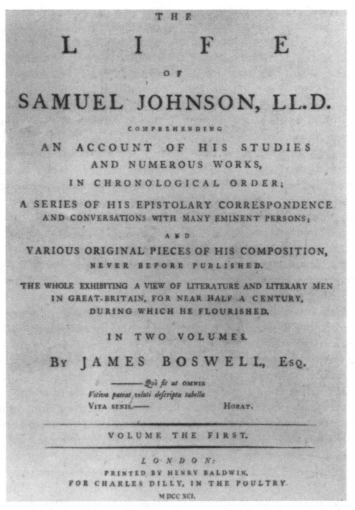

THE

LIFE

OF

SAMUEL JOHNSON, LL.D.

COMPREHENDING

AN ACCOUNT OF HIS STUDIES
AND NUMEROUS WORKS,

IN CHRONOLOGICAL ORDER;

A SERIES OF HIS EPISTOLARY CORRESPONDENCE
AND CONVERSATIONS WITH MANY EMINENT PERSONS;

AND

VARIOUS ORIGINAL PIECES OF HIS COMPOSITION,
NEVER BEFORE PUBLISHED.

THE WHOLE EXHIBITING A VIEW OF LITERATURE AND LITERARY MEN
IN GREAT-BRITAIN, FOR NEAR HALF A CENTURY,
DURING WHICH HE FLOURISHED.

IN TWO VOLUMES.

BY JAMES BOSWELL, ESQ.

————— *Quò fit ut OMNIS*
Vstiva pateat veluti descripta tabella
VITA SENIS.—————   HORAT.

VOLUME THE FIRST.

LONDON:
PRINTED BY HENRY BALDWIN,
FOR CHARLES DILLY, IN THE POULTRY.
M DCC XCI.

*Title page for volume one of the work that permanently influenced the art
of biography*

pass your door I cast many a longing look." Malone had therefore more than literary and editing assistance to offer: he also had to cheer his friend when he could and, failing that, had to see that Boswell did not give over to a complete breakdown.

Boswell's plans for publication were of necessity delayed from early to late March 1791 and then from early to late April, the book fortunately and ironically being further delayed until the anniversary date of 16 May. Once more a major work by Boswell was an instant success: *The Life of Samuel Johnson* sold half its initial run of 1,750 copies within the first month of publication. By the following summer almost all the copies had been purchased and a new, second edition was then in preparation. Although the new material was not as satisfactorily placed into the existing biography as it might have been, Boswell secured for this edition additional anecdotes by those who knew Johnson,

and he restimulated his own memory for further information and insights. The second edition was published the following summer (on 17 July 1793), and within a week 400 copies fell into the hands of an anxious public.

In the advertisement to the second edition Boswell remarks, "That I was anxious for the success of a Work which had employed much of my time and labour, I do not wish to conceal: but whatever doubts I at any time entertained, have been entirely removed by the very favourable reception with which it has been honoured." As in the case of *The Journal of a Tour of the Hebrides,* however, many complained about Boswell's apparently unbiased theory of biography: the overall impression of Johnson offended many for its "brutality" and eccentricity. In addition, Boswell's depiction of himself found disfavor among certain readers and critics: he appeared too conspicuous, too fawning, and too full of his own self-importance. Naturally some of those appearing in the book, such as Thomas Percy, were not overjoyed to be cast in an unfavorable light. Other "participants" in the biography had rather colorful responses – for example, that of Wilkes: "His book . . . is that of an entertaining madman." Friends of the deceased, most notably of Goldsmith, also took umbrage, but these criticisms did little to dampen the sheer pleasure the general public (and some writers for periodicals) took in reading the book.

The Life of Samuel Johnson commences with Boswell's introduction, in which he justifies his method, establishes his strong personal relationship with the subject, and attacks his most obvious rival, Hawkins's *Life of Johnson*. Boswell then quotes Johnson's own views on biographical writing as set forth in the *Rambler* (number 60, 1750): "The business of the biographer is . . . to lead the thoughts into domestick [sic] privacies, and display the minute details of daily life. . . . But biography has often been allotted to writers, who . . . have so little regard to the manners or behaviour of their heroes, that more knowledge may be gained of a man's real character, by a short conversation with one of his servants, than from a formal and studied narrative, begun with his pedigree, and ended with his funeral." Boswell was fortunate that his biographical subject made such a point, for over 80 percent of Boswell's *Life of Samuel Johnson* treats the period from 1763 to 1784, when he knew Johnson and recorded his conversations. Readers would soon recognize that they had before them substantial discussions between the biographical subject and his biographer. Even in death Johnson stood before the reader and justified Boswell's major focus, his major source materials, and his biographical theory. Few introductions have better established the authority and methods of the biographer. One detects as well an interesting mixture of shameless pride and self-assertion with sincere (or feigned) humility and modesty: "To write the Life of him who . . . has been equalled by few in any age, is an arduous, and may be reckoned in me a presumptuous task. . . . As I had the honour and happiness of enjoying his friendship for upwards of twenty years; as I had the scheme of writing his life constantly in view; . . . as I acquired a facility in recollecting, and was very assiduous in recording, his conversation; . . . and as I have spared no pains in obtaining materials concerning him, from every quarter where I could discover that they were to be found; . . . I flatter myself that few biographers have entered upon such a work as this, in which I am not vain enough to compare myself with some great names who have gone before me in this kind of writing." In other places, the self-congratulations emerge gushing: "Had his other friends been as diligent [in keeping Johnson's letters and recording his conversations] as I was, he might have been almost entirely preserved. As it is, I will venture to say that he will be seen in this work more completely than any man who has ever yet lived."

As one might predict, Boswell chose a chronological method of presentation; the reader is always cognizant (by conspicuous dates on the pages) of the year being reviewed. Modern biographies are more flexible in their chronology, with a facet of the subject's career being taken to its chronological termination, followed by a return of time to begin another aspect of the life. But in *The Life of Samuel Johnson* the method best suits Boswell's journal entries (even if they do not come fully into use until he reaches 1763), the method of composition with which he was most comfortable and proficient.

The Life of Samuel Johnson comprises facts; lists of works; anecdotes about Johnson from Boswell and a host of other contributors; many letters from Johnson and several from Boswell; excerpts of Johnson's writings; Boswell's estimation of those writings; Johnson's own commentary about his early life; Johnson's views on literary, political, social, and personal matters; recorded conversations of Johnson in the company of others or in the presence of Boswell alone; Boswell's own assessments of Johnson and others in the Johnson circle; and Boswell's observations about literary, moral, and social questions. The strengths of the book are readily apparent: it is for the most part lively and captivating; the reader is not tempted to skip ahead to escape boredom. Yet it is one of those rare books that rewards even the reader who dips into it at just about any place in the text. The reader develops a sense of intimacy with Johnson that a more traditional biography would not and could not allow. One also becomes fairly intimate with the biographer, whose presence in the work is almost always conspicuous, if not intrusive, and with other luminaries whose lives crossed paths with Johnson's. Accordingly, the reader easily detects and willingly responds to Boswell's gift of dramatic presentation; one is encouraged to anticipate with pleasure the next confrontation between Johnson and an adversary, whether it be with another animated acquaintance or with some inanimate idea or philosophy.

The work's shortcomings were observed at the time of publication but have been most strongly identified since the 1960s. First, one may likely take from *The Life of Samuel Johnson* a distorted (or con-

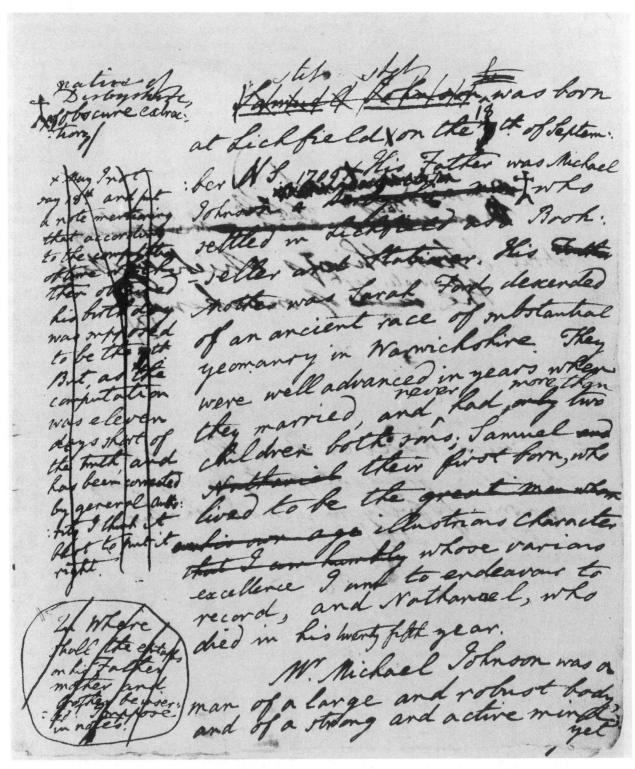

Page from the manuscript for Boswell's Life of Samuel Johnson, LL.D. (Yale University Library)

siderably distorted) picture of Johnson as a man who "talked the best literature of his century" – a witty respondent, a petulant debater, a pompous moralist, a humorous eccentric, and a literary monolith whose personality and opinions varied little over a long career. *The Life of Samuel Johnson,* critics also point out, provides an improper image of Boswell as Johnson's "best" friend or as the loyal and indefatigable "recorder" of Johnson's conversations who was almost always in his company throughout their twenty-one-year relationship. (This image remains firmly secured in the minds of more-casual readers of the book.)

A few critics have gone as far to conclude that this work, usually called the greatest biography in the language, is really no biography at all but rather an edited diary supplemented by letters and copious observations by the "biographer" himself. Thus the "strength" of accommodating even those readers who dip into it almost anywhere becomes a weakness when measured against the requirements of good biographical writing, one of those being the relationship of the past to the present. Others emphasize that *The Life of Samuel Johnson* lacks appropriate balance: as noted, over 80 percent treats the "Boswell years," 1763 to 1784. There are years for which the account is sketchy at best, even if buttressed by correspondence or the anecdotes provided by others – the inevitable result of Boswell's strong (and inhibiting) reliance on his journal entries; if he did not come to London, of course, there could be no journal account from which to draw. Critics also point to moments when Boswell's own opinions regarding literary, political, moral, or social matters either take up too much space in a purported biography of Johnson or actually end up being endorsed by Johnson himself. As a result, one is forced to question not only Boswell's trustworthiness but also the accuracy of so many of Johnson's recorded conversations.

Indeed, how accurate could Boswell be as a recorder? His method was to write down the memorable conversation he heard or overheard, but the actual moment of recording could be hours or days after the fact. Critics see the impossibility of accurate quotation given these circumstances, not to mention Boswell's conscious or unconscious wish to suppress, embellish, or dramatize his materials for literary impact, regardless of how these liberties might bruise or batter the truth. In response, advocates point to evidence of Boswell's remarkable memory, noting that this quality, honed by many years of practice, represented his strength as a biographer and more than justified his methodology in

The Life of Samuel Johnson. Other defenders argue that a comparison of the original journal entries with their final manifestations in the *Life of Samuel Johnson* reveals that Boswell was careful with the truth: on the whole he was with little question a trustworthy recorder of Johnson's conversation and, accordingly, a qualified biographer. Critics would counter, though, that if the journals themselves are flawed (that is, in relation to what Johnson actually said and in what context), then it matters little if the conversations in *The Life of Samuel Johnson* correspond letter for letter to those in the journals. Donald Greene, has, for example, cited Johnson's depiction of Lady Diana Beauclerk – "the woman's a whore and there's an end on't" – observing that such a remark does not even exist in the corresponding journal entry. Where then did it come from? The unflattering conclusion many have reached is that it sprang from Boswell's, not Johnson's, imagination.

Related to this matter is some critics' preoccupation with "Boswell's Johnson." That is, is the biographical subject of *The Life of Samuel Johnson* primarily a fictive construct of an imaginative author named Boswell? Those writing in recent years on biography and history note the many fictional techniques one may encounter in "factual" works. They have made readers accept more fully what should have been most obvious: that no biographer (or historian) can offer an untainted portrait of the subject, one that is purely factual or objective. The biographer's selection of details or emphases can make the biographical subject appear either more grand or more ridiculous in the eyes of the reader. Should Boswell be held any more accountable for simply doing what every biographer cannot help doing? Or is his Johnson so far removed from the Johnson that emerges from Johnson's own writings, autobiographical fragments, letters, and accounts of others that Boswell is guilty of biographical deception, giving the reader a literary impostor, a Johnson that either satisfies Boswell's own image of the man or provides more readable and entertaining copy? There is also the question of Boswell's attitude toward his biographical subject. Did he revere the man to the exclusion of any objective biographical perspective? Did he love and respect Johnson without losing that biographical distance necessary to provide the true-to-life portrait he promised to leave with the reader? Or did Boswell, for all the professed respect and affection, actually harbor resentment and jealousy, which may be detected in certain moments in *The Life of Samuel Johnson* in which he contradicts Johnson on literary and moral questions

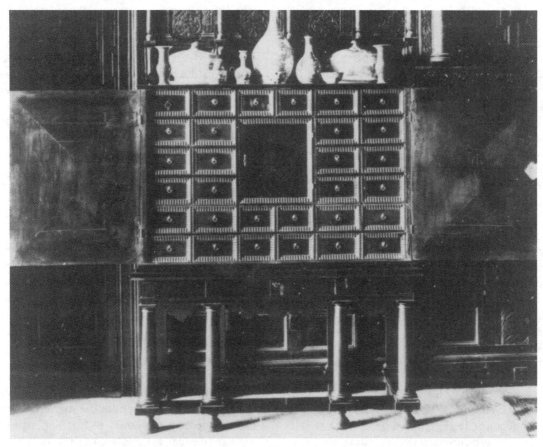

Boswell's ebony cabinet, in which some of his papers were stored at Auchinleck House. During the first decade of the twentieth century the papers and cabinet were taken to Malahide Castle, near Dublin, Ireland, where they remained inaccessible to scholars until Lt. Col. Ralph Heyward Isham bought them from Boswell's descendants in 1927 and published them as Private Papers of James Boswell *(1928–1934).*

or portrays him in embarrassing and comical ways? Students of *The Life of Samuel Johnson* have argued these points with considerable purpose and energy, particularly in the past thirty years.

To some, the matters of biographical accuracy and "Boswell's Johnson" have generally been ignored in favor of the literary qualities of the work deemed as shortcomings by many critics. *The Life of Samuel Johnson* continues to be subjected to various forms of critical analysis, at times serving as the text by which some recent literary theories may be tested. Boswell has been lauded for these "fictional techniques," his reputation as a writer increasingly enhanced by examinations of his style, dramatic sensibility, and other aspects of his presentation. Critics of the book, however, maintain that even conceding Boswell's skill as creative author, judgment of *The Life of Samuel Johnson* must ultimately be based on its portrait of Johnson, its contribution to the strong and apparently timeless image that seems so distorted, perverse, and unfortunate. Accord-

ingly, the recommendation of the critics has been to give appropriate weight to other biographical treatments of Johnson, from those of Hawkins and Piozzi to the more recent efforts of Walter Jackson Bate and James L. Clifford. In addition, the attack on Boswell's biographical shortcomings has been reinforced by a vigorous advocacy of Johnson's own writings as a way to wrench him free from Boswell's apparently Herculean grip. In response, defenders such as John Burke have argued that a careful examination of *The Life of Samuel Johnson* will show, perhaps to the chagrin of the detractors, that the reader does not in fact deal exclusively with "Boswell's Johnson," for Boswell's reliance on the accounts of others makes his biographical subject moreover "Langton's Johnson," "Maxwell's Johnson," "Garrick's Johnson," and so on.

Other topics that continue to intrigue students of *The Life of Samuel Johnson* are the relationship between the finished product and Boswell's journal entries as well as the ever-present autobiographical aspects of *The Life of Samuel Johnson*. Regarding the latter, Richard Schwartz contends that *The Life of Samuel Johnson* is "essentially a book about Boswell, a portion of his autobiography." Even without endorsing this particular conclusion, many have found "Boswell's Boswell" irresistible – that stimulating, though perhaps fictional, character created in his image and likeness. Still others, particularly Greene, have seen the book as a working out of Boswell's difficulties with his father, complete with a Johnson on whom Boswell seized "as a substitute father figure to support his shaky ego. But we all know, or by this time should know, how much suppressed resentment the poor father-figure is subjected to." The opposition, of course, forcefully rejects the notion that *The Life of Samuel Johnson* demonstrates any of this resentment; it is at its heart a labor of love and respect, regardless of any specific flaws. Even though the work is not a panegyric, Boswell still serves as a protector if not champion of Johnson's reputation.

Yet another avenue of approach has been to judge the work in the context of historicism and formalism. How correct have readers been in the methods by which they have approached the book? Others have examined the depiction of the secondary figures, most notably Goldsmith, as a way to judge Boswell's trustworthiness and accuracy. Some have chosen to focus on individual moments in *The Life of Samuel Johnson,* for example the dinner with Wilkes, as a way to emphasize Boswell's literary talents and to help explain the enduring popularity of the work.

But should its popularity justify use of *The Life of Samuel Johnson* as a research source? Students using the book may have little concern for its validity, its proper context, or the false impression of Johnson it may leave, while others have employed only that which can be corroborated by other biographical or anecdotal sources and by Johnson's own writings. How, then, should one use *The Life of Samuel Johnson*? And how should one teach it, especially to those who are still to understand adequately the complexity and limited value of such factual works? Yet the very intensity of the debate over the merits of *The Life of Samuel Johnson* only testifies to its enduring value. Regardless of how many errors, omissions, false impressions, and other forms of inaccuracy one may discover in its pages, Boswell's *The Life of Samuel Johnson* remains a classic of English literature. It stands up to the most intense scrutiny and is still able to provide any reader willing to suppress his or her critical instincts with immense pleasure and satisfaction.

Letters:

Letters of James Boswell, Addressed to the Rev. W. J. Temple, edited by Sir Philip Francis (London: Bentley, 1857 [i.e., 1856]);

The Letters of James Boswell, 2 volumes, edited by Chauncey Brewster Tinker (Oxford: Clarendon Press, 1924);

The Correspondence of James Boswell and John Johnston of Grange, edited by Ralph S. Walker (New York: McGraw-Hill, 1966; London: Heinemann, 1966);

The Correspondence and Other Papers of James Boswell Relating to the Making of the "Life of Johnson," edited by Marshall Waingrow (New York: McGraw-Hill, 1969; London: Heinemann, 1969);

Boswell's Correspondence with Certain Members of the Club, edited by Charles N. Fifer (New York: McGraw-Hill, 1976; London: Heinemann, 1976);

The Correspondence of James Boswell with David Garrick, Edmund Burke, and Edmond Malone, edited by George M. Kahrl, Rachel McClellan, Thomas W. Copeland, Peter S. Baker, and James M. Osborn (London: Heinemann, 1987; New York: McGraw-Hill, 1988).

Bibliographies:

Frederick A. Pottle, *The Literary Career of James Boswell, Esq., Being the Bibliographical Materials for a Life of Boswell* (Oxford: Clarendon Press, 1929);

Anthony E. Brown, *Boswellian Studies,* second edition, revised (Hamden, Conn.: Archon, 1972);

Marion S. Pottle, Claude C. Abbot, Frederick S. Pottle, eds. *Catalogue of the Papers of James Boswell at Yale University,* 3 volumes (New Haven, Conn.: Yale University Press, 1993).

Biographies:

Frederick A. Pottle, *James Boswell: The Earlier Years, 1740–1769* (New York: McGraw-Hill, 1966);

Frank Brady, *James Boswell: The Later Years, 1769–1795* (New York: McGraw-Hill, 1984);

Iain Finlayson, *The Moth and the Candle: A Life of James Boswell* (London: Constable, 1984).

References:

Harold Bloom, ed., *Dr. Samuel Johnson and James Boswell,* Modern Critical Views (New York: Chelsea House, 1986);

Bloom, ed., *James Boswell's "Life of Samuel Johnson,"* Modern Critical Interpretations (New York: Chelsea House, 1985);

Frank Brady, "Boswell's Self-Presentation and His Critics," *Studies in English Literature,* 12 (1972): 545–555;

Bertrand Bronson, "Boswell's Boswell," in his *Johnson and Boswell,* University of California Publications in English, volume 4, no. 9 (Berkeley: University of California Press, 1944); republished as *Johnson Agonistes & Other Essays* (Berkeley & Los Angeles: University of California Press, 1965), pp. 53–99;

A. R. Brooks, *James Boswell* (New York: Twayne, 1971);

David Buchanan, *The Treasure of Auchinleck: The Story of the Boswell Papers* (New York: McGraw-Hill, 1974);

John J. Burke, Jr., "The Documentary Value of Boswell's *Journal of a Tour to the Hebrides,*" in *Fresh Reflections on Samuel Johnson,* edited by Prem Nath (New York: Whitston, 1987), pp. 349–372;

James L. Clifford, ed., *Twentieth Century Interpretations of Boswell's "Life of Johnson"* (Englewood Cliffs, N.J.: Prentice-Hall, 1970);

Greg Clingham, *Boswell: The Life of Johnson* (Cambridge: Cambridge University Press, 1991);

Clingham, ed., *New Light on Boswell: Critical and Historical Essays on the Occasion of the Bicentenary of the "Life of Johnson"* (Cambridge: Cambridge University Press, 1991);

Leopold Damrosch, Jr., "The *Life of Johnson:* An Anti-Theory," *Eighteenth-Century Studies,* 6 (1973): 486–505;

William C. Dowling, *The Boswellian Hero* (Athens: University of Georgia Press, 1979);

Dowling, *Languages and Logos in Boswell's "Life of Johnson"* (Princeton, N.J.: Princeton University Press, 1981);

Joseph Foladare, *Boswell's Paoli* (Hamden, Conn.: Archon, 1979);

Donald Greene, "Johnson without Boswell," *Times Literary Supplement,* 22 November 1974, pp. 1315–1316;

Mary Hyde, *The Impossible Friendship: Boswell and Mrs. Thrale* (Cambridge, Mass.: Harvard University Press, 1972);

Allan Ingram, *Boswell's Creative Gloom: A Study of Imagery and Melancholy in the Writings of James Boswell* (New York: Barnes & Noble, 1982);

Donald Kay, "Boswell in the Green Room," *Philological Quarterly,* 57 (Spring 1978): 195–212;

Irma S. Lustig, "Fact into Art: James Boswell's Notes, Journals, and the *Life of Johnson,*" in *Biography in the Eighteenth Century,* edited by John D. Browning (New York: Garland, 1980), pp. 128–146;

Maximillian Novak, "James Boswell's *Life of Johnson,*" in *The Biographer's Art: New Essays,* edited by Jeffrey Meyers (London: Macmillan / New York: New Amsterdam, 1989), pp. 31–52;

Frederick A. Pottle, "James Boswell, Journalist," in *The Age of Johnson: Essays Presented to Chauncey Brewster Tinker* (New Haven: Yale University Press, 1949), pp. 15–25;

Pottle, *Pride and Negligence: The History of the Boswell Papers* (New York: McGraw-Hill, 1982);

Pottle, "The Power of Memory in Boswell and Scott," in *Essays on the Eighteenth Century Presented to David Nichol Smith* (Oxford: Clarendon Press, 1945), pp. 168–189;

Richard Schwartz, *Boswell's Johnson: A Preface to the "Life"* (Madison: University of Wisconsin Press, 1978);

William S. Siebenschuh, *Form and Purpose in Boswell's Biographical Works* (Berkeley & Los Angeles: University of California Press, 1972);

John A. Vance, ed., *Boswell's "Life of Johnson": New Questions, New Answers* (Athens: University of Georgia Press, 1985).

Papers:

Since 1949 (with the sale of Col. Ralph Isham's holdings to the university) the major repository for the Boswell papers has been at Yale. The next most important collection is at the Hyde Library at Four Oaks Farm in New Jersey. Other significant Boswell papers are in the National Library of Scotland.

Sir Samuel Egerton Brydges

(30 November 1762 – 8 September 1837)

Glyn Pursglove
University College of Swansea

See also the Brydges entry in *DLB 107: British Romantic Prose Writers, 1789–1832, First Series.*

BOOKS: *Sonnets and other Poems; with a Versification of the Six Bards of Ossian* (London: Printed for G. & T. Wilkie, 1785; enlarged, 1785; enlarged again, London: Printed for B. & J. White, 1795);

Mary De-Clifford, a Story Interspersed with Many Poems (London: Printed for H. D. Symonds, 1792);

Verses on the Late Unanimous Resolutions to Support the Constitution. To Which are added some other poems (Canterbury: Printed by Simmons, Kirkby & Jones, 1794);

Arthur Fitz-Albini, a Novel, 2 volumes (London: Printed for J. White, 1798);

Reflections on the Late Augmentations of the English Peerage (London: Printed for J. Robson & J. Debrett, 1798);

Tests of National Wealth and Finances of Great Britain in December 1798 (London: Printed for J. White, 1799);

Memoirs of the Peers of England During the Reign of James the First (London: Printed for J. White by Nichols & son, 1802);

Le Forester, a Novel, 3 volumes (London: Printed for J. White by T. Bensley, 1802);

Polyanthea; or, a Collection of Interesting Fragments in Prose and Verse (London: Budd, 1804);

Poems (London: Hurst, Rees & Orme, 1807);

A Biographical Peerage of the Empire of Great Britain, 4 volumes (London: Printed for J. Johnson, 1808–1817);

An Analysis of the Genealogical History of the Family of Howard (London: Printed & published for the author by H. K. Causton, 1812);

Letters on the Poor Laws (London: Longman, Hurst, Rees, Orme & Brown, 1813);

The Ruminator: Containing a Series of Moral, Critical and Sentimental Essays, 2 volumes (London: Longman, Hurst, Rees, Orme & Brown, 1813);

The Sylvan Wanderer; Consisting of a Series of Moral, Sentimental, and Critical Essays, 4 volumes (Kent: Printed at the Private Press of Lee Priory by Johnson & Warwick, 1813–1821);

Restituta; or, Titles, Extracts, and Characters of Old Books in English Literature, Revived, 4 volumes (London: Printed by T. Bensley for Longman, Hurst, Rees, Orme & Brown, 1814–1816);

Occasional Poems, Written in the Year MDCCCXI (Kent: Printed at the Private Press of Lee Priory by Johnson & Warwick, 1814); facsimile in *Samuel Egerton Brydges and Edward Quillinan* (New York & London: Garland, 1978);

Select Poems (Kent: Printed at the Private Press of Lee Priory by Johnson & Warwick, 1814);

Bertram, a Poetical Tale (Kent: Printed at the Private Press of Lee Priory by Johnson & Warwick, 1814); facsimile in *Samuel Egerton Brydges and Edward Quillinan* (1978); revised as *Bertram, A Poetical Tale in Four Cantos* (London: Longman, Hurst, Rees, Orme & Brown, 1816);

Desultoria: or Comments of a South-Briton on Books and Men (Kent: Printed at the Private Press of Lee Priory by Johnson & Warwick, 1815);

Fragment of a Poem, Occasioned by a Visit to the Old Mansion of Denton, July 23, 1815 (Kent: Lee Priory Press, 1815);

A Brief Character of Matthew, Lord Rokeby (Kent: Printed at the Press of Lee Priory by J. Warwick, 1817);

Arguments in Favour of the Practicability of Relieving the Able-bodied Poor (London: Printed by Bensley for Longman, 1817);

Reasons for a Farther Amendment of the Act 54 Geo. III. c. 156, being an act to amend the Copyright Act of Queen Anne (London: Printed by Nichols, son & Bentley, 1817); facsimile in *Four Tracts on Copyright, 1817–1818* (New York & London: Garland, 1974);

A Summary Statement of the Great Grievances imposed on Authors and Publishers; and the Injury done to Liter-

*Portrait of Sir Samuel Egerton Brydges, printed as the frontispiece
to volume one of his autobiography*

ature, by the Late Copyright Act (London: Printed for Longman, Hurst, Rees, Orme & Brown, 1818); facsimile in *Four Tracts on Copyright, 1817–1818* (1974);

A Vindication of the Pending Bill for the Amendment of the Copyright Act, from the Misrepresentations and Unjust Comments on the Syndics of the University Library, at Cambridge (London: Printed for Longman, Hurst, Rees, Orme & Brown, 1818); facsimile in *Four Tracts on Copyright, 1817–1818* (1974);

Answer to the Further Statement, ordered by the Syndics of the University of Cambridge to be printed and circulated (London, 1818); facsimile in *Four Tracts on Copyright, 1817–1818* (1974);

Five Sonnets, Addressed to Wootton, the Spot of the Author's Nativity (Kent: Printed at the Private Press of Lee Priory by John Warwick, 1819); facsimile in *Samuel Egerton Brydges and Edward Quillinan* (1978);

Lord Brokenhurst. Or, a Fragment of Winter Leaves: A Tragic Tale (Paris & Geneva: J. J. Paschoud / London: R. Triphook, 1819);

Coningsby, A Tragic Tale (Paris: J. J. Paschoud / London: R. Triphook, 1819);

The Population and Riches of Nations (Paris & Geneva: J. J. Paschoud / London: R. Triphook, 1819);

Tragic Tales: Coningsby, and Lord Brokenhurst, 2 volumes (London: Printed for Robert Triphook, 1820);

Sir Ralph Willoughby: An Historical Tale of the Sixteenth Century (Florence: I. Magheri, 1820);

Letters from the Continent, 2 parts (Kent: Printed at the Private Press of Lee Priory by J. Warwick, 1821);

What Are Riches? or, An Examination of the Definitions of this Subject Given by Modern Economists (Geneva: Printed by W. Fick, 1821; Kent: Printed at the Private Press of Lee Priory by John Warwick, 1822);

Portrait by Daniel Maclise in the Fraser's Magazine *"Gallery of Illustrious Literary Characters" (1830–1838)*

The Hall of Hellingsley: A Tale, 3 volumes (London: Longman, Hurst, Rees, Orme & Brown, 1821);

The Anti-Critic for August 1821, and March, 1822. Containing Literary, Not Political, Criticisms, and Opinions (Geneva: Printed by W. Fick, 1822);

Odo, Count Lingen: A Poetical Tale in Six Cantos (Geneva: Printed by W. Fick, 1824; facsimile, New York & London: Garland, 1978);

Gnomica: Detached Thoughts, Sententious, Axiomatic, Moral and Critical (Geneva: Printed by W. Fick, 1824);

Letters on the Character and Poetical Genius of Lord Byron (London: Longman, Hurst, Rees, Orme, Brown & Green, 1824);

An Impartial Portrait of Lord Byron (Paris: Published by A. & W. Galignani, 1825);

Recollections of Foreign Travel, on Life, Literature, and Self-Knowledge, 2 volumes (London: Printed for Longman, Hurst, Rees, Orme, Brown & Green, 1825);

Travels of my Nightcap, or Reveries in Rhyme (London: G. B. Whittaker, 1825);

Stemmata Illustria: Præcipue regia (Paris: Printed by J. Smith, 1825);

A Note on the Suppression of Memoirs announced by the author in June 1825; containing numerous strictures on contemporary public characters (Paris: Printed by J. Smith, 1825);

Who Was Ita, Countess of Hapsburg, Who founded the monastery of Muri in Switzerland, in 1018, and died in 1026? (Paris: Printed by J. Smith, 1826);

Lex Terrae. A Discussion of the Law of England, regarding Claims of Inheritable Rights of Peerage (Geneva: Printed by William Fick, 1831);

Modern Aristocracy, or, the Bard's Reception: The Fragment of a Poem (Geneva: Printed by A. L. Vignier, 1831);

The Lake of Geneva, a Poem, Moral and Descriptive, in Seven Books, 2 volumes (Geneva: Printed by A. L. Vignier for A. Cherbuliez, 1832);

The Autobiography, Times, Opinions, and Contemporaries of Sir Egerton Brydges, bart., 2 volumes (London: Cochrane & M'Crone, 1834);

Imaginative Biography, 2 volumes (London: Saunders & Otley, 1834);

The Life of John Milton (London: Printed for John Macrone, 1835);

Human Fate, and an Address to the Poets Wordsworth & Southey: Poems (Great Totham: Printed at C. Clark's Private Press, 1846).

OTHER: Edward Phillips, *Theatrum Poetarum Anglicanorum,* edited, with additions, by Brydges (Canterbury: Printed by Simmons & Kirkby for J. White, London, 1800);

Censura Literaria, 10 volumes, edited, with contributions, by Brydges (London: Printed by T. Bensley for Longman, Hurst, Rees & Orme, and J. White, 1805–1809; facsimile, New York: AMS Press, 1966);

The British Bibliographer, 4 volumes, edited, with contributions, by Brydges (London: Printed for R. Triphook by T. Bensley, 1810–1814; facsimile, New York: AMS Press, 1966);

Richard Edwards, *The Paradise of Dainty Devices,* edited by Brydges (London: Printed for Robert Triphook, 1810);

England's Helicon: A Collection of Pastoral and Lyric Poems, First Published at the Close of the Reign of Q. Elizabeth, edited by Brydges (London: Printed by T. Bensley for Robert Triphook, 1812);

Arthur Collins, *Collins's Peerage of England: Genealogical, Biographical, and Historical,* 9 volumes, edited and augmented by Brydges (London: Printed for F. C. & J. Rivington, Otridge & son, 1812);

Robert Greene, *Greene's Groatsworth of Wit,* edited, with a preface, by Brydges (Kent: Printed at the Private Press of Lee Priory by Johnson & Warwick, 1813);

Sir Henry Wotton, *The Characters of Robert Devereux, earl of Essex; and George Villiers, duke of Buckingham,* edited by Brydges (Kent: Printed at the Private Press of Lee Priory by Johnson & Warwick, 1814);

Michael Drayton, *Nymphidia: The Court of Fairy,* edited by Brydges (Kent: Printed at the Private Press of Lee Priory by Johnson & Warwick, 1814);

Thomas Stanley, *Poems by Thomas Stanley,* edited by Brydges (London: Longman, Hurst, Rees, Orme & Brown, 1814);

Margaret Cavendish, Duchess of Newcastle, *A True Relation of the Birth, Breeding, and Life of Margaret Cavendish, Duchess of Newcastle,* edited, with a critical preface, by Brydges (Kent: Printed at the Private Press of Lee Priory by Johnson & Warwick, 1814);

Excerpta Tudoriana; or, Extracts from Elizabethan Literature, edited, with a critical preface, by Brydges (Kent: Printed at the Private Press of Lee Priory by Johnson & Warwick, 1814–1818);

Archaica: Containing a Reprint of Scarce Old English Prose Tracts, 2 volumes, edited, with critical and biographical prefaces and notes, by Brydges (London: From the Private Press of Longman, Hurst, Rees, Orme & Brown, printed by T. Davison, 1815);

Richard Brathwaite, *Brathwayte's Odes; or, Philomel's Tears,* edited by Brydges (Kent: Printed at the Private Press of Lee Priory by Johnson & Warwick, 1815);

Nicholas Breton, *Breton's Melancholike Humours,* edited, with a critical preface, by Brydges (Kent: Printed at the Private Press of Lee Priory by Johnson & Warwick, 1815);

Breton, *Breton's Praise of Virtuous Ladies,* edited by Brydges (Kent: Printed at the Private Press of Lee Priory by Johnson & Warwick, 1815);

George Wither, *Hymns and Songs of the Church,* edited, with a preface, by Brydges (London: Longman, Hurst, Rees, Orme & Brown, 1815);

William Hammond, *Occasional Poems, by William Hammond, Esq.,* edited by Brydges (London: Printed by T. Bensley & son for Longman, Hurst, Rees, Orme & Brown, 1816);

John Hagthorpe, *Hagthorpe, Revived; or, Select Specimens of a Forgotten Poet,* edited by Brydges (Kent: Printed at the Private Press of Lee Priory by John Warwick, 1817);

William Percy, *Coelia: Containing Twenty Sonnets by W. Percy,* edited by Brydges (Kent: Printed at the Private Press of Lee Priory by J. Warwick, 1818);

Charles Fitz-Geffrey, *The Life and Death of Sir Francis Drake,* edited by Brydges (Kent: Printed at the Private Press of Lee Priory by J. Warwick, 1819);

Edward Quillinan, *Carmina Brugesiana: Domestic Poems by Edward Quillinan,* edited by Brydges (Geneva: Printed by W. Fick, 1822);

The Green Book; or, Register of the Order of the Emerald Star, edited by Brydges (Geneva?, 1822).

In the British Library are ten large manuscript notebooks containing more than two thousand sonnets along with miscellaneous notes written by Sir Samuel Egerton Brydges during three years of his

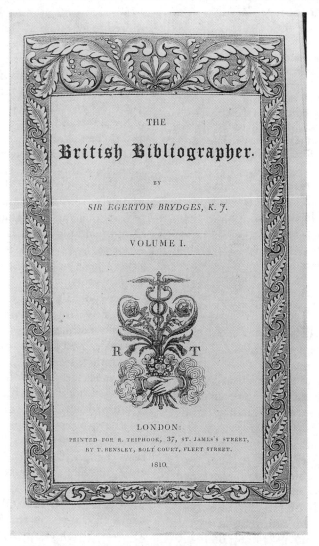

*Title page for one of the collections of British Renaissance works
for which Brydges and his friends supplied bibliographical and
historical commentaries (Special Collections, Thomas Cooper
Library, University of South Carolina)*

final "exile" in Geneva. There is something both fascinating and depressing about these untidily written volumes. Most of the poems are hastily written, the intermittent dating revealing several cases where Brydges has written as many as six or seven sonnets on a single day. There are some good and striking phrases irregularly scattered among much dross. A remarkable proportion of this collection of largely unpublished poetry is made up of sonnets about poets and poetry. There are poems, to take but a few examples, on Samuel Daniel, Edmund Spenser, Petrarch, Sir Walter Scott, Lord Byron, Robert Bloomfield, Thomas Chatterton, Torquato Tasso, and Abraham Cowley. There are sonnets on John Milton and on Milton's sonnets. Brydges's love of poetry is apparent on every page; so, too, is the sad inadequacy of his own efforts as a poet. His poetic ideals are lofty: "The Bard lives in ideal presences; / He calls up beings from the misty deep." In Brydges's case the "beings" rarely came when he called for them. For Brydges the true poet was a solitary figure, withdrawn from the everyday world: "Solitude is the poets' only sphere; / He cannot live amid the rude turmoils / Of the world's squabbling clamours." From poetry Brydges demands "deep moral thought, expanded comprehension." Time and again he returns to "the impotence of Art to produce poetry." His sonnets illustrate his propositions on poetry: "Poetry deals in immateriality"; "The Muse is best cultivated in woody solitudes";

and "Flowery language is not poetry." Brydges's generic "poets" are troubled romantic figures:

> Poets but children are of pain and want,
>   Like tender flowers, that in a climate rude
> Droop, and then perish: – frightful demons haunt
>   The deep recesses of their busy brain
> And torn with anguish they bring forth the strain –
>   Then in dark visions lost they sadly brood
>   Upon the death of pleasures they have wooed;
>   And shriek with stripes of foes that they disdain.

Brydges had his own reasons for seeing himself as just such a figure, and it was toward poets who fulfilled or who could be thought to fulfill such a stereotype that Brydges was most attracted as a literary biographer. He comes close to identifying himself with one of his heroes:

> Milton, the sword suspended by an hair
> Over his head, his mighty Epic Wrote!
> . . . .
> Amid misfortune, sorrow and despair
> My Tongue shall not be silent, nor my strain.

Though the comparison is, of course, absurd in poetical terms, it is not difficult to see why an embittered Brydges found in Milton an attractive analogy for his own situation. Brydges's *Life of John Milton* (1835) is perhaps his most substantial claim to serious attention as a literary biographer. It is perhaps best described as an "intellectual biography," concerned more with the development of Milton's mind and art than with the externals of his life. Elsewhere Brydges had already made a contribution to the scholarly rediscovery and rehabilitation of many obscure figures from earlier periods of English literature. In Brydges a romantic vision of poetry coexisted with an antiquarian fascination; the combination gives his work in biography a distinctive flavor.

Brydges was born on 30 November 1762 at Wootton Court in Kent. He was the second son of Edward Brydges and Jemima Egerton Brydges, daughter of William Egerton, LL.D., prebendary of Canterbury Cathedral, chancellor of Hereford Cathedral, and rector of Allhallows, Lombard Street, and Penshurst in Kent. The young Brydges was educated for some four years at Maidstone Grammar School and then for a further five at King's School, Canterbury. He was a student at Queen's College, Cambridge, from October 1780 until December 1782; he left without a degree, having by his own account devoted his time to the reading and writing of poetry rather than to his studies. In 1782 he began legal training at the Middle Temple in London, and he was called to the bar in November 1787. He never practiced, however, and in 1792 he retired to an estate at Denton in Kent. The purchase of this estate, and the considerable expense of necessary repairs to the property, began the financial worries which were to trouble him greatly for the rest of his life. He had married in January 1786, taking as his wife Elizabeth Byrche, daughter and heir of the Reverend William Dejovas Byrche. Two sons and three daughters were born before the death of Elizabeth in 1796. Brydges remarried the following year, his second wife being Mary Robinson, daughter of the Reverend William Robinson. By his second wife (who outlived him) Brydges was the father of five sons and six daughters. In 1810 Brydges left Denton and moved to Lee Priory, near Canterbury. From 1818 until his death Brydges spent all but two years (June 1826 to October 1828) abroad, mostly in Geneva.

Brydges's early literary ambitions as a poet and a novelist met with only modest success. His egotism led him to impute this relative failure to the jealousies and plots of others. Another kind of disappointment did much to further sour his life. In 1790 the last duke of Chandos had died; Bridges encouraged his elder brother, the Reverend Edward Tymewell Brydges, to claim the barony of Chandos on the grounds of his supposed descent from a younger son of the first Brydges who had held that title. Lengthy and confused legal wranglings ensued; in 1803 the House of Lords ruled against the claim. Tymewell Brydges died in 1807. The title out of which he felt himself to have been cheated became an obsession for Egerton Brydges. In work after work, relevantly or irrelevantly, he bemoaned his fate and accused the peers and others of assorted incompetencies and injustices. He sensed conspiracies all around him. His claim seems to have had little truth in it, and Brydges may even have tampered with some documents in pursuit of it. After his brother's death Brydges began signing himself (and proclaiming himself on title pages) "per legem terrae, Baron Chandos of Sudely."

There was much in Brydges's character that was absurd and vain; there was much, too, that was sensitive and intelligent. He was a man of learning and intellectual independence. The anonymous author of an obituary of Brydges, published in the *Gentleman's Magazine* (November 1837), suggests that in the hero of Brydges's novel *Arthur Fitz-Albini* (1798) one sees Brydges's portrait of himself as a young man:

> Himself he saw often neglected, and sometimes passed by with gross affront. The virtues he occasionally displayed, or the wisdom that at times burst from him, and

silenced all opposition, he saw followed by unwilling and extorted praise. And he saw a thousand tongues ready to burst forth and overwhelm him at the least deviations from rectitude, or even from the appearance of rectitude. An inequality of temper and of mind, an indignation and haughtiness at folly and meanness, which seemed by fits to possess him, he was conscious often raised the bitterest enmity against him. But, when he wished to please, and the softness and benevolence of his heart discovered themselves, it seemed strange that he should be the object of neglect and aversion.

When he was older, Brydges published his honest and moving autobiography (1834), which is by turns stirring, pathetic, pithy, and verbosely irrelevant. Its disorderly and excessive length is part of its meaning, even its charm. Brydges was well aware of some of the flaws in his character: "There are those who think me ungrateful and splenetic, when I complain of having been neglected; and call me avid of praise, and resentful of fancied wrongs. . . . I must repeat that I am fully conscious of the fault of my morbid sensitiveness; and that it has been my bane through life."

The Autobiography, Times, Opinions, and Contemporaries contains fascinating material on Brydges's dealings with "the book-hating squires of Kent," and with such contemporaries as Robert Bloomfield, John Gibson Lockhart, Thomas Medwin, Thomas James Mathias, Countess Teresa Guiccioli, and Jane Austen. Of the last (to whom Brydges was related) he says that "When I knew Jane Austen I never suspected that she was an authoress; but my eyes told me that she was fair and handsome, slight and elegant, but with cheeks a little too full." Brydges saw his book as a contribution to a genre he held in high esteem. Autobiographical accounts, or "self-written" memoirs, he takes to be "the best materials of biography . . . for these always bear with them internal evidence of authenticity, or vain disguise, which cannot be mistaken." Brydges was an enthusiastic reader of biographical works in general: "Of all sorts of reading, biography is the most generally attractive; and self-memoirs, if frank and sincere, are the most attractive of all. I scarcely know one publication of this latter class which one would be content to burn." Brydges's own autobiography is, in some ways, his greatest work of biography, his fullest realization of what he took to be the proper purposes of literary biography. The biography of a literary man, he insists, should be concerned with "the workings of the mind": "We desire to be told how far his pursuits make him happy and virtuous – how far they soften and refine his temper, his habits, and his heart; what have been his hopes and fears; and how he has

borne the sorrows and disappointments of life. Nor is it an irrational curiosity to wish to be acquainted with the lot into which he has been cast, and the circumstances which may have contributed to the colours of his mind."

Given such a conception of literary biography it follows logically that Brydges should believe that the poet (and Brydges believed himself preeminently to be a poet) is the ideal biographer. In his "Essay on the Genius and Poems of [William] Collins" (in an 1830 collection of Collins's poems) he affirms that "Poets of research are, of all authors, best qualified to write biography with sagacity and eloquence; they see into the human heart, and detect its most secret movements; and if there be a class of literature more amusing and instructive than another, it is well-written biography." Brydges's early efforts in biography, however, rarely show such psychological speculation.

In his edition of Edward Phillips's *Theatrum Poetarum Anglicanorum* (1800), in his many contributions to the ten volumes of *Censura Literaria* (1805–1809) and the four volumes of *The British Bibliographer* (1810–1814), in his editions of such miscellanies as *The Paradise of Dainty Devices* (1810) and *England's Helicon* (1812), as well as in his introductions to the many editions of early writers which he published at his private press at Lee Priory, Brydges's approach is firmly within the tradition of antiquarianism. In the brief biographies which appear in these books, facts are related, genealogies are traced, and bibliographical details are stated and analyzed. For example, *The British Bibliographer* contains a "Memoir of Sir Aston Cokayne" in which an accumulation of biographical and bibliographical information accompanies extensive quotation from Cokayne's poems. There is some limited analysis of the historical context and, superficially, of Cokayne's character: "His mind appears to have been much cultivated with learning; and it is clear that he possessed considerable talents: but he exhibits scarcely any marks of genius. He is never pathetic, sublime, or even elegant." Brydges's edition of Sir Walter Ralegh's poems, based on a seriously flawed notion of the canon of Ralegh's work, is prefaced by a straightforward rehearsal of the historical "facts" and with extensive quotation. Only occasionally does Brydges allow himself any speculative analysis, as in the suggestion that Ralegh's mind was characterized "by boldness, and freedom from nice scruples, either in thought or in action."

In Brydges's "Memoir of Sir Philip Sidney," which is split between volumes two and four of *The British Bibliographer,* one can perhaps see growing

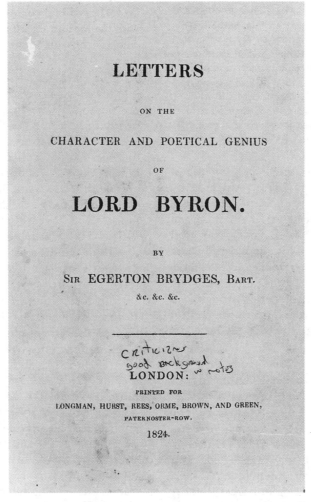

LETTERS

ON THE

CHARACTER AND POETICAL GENIUS

OF

LORD BYRON.

BY

Sir EGERTON BRYDGES, Bart.
&c. &c. &c.

LONDON:

PRINTED FOR
LONGMAN, HURST, REES, ORME, BROWN, AND GREEN,
PATERNOSTER-ROW.
1824.

*Title page for Brydges's book of speculations on Byron's life
and art*

signs of Brydges's later notion of literary biography. His memoir of Sidney, he says, does not exist to repeat facts already available elsewhere, and Brydges's reader is directed to previously published accounts of Sidney's life. Rather, Brydges offers his reader some "remarks naturally springing from so delightful and fertile an object of contemplation." In the process Brydges comes close to making of Sidney a prototype of that romantic conception of the poet which so attracted him. On the basis of a passage in one of Hubert Languet's letters to Sidney, Brydges identifies Sidney as essentially melancholy and proceeds to class this melancholy as the characteristic of literary genius, in terms which might describe Brydges's own nature and situation. Of Sidney's supposed melancholy, Brydges inquires: "Is not this melancholy almost always, if not constantly, the attendant of high genius? It is not necessary here to enter into the causes which produce this characteristic; but perhaps the acute feelings, without which genius cannot exist, are alone sufficient to account for it. The perpetual chills which that noble flame of ambition encounters in a coarse world; the murmurs of that solitude, which is the only field for the expanded thoughts it loves, must necessarily cherish the propensity."

In his two books on Byron, *Letters on the Character and Poetical Genius of Lord Byron* (1824) and *An Impartial Portrait of Lord Byron* (1825), Brydges is not, strictly speaking, writing biography. The two volumes, as Samuel Chew notes in *Byron in England: His Fame and After-Fame* (1924), are "primarily critical rather than biographical." Yet so much is Brydges concerned to delineate, as he says, "the character of the *Poet* and the *Man*" that he is led into precisely the kind of psychological speculation that he saw as the essence of literary biography. The works are biographies in essence if not in external form. There is, indeed, a basic chronological shape discernible in both of Brydges's accounts of Byron, the observations moving sequentially through Byron's works and places of residence, though so many and diverse are the digressions and additions that this sequence lies beneath the surfaces of the works. Byron is seen as a man governed by impulses rather than principles. His "ruling genius" is a somber melancholy, and Brydges wonders whether perhaps some "accidental circumstance may have given an impression of horror or bitterness to Lord Byron in his infancy," since Brydges has no doubt that "there are impressions sometimes made on a sensitive intellect or heart in early life, before reason has gained dominion, which nothing afterwards can efface." He finds Byron's work to be characterized by an inner antithesis. On the one hand is a fierceness and a "bitter and resentful misanthropy"; on the other is "an intense sensibility" to images of feminine beauty, solitude, and terror. Especially interesting, and closely related to Brydges's understanding of his own life, is the assertion that Byron's achievement was possible only because he lived largely outside "society," since "the invariable effect of society is to destroy originality, to produce sameness, to obliterate distinctions." Brydges states that the individual genius within society is invariably the victim of "that base artifice of *heartless sneer,* by which people of the world, of moderate abilities and acquirements, affect airs of superiority over the activity and vigour of those whom they are incapable of following." He believed himself to be such a genius (though he was not so sunk in egotism that he was entirely without periods of self-doubt) and to have received such treatment. His own career, he tells readers in *Letters on the Character and Poetical Genius of Lord Byron,* has been "a stormy, perilous and disappointed life." The Byron in exile, the Byron superior (and conscious of his superiority) to a society simultaneously disgusted and fascinated by him, is clearly a figure with whom Brydges was able to make a ready and comprehensive emotional identification.

Brydges's own self-imposed exile effectively began in 1818; he died on 8 September 1837 at Campagne, Gros Jean, near Geneva. Exile seems to have given to Brydges's work a new depth and maturity. Distanced, physically at least, from reminders of his disappointments, he was able to look both at himself and at others with a new clarity. His remarkable autobiography was the product of these exile years; so, too, was almost all of Brydges's most valuable work as a biographer and critic.

Where a younger Brydges had been content simply to memorialize and reprint, the mature Brydges aspired to theories of the poet and poetry which – while clearly influenced by, for example, Samuel Taylor Coleridge (as in the extensive discussion of the distinction between imagination and fancy and its application to Byron's poetry in the *Letters*) – were highly personal and deeply felt. In Byron, Brydges found fulfillment of his idea of the poetical genius. The best of Byron's poems "abound every where with that poetical INVENTION, which is sublime, pathetic, or beautiful." To distinguish this highest kind of poetry from that "sort of shadowy, bastard poetry, which is a mere poetry of *language*" is, in a sense, the ultimate purpose of Brydges's studies of Byron. Because Brydges locates the distinction in the different relationships between men and their writings, his books on Byron are, in great part, a kind of biographical inquiry, or at any rate inseparable from such inquiry. The two approaches – the critical or theoretical and the strictly biographical – sit rather uncomfortably side by side in the *Letters,* which is the more substantial and important of his two works on Byron. In the *Letters* forty-one "letters," occupying 451 pages, are largely devoted to the analysis of the nature of Byron's genius and character; there follows a "Note" of less than 5 pages which rehearses the biographical "facts" of his life, complete with all relevant dates and genealogical information. This "Note" might almost have come from one of Brydges's earlier antiquarian "lives." The preceding pages are biographical writing of an altogether different sort. It was in Brydges's *Life of John Milton* that he was to come closest to finding the means to combine the virtues of the two approaches.

Two intervening works deserve at least brief discussion. Brydges's "Essay on the Genius and Poems of Collins" is a brief but sensitive account of a poet with whom Brydges was temperamentally well able to sympathize. The essay is, however, just as valuable for the light it throws on Brydges's continuing consideration of the nature and problems of literary biography. This reflection that "the lives of poets would be the most amusing of all biography, if the materials were less scanty; it is strange that so few of them have left any ample records of themselves: of many not even a letter or fragment of memorials is preserved" leads him on to a survey of the surviving materials relevant to biographical knowledge of his contemporaries and immediate predecessors, such as Elizabeth Carter, James Beattie, Anna Seward, Charlotte Smith, and Byron. Brydges claims that biographical information con-

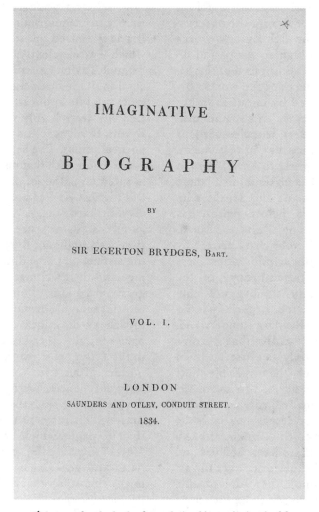

*Title page for the book of speculative biography inspired by
Brydges's impatience with "mere facts"*

cerning men of genius is valuable "in enabling us to contemplate how far the gifts of high intellect contribute to our happiness, or afford guides for the rest of mankind." His increasing impatience with mere "facts" led him to write *Imaginative Biography* (1834). By his title Brydges refers to "an Imaginary Superstructure on the known facts of the biography of eminent characters." Chafing at the inadequacy of bare facts, Brydges offers imaginative biographical explorations of a variety of people, from Petrarch to Charlotte Smith, from Charles Blount to Margaret Cavendish, Duchess of Newcastle. Readers are offered "imaginary conversations" between Samuel Daniel and the earl of Cumberland, between Horace Walpole and Thomas Gray, and between William Collins and Joseph Warton. There is much that is perceptive and lively in the two volumes, and the astuteness of Brydges's analysis of motive and emotion is frequently striking. When

the *Gentleman's Magazine* reviewed *Imaginative Biography* in its issue of January 1835 (not altogether favorably), the anonymous reviewer closed with a warm tribute to Brydges's "continued and zealous attachment to the literature of his country" and looked forward with some eagerness to Brydges's forthcoming biography of Milton. The critic observed that "from some pages in these volumes, we entertain no doubt of the judgment and temperance of opinion with which some difficult subjects connected with that biography will be discussed."

To note that Brydges's *Life of John Milton* might itself deserve the subtitle "an imaginative biography" is not to denigrate it. It is, rather, to point toward the essential nature and strategy of Brydges's most substantial and mature work of biography, unless his own autobiography is thought of as a rival for that title. He tells the reader that "all the facts of Milton's life have been laboriously

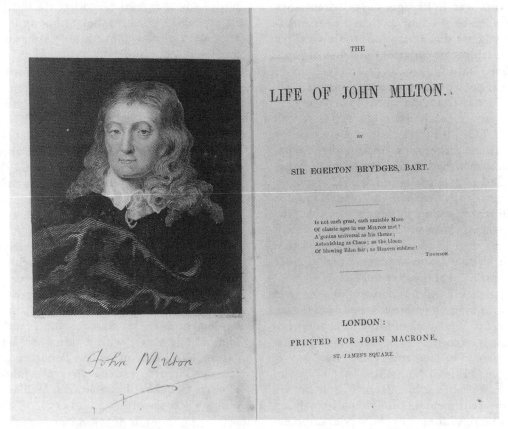

THE

LIFE OF JOHN MILTON.

BY

SIR EGERTON BRYDGES, BART.

Is not each great, each amiable Muse
Of classic ages in our MILTON met?
A genius universal as his theme;
Astonishing as Chaos; as the bloom
Of blowing Eden fair; as Heaven sublime!
                                                        THOMSON.

LONDON:
PRINTED FOR JOHN MACRONE,
ST. JAMES'S SQUARE.

Frontispiece and title page for the biography that was Brydges's last substantial work

searched for, and brought forward already: opinions upon them are not yet exhausted." What Brydges saw as the purpose of his biography, as the most relevant kind of opinion which had to be added to the facts, is clear from some of his prefatory remarks:

> Of a great poet's history we desire to know more than the leading facts, and the titles and dates of his works: we wish to know his private disposition, feelings, temper, habits, and manners. Milton's contemporaries have preserved little on these topics concerning him; and we are left to deduce them from incidental passages in his prose works, or from the tone and colour of his poems. Less in this way has been attempted by my predecessors in this task than seemed to me to be requisite. Perhaps I have been more copious in my own reflections and conjectures than many will approve; but if there is a raciness in my narrative – a freshness of tints, yet not over-coloured – a picture not dry, and barren, and faint; but distinct and prominent, yet natural – then I shall not have worked in vain.

In *The Romantics on Milton* (1970) Joseph Anthony Wittreich, Jr., notes that "Milton was, for the Romantics, a daring individualist who took his place outside the circle of conformists." As such, he naturally appealed to Brydges. In 1825, in *A Note on the Suppression of Memoirs announced by the author,* Brydges had presented himself as a man "sometimes . . . visited by the still small voice of genius, virtue and learning" who had been left "to struggle alone" by those who ought to have helped him; who had "been plotted against by treachery, fraud and corruption"; and who had been "persecuted and calumniated by the upstart power of hoary age." There was much in the story of Milton, particularly in the final years of his life, which struck a chord in the elderly Brydges.

Like many other Romantic critics and biographers, Brydges consciously wrote in reaction to the continuing influence of Samuel Johnson's "Life of Milton." Published in 1779 as part of the *Prefaces, Biographical and Critical, to the Works of the English Poets,* Johnson's account is in many ways unsympathetic to Milton. To many Romantic readers, such as Thomas de Quincey, Johnson's sketch appeared "a production grievously disfigured by prejudice" representative of "an odious spirit of malignity to Milton" (as quoted by Wittreich). For Brydges, too, Johnson's "Life of Milton" was characterized by "bad taste in literature [and] malignity of temper."

Johnson's work was, in Brydges's eyes, "derogatory to the unrivalled bard's fame, both as a poet and as a man." Brydges's dislike for Johnson's view led him to an intemperate judgment not just of Johnson's opinions but of his methods and techniques too: "There is not a particle of benevolence or candour in this furious and bitter piece of biography . . . nor is there any research; nor is the narrative well put together." Of Johnson's taste it is enough for Brydges to frame a rhetorical question as to what "rich and accomplished minds" can think of "him, who could find no true poetry in Lycidas." Brydges, who wrote more than two thousand sonnets in three years, could scarcely share Johnson's view that "the fabric of a sonnet, however adapted to the Italian language, has never succeeded in ours" and that only two of Milton's sonnets deserve the "slender commendation . . . that they are not bad."

With such a consideration of Johnson and other previous biographers of Milton, Brydges begins his own *Life*. The work of Milton's nephew Edward Phillips is, according to Brydges, the "foundation" for all would-be biographers of Milton, but he finds Phillips's "Life of Mr. Milton" (1694) "brief and bare" and wishes it had been written "in the amiable and sentimental, though half-gossiping style of old Isaac Walton." Brydges goes on to express his dissatisfaction, for various reasons, with the work of most of his other predecessors. Of Thomas Birch, for example (whose biographical notes introduced an edition of Milton's prose in 1738), Brydges says dismissively that he "was a laborious searcher into minute facts among original documents; but had neither the power of reflection, criticism, nor style." Thomas Newton's "Life" (1749) is called the work of a man of "excellent taste and judgement" but is found to be "languid and feeble." The *New Memoirs of the Life and Poetical Works of Mr John Milton* (1740), by Francis Peck, is said to be the work of "a mere antiquary; toilsome, but tasteless, frivolous, weak, and absurd." H. J. Todd's biography, prefaced to the first volume of his 1809 edition of Milton's poems, is similarly dismissed as excessively antiquarian and detailed, while the work of Charles Symmons (whose 1806 "Life" introduced an edition of Milton's prose) is judged to be coarse and heavy in style. Of a few other predecessors, notably Thomas Wharton (1785) and William Hayley (1794), Brydges is rather more generous. Yet it is clear that his own impulse to write his biography of Milton, insofar as his admiration for the poet was not a sufficient cause in itself, was his intense dislike of Johnson's "Life." He is disturbed that Johnson's work "by some strange chance, yet keeps its hold at least on part of the public," and in his preface he declares that "it has appeared to me not only a pleasure, but a duty, to endeavour to counteract its poison."

Brydges's "antidote" takes the form of an initial sixteen chapters of narrative and critical discussion organized along clear chronological lines; these occupy 183 of a total of 290 pages. They are succeeded by a further eleven chapters devoted to specific topics: some concern particular areas of Milton's work as a poet (on the sonnets, on *Paradise Regained,* and on *Samson Agonistes,* for example); others examine "The Merits of Milton Compared with Those of Other Poets" or contain "Observations on the Criticisms of 'Paradise Lost', by Addison and Johnson." In four appendixes Brydges addresses — in the best antiquarian fashion, though he had earlier used that word as a term of abuse — such matters as "The Family of Powell of Forest-Hill, Oxfordshire," "Descendants of Milton," and "Milton's Agreement with Mr Symons for Paradise Lost." The volume closes with a series of "Encomiastic Passages" on Milton, culled from the writings of Samuel Barrow, Andrew Marvell, John Dryden, Thomas Gray, William Collins, William Cowper, William Wordsworth, and others.

In his account of Milton's youth Brydges suggests that certain episodes and influences should be interpreted as "the preservatives of Milton's poetical genius against his *political* adoptions." He cites as examples Milton's connections with the countess of Derby and the earl of Bridgewater, and his Italian travels. This early suggestion of a tension between the poetical and the political inclinations is one that Brydges returns to several times. It proves a somewhat limiting strategy insofar as it precludes his seeking some sense of what united poetry and politics in Milton's mind, what gave the life and work the integrity they possess. Brydges sees Milton, in his years at Cambridge, as already torn between contrary impulses: "At this time . . . Milton's love of monarchical and aristocratical splendor was contending with his puritanic education, and his personal hatred of arbitrary power: his rich imagination and his stern judgement were at variance: his early poems rarely, if ever, touch upon sectarianism: Spenser and Shakespeare, courts, castles, and theatres, did not agree with Calvinistic rigours and formalities." The political realm, for Brydges, is necessarily wholly divorced from, and inferior to, the poetic. He declares himself entirely unable to understand, for example, how Milton could come "fresh" from all the artistic delights of Italy and "at once plunge into principles, which would destroy them all to the very root." Brydges comes close to suggesting that Milton's political involvement carried with it a punishment which effected a kind of "justice": "It is worthy of remark that as soon as Milton actively took the side of this cause of destruction, the Muses left him for twenty years." Milton's activities as secretary to the Council of State and as a controversialist are seen as his "evil days" because, in Brydges's eyes, they were of a sort guaranteed to "blind the imagination, and harden and embitter the heart." Brydges's Romantic conceptions of the poet and of poetic genius necessarily predispose him to believe that Milton could only have found his official duties irksome:

> How he must have fretted at the base intrigues of courts and councils, and the turpitudes of human ambition! — While immured within dark and close official walls, how he must have sighed and pined to be courting his splendid visions of a higher and more congenial world on the banks of some haunted stream! — The woods and forests, the mountains, seas, and lakes, ought to have been his dwelling-places. — The whispers of the spring, or the roaring of the winter-winds, ought to have soothed or excited his spirits. — In those regions aërial beings visit the earth; there the soul sees what the concourse of mankind puts to flight; there the mean passions, that corrupt the human bosom, have no abode.

In Milton's life after the Restoration, Brydges imagines him to have found, ironically, the conditions best fitted for the full articulation of this poetic genius. The life lived in poverty and solitude, as Brydges asserts Milton's to have been, is seen as peculiarly conducive to Milton's creative powers, since "the Muse can never live except feebly and languidly, amid material luxuries." Brydges, ever ready to speculate, feels sure that Milton must have achieved a greater happiness than he had known in the previous phase of his life: "Though now retired, neglected, and subject to many stings of disappointment, I doubt not he was altogether happier than when his mere memory, observation, and judgement were occupied in the coarse conflict of practical affairs." The governing conception of Brydges's Life is perhaps best located in this sense of a constant tension between the poetic and the practical. Milton's early years are seen as ones in which the two coexist in practice and in potential; his middle years are presented as being dominated by the political and practical; and his final years are characterized by a glorious return to his "true" poetical nature, outer "failure" being the cloak for inner triumph. One suspects that Brydges found consolation for his own limited popularity in the fact that Milton in his final years was able to disregard "the loud applause of the mob in favour of others." Milton was, for Brydges, "the greatest poet of our nation." That such an artist could have been the victim of relative neglect in his own time must have reassured Brydges that no great significance need be attached to the judgment of one's contemporaries in matters of literary achievement.

Brydges's critical accounts of individual poems are frequently of considerable interest; they include personal, committed, honest, and independent opinions. Of *Paradise Lost* he writes with particular skill of Milton's style, admiring what he thought of as a masculine sternness. Naturally Brydges is most attracted to all that is most Romantic in Milton. Such early poems as "L'Allegro" and "Il Penseroso" are, for Brydges, primarily of interest for the evidence they seem to him to offer of Milton's "love of nature, — of books, — of solitude, — of contemplation, — of all that is beautiful, and all that is romantic." Milton's creativity at its highest is understood as involving him in a kind of trance of inspiration: "While Milton was framing the 'Comus,' he, no doubt, lived in the midst of his own creation: he only clothed the tongues of his characters with what it appeared to him in his vision they actually spoke." It would be wrong, however, to imply that Brydges's method is always that of speculation, or that his Milton is always conceived of in such "unworldly" terms. The *Life* was written in Geneva, and Brydges made efforts, though unsuccessful, to gather information on Milton's visit to that city. He attempted an identification of the Deodati estate at the nearby village of Cologny, where Milton stayed.

Brydges's primary interest was in Milton's poetry. He also writes well of the prose, however, declaring it to constitute "a less explored, but not less magnificent domain." He quotes astutely and extensively from the prose, wherever there are items of direct biographical significance to be found. He appears to be the first biographer to quote in full the preface to the second book of *The Reason of Church Government*. All in all, Brydges's *Life of John Milton* is an impressive and sensitive piece of work. As Mark Longaker says, in his *English Biography in the Eighteenth Century* (1931), it is "more satisfactory for both thoroughness of information and for sympathetic character delineation than Johnson's brief *Life*." Beyond that it is a revealing testimony of much that is characteristic in the Romantic response to Milton. As Brydges's last substantial work it forms a fitting conclusion to a literary career which, even if it did not fulfill the high ambitions that Brydges had, was surely one of which most people could have been proud.

Brydges's work as a literary biographer is of two distinct types. His earlier work belongs firmly to the antiquarian tradition; his later writings are nearer to what one might think of as "intellectual biography." All phases of his work are informed, in necessarily different ways, by a love of poetry and a serious commitment to the effort to understand the nature of poetic genius. The mature Brydges was convinced of the intimate bond between writer and work, of the value of knowledge of the one as a means to the comprehension of the other. His own writing, including his work as a biographer, is fully expressive of his turbulent personality. As well as being a considerable biographer (most notably in his work on Byron and Milton), Brydges would be a rewarding subject for a modern biographer.

Biography:
Mary Katherine Woodworth, *The Literary Career of Sir Samuel Egerton Brydges* (Oxford: Blackwell, 1935).

References:
William Powell Jones, "New Light on Sir Egerton Brydges," *Harvard Library Bulletin,* 11 (1957): 102–116;

Jones, "Sir Egerton Brydges on Lord Byron," *Huntington Library Quarterly,* 13 (May 1950): 325–337;

Donald H. Reiman, Introduction to works by Brydges, in *Samuel Egerton Brydges and Edward Quillinan* (New York & London: Garland, 1978), pp. v–x.

Papers:
Collections of Brydges's papers are found in the British Library, London; the Houghton Library, Harvard University; the Bodleian Library, Oxford University; and the London Library.

James Currie

(31 May 1756 – 31 August 1805)

Leith Davis
Simon Fraser University

BOOKS: *A Letter, commercial and political, addressed to the Rt. Hon. William Pitt: in which the real Interests of Britain in the present crisis are considered, and some Observations are offered on the general State of Europe. By Jasper Wilson, Esq.* (London: Printed for G. G. J. & J. Robinsons, 1793);

Medical Reports, on the Effects of Water, Cold and Warm, as a Remedy in Fever, and Febrile Diseases; whether applied to the Surface of the Body, or used as a drink: with observations on the Nature of Fever; and on the Effects of opium, Alcohol, and inanition (Liverpool: Printed by J. M'Creery for Cadell & Davies, London, 1797; revised and enlarged edition, 2 volumes, London: Cadell & Davies, 1804; Philadelphia: Printed for James Humphreys, and for Benjamin & Thomas Kite, 1808).

OTHER: *The Works of Robert Burns; with an Account of his Life, and a Criticism on his Writings. To which are prefixed, some Observations on the Character and Condition of the Scottish Peasantry,* 4 volumes, edited, with an introduction and preface, by Currie (Liverpool: Printed by J. M'Creery for T. Cadell & W. Davies, London and W. Creech, Edinburgh, 1800; Philadelphia: Printed by Budd & Bartram for Thomas Dobson, 1801); revised and enlarged by Gilbert Burns (London: Cadell & Davies, 1820).

SELECTED PERIODICAL PUBLICATIONS –
UNCOLLECTED: "Commentary on *Essays on the Active Powers of Man* by Thomas Reid," *Analytical Review,* 1 (June 1778): 145–153, 521–529; 2 (November 1778): 265–270, 549–558;

"The African," anonymous [by Currie and William Roscoe], *World* (March 1788);

"The Recluse" [essay series], anonymous [by Currie and Roscoe], *Liverpool Weekly Herald,* 1790.

James Currie edited the first collection of the complete works of Robert Burns; he undertook the project primarily to raise money for Burns's widow and children. Along with the poems and letters of the poet, Currie provided a biography of Burns, in which he posited that the poet suffered from alcoholism and chronic melancholy. Currie died five years after the publication of this work and so did not realize the negative impact that it had on Burns's reputation. Charles Lamb found Currie "well-meaning" but a bad writer. Lamb advised, "*ne sutor ultra crepidam*" (let the cobbler stick to his rattling). William Wordsworth faulted Currie for his presentation of Burns's dissipation and suggested that Currie might have done well to have followed Burns's own dictum: "Who made the heart, 'tis *he* alone / Decidedly can try us." Currie's justification for including an account of Burns's failings is seen in his 8 February 1797 letter to John Syme: "The errors and faults, as well as the excellencies, of Burns' life and character, afford scope for painful and melancholy observation. This part of the subject must be touched with great tenderness; but it must be touched. If his friends do not touch it, his enemies will."

James Currie was born on 31 May 1756 in Kirkpatrick Fleming, Dumfriesshire. His father was minister of the parish, and James attended the lessons his father taught until the family moved in 1762 to Middlebie, where James continued his early education. Years later he described to a friend the awakening of his childhood passion for adventure. A relative of his father who had returned in 1763

James Currie

from serving in North America used to regale the Currie family with battle stories. Young James Currie set off one day "in hot pursuit" of a flock of geese which he had designated the French enemy. In the course of his game he charged over a bank into a bog. Upon returning home he was forced to tell the story of his mishap and was reprimanded by his father by being given a copy of Miguel de Cervantes' *Don Quixote* (1605) to read. According to William Wallace Currie, Currie later commented that, although the book proved a corrective to his impulsive behavior, "I never lost, and probably shall never lose, the influence of the early impressions which were made upon my mind." Accordingly, Currie's biography of Burns reflects both his admiration of the poet's boisterous nature and his disapproval of Burns's rashness. Other early impressions also had a profound effect on Currie. When he was eight he spent a year at Elderbeck with family friends. He attributed his love for nature and his sensibility – two characteristics he was

later to ascribe to Burns – to his experiences at that time. In order to spare him the pain of seeing his mother dying from consumption, Currie's father sent him to Dumfries to study with Dr. George Chapman in 1769. A schoolmate inadvertently informed Currie of his mother's death on the day he was supposed to sit a public exam before the presbytery and magistrates, and so he was unable to present his address. After his mother's death Currie remained with Chapman.

Fulfillment of his dream of adventure came in 1771, when he persuaded his father, who had intended that Currie study medicine, to let him sail to North America as an apprentice bookkeeper to William Cunninghame and Company, tobacco merchants from Glasgow. Currie settled at Cabin Point, Virginia, on the James River but soon afterward contracted the endemic fever that plagued him continually during his time there. Two years later his father died, and Currie, anxious about the welfare of his seven sisters but unable to support them on

36

~~[crossed out]~~ by the sailors calling
the watch at four o'clock — pleasing illusion —
a brisk trade wind —

    Saturday Octr 26th. Rose early —
the pain in my back returned tho' not very severe —
Quite weary of the voyage, & inclined to be splenetic —
No amusement — no books — no society — Played at
Backgammon as formerly — A fine trade wind from
the East — found ourselves at twelve o'clock in Lati-
tude 21° 10' North — A charming moonlight night.
Slept on Deck all the first watch, & got wet all over —
with a sea the Sloop ship'd —

    Sunday Octr 27th 1776 — Read the
book of Job in the forenoon — about 12 o'clock discover'd
a Ship to the leeward, steering due west, she lower'd her
topsails to give us an opportunity of speaking with her,
& hoisted French Colours, but as Capt Bryon did not
chuse to alter his course, we passed her without speaking her — Read the Song of Solomon in the afternoon — ~~[crossed out]~~
~~[crossed out]~~
~~[crossed out]~~
~~[crossed out]~~
~~[crossed out]~~ Great many of the images
in our modern love songs seem to have been borrow'd from it,
& particularly the principal beautys of Fixed Side, which
in my opinion is the finest song in our language, are

his salary, handed over his share of his father's inheritance to them.

Currie's letters to home during his time in Virginia indicate his growing apprehension regarding the unrest in the colonies and his concern about how political turmoil would affect the tobacco trade with Glasgow. He submitted to the *Virginia Gazette* a letter defending the Scots in North America. Published in the 23 March 1775 edition of the *Gazette,* Currie's letter purports to be from "an old gray headed fellow" who has lived in Virginia for twenty years. This "Scotchman" notes the prejudices of the English Virginians who accuse the Scots of unfair trading practices and Loyalist sympathies. He suggests that much of this animosity derives from people "blinded by selfish passions," and he advocates understanding and tolerance for all.

In March 1776 Currie obtained permission from the Convention of Virginia to return to Great Britain, but three days after he had embarked, the British vessel on which he was a passenger was seized. After being forced off the ship, Currie found his way back to Richmond, Virginia. He twice avoided being drafted into the Colonial army by paying a ten-pound fee. A later attempt to leave the colonies was precluded when another ship he was on was seized. Accusations of conspiracy were leveled against Currie and other passengers on the vessel, and they were required to travel by open boat to Edenton, North Carolina, and then to Nixonton. Eventually Currie left on board an American vessel, the *Betsy,* which was carrying cargo to the West Indies. Currie's journal indicates that he occupied himself during the six weeks of this journey by reading the Bible, John Home's play *Douglas* (1756), poetry by Joseph Addison, works by Jonathan Swift, and his own father's letters, which he admired for "the elegance of the diction, the beauty and tenderness of the sentiments, the excellence of their precepts, and the spirit of paternal regard and of true piety, which run through the whole." He arrived on the island of Saint Martin, received his pay for delivering the cargo, and worked in Antigua and Saint Eustatius for three months. But he lost all his profits, was struck again with fever, and at last, entrusted as a courier, sailed for Great Britain in February 1777. Due to storms he did not arrive in Deptford until 2 May, too late to collect the one hundred guineas promised to him upon successful completion of his mission.

Influenced perhaps by recollections of his father, Currie returned to Edinburgh in May 1777 and enrolled at the university to study medicine. At the same time he carried his literary and philosophical interests further. He was particularly intrigued by the philosophy of the human mind and wrote a commentary in 1778 on the *Essays on the Active Powers of Man,* by Thomas Reid, for the *Analytical Review.*

Currie completed his medical degree at the University of Glasgow, where exams were scheduled earlier than at the University of Edinburgh, and prepared to immigrate to take a position in Jamaica. But by the time he reached London, the position had been given to another man. Coinciding with the turmoil in his own life, the Gordon Riots which erupted in that city affected him deeply. He published letters advocating tolerance in the *Public Advertiser* (15 and 28 August 1780).

Currie moved to Liverpool in October 1780 on the advice of friends and started a practice at the Liverpool Infirmary. He also revived the Liverpool Literary Society and struck up what was to be a lasting friendship with William Roscoe. Roscoe, a politician as well as a writer and biographer himself (*The Life of Lorenzo de Medici, called the Magnificent,* 1795), later gave Currie advice and encouragement for the Burns project.

The unpublished "Dialogue on Melancholy," which Currie called "the best thing I ever wrote," dates from 1781. It presents a philosophical debate between the narrator and a character called Philocles. When the narrator offers his opinion that melancholy is a destructive state, Philocles intervenes with his own story. When he was sixteen, he relates, his inspiration and ideal was a woman named Ophelia. Their friendship lapsed when he reached maturity, but he renewed his acquaintance with her shortly before her death from consumption. Philocles suggests that his recurrent melancholy regarding her fate is in fact a positive influence because "where firmness of spirit and steadiness of judgment are united to tenderness of heart and delicacy of feeling, the melancholy which depends on these qualities will form the best ornament and support of virtue; and though it may incapacitate the possessor to shine in the circles of the great or the gay, it will give him an internal source of enjoyment which cannot be done away, and enable him to diffuse a charm over the scenes of domestic happiness." The effect of melancholy and the relationship between mind and body were subjects to which Currie returned often. The paper he presented upon being elected an honorary member of the Philosophical and Literary Society of Manchester concerned hypochondriasis considered as a mental as well as bodily affliction. Currie expressed a concern that the paper might be "rather metaphysical."

Currie married Lucy Wallace, the daughter of an Irish merchant, William Wallace, in Liverpool on 9 January 1783. He developed pleurisy the next year, traveled to Bristol for his health, and consulted with Erasmus Darwin. Currie's account of his case is published in Darwin's *Zoonomia, or the Laws of Organic Life* (1794–1796).

When he returned to Liverpool, Currie became involved in the abolition of slavery. The commerce of Liverpool depended heavily on the slave trade, so by adopting an abolitionist position, Currie was putting the success of his business at risk. In March 1788 he published anonymously with Roscoe a poem, "The African," in the *World*, a London newspaper. The poem presents the lamentations of a slave being transported to America who chooses to drown himself rather than live in misery.

Currie and Roscoe also joined forces to write a series of twenty essays under the title "The Recluse," which was published in the *Liverpool Weekly Herald* in 1790. The essays present the musings of a solitary aged man on such issues as the transience of material life and the benefits of delivering advice anonymously in print. Currie's literary and medical work won him the honor of being elected a fellow of the Royal Society in 1792. He subsequently purchased an estate in Dumfries, Scotland. It was on a visit to the estate in the same year that Currie had his first and only interview with Burns.

In June 1793 Currie published *A Letter, commercial and political, addressed to the Rt. Hon. William Pitt: in which the real Interests of Britain in the present crisis are considered, and some Observations are offered on the general State of Europe* under the name Jasper Wilson. The letter, in pamphlet form, attacks Pitt for his refusal to entertain French offers of peace. It also blames the origin of economic calamities on "the prevalence and extension of the war-system throughout Europe, supported, as it has been, by the universal adoption of the funding-system." As a result of the letter Currie found himself being assailed as a Jacobin and traitor to his country. He stayed out of politics for the remainder of his life. His biography of Burns takes pains to discount the rumors of Burns's antigovernment sentiments.

Currie's next publication, *Medical Reports, on the Effects of Water, Cold and Warm, as a Remedy in Fever, and Febrile Diseases* (1797), advocates the use of water to treat fever. The book is designed to be of use in institutions and on ships, places where "the usual means for prevention or cure are necessarily limited, and the imminence of the danger requires a remedy that operates with speed as well as efficacy." The case studies in the book include the shipwreck of an American vessel in the Irish Sea in

1790, an epidemic at the Liverpool Infirmary in 1787, and an ancient battle involving troops of Alexander the Great. From information on these cases and from his own experiments Currie derives the best measures for treatment. In the early stages of fever, he advises, the patient should be treated with cold water poured over the body. Later the fever should be reduced by bathing with lukewarm water. Throughout the treatment the patient should be required to drink large quantities of cold water.

While Currie was busy preparing his *Medical Reports* for publication, he took on the gargantuan task of editing and compiling Burns's poetry and letters. Currie became the official biographer more by default than by any natural affinity for the task. In 1787 he had been given a copy of Burns's poems by John Moore, author of *Zeluco* (1786) and biographer of Tobias Smollett, and became an ardent admirer of Burns. After Burns's death Currie helped raise a subscription fund for Burns's widow and children, after corresponding on the matter with Syme, whom Currie knew through college. At this time Currie offered his assistance in preparing a biography of the poet. Dugald Steward and Maria Riddell were first considered for the task, but eventually Burns's friends agreed on Currie. It took Currie almost four years to compile and edit the materials he was given: manuscripts and letters which were unsorted and, as Currie remarked, were "sent, with all their sins on their heads to meet the eye of an entire stranger." At one point he threatened to abandon the project, but a visit by Syme and Gilbert Burns convinced him to continue. In the book Currie notes the delicacy of his own undertaking: "In relating the incidents of his life, candour will prevent us from dwelling invidiously on those failings which justice forbids us to conceal; we will tread lightly over his yet warm ashes, and respect the laurels that shelter his untimely grave."

Volume one includes Currie's "Observations on the Scottish Peasantry" and the "Life of Burns." Volume two contains the "General Correspondence of Burns." Volume three features "Burns's Published and Additional Poems," while volume four includes "Burns's Letters to George Thomson and Additional Songs."

Currie's prefatory remarks in the first volume cover such topics as religion and education among the Scots, the absence of poor laws in Scotland, Scottish music and national songs, Scottish laws respecting marriage, and the "domestic and national attachments" of the Scots. Currie claimed that these observations on the character and condition of the Scottish peasantry were designed to help the reader

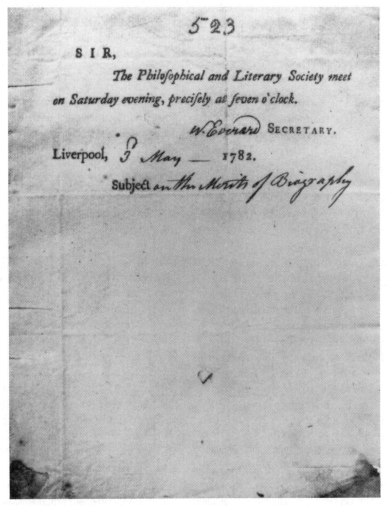

Notice of a lecture on "The Merits of Biography," which Currie attended on
3 May 1782 (City of Liverpool Public Libraries)

unfamiliar with Scottish people "form a more correct notion of the advantages with which he [Burns] started, and of the obstacles which he surmounted." At the end of the first volume Currie also provides a brief history of Scottish literature for the reader unfamiliar with the subject.

Currie builds his biographical sketch of Burns from the poet's own comments in letters and his commonplace book and from the observations of Burns's acquaintances. Currie paints a picture of Burns as a rustic genius who encountered much hardship in life. Letters from Burns's tutor, his friends, and his brother, Gilbert, are included to give the likeness of the real man. One of Currie's major concerns is to emphasize the extraordinary sensibility of Burns. A friend's account of Burns's response to the Highland scenery proves to Currie that "the imagination of Burns was constantly excited by the wild and sublime scenery." Neverthe-

less, Currie points out the dangers of sensibility, particularly among the poor or, in Burns's case, among those who lack a strong willpower: "delicacy of taste, though the source of many pleasures, is not without some disadvantages."

Currie notes that Burns was greatly distressed by the accusations brought against him by the government during the last stage of his life when he worked at the Excise. Although the accusations of Burns's Jacobinic sympathies were dismissed, the fiasco prevented Burns from being further promoted. But in Currie's assessment Burns's collapse was not a result of his persecution by government administration. Such troubles only "robbed the imagination of our poet of the last prop on which his hopes of independence rested," and "aggravated those excesses which were soon to conduct him to an untimely grave." Burns's own weakness for alcohol, Currie suggests, finally caused his death. Currie's final assessment of Burns provides an indication of what Lamb described as Currie's inclusion of "pathological and *medical* discussions":

> Though by nature of an athletic form, Burns had in his constitution the peculiarities and the delicacies that belong to the temperament of genius. He was liable, from a very early period of life, to that interruption in the process of digestion, which arises from deep and anxious thought, and which is sometimes the effect, and sometimes the cause of depression of spirits. Connected with this disorder of the stomach, there was a disposition to headache, affecting more especially the temples and eyeballs, and frequently accompanied by violent and irregular movements of the heart. Endowed by nature with great sensibility of nerves, Burns was, in his corporeal, as well as in his mental system, liable to inordinate impressions; to fever of body, as well as of mind. This predisposition to disease, which strict temperance in diet, regular exercise, and sound sleep, might have subdued, habits of a very different nature strengthened and inflamed. Perpetually stimulated by alkohol [*sic*] in one or other of its various forms, the inordinate actions of the circulating system became at length habitual; the process of nutrition was unable to supply the waste, and the powers of life began to fail.

Currie builds to an evangelical cadenza, worthy of one of his father's sermons: "He who suffers the pollution of inebriation, how shall he escape other pollutions?" However, he recovers his decorum, concluding: "But let us refrain from the mention of error over which delicacy and humanity draw the veil."

Two thousand copies of the first edition of Currie's *The Works of Robert Burns* (1800) were printed, costing £1 11s. 6d. for the set. The popularity of the works is evident from the fact that three more printings in Britain alone were needed within the next three years. A total of £1,300 was raised for Mrs. Burns, and Currie notes with satisfaction in one of his letters that all Burns's surviving sons had been provided with jobs.

Currie died of heart failure on 31 August 1805 at Sidmouth, where he is buried. He left behind six children. His son William Wallace Currie published a two-volume biography of his father (1831) which was intended to counter the accusations Gilbert Burns was then leveling against James Currie.

The second edition of *The Works of Robert Burns* (1801) includes a letter from Gilbert Burns approving the biography of his brother, but Gilbert was later to think differently. After Currie's death and after the copyright of the original work ran out in 1815, Gilbert sought to republish *The Works of Robert Burns* in a manner more sympathetic to Burns's reputation. Through James Gray, the master of the grammar school at Dumfries, Gilbert asked for the

advice of Wordsworth. Wordsworth's response to Gray, titled *A Letter to a Friend of Robert Burns: Occasioned by an Intended Republication of the Account of the Life of Burns, by Dr Currie; and of the Selection Made by Him from His Letters,* was published in pamphlet form in 1816. Wordsworth suggested positioning the letters before the biographical sketch in the new edition and providing notes correcting any misrepresentations. Gilbert Burns acted on this last recommendation but not on the first, and he produced a revised and enlarged edition of the works in 1820, with additional notes and an appendix. In his letter Wordsworth concurs with Currie's assessment of Burns's weaknesses, but he upbraids Currie for making them public and "revealing to the world the infirmities of the author." Lamb went further in his criticism, commenting that the biography is "very confusedly and badly written."

Currie has been blamed by other critics for his distortions of Burns's manuscripts. His adjustments of Burns's writing reflect his own sensitivity about bawdiness and political radicalness. For example, Currie tried to downplay Burns's association with the ribald *Merry Muses of Caledonia* (circa 1800). Whereas, in a letter to John M. Murdo dated December 1793, Burns comments on the *Merry Muses,* "I think I once mentioned something of a collection of Scots songs I have for some years been making," Currie, in his editorial process, added the phrase "A very few of them are my own," downplaying Burns's contribution. Similarly, Currie attempted to avert the accusation that Burns was sympathetic to the French Revolution by deleting the phrase "the rights of man" from Burns's letter to the *Evening Courant* published on 9 February 1789. J. W. Egerer comments that Currie was not "fitted to edit" the material and that as a result of his personal concerns he "forfeited the best opportunity that any editor has ever had to establish a definitive text." Robert Donald Thornton treats Currie's inaccuracies more sympathetically, suggesting that his main concern was to raise money for Burns's family. In fairness to Currie it must also be pointed out that procedures for editing were certainly not standard at the time he undertook his project.

More recent assessments of Currie have focused on his influence in forming the canon of Burns criticism. Carol McGuirk observes that "virtually every moralizing posture and mythic obliquity in the critical heritage" of Burns originated in Currie's edition of the works. In assessing the impact of Currie's biography of Burns, however, it is necessary to keep in mind that Currie was writing not just about one man but about the Scottish nation. As an expatriate Scot, he noted with distress the public inclination subsequent to Burns's death to blame the Scots for apathy toward the poet during his lifetime. Currie was concerned to counteract the "bitter invectives against Scotland, &c. which the extraordinary attractions and melancholy fate of the poet naturally provoke" in England. Consequently, almost half the material in the first volume is devoted to praising Scottish culture, law, and religion. More important, Currie's biographical sketch of Burns places the responsibility for the poet's fate on Burns himself, not on the nation he represented.

Biography:

William Wallace Currie, *Memoir of the Life, Writings, and Correspondence of James Currie, M.D. F.R.S of Liverpool,* 2 volumes (London: Printed for Longmans, 1831).

Bibliography:

J. W. Egerer, *A Bibliography of Robert Burns* (Edinburgh & London: Oliver & Boyd, 1964).

References:

William Findlay, *Robert Burns and the Medical Profession* (London: Alexander Gardner, 1898);

Donald Low, ed., *Robert Burns: The Critical Heritage* (London & Boston: Routledge & Kegan Paul, 1974);

Carol McGuirk, "The Politics of *The Collected Burns,*" in *Gairfish Discovery* (Bridge of Weir, Scotland: Gairfish, 1991), pp. 36–50;

Duncan M'Naught, "Dr. Currie and His Biography of Burns," *Annual Burns Chronicle and Club Directory* (1919): 5–34;

Robert Donald Thornton, *James Currie, The Entire Stranger, and Robert Burns* (Edinburgh & London: Oliver & Boyd, 1963);

William Wordsworth, "A Letter to A Friend of Robert Burns," in *The Prose Works of William Wordsworth,* 3 volumes, edited by W. J. B. Owen and Jane Worthington Smyser (Oxford: Clarendon Press, 1974), III: 111–136.

Papers:

Some of Currie's papers, including "The Journal kept by Dr. James Currie during a voyage from Nixonton, N. Carolina, to the Island of St Martin's, 1766," are at the City of Liverpool Public Libraries; the National Library of Scotland has many of Currie's letters.

Thomas Davies

(1712? – 13 April 1785)

William Over
Saint John's University

BOOKS: *Love Verses,* anonymous (London: Printed for T. Davies, 1761);

A Catalogue of Valuable and Curious Books, Including Several Libraries and Collections Purchased at Home and Abroad (London: Printed for T. Davies, 1769);

The Characters of George the First, Queen Caroline, Sir Robert Walpole, Mr. Pulteney, Lord Hardwicke, Mr. Fox, and Mr. Pitt, Reviewed. With Royal and Noble Anecdotes: and a Sketch of Lord Chesterfield's Character (London: Printed for T. Davies & T. Cadell, 1777);

A Genuine Narrative of the Life and Theatrical Transactions of Mr. John Henderson, Commonly called the Bath Roscius (London: Printed for T. Evans & sold by S. Leacroft, 1777);

Memoirs of the Life of David Garrick, Esq. Interspersed with Characters and Anecdotes of His Theatrical Contemporaries. The Whole Forming a History of the Stage . . . , 2 volumes (London: Printed for the author & sold at his shop, 1780);

Dramatic Micellanies [sic]: *Consisting of Critical Observations on Several Plays of Shakespeare . . . With Anecdotes of Dramatic Poets, Actors, &c.,* 3 volumes (London: Printed for the author & sold at his shop, 1783–1784); republished as *Dramatic Miscellanies . . .* (London: Printed for the author & sold at his shop, 1785).

OTHER: *The Works of William Browne . . . With the Life of the Author,* 3 volumes, edited, with a preface, by Davies (London: Printed for T. Davies, 1772);

The Poetical Works of Sir John Davies, edited, with a preface, by Thomas Davies (London: Printed for T. Davies, 1773);

Miscellaneous and Fugitive Pieces, 3 volumes, includes contributions by Davies (London: Printed for T. Davies, 1773–1774);

The Works of Dr. John Eachard . . . with Some Account of the Life and Writings of the Author, 3 volumes, edited, with a preface, by Davies (London: Printed for T. Davies, 1774);

The Works of George Lillo; With Some Account of his Life, 2 volumes, edited, with a preface, by Davies (London: Printed for T. Davies, 1775);

The Dramatic Works of Philip Massinger complete . . . with . . . a Short Essay on the Life and Writings, 4 volumes, edited, with a preface, by Davies (London: Printed for T. Davies, T. Payne & Son, L. Davis, J. Nichols, T. Evans, W. Davis & H. Payne, 1779);

John Downes, *Roscius Anglicanus, or, An Historical Review of the Stage . . . With Additions,* by the Late Mr. Thomas Davies, edited by F. G. Waldron (London: Printed for the editor, 1789).

Mentioned throughout James Boswell's *Life of Samuel Johnson* (1791) as a dinner and tavern companion, publishing adviser, actor, and friend to both Johnson and Boswell, Thomas Davies earned public esteem as both a biographer and publisher. The popular success of his biography about a well-known actor and manager, *Memoirs of the Life of David Garrick* (1780), ran through four printings and inspired other anecdotal collections and memoirs about actors; then it became the model for a second, more fully developed biography of Garrick by Arthur Murphy (1801). Davies's literary merit, however, was often underestimated or taken for granted. Throughout the 1770s his small publishing house and bookshop at 8 Russell Street, Covent Garden, produced important editions of works by English poets and playwrights, together with biographies of British stage figures. Conscientious in his plan to help publish a comprehensive body of English literature, Davies referred to himself in one advertisement as "the Bookseller who has employed himself in reviving the noblest monuments of the Dead." Part of this ambitious plan involved affixing a life of the author to most books, which detailed the chief events of his life and evaluated the significance of that writer in the literary world. These sketches would extend to several dozen pages or ap-

Thomas Davies

pear in a three- to four-page encapsulated form as a preface. Davies's editions were greatly appreciated by the literati for several decades after his death. William Hazlitt had particular regard for the thoughtfulness, comprehensiveness, and correctness of these complete works.

Johnson's high estimation of Davies led to his furnishing valuable material to him concerning the first years of Garrick's life in Lichfield, where Johnson and Garrick had spent their early years and attended school. In 1777 Davies became one of three distinguished London publishers deputed to convince Johnson to undertake his *Prefaces, Biographical and Critical, to the Works of the English Poets* (1779, 1781). Boswell expressed his regard for Davies directly: "his literary performances had no inconsiderable share of merit" (*The Life of Johnson*). But perhaps Boswell praised Davies best when he admitted dependence on Davies's diligent collections for many sayings and anecdotes of Johnson: "Tom was remarkably attentive to the most minute circumstance about Johnson." Boswell's *Life of Johnson*, of course, contains dialogues and stories from Davies's observations. Indicative of his contemporary influence is the fact that Davies introduced Boswell to Johnson in a 1763 meeting that has become legendary. In addition Davies encouraged Boswell in his

plan to follow up the first meeting by calling on Johnson at his chambers in the Inner Temple. Davies also arranged Boswell's introduction to Oliver Goldsmith during the same period.

Little is known of Davies's family, although his friend John Campbell described him as "a gentleman dealing in books," rather than simply as a bookseller. Born about 1712, Davies attended the University of Edinburgh (1728–1729) but was attracted to the stage, where he performed in London. He played the original role of Wilmot in George Lillo's domestic tragedy *The Fatal Curiosity* (1736) at the Haymarket Theatre, an experience he would draw on years later when writing his biography of Lillo. Shortly after, Davies began bookselling, first at a shop in Duke's Court, London, then at Round Court, but he "met with misfortunes in trade," according to John Nichols. During this period Davies's interest in writing increased. In his own words (as quoted by Nichols) he published "a silly pamphlet" in 1742 after "I was smit with the desire of turning Author." He then returned to the stage. In 1746 Davies played, for his benefit performance, the role of Pierre in a revival of Thomas Otway's *Venice Preserved* (1682) at Covent Garden. Becoming an itinerant actor, Davies performed at York, where he married the actress Susanna Yarrow, who was from a York acting family. Later Davies performed in Edinburgh, where he appears to have been an actor/manager, playing Romeo, Richard III, and other roles. However, a production dispute developed wherein he was accused of monopolizing the best parts. In Dublin, Davies performed several plays with his wife. He came to Drury Lane Theatre, London, as a replacement actor in 1753 and acted with Garrick, among others. Davies remained on the London stage with his wife for several years "in good estimation with the Town, and played many characters, if not with excellence, at least with propriety and decency," according to Nichols.

The Johnsonian circle of literati was also struck by the high moral example set by Thomas and Susanna Davies as theater personalities. In *Dramatic Miscellanies* (first published as *Dramatic Micellanies* [sic], 1783–1784; corrected, 1785) Davies writes modestly of himself playing Gloucester in William Shakespeare's *King Lear*: "the candour of the audience gave him much more encouragement than he expected." According to Johnson, Davies left the stage and resumed bookselling at 8 Russell Street subsequent to a slight published in Charles Churchill's *Rosciad* (1761):

> With him came mighty Davies. On my life
> That Davies hath a very pretty wife;
> Statesman all over – in plots famous drawn
> He mouths a sentence as ours mouth a drove.

An open letter in response was published in September 1761, which, according to Nichols, was written by another "comedian of inferior talents." In a letter to Garrick in 1763, however, Davies claimed that he left the stage on account of Garrick's unkindness, "who at rehearsals took all imaginable pains to make me unhappy." Wounded pride and impetuosity might indeed have motivated Davies's decision to quit the stage, since Johnson claimed that Davies and Susanna received five hundred pounds annually from acting and commented, "But what a man is he, who is to be driven from the stage by a line?" (quoted by Boswell). Whatever the problem, Davies continued to act for a few years after resuming bookselling in 1762. That same year he met the newly arrived Boswell through the biographer Samuel Derrick. Boswell found that Davies "increased my impatience . . . to see the extraordinary man [Johnson] whose works I highly valued." After Davies made repeated attempts to introduce Boswell to Johnson, they met on 16 May 1763 in the back parlor of Davies's bookshop. Boswell's *Life of Samuel Johnson* was published on the same day twenty-eight years later. Boswell once commented that he never

passed Davies's shop without mixed feelings of nostalgia and regret.

During the 1770s Davies began his major endeavor to republish noted British authors of the past. Isaac D'Israeli in *The Calamity of Authors* (1812) commented, "We owe to the late Thomas Davies . . . beautiful editions of some of our elder poets, which are now eagerly sought after, yet, though all of his publications were of the best kinds, and are of increasing value, the taste of Davies twice ended in bankruptcy." Hazlitt called Davies's *The Works of William Browne* (1772) "the only modern edition of value." Davies's biographical research on Browne was based on information sent him from Emanuel College, Cambridge, and, according to Hazlitt, was enhanced by "distinguished scholars," who were perhaps Richard Farmer and Thomas Warton, and the marginal notes – found by Davies in some manuscripts of Browne – by the Reverend William Thompson of Queens College, Oxford. Davies also mentioned assistance from the keeper of the Bodleian Library, Oxford, for certain poems in manuscript. The short biographical sketch on Browne seems to have been written entirely by Davies. *The Works of Dr. John Eachard* (1774) also includes a life of the author, wherein Davies states his preference for Eachard as satirist and critic over Jonathan Swift, who "turns his pen too frequently into a scalping-knife, and makes his wit the executioner of his ill-nature." Davies, apparently in financial distress, published *Miscellaneous and Fugitive Pieces* (1773–1774), in three volumes, advertised as "by the author of The Rambler." This work included writings mostly by Johnson without his knowledge and consent, and unacknowledged additions by Garrick, Goldsmith, and others. When it was brought to Johnson's attention after his return from Scotland, he showed little indignation toward Davies's unethical action: "I will . . . storm and bluster myself a little this time" (quoted by Hester Lynch [Thrale] Piozzi in *Anecdotes*, 1786). Making a special trip to London to confront Davies "in all the wrath he could muster," Johnson later commented, "I was a fierce fellow, and pretended to be very angry, and Thomas was a good-natured fellow, and pretended to be very sorry. . . . I believe the dog loves me dearly."

The Works of George Lillo; With Some Account of His Life (1775) includes a lengthy biography of the playwright, whom Davies had known as a young actor in rehearsal. On the title page Davies describes himself as "Bookseller to the Royal Academy." *A Genuine Narrative of the Life and Theatrical Transactions of Mr. John Henderson, Commonly Called the*

MEMOIRS
OF THE
LIFE
OF
DAVID GARRICK, ESQ.
INTERSPERSED WITH
Characters and Anecdotes
OF
HIS THEATRICAL CONTEMPORARIES.
THE WHOLE FORMING
A HISTORY OF THE STAGE,
WHICH INCLUDES A PERIOD OF THIRTY-SIX YEARS.

BY THOMAS DAVIES.

——Quem populus Romanus meliorem virum quam histrionem
esse arbitratur, qui ita dignissimus est scena propter artificium, ut
dignissimus sit curia propter abstinentiam.
CICERO pro Q. Roscio Comœdo.

A NEW EDITION,
WITH AMPLE ADDITIONS AND ILLUSTRATIONS,
IN THE FORM OF NOTES.

IN TWO VOLUMES.
VOL. I.

LONDON:
PRINTED FOR LONGMAN, HURST, REES, AND ORME,
PATERNOSTER ROW.
1808.

*Title page for a nineteenth-century edition of Davies's biography
of the best-known British actor and stage manager of the
eighteenth century*

Bath Roscius (1777) went through three printings in one year. (Henderson, a leading actor and sometime poet, was considered Garrick's successor on the London stage before Henderson's untimely death.) However, by 1778 the bookselling and publishing concern Davies had conceived with high standards went bankrupt (probably after years of financial woes), an event which prompted this newspaper verse: "For bankrupts write, when ruined shops are shut, As maggots crawl from out a perish'd nut" (as reported by Boswell). Johnson solicited money from mutual friends to rescue Davies's possessions, and Davies himself asked friends for five-guinea notes to redeem household furnishings. Johnson's chief contribution to Davies's financial recovery was his scheme to have Davies write a biography of Garrick for which Johnson would supply details and observations of Lichfield and the chief personalities they both knew in early life. *Memoirs of the Life of David Garrick*

(1780) begins with an epigram supplied by Johnson: "All excellence has a right to be recorded." Johnson also convinced Garrick's successor, Richard Brinsley Sheridan, then manager of Drury Lane, to give Davies a benefit performance. Davies then performed for the first time the role of Fainall in William Congreve's *The Way of the World* (1700) in 1778 and dedicated his first edition of *Garrick* to Sheridan. Davies's short biography of Philip Massinger in the first volume of *The Dramatic Works of Philip Massinger complete* (1779) was dedicated to Johnson for "his universal and active benevolence," an acknowledgement of his supervision of Davies's financial recovery. The popularity of *Garrick* encouraged Davies to write *Dramatic Miscellanies.*

As a respected London bookseller, a member of "The Trade," as they were known in London, Davies attended regular weekly social meetings with other booksellers and literati at the Devil Tavern, Temple Bar, and later at the Grecian Coffeehouse. After several years this club met only monthly at the Shakespeare. Included in the company were William Davenhill, a Cornhill bookseller; William Davis from Picadilly; Nichols the writer; and Thomas Evans, a Strand bookseller. Nichols described Davies's social manner as engaging: his "lively sallies of pleasantry were certain to entertain his friends by harmless merriment." Davies was conscious of his relation to the great literary figures of his day; in *Dramatic Miscellanies* he remarks of himself that he "was through life a companion of his superiors." Johnson's humorous observation (as reported by Nichols), that Davies had "learning enough to give credit to a clergyman," reflected a common opinion of Davies among Johnson's acquaintances. However, he was respected as both a publisher and an authority on the theater. Boswell, for example, depended on Davies's *Garrick* for knowledge of the increased interest in William Shakespeare among the middle classes and women during the first half of the eighteenth century. Boswell also respected Davies's ability to record dialogue and observe behavior. Davies's description in *Garrick* of Johnson's candor reveals this quality: "I never knew any man, but one, who had the honour and courage to confess that he had a tincture of envy in him. He [Johnson] . . . generously owed that he was not a stranger to it; at the same time he declared that he endeavored to subdue it." As a frequent dinner companion of the Johnsonian circle, Davies was the butt of many witticisms among his literary friends. Topham Beauclerk thought nothing more humiliating than to be "clapped on the back by Tom Davies" (quoted by J. L. Smith-Dampier). Still Johnson found him consoling and entertaining: "I know not whom I can see, that will bring more amusement on his tongue or more kindness in his heart." Johnson came to confide in both Susanna and Thomas Davies. According to Boswell, he "esteemed them, and lived in as easy an intimacy with them as with any family which he used to visit." When ill and left without visitors, Johnson depended on them for bedside attention and companionship. There is some evidence that Davies began a biography of Johnson shortly after his death. In her diary entry for 25 January 1785 Piozzi stated that Davies, among others, had "already undertaken" Johnson's biography. In a letter to her Samuel Lysons remarked that Davies was among six persons engaged to write Johnson's life. Perhaps his own death, following a year after Johnson's, explains the lack of evidence of such a biography.

His published biographies show talent. *The Works of George Lillo* was hailed by the *Monthly Re-*

view (1775) as including "a more critical and more perfect account of the life of that esteemed and popular Bard, than had before been given by any of our biographical compilers." Theophilus Cibber's work in *The Lives of the Poets* (1753) had been the only well-known account of Lillo's life until then. At his first meeting with Davies, during rehearsals of *The Fatal Curiosity,* Lillo offered directing notes to him and the other actors, an experience that must have clarified for Davies the playwright's intentions. This information may have helped Davies's critical approach toward Lillo's plays throughout the biography. Davies drew upon his own sensibilities as an actor when evaluating Lillo's language, which was "plain and easy, though vigorous and energetic," showing "a simplicity of style." In the dedication Davies situates Lillo at the forefront of a new development in dramatic literature, and Davies credits him with inventing "a new species of dramatic poetry . . . the inferior or lesser tragedy." According to Davies, Lillo went further than Otway and Nicholas Rowe in forming his plots around "private histories": "his characters seldom rose higher than the middle class of life." Davies, however, does not mention literary precedents for Lillo's middle-class tragedy, such as Samuel Richardson in narrative fiction, and, in theater, first French and later English middle-class comedy. Quoting Lillo's own views, Davies stresses the democratic and utilitarian foundations of Lillo's new drama. In justifying the publication of Lillo's collected works, Davies posits that biographical interpretation can be gleaned from an author's text: "Perhaps in reviewing the fate of Lillo's Plays we may strike out some sparks of intelligence, which may afford entertainment and illustrate our author's character." By the "character" of the author Davies might have been painting the particular moral agenda Lillo set for his audiences. Discussing the moral import of *Silvia: or the Country Burial* (1730), for instance, Davies stresses the strict moral division between competing choices: the play "was written to inculcate the love of truth and virtue, and a hatred of vice and falsehood."

Lillo's didactic purpose for drama, his revolutionary infusion of moral preachment into the British theater, seems to have been enthusiastically affirmed by Davies. As the composition of the theater audiences changed throughout the eighteenth century, the middle-class virtues of thrift, honesty, industriousness, and sobriety were replacing the more complacent, upper-class taste for amoral intrigue, laxity, and social indifference. Davies, who, along with his wife, was generally praised for maintaining in the theater a "uniform decency of character," as

Boswell put it, emphasizes Lillo's moral consciousness as playwright: "a love of truth, innocence, and virtue, a firm resignation to the will of Providence, and a detestation of vice and falsehood, are constantly insisted upon." As a credo of the newly formed sentimental drama, Davies's observations also articulate the underpinnings of nineteenth-century melodrama, with its advocacy of watchfulness in individual morality and particular abhorrence of obsessive love. The bourgeois or domestic tragedy began by Lillo electrified the British theater and spread to the Continent rapidly. Boldly innovative, it displayed reality in drama through the lens of didacticism. Yet Davies's comment on the sexual allusions in Lillo's stage adaptations of Shakespeare, *Pericles* and *Marina,* show an eighteenth-century concern with decorum at the expense of true character motivation: "A modern audience rejects with disgust the companions and language of a brothel. Though less virtuous than our ancestors, we are more refined and polite in our public entertainments." Such remarks throughout the account of Lillo's life reveal Davies's retreat from the playwright's full commitment to uncover social reality in all its manifestations. Davies criticized *Arden of Feversham* (1759), the Elizabethan domestic drama adapted by Lillo, for its improper subject matter: "Such subjects as will not bear to be seen, may yet be related to advantage. Detested characters . . . murderers and assassins, should be sparingly introduced upon the stage. . . . An audience will not long endure their company." At times withdrawing from Lillo's fuller social agenda, Davies's commentary often seems to prefer propriety to truthful depiction.

Lillo's most influential tragedy of bourgeois proportions, *The London Merchant: or, The History of George Barnwell* (1731), inspired domestic tragedy in France, Russia, and Germany, where Gotthold Ephraim Lessing's important *Miss Sara Sampson* (1755) showed a direct influence. Lillo's drama involves a young apprentice (Barnwell) who succumbs to temptation and ruins his life and those of others. Based on his own contact with the playwright, Davies found that Lillo's personal character resembled that of Barnwell's virtuous employer Thorowgood. Before Jeremy Bentham and John Stuart Mill articulated the utilitarian notion of "the greatest happiness for the greatest number," Davies in his biographical work comprehends Lillo's utilitarian moral strain. This moral principle Lillo himself best articulates in his dedication to *The London Merchant:* "Tragedy is so far from losing its dignity, by being accommodated to the circumstances of mankind, that it is more truly august in proportion to the extent of its influence, and the numbers that are properly affected by it." As a biographer of Lillo, Davies was limited in his opinions of the extent to which drama should uncover eighteenth-century social reality; nevertheless, he fully understood the democratic trajectory of Lillo's moral concerns.

In his *Memoirs of the Life of David Garrick* Davies gives full credit to Johnson for information about Garrick's early life and for other anecdotes throughout. These personal disclosures of Johnson, originally offered to Davies as part of a package of financial assistance, have proven important in understanding Johnson's own early years in Lichfield, where as a schoolteacher he began his first employment. Davies, however, was not hesitant to offer his own evaluation of Johnson's character as he had known him. Critiquing Johnson's teaching of young children, for instance, Davies observes, "he cannot, perhaps, easily descend to the minutiae adapted to young and uninformed minds."

Davies relied on his own experience as a stage actor for his presentation of the private lives and occupations of Garrick and other performers, theater managers, and dramatists: "A long acquaintance with the stage, and an earnest inclination to excel in the profession of acting . . . afforded me an opportunity to know much of plays and theatrical history." Davies's exceptional skill as a raconteur and mimic, together with his experience as a biographical researcher and publisher, enabled him to create a roughly chronological biography that fascinated readers. Noteworthy also is the frequency with which leading literary figures of the day referred to the Garrick biography. Still, the two volumes are uneven, at times only a patchwork of details and quotations often left unanalyzed and with few transitions. For example, in volume one Davies quotes in its entirety, but without comment, a prologue by Johnson, spoken from the stage by Garrick, on the development of English theater since Shakespeare, "When Learning's triumph o'er her barbarous foes."

Much of the popularity of the Garrick biography can be attributed to the particularly striking descriptions and keen observations that Davies had perfected during his years of collecting dialogue and stories among his literary and theatrical acquaintances. His special skill as an impersonator struck Boswell and others and must have been learned during his years in acting, a profession which in the eighteenth century was learned primarily by watching experienced performers and imitating their manners and methods.

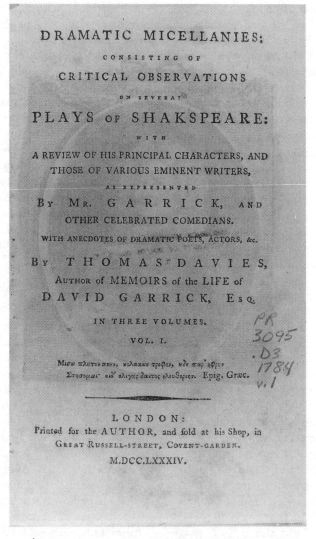

DRAMATIC MICELLANIES:
CONSISTING OF
CRITICAL OBSERVATIONS
ON SEVERAL
PLAYS OF SHAKSPEARE:
WITH
A REVIEW OF HIS PRINCIPAL CHARACTERS, AND
THOSE OF VARIOUS EMINENT WRITERS,
AS REPRESENTED
BY MR. GARRICK, AND
OTHER CELEBRATED COMEDIANS.
WITH ANECDOTES OF DRAMATIC POETS, ACTORS, &c.
BY THOMAS DAVIES,
AUTHOR OF MEMOIRS OF THE LIFE OF
DAVID GARRICK, ESQ.
IN THREE VOLUMES.
VOL. I.

LONDON:
Printed for the AUTHOR, and sold at his Shop, in
GREAT RUSSELL-STREET, COVENT-GARDEN.
M.DCC.LXXXIV.

Title page for the book that includes Davies's memoir of his years as an actor

Davies as biographer does attend to the considerable goals of literary "improvement" that Garrick set for himself. This aspect of Garrick's career as actor-manager Davies does not fully develop, however, handling Garrick's interpolations and adaptations of Shakespeare cursorily. Davies briefly mentions Garrick's intention to "restore" Shakespeare to "a genuine splendor and native simplicity" but does not expand this observation. Likewise, Davies offers only brief comments on Garrick's "improvements" on Otway, Rowe, and other Shakespearean adapters.

While leaving much unsaid about Garrick's transformations of Shakespeare, Davies often offers brief criticism on Garrick's stage adaptations of other popular playwrights. Davies devotes two pages to an analysis of the Garrick version of William Wycherley's *The Country Wife* (originally produced in 1675). For this Restoration comedy of manners Garrick "gave a more modern gloss" to Wycherley's characterizations. The play was adapted "to the present taste." Noting that Garrick changed Wycherley's ending, Davies does not discuss the reasons. Concerning other play adaptations, Davies writes cryptic literary remarks, speaking of a "deficiency of judgement" in many scenes and of dialogue "somewhat too swelling and boisterous." Comments such as the latter show the acting background of the biographer in his regard for the response of an audience. However, Davies seldom offers further explanation for the unfitness of such language in a theater situation.

Garrick includes evaluations of other playwrights and adapters contemporary with the main subject. These authors Davies often approaches thematically. He observes that the satirist Samuel Foote, for example, saw the "follies and vices of mankind with a quick and discerning eye . . . his humour pleasant, his ridicule keen, his satire pungent and exuberant." Foote's interest in parodying the sentimental drama tradition did not seem to offend the biographer of Lillo, evidence perhaps of Davies's broad vision of the theater.

Some degree of verisimilitude is assumed as a standard for both stage action and dialogue in Davies's brief evaluations of the Garrick stage performances. In such cases the biographer presents a literary analysis, however underdeveloped: "Let me admit the probability of the story, and the whole is consistent. The language is poetical, though not always dramatic, for it is generally too much raised for scenes of passion." A general summary of Garrick's literary merits covers two concise pages and gives a wide perspective on his epigrams, odes, comedies, farces, essays, letters, prologues, epilogues, and stage adaptations. Davies presents Garrick as "a perfect master of stage economy" whose adaptations appealed to the taste of his mid eighteenth-century public. This audience was aware that "poetical" language must resemble the speech of real life to some degree and that plots must demonstrate a credible "economy," attempting unity and causal connectedness. Davies often relies on traditional vocabulary to express standards of credibility in the range of social types presented on stage. He observes, for example, that Garrick's dramatic characters were generally "real" in that they displayed "discrimination of humour" but also at times parodied "fashionable folly, or some irregular gaiety of the times."

At the end of volume two Davies includes a list of thirty-five plays by Garrick. Here, also, he remains content to give brief critical commentary of a general nature or to evaluate Garrick's plays chiefly as vehicles for acting performances. As Garrick's biographer Davies perhaps most impresses the modern reader with his occasional insights into his subject's complex motivations and with his detailed explanations for certain career and personal decisions made by Garrick and other theater personalities.

The remarkable success of the Garrick biography inspired Davies to print and sell at his own shop a three-volume work consisting largely of commentary on Shakespeare's plays but also including large portions of stage anecdotes about noted Shakespearean performers. *Dramatic Miscellanies* includes a preface wherein Davies responds to Gar-

rick's widow, who had objected to the inclusion of several anecdotes in the Garrick biography that were unflattering to her husband. The response reveals Davies's interest in writing biography that seeks the truth beyond flattery: "In writing the life of a great and good man . . . the honest biographer must relate some circumstances of conduct which a tender and affectionate wife cannot peruse with complacency." Davies relied on a wide range of sources for his commentary in *Dramatic Miscellanies,* including facts and anecdotes from published works, but also personal knowledge of actors and critics, including John Roberts, Drib Morgan, Tony Aston, Nathaniel Clarke (who was prompter at Drury Lane Theatre), Ebenezer Forrest (attorney for Covent Garden Theatre), and the well-known actor Charles Macklin. Davies's usual diligence in collecting personal anecdotes was supplemented by his reliance on such scholars as William Thompson and Elizabethan sources such as the Stationers Register.

Davies combines eclectic methods of interpretation with an interest in biographical detail that modern Shakespearean scholars would find digressive and at times irrelevant. For example, Davies devotes much effort in attempting to demonstrate that Shakespeare was not a Roman Catholic, by reference to dialogue from *King John, Hamlet,* and *Henry VIII.* Interpretation of individual lines from Shakespeare are juxtaposed with historical background issues, and anecdotes of Shakespearean actors in specific roles are combined with evaluations of their performance styles and accomplishments. Discussions of tragedies also include recounting the histories of their performances on the English stage, with descriptions of the playhouses used. Justifications are offered for particular emendations and deletions by theater managers of Shakespeare's and Ben Jonson's plays, and the etymologies of selected words are traced, such as *weird,* found in *Macbeth* (1606). Davies also takes on certain controversies over authorship, such as Shakespeare's contribution to Jonson's *Sejanus* (1603), which Davies found was fact not conjecture. Stage production concepts are debated, as for example Davies's defense of then-recent representations of the witches in *Macbeth.*

The enthusiasm with which Davies pursued his publishing ideals threatened to lead to financial ruin and finally did. Nevertheless, he continued to publish many significant works regardless of projected sales. His conscientious approach was revealed in a 20 May 1770 letter to an author he was about to publish, reassuring him of a publication date: "I hope you are sensible that you have not mercenaries to deal with." Davies's 24 January 1769 letter to James Granger commenting on criticism of Granger's *Biographical History of England* (1769) — criticism which had attacked his attempt to reduce "our biography to system" — was an eloquent statement of Davies's high publishing standards for biography and collected works: "The candid, discerning and worthy part of the public will approve. . . . He that has least merit, and feels the weights of his own dullness, will be loudest in the cry against you."

The twin concerns of economics and literary standards in publishing were illustrated in Davies's careful handling of the corrections and additions to a later edition of his own Garrick biography from the eminent George Steevens, an editor of Shakespeare's collected works. Concurrently Davies was promoting sales of the biography by sending free examination copies to literary figures and other notables, asking for their comments. Such publishing issues as the form that future editions of *Garrick* should take — octavo or quarto — and the quality of paper used were also discussed, with Steevens and others.

The anonymous obituary of Davies in the *Gentleman's Magazine* (5 May 1785) is a succinct statement of his lifework: "Thomas Davies, bookseller; a man of uncommon strength of mind, and who prided himself on being through life 'a companion of his superiors,' suffered from cancer, presumably, buried in St. Paul's, Covent Garden."

Davies contributed a half-dozen significant, short literary biographies in comprehensive editions of the writing of British men of letters. The complete works of these authors were carefully selected and usually included previously unpublished and obscure pieces. His most influential writing was his biography of Garrick, which shows a brilliant ability to create short, dramatic scenes as well as vivid character vignettes, often of great subtlety. His other published works about the theater fed the popular passion of the day for stories of actors and dramatists. Davies's character observations impressed both Boswell and Johnson, and Boswell incorporated many of them in his own writings. As a respected London publisher, Davies nurtured and published many worthy authors at great financial risk to himself.

References:

James Boswell, *The Life of Samuel Johnson,* 6 volumes, edited by George Birkbeck Hill and L. F. Powell (Oxford: Clarendon Press, 1934);

James Peller Malcolm, ed., *Letters Between the Rev. James Granger . . . and Many of the Most Eminent Literary Men of His Time* (London: Longman, Hurst, Rees & Orme, 1805);

John Nichols, *Literary Anecdotes of the Eighteenth Century,* volumes 6 and 9 (London: Nichols, Bentley, 1812);

Hester Lynch [Thrale] Piozzi, *Anecdotes of the Late Samuel Johnson, LL.D., During the Last Twenty Years of His Life* (London: Printed for T. Cadell, 1786);

Piozzi, *Thraliana: The Diary of Mrs. Hester Lynch Thrale (Piozzi),* edited by Katharine C. Balderston (Oxford: Clarendon Press, 1951);

Bruce Redford, ed., *The Letters of Samuel Johnson,* 3 volumes (Princeton, N. J.: Princeton University Press, 1992);

J. L. Smith-Dampier, *Who's Who in Boswell?* (Folcroft, Pa.: Folcroft Press, 1935).

William Godwin

(3 March 1756 – 7 April 1836)

Gary Harrison
University of New Mexico

See also the Godwin entries in *DLB 39: British Novelists, 1600–1800* and *DLB 104: British Prose Writers, 1660–1800, Second Series.*

BOOKS: *The History of the Life of William Pitt, Earl of Chatham* (London: Printed for the author & sold by G. Kearsley, 1783);

An Account of the Seminary that will be opened on Monday the Fourth Day of August, at Epsom in Surrey, for the Instruction of Twelve Pupils in the Greek, Latin, French, and English Languages (London: Printed for T. Cadell, 1783); facsimile in *Four Early Pamphlets, 1783–1784,* edited by Burton R. Pollin (Gainesville, Fla.: Scholars' Facsimiles & Reprints, 1966);

A Defence of the Rockingham Party, in their Late Coalition with the Right Honorable Frederic Lord North (London: Printed for J. Stockdale, 1783); facsimile in *Four Early Pamphlets, 1783–1784;*

The Herald of Literature; or, A Review of the Most Considerable Productions that will be made in the Course of the Ensuing Winter: With Extracts (London: Printed for J. Murray, 1784); facsimile in *Four Early Pamphlets, 1783–1784;*

Sketches of History, in Six Sermons (London: Printed for T. Cadell, 1784);

Instructions to a Statesman. Humbly inscribed to the Right Honourable George Earl Temple (London: Printed for J. Murray, J. Debrett & J. Sewell, 1784); facsimile in *Four Early Pamphlets, 1783–1784;*

Damon and Delia: A Tale (London: Printed for T. Hookham, 1784);

Italian Letters; or, The History of the Count de St. Julian, 2 volumes (London: Printed for G. Robinson, 1784);

Imogen: A Pastoral Romance. In Two Volumes. From the Ancient British (London: W. Lane, 1784);

History of the Internal Affairs of the United Provinces from the Year 1780, to the Commencement of Hostilities in June 1787 (London: Printed for G. G. & J. Robinson, 1787);

An Enquiry Concerning the Principles of Political Justice, and its Influence on General Virtue and Happiness, 2 volumes (London: Printed for G. G. & J. Robinson, 1793); revised as *Enquiry Concerning Political Justice, and its Influence on Morals and Happiness,* 2 volumes (London: Printed for G. G. & J. Robinson, 1796; Philadelphia: Printed for Bioren & Madan, 1796; revised again [third edition], 1798); facsimile of third edition, 3 volumes (Toronto: University of Toronto Press, 1946);

Things as They Are; or, The Adventures of Caleb Williams (3 volumes, London: Printed for B. Crosby, 1794; 2 volumes, Philadelphia: Printed for H. & P. Rice and sold by J. Rice, Baltimore, 1795);

Cursory Strictures on the Charge Delivered by Lord Chief Justice Eyre to the Grand Jury, October 2, 1794 (London: Printed for & sold by D. I. Eaton, 1794);

A Reply to an Answer to Cursory Strictures, supposed to be wrote by Judge Buller. By the Author of Cursory Strictures (London: Printed for & sold by D. I. Eaton, 1794);

Considerations on Lord Grenville's and Mr. Pitt's Bills, Concerning Treasonable and Seditious Practices, and Unlawful Assemblies. By a Lover of Order (London: Printed for J. Johnson, 1795);

The Enquirer. Reflections on Education, Manners, and Literature. In a Series of Essays (London: Printed for G. G. & J. Robinson, 1797; Philadelphia: Printed for Robert Campbell by John Bioren, 1797);

Memoirs of the Author of a Vindication of the Rights of Woman (London: Printed for J. Johnson and G. G. & J. Robinson, 1798); republished as *Memoirs of Mary Wollstonecraft Godwin, Author of A Vindication of the Rights of Woman* (Philadelphia: Printed by James Carey, 1799);

St. Leon: A Tale of the Sixteenth Century, 4 volumes (London: Printed by R. Noble for G. G. & J.

*William Godwin, 1801 (portrait by James Northcote; National Portrait
Gallery, London)*

Robinson, 1799; Alexandria, Va.: Printed by
J. & J. D. Westcott for J. V. Thomas, 1801);

Antonio: A Tragedy in Five Acts (London: Printed by
Wilks & Taylor for G. G. & J. Robinson, 1800;
New York: D. Longworth, 1806);

*Thoughts. Occasioned by the Perusal of Dr. Parr's Spital
Sermon, preached at Christ Church, April 15, 1800:
being a Reply to the Attacks of Dr. Parr, Mr. Mac-
Kintosh, the Author of an Essay on Population, and
Others* (London: Printed by Taylor & Wilks
and sold by G. G. & J. Robinson, 1801);

*Life of Geoffrey Chaucer, the Early English Poet: Including
the Memoirs of his Near Friend and Kinsman, John
of Gaunt, Duke of Lancaster: With Sketches of the
Manners, Opinions, Arts and Literature of England
in the Fourteenth Century,* 2 volumes (London:
Printed by T. Davison for R. Phillips, 1803);

Fleetwood: or, The New Man of Feeling (3 volumes,
London: Printed for R. Phillips, 1805; 2 volumes, Alexandria, Va.: Published by Cotton &

Stewart, printed by Duane & Son, 1805; New
York: I. Riley, printed by S. Gould, 1805);

*Fables, Ancient and Modern, Adapted for the Use of Chil-
dren,* as Edward Baldwin (2 volumes, London:
Printed for T. Hodgkins, at the Juvenile Library, 1805; 1 volume, Philadelphia: Johnson
& Warner, 1811);

*The Looking-Glass. A True History of the Early Years of
an Artist; Calculated to Awaken the Emulation of
Young Persons of Both Sexes, in the Pursuit of Every
laudable Attainment: Particularly in the Cultivation
of the Fine Arts,* as Theophilus Marcliffe (London: Printed for T. Hodgkins at the Juvenile
Library, 1805);

*The Life of Lady Jane Grey, and of Lord Guildford Dud-
ley, her Husband,* as Marcliffe (London: Printed
for T. Hodgkins, 1806);

*The History of England, For the Use of Schools and Young
Persons,* as Edward Baldwin (London: T.
Hodgkins, 1806);

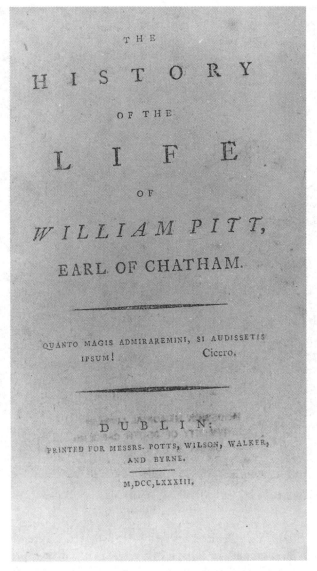

THE

HISTORY

OF THE

LIFE

OF

WILLIAM PITT,

EARL OF CHATHAM.

QUANTO MAGIS ADMIRAREMINI, SI AUDISSETIS
IPSUM!   Cicero.

DUBLIN:
PRINTED FOR MESSRS. POTTS, WILSON, WALKER,
AND BYRNE.

M,DCC,LXXXIII.

*Godwin's first biography, which includes some of his important
early statements on social philosophy and the art of biography*

*The Pantheon: or Ancient History of the Gods of Greece
and Rome. Intended to facilitate the Understanding of
the Classical Authors, and of the Poets in General,* as
Baldwin (London: Printed for T. Hodgkins,
1806);

Faulkener: A Tragedy (London: Printed for R. Phillips by R. Taylor, 1807);

*Dramas for Children. Imitated from the French of L. F.
Jauffret, by the editor of Tabart's popular stories*
(London: Printed for M. J. Godwin, at the Juvenile Library, 1808);

*Essay on Sepulchres; or, A Proposal for erecting some Memorial of the Illustrious Dead in All Ages on the Spot
where their Remains have been interred* (London:
Printed for W. Miller, 1809);

*The History of Rome: From the Building of the City to the
Ruin of the Republic,* as Baldwin (London: M. J.
Godwin, 1809);

*Mylius's School Dictionary of the English Language. To
which is prefixed A New Guide to the English
Tongue,* as Baldwin (London: Printed for M. J.
Godwin, 1809);

*Outlines of English Grammar, partly abridged from Mr.
Hazlitt's New and Improved Grammar of the English
Tongue,* as Baldwin (London: Printed for M. J.
Godwin, 1810);

*Lives of Edward and John Philips. Nephews and Pupils of
Milton. Including Various Particulars of the Literary
and Political History of their Times* (London:

Longman, Hurst, Rees, Orme & Brown, 1815);

Letters of Verax, to the Editor of the Morning Chronicle, on the Question of a War to be commenced for the Purpose of putting an End to the Possession of Supreme Power in France by Napoleon Bonaparte (London: Printed by Richard & Arthur Taylor, 1815);

Mandeville. A Tale of the Seventeenth Century in England (3 volumes, Edinburgh: Printed for A. Constable and Longman, Hurst, Rees, Orme & Brown, London, 1817; New York: Published by W. B. Gilley and C. Wiley, printed by Clayton & Kingsland, 1818; Philadelphia: Published by M. Thomas, printed by J. Maxwell, 1818);

Letter of Advice to a Young American, on the Course of Studies most advantageous for him to pursue (London: Printed for M. J. Godwin by Richard & Arthur Taylor, 1818);

Of Population. An Enquiry concerning the Power of Increase in the Numbers of Mankind; being an Answer to Mr. Malthus's Essay on that Subject (London: Printed for Longman, Hurst, Rees, Orme & Brown, 1820);

The History of Greece: From the Earliest Records of that Country to the Time in which it was reduced into a Roman Province, as Baldwin (London: M. J. Godwin, 1821);

History of the Commonwealth of England. From its Commencement, to the Restoration of Charles the Second, 4 volumes (London: Printed for H. Colburn, 1824-1828);

Cloudesley. A Tale (3 volumes, London: H. Colburn & R. Bentley, 1830; 2 volumes, New York: Printed by J. & J. Harper and sold by Collins & Hannay, Collins & Co., C. & C. & H. Carwill / Albany: O. Steele and Little & Cummings, 1830);

Thoughts on Man, his Nature, Productions and Discoveries, Interspersed with Some Particulars respecting the Author (London: Effingham Wilson, 1831);

Deloraine (3 volumes, London: R. Bentley, 1833; 2 volumes, Philadelphia: Carey, Lea & Blanchard, 1833);

Lives of the Necromancers: or, An Account of the Most Eminent Persons in Successive Ages, who have claimed for themselves, or to whom has been imputed by Others, the Exercise of Magical Power (London: F. J. Mason, 1834; New York: Harper, 1835);

An Essay on Trades & Professions by William Godwin, containing a Forcible Exposure of the Demoralizing Tendencies of Competition (Manchester: Heywood / London: Hetherington, 1842);

Essays Never Before Published, edited by Charles Kegan Paul (London: H. S. King, 1873);

Uncollected Writings (1785-1822), edited by Jack W. Marken and Pollin (Gainesville, Fla.: Scholars' Facsimiles & Reprints, 1968).

Editions: *The Adventures of Caleb Williams; or, Things as They Are,* edited by George Sherburn (New York: Rinehart, 1960);

Imogen: A Pastoral Romance from the Ancient British, edited by J. W. Marken (New York: New York Public Library, 1963);

Italian Letters; or, The History of the Count de St. Julian, edited by Burton R. Pollin (Lincoln: University of Nebraska Press, 1965);

Four Early Pamphlets (1783-1784) by William Godwin, edited by Pollin (Gainesville, Fla.: Scholars' Facsimiles & Reprints, 1966);

Enquiry Concerning Political Justice, edited by Isaac Kramnick (Harmondsworth, U.K. & Baltimore: Penguin, 1976).

OTHER: *Memoirs of the Life of Simon Lord Lovat. Written by Himself, in the French Language and now First Translated, from the Original Manuscript,* translated by Godwin (London: G. Nichol, 1797);

Mary Wollstonecraft, *Posthumous Works of the Author of a Vindication of the Rights of Woman,* 4 volumes, edited by Godwin (London: Printed for J. Johnson and G. G. & J. Robinson, 1798);

Mary Shelley, *Valperga; or, The Life and Adventures of Castruccio, Prince of Lucca,* 3 volumes, extensively revised by Godwin (London: G. & B. W. Whittaker, 1823);

"The Moral Effects of Aristocracy," in William Hazlitt, *The Spirit of Monarchy* (London: Wakelin, 1835).

For about a decade after the publication of his treatise on philosophical anarchism, *An Enquiry Concerning the Principles of Political Justice, and its Influence on General Virtue and Happiness* (1793), William Godwin enjoyed the kind of notoriety reserved for great literary figures and influential statesmen. Paying tribute to Godwin in *The Spirit of the Age* (1825), William Hazlitt describes that moment: "he was in the very zenith of a sultry and unwholesome popularity; he blazed as a sun in the firmament of reputation; no one was more talked of, more looked up to, more sought after, and wherever liberty, truth, justice was the theme, his name was not far off." In an age graced with great political minds such as those of Edmund Burke and Thomas Paine, Godwin not only held his own but, at least in Hazlitt's view, left them behind: "Tom Paine was considered for the time as a Tom Fool to him, [William] Paley an old woman, Edmund Burke a flashy sophist." Yet when the curtain fell on his fame, it fell swiftly and with an uncommon finality, so that today, despite Godwin's prodigious literary output that included biographies, novels, political essays, and children's books, he is best remembered for his two earliest important works, *Political Justice* and *Things as They Are; or, The Adventures of Caleb Williams* (1794). While hailed as an early anarchist writer, Godwin had more immediate and direct influence on the utopian socialism of Robert Owen and the utilitarianism of Jeremy Bentham and John Stuart Mill than he did on the classical anarchism of Pyotr Alekseyevich Kropotkin and Pierre Joseph Proudhon. Though Kropotkin does briefly mention Godwin in his *Encyclopaedia Britannica* entry on anarchism, Belgian anarchist Hem Day in 1953 probably best summed up Godwin's status in devoting the first issue of the *Cahiers de Pensée et Action* to "Un Précurseur Trop Oublié" – a precursor completely forgotten. Since the early 1950s, however, Godwin has regained his rightful place, in both the history of political thought and of literature, as a serious political philosopher and an innovative writer, the father, as some call him, of both philosophical anarchism and the contemporary detective novel.

William Godwin was born on 3 March 1756 in Wisbech, Cambridgeshire, the seventh of John and Ann Hull Godwin's thirteen children. John Godwin, whose Calvinist tenets were profoundly to influence William's early life, was minister of the Wisbech Independent Chapel, but as his son would be forced to do later, he left his situation in 1758 over a religious dispute, eventually settling in 1760 in Guestwick, just north of Norwich in Norfolk. Destined to be the third in a line of dissenting ministers, young William early took up reading the Bible, John Bunyan's *Pilgrim's Progress* (1678, 1684), and James Janeway's multivolume *A Token for Children* (1671–1672), a collection of tales about the glorious deaths of dutiful children. At eight years of age William was enrolled in a small private school with a master who had a reputation for being "the best, or second best, penman in the country of Norfolk"; later William went to Norwich to study under Samuel Newton, a follower of the extreme Calvinism of Robert Sandeman, whose dismal principles young William adopted under Newton's strict discipline.

The emphasis on guilt, justice, discipline, and punishment that emerges in Godwin's fiction and political writings may be traced in part to the years he spent with Newton, for it was then that the intel-

lectually curious, precocious, and diligent student met not with reward but with punishment despite his accomplishments. Of his time with Newton, Godwin remembers in one of the many autobiographical notes he collected, "It was scarcely possible for any preceptor to have a pupil more penetrated with curiosity and a thirst after knowledge than I was when I came under the roof of this man. All my amusements were sedentary; I had scarcely any pleasure but in reading. . . ." Despite his efforts, however, and perhaps because of Godwin's high opinion of himself, Newton subjected him to righteous harangues punctuated by the strokes of a birch rod. Godwin's astonishment was profound: "It had never occurred to me as possible that my person, which hitherto had been treated by most of my acquaintances . . . as something extraordinary and sacred, could suffer such ignominious violation. The idea had something in it as abrupt as a fall from heaven to earth." Sandeman taught that good works and even faith did not secure one a place among the handful of the saved, and Newton's actions probably were meant to humble his complacent pupil. Traces of some other Sandemanian ideas appear also in Godwin's later work, for Sandeman insisted that there was no New Testament authority for a national church or for the accumulation of property and wealth.

After the death of his father in 1772 Godwin enrolled at the well-known Dissenting Academy at Hoxton, where he came under the tutelage of two important radicals, Andrew Kippis, who was compiling the second edition of the *Biographia Britannica* (a liberal-leaning precursor to the *Dictionary of National Biography*), and Abraham Rees, editor of the multi-volume *The New Cyclopedia: or Universal Dictionary of Arts, Sciences, and Literature*. Both Kippis and Rees would later become members of the Revolution Society, and under their guidance Godwin – a self-professed Tory in politics at this time – began to scrutinize his religious and political beliefs under the scorching lamp of Enlightenment thought. While he clung to his Sandemanianism through his graduation from Hoxton in May 1778, Godwin would never abandon the rational questioning that these years inspired. His own comments show the power Hoxton exerted on him: "A little time before the period of my entering the Dissenting College at Hoxton, I had adopted principles of toryism in government, by which I was no less distinguished from my fellow-students than by my principles of religion. I had, however, no sooner gone out into the world than my sentiments on both these points began to give way; my toryism did not survive

Mary Wollstonecraft in 1797 (portrait by John Opie; National Portrait Gallery, London)

above a year, and between my twenty-third and my twenty-fifth year my religious creed insensibly degenerated on the heads of the Trinity, eternal torments, and some others."

Having left Hoxton at twenty-two, Godwin followed his father's and grandfather's footsteps to become a dissenting minister, at Stowmarket in Suffolk. When his ministry ended within the year over a controversy about his authority to administer the sacraments, Godwin moved to London in the spring of 1782. Fresh from reading Paul Thiry, Baron D'Holbach's *System of Nature* (1770) and Claude-Adrien Helvetius's *Of the Spirit* (1758) in 1782, Godwin was convinced, in the words of his biographer William St. Clair, to "embrace the ministry of enlightenment." Taking lodgings at Coleman Street, the haunt of many Grub Street writers who lived as best they could on small earnings, Godwin tried his hand at writing and teaching.

For his first project Godwin proposed to write a series of short biographies on prominent English political figures. The first of these, *The History of the Life of William Pitt, Earl of Chatham,* published anony-

mously in 1783 at Godwin's own expense, so much absorbed his attention that he abandoned the idea of a series in order to concentrate on this one book. As biography the *Life of Chatham,* as it is sometimes called, claims attention primarily as a fledgling effort; Godwin himself later referred to it as "a very wretched attempt." Written in an alternately affected and pedestrian style, the book focuses primarily on Pitt's parliamentary career, and even there it lacks a serious and detailed analysis of Pitt's private motivations and the convoluted party politics in which he was embroiled. Despite Godwin's claim in the introduction that the biographer/historian must be a "citizen of the world," personally disinterested from, yet morally engaged in, the life of his or her subject, the biography foreshadows some of the political ideas that inform Godwin's later writing. While largely generous to Pitt and praising his independence in the face of "the uniformity of fashion" and the "contagion of venality," Godwin charges Pitt with an excessive patriotism that led to a deficiency of universal benevolence – an opinion that Richard Price would espouse in the sermon that would set off the "Revolution Controversy" in England just six years later. Moreover, the introduction delivers one of Godwin's first testimonies of his belief in the perfectibility of humankind, as he claims that the disinterested biographer/historian must display frankly the subject's faults and accomplishments in order to lead his society "by imperceptible, never ceasing advances" to a truth and justice that would eventually bring about "the restoration of paradise."

Godwin was disappointed financially with his first book, which made him no money, even though an anonymous reviewer for the *Gentleman's Magazine* (April 1783) saw in its author a "poet, a painter, a philosopher, a friend of freedom, and a lover of mankind." With characteristic tenacity and resilience that would serve him throughout a life of many disappointments, he immediately took up other projects. When the school he advertised in *An Account of the Seminary* (1783) failed to materialize due to insufficient interest, Godwin became more fully dependent on his writing. Throughout the next two years he published various political pamphlets, such as *A Defence of the Rockingham Party* (1783) and *Instructions to a Statesman* (1784); edited a collection of his sermons, *Sketches of History, in Six Sermons* (1784); produced a rather lively parody of his contemporaries, *The Herald of Literature* (1784), which claims to be a review of works not yet written; and wrote three works of fiction: a romantic tale, *Damon and Delia* (1784); a pastoral romance, written in the style of Ossian, titled *Imogen* (1784); and an epistolary novel, *Italian Letters; or, The History of the Count de St. Julian* (1784).

In 1784, with the help of Kippis, Godwin received a permanent assignment to cover and summarize parliamentary debates for the *New Annual Register*. Shortly thereafter he met Gilbert Stuart, editor of the newly formed Opposition journal, the *Political Herald*, for which Godwin (under the name Mucius) wrote a series of letters on contemporary political questions, including English policy in India and Ireland. Through these summaries and essays Godwin began to shape some of the political ideas that would inform *Political Justice*, in particular demonstrating how gratitude serves oppression by puffing up the patron and debasing the grateful, thus compromising the latter's independence and humanity. Godwin was also contributing reviews to the *English Review* at this time, and his work in these prominent journals placed him on the guest list of many Opposition politicians and literary notables. Godwin's diary from this period shows that he met the Whig statesmen Burke and Charles James Fox;

the radical Dissenter and scientist Joseph Priestley; and other notables with liberal sentiments, such as Bentham, Elizabeth Siddons, Horne Tooke, Samuel Parr, Elizabeth Inchbald, and Fanny Burney.

Steeped from childhood in Dissent and newly transformed through his study of French Enlightenment philosophy, Godwin certainly had common cause with the promoters of reform in Parliament. As France, which Godwin studied for his annual essay on French politics for the *New Annual Register*, sped headlong toward revolution, England attempted to stay its course at home. Godwin shared the disappointment of many when the Test and Corporation Acts, which prevented Dissenters from holding office, failed to be repealed in 1787 and again in 1789. On 14 July 1789 the storming of the Bastille marked the beginning of the French Revolution. On 5 November 1789 Price alluded to that event in his sermon "A Discourse on the Love of Our Country," which ignited the so-called Revolution Controversy when it set Burke to writing *Reflections on the Revolution in France* (1790). In his 1789 contribution to the *New Annual Register* Godwin recorded his own optimistic forecast of events: "From hence we are to date a long series of years, in which France and the whole human race are to enter into possession of their liberties, when the ideas of justice and truth, of intellectual independence and everlasting improvement, are no longer to remain buried in the dust and obscurity of the closet, or to be brought forth at distant intervals to be viewed with astonishment, indignation, and contempt, but to be universally received, familiar as the light of day, and general as the air we breathe." Godwin's views departed radically from Burke's, and in the ideological ferment that followed the publication of *Reflections on the Revolution in France* — the attacks on Burke by Mary Wollstonecraft, James MacKintosh, and most notably Paine — Godwin proposed to the publisher George Robinson plans for a treatise on political principles that would correct the errors of previous political philosophers and set the world on a course toward truth and justice. With an advance from Robinson, Godwin left his position at the *New Annual Register*, and in September 1791 he began writing, in the words of the preface, "with unusual ardour," *An Enquiry Concerning the Principles of Political Justice*, which he completed sixteen months later and published in February 1793.

In *Political Justice* Godwin denounces the fraudulent principles of aristocracy and monarchy; attributes the decline of human civility to the growth of government institutions and laws; and celebrates the perfectibility of humankind and the inevitable, if gradual, liberation of humanity from its present institutional chains. A culmination of Enlightenment political philosophy, *Political Justice* exhibits Godwin's profound faith that the disinterested exercise of human reason will eliminate the need for arbitrary government, religion, and social institutions, such as property, marriage, and law. Free from the customary restraints, an enlightened people will act in the best interests of others, contributing toward the common good of all. Godwin's ideal society would abolish all government, because government itself, as it insinuates itself into human practices and ideology, is to blame for social corruption and moral error.

Because of its implicit anarchism Godwin's treatise has been hailed as the first full-length treatment of philosophical anarchism in English political thought, though scholars continue to dispute the originality of its doctrine and its place in the canon of English political philosophy. The almost irrational utopianism of some of its tenets, especially in the first edition – Godwin, for example, believed that through the increase in rational judgment one would eventually be able to achieve immortality – has led some to dismiss it altogether. But in the second and third editions Godwin did temper the more enthusiastic of his claims, allowing greater place in his philosophy for the operation of human sentiment and feeling. Of his revisions, though, Godwin always maintained, as he writes in the preface to the second, most substantively changed, edition, "the spirit and great outlines of the work . . . remain untouched."

Political Justice placed Godwin at the forefront of public attention. With its publication he became known as the founder of "The New Philosophy" and exerted considerable influence in English Jacobin circles. His treatise influenced many young radical reformers and Dissenters among his contemporaries and inspired some – including Samuel Taylor Coleridge, Robert Southey, and later Robert Owen – to plan utopian communities based on the equitable, if not equal, distribution of property and wealth, intellectual freedom, and absolute freedom of speech (all ideas advanced in Godwin's work). In *Political Justice* Godwin denounced violent revolution, arguing that the gradual advance envisioned in his work would come about by means of education, literature, and debate; like many liberals in England he was much chagrined at the 1793 executions of Louis XVI, Marie Antoinette, and the Girondin leaders.

When the first edition was published, England was charged with unwarranted fears of revolution. The popularity of Paine's *Rights of Man* (1791–

1792), which similarly denounced fraudulent principles of aristocracy and monarchy, raised an alarmist reaction from the William Pitt administration, and Paine had been convicted (in absentia) of seditious writing and treason just months before Godwin's treatise appeared. Nonetheless, at a cost of three guineas, about two months' wages for the average workingman and sixty times the cost of Paine's pamphlet, which sold for a mere sixpence, *Political Justice* circulated without government reprisal.

Godwin did not, however, stand aside from the high political theater that played in London during the mid 1790s. As the Pitt administration took severe measures to suppress any writings sympathetic to the Jacobin cause, Godwin argued in letters to the *Morning Chronicle* in February and March 1793 that the English Constitution supported free speech. When Thomas Muir and Thomas Palmer, two Scottish radicals, were exiled to Botany Bay after being convicted of sedition, Godwin visited them in their prison ships before they left and protested their punishment in another letter to the *Morning Chronicle*. During the 1794 trials of Godwin's friends Thomas Holcroft, Thomas Hardy, and Horne Tooke, Godwin wrote *Cursory Strictures on the Charge Delivered by Lord Chief Justice Eyre to the Grand Jury, October 2, 1794* (1794), which effectively crippled support for the prosecution's attempt to broaden the definition of treason to include advocating the reform of Parliament. Of the charges against his friends Godwin noted in his diary, "The accusation, combined with the evidence adduced to support it, is not to be exceeded in vagueness and incoherence by anything in the annals of tyranny."

When in 1795 the hated Two Acts – extending the range of treason and placing tight governmental restrictions on assembly – were proposed, Godwin replied with another powerful pamphlet, *Considerations on Lord Grenville's and Mr. Pitt's Bills concerning Treasonable and Seditious Practices, and Unlawful Assembies* (1795), which again defended the right to free speech but also appealed for moderation among the reformers. This time Godwin's argument had no effect, and the acts passed in December, ironically just after the publication of the second edition of *Political Justice*. In the years that followed, the voices of radical reform were successfully muted, and in the wake of increasing brutality in, and the threat of invasion from, France, many English liberals became disillusioned or gave up hope for reform; some, including Southey, became ardent Tories.

As the treason trials got underway, Godwin's most important novel, *The Adventures of Caleb Wil-*

MEMOIRS

OF THE

AUTHOR

OF A

VINDICATION OF THE RIGHTS OF WOMAN.

By WILLIAM GODWIN.

LONDON:
PRINTED FOR J. JOHNSON, NO. 72, ST. PAUL's
CHURCH-YARD; AND G. G. AND J. ROBINSON,
PATERNOSTER-ROW.
1798.

Title page for Godwin's biography of Mary Wollstonecraft,
which shocked eighteenth-century readers with its frank
discussion of her love relationships

liams, appeared to a highly receptive audience. Begun just ten days after he had finished his great treatise, this popular thriller about spying, guilt, punishment, and misplaced chivalry has sometimes – justifiably – been called *Political Justice* in fiction. A political and psychological analysis of the obsessive behavior of its central characters – the fallen, guilt-ridden nobleman, Falkland, and his overly curious, equally guilt-ridden servant, Caleb – this precursor to the modern detective novel dramatizes the conflict arising from the stubborn persistence of an outmoded and mystifying feudal code of honor, even among the enlightened aristocracy, in a society seeking moral guidance in independent reason and rational discourse. One of the strengths of the novel is the way Godwin refuses merely to simplify these questions, so that both Falkland and Caleb, representatives of the aristocracy and the middle class, end up compromising their own values and are driven to remorse. Images of prisons abound in the novel, as Godwin paints English society as a tangle of disciplinary mechanisms that limit the freedoms of, and punish, the innocent so as to render the guiltless guilty.

Obviously the novel appeared tendentiously impolitic to the enemies of Jacobinism in England, and it was duly parodied and criticized, even as it received an enthusiastic reception, as recorded by Hazlitt in a review of Godwin's *Cloudesley* for the *Edinburgh Review* (April 1830): "Few books have made a greater impression than *Caleb Williams* on its first appearance. It was read, admired, parodied and dramatized. . . . It was a new and startling event in literary history for a metaphysician to write a popular romance. Mr. Godwin was thought a man of very powerful and versatile genius; and in him the under-standing and the imagination reflected a mutual and dazzling light upon each other." Subsequent critics have sustained the interest in, if not always the praise for, *Caleb Williams,* which went through thirteen printings by 1800; was adopted (and depoliticized) by George Coleman as a successful play, *The Iron Chest,* first performed on 12 March 1796 at the Drury Lane Theatre; and was reprinted in 1831 as the second novel in Richard Bentley's "Standard Novels" series. Two of Godwin's later novels, *St. Leon: A Tale of the Sixteenth Century* (1799) and *Fleetwood: or, The New Man of Feeling* (1805) would also achieve "classic" status among the early Victorians, appearing as numbers 5 and 22 in Bentley's popular series.

What these novels have in common, with varying degrees of emphasis and success, is a primary interest in the psychological and moral dilemmas of their characters, who are placed in historical situations that draw out the moral and social dimensions of their interactions with the political institutions of their own times. These conflicts always allude to or parallel the political conditions faced by Godwin's contemporaries. As Gary D. Kelly puts it in his chapter on Godwin in *The English Jacobin Novel* (1976), Godwin hoped to show in these three novels "the continuity between 'things as they were' and 'things as they are.' " In the dynamic interaction among historical incident, social institutions, and individual character, Godwin's novels look backward to the novels of sensibility and manners by Samuel Richardson and Fanny Burney, and forward to the historical novels of Sir Walter Scott and Charles Dickens. Nonetheless, with the exception of such minor writers as Edward George Bulwer-Lytton, Godwin exerted little direct influence on the history of the novel, as B. J. Tysdahl rightly observes in *William Godwin as Novelist* (1981): "Godwin's importance lies not so much in direct influence as in the fact that in him we find early and sensitive reaction to the intellectual and emotional climate in which the Victorians found themselves. Sharply, his fiction outlines a number of problems and themes (e.g., the plight of the poor, the self-tormented character struggling against the social custom) that were to occupy new generations of novelists."

In 1795, at the height of his success, the cause for which Godwin had written came under increased censure and censorship. In January 1795 Godwin met for the second time Mary Wollstonecraft, author of *A Vindication of the Rights of Woman* (1792), one of the most powerful and earliest feminist treatises in England. On 29 March 1797 the two "New Philosophers," contrary to their reasoned injunctions against marriage, joined hands in wedlock. Wollstonecraft's influence on Godwin, his experience firsthand of a genuine love, effected a change in this man whose calculated rationality led Charles Lamb to call him "the professor." Unfortu-

nately Godwin was also to learn from Wollstonecraft the depths of grief, for within six months of their marriage she died of a puerpural infection, ten days after giving birth to their daughter, Mary, who would later be known as the author of *Frankenstein* (1818) and other novels. In his grief Godwin began work almost at once on his most important biography, *Memoirs of the Author of a Vindication of the Rights of Woman* (1798), and an edition (1798) of her then-unpublished works.

Heretofore Godwin's writing had been instrumental in forwarding the cause of liberty and human rights; in this case, however, his biography of Wollstonecraft retarded, if it did not reverse, the efforts of liberal reformers, especially those who advocated women's rights. Perhaps taking his cue from Jean Jacques Rousseau's *Confessions* (1781–1788), Godwin presented Wollstonecraft with all her virtues and vices, believing (as he had noted in the introduction to the *Life of Chatham*) that the biographer or historian must take a disinterested stance so far as the facts of his or her subject's life go. Godwin sketches his objective in the introduction, hoping that a just and full portrayal of Wollstonecraft, or indeed of any of the "illustrious dead," would become "the fairest source of animation and encouragement to those who would follow them in the same carreer [*sic*]." Moreover, such an account, Godwin hoped, would lead the reader to sympathize with the subject of the biography and to place his or her faults in the shadow of his or her "excellencies."

As he did not do in the earlier biography of Pitt, Godwin attempts in *Memoirs* to contextualize fully Wollstonecraft's development as a writer and thinker, beginning with her memories of her childhood, plagued as it was with an abusive, often drunken father, and following her through the most critical incidents of her life, including their own relationship – "a friendship melting into love" – up to her death. With characteristic honesty and frankness Godwin discusses in some detail Wollstonecraft's love for Henry Fuseli, her relationship with the American businessman Gilbert Imlay, and her despair and attempted suicides. Always the philosopher, Godwin contemplates the complex feelings of the jilted lover, the suicide attempter, and the woman (and man) in love, hoping to help his reader both to understand and to sympathize with Wollstonecraft.

Despite warnings from his publisher and friend Joseph Johnson, Godwin reprinted in his collection of Wollstonecraft's posthumous works, published at the same time as the *Memoirs,* her love letters to Imlay. (Fuseli refused Godwin's request for his letters from Wollstonecraft.) Though lightly edited, the intimacy of these revealing letters and the hitherto private details about Wollstonecraft's life contained in the *Memoirs* sent shockwaves through England: Wollstonecraft's sisters were furious with Godwin, his acquaintances were puzzled at his candor, and opponents of liberalism and feminism quickly seized the opportunity to discredit both publications. Shocked that he could publicize, in the words of Charles Lucas's parody of Godwin, *The Infernal Quixote* (1801), "The History of the Intrigues of his own Wife," reviewers denounced Godwin and his book as well as his wife, whose death was seen as just retribution for her licentiousness. While the scandal over the biography sped the demise of Godwin's popularity, it so ruined Wollstonecraft's reputation that it took over a century for it to recover.

From a historical distance, however, the *Memoirs*, as Mitzi Myers puts it in her 1981 essay on his *Memoirs*, still remains "in some ways the best of all the lives" of Wollstonecraft and provides a thoughtful account of the formative incidents in her life, a balanced assessment of her thought, and – for someone so close to her – a sensitive analysis and appreciation of her character, though Godwin could not help but see her as a symbol of Enlightenment perfectibility. For these qualities Donald A. Stauffer sees in the *Memoirs* the "fine essence of eighteenth century romantic biographies" and calls it "the noblest subjective record of a life to be found in the . . . century outside . . . religious biography." Overall Godwin's *Memoirs* offers a fine example of Romantic biography, which, as Myers has shown, because of the close connection between Wollstonecraft and Godwin, includes elements of Romantic autobiography as well. Indeed Godwin concludes his memoir with an examination of her contributions to his own understanding, attributing to her influence a greater appreciation of the place that sentiment, beauty, and passion play in human actions. While he long had "an ambition for intellectual distinction," he writes, he had little "intuitive perception of intellectual beauty." What he lacked, he concludes, Wollstonecraft made up and possessed in high degree.

His reputation quickly sinking in an atmosphere in which liberal thinkers were held in a high degree of suspicion and even contempt, Godwin had become the butt of attacks from the reviewers; novels such as Amelia Alderson Opie's *Adeline Mowbray* (1805) were published that criticized and parodied his and Wollstonecraft's lives. As biogra-

pher William St. Clair aptly notes, "Like Lord Byron in 1816, Godwin suddenly found himself the astonished victim of one of the British public's ridiculous fits of morality." He was also in search of a wife to care for his two young children: Mary, his own daughter; and Fanny Imlay, whom Godwin adopted after his wife's death. Eventually, in December 1801, he married Mary Jane Clairmont, who had two children of her own. Before their marriage, however, Godwin demonstrated his typical resilience by continuing his writing, producing another novel, *St. Leon* (1799); one of the few plays Godwin wrote, *Antonio* (1800); a collection of essays, *The Enquirer. Reflections on Education, Manners, and Literature* (1797), in which Godwin advances a progressive system of education and speculates in general on morality, poverty, wealth, the trades and professions, manners, and English prose style; and an important pamphlet defending his ideas against a former friend's hostile repudiation of them in *Thoughts. Occasioned by the Perusal of Dr. [Samuel] Parr's Spital Sermon* (1801).

A romance set during the Spanish Inquisition, *St. Leon* shows Godwin returning to the question of political, philosophical, and religious intolerance, a topic then close to Godwin's heart. The novel holds up the virtues of marriage and so offers a sort of public retraction of the condemnation of that institution in *Political Justice*. Godwin calls attention to this point in his preface, noting that "Some readers of my graver productions will perhaps . . . accuse me of inconsistency; the affections and charities of private life being every where in the publication a topic of the warmest eulogium, while in the enquiry concerning Political Justice they seemed to be treated with no great degree of indulgence and favour." While arguing that he again does not see this "modification" as a change of the system offered in the treatise, he does claim that he now finds the "domestic and private affections inseparable from the nature of man, and from . . . the culture of the heart," and he is "fully persuaded that they are not incompatible with a profound and active sense of justice in the mind of him that cherishes them." This new interest in feeling would form the substance of his next novel, *Fleetwood: or, The New Man of Feeling*, in which Godwin sets out to improve upon Henry MacKenzie's Harley, the man of feeling from the 1771 novel, by presenting Casimir Fleetwood as a solitary but sensitive man who practices universal benevolence and disinterested charity. One unfortunate outcome of this book was that Godwin's most enduring friend, Holcroft, broke off contact because he thought that Godwin was paro-

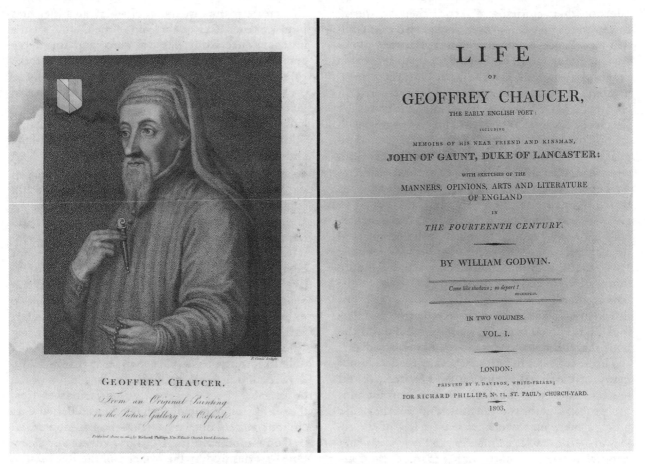

LIFE
OF
GEOFFREY CHAUCER,
THE EARLY ENGLISH POET:
INCLUDING
MEMOIRS OF HIS NEAR FRIEND AND KINSMAN,
JOHN OF GAUNT, DUKE OF LANCASTER:
WITH SKETCHES OF THE
MANNERS, OPINIONS, ARTS AND LITERATURE
OF ENGLAND
IN
THE FOURTEENTH CENTURY.

BY WILLIAM GODWIN.

Come like shadows; so depart!
SHAKESPEAR.

IN TWO VOLUMES.
VOL. I.

LONDON:
PRINTED BY T. DAVISON, WHITE-FRIARS;
FOR RICHARD PHILLIPS, N°. 71, ST. PAUL's CHURCH-YARD.
1803.

GEOFFREY CHAUCER.
*From an Original Painting
in the Picture Gallery at Oxford.*

Frontispiece and title page for Godwin's biography of the author of The Canterbury Tales

dying him in the unsympathetic character Mr. Scarborough. This novel also marks a decline in Godwin's powers as a novelist, from which he never recovered, though he went on to publish three more novels in his lifetime: *Mandeville. A Tale of the Seventeenth Century in England* (1817), *Cloudesley* (1830), and *Deloraine* (1833). While Godwin shows further experimentation with form in these later novels, as critics such as Tysdahl have noticed, "there is a marked unity in themes and mood – in an underlying sensibility which is recognizably the same throughout, but in which there is a slow growth." Social critique and a checkered atmosphere of hope and failure, guilt and innocence, prevail throughout all of his novels, though his social criticism appears tempered in the later novels, and his narrative gives way to periodic digressions and diffusiveness.

More important from the perspective of biography, fresh from his researches on sixteenth-century literature and history for the writing of *St. Leon* and with his financial situation steadily worsening, Godwin tried his hand at writing a biography of Geoffrey Chaucer. Godwin, of necessity, turns from the intimate portrait and subjective engagement with his subject that characterizes the *Memoirs* and instead attempts to depict Chaucer as a sort of product of his age. In Godwin's words, "Chaucer, however superior he may be considered to the age in which he lived, had yet the frailties of a man . . . and was acted upon, like other men, by what he heard and saw, by what inspired his contemporaries with approbation or with rapture." The full title of the book characterizes at least what Godwin attempted to produce: *Life of Geoffrey Chaucer, the Early English Poet: Including the Memoirs of his Near Friend and Kinsman, John of Gaunt, Duke of Lancaster: With Sketches of the Manners, Opinions, Arts and Literature of England in the Fourteenth Century* (1803). Readers looking for a colorful picture of Chaucer will be disappointed with the result of Godwin's three-year labor, as will those looking for accurate details about Chaucer's life or fourteenth-century England. Godwin had hoped, as he puts it, "to rescue for a moment the illustrious dead from the jaws of the grave, to make them pass in review before me, to question their spirits, and record their answers." But even his contemporaries recognized that Godwin was no necromancer with a crystal view of the past, and they found his history too speculative, his biography too fanciful, and both too thinly documented, despite a great deal of original research on Godwin's part, a trip to what was thought to be Chaucer's home at Woodstock, and learned consultations on minstrel traditions and Chaucer's language with Joseph Ritson and Horne Tooke. Godwin went so far as to invent an exchange, based on an apocryphal story, between Chaucer and Petrarch. Nonetheless, Peter H. Marshall is right to give Godwin's massive work credit as "an antiquarian's feast day," though so is Scott, who complained in his review for the *Edinburgh Review* (January 1804) that the antiquarianism dwarfed the minute figure of Chaucer that managed to surface at all: "the incidents of Chaucer's life, serving as a sort of thread upon which to string his [Godwin's] multifarious digressions, bear the same proportion to the book that the alphabet does to the Encyclopaedia. . . ." The heavy sales indicate that many readers, if not many professional reviewers and writers, found much of interest in the work. Even if Scott found it too prolix; Lamb, too fanciful; and Southey, too much a mere patchwork, at least a few of the reviewers – for the *Monthly Review, Literary Journal* and *Imperial Review,* in particular – granted cautious praise to Godwin's style and applauded his historical approach to Chaucer's life and work.

What Godwin does accomplish amounts to a history of English literature up to the fourteenth century, linking Chaucer's poetry to, and differentiating it from, the poetic practices of the earlier bards, skalds, and minstrels. Along the way Godwin discusses the origin of the English stage in the miracle and mystery plays, pageants, and masks, and gives a colorful account of the shows and spectacles of the fourteenth century – the burlesques, sports, feasts, festivals, tournaments, and duels of the feudal period. Godwin notes that the condemnation of the brutality of once-acceptable and even "virtuous" blood sports (such as bearbaiting and dueling) offers evidence of the progress of humanity: "There are few truths more striking in the history of human affairs than that things which may be hurtful and injurious in one stage of society, had probably their period in a different stage when they were eminently advantageous and salutary." Thus Godwin cautions the historian or biographer to be wary of applying the standards of judgment of his or her own age to the subjects of another. Other topics Godwin discusses in the volume include Gothic ar-

chitecture, in the discussion of which he anticipates John Ruskin's later celebration of the Gothic artist's independence from classical rules and form; the connection between chivalry and romance; and the role of the Reformation in England – especially as presaged by John Wycliffe and his patron John of Gaunt – to lift "that night and torpor in which we had so long been involved" (Catholicism) and so to initiate a period favorable to independent thinking and innovation.

Interwoven into this historical panorama of the Middle Ages are details, as far as Godwin could supply them, of Chaucer's private and public life, and descriptions and critical assessments of Chaucer's major and minor literary works. From Godwin, Chaucer receives the kind of praise that eighteenth-century criticism reserved for "primitive" poetic geniuses such as Homer and William Shakespeare. Chaucer's work, to Godwin, offers an immediacy and vividness of scene and character, partly because of his fortune to write at a time when "the mind of man was not yet broken down into a dull uniformity." The *Canterbury Tales* (1387–1400), in particular, is remarkable for its conception of the pilgrimage, the representation of various classes, the perfect suitability of each tale to its teller, and its "infinite variety of character." Although the Puritan in Godwin objects to the "filthy, vulgar and licentious" stories told by the Miller and the Reeve, true to his historicist position Godwin nonetheless praises them for their display of "eloquence and imagination" and recommends they be read and reread even by those with the most exacting of taste.

Often in his depiction of Chaucer's character, Godwin seems to project himself into the mirror of his subject so that some of his own traits blur with those of Chaucer, as when he notes that Chaucer "was not less fond of study than of convivial intercourse." Godwin himself spent his mornings in study, then always sought company in the afternoons and evenings among his friends, for he believed that discussion as well as study was essential to the formation of character and helped to sharpen one's thinking. In addition one can see in Godwin's fascination with the "romantic" and "sublime" – the emotional aspects of Chaucer's work and the scenes in which he put forward his ideas – Godwin's own expanded emphasis on the role of imagination and feeling and their influence on the development of the mind. This sentiment is much akin to William Wordsworth's in his great autobiographical epic *The Prelude* (1850). The author of the rational system of *Political Justice* makes the somewhat startling claim that "He who trusts much to sentiment, to im-

Godwin at age seventy-four (portrait by Henry W. Pickersgill; National Portrait Gallery, London)

pulse, to intuition will often be freest from absurdities, and be conducted to the most useful and beautiful modes of viewing either nature or man." It seems that the Enlightenment philosopher found a kindred spirit in the Romantic poet, though *Life of Geoffrey Chaucer* is no Romantic biography, but rather what Waldo Dunn once called in his early study *English Biography* (1916) a reconstructive biography, "that is, the gathering together of all available historical documents, facts, and traditions relative to some person and from these distilling something like the true story of this person's pilgrimage through life."

Like most twentieth-century critics of biography and of Chaucer, Dunn sees Godwin's "large scale" effort as an inauspicious beginning for reconstructive biographies. Altick agrees. Recalling Scott's censure of Godwin's prolixity, Altick writes in *Lives and Letters,* "In the 1,100 pages of his life of Chaucer, the poet appeared only at long intervals; for the most part, he was lost to view behind Godwin's survey of life and manners in fourteenth-

century England." Although most recent literary criticism has largely neglected Godwin's *Chaucer,* a scholar of no less stature than D. W. Robertson, Jr., in *A Preface to Chaucer* (1962), cites Godwin's assessment of *Troilus and Cressyde* as a "sound" example of the Romantic approach to the poem. In "Images of Chaucer 1386–1900," included in his *Chaucer and Chaucerians* (1966), D. S. Brewer also remembers Godwin, though he condemns what he calls Godwin's "mainly unsuccessful effort" at cultural criticism, and in his role as a New Critic Brewer suggests that one should simply "look into a poem, not all around it, for its meaning and value." Brewer does, nonetheless, include a selection from Godwin's *Chaucer* in his anthology of Chaucer criticism, *Chaucer: The Critical Heritage* (1966). Finally, Chaucer's recent biographers, more than the critics, remember Godwin's pioneering effort, though primarily, as in John Gardner's *The Life and Times of Chaucer* (1977) and in Donald R. Howard's *Chaucer: His Life, His Works, His World* (1987), in connection with Tyrwhitt, Chaucer's late-eighteenth-century editor (whose edition of Chaucer inspired Godwin to write the biography), and the dating of the story of Palamon and Arcite. Thus, while it may be too harsh to find Godwin's *Chaucer* worth mentioning only as the worst example of what kind of biography might result from late-eighteenth-century "antiquarian zeal," as Joseph W. Reed calls it in his *English Biography in the Early Nineteenth Century* (1966), Godwin's book is perhaps best viewed as an early example of the "life and times" approach of later Victorian autobiographies, as Harold Nicolson observes in *The Development of English Biography* (1928). In Godwin's *Memoirs* and *Chaucer* readers have something like the relationship between Wordsworth's *Prelude* and *The Excursion* (1814): the insightful blend of deep feeling, keen observation, and philosophical meditation of the former give way to the tangled profusion and pedestrian discursiveness of the latter.

Although Godwin received six hundred pounds for his *Chaucer,* that sum was insufficient for him to surmount what would soon become a chronic debt. Just before Godwin finished *Chaucer,* his wife, Mary Jane, had given birth to their son, William, Jr., and Godwin found himself with five children to support. While *Fleetwood* met with mild success when it was published in the spring of 1805, Godwin took the advice of his wife, who had been writing translations to supplement their income, and set up shop publishing, writing, and selling children's books and stationery. Because his name might put off prospective buyers, he wrote under the pseudonyms Theophilus Marcliffe and Edward Baldwin and published several books for children over the next few decades, including *Fables, Ancient and Modern, Adapted for the Use of Children* (1805); *The Life of Lady Jane Grey, and of Lord Guildford Dudley, her Husband* (1806); *The Pantheon: or Ancient History of the Gods of Greece and Rome* (1806); three histories (of England, Greece, and Rome); and *Lives of Edward and John Philips. Nephews and Pupils of Milton* (1815). Continuing financial difficulties forced Godwin and his wife to move to 41 Skinner Street, where business might be better and where he got free rent, after which their enterprise became known as the Juvenile Library, under the ownership of the thinly but successfully veiled name of M. J. Godwin and Company. The business prospered, but costs escalated, eventually forcing bankruptcy, so that Godwin had to sell the Juvenile Library and close up shop in 1825. In the meantime Godwin continued to publish novels under his own name and found occasion to engage publicly in a few political and philosophical controversies, most notably (outside

the scandal caused when his daughter, Mary, eloped with a nineteen-year-old married man, Percy Bysshe Shelley) with his *Letters of Verax* (1815), protesting the Congress of Vienna's decision to depose Napoleon, and his *Of Population . . . an Answer to Mr. Malthus's Essay* (1820), in which he rejects Thomas Robert Malthus's dismal ratio of food resources to population and Malthus's claim that humans are incapable of restraining sexual desire. Although Godwin in neither case effectively altered the course of events or won the public to his side, both arguments earned high praise, especially from those such as James MacKintosh and Henry Crabb Robinson who wished to preserve the discourse of political philosophy from the cold calculus of political economy.

As creditors and solicitors representing the owners of the building at 41 Skinner Street closed in, Godwin was at work on a history of the English Commonwealth. In May 1822 Godwin was forced to move his business to 195 the Strand, where he and Mary Jane continued what was then called the French and English Juvenile Library and School Library. With the incredible tenacity with which he was blessed, Godwin made time to complete his four-volume *History of the Commonwealth of England* (1824–1828). Godwin's history attempts to explain why the Glorious Revolution failed and devotes much attention and praise to the forebears of the dissenting and republican tradition from which he drew much of his strength and youthful ideas. Marshall observes that Godwin's history was "the first substantial history written from the republican side," and he commends its originality, clarity, and documentation. While it sold well, the proceeds from the history were insufficient to put Godwin's finances in order, so in May 1825 he sold the bookshop and the Juvenile Library and moved to Gower Place in order to be closer to his daughter, Mary Wollstonecraft Shelley, who had returned to London two years before, after the death of Shelley.

Godwin was then almost seventy years old; at a time when many would retire, necessity and habit kept Godwin at the writing table. In the last years of his life Godwin wrote two rather undistinguished novels, *Cloudesley* and *Deloraine;* two series of essays, *Thoughts on Man* (1831) and "The Genius of Christianity Unveiled" (included in *Essays Never Before Published,* 1873), which was left unfinished at his death and in which Godwin demonstrates the hazards of religious prejudice and its power to retard the progress of the mind; and *Lives of the Necromancers* (1834), which, despite its title, is less a series of short biographies than a study of the way the mind is readily deceived by the overwrought imagination and the desire for immortality. Biographer Don Locke describes *Lives of the Necromancers* as a series of "tales of sorcery . . . culled from the Bible, the Ancient World and the Far East as well as from medieval Europe," and he notes, too, that one of the admirers of the book was none other than Edgar Allan Poe.

As Godwin labored on his books with the specter of poverty haunting his study, political fortunes in England shifted at last in his favor. Godwin saw Catholic Emancipation, the repeal of the Test and Corporation Acts, and the ascendence of a Whig government, which included some, such as MacKintosh and Bulwer-Lytton, who remembered the aging radical philosopher. In 1833 Godwin was appointed office keeper and yeoman usher in the Receipt of the Exchequer, for which he received a pension of two hundred pounds per annum and a residence at 13 New Palace Yard, where he and Mary Jane lived from May 1833 until Godwin's death on 7 April 1836.

While Godwin included biography among the many genres in his repertoire, it is fair to say that his reputation rests on his works of political philosophy and his earliest novels, although his *Memoirs of Mary Wollstonecraft Godwin* (as it was retitled in 1799), which critics of literary biography have largely left unnoticed, deserves more attention as an early example of Romantic biography than it has so far received. *Political Justice* remains one of the key documents of Enlightenment rationalism in England, and its companion piece in fiction, *Caleb Williams,* deserves recognition not only as an important precursor to the detective novel but as the finest and most popular of the many "Jacobin" novels that combine psychological realism with a trenchant critique of society. If the philosophical anarchism implicit in Godwin's works seems at times both utopian and excessively rationalistic, the humanitarian character of his work, his tireless defense of human rights, his insistence on civil and sexual equality, and his insight into the mutually determining nature of the relationship between individual character and institutional practices give his work a continuing relevance and importance. Finally, *Political Justice, Caleb Williams,* and the *Memoirs,* as Raymond Williams observes in *Problems in Materialism and Culture* (1980), provide one with "a remarkable evocation" of the crisis in England during the 1790s, when "the rational and civilizing proposals" of a handful of liberal thinkers "were met by the crudest kind of repression." Even if the time has passed when a young Wordsworth could say, "Throw aside your books of chemistry and read Godwin on

Necessity," one may nonetheless still benefit from reading Godwin's work, especially in the critical spirit that he advised in volume one of *Political Justice:* "Let us look back, that we may profit by the experience of mankind; but let us not look back, as if the wisdom of our ancestors was such as to leave no room for future improvement."

Letters:

Shelley and His Circle, 1773–1822, Carl H. Pforzheimer Library, 8 volumes, volumes 1–4 edited by Kenneth Neill Cameron, volumes 5–8 edited by Donald H. Reiman (Cambridge, Mass.: Harvard University Press, 1961–1986);

Godwin & Mary: Letters of William Godwin and Mary Wollstonecraft, edited by Ralph M. Wardle (Lawrence: University of Kansas Press, 1966).

Bibliographies:

Francesco Cordasco, *William Godwin: A Handlist of Critical Notices and Studies* (Brooklyn: Long Island University Press, 1950);

Burton R. Pollin, *Godwin Criticism: A Synoptic Bibliography* (Toronto: University of Toronto Press, 1967).

Biographies:

Charles Kegan Paul, *William Godwin: His Friends and Contemporaries,* 2 volumes (London: Henry S. King, 1876);

Ford K. Brown, *The Life of William Godwin* (London: Dent, 1926);

George Woodcock, *William Godwin: A Biographical Study with a Foreword by Herbert Read* (London: Porcupine Press, 1946);

Don Locke, *A Fantasy of Reason: The Life and Thought of William Godwin* (London, Boston & Henley: Routledge & Kegan Paul, 1980);

Peter H. Marshall, *William Godwin* (New Haven & London: Yale University Press, 1984);

William St. Clair, *The Godwins and the Shelleys: The Biography of a Family* (London & Boston: Faber & Faber, 1989).

References:

Richard Altick, *Lives and Letters* (New York: Knopf, 1965);

H. N. Brailsford, *Shelley, Godwin, and Their Circle* (London: Williams & Norgate, 1913);

Marilyn Butler, "Godwin, Burke, and Caleb Williams," *Essays in Criticism,* 32 (July 1982): 237–257;

Butler, *Jane Austen and the War of Ideas* (Oxford: Oxford University Press, 1975);

John P. Clark, *The Philosophical Anarchism of William Godwin* (Princeton: Princeton University Press, 1977);

David Fleisher, *William Godwin, a Study in Liberalism* (London: Allen & Unwin, 1951);

Albert Goodwin, *The Friends of Liberty: The English Democratic Movement in the Age of the French Revolution* (Cambridge, Mass.: Harvard University Press, 1979);

Rosalie Glynn Grylls, *William Godwin and His World* (London: Odhams Press, 1953);

Elie Halevy, *The Growth of Philosophic Radicalism* (New York & London: Monthly Review Press, 1970);

William Hazlitt, *The Spirit of the Age: or Contemporary Portraits* (1825), in volume 11 of *The Complete Works of William Hazlitt*, 21 volumes, edited by P. P. Howe (London: Dent, 1932);

Jerrold E. Hogle, "The Texture of the Self in Godwin's *Things as They Are*," *Boundary*, 2 (Winter 1979): 261–281;

Chris Jones, "Godwin to Mary," *Keats-Shelley Review*, 1 (Autumn 1986): 61–74;

Gary D. Kelly, *The English Jacobin Novel* (Oxford: Oxford University Press, 1976);

Robert Kiely, *The Romantic Novel in England* (Cambridge, Mass.: Harvard University Press, 1972);

Isaac Kramnick, "On Anarchism and the Real World: William Godwin and Radical England," *American Political Science Review*, 69 (March 1972): 114–128;

Don Locke, *A Fantasy of Reason: The Life and Thought of William Godwin* (London: Routledge & Kegan Paul, 1980);

D. H. Munro, *Godwin's Moral Philosophy, an Interpretation of William Godwin* (London: Oxford University Press, 1953);

John Middleton Murry, *Heaven ——and Earth* (London: Cape, 1938);

Mitzi Myers, "Godwin's Memoirs of Wollstonecraft: The Shaping of Self and Subject," *Studies in Romanticism*, 20 (Fall 1981): 299–316;

Mark Philp, *Godwin's Political Justice* (Ithaca, N.Y.: Cornell University Press, 1986);

Burton R. Pollin, *Education and Enlightenment in the Work of William Godwin* (New York: Las Américas, 1963);

James Arthur Preu, *The Dean and the Anarchist*, Florida State University Studies, no. 33 (Tallahassee: Florida State University Press, 1959);

Henry Crabb Robinson, *Diary, Reminiscences, and Correspondence*, edited by Thomas Sadler, second edition (3 volumes, London: Macmillan, 1869; 2 volumes, Boston: Fields, Osgood, 1870);

A. E. Rodway, ed., *Godwin and the Age of Transition* (London: Harrap, 1952);

Andrew J. Scheiber, "Falkland's Story: Caleb Williams' Other Voice," *Studies in the Novel*, 17 (Fall 1985): 255–266;

Elton Edward Smith and Esther Greenwell Smith, *William Godwin* (New York: Twayne, 1965);

Donald A. Stauffer, *The Art of Biography in Eighteenth Century England* (Princeton, N. J.: Princeton University Press, 1941);

B. J. Tysdahl, *William Godwin as Novelist* (London: Athlone, 1981);

George Watson, "The Reckless Disciple: Godwin's Shelley," *Hudson Review*, 39 (Summer 1986): 212–230;

Donald R. Wehrs, "Rhetoric, History, Rebellion: *Caleb Williams* and the Subversion of Eighteenth-Century Fiction," *Studies in English Literature, 1500–1900*, 28 (Summer 1988): 497–511.

Papers:

The Abinger Collection, on loan to the Bodleian Library, Oxford, includes Godwin's diaries and memoirs as well as manuscripts, notes, and correspondence. The Forster Collection in the Victoria and Albert Museum Library includes manuscripts for *Political Justice, Caleb Williams, Life of Geoffrey Chaucer,* and *History of the Commonwealth of England* as well as miscellaneous correspondence. The Carl H. Pforzheimer collection, now at the New York Public Library, includes the manuscript for *Fleetwood,* revisions for *St. Leon,* drafts, notes, and miscellaneous correspondence. The Keats-Shelley Memorial House, Rome, also has various Godwin papers and manuscripts.

Oliver Goldsmith

(10 November 1730? – 4 April 1774)

Mark Loveridge
University of Swansea

See also the Goldsmith entries in *DLB 39: British Novelists, 1660–1800; DLB 89: Restoration and Eighteenth-Century Dramatists, Third Series;* and *DLB 104: British Prose Writers, 1660–1800, Second Series.*

BOOKS: *An Enquiry into the Present State of Polite Learning in Europe* (London: Printed for R. & J. Dodsley, 1759);

The Bee, nos. 1–8 (London, 6 October–24 November 1759); republished as *The Bee. Being Essays on the most Interesting Subjects* (London: Printed for J. Wilkie, 1759);

The Mystery Revealed: Containing a Series of Transactions and Authentic Testimonials Respecting the Supposed Cock-Lane Ghost (London: Printed for W. Bristow, 1762);

The Citizen of the World; or, Letters from a Chinese Philosopher, Residing in London, to His Friends in the East, 2 volumes (London: Printed for the author & sold by J. Newbery & W. Bristow; J. Leake & W. Frederick, Bath; B. Collins, Salisbury; and A. M. Smart, Reading, 1762; Albany, N.Y.: Printed by Barber & Southwick for Thomas Spencer, 1794);

Plutarch's Lives, Abridged from the Original Greek, Illustrated with Notes and Reflections, 7 volumes, by Goldsmith and Joseph Collier (London: Printed for J. Newbery, 1762);

The Life of Richard Nash, of Bath, Esq., Extracted Principally from His Original Papers (London: Printed for J. Newbery and W. Frederick, Bath, 1762);

An History of England in a Series of Letters from a Nobleman to His Son, 2 volumes (London: Printed for J. Newbery, 1764);

The Traveller; or, a Prospect of Society (London: Printed for J. Newbery, 1764; enlarged, 1765; Philadelphia: Printed by Robert Bell, 1768);

Essays. By Mr. Goldsmith (London: Printed for W. Griffin, 1765; enlarged, 1766);

Edwin and Angelina: A Ballad by Mr. Goldsmith, Printed for the Amusement of the Countess of Northumberland (London: Privately printed, 1765);

The Vicar of Wakefield: A Tale, 2 volumes (Salisbury: Printed by B. Collins for F. Newbery, London, 1766; second edition, revised, London: Printed for F. Newbery, 1766; Philadelphia: Printed for William Mentz, 1772);

The Good Natur'd Man: A Comedy (London: Printed for W. Griffin, 1768);

The Roman History, from the Foundation of the City of Rome, to the Destruction of the Western Empire, 2 volumes (London: Printed for S. Baker & G. Leigh, T. Davies & L. Davis, 1769);

The Deserted Village: A Poem (London: Printed for W. Griffin, 1770; Philadelphia: Printed by William & Thomas Bradford, 1771);

The Life of Thomas Parnell, D.D. (London: Printed for T. Davies, 1770);

The Life of Henry St. John, Lord Viscount Bolingbroke (London: Printed for T. Davies, 1770);

The History of England, from the Earliest Times to the Death of George II, 4 volumes (London: Printed for T. Davies, Becket & De Hondt and T. Cadell, 1771);

Threnodia Augustalis: Sacred to the Memory of the Princess Dowager of Wales (London: Printed for W. Woodfall, 1772);

Dr. Goldsmith's Roman History, Abridged by Himself for the Use of Schools (London: Printed for S. Baker & G. Leitch, T. Davies & L. Davis, 1772; Philadelphia: Printed for Robert Campbell, 1795);

She Stoops to Conquer; or, The Mistakes of a Night: A Comedy (London: Printed for F. Newbery, 1773; Philadelphia: Printed & sold by John Dunlap, 1773);

Retaliation: A Poem (London: Printed for G. Kearsly, 1774);

The Grecian History, from the Earliest State to the Death of Alexander the Great (2 volumes, London: Printed for J. & F. Rivington, T. Longman, G. Kearsly, W. Griffin, G. Robinson, R. Baldwin, W. Goldsmith, T. Cadell & T. Evans, 1774; 1 volume, Philadelphia: Printed for Mathew Carey, 1800);

*Oliver Goldsmith (portrait by Sir Joshua Reynolds or one of his students;
National Portrait Gallery, London)*

An History of the Earth, and Animated Nature (8 volumes, London: Printed for J. Nourse, 1774; 4 volumes, Philadelphia: Printed for Mathew Carey, 1795);

An Abridgement of the History of England from the Invasion of Julius Caesar to the Death of George II (London: Printed for B. Law, G. Robinson, G. Kearsly, T. Davies, T. Becket, T. Cadell & T. Evans, 1774; Philadelphia: Printed for R. Campbell, 1795);

The Haunch of Venison: A Poetical Epistle to Lord Clare (London: Printed for J. Ridley & G. Kearsly, 1776);

A Survey of Experimental Philosophy, Considered in Its Present State of Improvement, 2 volumes (London: Printed for T. Carnan & F. Newbery jun., 1776);

The Grumbler: A Farce, adapted by Goldsmith from Sir Charles Sedley's translation of David Austin de Brueys's *Le Grondeur,* edited by Alice I. Perry Wood (Cambridge, Mass.: Harvard University Press, 1931).

Editions: *The Miscellaneous Works of Oliver Goldsmith, M.B.,* 4 volumes, edited by Thomas Percy (London: Printed for J. Johnson by H. Baldwin & Sons, 1801);

Collected Works of Oliver Goldsmith, 5 volumes, edited by Arthur Friedman (Oxford: Clarendon Press, 1966).

OTHER: *The Memoirs of a Protestant, Condemned to the Galleys of France for His Religion,* by Jean Marteilhe, translated by Goldsmith as James Willington, 2 volumes (London: Printed for R. Griffiths & E. Dilly, 1758);

Richard Brookes, *A New and Accurate System of Natural History,* 6 volumes, preface and introductions to volumes 1–4 by Goldsmith (London: Printed for J. Newbery, 1763–1764);

William Guthrie, John Gray, and others, *A General History of the World from the Creation to the Present Time,* 13 volumes, preface to volume 1 by Goldsmith (London: Printed for J. Newbery, R. Baldwin, S. Crowder, J. Coote, R. Withy, J.

Statue of Goldsmith by Foley, at the gate of Trinity College, Dublin

Wilkie, J. Wilson & J. Fell, W. Nicoll, B. Collins & R. Raikes, 1764);

C. Wiseman, *A Complete English Grammar on a New Plan,* preface by Goldsmith (London: Printed for W. Nicoll, 1764);

A Concise History of Philosophy and Philosophers, by M. Formey, translated by Goldsmith (London: Printed for F. Newbery, 1766);

Poems for Young Ladies. In Three Parts. Devotional, Moral and Entertaining, edited by Goldsmith (London: Printed for J. Payne, 1767);

The Beauties of English Poesy, 2 volumes, edited by Goldsmith (London: Printed for William Griffin, 1767);

Charlotte Lennox, *The Sister: A Comedy,* epilogue by Goldsmith (London: Printed for J. Dodsley & T. Davies, 1769);

Thomas Parnell, *Poems on Several Occasions,* includes Goldsmith's biography of Parnell (London: Printed for T. Davies, 1770);

Henry St. John, Lord Viscount Bolingbroke, *A Dissertation upon Parties,* includes Goldsmith's biog-

raphy of Bolingbroke (London: Printed for T. Davies, 1770);

Joseph Cradock, *Zobeide: A Tragedy,* prologue by Goldsmith (London: Printed for T. Davies, 1770);

The Comic Romance of Monsieur Scarron, translated by Goldsmith, 2 volumes (London: Printed for W. Griffin, 1775).

Since its first night on 15 March 1773, Oliver Goldsmith's second play, the comedy *She Stoops to Conquer,* has appeared in over three hundred different editions and has been produced in the London West End approximately once every three years. Tom Davis, a recent editor, refers to it as "the most popular play outside Shakespeare." Goldsmith's one novel, *The Vicar of Wakefield* (1766), averaged two printings a year during the nineteenth century, thirty printings being published in France in the period from 1830 to 1870 alone. It "found entry into every castle and every hamlet in Europe," said William Makepeace Thackeray, in his *English Humourists of the Eighteenth Century* (1851). But in Goldsmith's own age his fame rested on the reputation of his two major poems, *The Traveller; or, A Prospect of Society* (1764) and *The Deserted Village* (1770), which were immediately taken to be the best, most representative English poems of their age: "a production to which, since the death of Pope, it will not be easy to find any thing equal," as Samuel Johnson's review of *The Traveller* put it (*Critical Review*, December 1764). In short, Goldsmith was a writer of what became popular classics, though his contemporaries were sometimes reluctant to acknowledge that such a transparently naive and apparently absurd Irishman could achieve such status. As well as poems, plays, and novels, he wrote classical, natural, and philosophical history; criticism; light topical essays; biographical sketches; and full-length biographies. Most of these biographies, including his only literary biography, *The Life of Thomas Parnell, D.D.* (1770), are rather casual performances, though Samuel Johnson abridged *The Life of Thomas Parnell* for use in his *Prefaces, Biographical and Critical, to the Works of the English Poets* (1779–1781), rather than writing one of his own. But Goldsmith's *The Life of Richard Nash* (1762), the "King of Bath," has a claim to being regarded as one of the major works of an author who is referred to by his biographer Ralph Wardle as the "most versatile genius of all English literature." In addition, Goldsmith's habit of using apparently autobiographical elements in his imaginative writing raises important critical questions about his work.

The leaf of the lost Goldsmith family Bible, seen by biographer John Forster, was torn away at the point where the year of Oliver's birth was recorded; the date is 10 November. The most likely year is 1730, though 1728, 1729, and 1731 are all possible. He was born in central Ireland, either at Pallas, county Longford, or at his maternal grandmother's house near Elphin, and was the second son and fifth child of Charles Goldsmith, a genial but improvident Protestant clergyman and tenant farmer, and Ann Jones Goldsmith, daughter of the Reverend Oliver Jones, master of the Diocesan School at Elphin. Oliver Goldsmith was conspicuously reticent about the facts of his birth, preferring to tell friends that he was named after Oliver Cromwell, rather than after his own Irish grandfather.

Soon after Oliver's birth, Charles Goldsmith succeeded his wife's uncle as curate of the parish of Kilkenny West, and the family moved to a larger house just outside the village of Lissoy (or Lishoy). Though Oliver's childhood was settled, rural, and relaxed, it was marred by his contracting smallpox when he was eight or nine. This left him badly pockmarked and even more disconcerting in appearance than he would otherwise have been: a letter in the *London Packet* of 24 March 1773 referred to his "monkey face" and "grotesque orang-outang figure." Together with the exclusive but parochial nature of a Protestant upbringing in rural Ireland (90 percent of his father's parish likely being Catholic), which seems to have fostered his mercurial and eccentric temperament, this disfigurement ensured that it would be hard for the metropolitan English society in which he later moved to respond to Goldsmith as anything but a very unusual man.

His early education, first at the village school and later the Diocesan School at Elphin, revealed a talent for writing light verse and a capacity for repartee. After spending two years at a school in Athlone, he was moved at about age thirteen to another at Edgeworthstown, run by the Reverend Patrick Hughes. Hughes was humane and sensitive, and he seems to have treated Goldsmith as an intellectual equal: "the Master conversed with him on a footing very difft. from that of a young Scholar," according to the memoir Goldsmith dictated to his friend Thomas Percy in 1773. Previously rather unsure of himself, Goldsmith became more confident and independent, and on 11 June 1745 he successfully presented himself for the entrance examination (on Homer, Virgil, and Horace) at Trinity College, Dublin.

Unfortunately two recent family marriages had drained the Goldsmiths' financial resources. Oliver's elder brother, Henry, had married before graduating from Trinity, thus reducing his chances of a materially successful church career. Catherine, the eldest surviving daughter, had eloped with Daniel Hodson, a young man of good family who had been admitted to the Goldsmith household as a tutorial pupil of Henry's; her father had felt obliged to provide a cripplingly generous dowry. Charles's prestigious brother-in-law, the Reverend Thomas Contarine, proposed that Oliver should attend Trinity as a sizar, a semimenial rank of student entitled to charitable subsidy. The perceived lack of status and of money, together with an antiquated curriculum and a bullying tutor, meant that Goldsmith derived few academic benefits from Trinity College. He did achieve a small award, an exhibition of thirty shillings, in 1747 shortly after his father's death, but this presentation was by way of a consolation prize for missing the expected scholarship. With family money drying up, Goldsmith found he could spin out his resources by selling ballads on

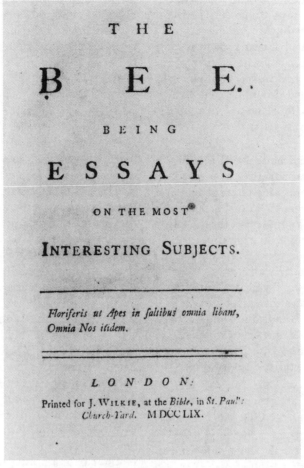

Title page for the collected edition of the weekly periodical in which Goldsmith published several of his earliest biographical sketches

contemporary events to the owner of a local shop at five shillings each; none of these ballads survives. A constitutional fondness for gambling and for impulsive acts of generosity compounded his predicament. Eventually, having been reduced to penury and humiliated by his tutor to the extent that he sold his books and absconded for several days, he managed to fulfill the residence requirements for an A.B. degree, which he eventually earned in February 1750.

Custom and Uncle Contarine dictated a career in the church, but Goldsmith contrived to convince the bishop of Elphin, during an interview, that he was an unsuitable candidate for the ministry. His uncle found him a post as tutor with a family in Roscommon, but after a year Goldsmith left, supposedly having resigned when he found that he had been cheated at cards. With thirty pounds and a good horse he set out from home for Cork and foreign shores, but in six weeks he returned, penni-

less and on a horse so decrepit he had named it Fiddleback. His exasperated mother demanded an explanation, and Goldsmith (according to the narrative of his sister Catherine, written in the 1770s, which is the only authentic source of the episode and which is published in *The Collected Letters of Oliver Goldsmith,* 1928) proceeded to tell a detailed, circumstantial, but fantastic story about his adventures. Having reached Cork, sold the horse, and paid for his passage, he missed the boat ("unfortunaty the day the wind served he hapened to be on a party in the Country with some Freinds" [*sic*]), bought the nag, was successfully importuned on his journey by "a poor Woman with eight little Clean children" who "told him a long melocholy [*sic*] tale," visited a friend who offered to buy his horse and lend him another which then turned out to be "an oak stick," and had then been providentially rescued by a "Councelor F. G.," whose daughters, who were mourning the death of their mother, provided sentimental musical entertainment. The counsellor gave him money for his return home. Catherine continues: "And pray says the Mother have you ever wrote a letter of thanks to that dear good man . . . no says the Dr. I have not then says the Mother you are an ungratefull Savage a Monster." When his mother and his family cooled down, he told them that the whole story was fabricated "to amuse them," but later he assured his sister that it was all true.

Some of the motifs and patterns of this biographical or autobiographical narrative bear resemblance to those found in Goldsmith's later imaginative work. For example, in chapter 12 of *The Vicar of Wakefield,* Moses, the Vicar's son, leaves for the fair with a good horse and returns with a gross of green spectacles: "Marry, hang the ideot [*sic*]," cries his mother. Mrs. Hardcastle similarly abuses her son at the end of *She Stoops to Conquer:* "you graceless varlet." Providential rescues from distress, benevolent father figures, sentimental ballads and songs, foolish generosity, episodes inside narratives which replicate the overall pattern, and transitions of tone and effect are all very characteristic of Goldsmith's writing.

Catherine's narrative also includes an anecdote in which Goldsmith suffered the indignity of being sent to a private house he believed to be an inn, which, as she points out, is what happens to Marlowe and Hastings in act 1 of *She Stoops to Conquer.* She also included injunctions to interpret the characters of the Vicar in the novel and the Man in Black in *The Citizen of the World* (1762) as that of Charles Goldsmith: "I am sartain that character is his"; and her narrative reminds the reader that Goldsmith dedicated *The Traveller* to his brother Henry. Such congruities started a persistent tradition of reading Goldsmith's works as if they were in large measure naive transcriptions of episodes from his own experience. His contemporaries' reaction to his character as that of an "inspired idiot" (Horace Walpole), a socially inept genius who somehow "wrote like an angel, but talked like poor Poll" (David Garrick), further legitimated this tradition. But since the publication of Ricardo Quintana's *Oliver Goldsmith: A Georgian Study* (1967) critics have begun to stress the qualities in Goldsmith's work which counterbalance these autobiographical aspects, qualities of great aesthetic and rhetorical poise together with a remarkable control of ironic and argumentative tones of voice. This balance suggests that the strength of Goldsmith's art lies in its combination of personal charm with what Quintana calls the "strength and firmness of impersonal state-ment," and it allows a reading of his works that grants his ability to play off his own characteristics against some of the most important cultural stereotypes of his day, such as the Amiable Spendthrift (Charles Surface in Richard Brinsley Sheridan's *The Rivals,* 1775) and the Innocent Abroad (Laurence Sterne's *Sentimental Journey,* 1768).

Uncle Contarine eventually, in 1752, provided Goldsmith with fifty pounds in order that he should study law at the Temple in London, but he lost it all gambling in a Dublin coffeehouse and returned home in deep disgrace. Finally, in the second half of 1752, he was sent to the University of Edinburgh to study medicine, with less cash in hand but the promise of ten pounds a year from the ever-hopeful Contarine. At the age of about twenty-four Goldsmith had left Ireland never to return.

Goldsmith studied in Edinburgh for about eighteen months, apparently taking some real interest in medicine, then decided that, as he knew French, he should complete his studies at Paris. Going instead to Leiden in Holland, he studied medicine and the Dutch without enthusiasm: the experience seems to have given him a dislike for the colonializing bourgeoisies of the day. He then decamped, probably in late 1754 or early 1755, for a wandering tour of the Continent, which took him through Belgium, France, Germany, and Switzerland to Italy. How he supported himself on this trip is unclear. Gambling has been suggested, and his description of the roughly similar travels of George Primrose in chapter 20 of *The Vicar of Wakefield* hint at flute playing, public disputations in universities, and casual employment as traveling tutor. All except the last have an air of fantasy about them but may be true. He stayed six months at Padua before returning through France to England, reaching Dover in early February 1756 and London shortly thereafter, "without Friends, recommendations, money, or impudence," as he wrote in a 27 December 1757 letter to Daniel Hudson.

For a year he struggled at various forms of employment, beginning as an assistant in an apothecary's shop between the monument and Lower Thames Street. Then, with the aid of a loan from Fenn Sleigh, an acquaintance from his Edinburgh days, and claiming to possess a medical degree, he set up briefly as a physician in Bankside, just across the river in Southwark. He had, he told Bishop Percy, "plenty of Patients, but got no Fees." Near the end of 1756 he took a temporary post as schoolmaster in a Presbyterian establishment in Peckham run by the Reverend Dr. John Milner, the father of another Edinburgh friend. At Milner's house he

Letter to John Newbery in which Goldsmith announced his inability to complete his abridgment of Plutarch's Lives *(from*
Temple Scott, Oliver Goldsmith Bibliographically and Biographically Considered, *1928)*

met Ralph Griffiths, bookseller and proprietor of
the *Monthly Review;* Griffiths offered him a position
as reviewer, at an annual salary of one hundred
pounds, and by April 1757 Goldsmith's literary career was under way.

For over six months he lived above Griffiths's
bookshop in Paternoster Row and wrote assiduously for five hours a day on books covering a wide
variety of topics. Although these reviews are only
casual and occasional productions, they sometimes
reveal settled views and principles and a composed
and flexible prose style which he would cultivate in
later works. Reviewing Thomas Gray's *Odes* (1757),
for example, Goldsmith displays a characteristic allegiance to the classical Augustan tradition in arguing that the Pindaric exoticism of Gray's effects
will find little response in the native English temperament. Be more original, Goldsmith tells Gray:
adapt foreign effects to the new context, "study the
people," and show yourself "capable of giving pleasure to all." The paradox shows that this advice is
not mere nerveless classicism but the result of an in-

dividual mind working through subtle and carefully
judged transitions of thought.

Goldsmith left the *Monthly Review* and Griffiths's accomodation after about seven months, apparently objecting, according to Thomas Percy in
his "Memoir of Goldsmith" (1801), to "Griffith and
his wife continually objecting to everything he
wrote & insisting on his implicitly submitting to
their corrections." He was still eager to pursue a
medical career, and for a time he had hopes of an
appointment as a physician with the East India
Company near Madras. This plan eventually came
to nothing on 21 December 1758, when he was examined at the College of Surgeons for a license that
would have entitled him to apply for the relatively
low position of surgeon's mate on one of the company's ships. "Doctor" Goldsmith was found to be
unqualified.

After having lodged for a few months in late
1757 near Salisbury Square, just south of Fleet
Street, he moved briefly back to Peckham, to help in
Milner's school. He then moved again in 1758 to

Green Arbour Court, Old Bailey. As well as the East India scheme and other ideas, he had several literary projects in mind. Griffiths had commissioned a translation of Jean Marteilhe's gory and prolix *Memoires d'un Protestant* (1757). Goldsmith renovated and embellished the style, tidied up the structure, made it more dramatic, and effectively "translated" Marteilhe's crude account of his persecutions into a vivid and moving narrative, which was published on 9 March 1758. Griffiths and another bookseller, Edward Dilly, paid him twenty pounds, but the book appeared under an assumed name.

By 1759 his circle of contacts was expanding rapidly to include Archibald Hamilton and Tobias Smollett, proprietor and editor of the *Critical Review*, and Robert and James Dodsley of the Tully's Head bookshop in the West End. The Dodsley clientele was distinctly upscale, and Goldsmith's contract to produce an extended survey of "The Present State of Taste and Literature in Europe" was something of a coup. Other projects also had a distinctly European flavor: he engaged with Griffiths to produce a "Life of Voltaire," which was ready and paid for (twenty pounds) by early 1759, but which was not published until 1761, when it appeared in installments between February and November in the *Lady's Magazine* as "Memoirs of M. de Voltaire" at a time when Goldsmith was probably editing the magazine himself.

The Dodsley brothers published *An Enquiry into the Present State of Polite Learning in Europe* on 2 April 1759 to very mixed reviews. Even the *Critical Review*, for which Goldsmith was then working, found it laudable only for its lively and agreeable manner. *An Enquiry* is a curious, composite work, mixing quite promising semi-sociological arguments about the decay and possible renewal of the arts with snippets of information about ancient and modern authors. Dante rates one hundred words of rather derogatory comment, and the Danish baron Holberg, whose early career bears a striking resemblance to Goldsmith's own, gets four hundred words of fulsome praise. Goldsmith may well have hoped for a similar fate as that of Holberg: "honoured with nobility, and enriched with the bounty of the king . . . opulence and esteem." Furthermore, *An Enquiry* insults the "dull and dronish . . . Monthly Reviews and Magazines," pedantic critics, actor-managers, and mercenary booksellers who commission "tedious compilations": the whole contemporary, middle-class, metropolitan, literary culture, just the culture in which he was beginning successfully to immerse himself. His acquaintance

with Hamilton and Smollett had led, in January 1759, to a position as reviewer on the Tory-oriented *Critical Review*, to which he contributed for about a year, and again in 1763. Goldsmith, who was more of a Tory than a Whig (though he refused on principle to engage in partisan political writing), may have felt more at home than at the Whiggish *Monthly Review*. In October 1759 another bookseller, John Wilkie, set up the *Bee* and the *Lady's Magazine*, and Israel Pottinger started the *Busy Body* and the *Weekly Magazine*. Goldsmith compiled virtually the whole of the *Bee* for its short run of eight numbers, and he contributed to the latter three; indeed, between 1757 and 1763 (if one counts the "Chinese Letters" – later included in *The Citizen of the World*, 1762 – as separate essays) he wrote over two hundred essays and reviews in at least a dozen magazines.

At this point, when his enhanced professional status was beginning to result in a degree of editorial independence, Goldsmith's interests in biography began to develop. As well as writing the "Memoirs of M. de Voltaire," he published in the first number of the *Bee* (6 October 1759) his short account of the French scientist and writer Pierre Louis Moreau de Maupertuis. The second number (13 October) includes a letter, borrowed from the Dutch author Justus Van Effen, with anecdotes about King Charles XII of Sweden. In the *Weekly Magazine* (5 January 1760) Goldsmith published a short "Life of the Hon. Robert Boyle," about the Irish philosopher, which he largely borrowed from the *Biographia Britannica*. He then wrote two more original biographical sketches. The first is the "Memoirs of the Late Famous Bishop of Cloyne," about the philosopher George Berkeley, for which he probably used anecdotal material gleaned from Uncle Contarine and another relative, the Reverend Isaac Goldsmith: Contarine was at Trinity at the same time as Berkeley, and Isaac Goldsmith was dean of Cloyne from 1736 to 1769. This sketch was published in the *Weekly Magazine* on 29 December 1759 and 5 January 1760. The second is letter 59 of the "Chinese Letters" (letter 62 in Arthur Friedman's 1966 edition), published in the *Public Ledger* for 28 July 1760; it is a brief, romanticized history of "Catherina Alexowna, wife of Peter the Great," which Goldsmith refers to as an "Authentic History."

In personal letters Goldsmith himself said that these "Memoirs" were "no more than a catch penny," and that he "spent but four weeks on the whole performance." Donald A. Stauffer characterizes Goldsmith as being a biographer "by chance rather

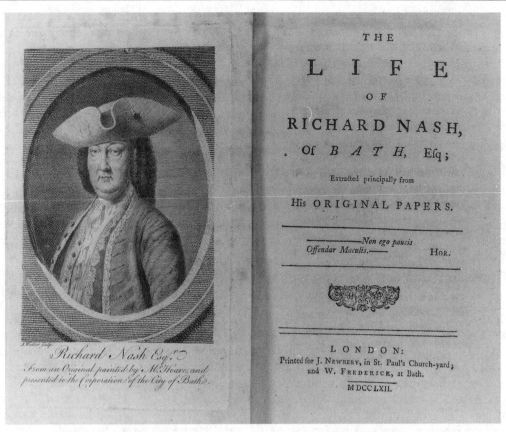

Frontispiece and title page for Goldsmith's biography of the "Little King" of Bath society

than by choice" and ascribes the composition of the short pieces primarily to the vogue for such sketches in periodicals. But while it is true that Goldsmith reprinted none of these when he collected his *Essays* in 1765, taken collectively they point toward the distinctive nature of many of his later writings and contain hints of the originality and coherence of *The Life of Richard Nash*. Of particular interest are the underlying attitudes to biography that emerge through the mixing of naturalism and romance, and biography and fiction.

All Goldsmith's biographies appear to rest on the general premise of truth — fidelity to the details of the facts — which is characteristic of later eighteenth-century biography. By 1750 this premise was replacing the earlier attitude which had imbued biographies that were either formal panegyrics, praise of the power and virtue of great men, or scurrilous and satiric attacks on villains and malefactors. Genuine biography (as opposed to the casual and sensational tales of the lives of criminals or courtesans) came to stress the mixture of good and evil, and strength and frailty, in the interests of producing a realistic effect. Late-eighteenth-century biography still had a moral or educative function, but

to fulfill this goal it had to be probable, convincing, and judicious in order to establish a degree of imaginative sympathy between the reader and the biographical subject.

There is some disagreement over the speed and completeness with which this transition occurred. Stauffer represents the more modern attitude as having "gained wide currency" by the latter part of the century, to the extent of having become a "truism." But Wardle, in his biography of Goldsmith, says that the notion of a balanced, detailed biography was still "provocative" and "new" in 1761, and he isolates its origins in Johnson's essays in the *Rambler* (number 60) and the *Idler* (number 84) and in his *The Life of Mr. Richard Savage* (1744). Goldsmith knew Johnson's essays and indeed closed his introduction to his abridged translation of *Plutarch's Lives* (1762) by quoting the *Rambler* (number 60) in its entirety. To some critics, such as Joseph Brown, this fact indicates that Goldsmith borrowed Johnson's view of biography more or less wholesale. But more recently, critics such as G. W. Bowersock and Quintana have pointed out that the detailed presentation of human character in terms of a balance or tension between antithetical characteristics is common to classical biographers such as Suetonius and Plutarch and is also a feature of the Augustan verse tradition of which Goldsmith saw himself as a late representative. So Goldsmith may deserve the epithet of *pioneer* of biography which Stauffer and Wardle bestow on him for following Johnson, or he may deserve it because of the individual nature of his achievement in biography.

Goldsmith articulates the more modern view of biography as early as in his translation of Marteilhe: "all here wears the Face of Sincerity," he says, warning the readers that they should expect to "be content with the simple Exhibition of Truth." Similarly, in the "Memoirs of M. de Voltaire" Goldsmith breaks off from an anecdote to apologize for giving the "trifling particulars of a great man's life" and to explain that "these generally best mark a character." He states his aim as being neither to "compose a panegyric" nor "draw up an invective; truth only is my aim." But the Marteilhe translation wears the gloss of conscious artistry, and the biography of Voltaire is a mixture of genuine data, anecdotes borrowed from Goldsmith's other writings and elsewhere, and allusions to Voltaire's conquests and liaisons. It also includes supposedly firsthand accounts of episodes which could not have taken place, such as the report of an energetic disputation in Paris among Voltaire, Bernard le Bovier de Fontenelle, and Denis Diderot, at a point in time when Voltaire was not in Paris and Fontenelle was ninety-eight. This example may be invention, or it may be a borrowing from a presumed but unlocated source.

So the "truth" in Goldsmith's biographies is partly an artistic truth conveyed by effects akin to fictional effects, though still capable of balance and evenhandedness. The "Authentic History" of Catherina Alexowna turns out to be a brief, apparently original romance narrative of a young maiden of low degree who suffers hardships and distresses virtuously and is then transformed at a stroke into an empress. A supporting essay, "Of the Assemblies of Russia," published two months later in the *Lady's Magazine* (September 1760), shows an entirely nonromantic Catherina providing rules for the embryonic polite society of Russia, introducing mixed assemblies, and socializing the "savage people." Change maiden to man and empress to "King" and one has the outline of the life history of Nash, who similarly harmonized the rude society of Bath. The climax of *The Vicar of Wakefield* comes when the Vicar has socialized and regulated another society, that of the chaotic prison: he has formed the prisoners "into something social and humane, and had the

pleasure of regarding myself as a legislator, who had brought men from their native ferocity into friendship and obedience."

As well as the themes and motifs of Goldsmith's later work being present in the early biographies, there are hints of his later development of character in fiction. One of the central critical problems of *The Vicar of Wakefield,* for example, is the question of whether the Vicar is being lauded or satirized by Goldsmith. Sometimes the Vicar's narration is perspicacious and witty, but sometimes it is transparently obtuse and ridiculous past the point of absurdity. This combination replicates the effect that Goldsmith's own personality made on his contemporaries, but it is also anticipated in the biographical sketches. Writing of Maupertuis, who popularized Newtonian physics for the French, Goldsmith produces three short paragraphs which use secondary sources to identify and praise his subject's achievements as writer and "good citizen" in straightforward terms, and then he begins the fourth: "That oddity of character which great men are sometimes remarkable for, Maupertuis was not entirely free from. If we can believe Voltaire, he once attempted to castrate himself; but whether this be true or no, it is certain he was extremely whimsical." Here Goldsmith forces his defining premise, that biography should show strength and frailty, greatness and peculiarity, so hard as to transform it from a truism into an oxymoron. The public figure becomes for a moment outlandish and incapable of definition: "whimsical" hardly covers the case just mentioned. Similarly, Berkeley may be seen by fellow students as "the greatest genius or the greatest dunce in the whole university," passing examinations "with the utmost applause" but nearly killing himself by experimenting with a mock hanging in order to "know what were the pains and symptoms" felt by criminals at their execution. His genius for metaphysics and a praiseworthy bent for charitable works go hand in hand with an absurd faith in the medical efficacy of tar water. Goldsmith may have dramatized his own characteristics in his writing, but his view of biography allowed him also to see such antithetical qualities in many of his biographical subjects.

In 1759 Goldsmith made the acquaintance of the publisher John Newbery, part owner of two magazines and a specialist in educational literature. Early in 1760 Newbery set up another newspaper, the daily *Public Ledger,* which specialized in business and financial news, and invited Goldsmith to contribute a twice-weekly column along the lines of Johnson's *Idler* at an annual salary of one hundred

Caricature of Goldsmith by Henry Bunbury (British Museum)

pounds. Over the next nineteen months, initially on an inside page but then as a front-page feature, Goldsmith's "Chinese Letters" appeared, a series of 119 letters purportedly containing the observations of an oriental traveler, Lien Chi Altangi, on the London scene. A revised version of these, together with four additional letters, was published by Newbery in a collected edition on 1 May 1762 under the title *The Citizen of the World*. The form was an established one, derived from models such as Montesquieu's *Lettres persanes* (1721), which had been widely imitated in English, but Goldsmith's series has a distinctive freshness and variety. Day-to-day events in London are brought vividly to life in Altangi's sharp but bemused observation of a gallery of wholly plausible incidental and recurring characters. Topical satire, moral essay, and burlesque are presented in a loose, seminarrative framework and with Altangi's less worldly philosophical attitude. The effect involves deft control of comic, argumentative, and ironical tones inside a freewheeling structure. The letters were popular

enough to be reprinted, plagiarized, and parodied in other periodicals, and *The Citizen of the World* attracted favorable reviews, but a second London edition was not called for until July 1774.

In the middle of 1760 Goldsmith moved from his seedy-genteel lodgings in Green Arbour Court to two rooms at the more prepossessing Wine Office Court, just off Fleet Street. His landlady was a relative by marriage of Newbery, who continued to take a paternalistic interest in Goldsmith. The "Memoirs of Voltaire" were published in 1761, and he continued to write for Newbery and others in magazines. But his output slackened as the year wore on, and 1761 was remarkable more for his varied social life than for artistic progression. On 31 May Johnson was among the "much Company" that Percy records as having spent the evening at Goldsmith's, and Johnson and Goldsmith were soon close friends. Soon afterward he met and formed a lifelong friendship with the painter Joshua Reynolds.

For Newbery he revised his "Chinese Letters" and assisted in what Newbery hoped would be the first volume of a "Compendium of Biography," a seven-volume abridgment of *Plutarch's Lives.* Goldsmith was charged with abridging six or seven "Lives" in each volume but was growing as dissatisfied with this form of hackwork as he was with the periodicals. He completed four volumes but cried off the fifth, pleading illness, and the rest were prepared by Joseph Collier. Newbery published the seven-volume set from May to November 1762; Goldsmith received twenty-three and a half guineas for his efforts. His illness was genuine, though, and necessitated visits to Tunbridge and Bath to recuperate. The visit to Bath was timely, as he had probably already been commissioned by Newbery to write a biographical sketch of Nash. George Scott, Nash's executor, allowed Goldsmith access to Nash's papers, and *The Life of Richard Nash* was published on 14 October 1762. Goldsmith had already received fourteen guineas as payment "in full for the copy" in March, only thirteen months after the death of his subject. *The Life of Richard Nash* sold well at first and was widely excerpted in newspapers and magazines. A second edition, lightly revised and titled *The Life of Richard Nash, Esq.: Late Master of the Ceremonies at Bath,* followed in December, but, apart from a Dublin edition in the same year, it was not printed again until 1837. *The Life of Richard Nash* is, according to R. E. M. Peach, "the quarry from which all succeeding biographies of Nash have been hewn."

Apart from the fact that he disliked writing (his pen "numbed all his faculties"), Nash was almost the ideal subject for a Goldsmith biography; he was a ready-made Goldsmithian character. Nash was as reticent as Goldsmith about his obscure early life, but it is known that he went to Oxford as a "batteler" or "demi-commoner," a status equivalent to Goldsmith's at Trinity, and left in some disgrace. His gradual transformation into the social legislator and "little king" of his "little people" at Bath revealed many traits in common with Goldsmith: "kindheartedness . . . generosity of a somewhat reckless kind . . . neglect of strict obligations, carelessness and prodigality . . . unfailing good humour, and certain puerile vanities, such as a love of fine clothes." In some respects he was what Goldsmith would have liked to have been: successful at gambling; honored by the monarch (Nash had had to refuse an expensive knighthood from William III after staging an entertainment for him); and prominent in a distinctive society. In terms of personality he was what Goldsmith was seen as: sometimes admirable, sometimes reprehensible, and sometimes ridiculous.

But *The Life of Richard Nash* is remarkable for its poise and control rather than for any sense of full identification with its subject. Goldsmith begins by coolly presenting himself as the "Editor" of Nash's papers and by asserting that the book is a "genuine and candid recital," not a "romantic history." The critic for the *Monthly Review* (November 1762) noted the parallel with "Johnson's Admirable Life of Savage," and Goldsmith does indeed develop an authoritative Johnsonian stress on the common qualities of humanity in order to justify the selection of a subject from "the middle ranks of life." But as Nash was "placed in public view" in his career, Goldsmith adapts Johnson's emphasis on the revelation of individual moral nature in biography (in *Idler,* number 84): "how he became discontented with himself") to a more social one: "how [he] acquired the esteem of [his] friends and acquaintance." Nash's is "a mind without disguise": his vices and virtues were transparent, "open to the eye."

In order to reinforce this public, social quality and to lend an air of documentary realism, Goldsmith devotes about one-tenth of *The Life of Richard Nash* to information about the social and architectural history of Bath, gleaned from the architect John Wood's *Essay towards a Description of Bath* (second edition, 1749). In the later stages Goldsmith includes panegyrical epitaphs on Nash, the hymn sung at his funeral, letters written to and by him, and an epigram satirizing his portrait in Wiltshire's Ballroom. These additions diffuse the narrative but further establish the sense that Nash's identity was primarily a social one, conferred on him by others.

The story of a commoner of obscure origins who rises to be honored by a monarch and himself becomes a "king," even if a little one, is not without its romantic aspects, but Goldsmith keeps these under careful control. Indeed, they were already present in the public, social account of Nash. The motif of the mythic hero who, as described by critic Richard Wendorf, "establishes his authority (and thereby confirms his identity) by resolving a crisis as he enters the city" is relayed in a paragraph derived closely from Wood's *Essay towards a Description of Bath,* which recounts the story of how Nash combatted Dr. John Radcliffe (who had said he would "*cast a toad into the spring*") by writing a pamphlet against the medicinal powers of the waters. Mock threats of magic spells require a counterspell, so Nash is shown as driving the toad out with music, "as they usually charmed the venom of the Tarantula," and the number of visitors to the area increased when Nash set up regular concerts. As in

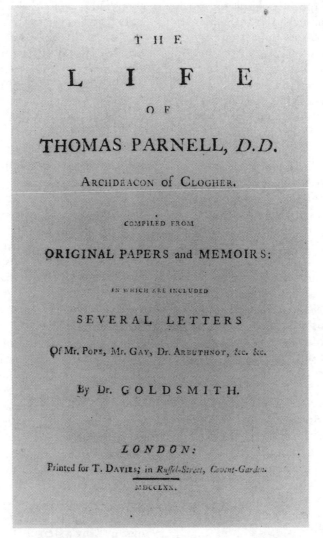

THE

LIFE

OF

THOMAS PARNELL, *D.D.*

ARCHDEACON of CLOGHER.

COMPILED FROM

ORIGINAL PAPERS and MEMOIRS:

IN WHICH ARE INCLUDED

SEVERAL LETTERS

Of Mr. POPE, Mr. GAY, Dr. ARBUTHNOT, &c. &c.

By Dr. GOLDSMITH.

LONDON:

Printed for T. DAVIES; in *Ruſſel-Street, Covent-Garden.*

MDCCLXX.

Title page for the first separate edition of Goldsmith's biography of a poet he admired for his straightforward, unaffected language

the earlier sketches, history and romance are blended with fiction in the form of dramatized anecdotes about Nash which Goldsmith often claims to be transmitting firsthand and verbatim, even though he never met Nash. Indeed, a few of these anecdotes are borrowed from Goldsmith's earlier works or are duplicated in *The Vicar of Wakefield.*

This composite method in *The Life of Richard Nash* is held together by an understated moral attitude which demonstrates Goldsmith's full awareness of the functions of biography. The inflation of the subjects (Nash and Bath) achieved through sociohistorical and romantic qualities is set against a reductive attitude implicit in words such as *little, stupid trifles,* and *foibles,* and explicit in such anecdotes as Nash's winning a bet by "riding naked through a village upon a cow." Nash's regulation of the emer-

gent Bath society, his care for the individuals who were threatened with ruin by gambling, and his charitable donations to institutions such as the new Bath hospital are presented as genuine and admirable achievements. Bath society is exposed to a reductive gaze. Nash may be a poor letter writer, for example, but the duchess of Marlborough "seems not to be a much better . . . but she was worth many hundreds of thousands of pounds, and that might console her." Charity itself is not merely commended but subtly set in perspective through the epithets of "reigning and fashionable virtue." The vivid anecdotes about Nash are set against a breadth of satiric application so that his individual peculiarities are seen as belonging to a universal human nature. As Nash grows older, he becomes ineffectual, outmoded, and partly discredited: "his mind shrunk to the size of the little objects on which it was employed." Goldsmith changes the accent toward pathos, but this sentimental tone is quickly replaced by the more formal manner of the public manifestations of regret at Nash's death, and then by a dispassionate view of Nash in his domestic routine. This shifting of perspectives stops *The Life* just short of full artistic coherence, but the book remains, to quote the *Monthly Review,* "lively, ingenious, and entertaining."

Toward the end of 1762 Goldsmith moved from Wine Office Court to Canonbury House, Islington, just outside London, where Newbery lived for part of the year. For two years Newbery was his patron and banker. In an attempt to regularize Goldsmith's sometimes disastrous finances, Newbery gave him a strict allowance, which was to be repaid by literary commissions. The projects included prefaces, reviews, and abridgments, which he drudged at through 1763. A lucrative contract in March 1763 (three guineas per printed sheet) with James Dodsley for a "Chronological History of the Lives of Eminent Persons of Great Britain and Ireland" was never completed; nineteen months later Goldsmith sold the few completed sheets, which Dodsley had returned, to Newbery for eight guineas. This abortive enterprise was probably the origin of *The Life of Thomas Parnell* and the life of Bolingbroke, which seem to have been available in 1770 to accompany a printing of Parnell's *Poems* and Bolingbroke's *Dissertation upon Parties.* But Goldsmith was never to be a systematic biographer; instead, he was to achieve a remarkable double apotheosis, social and literary.

On the strength of Goldsmith's work to date and a friendship of two years' standing, Johnson was happy to assert to James Boswell in 1763 that Goldsmith was "one of the first men we have as an authour ... and a very worthy man too." When in the winter of 1763–1764 Reynolds suggested to Johnson that they form a literary club, Goldsmith was invited to be one of the founding members. "The Club," which met for supper every Monday at the Turk's Head on Gerrard Street in Soho, quickly became the most prestigious of its kind. Goldsmith was happy to play the fool for the company, but the publication by Newbery of his poem *The Traveller: or, A Prospect of Society* on 19 December 1764 meant that they had to begin taking him seriously. Nothing in the literary world carried more prestige and status than reflective, Augustan heroic couplets which blended personal sincerity with considered social utterance in dignified but accessible diction, and

this goal is what Goldsmith achieved. The poem puts forward virtually all the cultural positions he had developed in his earlier prose writings, in the course of just over four hundred lines. Johnson paid Goldsmith the compliment of improving the ending, and Newbery paid him twenty guineas. The critical reception was almost universally admiring; the sale, after a slow start, sufficient to require nine printings in Goldsmith's lifetime; and the author, to quote Reynolds, was "sought after with greediness" by social and literary London.

Goldsmith's only other large-scale publication in 1764 was *An History of England in a Series of Letters from a Nobleman to His Son,* published by Newbery on 26 June for the same payment as for *The Traveller.* This book is another compilation, but the style was plausible enough to persuade the reviewers that the author was a genuine nobleman. It ran to twenty-five printings by 1824 and was used, as were Goldsmith's other histories, as school texts throughout the nineteenth century.

The author was not, of course, a nobleman, but he could count nobility among his friends: Robert Nugent (later Lord Clare) and the earl and countess of Northumberland, to whom he dedicated his ballad *Edwin and Angelina* in 1765. In the same year his new status led to the publication of a selection of his periodical pieces as *Essays. By Mr. Goldsmith.* Newbery and Griffin paid ten guineas each, and the volume sold reasonably well. In 1764 Goldsmith had left Canonbury House for the Temple, at first moving to temporary lodgings in Garden Court, and in 1765 he moved to superior lodgings in King's Bench Walk, where he could eventually afford to employ a manservant. A final attempt to work as a physician met with little success, even though he equipped himself with new purple silk trousers, a scarlet knee-length coat, a full-dress wig, and a cane. On one occasion a patient's appalled apothecary refused to make up a prescription Goldsmith had ordered for her. The financial implications of this abortive project led him briefly back toward hackwork, compilation, and translation, but there was one other effect of his recent experiences. In 1762 Johnson had rescued Goldsmith from an unpaid and importunate landlady by taking to Newbery's shop the manuscript of a short novel, which Goldsmith had showed him. According to Boswell, Newbery gave sixty pounds for it, but it is more likely that he bought a third share for twenty guineas. The publishers William Strahan and Benjamin Collins later paid the same amount each for the other two shares. The novel, *The Vicar of Wakefield,* had become the work of a prestigious

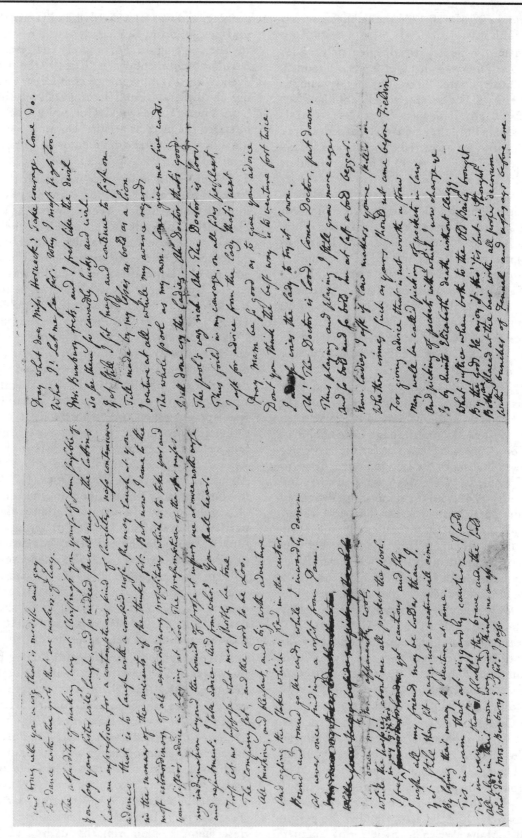

Pages from Goldsmith's circa 25 December 1773 verse letter accepting Catherine Horneck Bunbury's invitation to join the Horneck family's New Year's festivities at Barton Hall in Suffolk (MA 1297; Pierpont Morgan Library)

author, and on 27 March 1766 the publishers tried their luck with it.

Goldsmith's poetry is conspicuously of its time, but *The Vicar* was ahead of it: it sold moderately well at first, after mixed but largely complimentary reviews, but became widely popular after Goldsmith's death. It was usually read as a moral, sentimental tale until the mid twentieth century, at which point it was discovered to be susceptible (as was much of Goldsmith's work) to an interpretation which stressed its sophistication and irony. More recently critics have stressed the story's characteristically Goldsmithian double nature, its combination of naiveté and knowingness. It is a disarming, subtle story, the Book of Job rewritten as provincial English domestic comedy. Its brevity is important: at only 170 pages, and in thirty-two chapters, it is a hybrid of a full, naturalistic novel and a short *conte philosophique* such as those of his philosophic and literary mentors, Voltaire's *Candide* (1759) and Johnson's *Rasselas* (1759). Hence it is, as Wardle remarks, an "anomaly" like its author, but its durability proves its integrity.

The Vicar of Wakefield brought in no new money for Goldsmith, and he had a reputation to keep up. The most fashionable and lucrative form of writing was drama, and although Goldsmith had on occasion expressed contempt for the insipidity and conventionalism of the London stage, he set to work on a comedy. *The Good-Natur'd Man* was finished by early 1767, and the manuscript deposited with David Garrick, the current theatrical leader. Garrick took no action for several months and eventually returned the manuscript after a prickly conversation with Goldsmith, who was possibly already negotiating with Garrick's rival, George Colman. Reynolds and others in Goldsmith's circle lobbied hard for the play, and Colman agreed to schedule it for production shortly before Christmas 1767. Garrick essayed a spoiling tactic by arranging the first night of Hugh Kelly's genteel comedy *False Delicacy* for the same date, and Goldsmith's play eventually appeared on stage on 29 January 1768, with the printed text published on 5 February.

The Good-Natur'd Man was a moderate success, running for ten nights and through five impressions; Goldsmith netted four or five hundred pounds. The first night had almost been ruined by the audience hissing at a scene it considered "low," meaning below the social level considered appropriate for comedy. But the actors pulled the performance off, and the play ended by inspiring laughter. Goldsmith, just as volatile as the audience, attended his celebratory Club supper, sang comic songs, ate

nothing, and was later discovered in tears by the astonished Johnson; Goldsmith vowed never to write for the stage again. Fortunately the reviews were mostly complimentary. Artistically the play is uneven, with several vigorous comic characters playing ebulliently around a comparatively indistinct hero, Young Honeywood. Goldsmith seems to have intended the piece as a satiric comment on the fashionable sentimental drama but then to have partly deferred to the taste of the audience.

Goldsmith now purchased, with the money from his play, a long lease on a fine set of chambers in Brick Court, Middle Temple, which he kept until his death. To try to keep himself in the ostentatiously sociable manner to which he had become accustomed, he undertook several large literary projects for the booksellers. In 1768 he was commissioned by Thomas Davies to write a history of Rome for 250 guineas; this work was published on 18 May 1769. For Griffin he agreed in February 1769 to compile a huge natural history, *An History of the Earth, and Animated Nature* (1774), in eight volumes, which was worth the vast sum of eight hundred guineas, paid in advance installments. Goldsmith took three years to complete it, and the work was not published until shortly after his death. Other projects included *The History of England,* in four volumes – promised to Davies in June 1769 for five hundred pounds and finished and published in August 1771 – and *The Grecian History* (1774), begun for Griffin in 1773 but not published until after Goldsmith's death. In order to complete his tasks he partly withdrew from London in spring 1768 and took a cottage in the village of Edgeware, to the northwest of the city; he also made several extended rural excursions. His hugely increased income did nothing for Goldsmith's finances: however much money he had coming in, he always contrived to spend and give away more. He was two thousand pounds in debt at his death.

Apart from the Grecian and Roman histories, the works of Goldsmith's last years are notably preoccupied with British themes, at the expense of the earlier stress on European culture. His second major ethical poem, *The Deserted Village,* written in 1769 and published on 26 May 1770, describes the effects of rural depopulation and of "luxury" on English society and on morality. The Goldsmith family tried strenuously to relate the poem to the rural Ireland of Goldsmith's own background, and, as before, this move legitimated a critical tradition which described the poem primarily in terms of the poet's personal feelings, in this case feelings of nostalgia and of guilt at deserting his family. This biographical reading is wholly at odds with the way the poem was perceived by the critics of Goldsmith's own time, who responded to it as an extremely carefully composed poem in the neo-Augustan manner and a forceful contribution to an important public debate. There were wide and prolonged discussions about the issues raised by the poem and some cavilling at its political message: Englishmen did not like to be reminded of the retrograde effects of aspects of contemporary social "progress." But although its drift was opposed by other poems it was supported by John Robinson's *The Village Oppress'd* (1771) and by an anonymous writer in the *London Magazine* (October 1772), who asserted that "a *deserted village* and an *oppressed village* are not the fictions of poetry." The poem ran through six authorized and four pirated printings in 1770. Goldsmith is reported to have returned one hundred guineas to Griffin after deciding that Griffin had overpaid him for the 430-line work, but he made at least that sum from the profits that quickly accrued.

In the same year, Goldsmith published his two final biographical works: "The Life of Dr. Parnell," prefixed by Davies to a new edition of Parnell's *Poems on Several Occasions* in June 1770 and published separately as *The Life of Thomas Parnell, D.D.* on 5 July, and *The Life of Henry St. John, Lord Viscount Bolingbroke*, which was prefixed by Davies to the ninth edition of Bolingbroke's *Dissertation upon Parties* on 1 December 1770 and published separately a few days later. Both publications were anonymous.

Bolingbroke is a strikingly poor piece of work and was reviewed as such: 80 percent of it is transcribed or paraphrased from the entry on Bolingbroke in the fifth edition (1760) of the *Biographia Britannica*. This fact may be taken as evidence that Goldsmith had begun to attach little importance to biography, as Bolingbroke's *The Idea of a Patriot King* (1749) was one of his favorite political works, representing the monarch as a patriarchal figure akin to the father figures in Goldsmith's imaginative work. The king should be above the reach of party politics, "equally the friend and the father of all."

Nor did Goldsmith make anything of the connection between Parnell and Bolingbroke: Parnell dedicated his verse *Essay on the Different Stiles of Poetry* (1713) to Bolingbroke, but Goldsmith does not mention this work when recording Parnell's life. He was fully aware that he could not do what a biographer should: Parnell's "peculiarities are gone to the grave with him" (Parnell having died in 1718), so the biography must be given in "very unpoetical detail." *The Life of Thomas Parnell* also attracted disparaging reviews, though the anonymous writer for the

Critical Review (July 1770) praised the style and noted shrewdly that Goldsmith's aim was critical as much as biographical. Parnell's poetic language is a model of what Goldsmith tried to achieve in his own verse, being straightforward, unaffected, and accessible. It "conveys the warmest thoughts in the simplest expression." The writer for the *Critical Review* took the point but was uneasy about the implicit rebuke to contemporary forms of poetry: "we are afraid the doctor is growing intoxicated with fame, and insensible to all living eminence except his own." *The Life of Thomas Parnell* is evidence of the coherence of Goldsmith's aesthetic, though, and replicates the attitude of his earlier criticism of Gray in the *Monthly Review* (September 1757) in the remarks about the "licentious transpositions" of modern poets and their "follies and affectations."

By 1770 Goldsmith was at the zenith of his professional and social life. At the end of 1769 he had been nominated and accepted for the position of professor of ancient history in the Royal Academy; he was having his portrait painted by Reynolds; and at "The Club" and elsewhere his public persona of a humorous, zany individual was as firmly established as Laurence Sterne's had been when he presented himself as Tristram Shandy to the London of the 1760s. This persona was probably an exaggeration of the real Goldsmith, though Hester Lynch [Thrale] Piozzi attributed it to a pathological and "unequall'd rage of shining in Conversation." Reynolds, who was closer to him than almost anyone, felt sure that a "great part of Dr. Goldsmith's folly and absurdity proceeded from principle," that his effectively abasing himself in company was the result of a strong desire to be liked. Goldsmith was aware of this persona, even though he may not have had full control over it: in his posthumously published poem *Retaliation* (1774), after drawing humorous and devastatingly accurate character sketches of his friends in mock epitaphs, he characterizes himself as a "gooseberry fool."

In 1771 Goldsmith visited Bath at least twice as the guest of Lord Clare, and he spent part of the summer writing his volumes on natural history at one of his rural hideaways at Hyde, six miles northwest of London. But he had also, as he explained to Bennet Langton – a founding member of "The Club" – in September, been "quite alone trying to write a Comedy," which was "now finished." The manuscript was given to Colman the following year, but the producer and others had such serious doubts about its viability that the piece did not appear at Covent Garden until 15 March 1773, titled (at the last moment) *She Stoops to Conquer; or, The*

Mistakes of a Night, which was published later that year.

Goldsmith was badly in need of a success: he had been borrowing money in 1772 and had also been suffering from an inflammation of the bladder serious enough to require surgery. The theatrical management's contagious gloom and the perverse whims of some of the acting company meant that his "ease and comfort" had deserted him, but the play was a triumph. The first performances were accompanied throughout, according to the *Public Advertiser,* by "uninterrupted Laughter or clamorous Plaudits." The run extended for the twelve nights of the season for which the house remained available, and the "Orange-women" (vendors at the theater), according to the *Morning Chronicle,* sold more copies of the published play in half an hour on the fourth night than they had ever sold "of any new piece during its whole run." The critics did not know how to respond to the blend of comedy and near farce in the play, but they applauded Goldsmith's attempt to reintroduce laughing comedy to an audience which had previously been more committed to the sentimental drama.

The plot of *She Stoops to Conquer* evolves from two deceptions. Tony Lumpkin, the ebullient and ungenteel son of a country family, persuades two visiting London gallants that his father's house, to which they have been invited, is really an inn. Kate, the daughter, succeeds in persuading Marlow, one of the visitors, that she is a barmaid. Complications follow unrelentingly, Tony inventing stratagems with great facility and Kate drawing out Marlow's character, until all is resolved. Modern critics ascribe the success of the play to its mixture of what Quintana calls "artificialities" and "naturalism" and to the way Goldsmith achieves the difficult feat of unobtrusively blending satire with good-natured comedy, so that the farcical elements are transcended. Tony's "satirical" plots are taken over by Kate's, which are ameliorative and educational: what might have been simply a "comedy of deceptions," according to Quintana, ends as a "comedy of discovery."

Goldsmith's health continued to worsen: the infection in his urinary system was developing into strangury. His debilitated physical condition began to be accompanied by signs of irritability and depression, though there were still long intervals of cheerfulness. By June 1773 he had completed the first volume of his *Grecian History,* but rather than retreating to the country to work, he stayed in London for the summer and threw himself determinedly into the distractions of social life. By Christmas he had done very little, and Garrick had to lend him sixty pounds to finance a New Year's visit to the Horneck family, with whom he had a longstanding friendship, at Barton Hall in Suffolk. Briefly he returned to London to promote various projects, but the only spark to his imagination occurred at a meeting of a new, informal, dining club. Garrick's impromptu spoken epitaph – "Here lies NOLLY Goldsmith, for shortness call'd Noll, Who wrote like an angel, but talked like poor Poll" – silenced Goldsmith for a moment. A brief break in Hyde in March 1774 allowed him to write seventy-three couplets of *Retaliation,* which was published on 19 April. Toward the end of March he was forced to return to town for medical treatment in his rooms in the Temple, but his death was precipitated by his dosing himself repeatedly with Dr. James's Fever Powder, a nostrum in which he placed an entirely misguided faith. Worn out by repeated vomiting and diarrhea, he died on 4 April 1774 with only a doctor in attendance.

His debts meant that a planned expensive burial in Westminster Abbey had to be replaced by a private interment in the Temple burying ground on 5 April. The subsequent outburst of public obituary and printed anecdotal reminiscence surpassed even that occasioned by the death of Nash. Goldsmith's friend Percy had promised in 1773 to write his biography, but when he turned the task over to Johnson in 1777, Johnson was unable to complete it. Percy's flimsy "Memoir of Goldsmith" was not published until 1801. This circumstance left Goldsmith's life story at the mercy of what later biographers have come to call the Goldsmith "legend," the accretion of printed gossip and illustrative anecdote. Boswell compounded the problem by casting him as a foil to Johnson in *The Life of Samuel Johnson* (1791), depicting him largely as a whimsical curiosity set against Johnson's solidity. Goldsmith becomes thus important as a subject of biography as well as a creator of it, though it is ironic that he appears in the service of a sophisticated aesthetic "truth" in Boswell, given the complicated status of "truth" in Goldsmith's own biographies.

Johnson did not want Goldsmith to write his biography, being suspicious of what he termed his "general disregard for truth" – a revealing remark in view of Goldsmith's supposed reliance on Johnsonian criteria in his biographies. Indeed, Boswell used a discussion with Johnson on 31 March 1772 of *The Life of Thomas Parnell* to insinuate his own merits as a prospective biographer, and Johnson showed his approval. Nor did Johnson include Goldsmith in his *Prefaces, Biographical and Critical, to* the *Works of the English Poets* (1779–1781), which, given his admiration of Goldsmith's verse, is a conspicuous omission. It is notable, however, that Johnson pays more wholehearted tribute to Goldsmith's overall achievement in the preamble to his abridgment of *The Life of Thomas Parnell* than he does almost anywhere else, even though he was fully aware of the deficiencies of that particular work. The Latin epitaph Johnson wrote for Goldsmith's monument in Westminster Abbey praises the power, spirit, and style of Goldsmith's writing and testifies to the love that his friends bore for him. Indeed, to William Makepeace Thackeray (in *The English Humourists of the Eighteenth Century,* 1851) Goldsmith was "the most beloved of English writers" – a eulogy that Goldsmith, who loved to please and be liked, would have appreciated. Much of his work is merely good journalism, compilation, or rewriting, and this fact has meant that critical interest in him has been less intense than for some of his contemporaries. But his two long poems, his novel, and his two plays are among the most interesting work of his generation, and *The Life of Richard Nash* and *The Life of Thomas Parnell* were significant contributions to the development of biography in the second half of the eighteenth century.

Letters:

The Collected Letters of Oliver Goldsmith, edited by Katherine C. Balderston (Cambridge: Cambridge University Press, 1928).

Bibliographies:

Temple Scott, *Oliver Goldsmith Bibliographically and Biographically Considered* (New York: Bowling Green Press, 1928);

Samuel Woods, *Oliver Goldsmith: A Reference Guide* (Boston: G. K. Hall, 1982).

Biographies:

Thomas Percy, "Memoir of Goldsmith," in volume 1 of *The Miscellaneous Works of Oliver Goldsmith, M.B.* (London: Printed for J. Johnson by H. Baldwin & Sons, 1801); modern edition of Percy's memoir: *Thomas Percy's Life of Dr. Oliver Goldsmith,* edited by Richard L. Harp (Salzburg: Institut für Englische Sprache und Literatur, 1976);

James Prior, *The Life of Oliver Goldsmith, M.B.,* 2 volumes (London: Murray, 1837);

John Forster, *The Life and Adventures of Oliver Goldsmith* (London: Bradbury & Evans, 1848); third edition as *The Life and Times of Oliver Goldsmith* (London: Bradbury & Evans, 1848);

Henry Austin Dobson, *The Life of Oliver Goldsmith* (London: Scott, 1888);

Ralph M. Wardle, *Oliver Goldsmith* (Lawrence: University of Kansas Press, 1957);

A. Lytton Sells, *Oliver Goldsmith: His Life and Works* (London: Allen & Unwin, 1974);

John Ginger, *The Notable Man: The Life and Times of Oliver Goldsmith* (London: Hamilton, 1977).

References:

Sven Bäckman, "The Real Origin of One of the 'Manufactured Anecdotes' in Goldsmith's *Life of Nash,*" *Modern Philology,* 72 (February 1975): 277–279;

Katherine C. Balderston, *The History and Sources of Percy's Memoir of Goldsmith* (Cambridge: Cambridge University Press, 1926);

John Bender, "Prison Reform and the Sentence of Narration in *The Vicar of Wakefield,*" in *The New Eighteenth Century,* edited by Felicity Nussbaum and Laura Brown (New York & London: Methuen, 1987), pp. 168–188;

G. W. Bowersock, "Suetonius in the Eighteenth Century," in *Biography in the Eighteenth Century,* edited by J. D. Browning (New York & London: Garland, 1980), pp. 28–42;

Joseph E. Brown, "Goldsmith and Johnson on Biography," *Modern Language Notes,* 42 (March 1927): 168–171;

James L. Clifford, "How Much Should a Biographer Tell? Some Eighteenth-Century Views," in *Essays in Eighteenth-Century Biography,* edited by Philip B. Daghlian (Bloomington & London: Indiana University Press, 1968), pp. 67–95;

John A. Dussinger, "Philanthropy and the Selfish Reader in Goldsmith's *Life of Nash,*" *Studies in Burke and His Time,* 19, no. 3 (1978): 197–207;

Oliver W. Ferguson, "The Materials of History: Goldsmith's *Life of Nash,*" *PMLA,* 80 (September 1965): 372–386;

Arthur Friedman, "Goldsmith's *Life of Bolingbroke* and the *Biographia Britannica,*" *Modern Language Notes,* 50 (January 1935): 25–29;

Morris Golden, "Goldsmith's Reputation in His Day," *Papers on Language and Literature,* 16 (Spring 1980): 213–238;

Mary Elizabeth Green, "Oliver Goldsmith and the Wisdom of the World," *Studies in Philology,* 77 (Spring 1980): 202–212;

Frances M. Haydon, "Oliver Goldsmith as a Biographer," *South Atlantic Quarterly,* 39 (1940): 50–57;

Richard Helgerson, "The Two Worlds of Oliver Goldsmith," *Studies in English Literature,* 13 (Summer 1973): 516–534;

Robert H. Hopkins, *The True Genius of Oliver Goldsmith* (Baltimore: Johns Hopkins Press, 1969);

Robert D. Hume, "Goldsmith and Sheridan and the Supposed Revolution of 'Laughing' Against 'Sentimental' Comedy," in *Studies in Change and Revolution,* edited by Paul Korshin (London & Menston: Scolar, 1972), pp. 237–276;

Richard J. Jaarsma, "Biography as Tragedy: Fictive Skill in Oliver Goldsmith's *The Life of Richard Nash, Esq.,*" *Journal of Narrative Technique,* 1 (1971): 15–29;

D. W. Jefferson, "*The Vicar of Wakefield* and Other Prose Writings: A Reconsideration," in *The Art of Oliver Goldsmith,* edited by Andrew Swarbrick (London: Vision, 1984), pp. 17–32;

W. J. McCormack, "Goldsmith, Biography, and the Phenomenology of Anglo-Irish Literature," in *The Art of Oliver Goldsmith,* pp. 168–194;

R. E. M. Peach, *The Life and Times of Ralph Allen* (London: D. Nutt, 1895);

Ricardo Quintana, *Oliver Goldsmith: A Georgian Study* (New York: Macmillan, 1967);

Quintana, "Oliver Goldsmith: Ironist to the Georgians," in *Eighteenth-Century Studies in Honor of Donald F. Hyde,* edited by W. H. Bond (New York: Grolier Club, 1970), pp. 297–310;

Joshua Reynolds, *Portraits by Sir Joshua Reynolds, Character Sketches of Oliver Goldsmith, Samuel Johnson, and David Garrick, together with Other Manuscripts of Reynolds Discovered among the Boswell Papers and now First Published,* edited by Frederick W. Hilles (New York: McGraw-Hill, 1952), pp. 44–59;

Allen Rodway, "Goldsmith and Sheridan: Satirists of Sentiment," in *Renaissance and Modern Essays Presented to Vivian de Sola Pinto,* edited by G. R. Hibbard (London: Routledge & Kegan Paul, 1966), pp. 65–72;

G. S. Rousseau, ed., *Goldsmith: The Critical Heritage* (London & Boston: Routledge & Kegan Paul, 1974);

Arthur Sherbo, "A Manufactured Anecdote in Goldsmith's *Life of Richard Nash,*" *Modern Language Notes,* 70 (January 1955): 20–22;

Donald A. Stauffer, *The Art of Biography in Eighteenth Century England* (Princeton: Princeton University Press, 1941);

Richard Wendorf, *The Elements of Life: Biography and Portrait-Painting in Stuart and Georgian England* (Oxford: Clarendon Press, 1990);

Virginia Woolf, "Oliver Goldsmith" (1934), in her *Collected Essays,* 2 volumes (London: Hogarth Press, 1966), I: 106–114.

Papers:

Few Goldsmith manuscripts survive; the largest concentration is in the British Library (Add. MSS 42515–42517). That of *The Haunch of Venison* is held by the New York Public Library. Margaret M. Smith supplies a full list of surviving autograph manuscripts in the eighteenth-century volume of *The Index of English Literary Manuscripts.*

John Hawkesworth

(October 1720 – 17 November 1773)

Karina Williamson
University of Edinburgh

BOOKS: *A Letter to Mr. David Hume, On the Tragedy of Douglas,* anonymous (London: Printed for J. Scott, 1757);

Almoran and Hamet: An Oriental Tale, anonymous, 2 volumes (London: Printed for H. Payne & W. Cropley, 1761);

Edgar and Emmeline; A Fairy Tale: In a Dramatic Entertainment of Two Acts (London: Printed for H. Payne & W. Cropley, 1761).

PLAY PRODUCTIONS: *Amphitryon; or, The Two Sosias: A Comedy,* adapted from John Dryden, London, Theatre Royal, Drury Lane, 15 December 1756;

Oroonoko: A Tragedy, adapted from Thomas Southerne, London, Theatre Royal, Drury Lane, 1 December 1759;

Zimri: An Oratorio, with music by Thomas Stanley, London, Theatre Royal, Covent Garden, 12 March 1760;

Edgar and Emmeline: A Fairy Tale, London, Theatre Royal, Drury Lane, 31 January 1761;

The Fall of Egypt: An Oratorio, with music by Stanley, London, Theatre Royal, Drury Lane, 23 March 1774.

OTHER: *The Adventurer,* 2 volumes, edited, with many contributions, by Hawkesworth (London: Printed for J. Payne, 1753, 1754);

The Works of Jonathan Swift . . . with Some Account of the Author's Life and Notes Historical and Explanatory, 16 volumes, edited by Hawkesworth (London: Printed for C. Bathurst, C. Davis, C. Hitch & L. Hawes, J. Hodges, R. & J. Dodsley & W. Bowyer, 1754–1765);

François Fénelon, *The Adventures of Telemachus,* translated by Hawkesworth (London: Printed for W. Strahan, 1768);

An Account of the Voyages undertaken by the Order of His Present Majesty for making Discoveries in the Southern Hemisphere . . . by Commodore Byron, Captain Wallis, Captain Carteret, and Captain Cook, in the Dolphin, the Swallow, and the Endeavour, 3 volumes, edited by Hawkesworth (London: Printed for W. Strahan & T. Cadell, 1773).

SELECTED PERIODICAL PUBLICATIONS – UNCOLLECTED: "The Fop, Cock and Diamond," *Gentleman's Magazine* (June 1741);

"Life," *Gentleman's Magazine* (July 1747);

"Death of Arachne," *Gentleman's Magazine* (August 1747).

John Hawkesworth wrote only one biography, the life of Jonathan Swift, prefixed to his edition (1754–1765) of Swift's works. Better known as an essayist and the editor of *An Account of the Voyages,* by Capt. James Cook and others (1773), Hawkesworth nevertheless deserves a modest place in the history of literary biography. His "Account of the Author's Life" was the first major attempt at a balanced and objective portrayal of an author's character through judicious weighing of published evidence and opinion.

Hawkesworth spent his childhood in London, where he was born in October 1720, and was the second child of John and Ann Cornford Hawkesworth, who were then living at Tottenham Court. His precise date of birth is unknown, but he was baptized in Old Saint Pancras Church on 28 October 1720. His sister, Honor, was born about a year earlier. His father, a skilled watch engraver by trade, was brought up as a Dissenter and acquired a thorough knowledge of French and some Latin and Greek. As a consequence of the collapse of the South Sea scheme in 1720, the elder John Hawkesworth's business and health declined, and he eventually took a job as French usher in a small academy. Presumably because of the family's reduced circumstances, the young John Hawkesworth had no formal schooling: near the end of his life, as Fanny Burney reports (in her *Early Journals and Letters,* as published in 1988), "he had had no education or advantage but what he had given himself."

*John Hawkesworth (engraving by James Watson, after a
portrait by Sir Joshua Reynolds)*

According to the author of an anonymous biographical account referred to as the "Osborn Sketch," he "learned only to write a fine hand, and the first rules of arithmetic, with a competent knowledge of his own language, chiefly from the Bible, from which text his parents diligently inculcated religious principles on his mind."

In March 1737 the sixteen-year-old Hawkesworth was apprenticed as a clerk to an attorney, but he found the occupation unsatisfying. According to Rowland Freeman, he escaped as soon as he could into "the more congenial pursuits of literature." By 1738 he was already writing poetry and consorting with friends who had literary tastes, particularly a young merchant, John Ryland, who married Hawkesworth's sister in 1742. Hawkesworth was married in Old Saint Pancras Church on 12 May 1744 to Mary Brown, whom he met in 1742 or earlier, probably at the boarding school she ran with her mother at Sydenham in Kent, where Hawkesworth was a writing master. It was evidently a happy marriage, founded on mutual affection and respect. Mary was a woman of intelligence, capability, and good nature who is said to have been a valuable help to her husband in his literary work. She impressed Burney in 1773 as "very well-bred, obliging, and sweet tempered." The daughter of a prosperous butcher, Mary also helped Hawkesworth materially. The young couple moved immediately into a handsome

Tudor house with extensive grounds, Thornhill Mansion in Bromley, Kent, where Mary kept a girls' schools. The Hawkesworths remained there for the whole of their married life. They lived well and became known in their wide circle of friends for their warm hospitality.

Samuel Johnson and his wife were frequent guests in the 1740s and 1750s. Hawkesworth was familiar with Johnson in these years ("though I think there was not much affection," Johnson later told Hester Lynch [Thrale] Piozzi – as reported in her *Anecdotes* of Johnson, 1786). According to an anonymous account of Hawkesworth's life in the *Universal Magazine* (1802), he was introduced to Johnson by Edward Cave, a proprietor of the *Gentleman's Magazine,* for whom Johnson was working as a writer and editor. Hawkesworth made his first appearance in print in the magazine, with "The Fop, Cock and Diamond," a verse fable published in June 1741. Several more of his fables were printed there in the following twelve months. This series was the beginning of his lifelong association with the magazine.

Hawkesworth's poetry has never been collected and remains largely unread. His first known effort, in a letter of 1738, was a set of impassioned heroic couplets, but on the evidence of his poems in the *Gentleman's Magazine* Hawkesworth's chief talent was for comic and satirical verse. His poems in this vein, especially the mock-epic "Death of Arachne" (August 1747), are spirited and well written. He also wrote serious moral and reflective poems, one of which, the pessimistic ode "Life" (July 1747), was much admired by Johnson. After Hawkesworth's death preparations were made by Johnson and Ryland, in collaboration with Mary Hawkesworth, for a collected edition of his works, which (on Johnson's recommendation) would have included all his poems, but for reasons unknown the collection was never published.

From 1744 to 1752 Hawkesworth's main employment was with the *Gentleman's Magazine*. When Johnson gave up his editorial duties after 1743, Hawkesworth gradually took them over, writing up parliamentary debates; compiling the poetry section; contributing essays, reviews, poems, and other pieces of his own; and editing the contributions of other authors. In 1749 he was invited to join Johnson's Ivy Lane Club, which met every week at a steak house near Saint Paul's Cathedral for literary discussion. Fellow members included the lawyer John Hawkins, later knighted as a magistrate, and the physician and writer Richard Bathurst.

Encouraged by these new friends, Hawkesworth took up where the *Rambler* had left off in March 1752 by starting a new essay paper, the *Adventurer*. It ran twice weekly, from 7 November 1752 until 9 March 1754. Hawkesworth was editor and wrote 70 of the 140 papers, but several members of the Ivy Lane Club, including Hawkins and Johnson, also contributed. Among other writers for the paper were Joseph and Thomas Warton; George Colman; and three talented women, Hester Mulso, Catherine Talbot, and Elizabeth Carter. Like its predecessors, such as the *Spectator* and the *Rambler*, the *Adventurer* offered essays on moral, critical, and philosophical subjects. The general aim, as Hawkesworth explained, was to steer "the young and the gay" away from the paths leading to vice, but to steer them by indirect persuasion more than reasoning or exhortation: "I knew it would be necessary to amuse the imagination while I was approaching the heart" (*Adventurer,* no. 140). Of his own papers 54 were in the form of stories: narratives of middle-class life in England or oriental tales, a genre in which he excelled. His formula – moral fables with exotic trappings, spiced with fantasy, magic, and melodrama – found a ready audience; one of these tales, "Amurath: An Eastern Story" (*Adventurer*, nos. 20–22), was frequently reprinted. Essayist Nathan Drake thought Hawkesworth's imagination "uncommonly fertile and glowing, his language clear and brilliant," while also praising him for mak-

ing "the moral prominent and impressive." Hawkesworth emulated Johnson's essay style with uncanny aptitude, as John Courtenay observed in his *Poetical Review of the Literary and Moral Character of Dr. Johnson* (1786): "Ingenious HAWKESWORTH to this school we owe, / And scarce the pupil from the tutor know." Critic Hugh Walker's comment that Hawkesworth's "touch is lighter" than Johnson's and his themes more varied is fair as a generalization, but Hawkesworth was capable also of Johnsonian force and acerbity, as he shows, for example, in the *Adventurer* number 47, in which he draws a parallel between Alexander the Great and Bagshot, a notorious highwayman, to prove that morality is not a matter of motives and consequences alone.

The popularity of the *Adventurer* established Hawkesworth as a rising author and man of letters. With his edition of *The Works of Jonathan Swift* he staked his claim as a serious scholar. Hawkesworth's edition was intended to rectify the faults of predecessor George Faulkner's Dublin edition of 1735, and it supplanted Faulkner's as the authoritative text in England for a century. However, modern scholarship has revealed that Hawkesworth himself was not a reliable editor. His critical annotations and his "Account of the Author's Life," have fared better than his editing. The notes remain of interest as specimens of an eighteenth-century reading of Swift. Hawkesworth's concern is primarily to clarify or emphasize the moral impact of Swift's satire, but Hawkesworth's attitude is not narrowly moralistic. He defends Swift's scatological poems, such as "Strephon and Chloe" (1734), against charges of "indelicacy," and he comments sympathetically on Swift's use of "disgusting images" in *Gulliver's Travels* (1726), pointing out their effectiveness as satiric weapons.

Hawkesworth's life of Swift was said by Johnson in *Prefaces, Biographical and Critical, to the Works of the English Poets* (1779–1781) to have been based on "a scheme which I laid before him," but it is not obvious what Johnson meant by that. Hawkesworth does not adopt the tripartite pattern of events, character, and writings favored by Johnson; nor does he attempt to enrich his record with anecdotes or reminiscences collected from people who had known the author personally, as Johnson recommended. His biography is in fact a skillful compilation based on published accounts of Swift's life, mainly those by Lord Orrery, Patrick Delany, and Deane Swift. Johnson's "scheme," as Robert Folkenflik suggests in *Samuel Johnson, Biographer* (1978), may have been to make a synthesis of Delany's and Orrery's conflicting reports. James Boswell reports Johnson's comment in 1778 "that his [Delany's] book and Lord Orrery's might both be true, though one viewed Swift more, and the other less favourably; and that between both, we might have a complete notion of Swift." Hawkesworth does indeed balance the accounts with considerable ingenuity, and he offers a coherent view of a notoriously complex and problematic personality.

Hawkesworth's stated intention was not "to relate every trifling particular that has been recorded" about Swift but to select enough to show "the peculiarities of his character and manners, and transmit a knowledge of him to posterity, of the same kind, if not in the same degree, as was obtained by those among his contemporaries, who were admitted to his conversation and friendship." Hawkesworth does not conceal the less attractive aspects of Swift's character or conduct, but his approach is basically sympathetic. Where he cannot withhold criticism, he offers extenuation. Swift's "love of money," for example (bluntly called "avarice" by Johnson), is explained as an inborn tendency to frugality, driven to excess by his "naturally high-spirited" wish for independence. Swift's "natural propensities," moreover, were counteracted by his Christian principles; hence "his love of money did not contract his charity to the poor, or defraud his successors to enrich himself." The final summary of Swift's character, from which this comment comes, is a masterly exercise in evenhanded judgment. However, Swift's treatment of "Stella" (Esther Johnson) was an insuperable problem to Hawkesworth. In the then-current belief that Swift married her late in his life but never lived with her, Hawkesworth ponders "why the dean did not sooner marry this most excellent person; why he married her at all; why his marriage was so cautiously concealed." Unable to offer a solution, Hawkesworth prefers to put a lid on conjecture, concluding that these are "enquiries which no man can answer, or has attempted to answer without absurdity, and are therefore unprofitable objects of speculation."

Discussion of Swift's writings are deliberately omitted from the history of his life, on the grounds that it would have meant disturbing the narrative sequence with "frequent references and quotations." Hawkesworth's concern with literary form is manifest in other ways as well — in his habit of interspersing events with philosophical reflections, for example, and marking the stages of Swift's life with narratorial interjections. The overarching pattern is resolutely moral: the studied rhetoric of the concluding paragraph sets Swift's career in marble as an example of the vanity of human aspirations. His life, says Hawkesworth, "with all the advantages of genius and learning, was a scale of infelicity" gradually leading to physical and mental decay, friendlessness, and unjust vilification after his death. The lesson drawn from this tale is nevertheless positive: "to the wise it may teach humility, and to the simple content."

The sententiousness of Hawkesworth's style does not make for lively reading, but it appealed to contemporary readers. Johnson praised Hawkesworth's life of Swift for its dignity, its "elegance of language," and its "force of sentiment." Thomas Sheridan, in his *Life of the Rev. Dr. Jonathan Swift* (1784), paid generous tribute to Hawkesworth even while recognizing shortcomings in his account due to the lack of original material. Hawkesworth, he wrote, was "a man of clear judgment, and great candour. He quickly discerned the truth from the falsehood; wiped away many of the aspersions that had been thrown on Swift's character; and placed it, so far as he went, in its proper light." Modern commentators such as Harold Williams and Wayne Warncke have also praised Hawkesworth's judicious approach: he "cites authority for his statements, and shows critical discrimination," writes Williams; and Warncke considers that he "presents a picture of Swift which might stand for the eighteenth century as the most levelheaded and just description of the man."

This work was a turning point for Hawkesworth. In 1756 he received the degree of doctor of laws from Lambeth Palace, awarded by the archbishop of Canterbury in recognition of the merit of his *Adventurer* essays and the probity of his character. In the same year he was offficially made literary editor of the *Gentleman's Magazine,* on terms shrewdly negotiated with Cave's successor, David Henry. The "Osborn Sketch" records "a considerable change" in Hawkesworth's way of life at this time: he applied himself assiduously to his duties, "became a man of the world in his dress," and was increasingly sought after in society. Two of his warmest friendships – with Charles Burney and Benjamin Franklin – were formed in this period. Hawkesworth probably first met Burney in about 1755, and this friendship was to last for the rest of his life.

Comments by people who knew Hawkesworth indicate that he was sociable by nature, honest, high principled, and kindhearted. Franklin's friend Polly Stevenson, who stayed with the Hawkesworths in 1760, wrote glowingly of his piety and benevolence in a letter to a cousin in 1761: "His disposition is such that he is beloved by all who know him" (quoted by John Lawrence Abbott in his 1982 biography of Hawkesworth). Her view is echoed in a memorial tribute to him in the *Gentleman's Magazine* in December 1773 (probably by Francis Fawkes), which concludes: "Belov'd by all – to virtue's precepts true, / Thou lively, cheerful, social friend, adieu!" His loyalty to friends is illustrated by his kindness to poet Christopher Smart, whom he visited in 1764, when Smart had fallen on hard times. Hawkesworth was among those who helped Smart by subscribing to his *Translation of the Psalms of David* (1765).

However, Hawkesworth also had a strong streak of ambitiousness. In the *Adventurer* number 1 he compares an author to a knight-errant who does good for the sake of fame. The cost of failure was not death but dishonor, and "the ignominy which falls on a disappointed candidate for public praise, would by those very knights have been deemed worse than death." The tone is jocular, but Hawkesworth's pursuit of public praise and status was earnest. Achievement of these goals had an unfortunate effect on his character, as the "Osborn Sketch" hints. Johnson told Edmund Malone that Hawkesworth – "who had set out as a modest, humble man – was one of the many whom success in the world had spoiled" (quoted by James Prior in his 1860 biography of Malone). Friends such as Oliver Goldsmith and Joshua Reynolds commented on Hawkesworth's dandyish and affected manners. Reynolds told Malone that "he was latterly . . . an affected insincere man, and a great coxcomb in his dress." The portrait of Hawkesworth painted by Reynolds (1769–1770) shows him seated writing in a book-lined room and stern faced but conspicuously well dressed. The pose conceals the fact that he was a small man; Fanny Burney referred to him as "little" Hawkesworth. On first meeting him in 1769, she found his conversation stilted ("I never heard a man speak in a style which so much resembles writing") but thought him "remarkably well bred and attentive, considering how great an Author he is." Though anxious to think well of her father's distinguished friend, she also noticed "a small tincture of affectation" in his manner.

Beginning in 1756, he was active in the theater world. Over the next five years he worked closely with David Garrick: giving literary advice, adapting plays by Restoration dramatists to suit the primmer tastes of the period, supporting Garrick in his theatrical quarrels, and writing plays and oratorios of his own. His *Edgar and Emmeline; A Fairy Tale: In a Dramatic Entertainment of Two Acts* was first staged with music by Michael Arne on 31 January 1761 and was restaged several times. A sprightly mixture of romance, farce, and comedy of manners, it drew appreciative comments from playwright Arthur Murphy, who described it in his *Life of David Garrick* (1801) as "a whimsical, but beautiful little piece."

Hawkesworth's novel, *Almoran and Hamet: An Oriental Tale* (1761), was also written originally for the stage, but the costs of production were so forbidding that Hawkesworth rewrote it as prose fiction. Although in theme (the choice of life) the tale resembles Johnson's *The History of Rasselas* (1759), liberal injections of magic, melodrama, and romance give it an un-Johnsonian extravagance. It was widely read and reprinted in the eighteenth and early nineteenth centuries, but as a work of exotic invention and surreal fantasy it was eclipsed for modern readers by William Beckford's *Vathek* (1786). *Almoran and Hamet* initially received mixed reviews. Owen Ruffhead in the *Monthly Review* (1761) rejoiced to find the "Genius of Romance" in a composition so "chaste, elegant and moral." Shrewder criticism came from Thomas Percy, in a letter to William Shenstone in June 1761 (in *The Correspondence of Thomas Percy and William Shenstone*, volume seven, 1977). He thought *Almoran and Hamet* inferior to *Rasselas* and found the style uneven ("whenever he affects the oriental manner, turgid"), the characters too black and white, and the moral effect undermined by devices "out of nature" such as genies and enchantments: "no reader finds anything to apply to himself." But Hawkesworth had one advantage over Johnson in that he "contrived to interest his readers more, by introducing a very pleasing love-story."

Throughout the 1760s Hawkesworth was busy editing, writing, and reviewing for the *Gentleman's Magazine* and other journals. He translated various French articles and in 1768 published a full-scale translation of François Fénelon's *Aventures de Télémaque* (1699). This translation was highly praised: "the spirit and genius of the Author have never been so effectively represented," wrote an anonymous critic in the *Monthly Review* (August 1768). Hawkesworth was one of the leading reviewers on the *Monthly Review* from 1768 to 1771. However, his activities during this time were not only literary. His election in 1761 to the Society for the Encouragement of Arts, Manufactures, and Commerce shows his scientific interests, and his association with Sir James Caldwell, soldier and politician, brought him into parliamentary circles. From 1759 onward he helped Caldwell with his political writings and thereby gained aristocratic friends of whom he was naively proud.

In 1771 he secured his most prestigious literary commission. On Charles Burney's recommendation, backed up by Garrick, he was authorized by Lord Sandwich, first lord of the Admiralty, to compile the official account of the voyages to the South Pacific made between 1764 and 1771 by Commodore John Byron and Captains Samuel Wallis, Philip Carteret, and James Cook. Negotiations for publication were left to Hawkesworth, who sold the copyright to William Strahan and Thomas Cadell for the staggering sum of six thousand pounds (nearly four times what Johnson received for his 1755 dictionary). In April 1773, when the work was nearly complete, he was honored by election to a directorship of the East India Company. The edition, handsomely illustrated and dedicated to the king, was published in June 1773.

This work should have been the climax of Hawkesworth's career, but it was a calamity for him. Even before publication of *An Account of the Voyages* he was involved in disputes harmful to his good name. His sale of the copyright caused a quarrel with Garrick, who believed that another publisher should have shared in the deal and that Hawkesworth had put financial gain before friendship. Hawkesworth was also party to a lawsuit in January 1773 to prevent publication of a rival account of Cook's voyages. In both affairs he may have acted within his rights, but as Abbott remarks, he "conducted himself less like the benign moralist of the *Adventurer* papers and more like a hardheaded businessman."

Worse was to come. Hawkesworth edited the manuscripts thoroughly, altering the text to bring it into line with the standards of style and decorum he judged appropriate and to promote the patriotic image of Great Britain as a great and magnanimous trading nation. But he imprudently chose to retain the first-person narrative mode, which meant that he was putting his own words into the captains' mouths. They justifiably protested against this interference with their text, and Hawkesworth was accused of misrepresentation, lack of editorial integrity, and profiteering. In spite of his attempts to bowdlerize the text, he was blamed for immorality by allowing reports of the sexual freedoms of the South Sea islanders to be printed. Finally he was attacked for want of piety because of a passage in the general introduction in which he rashly challenges the doctrine of providential intervention.

Nevertheless, Hawkesworth's edition of *An Account of the Voyages* was a best-seller in its time, reaching its second English and first American printing by the end of 1773, with French and German editions following in 1774. This success was no consolation to Hawkesworth. He was deeply wounded by the barrage of hostile criticism, and his health broke down. Fanny Burney described him in October as looking ill and thought "the abuse so illiberally cast on him" was preying on his mind. He died in London a month later, on 17 November 1773, of a "slow fever" according to the *Gentleman's Magazine,* and was buried in Bromley. Malone's hearsay report that Hawkesworth killed himself with an overdose of opium remains uncorroborated, but Burney's belief that his health was undermined by the vilification he suffered seems incontestable: "his 6000 l. was dearly purchased, at the price of his character and peace," she commented. The knight-errant had failed, and the ignominy was unendurable.

The neglect of Hawkesworth's writings in the twentieth century is difficult to explain. He was indisputably a talented and versatile author, highly regarded by discerning critics in his own day. The fact that he was overshadowed by greater or more-original authors does not rob his writings of their intrinsic value and interest. As a literary biographer he may not have shown the powerful critical intelligence of Johnson or the tireless inquisitiveness of Boswell, but he set new standards of scholarliness and objectivity. Full understanding of a period depends on knowledge of its representative figures as well as its giants: without closer study of Hawkesworth's work than it has yet received, the eighteenth-century literary map remains incomplete.

Biographies:

Anonymous, "Memoirs of the Life of Dr. John Hawkesworth," *Universal Magazine,* 111 (1802): 233–239;

John Lawrence Abbott, *John Hawkesworth: Eighteenth-Century Man of Letters* (Madison: University of Wisconsin Press, 1982).

References:

John Lawrence Abbott, "Dr. Johnson and Dr. Hawkesworth: A Literary Friendship," *New Rambler,* 111 (Autumn 1971): 2–21;

Abbott, "Samuel Johnson, John Hawkesworth, and the Rise of the *Gentleman's Magazine,* 1738–1773," in *Studies on Voltaire and the Eighteenth Century* volume 151, edited by Theodore Besterman (Oxford: Voltaire Foundation, 1976), pp. 31–46;

"F.F.," Tribute to Hawkesworth, *Gentleman's Magazine* (December 1773);

Martha Pike Conant, *The Oriental Tale in England in the Eighteenth Century* (New York: Columbia University Press, 1908), pp. 70, 89–97;

Nathan Drake, *Essays, Biographical, Critical, and Historical, Illustrative of the Rambler, Adventurer, and Idler*, 2 volumes (Buckingham & London: J. Seeley, for W. Suttaby, 1809–1810), II: 1–34;

Donald B. Eddy, "John Hawkesworth: Book Reviewer in the *Gentleman's Magazine*," *Philological Quarterly*, 43 (April 1964): 223–238;

R. Freeman, *Kentish Poets*, 2 volumes (Canterbury: Wood, 1821), II: 176–234;

Philip Mahone Griffith, " 'A Truly Elegant Work': The Contemporary Reputation of Hawkesworth's *Adventurer*," in *The Dress of Words: Essays on Restoration and Eighteenth-Century Literature in Honor of Richmond P. Bond*, edited by Robert White, Jr. (Lawrence: University of Kansas Press, 1978), pp. 199–208;

Robert D. Mayo, *The English Novel in the Magazines 1740–1815* (Evanston, Ill.: Northwestern University Press, 1962), pp. 105–117;

Edward E. Morris, "Doctor John Hawkesworth, Friend of Dr. Johnson and Historian of Captain Cook's First Voyage," *Gentleman's Magazine*, 289 (1900): 218–238;

W. H. Pearson, "Hawkesworth's Alterations," *Journal of Pacific History*, 7 (1972): 45–72;

James E. Tierney, "Edmund Burke, John Hawkesworth, the *Annual Register*, and the *Gentleman's Magazine*," *Huntington Library Quarterly*, 42 (1978): 57–72;

Hugh Walker, *The English Essay and Essayists* (London: Dent, 1915), pp. 136–142;

Helen Wallis, "John Hawkesworth and the English Circumnavigators," *Commonwealth Journal*, 6 (August 1963): 167–171;

Wayne Warncke, "Samuel Johnson on Swift: the *Life of Swift* and Johnson's Predecessors in Swiftian Biography," *Journal of British Studies*, 7 (May 1968): 56–65;

Harold Williams, "Swift's Early Biographers," *Pope and His Contemporaries: Essays Presented to George Sherburn* (Oxford: Clarendon Press, 1949), pp. 114–128.

Papers:

The major repository of John Hawkesworth's papers is the James Marshall and Mary-Louise Osborn Collection at the Beinecke Library, Yale University. It includes personal letters and an anonymous biographical account of Hawkesworth, evidently based on firsthand knowledge (the "Osborn Sketch"). Other important deposits of Hawkesworth papers are at John Rylands University Library, Manchester; the Hyde Collection, New Jersey; the British Library, London; Westminster Abbey Muniment Room and Library, London; the Huntington Library, California; and the National Library of Australia, Canberra. A collection of manuscript notes by Philip Norman at Bromley Central Library, Kent, provides information about the Hawkesworths in Bromley.

Sir John Hawkins

(9 April 1719 – 21 May 1789)

John H. Rogers
Vincennes University

See also the Hawkins entry in *DLB 104: British Prose Writers, 1660–1800, Second Series.*

BOOKS: *The English Protestant's Answer to the Wicked Sophistry of Some Late Treasonable Papers* (London: Printed for J. Roberts, 1745);

Observations on the State of the Highways, and on the Laws for Amending and Keeping Them in Repair; with a Draught of a Bill for Comprehending and Reducing into One Act of Parliament the Most Essential Parts of All the Statutes in Force relating to the Highways, and for Making Provision for the More Easy and Effectual Repair of the Highways (London: Printed for J. Worrall, 1763);

A Charge to the Grand Jury of the County of Middlesex (London: Printed for J. Worrall & B. Tovey, 1770);

An Account of the Institution and Progress of the Academy of Ancient Music, with a Comparative View of the Music of the Past and Present Times. By a Member (London: Privately printed, 1770);

A General History of the Science and Practice of Music, 5 volumes (London: Printed for T. Payne & Son, 1776);

A Charge to the Grand Jury of the County of Middlesex (London: Printed for E. Brooke, 1780);

The Life of Samuel Johnson, LL.D. (London: Printed for J. Buckland and others, 1787).

Edition: *The Life of Samuel Johnson, LL.D.*, edited and abridged, with an introduction, by Bertram H. Davis (New York: Macmillan, 1961; London: Cape, 1961).

OTHER: John Stanley, *Six Cantatas, for a Voice and Instruments,* includes a preface and lyrics for five of the cantatas by Hawkins (London: Printed for J. Walsh, 1742);

Izaak Walton and Charles Cotton, *The Complete Angler, or, Contemplative Man's Recreation,* edited, with a life of Walton, by Hawkins and, with a life of Cotton, by William Oldys (London: Printed for T. Hope, 1760); revised and en-larged with Hawkins's life of Cotton replacing Oldys's (London: Printed for John, Francis & Charles Rivington, 1784);

The Works of Samuel Johnson, LL.D., Together with His Life, and Notes on His Lives of the Poets by Sir John Hawkins, Knt., 11 volumes (London: Printed for J. Buckland and others, 1787);

"Memoirs of Dr. William Boyce," in *Cathedral Music,* second edition, edited by William Boyce (London: Printed for J. Ashley, 1788).

SELECTED PERIODICAL PUBLICATIONS – UNCOLLECTED: "Essay on Honesty," *Gentleman's Magazine,* 9 (March 1739): 117–118;

"Remarks on the Tragedy of the Orphan," *Gentleman's Magazine,* 18 (November 1748): 502–506; (December 1748): 551–553;

Imitation of John Donne's "The Canonization," *Gentleman's Magazine,* 31 (October 1761): 472;

"Memoirs of the Life of Sig. Agostino Steffani," *Gentleman's Magazine,* 31 (November 1761): 489–492.

For over two centuries Sir John Hawkins has been known as a "most unclubable man." That Hawkins deserved this epithet bestowed on him by his friend Samuel Johnson cannot be denied, for his personality was aloof and abrasive, earning him the enmity of many of the most eminent and influential men of his time, and there is considerable truth underlying Johnson's fuller analysis of Hawkins's character, delivered with his usual humorous exaggeration to Hester Lynch [Thrale] Piozzi and reported by Fanney Burney: "As to Sir John, why really I believe him to be an honest man at the bottom: but to be sure he is penurious, and he is mean, and it must be owned he has a degree of brutality, and a tendency to savageness, that cannot easily be defended." Hawkins indeed devoted a large part of his personal, professional, and literary life to quarreling with his friends and his rivals. Personal arguments and literary feuds were, of course, common-

Sir John Hawkins, 1785 (portrait by James Roberts; Oxford Music Faculty)

places of the eighteenth century, but in no other instance has a writer's unpleasant personality so thoroughly eclipsed his work. Hawkins's multitude of enemies has so poisoned his reputation that he has never been given the credit due him for his pioneering efforts as an editor, a musical historian, and a biographer.

Sir John Hawkins was born in London on 9 April 1719 to Elizabeth Gwatkin Hawkins and John Hawkins, an impecunious carpenter and, according to his granddaughter Laetitia-Matilda Hawkins, a man "of no eminence" who frequently lent money to the needy without interest, security, or, at times, repayment. Despite the elder John Hawkins's financial circumstances, he sent his son to two schools, the names of which are unknown. After this early education Hawkins in 1736 began training under the architect Edward Hoppus. The following year Hawkins's cousin Thomas Gwatkin, a clerk to the attorney John Scott, persuaded him to take up the law, and Hawkins became articled to Scott, with whom he spent the next five years. They were most unhappy years, for Scott was parsimonious and de-

manding. The attorney seemed more concerned with his apprentice's handwriting, necessary to a copy clerk, than in his education as an attorney, and Hawkins was kept so busy that he had little time for the necessary reading. Hawkins, however, early displaying the diligence he retained throughout his life, rose at four o'clock every morning to read not only works by the essential legal writers but also by the essential poets and essayists. On 15 November 1742 Hawkins passed his examinations and became an attorney admitted to practice in the Court of King's Bench and the Court of Common Pleas.

Although becoming an attorney was quite an achievement for a man of Hawkins's background, the profession was by no means held in high esteem. No university education was required, as it was for a solicitor, and Hawkins himself later wrote (in his *Life of Samuel Johnson, LL.D.,* 1787) that "men of low extraction, domestic servants, and clerks to eminent lawyers" became attorneys who "by an unrestrained abuse of the liberty of speech, have acquired popularity and wealth." Whatever the profession's shortcomings, however, becoming an at-

torney provided Hawkins a means of social eleva-
tion and gave him entry to an upper-middle-class
world, in which he soon found a wife and, correla-
tively, the economic independence necessary for his
writing.

Richard Hare, a Limehouse brewer, introduced Hawkins to Peter Storer of the Inner Temple.
Hawkins became the attorney and friend not only
of Storer but of his son, Peter Storer, Jr., and of his
daughters, Martha and Sidney. Sidney Storer soon
became more than a friend, and Hawkins married
her on 24 March 1753. With his new wife came new
wealth, for Sidney had received a legacy of five
thousand pounds worth of stock in the Bank of England, a legacy which apparently enabled Hawkins
to become a serious collector of rare musical works,
including the library of John Christopher Pepusch.
After Peter Storer, Jr.'s death in 1759, Sidney inherited further money and property worth about thirty
thousand pounds, leaving Hawkins, as he noted in
the preface to his *General History of the Science and
Practice of Music* (1776), "in a situation that left his
employments, his studies, and his amusements in a
great measure to his own choice." Hawkins's choice
was to sell his legal practice to his clerk Richard
Clark, later lord mayor of London, and devote himself to other matters. Hawkins bought a country
house in Twickenham and rented a town house in
Hatton Garden, where for the next several years he
annoyed his neighbors with a series of petty law-
suits, including one in 1763 over twenty thousand
nail holes supposedly made in his greenhouse wall
by a neighbor who was an overzealous gardener.
Hawkins later moved from Hatton Garden because
he became, according to his friend Horace Walpole
in his journal, "uneasy over the uneasiness he gave
his neighbors," but during his residence there Hawkins used his abundant leisure time to indulge in
personal interests which served as the basis for his
major literary efforts.

Hawkins's interest in literature predated his
interest in law, for his first published writing had
appeared in the *Gentleman's Magazine* in March 1739.
His first essay was apparently an "Essay on Swear-
ing," but his first known work was his "Essay on
Honesty" in the *Gentleman's Magazine;* it led to the
first and least serious of the many literary controversies that so strongly marked Hawkins's career.
Hawkins's essay sparked a reply from Adam Calamy, Hawkins's fellow clerk and housemate at
Scott's. Hawkins responded to Calamy's criticism
by suggesting that "candidly to point out the Mistakes of another, is the Part of a generous Adversary, and is by many Degrees more prevailing than

the ill-natur'd Snarling of a carping Momus."
Shortly after this exchange, Calamy became an attorney and left Scott's house in 1740, a move which
improved the degree of tranquillity in the household.

After publishing several of Hawkins's essays,
Edward Cave, editor of the *Gentleman's Magazine,*
wrote Hawkins that "whatever you shall please to
send will be acceptable." Among the work Hawkins
was pleased to send were an "Essay on Love" (November 1743) and a poem in imitation of John
Donne's "The Canonization," an imitation the poet
Moses Brown admired. Brown found Hawkins's version somewhat superior and rendered the judgment
that the poems (including another imitation by Foster
Webb) are "each of them Improvements on the
Dr.'s." Hawkins contributed an "Essay on Politeness"
(1741) and an "Essay on Business" (1742) to the *Westminster Journal,* and, after the death of his friend Webb,
a 26 February 1744 letter to the *Gentleman's Magazine.*

Sometime during the 1740s Hawkins met Johnson, another regular contributor to the *Gentleman's
Magazine.* Hawkins was sufficiently friendly with Johnson by 1749 to become a member of Johnson's Ivy
Lane Club, formed during the year.

Hawkins's next literary venture involved
Johnson and, again, the egregious Brown, who this
time provided a less pleasant stimulus. In 1750
Brown, at Johnson's suggestion, had published an
edition of Izaak Walton's *Complete Angler,* an edition
in which he revised and modernized some of Walton's passages and rewrote some of Walton's
verses, "to file off that Rust, which Time fixes on
the most curious and finished Things." In 1759
Hawkins offered Brown some material from his
own collection for the second edition and suggested
that Brown use Walton's own fifth edition, which
includes his final additions and corrections. Brown
ignored these valuable suggestions and continued to
use the inferior fourth edition of Walton's work.
Hawkins then decided to produce his own edition
of the *Complete Angler,* which was advertised by publisher Thomas Hope as "the only correct and complete edition." Hope's advertisement was essentially
correct, for Hawkins did provide a much more correct and complete edition, one that was considerably more faithful to Walton. Brown, of course,
took serious exception to both the book and the
publisher's blurb, stating in the *Public Advertiser* (25
and 29 September 1760) and the *Evening Post* (28–30
September 1760) that, had his rival editor confined
himself within the bounds of modesty and common
sense, he would have left Hawkins "quietly exulting
in those many Blunders he has inserted and boasts

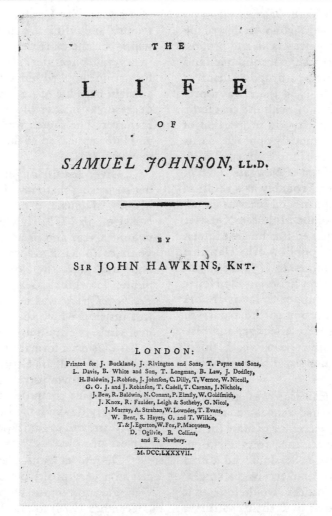

THE

LIFE

OF

SAMUEL JOHNSON, LL.D.

BY

Sir JOHN HAWKINS, Knt.

LONDON:

Printed for J. Buckland, J. Rivington and Sons, T. Payne and Sons,
L. Davis, B. White and Son, T. Longman, B. Law, J. Dodfley,
H. Baldwin, J. Robfon, J. Johnfon, C. Dilly, T. Vernor, W. Nicoll,
G. G. J. and J. Robinfon, T. Cadell, T. Carnan, J. Nichols,
J. Bew, R. Baldwin, N. Conant, P. Elmfly, W. Goldfmith,
J. Knox, R. Faulder, Leigh & Sotheby, G. Nicol,
J. Murray, A. Strahan, W. Lowndes, T. Evans,
W. Bent, S. Hayes, G. and T. Wilkie,
T. & J. Egerton, W. Fox, P. Macqueen,
D. Ogilvie, B. Collins,
and E. Newbery.

M. DCC. LXXXVII.

Title page for Hawkins's biography of Samuel Johnson, with
whom Hawkins became acquainted in the 1740s, about two
decades before Johnson met his best-known
biographer, James Boswell

of," but he was now forced to object to the "last gas-conading insolent advertisement," which stated that the biography of Walton (in the preface) had never been done before, whereas Brown claimed he himself had published one. Hawkins responded, in the same two publications, that Brown had continued to use the fourth edition, although he knew the fifth was more accurate, and that the life of Walton in Hawkins's edition included forty pages from information in his possession, as opposed to Brown's shorter life of Walton.

In this case Hawkins easily had the best of the controversy because his was the best edition. The book includes an admirable short biography of Walton based on Walton's works, his will, and notes supplied by William Oldys, the writer of William Cotton's life story for the 1760 edition. Hawkins also provides necessary explanations of references and allusions, as well as much supplementary information on baits, types and habits of fish, and especially directions on fly-fishing, a sport in which Hawkins took great delight. Hawkins's first edition went through several printings, and the popular revised edition was published in 1784. Between 1791 and 1826 there were ten more printings of the revised version, printings directed by his son John Sidney Hawkins; and between 1833 and 1857 James Rennie published twenty more.

Shortly after this successful literary work Hawkins returned to the law in a new capacity when in August 1761 he became a magistrate for Middlesex. A man of considerable wealth, he at first returned his fees, but when he found that this practice encouraged litigation, he began to collect fees and then give them to parish clergymen for relief work among the poor. In May 1763 he addressed to

Parliament and then published *Observations on the State of the Highways,* a 143-page pamphlet describing problems of the current highway laws and proposing that all highway acts be consolidated and adapted to modern conditions, a proposal that was passed into law in 1767. In 1764 there was a proposal to move Newgate Prison, with the cost to be assessed to the county and city "in proportion of two to one." Hawkins, strenuously opposed to this proposal, wrote "The Case of the County of Middlesex with respect to the Gaol of Newgate" (1765), another successful address. Probably as a result of this work, Hawkins in September 1765 was unanimously elected chairman of the Middlesex Quarter Sessions, a position he retained for the next fifteen years. In addition to these public works Hawkins also assisted his neighbors when in 1769 the city of London planned to move Fleet Prison to Ely House and Hawkins's horrified upper-class neighbors asked him to prepare petitions to the House of Commons. The petitions were effective, and residents gave Hawkins a silver cup worth thirty pounds, with an inscription by Bishop William Warburton.

A few years later Hawkins was granted a knighthood, an honor he had requested. He reasoned to Lord Rochford, secretary of state for the Northern Department, that since John Fielding, chairman of the Westminster Sessions and a man Hawkins considered a rival, had received a knighthood, then the Middlesex justices "would look on it as a sanction to their choice, if I, their chairman, might receive at his Majesty's hands, the same mark of his royal favor." The knighthood was granted on 23 October 1772 and naturally pleased Hawkins but also gave ammunition to his enemies. Hawkins's judicial career ended when the justices elected William Mainwaring as chairman of the Quarter Sessions on 22 February 1781. Hawkins never again attended the sessions.

Hawkins's duties as a magistrate did not prevent his continuing to write in his various areas of interest, including music. An amateur singer since his youth, Hawkins had begun writing on musical subjects early in his career with a poem to the composer and blind organist John Stanley. It was published in the *Gentleman's Magazine* on 21 February 1741. One of Hawkins's songs was set to music by William Boyce in the same year, and in 1742 Hawkins supplied the poems for six solo cantatas composed by Stanley. In 1748 Hawkins was elected a member of the Academy of Ancient Music, of which he later wrote a pamphlet history, and a member of the Madrigal Society. In 1743 Hawkins wrote a sec-

ond set of "Six Cantatas for a Voice and Instruments," including the song "Who'll Buy a Heart," which became extremely popular and was reprinted in several collections. Hawkins also wrote, with information supplied him by George Frideric Handel, an eight-page life of Agostino Steffani, Handel's predecessor as master of the Chapel at the Court of Hanover. The sketch was privately printed in 1758 and later appeared in the *Gentleman's Magazine* (November 1761).

Given his lifelong interest in the subject, it is not surprising that Hawkins decided to undertake a history of music, a project he apparently began sometime in 1770. Hawkins completed about one volume a year and presented the first set of the five volumes to King George III in November 1776. Nine days later the work became available to the public. Hawkins's *General History of the Science and Practice of Music* was a pioneering effort, for there was little on which to base his work, except Peter Prelleur's twenty-four-page *Brief History of Music* (1730). Using information from such acquaintances as Walpole, William Gostling, and George Steevens and from his own private collection of musical treatises, Hawkins composed a history filled with good, previously unavailable information, but the book lacks form and organization and is far from a masterpiece of style.

Despite its faults, Hawkins's history at first received a very positive reception. In a five-part review an anonymous writer for the *Critical Review* (December 1776) found the factual information intriguing and the arguments "convincing and decisive"; he added that all elements of the work give such an idea of the dignity of music as "can only be excited by one who is intimately conversant with the beauties and principles of the art." The critic for the *Gentleman's Magazine* (January 1777) agreed with Hawkins's negative view of modern music and suggested that all curious readers, not just musical ones, would find Hawkins's work "a museum of interesting history and amusing particulars." The writer for the *Young Gentleman's Magazine* remarked, "in how masterly a manner he has executed his plan, and how well he has deserved of the republic of letters."

A General History of the Science and Practice of Music was not, however, greeted with universal enthusiasm. The reviewer for the *Morning Post* (4 January 1778) called the book "a collection of trash and falsehoods" and Hawkins's anecdotes "a load of nonsense," although the review mentioned only one factual error. The truly damning response to the book, however, came from Hawkins's rival Charles

Burney, who was writing his own history of music at the time, the first volume of which was published a few months before Hawkins's history. Burney has often been seen as a foil to Hawkins because of Burney's sweet, gracious personality, but Hawkins at his worst could hardly have imagined such a plot as the one that Burney instigated. Burney compelled William Bewley, a friend who had reviewed some of Burney's books in the *Monthly Review* and who shared Burney's taste in music, to review Hawkins's history, using his review to condemn Hawkins and reflect Burney's own ideas. Bewley began his attack in the February 1777 issue of the *Monthly Review* and continued this attack through the August 1777 issue, which includes his sixteen-page diatribe against Hawkins's supposed lack of plan, excessive use of detail, and preference for ancient music. Bewley concluded that despite a few interesting facts Hawkins's history was a disaster to which Bewley "cannot honestly bestow a more favorable appellation than that of *rubbish*." Burney wrote a crude and unpublished satire, "The Trial of King Midas the Second," which ended with Hawkins's history being thrown into Fleet Ditch and sinking under its own weight, and a popular song at the time included these lyrics: "Sir John Hawkins, Burn 'is history! How d'ye like him? Burn 'is history! Burney's history pleases me."

These attacks, for all their vehemence, did little immediate damage to Hawkins's *General History*. The relative lack of sales may be more reasonably attributed to the then-astonishing price of six guineas. The attacks did, however, seriously affect Hawkins's reputation by making him fair game for ridicule, a ridicule in which Burney seldom failed to indulge among his influential friends. Despite Burney's attempt to laugh the book out of existence, however, Hawkins's history was republished by Novello in 1853 and reprinted in 1875. Burney's history was not reprinted until 1933. Both of these histories of music have now been superseded by more informed works, but both still have value to music historians. Hawkins's history remains in some ways an essential reference work because of his discussions of ancient music, the one aspect that was most derided at the time of publication, and for his excellent portrayal of the eighteenth-century music milieu. Hawkins's work, however, is that of a gifted amateur, while Burney's is the work of a professional musician who had a wider knowledge of European sources and music and provided better analyses in a greatly superior writing style. Now that the conflicts of personality and self-interest are past, the works can be more rationally judged as complementary rather than conflicting early sources of music history, and both include valuable historical material.

For the next few years Hawkins continued to serve as a magistrate and to participate in family and social life. In 1764 he became an original member of Johnson's Literary Club, but he left the club in 1768 apparently as a result of his rudeness to Edmund Burke, which caused the other members to greet him coolly. James Boswell used this departure as evidence that Johnson and Hawkins were never really close, but in 1783 Johnson proposed to Hawkins that members of the old Ivy Lane Club dine together for old times' sake. In 1784 Johnson wrote from Lichfield to ask Hawkins to visit him in Bolt Court and give him "the benefit of your advice and the consolation of your company," and later that same year he made Hawkins one of the executors of his will. Hawkins's actions as executor were, inevitably, condemned by Johnson's other friends. He was accused of trying to steal a manuscript (although he explained this action to Johnson's complete satisfaction), of giving Johnson a less elaborate funeral than he deserved (to save expenses), and of asking payment for his work as executor. Hawkins's activities as executor and the criticism he received for these activities led to his next major work and to the type of reception it met.

Hawkins's *Life of Samuel Johnson, LL.D.* is, despite its admittedly ponderous fashion, of considerable value, but one would hardly realize this fact by judging from both the contemporary and subsequent response to the work, which has been roundly damned from the moment of publication. Exactly when Hawkins decided to write his life of Johnson is unclear, but Laetitia-Matilda Hawkins, his daughter, wrote in *Memoirs, Anecdotes, Facts, and Opinions* (1824) that she had heard her father say "He has left me his executor, and I will write his life." So when Thomas Cadell and William Strahan, representing a large group of London booksellers, asked Hawkins to write Johnson's life story and to supervise their edition of Johnson's works, Hawkins agreed. The *St. James Chronicle* announced on 16 December 1784, three days after Johnson's death, that "Biographers are very busy in preparing materials for the life of Dr. Samuel Johnson" and that the principal candidates were Hawkins and Boswell.

The remark that "biographers are very busy" was an understatement: Johnson was a figure of such imposing interest that soon after his death biographies began appearing with unseemly haste. William Cooke's life of Johnson was for sale two weeks after the subject's death, and it was soon fol-

Letter from Hawkins to John Nichols, publisher of Gentleman's Magazine, *in which Hawkins published biographical essays (Osborn Collection, Beinecke Rare Book and Manuscript Library, Yale University)*

lowed by biographical effusions by Thomas Tyers, William Shaw, Joseph Towers, and, more notably, Boswell's *Tour of the Hebrides* (1785) and Piozzi's *Anecdotes of the Late Samuel Johnson* (1786). Given the welter of Johnson biographies, readers began to grow weary of them. An anonymous writer for the *Morning Herald* (9 January 1787) hoped that Boswell and Piozzi's books would change "the long procession of dulness which has followed the exit of the unfortunate doctor," and the *Morning Chronicle* on the same day declared that "Whenever Johnson is mentioned, the general exclamation is – Something too much of this!"

The general climate, then, was hardly auspicious for the appearance of yet another book on Johnson, and, in addition to the public weariness of Johnsoniana, other circumstances seemed to conspire against Hawkins and his book. Hawkins's publishers did him little service when they warned the public in the *St. James Chronicle* (21 December 1784) against "giving Credit to any Particulars respecting him, or any Posthumous Works pretending to be his, that may hereafter be published by anonymous Authors or Editors" and noted that a life of Johnson by "one of his executors" would be published "with all convenient speed." Hawkins's enemies were quick to take exception to this notice and to the proposed work itself. George Steevens, who had earlier been one of the more venomous

critics of Hawkins's history of music, again attacked. In the 15 January 1784 *St. James Chronicle* he criticized the booksellers' plan to publish the biography as the first volume of Johnson's works, noting that the works of Johnson must then be bought with a "disgusting Incumbrance – The Husband must be endured for the sake of the Wife." Steevens was enthusiastic, though, about Boswell's forthcoming biography. In 1785 poet Richard Tickell's *Probationary Odes for the Laureateship,* a satire against the William Pitt ministry, included a "Preliminary Discourse by Sir John Hawkins, Knt," a parody of Hawkins's preface to his *General History of the Science and Practice of Music.* The poem ran through eight printings before Hawkins's *Life of Samuel Johnson* was published, and it further prepared the climate of ridicule. When Peter Pindar (John Wolcot) wrote his "town eclogue" *Bozzy and Piozzi* (1786), concerning two biographers (Boswell and Piozzi) who swapped trivial stories to see which "bore the palm of anecdote away," he added on the last page that Hawkins's *Life of Samuel Johnson* would soon appear and was "likely to *distance* his formidable competitors," but the compliment was almost lost in the sea of criticism.

More serious than such literary quarrels was a fire at Hawkins's Queen's Square House on 23 February 1785. The house was destroyed, and, according to the *London Chronicle* (26 February 1785),

"Scarcely any article was saved." After the fire Hawkins wrote Cadell that he had "saved a box containing Dr. Johnson's papers and manuscripts" and that "all that is already written of the life is preserved and there is no want of materials" for finishing it. Using the materials still at his disposal, Hawkins completed his *Life of Samuel Johnson,* which was first presented to the king on 12 February 1787 and was offered for sale to the public in March of that year.

Given the climate of opinion, when Hawkins's *Life of Samuel Johnson* was published, many readers immediately seized on the negative qualities, of which there are several. The most frequent and most serious criticisms were that the book was unoriginal, inaccurate, turgid, digressive, and malevolent. All these criticisms have some basis in fact. Much of the factual material was taken directly from newspapers, magazines, and the *New and General Biographical Dictionary* (1761–1767), a common practice at the time (and one Johnson himself had used in his "Life of Pope"). There are also some incorrect dates, incorrect attributions, misreadings of Johnson's notoriously bad handwriting, and several factual and textual errors. More substantially, certain parts of the book clearly reflect some of Hawkins's more-notable prejudices. He completely misunderstood the nature of satire and so had little respect for Johnson's work in this area. Hawkins also indulged in attacks against the theater and included a lengthy diatribe against several novelists, one of the many digressions that so exercised the book's critics. He also disliked Johnson's edition of the works of William Shakespeare, published in 1765, except for the preface. (So did many other readers, but Hawkins's criticism aroused the ire of Malone, another powerful enemy.) Perhaps more troubling to modern readers than these flaws in content is the style of the book. Hawkins's writing is full of words such as *whereof, thereto,* and *herein-before,* as well as other legalistic encumbrances. The style runs to lengthy sentences and is marked by an excessive use of the passive voice and antiquated diction, traits which produce an overall monotony.

Hawkins was the supervisor, not the editor, of Johnson's collected works, but his work in that regard was more seriously flawed than his biography. He omitted from the collected works Johnson's parliamentary debates, *Marmor Norfolciense* (1739), and *Complete Vindication of the Licensers of the Stage* (1739), indeed any works of which he felt the mature Johnson (or perhaps more to the point the mature Hawkins) would not approve. Despite these inexcusable omissions, Hawkins's edition with his notes remained useful, indeed essential, for the next 150 years, until the Yale edition of Johnson's writings began to appear.

In spite of its notable faults, and despite the almost-universal opprobrium heaped upon the book, Hawkins's *Life of Samuel Johnson* also has several merits. The main interest of the book is referred to in the opening, where Hawkins apologizes for his overuse of the first person but explains that he is going to "relate facts to which I was a witness, conversation in which I was a party, and to record memorable sayings uttered only to myself." Hawkins had known Johnson much longer than Boswell did, at least since 1749, when the Ivy Lane Club began, and probably earlier, almost from the beginning to the end of Johnson's literary career. This longer and in some ways more intimate knowledge of his subject made Hawkins well informed on Johnson's early life and his career in the 1740s and 1750s, aspects Boswell treats only glancingly. Hawkins also had more knowledge than Boswell on Johnson's final days, for from 27 November to 13 December 1784, while Boswell was in Scotland, Hawkins was in almost constant attendance on Johnson and apparently kept a diary. Moreover, what were at the time seen as the book's greatest faults – Hawkins's digressiveness and his supposed malevolence toward his subject – from a modern perspective become in some ways its greatest strengths.

Only about half of the six hundred pages of the book is a direct narrative of Johnson's life, and few readers would miss Hawkins's speculations concerning such arcane matters as a Portuguese mission to Abyssinia, the decline of British watchmaking, the proportions of columns, and the first prayer book of Edward VI, just as few would care to read the twelve pages of Lord Hardwicke's speech on Carteret's address to the Crown or the nine pages concerning Walpole's speech about the retailing of liquor. However, some of the other digressions considered superfluous by Hawkins's contemporaries are now of considerable interest. His characterizations of the periodicals for which Johnson wrote, of the political movements in which Johnson was involved, and of the contemporaries with whom Johnson associated – vicious though some of these are – have a certain intrinsic historical interest and, more important, add to a full understanding of Johnson by placing him firmly in the context of his time.

The other major criticism of the book, concerning Hawkins's malevolence toward Johnson, is in fact one of its strongest points. What Johnson's friends considered malevolent readers now usually see as honest, for Hawkins provides a picture of Johnson the man rather than Johnson the literary symbol. Hawkins believed that to perform properly his duty as a biographer he was compelled to "make public as well those particulars of Johnson that may be thought to abase as those that exalt his character," and so he included descriptions of Johnson's indolence, his unhappy marriage, his disgusting manners of dress and eating, and other personal flaws. Such discussions, which so angered and upset Johnson's friends, give a fuller view of Johnson the man than readers get elsewhere, and Hawkins could perhaps take comfort in knowing that Johnson would have certainly approved of this approach, an approach Johnson himself had used in his *Prefaces, Biographical and Critical, to the Works of the English Poets* (1779–1781).

While modern readers may approve such an approach to biography, with few exceptions eighteenth-century readers decidedly did not. The book did receive some favorable attention at the time of publication. The *St. James Chronicle, London Chronicle, Political Magazine, Country Magazine, European Magazine, Universal Magazine,* and *Scots Magazine* all printed lengthy excerpts from Hawkins's *Life* during March 1787, reflecting considerable public interest in the work, an interest further evidenced by a second printing being required three months after publication. The editor of the *Universal Magazine* wrote that in Hawkins's *Life* were "many Particulars, both of the Doctor and others, no less interesting" than those found in the works by Boswell and Piozzi, and the reviews for the *Public Advertiser* (10 March 1787), while admitting that Hawkins "is no elegant writer, nor does he possess the 'soul of wit,' brevity," nonetheless concluded that he "is not like Boswell, the panegyrist of Dr. Johnson, nor does he, like Mrs. Piozzi, draw a frightful figure, and call it an Adonis – Sir John mixes, with a high opinion of Dr. Johnson, a regard for truth and justice; and we confess, that a better idea of the Doctor may be gathered from this book than any former publication."

This reasonable and accurate assessment was nearly the last Hawkins's work was to receive. Remarking on a recent suicide by arsenic, Sir Herbert Croft wrote John Nichols that such a fate is "almost better than Sir John Hawkins. Boswell, and co. will torture the poor Knight half an inch at a time, to literary death" (quoted in Nichols's *Illustrations of the Literary History of the Eighteenth Century,* 1817–1858). Croft proved a true prophet, for Hawkins's enemies, busy enough before the book's publication,

began more serious and lasting attacks as soon as it appeared.

Arthur Murphy, writing anonymously for the *Monthly Review* (July 1787), had nothing good to say about Hawkins's book. He devoted most of his four-part review to presenting his own short narrative of Johnson's life and wondered, if Johnson could read Hawkins's work, where Hawkins would "hide himself from the indignation of an injured friend." The *English Review* (April 1787) suggested that if Johnson treated his friends with "arrogance and contempt" while he was alive, "they have taken full vengeance on his ashes." The *Critical Review* (June 1787) in turn suggested that Hawkins "sinks under the weight of his subject" and that because he is unable to write effectively of Johnson himself, he "is glad to escape to scenes more congenial to his disposition, and more suitable to his talents, the garrulity of a literary old man." Hawkins's legalistic style was universally deplored and often parodied, most effectively by Richard Porson, who, using the pseudonym "Sundry Whereof," ironically praised the faults of the book in a three-part satiric "Panegyric Epistle" in the *Gentleman's Magazine* (August 1787). The *English Review* harshly dismissed both Hawkins and his subject, suggesting that six hundred pages devoted to a literary man whose life could be written in thirty was "the most multifarious, miscellaneous, tedious, and minute composition that has ever been submitted to the public view." The contemporary response to Hawkins's *Life of Samuel Johnson* was most succinctly expressed by Lady Eleanor Butler, who wrote in her diary on 9 February 1788: "Sir John Hawkins' life of Johnson. Wretched performance" (quoted by Davis in his 1973 biography of Hawkins).

Not all readers responded as biliously as Johnson's friends. William Cowper and Elizabeth Carter, who were not subject to the personal rivalries and petty jealousies of the Johnson circle, were impressed by the book. Cowper wrote to Samuel Rose that, after reading Hawkins and Boswell, he felt himself "almost as much a master of Johnson's character, as if I had known him personally," and he regretted that older writers had no such biographers, for "such a history of Milton or Shakespeare, as they have given of Johnson – O how desirable" (quoted by Davis). Carter, who had known Johnson personally from his first years in London, wrote in a letter to her friend Elizabeth Montagu that Hawkins's *Life* was "much less exceptionable than the other two. Indeed there are but very few passages that are likely to give pain to anyone. His character of Dr. Johnson is impartially, and very decently and candidly represented" (quoted by Davis). And Dr. George Horne, dean of Canterbury Cathedral, wondered if anyone really imagined that Johnson was a perfect character and concluded that all the memoirs contained so many witty and wise sayings that readers "may be at once entertained and improved" (also quoted by Davis). Horne's, however, was a small voice of reason drowned by the literary and personal virulence surrounding it.

As might have been expected, the strongest response and challenge to Hawkins's work came from Boswell. When Malone suggested that Johnson's friends sign a protest for posterity declaring Hawkins's book "a false and injurious account," Boswell thought it an admirable plan and "resolved it should not sleep." But Sir Joshua Reynolds hesitated, and no action was taken by members of "The Club." Action was, however, taken by Boswell, who, ever fearful of possible rivals, ever mindful of his literary reputation, and ever jealous of Johnson's other friends, announced in several newspapers that one of his principal objectives in his promised *Life of Samuel Johnson* would be to correct erroneous accounts, and he hoped that the public would not be taken in by "the light effusions of carelessness and pique, or the ponderous labours of solemn inaccuracy and dark uncharitable conjecture" of Piozzi and Hawkins. More seriously, in the opening pages of his *Life of Samuel Johnson,* Boswell codified and made permanent the many and various criticisms of Hawkins's *Life of Samuel Johnson.* He lastingly influenced the reputation of Hawkins's book when he dismissed Hawkins as a man "whom, during my long intimacy with Dr. Johnson, I never saw in his company, I think but once, and I am sure not above twice," and he described Hawkins's book as "a *farrago,* of which a considerable portion is not devoid of entertainment to the lovers of literary gossiping; but besides its being swelled out with long unnecessary extracts from various works . . . a very small part of it relates to the person who is the subject of the book; and, in that, there is such an inaccuracy in the statement of facts, as in so solemn an authour is hardly excusable, and certainly makes his narrative very unsatisfactory. But what is still worse, there is throughout the whole of it a dark uncharitable cast, by which the most unfavourable construction is put upon almost every circumstance in the character and conduct of my illustrious friend." Although Boswell's description is clearly self-serving and in many ways inaccurate, there was enough truth in his words to establish this attitude toward Hawkins's book in the public mind, and Hawkins's *Life of Samuel Johnson* has from that time remained, as Davis terms it, "a study in oblivion."

Hawkins's final piece of writing was "Memoirs of Dr. William Boyce," prefixed to the 1788 reissue of Boyce's *Cathedral Music.* During May 1789 Hawkins felt ill and went to Islington Spa for the waters; on 14 May he apparently had a stroke. After returning home he had a second and fatal stroke on 21 May 1789. Hawkins was buried in the cloisters of Westminster Abbey, where, by his instructions, the grave lists only his initials, his date of death, and his age.

The almost total lack of recognition and respect accorded Hawkins since his death is curious, for his life was one of considerable accomplishment. Hawkins rose from dire poverty to become a successful attorney and magistrate; his edition of *The Complete Angler* set new standards for accuracy and established the lasting popularity of Walton's book; his history of music, the first such work in English, is a source from which other musical historians from Burney to the present have freely drawn; and his *Life of Samuel Johnson,* though lacking the pleasing style and incomparable dramatic flair of Boswell's biography, still provides an admirable portrait of Johnson and his age. But Hawkins paid a heavy price for those personality traits that alienated and infuriated so many of his contemporaries. Boswell and company have so firmly fixed the idea of Hawkins as a soporific writer and contemptible human being that Hawkins is likely to be regarded by most readers as no more than Johnson's "most unclubable man," rather than the impressive though flawed writer he was. Isaac D'Israeli, in the July 1814 *Gentleman's Magazine,* offers perhaps the most accurate and succinct analysis of Hawkins's work: "Of Hawkins's literary character I am inclined to think far better than the criticks have hitherto allowed; the confused statements of objects which had passed under his eye, his feeble taste, his imperfect views, originate in the contraction of his intellect, and will for ever exclude him from the order of genius; but his fervent researches, his literary habits, and that passion for Literature he inspired through his family, excite our respect, and rank him among the esteemable men of letters."

Biographies:

Laetitia-Matilda Hawkins, *Anecdotes, Biographical Sketches and Memoirs* (London: F. C. & J. Rivington, 1822);

Hawkins, *Memoirs, Anecdotes, Facts, and Opinions,* 2 volumes (London: Longman, Hurst, Rees, Orme, Brown & Green, 1824);

Austin Dobson, "Sir John Hawkins, Knight," in his *Old Kensington Palace and Other Papers* (London: Chatto & Windus, 1910), pp. 112-139;

Clarence A. Miller, *Sir John Hawkins, Dr. Johnson's Friend-Attorney-Executor-Biographer* (Washington: Privately printed, 1951);

Percy A. Scholes, *The Life and Activities of Sir John Hawkins* (London: Oxford University Press, 1953);

Bertram H. Davis, *A Proof of Eminence: The Life of Sir John Hawkins* (Bloomington & London: Indiana University Press, 1973);

Davis, "Dr. Johnson and Sir John Hawkins: A Friendship of Four Decades," *South Atlantic Quarterly,* 74 (Spring 1975): 212-223.

References:

Edward Boyle, "Johnson and Sir John Hawkins," *National Review,* 87 (1926): 77-89;

Bertram H. Davis, *Johnson Before Boswell: A Study of Sir John Hawkins' Life of Samuel Johnson* (New Haven: Yale University Press, 1960);

Austin Dobson, "Boswell's Predecessors and Editors," in his *A Paladin of Philanthropy* (London: Chatto & Windus, 1899), pp. 137-172;

A. Hyatt King, *Some British Collectors of Music c. 1600-1960* (Cambridge: Cambridge University Press, 1963);

Lawrence Lipking, *The Ordering of the Arts in Eighteenth Century England* (Princeton: Princeton University Press, 1970), pp. 229-324;

Roger Lonsdale, *Dr. Charles Burney: A Literary Biography* (Oxford: Clarendon Press, 1965), pp. 189-225;

Frederick A. Pottle, "The Dark Hints of Sir John Hawkins and Boswell," *Modern Language Notes,* 56 (1941): 325-329;

Donald A. Stauffer, *The Art of Biography in Eighteenth Century England* (Princeton: Princeton University Press, 1941);

Robert Stevenson, "The Rivals – Hawkins, Burney, and Boswell," *Musical Quarterly,* 36 (1950): 67-82.

Papers:

Few Hawkins papers have survived, and most of those concern his work with the Middlesex Quarter Sessions. The largest group is housed in the Greater London Record Office. Most of the rest are in the Public Record Office. The locations of individual letters and other documents are recorded in Bertram H. Davis's *A Proof of Eminence: The Life of Sir John Hawkins.*

William Hayley

(29 October 1745 – 12 November 1820)

Paul Baines
University of Liverpool

See also the Hayley entry in *DLB 93: British Romantic Poets, 1789–1832, First Series.*

BOOKS: *A Poetical Epistle to an Eminent Painter* (London: Printed for T. Payne & Son, J. Dodsley, and Robson & Co., 1778); republished as *An Essay on Painting: In Two Epistles to Mr. Romney* (London: Printed for J. Dodsley, 1781);

An Elegy, on the Ancient Greek Model (Cambridge: Printed by Francis Hodson; sold by T. Payne, London, and T. & J. Merrill, Cambridge, 1779);

Epistle to Admiral Keppel (London: Printed for Fielding & Walker, 1779);

Epistle to a friend, on the death of John Thornton, Esq. (London: Printed for J. Dodsley, 1780);

An Essay on History; in Three Epistles to Edward Gibbon, Esq., with Notes (London: Printed for J. Dodsley, 1780);

Ode Inscribed to John Howard (London: Printed for J. Dodsley, 1780; Philadelphia: Printed & sold by Enoch Story, 1780);

The Triumphs of Temper; a Poem. In six cantos (London: Printed for J. Dodsley, 1781; Newburyport, Mass.: Printed by John Mycall for Joseph H. Seymour, Boston, 1781);

An Essay on Epic Poetry; in Five Epistles to the Rev. Mr. Mason. With Notes (London: Printed for J. Dodsley, 1782);

Ode to Mr. Wright of Derby (Chichester: Printed by Dennet Jacques, 1783);

Plays of three acts, written for a private theatre (London: Printed for T. Cadell, 1784) – comprises *The Happy Prescription, Marcella, The Two Connoisseurs, Lord Russel,* and *The Mausoleum;*

Poems and Plays, 6 volumes (London: Printed for T. Cadell, 1785);

A Philosophical, Historical and Moral Essay on Old Maids. By a Friend to the Sisterhood, 3 volumes (London: Printed for T. Cadell, 1785);

Two Dialogues; Containing a Comparative View of the Lives, Characters, and Writings of Philip, the Late Earl of Chesterfield, and Dr. Samuel Johnson (London: Printed for T. Cadell, 1787);

Occasional Stanzas, Written at the Request of the Revolution Society, and Recited on their Anniversary, November 4, 1788. To Which is Added, Queen Mary to King William, During his Campaign in Ireland, 1690, a Poetical Epistle (London: Printed for T. Cadell, 1788);

The Young Widow; or, the History of Cornelia Sedley, in a Series of Letters, 3 volumes (London: Printed for G. G. J. & J. Robinson, 1789);

The Eulogies of Howard, a Vision (London: Printed for G. G. J. & J. Robinson, 1791);

The National Advocates; a Poem, Affectionately Inscribed to the Honourable Thomas Erskine, and Vicary Gibbs, Esquire (London: Printed for J. Debrett, 1795);

An Elegy on the Death of the Honourable Sir William Jones, a Judge of the Supreme Court of Judicature in Bengal, and President of the Asiatic Society (London: Printed for T. Cadell, Junior & W. Davies, 1795);

The Life of Milton, in Three Parts. To Which are Added, Conjectures on the Origin of Paradise Lost: with an Appendix (London: Printed for T. Cadell, Junior & W. Davies, 1796);

An Essay on Sculpture, in a Series of Epistles to John Flaxman, with Notes (London: Printed by A. Strahan for T. Cadell, Junior & W. Davies, 1800);

Little Tom the Sailor. Printed for & Sold by the Widow Spicer of Folkstone for the Benefit of her Orphans, October 5, 1800 [broadside], by Hayley, with engravings by William Blake (Felpham: Printed by William Blake, 1800);

A Series of Ballads, nos. 1–4, by Hayley, with engravings by Blake (Chichester: Printed by J. Seagrave, 1802);

The Life and Posthumous Writings of William Cowper, Esqr. (3 volumes, Chichester: Printed by J. Seagrave for J. Johnson, London, 1803, 1804; 2 volumes, Boston: Published by W. Pelham, Manning & Loring, and E. Lincoln, 1803);

William Hayley, circa 1779 (mezzotint by J. Jacobe, after a portrait by George Romney)

The Triumphs of Music; a Poem: in Six Cantos (Chichester: Printed by & for J. Seagrave and sold by T. Payne, London, 1804);

Ballads, By William Hayley, Esq., Founded On Anecdotes Relating To Animals, With Prints, Designed and Engraved by William Blake (London: Printed by J. Seagrave for Richard Phillips, 1805);

Supplementary Pages to the Life of Cowper, Containing the Additions Made to that Work, on Reprinting it in Octavo (Chichester: Printed by J. Seagrave for J. Johnson, London, 1806);

The Stanzas of an English Friend to the Patriots of Spain (London: Printed for Westley & Parish, 1808);

The Life of George Romney (Chichester: Printed by W. Mason for T. Payne, London, 1809);

Eudora. A Tragedy (London: Printed by William Mason for T. Cadell & W. Davies, 1811);

Three Plays (Chichester: Printed by W. Mason for T. Cadell & W. Davies, London, 1811) – comprises *Eudora, The Viceroy,* and *The Heroine of Cambria;*

A Patriot Song for the Amicable Club of Felpham [broadside] (Chichester: Printed by W. Mason, 1814);

Song for the Amicable Fraternity of Felpham [broadside] (Chichester: Printed by W. Mason, 1817);

Poems on serious and sacred subjects, printed only as private tokens of regard, for the particular friends of the author (Chichester: Printed at the private press of W. Mason, 1818);

Memoirs of the life and writings of William Hayley, Esq. The Friend and Biographer of Cowper, written by himself, 2 volumes, edited by John Johnson (London: Printed by Henry Colburn and Simpkin & Marshall, 1823).

PLAY PRODUCTIONS: *Lord Russel,* London, Theatre Royal, Haymarket, 18 August 1784;

The Two Connoisseurs, London, Theatre Royal, Haymarket, 2 September 1784;

The Trial of the Rock, London, Theatre Royal, Covent Garden, 1788;

Marcella, (unauthorized production) London, Theatre Royal, Drury Lane, 7 November 1789; authorized version, London, Theatre Royal, Covent Garden, 10 November 1789;

Eudora, London, Theatre Royal, Covent Garden, 29 February 1790;

Zelma; Or, The Will O' Th' Wisp, London, Theatre Royal, Covent Garden, 17 April 1792.

OTHER: "An English Ode," in *Gratulatio academiae cantabrigiensis natales auspicatissimos Georgii Walliae principie agustissimi Georgii III. Magnae Brittanicae regis et serenissimae Charlotte reginge tillii celebrantis* (Cambridge: Printed by Joseph Bentham, 1762);

Andrew Kippis, *Biographia Britannica,* second edition, volumes 3 and 4 (London: Printed by W. & A. Strahan, for C. Bathurst, W. Strahan [etc.], 1784, 1789) – include biographies of William Clarke and Richard Crashaw by Hayley;

"Impromptu on Miss Sewerd's Louisa," in *An Asylum for Fugitive Pieces,* edited by John Almon (London: Printed by J. Debrett, 1785);

The Poetical Works of John Milton. With a Life of the Author by William Hayley, 3 volumes (London: Printed by W. Bulmer & Co. for John & Josiah Boydell, 1794–1797);

Extracts from the Works of the most celebrated Italian Poets, includes translations by Hayley (London: Printed for F. & C. Rivington, and J. Hatchard, 1798);

Anonymous, *Miranda, or The discovery. A Tale. To which are added, Chariessa, or A pattern for her sex* [by Haley]. *Also, an original story, founded on fact* (Norwich, Conn.: Printed by J. Trumbull, 1800);

The Latin and Italian Poems of Milton Translated into English Verse, and a Fragment of a Commentary on Paradise Lost, By the late William Cowper, Esq., edited by Hayley (Chichester: Printed by J. Seagrave, for J. Johnson and R. H. Evans, London, 1808);

"Impromptu to the Author," in F. N. C. Mundy, *The Fall of Needwood* (Derby: Printed by J. Drewry, 1808);

Thomas Bradford, *Poetical Pieces,* includes a sonnet and an epitaph by Hayley (Chichester: Printed by William Mason, 1808);

Select Poems, &c., by the Late John Dawes Worgan, of Bristol, edited, with a preface, by Hayley (London: Printed by Gosnell for Longman, Hurst, Rees & Orme, 1810; Philadelphia: Printed by Merritt for Kimber & Richardson, 1813);

Cowper's Milton, 4 volumes, edited by Hayley (Chichester: Printed by W. Mason for J. Johnson, London, 1810);

"Hymn for the children of Petworth," in *Psalms and Hymns for Petworth Church* (Petworth: Printed by and for James Goldring, 1820).

William Hayley was one of the most popular poets of the period from 1780 to 1800, but even in his own lifetime he dropped out of the accepted canon. He is known today as the generous but bemused patron of William Blake, but on the title page of his *Memoirs of the life and writings of William Hayley, Esq.* of 1823 he styled himself "the friend and biographer of Cowper." He wrote biographies of John Milton, George Romney, William Cowper, and of his own son (included in the *Memoirs*), and all these works present the subjects in a tone of elegiac hyperbole. In his *Memoirs* he uses the same style for his own life. His genius for friendship combined with commemoration was the essence of Hayley's sensibility.

Hayley was born in Chichester on 29 October 1745 and christened there on 25 November. His grandfather had been dean of Chichester Cathedral. William's father, Thomas Hayley, had acquired financial independence with his first marriage, which ended in the early death of his wife. His second wife was Mary Yates Hayley, the daughter of the local member of Parliament, and they had two sons, Thomas and William. Thomas Hayley, Sr., died when William was only three, but by then the family had bought an estate at Eartham, a few miles from Chichester, and rebuilt the house there; this estate was to be a place of great importance to William. Thomas, Jr., died two years after his father, leaving William and his mother alone in the world. The bond was very close, and Hayley wrote several public tributes to her "with the highest degree of filial love and veneration," as well as beginning a biography (portions of which are printed in his *Memoirs*) of her, perhaps his first exercise in that genre. After a brief period at local schools Hayley was sent to a boarding school in Kingston, and his mother moved to London. He nearly died of a fever but was rescued by his mother, who nursed him slowly back to health. Eventually he recovered from his illness but was left with a permanent limp. During this enforced absence from school, he read plentifully, was taught Greek and Latin by a tutor, and acquired a liking for horseback riding. In 1757 he was sent to Eton; in his *Memoirs* he says little of his time there, except that he was severely beaten on a couple of occasions, experiences which remained vivid.

In 1763 he left Eton to live with his mother at her house in London. He found his father's library well arranged, and he indulged in luxurious reading. He entered Trinity Hall, Cambridge, because that college then enjoyed certain exemptions from university regulations, and he could spend more time in private study. He had formed a secret attachment to Frances (Fanny) Page, daughter of a rich but difficult old friend of the family. To her he began writing copious verses. But his first published poem was "An English Ode" on the birth of the Prince of Wales, which was printed in a 1762 anthology and in the *Gentleman's Magazine* (January 1763); he presented his mother with the inscribed proof sheet in recognition of her encouragement of his literary studies. At Cambridge he did almost no official work (he never took a degree) but set about educating himself. He learned Spanish, Italian, drawing, and painting, and he met the well-known miniaturist Jeremiah Meyer, who was to remain a lifelong friend. In 1766 he enrolled at the Middle Temple with no intention of actually studying there; he was already devoted to a literary career. He was still passionately attached to Page, but (by his account) she was turned against him by the secret machinations of others and married someone else. Instead, on 23 October 1769, Hayley married Eliza Ball, the daughter of another dean of Chichester; she was an old friend and confidante and had acted as go-between in his courtship of Fanny. His mother warned him that there was insanity in the Ball family, but he nobly brushed this warning aside. At first, as Hayley writes in his *Memoirs,* the marriage appeared to match his conception of "purest felicity." They had health, enough money, and "a very uncommon portion of reciprocal esteem and affection."

Even so, Hayley began to write a tragedy, under the naive impression that a couple of plays per year would bring him an annual salary of a thousand pounds. His first effort was called "The Afflicted Father," a sadly ironic title in view of Hayley's troubled later life, and in any event too saturated with moralistic sensibility to be very interesting on stage. Hayley sent it to David Garrick, who at first appeared delighted with it but later changed his mind – an episode of which Hayley tells with restraint in his *Memoirs.* The play was never published. His father-in-law died

in 1770, and the inheritance provided a slightly increased income for the Hayleys. Then Hayley wrote another play, this time a "safe" adaptation of Pierre Corneille's *Rodogune* (1644), titled "The Syrian Queen." George Colman the Elder rejected it with a courteous but firm note which Hayley reprints in his *Memoirs.* He soon turned to the idea of a patriotic epic on the theme of the Magna Carta, meanwhile honing his technique with lesser poems about public good works. Progress was slow, various passages were accidentally lost, and Hayley's eyes were permanently damaged by an inflammation.

After some leisurely country tours, in 1774 Hayley decided to leave London and restore the family villa at Eartham. His mother, whose health had been in decline for some time, died in December of that year in London, and Hayley had her buried at Eartham under a lavish monumental tablet on which his epitaph for her was engraved, including the words *Parens amantissima* (most loving parent). It was the first of many epitaphs he wrote for people he loved.

Hayley began to fill the parental home with visitors, making his place of retreat also a place of gregarious chatter. He wrote poems on marriage for the benefit of some of these young friends. He also expanded his contacts with the art world, Joseph Wright of Derby and Romney being the two best-known artists he knew. Romney in particular became a regular visitor, recuperating from fits of nervous exhaustion and painting to Hayley's advice and suggestions in the peaceful environment Hayley had put together. It was to Romney that Hayley dedicated his first major work, *A Poetical Epistle to an Eminent Painter* (1778). He also wrote several minor pieces on public occasions and four tragedies, all rejected. But he made new ones, publishing *An Essay on History* (1780), dedicated and sent to Edward Gibbon; and an *Ode Inscribed to John Howard* (1780), written in praise of John Howard. Both succeeded in winning the friendship of the recipients. In 1780 his close friend John Thornton died, and Hayley wrote the elegy to his friend.

Meanwhile Hayley's marriage was faltering, and on 5 October 1780, his son Thomas Alphonso Hayley was born to the housemaid, a daughter of his old nurse. According to Hayley's friend Anna Seward (as cited by biographer Morchard Bishop), Eliza Hayley adored Hayley, praised him, and desperately needed his esteem, but she was sexually frigid. Hayley tried to account for her frigidity in psychological terms, adding that he considered himself "singularly exempted from a strict observance

Broadside by Hayley, illustrated by William Blake. This copy, in the George C. Smith Collection at the Princeton University Library, has been cut in half to form two leaves.

of the nuptial vow." According to Bishop there is some evidence that Eliza herself nominated the housemaid as her substitute, and Eliza took more interest in Thomas Alphonso than one might have expected. The presence of the son was not the source of their separation. She evidently experienced depression and boredom, and she was sent to Bath to recuperate. She seems to have enjoyed the social aspects of Bath, being looked after by Gibbon and other friends, to the extent that it took Hayley five months to get her back again, and even then she soon returned to Bath. Their letters indicate how much better they were apart than together. At the same time Hayley made the acquaintance of Seward, with whom he corresponded in a rather quaint style of mutual congratulation.

In 1781 Hayley published *The Triumphs of Temper,* a sub-Popean exercise in educating the female mind against the dangers of the melancholy condition known as "the spleen." The poem grafts sensibility onto neoclassicism, but for all its patronizing tone and lukewarm creativity, it was immensely popular, running into some sixteen English printings in Hayley's lifetime, not to mention Irish and American editions and translations; Emma Hamilton, oddly enough, paid tribute to its effects on her own temper. It made him famous, almost everyone except Samuel Johnson praised it. There soon followed *An Essay on Epic Poetry* (1782), in which Hayley exhorted the Reverend William Mason to write a national epic (his own attempt having broken down).

His friendship with Gibbon blossomed, the historian making several visits to Eartham, and John Flaxman came to design part of Hayley's new library and stayed as a friend. Charlotte Smith

137

found a ready sympathizer in Hayley, who helped her with recommendations to publishers. In a mood of positive buoyancy Hayley recommenced his abandoned career as playwright, and having bought back his copyrights from the Dodsley publishing house and transferred them to Thomas Cadell, he published *Plays of three acts, written for a private theatre* (1784). Such was Hayley's eminence then that later in 1784 Colman produced two of the plays at the Haymarket with some success: the two were occasionally staged until 1787. Another successful work, this time in prose, was *A Philosophical, Historical and Moral Essay on Old Maids* (1785), a comic defense of such women which certain of them (such as Seward) not surprisingly found offensive, but which went down well in other quarters and which may indicate a certain chauvinism which cannot have helped Hayley's domestic life.

Around 1785 Hayley wrote to his friend William Long that his only company was a "parcel of querulous & half crazy Females" and that Eliza was so mad everyone kept away. Other letters to Long give more details and suggest that Long is better off unmarried as certain amorous satisfactions may be found in other ways. In 1786 Hayley's marriage virtually broke down; his version was that Eliza's mercurial depressions simply got too much for him, that her constant need for stimulation and society could not be catered for at Eartham. He felt her instability could easily degenerate into insanity, and he found he did not have the strength he once nobly declared he would devote to caring for her. He attempted to find a home for her with his friend Dr. Beridge at Derby, who in the end refused the charge, and Hayley was forced to try to get along with her at home. His son seems to have become something of a buffer zone between the two, a focus for affection which they could no longer express to each other. Hayley's literary output dwindled somewhat during the mid 1780s, though he produced some patriotic *Occasional Stanzas* on the centenary of the Glorious Revolution and supplied some biographical sketches on his friend the Reverend William Clarke and the poet Richard Crashaw for Andrew Kippis's *Biographia Britannica* (second edition, 1784, 1789). He spent much of his time educating the precocious Thomas and a few other companion children. He also spent time in London, visiting Gibbon and avoiding home life. In 1789, Dr. Beridge having died in 1788, Haley moved Eliza to the house at Derby with Beridge's widow. There was a terrible parting scene, and a great deal of affectionate (if sometimes argumentative) correspondence followed, but they never saw each other again.

Hayley was now an eminent man, attracting protegés and some satirists. He published a novel, *The Young Widow; or, the History of Cornelia Sedley, in a Series of Letters* (1789), which was so unassailably moral that he sent it to the archbishop of Canterbury. There was also *The Eulogies of Howard, a Vision* (1791), a commemoration of the prison reformer John Howard, of one of Hayley's heroes of public sensibility. Another play (*Marcella,* 1789) and an opera (*Eudora,* 1790) were performed, and in 1790 (on the death of Thomas Warton) Hayley was offered the laureateship. He turned it down, apparently for political reasons, and set out for France with his son and Romney. Despite the French Revolution, they moved in high society, enjoying parties and visits to eminent painters. Hayley also acquired a French governess for Thomas, though this arrangement only lasted long enough for her to inspire and copy out a drama by Hayley in French which was rejected by Parisian managers for its indelicate portrait of a courtesan. But this play, *Zelma; Or, The Will O' Th' Wisp,* as revised and translated in collaboration with the painter Meyer, lasted four nights at Covent Garden in 1792.

After these efforts Hayley began the work and the friendship for which he is most celebrated. He undertook to write a biography of John Milton to front the magnificent edition proposed by John and Josiah Boydell, and when he found that Cowper was engaged in a related project for other publishers, Hayley wrote to him to introduce himself and to discuss their respective works. The two men quickly formed an intense friendship, despite the reservations of Lady Hesketh about Hayley's religious character. Cowper was sixty-one and well established at the house of Mary Unwin, his companion; Hayley was perhaps the last to penetrate his retirement before his final descent into madness. Within weeks Cowper was writing to Hayley: "I feel a disposition of heart toward you, that I never felt for one whom I had never seen" (6 April 1792); on 7 June he began, "Love you? Yes to be sure I do." Some fifty warm and brilliant letters to the "dear friend and Crony-bard" followed in the next two years. Hayley for his part felt that Cowper was just the sort of man to sympathize with his exceptionally difficult life (knowing at this stage nothing of Cowper's own far more desperate problems). He went to visit Cowper in May of this year and deepened the friendship by being present when Mrs. Unwin's near-fatal stroke reduced Cowper almost to idiocy. Hayley managed to calm Cowper, to make him believe that it was possible to find once again the God who seemed to have deserted him, and Cowper thereafter regarded Hayley as a providential preserver, "the most benevolent and amiable of his kind" (to Lady Hesketh, 24 May 1792). Hayley tried all kinds of medical nostrums (he was fanatical about the benefits of static electricity), but his most important function was simply to be there and to support Cowper. Once the older man had regained some steadiness, Hayley set about providing for Cowper's future in the event of Mrs. Unwin's death, and for the next four years he doggedly and passionately pursued the goal of a public pension for Cowper. He badgered everyone he knew, and many he did not know, with a reckless and often tactless enthusiasm. "In short," wrote Cowper to Lady Hesketh, "if any thing can be squeezed out of the Wooll-sack in the shape of emolument for me, now is the time and Hayley will be the Squeezer" (26 May 1792).

Meanwhile Hayley somehow persuaded Cowper to overcome the "thousand Lions, monsters and giants" in the way and bring Mrs. Unwin to Eartham, where they were joined by Romney, Smith and John Johnson. This was the kind of company of which Hayley dreamed, and for a while the arrangement was a great success. Cowper enthused about the house and garden and told Lady Hesketh, "here we inhabit a paradise" (11 August 1792). Johnson wrote enthusiastically to Lady Hesketh of Hayley's library, with the portrait of Lady Hamilton "in the character of Sensibility" over the fireplace, and most of all of his tender care for Cowper. Hayley and Cowper revised translations of Milton and worked on a translation of Giovanni Battista Andreini's *L'Adamo* (1613), which Hayley argued was a main source for Milton's *Paradise Lost;* Smith read aloud her new novel, *The Old Manor House* (1793), and Mrs. Unwin's health slowly improved. Cowper wanted to be made to study, but Hayley may have organized things for him a little too rigorously. Both Cowper and Johnson wrote that after a while the landscape had a depressing effect, although the arrival of the poet James Hurdis, grieving for the death of his sister did not help either. Johnson also told Lady Hesketh that Hayley's revision of Cowper's translations of Milton's Latin and Italian poems was extremely detrimental: "there is scarcely a page but he has *murdered* in *my* opinion." After Cowper went home his depression deepened, and Hayley wrote almost continuously to try to raise his spirits. Cowper told Hayley about his dreams, his nocturnal voices, and his "Monitor," and eventually his humor returned: he even teased Hayley about his poor moral and political reputation and addressed him as "Dear Architect of fine

Chateaux in the air" (29 June 1793). Hayley went back to Weston to see Cowper in November 1793, and Cowper wrote to his friend Mrs. Catharine Courtenay of an amusing scene of their labors on Homer and Milton, while Mrs. Unwin babbled in a corner (4 November 1793). But despite progress on their literary projects, Hayley was so alarmed by Cowper's worsening depression and Mrs. Unwin's evident senility that he sped off to London to pursue Cowper's pension. Eventually, after interviewing everyone he knew with any trace of power, he managed to get an interview with William Pitt the Younger, in which the pension seemed to be promised, but it took several more months and several more appeals, each rising in desperation as Cowper's condition slid toward madness, before the pension was finally (though, as it turned out, ineffectually) granted.

At Eartham other visitors came and enjoyed themselves: Romney, as usual finding support and ideas in Hayley's company, and Gibbon, delighting Hayley with his conversation if not his politics. Hayley managed to finish his *Life of Milton in Three Parts* in 1793, but his publishers refused to print during the Reign of Terror a work which so highlighted Milton's republicanism. Cowper, who had been enthusiastic about Hayley's plan, commiserated with Hayley on the necessary compromise, whereby an expurgated version of his biography of Milton formed the first volume of the glossy but forbidding edition of Milton's works published in 1794, while Hayley retained five hundred copies of the plates in order to illustrate his full-scale *Life of Milton,* published in 1796 (though he did not use them). The 1796 version, besides some verbal polishing, is substantially more political in character.

Hayley's *Life of Milton* was expressly written to counter the antirepublican biography by Samuel Johnson. There were already several biographies available, as Milton's reputation soared in the eighteenth century. Apart from the early lives, there was (in Johnson's phrase) Elijah Fenton's "elegant abridgement," attached to a 1725 edition of *Paradise Lost;* Thomas Birch's ponderous edition of the *Prose Works* (1753), published in two volumes; and Thomas Newton's many editions of the poems. Then came Johnson's admiring but politically conservative account, which brought many protests, and Hayley's is the best example of the Whig hagiography of Milton. What Hayley called Johnson's "detractive sarcasms" and "malevolent prejudices" are contrasted signally with Milton's high-minded radicalism, though Hayley praises Johnson's "powerful mind" and his charitable work on behalf of Milton's granddaughter. Hayley's biography of Milton offers no new material or evidence, rather it recycles and recharacterizes the material already available (just as Johnson had done). However, the rebuttal is detailed and fairly accurate, though there is also much conjecture and interpretation: Gibbon told Hayley that the book sounded like a brilliant piece of advocacy, a juridical defense.

Hayley divides Milton's life into three phases: lyric, polemic, and epic. The polemic writing is not buried but highlighted, showing Milton's intellectual energy as being behind a creative principle: Milton was a "constant advocate for freedom, in every department of life," and this aspect of his personality was inextricably linked to that "inextinguishable fire of imagination, which gave existence and perfection to his Paradise Lost." In Hayley's view Milton's political tracts must be treated alongside Milton's revolutionary Christianity, and both are fused in his epic form. Though the artist Joseph Farington called Hayley "a violent Republican" on account of his *Life of Milton,* the book merely shows devout Whiggism: Hayley thought Milton would have applauded the Glorious Revolution, but this judgment is now scarcely credible.

Much of the book is not actually biographical: rather Hayley uses criticism to establish a Milton "of accomplished mind, in which sensibility and judgment were proportioned to extraordinary imagination." This sensibility is uncompromisingly virtuous – Milton's work "displays at full length, the delicious tranquillity of innocence, the tormenting turbulence of guilt, and the consolatory satisfaction of repentance" and therefore "has surely abundance of attraction to awaken sympathy." A large appendix discusses the origins of *Paradise Lost,* which Hayley (and Cowper) sought in Adreini's *L'Adamo,* a source already rejected by Johnson. Hayley presents Milton's building of this epic as analogous to God's creation of the world, and Hayley idolizes the work of the poet in a proto-Romantic vein.

The Life of Milton was moderately successful and was reprinted several times. The anonymous critic for the *Monthly Review* (January–April 1795) liked Hayley's "manly and liberal sentiments," but he thought Hayley's effort to "obliterate every moral stain" was both overdone and unnecessary. In the critic's view Hayley's "amiable ardour" led him to take as sincere phrases which were conventional and literary, and Hayley's defense of Milton's attitude toward Oliver Cromwell and of Milton's conduct in his marital problems was presented "with more ingenuity than solidity." A writer for

the *Gentleman's Magazine* (May 1796) judged that Hayley wrote "in the ardour of enthusiastic friendship" (something he would not have denied); T. J. Mathias carped at Hayley's eulogistic tendency. Samuel Taylor Coleridge's annotated copy survives and shows his close reading of the book, with which he was not always in agreement. The book is now treated rather as a document of its time, a stimulus for a Romantic view of Milton. Certainly it celebrates rather than deprecates Milton's political life, and this stance was a departure for Milton criticism; the Romantics no doubt drew inspiration from it and the revaluation it represented. It is not itself a Romantic book, though, as comparison with Blake's *Milton,* written and edited between 1804 and 1808, written nearly a decade later, partly under Hayley's patronage, demonstrates; it is instead an expressive transition between the classic and the Romantic views of Milton.

Cowper's letters to Hayley (and everyone else) stopped abruptly in January 1794. In April Hayley was summoned to Weston by Cowper's friends in an effort to rouse Cowper from total despondency; though ill, Hayley went, later describing in his *Memoirs* the "spectacle" of the "interesting sufferer" as "grievous and terrible." Cowper showed little recognition. Hayley sent for his son Thomas to whom Cowper had already shown some kindness, in a vain attempt to awaken his sympathy; but Hayley was himself too ill to stay and had to abandon Cowper to his depression. Meanwhile Gibbon had died, and Hayley was engaged in another biographical project, assisting Lord Sheffield in the editing of the "Memoirs of my Life and Writings," published in the *Miscellaneous Works of Edward Gibbon, Esq.* (1796). Part of the work was done at Eartham. As elsewhere in his biographical work, Hayley seems to have wanted to tone down things which showed the subject in a poor light; he wanted to hear the private voice, to be "introduced to a great author, not expressly *writing* a Book but rather *thinking aloud* "; yet he also felt that any "lamentable defect" should be "veiled."

In the meantime his wife Eliza was threatening to return to Sussex, though she eventually chose London, perhaps in deference to Hayley's alarmed letters. The situation was complicated by the apprenticeship of Thomas to the sculptor Flaxman, which required a lodging in London. Hayley asked Eliza to "avoid an interview," but she was increasingly restive about her independence and demanded a formal settlement of her income. Hayley refused and threatened to stop her from seeing Thomas, though he soon relented on this point. But their correspondence ceased with a stiff letter from

THE

LIFE OF MILTON,

IN THREE PARTS.

TO WHICH ARE ADDED,

CONJECTURES ON THE ORIGIN OF PARADISE LOST:

WITH AN APPENDIX.

By WILLIAM HAYLEY, Esq.

Ολϐιος, ὅς μέγα ἔργον ἐν ἀθανάτοισιν ἀνύσσας,
Ναίει ἀπήμανῖος καί ἀγήραος ἤματα πάντα.
HESIOD. THEOGONIA, v. 953.

Magnarum virium est tractare sacra tam splendide, simplicia tam erudite, inculta tam polite, retrusa tam dilucide, a sensu communi abhorrentia tam populariter, periculosa tam libere, severa tam plausibiliter. Et tamen hunc virum, quem ne summi quidem queant assequi, non verentur calumniari et mediocres.
ERASMUS.

LONDON:

Printed for T. CADELL, Junior, and W. DAVIES, (Successors to Mr. CADELL) in the Strand.

M. DCC. XCVI.

Title page for the biography Hayley wrote to counter the interpretation of Milton's life and works put forth by Samuel Johnson in Prefaces, Biographical and Critical

Hayley insisting on his financial probity and refusing to change his arrangements on her behalf. All his emotional energy was now focused on his son, by Hayley's account a prodigy in all arts, but still likable. Thomas, called Tom, seems to have charmed all Hayley's adult friends, and a good deal of his character emerges from Hayley's mawkish and overprotective account of him. Hayley's letters to his son from this period are filled with advice – on books, art, health, and London. Hayley acknowledges that even the affectionate Tom was tried by the relentless pressure of paternal ideas. In 1796 he fell ill, and Flaxman sent him home to recuperate. Doctors told Hayley nothing was wrong, and he treated the boy to what one suspects were fairly interminable readings. In fact Tom was already suffering from the disease that was to kill him – some sort of curvature of the spine, perhaps the same disease that killed Alexander Pope. Tom recovered

sufficiently to resume his training and indeed responded enthusiastically to Hayley's multiple suggestions. Hayley was building a "Marine Villa" (complete with a recluse's turret) at Felpham, where he already had a cottage, and he and Tom exchanged designs for the decor of the library to be constructed there. But by the middle of 1797 Tom had relapsed and was back at Eartham, where Hayley once more nursed him with a mixture of books and sea bathing.

At the same time, Hayley received a brief note from Cowper, the first for many years. It was in dark contrast to the long and amusing letters of 1792 and 1793: it expressed "Perfect Despair." Hayley's response to this desperate communication has a kind of ludicrous magnanimity which illustrates as well as anything Hayley's character. He immediately wrote back to Cowper an account of an "ecstatic Vision" he had had, in which Cowper's mother and his own were seen on the steps of the throne of God. Cowper's mother had prophesied that her son's recovery would be slow but preceded by "extraordinary circumstances of signal Honour on earth" – notably letters from members of Parliament, bishops, judges, the prime minister, and the king, all thanking Cowper for his services to Christianity. When these arrived Hayley was enjoined to tell him, he would receive his "celestial Emancipation from Despair." Hayley innocently requested Cowper to let him know if any of the portents should come to pass. Hayley had no means of knowing how he was going to get the letters out of the specified people, but he felt that Cowper was so deranged as to be receptive only on this level. John Johnson, who had by now removed Cowper to his own house at Dereham, said that the letter appeared to have done some good at any rate. Hayley now set about getting the requisite letters to arrive, with some success; William Wilberforce and the bishops of London and Gloucester duly complied with Hayley's fervent requests, and Johnson and Lady Hesketh tried hard to make the plot work. But the effort failed to rouse Cowper beyond a few emendations to his Homer translation, and Hayley heard little more until Cowper's death.

In 1797 Eliza died, and it is not difficult to sense Hayley's relief; he did, of course, all that was fitting by way of funeral arrangements. His finances were now sufficient to press on with the building at Felpham. But Tom, who had tried to resume studies once more, was desperately ill, and early in 1798 Hayley took him home to Eartham. Treatment was useless; the disease is charted in Hayley's *Memoirs* and also in his series of letters to William Long written from 1793 to 1812. Tom gradually lost the use of his limbs, while Hayley drove himself frantic trying to amuse him. Hayley had a wheelchair made, got hold of various other mechanical contrivances, and doctored Tom with his own remedies. His *An Essay on Sculpture* (1800) – another art-historical poem with many notes – inspired by Tom's choice of career, was now finished, and Tom proofread it, expressing particular gratification about the plate of his own design (engraved by Blake) which accompanied it. But *An Essay on Sculpture* turned into an epitaph, and the postscript records Tom's final sufferings. By Hayley's account, his son remained astoundingly cheerful and noble; he died on 2 May 1800, a week after Cowper.

It was a terrible year, compounded by the loss of Romney from Eartham. His mental state had deteriorated, and he had finally gone home to Kendal to be nursed by his long-neglected wife; he died in 1802. But it was also a new beginning – not only because Hayley began to write biographies of Cowper and Tom but because in July 1800 Blake visited Felpham for the first time. Hayley's main preoccupation for the next three years was the Cowper biography, though history has concentrated in a rather unbalanced fashion on Blake's life under Hayley's patronage at Felpham, where Hayley now lived as a self-styled hermit. He became the "official" biographer of Cowper through a mixture of John Johnson's indolence and Lady Hesketh's need to find an editor she could control. After accepting the task with some reluctance (or polite show of it), Hayley busied himself with research, extracting as many letters and as much information as possible from Johnson and Lady Hesketh (the latter proving particularly resistant) and pestering them for introductions to people connected with Cowper. Hayley did in fact obtain an interview with Lady Austen, though in the end he could make little of it. Lady Hesketh's original plan had been for something short, plain, and sedate; Hayley wanted something long, ornate, and emotional. Their correspondence, which survives in two bound volumes in the British Library, is a record of struggle, and it is to Hayley's credit that he managed to get the biography published at all. Lady Hesketh forced Hayley to curb or omit material which gave any indication of republican views in Cowper and also had him tone down the account of Cowper's insanity and his private religious life. Nothing should appear that would suggest Cowper was "a Visionary! an Enthusiast! or a Calvinist." She was worried about Hayley's own radical sympathies (not to mention his reputed atheism and actual adultery) and gave a fearsome example of her displeasure when Samuel Greatheed revealed some of the skeletons in Cowper's closet. Early romances, comments on the family, and even minor humorous remarks were all expunged. What Hayley would have produced given a free hand one can only speculate. All his biographies have something defensive and lionizing about them, and it is quite likely he would have omitted much even if unprompted. But his biography of Romney and his autobiography make no secret of marital problems, for example, and it seems likely that what Lady Hesketh wanted concealed would have struck Hayley as too emotionally interesting to ignore; he was much more tolerant toward Greatheed's indiscretion.

In March 1802 Hayley handed over the manuscript of *The Life and Posthumous Writings of William Cowper, Esqr.* to a local printer, James Seagrave of Chichester, and the two volumes were published in

1803. The main text of the work consists of more than 250 letters by Cowper arranged chronologically and intercut with a brief biographical narrative especially where large gaps appeared in the letter record, during Cowper's periods of insanity. The overall scheme is tripartite, covering the time before Cowper's first book of poems, the time up to his translation of Homer, and his last years. The correspondents include Hayley himself, Joseph Hill, Samuel Rose, Lady Hesketh, James Hurdis, John Johnson, and Greatheed. There are also several posthumous poems, including "The Castaway." Hayley insists several times on the reliability of the letters as a index of character; they offer "an insight into the pure recesses of Cowper's wonderful mind at some remarkable periods of his life"; they are more spontaneous than those of Pope; and they make up "a faithful representation of him . . . where the most striking features will appear the work of his own inimitable hand." However, readers also learn that Hayley thinks that only those who feel "the influence of tenderness and truth" should become biographers, and "tenderness" may sometimes offset "truth." Just as William Mason, whose biography of Thomas Gray was admired by Hayley, rearranged and "edited" that correspondence, so Hayley, under the combined pressure of Lady Hesketh's tyranny and his own sensibility, set about cutting the letters to an appropriate form. Some cuts were indicated by asterisks, and Hayley also argued that "many of them are of a nature, not suited to publication"; but there were many silent cuts, mutilations, and conflations, as well as "improvements" and simple errors. The work formed the basis of most nineteenth-century editions, though modern editors have completely reedited the letters.

As far as Hayley was concerned, the purpose of biography was to provide a living portrait of a dead friend. This attitude was one reason he collected portraits, and why he was so disappointed with the engraving Blake did of the portrait of Thomas in *An Essay on Sculpture*. Most of Hayley's poems have an individual addressee, and he adopts a hortatory tone toward leading professors of particular arts. Much of the rest of his verse consists of elegies or (more accurately) eulogies on similar individuals. In *A Poetical Epistle to an Eminent Painter* Hayley tells how portraits of lost friends soothe and console audiences by providing a focus for affection. In poems published toward the end of his life Hayley spoke of Cowper and Thomas as always present at Felpham because of his labor there on the biographies. *The Life of William Cowper* remains the best example of Hayley's attempt to preserve in

word and image the presence of a close friend. Hayley seeks to give the reader "intimate acquaintance" with Cowper and thus tries to establish certain psychological bases: notably Cowper's loss of his mother, which "contributed perhaps in the highest degree to the dark colouring of his subsequent life." Hayley attempts to "trace the rise and progress of genius" and the "degree of influence, which the warmth of his heart produced on the fertility of his mind." The biography leads up to and ends with a "character," described in terms of physiognomy, "constitution" (warm but thwarted in love – as was Hayley himself), benevolence and moral life, and conversation (characterized, not recorded). Hayley had a tendency to label and judge, rather than report in detail. Cowper's break with Lady Austen, which Hayley certainly knew more about than he could or would tell, is dealt with in the blandest of terms. But there are touches of vivid if melodramatic writing, particularly about the death of Mrs. Unwin; and for all the editorial meddling, the book does at least present large quantities of Cowper's letters. Hayley worries in print about egotism in reprinting letters to himself detailing his own good works, though he is probably right not to misrepresent Cowper by omitting them. Hayley was drawn to Cowper not only by mutual admiration of Milton but by the sensibility of a melancholy but benevolent poet in an unusual domestic ménage, and there could easily be a kind of narcissism in the biography. But the picture of their mutual study at Eartham seems pleasantly devoid of vanity; Hayley tones down his role in calming Cowper after Mrs. Unwin's stroke and all but erases his activity in getting him a pension. In all, the Haylean elements are well controlled, and this restraint may be one reason the book proved to be a fantastic success, one of the few works that brought Hayley financial success. Lady Hesketh was ecstatic: "The elegance and animation of the style can only be equalled by the extreme tenderness and delicacy with which you touch on particular subjects, too affecting in their nature not to be seen with real pain by me, and which would indeed have been *insupportable,* had they been drawn by a rougher pencil."

One of the results of this success was that Lady Hesketh turned up some more letters, and important letters to William Unwin and John Newton were found; another 150 letters formed volume three of the biography, published in 1803. Also included was the recently discovered "Yardley Oak," in a variorum text, and Hayley padded out the volume with a criticism on letter writing, in which he declares himself unrepentant for what some, notably Seward, regarded as his excessive praise of Cowper. More was to come, and in 1806 Hayley published *Supplementary Pages to the Life of Cowper,* with corrections and additional letters most of which were written to William Bagot; the new material was included in a fully revised edition of the *The Life of William Cowper* which also came out that year.

Hayley had tried to deal cautiously with the problematic question of Cowper's religion, which by some accounts was the direct cause of his madness. He tried to adduce additional psychological factors and also to meliorate the general question: "if the charitable and religious zeal of the Poet led him into any excesses of devotion, injurious to the extreme delicacy of his nervous system, he is only the more entitled to admiration and to pity." But Hayley's evenhandedness was thought too soft: "Mr. Hayley seems to have exerted himself to conciliate readers of every description, not only by the most lavish and indiscriminate praise of every individual he has occasion to mention, but by a general spirit of approbation and indulgence towards every practice and opinion which he has found it necessary to speak of" (anonymous, *Edinburgh Review,* April 1803). The reviewer for *Gentleman's Magazine* (January–June 1803) found the work too revealing. The writer for the *British Critic* (July–December 1803) liked the letters but thought those that showed the influence of "wretched Calvinism" should have been omitted; as did the critic for the *Monthly Review* (May–August 1803), who further felt the whole book was too panegyrical, "over-loaded and bedecked with praise." As the supplements came out, the reviews grew warmer, but later in the century Hayley was attacked by both Anglicans and Nonconformists. Some of the worst reinterpretation of his text was done by Victorian clergy anxious to find evidence for their own causes. The letters have long since been represented in purer editions, and the biographical narrative has been adapted and absorbed by later ones; but Hayley's material is still used as a primary document, and it remains his best piece of work.

The first edition of *The Life of William Cowper* is illustrated with three engraved plates by Blake, followed by more in the supplement. Blake's troubled relationship with Hayley remains the best-known element of Hayley's life. Flaxman was responsible for introducing Blake to Hayley as a potential benefactor. Flaxman had sent Hayley Blake's *Poetical Sketches* of 1783 and recommended him as a painter rather than an engraver. There is some evidence of meetings before 1800, when Blake was invited to rent the cottage Hayley found for him at Felpham;

certainly the tone of Blake's first surviving letters to Hayley is warmly sympathetic and familiar. Blake consoles Hayley on the death of his son by assuring him that his own dead brother is still an active presence in his life: "I hear his advice & even now write from his Dictate." Hayley represented Blake to Lady Hesketh as having "infinite Genius, with a most engaging simplicity of character," not to mention "an excellent wife," whom Hayley apparently thought was all Eliza had not been. Blake was keen to leave Lambeth, and Hayley no doubt promised him work and other kinds of help; Blake's initial reactions were ecstatically thankful, both to Flaxman and Hayley, the "Leader of my Angels." The first fruit of Blake's sojourn at Felpham was a single-sheet ballad, *Little Tom the Sailor* (1800), which Hayley wrote and Blake illustrated; it was, typically, sold for charitable purposes. Blake was then commissioned to provide a set of "heads of the poets" for Hayley's library at the Turret — a series containing many obvious choices but also many individual ones: Luiz vaz de Camões, Ercilla y Zúñiga, and Hayley's son. Hayley also encouraged various aristocratic friends to ask Blake for their portraits in miniature, a job to which Blake was surprisingly amenable. Hayley "acts like a Prince," Blake wrote to Thomas Butts, "I am at complete ease" (10 May 1801). When the frieze of heads was finished, Hayley started composing ballads for children on animal themes, which Blake was to illustrate. Some of these now look very odd: a poem about a dog called Fido seems hardly likely to inspire Blake, and his designs are rather more creative than the poems. But they, too, brought in some money when published in 1805 under the title *Ballads, By William Hayley, Esq.* Even more bizarre is the idea of Blake illustrating Hayley's *Triumphs of Temper;* but he did, to designs by Maria Flaxman, for the twelfth edition of 1803. He was also being used as an amanuensis, and Hayley even taught him Greek.

Just as Lady Hesketh did not much care for Blake's work, Hayley was not pleased by Blake's engraving of his son's portrait for the *Essay on Sculpture* and made him redo it, although Blake's other engraving in that work, from Thomas's "Death of Demosthenes," pleased Thomas himself. Hayley vigorously defended Blake's "great spirit and sentiment" and "true Genius." In his *Memoirs* Hayley writes of Blake's "wonderful talents for original design," and Blake is described as "interesting," "alert," and "indefatigable." Hayley never spoke badly of his "kind-hearted Brother of Parnassus" in letters to others, though comments about "our poor industrious Blake" do have a patronizing ring. He

William Hayley (engraving after a portrait by Engleheart)

saw Blake as another Cowper, "in the Tenderness of his Heart, and in the perilous powers of an imagination utterly unfit to take due care of Himself." He thought Blake's acute sensibility, if challenged with criticism, liable to reduce him to depression and madness, and Hayley did his best to avoid ruffling "our quick-sprited" Blake. But Blake was ruffled, largely by Hayley's insistence on his doing remunerative work rather than the free imaginative projects he had within him. There were disagreements over money, Blake apparently demanding more as he thought Hayley needed him more. Blake came to see Hayley as more Satan than Milton, Felpham another trial between imagination and reason. His own prophetic book *Milton* was begun at Felpham. The understanding between Blake and Hayley broke down early in 1803, and Blake wrote to his brother accusing Hayley of jealousy and incomprehension (30 January 1803). Blake felt he had the measure of Hayley and some control over him, and Blake claimed money was about to start pouring in, that he would be able to start publishing his own "formidable works." It is a babbling, almost feverish letter, but Blake acknowledges and takes pride in the remuneration his work for Hayley was bringing in. The plates for Hayley's *The Life of William Cowper* were perhaps the most calculatedly "ordinary" style Blake ever contrived and may have

been a strain, but Blake had had no complaints about the project and had praised Hayley's "matchless industry." He thought the plates, which his wife printed, were "as fine as the French prints and please everyone." Nonetheless in a letter to Butts (6 July 1803) he was storming: "I am determin'd to be no longer Pester'd with his Genteel Ignorance & Polite Disapprobation. I know myself both Poet & Painter, & it is not his affected Contempt that can move me to any thing but a more assiduous pursuit of both Arts." Blake never knew of Hayley's defense of his genius.

In August 1803, after an ugly fracas with a soldier, Blake was put on trial for sedition. This problem was exactly the kind of situation at which Hayley excelled, and he and his friend the printer Seagrave got Blake out on bail and paid for his defense by Samuel Rose, whom Hayley had gotten to know through Cowper. Hayley gave evidence at the trial and sent a letter of rejoicing to Lady Hesketh at Blake's acquittal. Blake's own impatience with Hayley was understandably tempered by a recognition of his "generous & tender solicitude," and he apologized to Hayley for having misunderstood his motives. Blake began carrying out various commissions for Hayley, including plates for extended editions of *The Life of William Cowper* and research for Hayley's new biographical project, *The Life of George*

Romney (1809). Hayley was still sending money, and Blake's letters are full of affectionate thanks. Blake even contrived to be polite about Hayley's *Triumphs of Music* (1804), a melodramatic Venetian tale showing how decayed Hayley's style had become. Over a third of Blake's surviving letters were written to Hayley, and most of those date from the two years after he left Felpham. In the last letter which survives, Blake wistfully commends "our Beautiful, Affectionate Ballads," which had just been published as a book, and tells Hayley of his spiritual sufferings in a way which can only have confirmed Hayley's view of the similarity between Blake's mental condition and Cowper's: "You Dear Sir are one who has my Particular Gratitude, having conducted me thro' Three that would have been the Darkest Years that ever Mortal Suffer'd, which were render'd thro' your means a Mild & Pleasant Slumber. I speak of Spiritual Things, Not of Natural; Of Things known only to Myself & to Spirits Good & Evil, but Not known to Men on Earth.... *I know* that if I had not been with You I must have Perish'd."

Nonetheless their relationship grew less firm; Hayley replaced Blake with Caroline Watson as his favorite engraver, though he subscribed to Blake's illustrated version of Robert Blair's *The Grave* (1808). Blake's sufferings continued, and his lack of success seems to have convinced him that there was a conspiracy against him and that Hayley was involved. A much-quoted series of deadly couplets and epigrams dating from 1808 to 1811 accuses Hayley and more or less everyone else Blake knew of enmity and stupidity; the poems seem to have been motivated by nothing more aggressive than neglect.

The ensuing years were quieter for Hayley. More friends died and were memorialized in song; his *The Life of George Romney* proceeded slowly, thanks to works on new editions of *The Life of William Cowper;* and Hayley was badgered by people less talented and honest than Blake in search of patronage – notably the poet William Hersee. Hayley edited or otherwise helped several other now-forgotten poets. He also published two more volumes in memory of his collaboration with Cowper: the translations of Milton's Latin and Italian poems (1808) and *Cowper's Milton* (1810), an assemblage of all their mutual work on the subject. In 1809 *The Life of George Romney* was finally published as a testimony to the twenty years of friendship they had enjoyed. Romney had been the subject of Hayley's first major poem, which he reprinted in the biography. Every year Romney had come for a visit, and Hayley had partitioned his riding room to provide

Romney with a studio. He had also witnessed Romney's difficult mental situation, but the book is much more of a "Romney as I knew him" biography than the work on Cowper. It is chronologically arranged around a stock of some sixty-five letters, some given in extract, from Romney mostly to Hayley. (A promised cache of personal material from Romney's brother never materialized.) The narrative is a somewhat loose introduction to each letter. Though Hayley proposed that "extracts from these, will afford a clear insight into the heart and mind of a man, who had received from nature, that inestimable, though perilous gift, extreme sensibility," the letters themselves are not in Cowper's class and rather fail to confirm the image of Romney as "one of the most singular and interesting mortals, who ever enlivened and embellished human life by the successful cultivation of extraordinary talents." Gaps are filled in with letters written by Hayley (who presumably kept archive copies) or by his son, or by Hayley's own verse – all of which makes for a rather egotistical presentation. Since many of Romney's letters are written in praise of Hayley's own goodness, and since Hayley spends much of the book recounting his multiple suggestions for subjects for Romney's brush, the effect can be one-sided. An incident which Hayley relates tells readers much about his own character and his relationship with Romney:

> During my visit to Romney in November, I happened to find him one morning contemplating by himself, a recently coloured head, on a small canvas. I expressed my admiration of his unfinished work in the following terms: "This is a most happy beginning: you never painted a female head with such exquisite expression; you have only to enlarge your canvas, introduce the shrub mimosa, growing in a vase, with a hand of this figure approaching its leaves, and you may call your picture a personification of Sensibility." – "I like your suggestion," replied the painter, "and will enlarge my canvas immediately." – "Do so (I answered with exultation, on his kindly adopting my idea), and without loss of time I will hasten to an eminent nursery-man at Hammersmith, and bring you the most beautiful plant I can find, that may suit your purpose."

Hayley tries to defend himself against the charge of egotism ("I found it impossible to do justice to all the affectionate feelings of my companion and correspondent, without introducing much of myself, and much of my son, whose talents as a very young artist, Romney was ever inclined to encourage and commend"), but the effect is often comic. The biography is defensive in other ways: principally it attacks the "coarse misrepresentation"

146

of Romney given by George Cumberland in the *European Magazine* (June 1803) and claims "official" status against that memoir. Cumberland had referred to Romney's "failings," but Hayley is more circumspect: "It is a moral question of great delicacy, how far it may be incumbent on a confidential biographer to display, or to conceal, the imperfections of his departed friend." In the epitaph he provided for Romney, he wrote "thou on lost friends could'st such a life bestow, / That all their virtues on thy canvas flow," and the biography aims at something like that: a static character portrait, a four-hundred-page elegy. Hayley and Romney found sympathy in each other because of their marital estrangements, nervous hypochondria, frank benevolence, and insistence on friendship itself. Hayley dwells with particular wistfulness on the occasion of Cowper's meeting with Romney at Eartham in 1792. Romney painted Cowper; Cowper wrote a sonnet to Romney; and Hayley watched. His regret is tinged with the hope "that I may a little contribute 'to keep their memories green on earth,' by tender and faithful records of those particular talents and virtues in each, which excited my constant solicitude for the welfare of both during many years, and rendered them objects of my indelible affection." Several other scenes are "frozen" with this same note of pointed threnody: when Hayley writes of Romney's visit to Hayley's new building at Felpham, with Hayley's son and the architect, readers learn that within six years all except Hayley himself were dead: "I am now sitting alone in the dwelling, which their kindness has endeared, and which their ingenuity has adorned; and I feel a tender gratification in employing the uncertain remnant of my days on such literary works, as may faithfully commemorate the talents and the virtues of those who still speak to me in their works, and here daily remind me both of their genius and their affection."

The Life of George Romney offers critical views on Romney by Flaxman and others and is well illustrated, mostly with stipple engravings, in Romney's style, by Watson (though there is one print by Blake). Mrs. Flaxman, whose husband had helped collect materials for the biography, told Hayley the prints would need to be good, because "from the Life I do not see how you can give us much Morality, or delight." The critic for the *Gentleman's Magazine* (December 1809) called the book "one of the most ingenious and affectionate tributes ever paid to the memory of a departed friend" and praised Hayley's skill in making sympathetic a character much less interesting than Cowper's. The reviewer for the *British Critic* (October 1809) thought the engravings alone were worth the price; he also praised Hayley's affectionate zeal. But the writer for the *New Annual Register* (1809) damned the book as having been written in Hayley's "usual style of plenary verbiage, and rather characterized by warmth of friendship than chasteness or elegance of style." The critic for the *Monthly Review* (December 1809) said it spoke too much of Romney's infirmities and not enough of his powers. Hayley admitted it was not a success. His reputation has never really recovered from the malicious *Memoirs* Romney's son John – whom Hayley celebrated as his talented and intelligent friend – published in 1830. This book accuses Hayley of all manner of malevolent dealings with Romney: stealing paintings, encouraging Romney to waste money on building projects, and even causing Romney to desert his wife, which occurred before Romney and Hayley had met. The image persists of Hayley exercising a malign influence over Romney's depressed spirits.

Hayley's final biographical project was a life of himself, and he managed to sell the prospective *Memoirs* to his publisher in return for a substantial annuity. On 28 March 1809 Hayley married Mary Welford, the twenty-eight-year-old daughter of a retired merchant, and once again looked forward optimistically to a life of quiet retirement and reading. For a time all went well, despite the limited success of *The Life of George Romney* and a final volume of plays, *Three Plays* (1811). Mary evidently helped Hayley with his writing and proofreading. Hayley's retreat was less often invaded by visitors, though William Godwin passed an uncomfortable afternoon there in August 1811. As quoted by Morchard Bishop, he describes Hayley's Turret routine, which involved crawling into an attic gallery once a day "for the sake of the prospect," and his luxurious decor: "Pictures, drawings, splendid books, and splendid bindings adorn every room in the house." Like the younger Romantics, Godwin hated this kind of thing and concluded, "Damn him." Mary, whom Godwin saw as a "pleasant, unaffected, animated girl," left Hayley in 1812 for unexplained reasons. Hayley is uncharacteristically silent on the subject. Perhaps the life of seclusion was simply too much of a strain for her. Afterward he attempted to reopen the walls of his solitude, and a few songs printed for the "Amicable Fraternity of Felpham" survive in the Fitzwilliam Museum, Cambridge. He flirted ineffectually with Flaxman's wife and in a rather more serious fashion with a widow, the novelist Amelia Opie. Hayley's letters to Opie show his continuing need for sympathetic company, and after some worry about her reputation she accepted an invitation to Felpham. She found his habits regular to the point of obstinacy, and the whole month was spent reading, singing, praying, and taking temperate exercise in the garden. She seems to have enjoyed the hint of impropriety in the liaison, and there is certainly something coquettish about her letters. Reports from her second visit in 1815 show the increased influence of Quaker propriety on her judgments, and how Hayley evidently went too far, taking the Lord's name in vain, reading "exceptional passages" from books to her, and persisting in defending his having a son by his servant when there was no offspring from his marriage. She was curious about Hayley's marital troubles and upset him by asking for too much information about Mary, but in the end she accepted his version, lambasted the absent wife, and resumed her role as *carissima figlia* (dearest daughter) to Hayley.

Other visitors during Hayley's final years included Henry Cary, whose translation of Dante owes much to Hayley's pioneering work and encouragement. In 1818 Hayley published a book of serious, pious poems, many of them hymns, and some of which reassert his idea of biography as essentially elegiac recollection. Hayley was slowly dying of kidney disease, and he made a detailed will in which all his pictures and portraits were assigned to appropriate new owners. He survived a stroke in 1819, but a fall in 1820 shifted a large stone in his bladder, and he died on 12 November. An obituary in the *Gentleman's Magazine* (July–December 1820), probably by his friend John Nichols, defends his religious character and praises his "spirit of benevolence and good humour." His biographies are praised, though the verse comes off quite badly in comparison with younger writers: "he seems to have studied a chaste and classical correctness, rather than indulged an inborn fire and spirit." The obituarist hoped all Hayley's work on behalf of Cowper would soon be made public and felt that "a judicious selection from his Poems would . . . be acceptable to a numerous class of readers."

Hayley's *Memoirs* which includes a narrative about his son was published in 1823. The memoirs about Thomas had been written first, apparently concurrently with his *The Life of William Cowper*. This part alone runs to five hundred pages, for the most part consisting of the full and regular correspondence between Hayley and his son while the latter was training as a sculptor with Flaxman. Hayley says, "this son and father resembled a pair of youthful lovers in the frequency and tenderness of their correspondence." For some reason Hayley

chose to put the most disagreeable letters between him and his wife – on the subject of her income and the terms of the separation – in this biography rather than in his own. There are also extracts from Tom's diary, and from Hayley's, and much verse, which became increasingly more pious as Tom's illness worsened. Hayley refers to himself in the third person and acts as editor to a beautifully kept archive. Eliza's manuscripts are all in neat order, as are Tom's. The biography is dedicated to rendering Tom as "enchanting" to the reader as he evidently was to his father: "there never existed a mortal, to whose talents and manners the word enchanting might be applied with greater propriety. This singular youth possessed such a rare union of good-natured simplicity and of intelligent sweetness in his character, that without any appearance of endeavouring to ingratiate himself with the persons around him, he became endeared to them with a sort of magical celerity." Readers see every one of the birthday poems that Hayley wrote for Tom, as many anecdotes as Hayley can remember (and these were not enough for him), and a succession of appraisals from great men on Thomas's amazing charm and precocity. The final months in his life are lingered on: the quiet sufferings of "the filial angel" contrast with Hayley's alternation between hope and despair. The effect of the narrative is in many ways oppressive, and one almost sympathizes the more with Thomas for having to cope with the enormous weight of Hayley's love and perpetual, smothering officiousness. Hayley is aware that the claims he makes are sometimes "preposterous" and even tries to justify the work as a medical admonition to parents to watch out for the early symptoms of spinal curvature in their children, but there was no other way for him to deal with grief than by this testimony: "Perhaps the records of mankind could afford very few examples of a father and a son in whom their reciprocal affection rose to such a height, and supported itself in so striking a manner, through a series of chequered years."

Hayley's account of his own life begins with a defense of its importance. It might have been a simple life, but "incidents, very singular in themselves, and productive of consequences no less extraordinary, befel the subject of this Memoir." He had known many great men. The life is divided into books and chapters, "each book terminating with some remarkable event," and this approach also leads Hayley to relate many conversations which could only have happened in a novel and to terminate the *Memoirs* at his second marriage, so as to liken his story to those "most agreeable romances" which "are apt to terminate, with a wedding." It is, of course, also a gesture of self-importance, an effect heightened by the succession of narrow escapes from death Hayley contrives for himself: starved of milk by his nurse, almost dead from fever, just missing the flawed inoculation which killed his brother, accidentally stabbing himself while acting in William Shakespeare's *Othello,* and in adult life continually falling off his horse. He was ever "in imminent danger of being destroyed." Hayley talks about himself in the third person, perhaps in an attempt at objectivity, but the result is a stiff and pompous style, often requiring awkward shifts of perspective. Hayley's continual discovery of himself through his own archive is often disconcerting and sometimes seems no more than a blind for self-praise: "Hayley had indeed just grounds for self-approbation upon all his conduct in these occurrences." He prints all his letters to great men and their letters back to him. When his literary works fail, he tells us how much Gibbon or Cowper had praised them.

The book is not without candor and a certain integrity: documents are printed which do not show him in a good light. Hayley tells many stories against himself and seems anxious that readers see his true character. But the overall effect is that something is being suppressed, that readers are not really getting both sides of the story. Not only do Eliza's letters not show the melancholy irritability that Hayley assures readers she suffered from, there is always the sense that he makes his suffering more vivid than hers: "Perhaps no man, on the point of removing from him a wife, with whom he felt it impossible to live, ever shewed more tender or more sincere anxiety, to promote her ease, comfort, and welfare, to the utmost of his power, than Hayley manifested, in conducting all this painful business." He selects passages from her letters which "forcibly display some of her most admirable mental peculiarities" and tells readers that "there were, in her marvellous organization, inscrutable sources of suffering, which rendered her occasionally one of the most truly pitiable mortals, that sympathetic humanity could wish to relieve." But he praises her only when she is doing what he wants her to do, and his stubbornness in refusing to let her leave her distant prison in Derby reflects badly on him.

Hayley's name for himself is "the Sussex Bard" or "the poet of Eartham," or simply "Hermit," and hermits who shut themselves in the study may tend to regard everyone else (even in charity) in a narcissistic fashion. Certainly, for all Hayley's reading, there is not the least sign that he knew anything at all about what was going on outside his own literary concerns: he never mentions William Wordsworth, Samuel Taylor Coleridge, or George Gordon, Lord Byron (who repeatedly ridiculed him), or even Robert Southey or Samuel Rogers (who both liked him). Blake is the only Romantic mentioned in *Memoirs* and then only as a quaintly eccentric artist.

The manuscript of Hayley's *Memoirs* had been given to Cowper's kinsman John Johnson to edit. Johnson had been as regular a visitor as any during Cowper's final years, and he added to Hayley's book the letters Hayley wrote to him about Cowper and Thomas, as well as information about Hayley's final years (and, at some length, his death) from various friends. He also cut what he calls "irksome" details relating to Hayley's first romance, and he refused to add anything on the subject of Hayley's second marriage and its failure. Johnson's own view of Hayley is positive: "As the preceding Letters exhibit the sympathy of the Author in the sufferings of his friend Cowper, and the measures resorted to by his affectionate spirit, in the hope of relieving him under the pressure of his malady, so the present discover an equal earnestness to promote the interests of his posthumous reputation." He also did his best to stress the better qualities of Hayley's verse and prose. The occasional "feebleness of diction" Johnson notes "may be traced to an amiable source – to that exuberance of feeling, which, at the expense of his better judgement, impelled him to invest with endearing epithets, every person and every thing, of which he had occasion to speak – an impulse very creditable to his heart, no doubt, though prejudicial to the development of his conceptions as an author." This statement is not unfair, and it adequately places Hayley at the fading end of a tradition of sensibility which had been his main literary vehicle and mode of existence.

The book received a pleasant notice in the *Gentleman's Magazine* (June 1823), the critic for which did not doubt "the work will be considered as an acquisition to our stores of National Biography and Literary History"; but Leigh Hunt, writing in the *Literary Examiner* (5 July 1823), saw Hayley as a relic of a completely outmoded kind of writing, most of which now seemed mawkish or puerile, and his *Memoirs* "as fine an illustration of the importance of a man to himself as we ever beheld." Another negative review appeared in *Blackwood's Edinburgh Magazine* (July–December 1823). After poking fun at the "posthumous square yards of autobiography" and quoting the book against itself (which is not difficult) the reviewer settled into lacerating "the most distinguished driveller of his age" for his treatment of his wife, both in life and in *Memoirs:* "He has meanly, basely, and falsely striven to build up for himself a reputation for the finest feeling and most thoughtful humanity, at the expense of the most shameful violation of natural duties to the injured dead . . . the heartless hypocrite stands confessed on every page." The reviewer is seized with a "loathing disgust with this heartless, brainless versifier." The moral outrage was heightened by the impression that Eliza was the mother of Hayley's son, though many people knew the truth of the matter. One who did was Southey, whose own much more temperate essay appeared in the *Quarterly Review* (December 1824–March 1825): "These Memoirs are to be censured for nothing so much as for leaving the relationship in which Mrs. Hayley stood to her husband's child doubtful. His character required no such tenderness; and it was injuring her's to deprive her of the high credit which, upon that score, is her due." Southey also disliked the third-person style and found the book disappointingly deficient in literary anecdote. But he found things to value: "we may gather from it, however, an account, amusing in some points, and not uninteresting in others, of one so conspicuous in his day, that he must always hold a place in the history of English literature." There was no defending that style of writing which "in the course of time and of nature is defunct," but Southey praises Hayley's influential work on Spanish and Italian vernacular poetry, as represented by the notes to *An Essay on Epic Poetry,* and he finds touches of feeling even in the *Essay on Old Maids.* Southey regards the biography of Thomas as the most interesting part of Hayley's last book, both the correspondence and the devotional poems rising to some sublimity: "surely there are few persons who can read these most affecting poems without feeling some respect for Hayley." In the end Hayley is judged in personal terms he would not have refused: "there are few better criteria of a man's worth than the choice and stability of his friendships: few men could boast of more distinguished friends than Hayley, and no one was ever more lastingly attached to them, or more cordially esteemed in return." Sentiment is the key. Southey quotes a letter of Seward's in which she doubted that Hayley's grief would drive him insane because, in effect, he derived a kind of life from it. Nonetheless, "the judgment of that reader must be strangely warped by a censorious disposition who does not agree with him in admiring Hayley as a truly generous and gentle-hearted man." In "the outpourings of an afflicted heart" the reader may find "a strain of thought and feeling, which will find sympathy and may afford consolation, and which entitles him to respect, both as a poet and a man."

Hayley would have wanted no better testimony. But usually he got much worse. He was regarded as a "lady's poet" as early as 1803, and the Romantics were mostly rather snide about his talents. Byron was openly and wittily hostile in *English Bards and Scotch Reviewers:* "Triumphant first see 'Temper's Triumphs' shine! / At least I'm sure they triumphed over mine." The Blake industry which began in the late nineteenth century found Hayley ridiculous in proportion as it found Blake divine. Hayley still owes much of his hold on a place in the textbooks to Blake, but recently his role in the wider sphere of late eighteenth-century art has received more attention, and there have been a few exhibitions concerning his circle. Most of his poems have been made available in facsimile as documents of literary history. But his own view of himself was the one he put on the title page of his *Memoirs:* "the friend and biographer of Cowper"; both descriptive nouns had equal weight with Hayley.

Bibliography:

Nicholas Barker, "Some Notes On the Bibliography of William Hayley," *Transactions of the Cambridge Bibliographical Society,* 3 (1959–1963): 103–112, 167–176, 339–360.

Biographies:

W. T. Le Viness, *The Life and Works of William Hayley 1745–1820* (Santa Fe, N.Mex.: Rydal Press, 1945);

Morchard Bishop, *Blake's Hayley: The Life, Works, and Friendships of William Hayley* (London: Gollancz, 1951).

References:

Gerald E. Bentley, Jr., "Blake, Hayley, and Lady Hesketh," *Review of English Studies,* 7 (July 1956): 264–268;

William Blake, *Blake: Complete Writings With Variant Readings,* edited by Geoffrey Keynes (London & New York: Oxford University Press, 1969), pp. 536–559, 796–863;

Victor Chan, *Leader of My Angels: William Hayley and His Circle* (Edmonton, Alberta: Edmonton Art Gallery, 1982);

William Cowper, *Letters and Prose Writings,* volume 4, edited by James King and Charles Ryskamp (Oxford: Clarendon Press, 1979–1986);

James King, "Cowper, Hayley, and Samuel Johnson's 'Republican' Milton," *Studies in Eighteenth-Century Culture,* 17 (1987): 229–238;

John Nichols, *Illustrations of the Literary History of the Eighteenth Century,* 8 volumes (London: Nichols, Son, & Bentley, 1817–1858), IV: 741–745;

Donald Reiman, Introduction to the five volumes of Hayley's poetry printed in facsimile in the series Romantic Context: Poetry. Significant Minor Poetry, 1789–1830 (New York & London: Garland, 1978–1979);

Judith Wardle, " 'Satan not having the Science of Wrath, but only of Pity,'" *Studies in Romanticism,* 13 (Spring 1974): 147–154;

William Wells, *William Blake's "Heads of the Poets" For Turret House, The Residence of William Hayley Felpham* (Manchester: Manchester City Art Gallery, 1969);

Joseph A. Wittreich, Jr., "Domes of Mental Pleasure: Blake's Epics and Hayley's Epic Theory," *Studies in Philology,* 69 (January 1972): 101–129;

Wittreich, "'Far Yet extend that biographic Page!': Some Thoughts on Donald Reiman's Hayley,'" *Blake: An Illustrated Quarterly,* 15 (Summer 1981): 48–50.

Papers:

Hayley's letters and manuscripts are in several major collections: at the British Library (which has the correspondence with Lady Hesketh and several others, as well as Hayley's "Memorials" of his relationship with Cowper); the Fitzwilliam Museum, Cambridge; the West Sussex Record Office; the Cowper Memorial Library; Cambridge University Library; the Houghton Library at Harvard; the Larpent Collection, Huntington Library; and the Beinecke Library at Yale. Smaller groups of letters and poems are at the National Library of Scotland, the Bodleian Library, Lancashire Record Office, the Folger Shakespeare Library, Princeton University Library, Cornell University Library, and the Historical Society of Pennsylvania at Philadelphia. The manuscript of *The Life of George Romney* is in the Rosenwald Collection, Library of Congress.

Mary Hays
(1760 – 1843)

Eleanor Ty
Wilfrid Laurier University

BOOKS: *Cursory Remarks on an Enquiry into the Expediency and Propriety of Public or Social Worship: Inscribed to Gilbert Wakefield,* as Eusebia (London: Printed for Thomas Knott, 1791; enlarged, 1792);

Letters and Essays, Moral and Miscellaneous, by Mary and Elizabeth Hays (London: Printed for T. Knott, 1793);

Memoirs of Emma Courtney, 2 volumes (London: Printed for G. G. & J. Robinson, 1796; New York: Printed for Hugh M. Griffith, 1802);

Appeal to the Men of Great Britain in Behalf of Women, anonymous (London: Printed for J. Johnson & J. Bell, 1798);

The Victim of Prejudice, 2 volumes (London: Printed for J. Johnson, 1799; facsimile, Delmar, N.Y.: Scholars' Facsimiles & Reprints, 1990); modern edition, edited by Eleanor Ty (Peterborough, Ont.: Broadview, 1992);

Female Biography; or, Memoirs of Illustrious and Celebrated Women, of all Ages and Countries (6 volumes, London: Printed for R. Phillips, 1803; 3 volumes, Philadelphia: Printed for Byrch & Small, 1807);

Harry Clinton: A Tale for Youth (London: Printed for J. Johnson by T. Bensley, 1804);

History of England, from the Earliest Records, to the Peace of Amiens: In a Series of Letters to a Young Lady at School, 3 volumes: volumes 1 and 2 by Charlotte Smith; volume 3 by Hays (London: Printed for Richard Phillips, by J. G. Barnard, 1806);

Historical Dialogues for Young Persons, 3 volumes (London: J. Johnson & J. Mawman, 1806–1808);

The Brothers; or, Consequences: A Story of What Happens Every Day; With an Account of Savings Banks (Bristol: Prudent Man's Friend Society, 1815);

Family Annals; or, The Sisters (London: Printed for W. Simpkin & R. Marshall, 1817);

Memoirs of Queens, Illustrious and Celebrated (London: Printed for T. & J. Allman, 1821).

OTHER: Obituary of Mary Wollstonecraft, in *The Annual Necrology, for 1797–8, Including also, Various Articles of Neglected Biography* (London: Printed for R. Phillips, 1800);

"Life of Charlotte Smith," by Hays (anonymous) and Charlotte Smith, in *Public Characters of 1800–1801* (London: Richard Phillips, 1807).

SELECTED PERIODICAL PUBLICATIONS –
UNCOLLECTED: "The Hermit, An Oriental Tale," *Universal Magazine of Knowledge and Pleasure* (April 1786): 204–208; (May 1786): 234–238;

"Reply to J. T. on Helvetius," as M. H., *Monthly Magazine,* 1 (June 1796): 385–387;

"Remarks on A. B. Strictures on the Talents of Women," as A Woman, *Monthly Magazine,* 2 (July 1796): 469–470;

"The Talents of Women," *Monthly Magazine,* 2 (November 1796): 784–787;

"Defence of Helvetius," as M. H., *Monthly Magazine,* 3 (January 1797): 26–28;

"Improvements Suggested in Female Education," as M. H., *Monthly Magazine,* 3 (March 1797): 193–195;

"Are Mental Talents Productive of Happiness?," as M. H., *Monthly Magazine,* 3 (May 1797): 358–360;

"On Novel Writing," as M. H., *Monthly Magazine,* 4 (September 1797): 180–181;

Obituary of Mary Wollstonecraft, anonymous, *Monthly Magazine,* 4 (September 1797): 232–233.

Though Mary Hays is not primarily known as a biographer, she published two major works which established her as one of England's early feminist biographers. Both *Female Biography; or, Memoirs of Illustrious and Celebrated Women, of all Ages and Countries* (1803), published in six volumes, and *Memoirs of Queens, Illustrious and Celebrated* (1821) focus exclusively on women and are indicative of Hays's life-

FEMALE BIOGRAPHY;
OR,
MEMOIRS
OF
ILLUSTRIOUS AND CELEBRATED
WOMEN,
OF ALL AGES AND COUNTRIES.
Alphabetically arranged.

BY MARY HAYS.

IN SIX VOLUMES.

VOL. I.

LONDON:
PRINTED FOR RICHARD PHILLIPS, 71, ST. PAUL'S
CHURCH-YARD.
By Thomas Davison, White-Friars.
1803.

*Title page for volume one of Hays's biographical series written
"in the cause, and for the benefit of my own sex"
(courtesy of Research Publications, Inc.)*

long commitment to such important issues relating to women as education, employment or career opportunities, and the proper mode of conduct. Unlike her essays and novels published before 1800, her biographies are not polemic and do not represent original research; rather they support her contention that it is circumstances, not inherent capabilities, which define and create a woman.

Born in 1760 to a large family of Dissenters in Southwark, near London, Mary Hays lived quietly for the first seventeen years of her life. In 1777 she met and fell in love with John Eccles, a young man of similar background who lived across the road from her home. The relationship was frowned upon by both families, and the couple began a secret, intimate correspondence which lasted for more than a year. In a letter dated 28 October 1779, Eccles describes his initial impression of Hays: "the first time I saw a little girl with dark hair and features soft as those of the peaceful messengers of heaven . . . I saw everything

that was engaging and amiable in her face." This portrait of Hays is the only complimentary description of her that survives. However, Eccles was more than just a lover; he was a friend and Hays's mentor, often influencing her studies and choice of reading materials. In 1780 the engagement finally met the approval of both families, and the couple made plans to be married. Before their love could be consummated, though, John's health began to fail, and he died from fever on 23 August 1780.

Hays was devastated by his demise and wrote afterward that the fatal day "blasted all the fond hopes of youth." To his sister she wrote: "he was the friend of my heart, the best beloved of my soul! all my happiness – all my pleasure – and every opening prospect are buried with him!" In some ways her sense of hopelessness was accurate. At twenty-two she had already experienced the only mutually reciprocated love with a man that she would enjoy for the rest of her life. After Eccles's death she turned to intellectual pursuits — to reading, writing, and corresponding with religious and political reformers. Between 1782 and 1789 Hays exchanged letters with the Baptist preacher and philanthropist Robert Robinson, who acted as confessor, healer, friend, and mentor, helping Hays through a difficult period of her early life.

Her first publication was "The Hermit, An Oriental Tale," which was published in two parts in the *Universal Magazine of Knowledge and Pleasure* (April and May 1786). Similar to Samuel Johnson's *Rasselas* (1759), it is set in an exotic place and is didactic in tone. The hermit's lessons about excess passion are comparable to the theme of Hays's first novel, *Memoirs of Emma Courtney* (1796). The hermit's warning that strong passions "too often accompany superior talents, and endanger the most amiable and elevated minds" is subsequently echoed by Hays's autobiographical heroine, Emma. Both Emma and the hermit discover after losing their loved ones that bliss is to be found in nature and social affection, in well-ordered conduct, in regulated passions, and in a "tranquillized" temper. These ideas of moderation and conduct based on reason reveal the influence of eighteenth-century thinking on Hays.

Through Robinson, Hays was exposed to the teachings of leading Rational Dissenters, or Nonconformists, such as Theophilus Lindsey, John Disney, and Joseph Priestley. She also met George Dyer and William Frend, probably in the early 1790s. Her *Cursory Remarks on an Enquiry into the Expediency and Propriety of Public or Social Worship: Inscribed to Gilbert Wakefield* (1791) was a result of her involvement with this group of liberal reformers. In the pamphlet Hays addresses Wakefield's objections to communal prayer, and she argues that public worship was necessary for the majority of men and women, who, she believed, were not ready for a purely mental and contemplative religion. Although she admits that she may have "ventured beyond" her depth on this controversial issue, her ideas are convincingly argued. Occasionally she uses her own positive experience with worship to strengthen her case. Hays's pamphlet was very warmly received, and in a second edition of his *Public Worship* (1792) Wakefield included a reply to her ideas. Subsequently, in 1792 the second edition of Hays's pamphlet was published with a postscript in answer to Wakefield's remarks to her.

The success of the second edition brought her the attention and friendship of Frend, a Cambridge mathematician and reformer, who wrote to her in April 1792 that he was impressed with her "can-

dour" and "sound reasoning." He provided Hays with some romance during the next few years. Hays also became involved with the London circle of Jacobinic intellectuals, including Dyer, Mary Wollstonecraft, and the publisher Joseph Johnson. Dyer was sympathetic to the French republicans, and in 1792 he published his *Poems,* which include reflections titled "On Peace" and "On Liberty." He encouraged Hays by reading her work and corresponding with her. However, the most influential person of this group was Wollstonecraft, whose *Vindication of the Rights of Woman* (1792) inspired Hays to publish her next book, to which her sister, Elizabeth, also contributed. After reading *Vindication of the Rights of Woman,* Hays wrote to Wollstonecraft expressing her deep admiration. At Hays's request they met in the late summer of 1792, and soon afterward Hays wrote Wollstonecraft seeking advice on writing *Letters and Essays, Moral and Miscellaneous,* which was published the next year. Hays is credited with bringing together through a tea party at her home Wollstonecraft and the philosopher William Godwin, whom Wollstonecraft eventually married in 1797.

Though most of *Letters and Essays* was already written before Hays met Wollstonecraft, Hays pays tribute to her in the preface as the writer who "hath endeavoured to rescue the female mind from those prejudices by which it has been systematically weakened." As the title suggests, the work is made up of miscellaneous epistles on subjects ranging from civil liberty to the female mind and manners to reading romances to friendship. The style is mixed: sometimes it takes the form of conversational essays; at other times, that of didactic narratives. Hays returns to the subject of female education in several of the letters, protesting against the "degrading system of manners by which the understandings of women have been chained down to frivolity and trifles." She defies "Authority," which, she feels, limits women, and, using language suggestive of those who supported the French Revolution, she boldly asserts: "bolts and bars may confine for a time the feeble body, but can never enchain the noble, the freeborn mind; the only true grounds of power are reason and affection." In practical terms the consequence of the eighteenth-century system of education was that women had few employment opportunities: "Young women without fortunes, if they do not chance to marry . . . have scarce any other resources than in servitude or prostitution."

This concern for opportunities for single women without fortunes resurfaces in her first novel, in her essays in the *Monthly Magazine,* and, to a lesser extent, in her second novel, *The Victim of Prejudice*

(1799). *Memoirs of Emma Courtney* was based on Hays's love and pursuit of Frend. Frend admired her work and carried on a correspondence with her but evidently did not fully reciprocate her passionate feelings for him. The disappointed Hays turned to Godwin for consolation and advice. In October 1794, after reading his novel *Caleb Williams* (1794), Hays wrote to Godwin to ask him for his copy of his *Enquiry Concerning Political Justice* (1793), which she had not been able to obtain. He agreed to lend her the book, and this exchange began a strong intellectual bond and friendship between them. Godwin played the role of her mentor in the same way that Eccles, Robinson, and Dyer had earlier. Godwin was a sympathetic listener, and Hays poured out to him her unhappiness regarding Frend.

On Godwin's recommendation she gathered together her letters to Frend and to Godwin and used them in *Memoirs of Emma Courtney,* a philosophical novel in which she attempts to explore the link between reason and a woman's passion. Structurally as well as thematically Hays demonstrates her contention that women are prevented from participating in many of the important functions of society or, to use one of her metaphors, they are "confined within a magic circle." Written partly in an epistolary form, partly in the form of memoirs, the book traps both the reader of the novel and the reader within the story, young Augustus, in an endless circle of suffocating repetition. Emma's sexual and intellectual disappointments are mirrored by an incessant and stifling pattern of frustrated desire and unfulfilled expectations in the novel. As an epistolary work the book is deliberately unbalanced and one-sided. Through a strong first-person narration readers hear Emma's story of exclusion, rejection, and self-torture. Hardly anyone else's voice is heard in the narrative, so the reader's attention is focused on Emma's plight. What Hays believes to be the female experience of confinement by the "constitutions of society" becomes literal in the novel as readers experience narrative entrapment.

Another important achievement of the novel is that Hays's heroine, Emma Courtney, like Wollstonecraft's Maria in *The Wrongs of Woman* (1799), dares to assert female sexuality and desire. The notion that women had or could express sexual feelings was one that eighteenth-century moralists and authors of conduct books tried to deny or ignore. Emma announces: "I feel that I am neither a philosopher, nor a heroine – but a *woman, to whom education has given a sexual character.*" Unfortunately this assertion of female desire was condemned by conservative thinkers and moralists who equated female phi-

losophers, such as Hays and Wollstonecraft, with licentiousness and sexual liberality.

After the publication of her first novel, Hays contributed to the *Monthly Magazine* short articles on topics including women's education, gender differentiation, political philosophy, and novel writing. One such piece, published in June 1796, shows some of Hays's ideas about the importance of biography: "were every great man to become his own biographer, and to examine and state impartially, to the best of his recollection, the incidents of his life, the course of his studies, the causes by which he was led to them, the reflections and habits to which they gave birth, the rise, the change, the progress of his opinions, with the consequences produced by them on his affections and conduct, great light might be thrown on the most interesting of all studies, that of moral causes and the human mind." She also reviewed novels for the *Analytical Review,* where the fiction editor in 1796 and early 1797 was Wollstonecraft.

Hays's next major work was *Appeal to the Men of Great Britain in Behalf of Women* (1798), which was published anonymously. The book stresses the necessity of reforming the system of education for women and refutes the claim that women are naturally inferior to men. Its style is more spirited and direct rather than anecdotal and illustrative, as *Letters and Essays* is. As in her earlier works, Hays attempts to point out that woman are socially and culturally constructed rather than inherently weak and lacking in abilities: "Of all the systems . . . which human nature in its moments of intoxication has produced; that which men have contrived with a view to forming the minds, and regulating the conduct of women, is perhaps the most completely absurd." Critic Katherine M. Rogers suggests that, compared to Wollstonecraft's *Vindication of the Rights of Woman,* Hays's *Appeal to the Men of Great Britain* is less theoretical and more pragmatic: "Hays's basic strategy . . . is to confront conventional formulas with daily experience, so as to demonstrate by common sense their internal inconsistencies and their deviations from what actually happens and what is obviously desirable."

The ability to particularize and render concrete her feminist assertions is what makes her second novel, *The Victim of Prejudice* (1799), so powerful an indictment of patriarchy. Similar to her first novel, *Victim of Prejudice* is concerned with female economic and social dependence, sexuality, and subjectivity. But Hays adds another important dimension to this novel: a critique of social hierarchy based on class. Written at the end of the revolutionary decade, *Victim of Prejudice* exploits the politicized

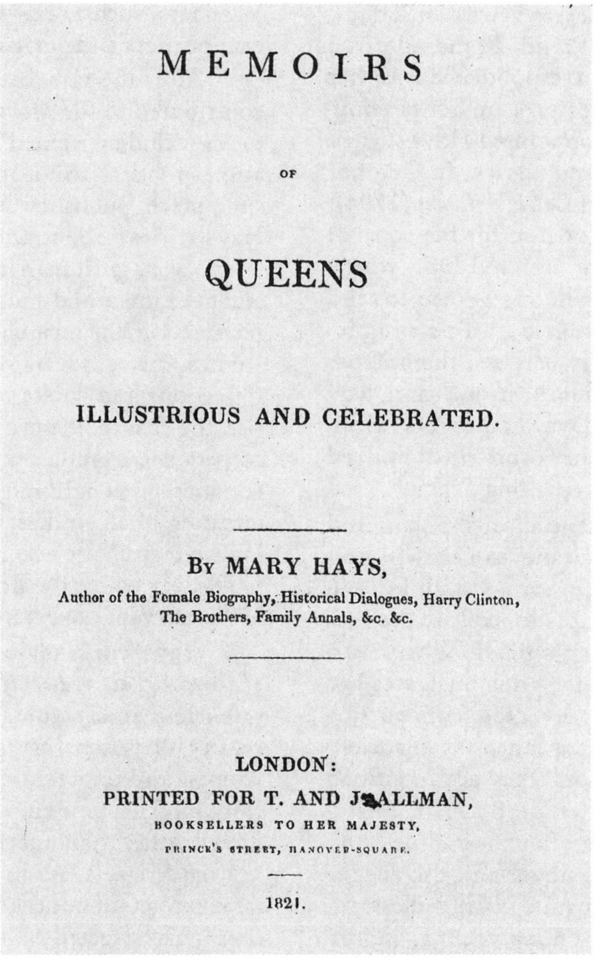

MEMOIRS

OF

QUEENS

ILLUSTRIOUS AND CELEBRATED.

By MARY HAYS,

Author of the Female Biography, Historical Dialogues, Harry Clinton,
The Brothers, Family Annals, &c. &c.

LONDON:

PRINTED FOR T. AND J. ALLMAN,

BOOKSELLERS TO HER MAJESTY,

PRINCE'S STREET, HANOVER-SQUARE.

1821.

*Title page for Hays's volume of biographical sketches intended as
models for the "intellectual advancement of woman"
(courtesy of Research Publications, Inc.)*

climate and demonstrates the uneasy tensions and potentially explosive situations between those with power and those without, between male and female, and between oppressor and victim. The heroine of the novel, Mary, despite her determination not to fall prey to seduction as her mother (also named Mary) did, ends up with an equally tragic fate. The younger Mary's worst nightmares become real in the novel, giving the work a dreamlike, Gothic quality. This mother/daughter link and the subsequent literal reenactment of the mother's written memoirs create much of the force and the sense of foreboding in the novel. Young Mary's life follows that of her mother as she is systematically seduced, abandoned, and cast out of society. Through a replication of the mother's life in the daughter's, Hays shows that challenging the patriarchal system can become a form of female punishment in contemporary eighteenth-century culture. The attempts of both the first- and the second-generation Mary to rebel against, oppose,

and curtail masculine will and desire only create further constraints in their lives. Yearning for more space and freedom, they become physically and spiritually more constricted and circumscribed.

After Wollstonecraft's death in 1797 and Godwin's publication of *Memoirs of the Author of a Vindication of the Rights of Woman* (1798) – which offers accounts of her suicide attempts, her illegitimate daughter, and her love affairs – there was an increasing wave of antifeminist sentiment in England. At the same time, the atrocities of Maximilien Robespierre and the Reign of Terror in France made the supporters of the revolution extremely unpopular. Along with Anna Laetitia Barbauld, Mary Robinson, Charlotte Smith, Helen Maria Williams, and others, Hays is cited in the Reverend Richard Polwhele's poem *The Unsex'd Females* (1798) among Wollstonecraft's female band of rebels who despise "Nature's law." Hays was also caricatured in at least two novels published at this time. In Charles

Lloyd's *Edmund Oliver* (1798), which satirizes Samuel Taylor Coleridge and the English Jacobins, Hays appears as Lady Gertrude Sinclair. Similarly, Elizabeth Hamilton modeled the comic female philosopher Bridgetina Botherim after Hays and after Emma Courtney in *Memoirs of Modern Philosophers* (1800). Coleridge wrote of Hays in a letter to Robert Southey, dated 25 January 1800: "Of Miss Hays' intellect I do not think so highly as you, or rather, to speak sincerely, I think, not contemptuously, but certainly very despectively thereof. – Yet I think you likely in this case to have judged better than I – for to hear a Thing, ugly & petticoated, ex-syllogize a God with cold-blooded Precision, & attempt to run Religion thro' the body with an Icicle . . . I do not endure it!"

With the turn of the century and possibly as a result of this antifeminist backlash, Hays's radicalism and her criticism of society seem to have mellowed. *Female Biography; or, Memoirs of Illustrious and Celebrated Women, of All Ages and Countries* is a work commissioned by Richard Phillips, who agreed to pay Hays ten shillings and six pence per sheet. As the title indicates, it was an ambitious project, one which took nearly three years to complete. The work consists of the biographies of about 290 women, approximately one-third of whom were Englishwomen. In her preface Hays implies that the work treats "every woman who, either by her virtues, her talents, or the peculiarities of her fortune, has rendered herself illustrious or distinguished." She wishes to be objective, to "serve the cause of truth and of virtue," yet her stance is feminist: "My pen has been taken up in the cause, and for the benefit of my own sex. For their improvement, and to their entertainment, my labours have been devoted. . . . I have at heart the happiness of my sex, and their advancement in the grand scale of rational and social existence." She acknowledges that there is "little new" in the work; however, the aim is to "collect and concentrate in one interesting point of view, those engaging pictures, instructive narrations, and striking circumstances that may answer a better purpose than the gratification of a vain curiosity."

For the most part she uses previously published history books and earlier biographical compendiums and dictionaries as sources, including David Hume's *The History of England from the Invasion of Julius Caesar to the Revolution of 1688* (1778); Pierre Bayle's *Historical Dictionary; Biographium Faeminium: The Female Worthies, or, Memoirs of the Most Illustrious Ladies of All Ages and Nations* (1766); George Ballard's *Memoirs of Several Ladies of Great Britain, who have been celebrated for their writings of skill in the learned languages, arts* (1752); and works by classical writers such as Tacitus, Suetonius, and Plutarch. She also consulted memoirs and lives of individual women, such as Robert Southey's *Joan of Arc* (1796), Sarah Fielding's *Lives of Cleopatra and Octavia* (1757), and C. F. P. Masson's *Secret Memoirs of the Court of Petersburg* (1800). In most cases she simply transcribed the information from the various sources. For example, in her entry for Anne Boleyn, Hays copied not only the factual materials from Bayle, but also his moralistic tone. Like Bayle, Hays saw Boleyn as a usurper: "in becoming the concubine of the king, she would perhaps have committed an action less reprehensible, than in being the cause of the dethronement and humiliation of the queen." Hays's entry contains Boleyn's letter to the king, which is found in Hume's *History of England* but not in Bayle's book. Her skill in *Female Biography* comes largely from her ability to compile and weave materials into interesting narratives.

However, what is striking about *Female Biography* is its inconsistency, and this inconsistency, in choice of subject matter and length of each entry, reveals much about Hays as a woman who was grappling with the cultural ideologies of her time. By far the longest entry is that on Catherine II, Empress of Russia, which takes up almost an entire volume. The other two long entries are those on Queen Elizabeth I and Mary, Queen of Scots. The fact that these women's lives were not uniformly "virtuous" or chaste suggests that, for Hays, what was fascinating or useful about these women was not their excelling in traditional female roles as wives, mothers, or daughters but their talents or their extraordinary circumstances. In Hays's account they were outstanding because they were ambitious and independent women who were skillful as politicians and had strength of character. Hays admired leaders and women who overcame great obstacles to succeed. Of Catherine she writes, "ambition triumphed in her mind over every inferior propensity," yet "the empress neglected not her domestic regulations: she studied the duties of a sovereign, and considered herself as the mother of her people, whom she treated with confidence, and whose condition she ameliorated." Hays was willing to overlook her sexual promiscuity and her love of glory: "Whatever may have been her faults, and doubtless they were great, her genius, her talents, her courage, and her success must ever entitle her to a high rank among those women whose qualities and attainments have thrown a lustre on their sex."

In a similar way Hays's defense of some of Queen Elizabeth's "unfeminine" characteristics reveals Hays's disapproval of conventional eighteenth-century virtues of female docility and submission: "Those who require more softness of manners, greater lenity of temper, and more feminine graces to form the character of a woman, to whom they could attach themselves as a mistress and a wife, must be reminded, that these amiable weaknesses, which arise out of a state of subjection and dependence, are utterly incompatible with the situation of an absolute sovereign." In her portrait of Boudicca, Hays offers an instance of female courage which surpasses that of men: Boudicca, "who though a *woman,* had determined on victory or death – 'Let the *men* who prefer life,' added she, in a raised and dignified tone, 'live dishonoured and slaves.'" Through the many portraits of women distinguished for their strength or their convictions, Hays demonstrates the thesis found in many of her earlier works, that the characters of women are formed by external circumstances and not by inherent gender deficiencies. Women could therefore surpass men in intellect and action when given the opportunity.

Some of the entries in *Female Biography,* particularly those from antiquity, are extremely brief. Two examples of entire entries are as follows: "Polla Argentaria, the wife of Lucan, assisted her husband in his *Pharsalia.* She is praised by Martial, and also by Statius." Equally short is the account of Charixena: "Charixena, a learned Greek lady, the author of several compositions both in prose and verse; particularly of a poem entitled 'Crumata.' This lady is mentioned by Aristophanes." Usually Hays expanded on the factual materials of her sources and gave anecdotal illustrations; however, occasionally she did censor materials she thought would offend. For example, while her account of Héloïse is more romanticized than is Bayle's, it is also edited. Bayle's narrative gives facts, including Peter Abelard's castration: "They surprised him in his sleep and cut off those parts which are not to be named." Hays's version reads: "ruffians were introduced during the silence and darkness of the night. The consequences of this treachery are too well known to require a repetition." Similarly Bayle includes the fact that Sappho's "amorous passion extended even to persons of her own sex, and this is that for which she was most cried down." Hays's version states that Sappho, "like all persons of talents (women more especially)," was "exposed to envy and slander." It does not mention her lesbianism explicitly.

One prominent woman whose life does not appear is Wollstonecraft. Hays had written two obituaries of her, which were published in the September 1797 issue of the *Monthly Magazine* and *The Annual Necrology, for 1797–8* (1800). In the former she praises Wollstonecraft as an "extraordinary woman, no less distinguished by admirable talents & a masculine tone of understanding, than by active humanity, exquisite sensibility, and endearing qualities of heart." The omission of Wollstonecraft in *Female Biography* is striking and reveals Hays's fear of the public's less tolerant attitude toward those who had spoken on behalf of women's rights following the French Revolution. Finally, what is noticeably disproportionate about *Female Biography* is that the number of entries for each letter of the alphabet decreases as one gets closer to the end of the alphabet. The number of biographies under *a, b,* and *c* is 43, 33, and 35 respectively, while the number of entries under *r, s,* and *t* is 11, 19, and 8. It seems as if Hays started with much more ambition and scope than was practical or necessary for the work. Most of the contemporary reviews of the *Female Biography,* however, saw it as a useful compilation and as a vindication of women through lives of females of the past.

During the second half of her life Hays continued to write novels, but the works were more didactic and conservative than her earlier productions. In 1804 Johnson published Hays's *Harry Clinton: A Tale for Youth,* a reworking of Henry Brooke's popular sentimental novel, *The Fool of Quality* (1765–1770). Hays edited out much of what she termed "fanaticism and extravagance" from the original, and in the advertisement she says that her interest in the work lies in its "exhibiting a history of the practical education and culture of the *heart.*" In about 1804 she moved out of her London lodgings and into a small house in Camberwell, Surrey, where she lived a quieter and more retired life than previously. Her faithful correspondents during this period were Henry Crabb Robinson and Eliza Fenwick, both of whom remained devoted to Hays through her later years. In Fenwick's letters Hays emerges as a faithful and generous friend who willingly helps her through various domestic and financial crises.

Hays's last two novels show the influence of the evangelical movement, especially the teachings and works of Hannah More and Hamilton. *The Brothers; or, Consequences* (1815) and *Family Annals; or, The Sisters* (1817) are didactic works, designed in their simplicity to teach the lower classes the values of economy, frugality, and self-discipline. Both novels contain a pair of contrasting characters, brothers in the former and sisters in the latter work. In the preface to *Family Annals* Hays gives credit to Maria Edgeworth, who inspired her with literature which happily blends "amusement and instruction." The story of the two sisters, one who is romantic and the other who is sensible, is reminiscent of Jane West's *A Gossip's Story* (1796), which Hays had reviewed for the *Analytical Review* in January 1797, and of Jane Austen's *Sense and Sensibility* (1811), which was also influenced by West's novel.

Hays's final publication, *Memoirs of Queens, Illustrious and Celebrated,* was written when she was already in her sixties. In the preface Hays speaks of herself "declining in physical strength and mental activity" and of compiling *Memoirs of Queens* only at the "request of the publishers." The work contains more than seventy biographies of queens, more than half of them already found in *Female Biography.* Hays insists on the assertions she had made earlier about the capabilities of women: "I maintain, and while strength and reason remain to me, ever will maintain, that there is, there can be but *one moral standard of excellence for mankind,* whether male or female, and that the licentious distinctions made by the domineering party, in the spirit of tyranny, selfishness, and sensuality, are at the foundation of the heaviest evils that have afflicted, degraded, and corrupted society." She claims that "the powers and capacity for woman for rational and moral advancement are . . . no longer a question," yet she laments that, for the most part, "the education of woman is yet directed only towards the embellishment of the transient season of youth."

Hays's opinions about the importance of knowledge to the progress of society are clear. According to her, "Knowledge, virtue, happiness, are inseparably connected: wisdom must be the *mean,* moral improvement the *end.*" With *Memoirs of Queens* she intended to demonstrate the pervasiveness of illustrious women of the past. She reminds readers that she has more than once taken up her pen for the "honour and advantage of my sex" and has the "moral rights and intellectual advancement of *woman*" at heart. Though not all the lives can act as models for young women, understanding the reasons why human beings, especially women, act the way they do is enlightening. There is an implicit suggestion that women of all classes are united to some degree by their state of oppression: "The throne itself, with but few exceptions, secures not woman from the peculiar disadvantages that have hitherto attended her sex."

One critic, Gary Kelly, believes that Hays was attacking the "corrupting effect of court culture, the trivialization of women in courtly 'gallantry,' and the 'mistress system'" (*Women, Writing, and Revolution,* 1993). Two biographies Hays wrote in response to then-recent political events depict women

as victims. Queen Caroline of Brunswick, wife of George IV, is portrayed as an unfortunate pawn in a political marriage. Hays criticizes this type of alliance as unnatural: "Marriages in [this] rank of life are not formed upon the sympathies and affections by which hearts and hands are united in humbler, more natural, happier stations; yet, even when tenderness is wanting, respect and consideration for the feelings and claims of others are assuredly due, and ought to be observed." Hays condemns George IV's indiscretions, his capriciousness, and his irresponsibility toward his family. Her argument is that the king gets away with things commoners cannot: "in a private station . . . a husband and a father is not authorised to withhold his countenance and protection from the wife to whom he has pledged his faith, from the child to whom he has been the means of giving life." In her discussion of the popularity of the queen and the public's reluctance to persecute her and drive "a desolate unprotected female from her family," Hays harks back to the liberal sentiment of the revolutionary age of the 1790s. She comments that "[Edmund] Burke, had he now lived, would have retracted his assertion, that the age of chivalry had passed away." She contends that "brute force may subjugate, but in knowledge only is real strength, and to truth and justice is the last and only legitimate appeal."

Similarly, in her biography of Marie-Antoinette, Hays makes the queen an object of pity despite her "extravagance, dissipation, and levity." In the 1790s Hays and her circle of Jacobinic intellectuals would have viewed Marie-Antoinette as a symbol of aristocratic decadence; in 1821 Hays depicted her as the ill-fated target of the people of France. Hays describes the queen's "shrieks and sobs" and her dungeon "eight feet square," with its "hard straw bed and scanty covering." Hays makes Antoinette a heroine whose character "rose to respect and dignity" in adversity. The account becomes a narrative of loss and female suffering: "From the highest pinnacle of worldly glory she sunk into the lowest abyss of misery and wretchedness. Her history has scarcely a parallel in the annals of mankind; it affords an affecting and impressive lesson."

Most of the other entries in *Memoirs of Queens,* however, are not so dramatic. Many of them, such as the biography of Jane D'Albert, Queen of Navarre; Boudicca; Boleyn; and Catherine II, Empress of Russia, are just shortened or more-concise versions of entries in *Female Biography.* Occasionally Hays wrote a different text, such as the account of Agrippina the Younger, where she seems to have used new sources and worded the sequence of events differently. As in *Female Biography* there are some short, factual entries with no commentaries. For example, "Fritigilia, queen of the Marcomans, became a Christian through the writings of Ambrose. She converted her husband and her nation to her faith. Through her persuasion her husband formed an alliance with the Romans. She flourished in the fourth century." Obviously Hays was not concerned with the uneven length of the entries.

Hays lived for more than twenty years after the publication of *Memoirs of Queens*. She complained more than once that "the world forsakes me," as her circle of friends and correspondents grew smaller. In her final letter to Robinson, written sometime in March 1842, she told him that should he fail to see her soon, he could next "seek my remains in a humble grave in the Newington *cemetery* with the simple memorial *Mary Hays* engraven on the headstone." Hays died quietly the next year, in the early months of 1843.

Letters:

The Love-Letters of Mary Hays (1779–1780), edited by A. F. Wedd (London: Methuen, 1925).

Biography:

Gina Luria, "Mary Hays: A Critical Biography," Ph.D. dissertation, New York University, 1972.

References:

Marilyn Butler, *Jane Austen and the War of Ideas* (Oxford: Clarendon Press, 1975);

Terence Allan Hoagwood, Introduction to Hays's *Victim of Prejudice* (Delmar, N.Y.: Scholars' Facsimiles & Reprints, 1990);

Claudia L. Johnson, *Jane Austen: Women, Politics, and the Novel* (Chicago: University of Chicago Press, 1988);

Gary Kelly, *English Fiction of the Romantic Period 1789–1830* (London: Longman, 1989);

Kelly, *Women, Writing, and Revolution: The 1790s to the 1820s* (Oxford: Clarendon Press, 1993);

Gina Luria, "Mary Hays's Letters & Manuscripts," *Signs: Journal of Women in Culture and Society,* 3 (Winter 1977): 524–530;

Burton R. Pollin, "Mary Hays on Women's Rights in the *Monthly Magazine,*" *Etudes Anglaises,* 24, no. 3 (1971): 271–282;

Katherine M. Rogers, "The Contribution of Mary Hays," *Prose Studies,* 10 (September 1987): 131–142;

Jane Spencer, *The Rise of the Woman Novelist: From Aphra Behn to Jane Austen* (Oxford: Blackwell, 1986);

Dale Spender, *Mothers of the Novel: 100 Good Women Writers before Jane Austen* (New York: Pandora, 1986);

Janet Todd, *The Sign of Angellica: Women, Writing and Fiction, 1660–1800* (London: Virago, 1989), pp. 236–252;

Eleanor Ty, *Unsex'd Revolutionaries: Five Women Novelists of the 1790s* (Toronto: University of Toronto Press, 1993);

A. F. Wedd, ed., *The Fate of the Fenwicks; Letters to Mary Hays (1796–1828)* (London: Methuen, 1927).

Papers:

The largest concentration of Hays's manuscripts and letters is in the Carl H. Pforzheimer Collection in the New York Public Library. Hays's letters to and from William Frend are at Cambridge University.

Robert Heron

(6 November 1764 – 13 April 1807)

Paul Baines
University of Liverpool

BOOKS: *Scotland Delineated, or A Geographical Description of Every Shire In Scotland, Including the Northern and Western Isles* (Edinburgh: Printed for James Neill; sold by Bell & Bradfute, W. Creech, and G. G. J. & J. Robinson, London, 1791; enlarged edition, Edinburgh: Printed for Bell & Bradfute, and G. G. J. & J. Robinson, London, 1799); republished as *Scotland Described: or, A Topographical Description of all the Counties of Scotland: With the Northern and Western Isles belonging to it* (Edinburgh: Printed by John Moir, for T. Brown, and sold by Mudie & Murray, London; Brash & Reid, and Cameron & Murdoch, Glasgow; T. Hill, Perth; and A. Brown, Aberdeen, 1797; revised edition, anonymous, Edinburgh: Printed by John Moir, for T. Brown, and Vernor & Hood, London, 1799);

Elegant Extracts of Natural History, 2 volumes (Edinburgh: Printed for E. Balfour, and G. G. J. & J. Robinson, and C. Dilly, London, 1792);

Facts, Reflections, and Queries, Submitted to the Consideration of the Associated Friends of the People, anonymous, attributed to Heron (Edinburgh, 1792);

Observations made in a Journey through the Western Counties of Scotland; in the Autumn of M,DCC,XCII, 2 volumes (Perth: Printed for R. Morison & Son; Bell & Bradfute, Edinburgh; and Vernor & Hood, London, 1793; enlarged edition, Perth: Printed for W. Morison, and Stewart & Meikle, and John Murdoch, Glasgow, 1799);

Information concerning the Strength, Views, and Interests of the Powers presently at War (Edinburgh: Printed for R. Morison & Son, G. Mudie, and Manners & Miller; Ja. Gillies, and Brash & Reid, Glasgow; J. Burnet, Aberdeen; and for Vernor & Hood, London, 1794);

General View of the Natural Circumstances of those Isles, adjacent to the North-West Coast of Scotland, which are distinguished by the common name of Hebridae or Hebrides (Edinburgh: Printed by John Paterson, 1794);

A New General History of Scotland, from the Earliest Times to the Æra of the Abolition of the Hereditary Jurisdictions of Subjects in Scotland, in the year 1748, 5 volumes (Perth & Edinburgh: Printed by R. Morison, Jr., for R. Morison & Son, and Vernor & Hood, London, 1794–1799);

Account of the Proceedings and Debate in the General Assembly of the Church of Scotland, 27th May 1796; on the Overtures from the Provincial Synods of Fife and Moray, respecting the propagation of the Gospel among the Heathen, anonymous (Edinburgh: Printed for Alex. Lawrie, 1796);

Philosophical Views of Universal History. From the Creation of the World to the Christian Æra (Edinburgh: Printed for R. Morison and Son, Perth, 1796);

Abstract of a Course of Lectures on Law, Natural and Positive (Edinburgh: Sold by Bell & Bradfute, W. Creech, A. Guthrie, Arch. Constable & H. Mitchel, 1797);

A Memoir of the Life of the late Robert Burns (Edinburgh: Printed for T. Brown, 1797);

A Letter from Ralph Anderson, Esq. [pseudonym] *to Sir John Sinclair, Bart. M.P. &c. on the Necessity of an Instant Change of Ministry, and an Immediate Peace* (Edinburgh: Printed for G. Mudie & Son, 1797);

St. Kilda in Edinburgh; or, News from Camperdown: A Comic Drama, in Two Acts, anonymous (Edinburgh, 1798);

Elements of Chemistry: Comprehending all the most important facts and principles in the works of Fourcroy and Chaptal (London: Printed for T. N. Longman & O. Rees by J. Rider, 1800);

Sketch of a Plan for the perpetual prevention of dearth and scarcity of provisions in Great Britain and Ireland (London: Printed for the author, by V. Griffiths, 1802?);

Letter to William Wilberforce, Esq., M.P., on the Justice and Expediency of Slavery and the Slave Trade (London: Printed for Jordan & Maxwell, 1806);

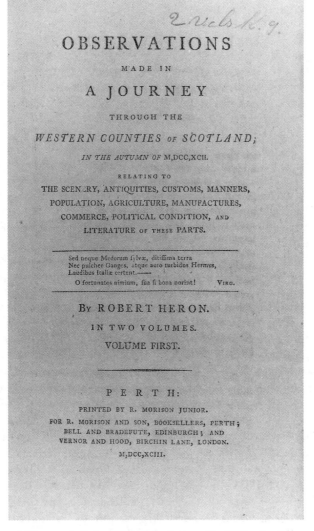

Title page for Robert Heron's book about his 1792 tour of the
West Highlands of Scotland

The Comforts of Human Life; or, Smiles and Laughter of Charles Chearful and Martin Merryfellow: In Seven Dialogues (London: Printed for Oddy by J. & W. Smith, 1807).

PLAY PRODUCTION: *St. Kilda in Edinburgh, or News from Camperdown,* Edinburgh, Theatre Royal, 21 February 1798.

OTHER: *Thomson's Seasons, with a Criticism on his Poetry,* edited by Heron (Perth: Printed for R. Morison & Son, 1789); revised and enlarged as *The Seasons, by James Thomson. A New Edition . . . Together with An Original Life of the Author, and a Critical Essay on The Seasons. By Robert Heron* (Perth: Printed by R. Morison, Jr., for R. Morison & Son, 1793; New York: Printed for T. B. Jansen, 1803);

Robert Burns, *Poems, Chiefly in the Scottish dialect,* edited by Heron (Cork: Printed by A. Edwards, 1804).

TRANSLATIONS: *The New Universal Traveller: or A Collection of late Voyages and Travels through Europe, Asia, Africa, America, and the South-Sea Islands; chiefly translated and abridged from the French and other foreign languages,* 2 volumes (Edinburgh: Printed for G. Mudie, and James Watson & Company, 1791–1792);

Louis-Pierre Anquetil, *Memoirs of the Court of France, during the reign of Louis XIV. and the Regency of the Duke of Orleans,* 2 volumes (Edinburgh: Printed for Bell & Bradfute; and G. G. J. & J. Robinson, London, 1791);

Dom Chavis and M. Cazotte, *Arabian Tales: or, A Continuation of The Arabian Nights Entertainments,* 4 volumes (Edinburgh: Printed for Bell & Bradfute, J. Dickson, E. Balfour & P. Hill; and G. G. J. & J. Robinson, London, 1792);

Jean-Pierre Claris de Florian, *Gonsalvo of Cordova: or, The Conquest of Granada . . . To which is prefixed, A Sketch of the History of the Moors in Spain,* 3 volumes, translated, with a preface, by Heron (Perth: Printed for R. Morison & Son, and sold by A. Guthrie, Edinburgh; and Tho. Vernor, London, 1792);

Carsten Niebuhr, *Travels through Arabia, and other Countries in the East,* 2 volumes, translated, with notes, by Heron (Edinburgh: Printed for R. Morison & Son, G. Mudie; and T. Vernor, London, 1792);

Jean-François Marmontel, *A New Collection of Moral Tales,* 3 volumes (Perth: Printed for R. Morison & Son; and W. Lane, London; and A. Guthrie, Edinburgh, 1792); abridged as *The Widow of the Village* (Hartford, Conn.: Printed by John Babcock, 1797);

Letters, which passed between General Dumourier, and Pache, Minister at War to the French Republic, during the Campaign in the Netherlands, in 1792 (Perth: Printed for R. Morison & Son, 1794);

Jean-Baptiste Louvet de Couvray, *An Account of the Dangers to which I have been exposed, since the 31st of May, 1793,* anonymous translation attributed to Heron (Perth: Printed for R. Morison & Son, 1795);

Antoine-François de Fourcroy, *Elements of Chemistry, and Natural History,* 4 volumes (London: Printed for J. Murray & S. Highley; J. Cuthell; and G. Mudie & Son, Edinburgh, 1796);

An Account of the Life of Muley Liezit, Late Emperor of Morocco. Written by a Spanish Agent at the Moorish Court . . . To which is prefixed, A Short Review of the Moorish History, translated, with a preface, by Heron (Edinburgh: Printed for R. Morison & Son, 1797);

Dominique-Joseph Garat, *Memoirs of the Revolution; or, An Apology for my Conduct, in the Public Employments which I have held* (Edinburgh: Printed for G. Mudie & Son, 1797);

The Letters of Junius, 2 volumes, edited, with notes and illustrations, by Heron (London: Printed by W. Justins, for Harrison, 1802; Philadelphia: Samuel F. Bradford, 1804).

SELECTED PERIODICAL PUBLICATIONS – UNCOLLECTED: *The Ghost: Number Twenty-Fourth and Last* (14 July 1796);

"Memoirs of the Life of the late Robert Burns," anonymous, *Monthly Magazine, and British Register,* 3 (January–June 1797): 213–216, 552–562.

If it were not for Robert Burns, one would hardly know the name of Robert Heron. His work as a journalist, translator, and miscellaneous writer has all but vanished, but *A Memoir of the Life of the late Robert Burns* (1797), which Heron published soon after the poet's death, has continued to attract attention and dispute. Nearly two hundred years later the man who wrote it remains in virtual obscurity.

Robert Heron was born in Creehead, New Galloway, Scotland, on 6 November 1764. His family was one of exceptional, if strict, piety and industry. His father, John Heron, was a weaver; Robert's maternal grandmother, Margaret Murray, was an aunt of Dr. Alexander Murray, the philologist; and there seems to have been a strong educational impetus within the family. Heron's mother tutored him at home until he was nine, when he went to the parish school. After two years of rapid progress he began to earn a living by teaching the children of local farmers, and by the age of fourteen he became master of the parochial school of Kelton. By 1780 he had managed to save enough money to register at the University of Edinburgh for theological training. He received some financial aid from his family but also supported himself by teaching anything and everything and by hackwork for booksellers. He was also employed as an amanuensis by Hugh Blair and later acted as assistant preacher at the high church.

Historian John Nichols reports that when John Pinkerton used "Robert Heron" as a pseudonym for his *Letters of Literature* (1785), some of the resulting odium fell on the real Heron. Some undated letters to his parents were perhaps written during this time in Edinburgh; they indicate some strain in the familial relationship, presumably as a result of Heron's failure to advance in the church: "I hope by living more pious and carefully, by managing my income frugally, and appropriating a part of it to the service of you and my sisters, and by living with you in future at least a third part of the year, to reconcile your affections more entirely to me, and give you more comfort than I have yet done. Oh forget and forgive my follies; look on me as a son who will anxiously strive to comfort and please you, and, after all your misfortunes, to render the evening of your days as happy as possible."

In 1789 Heron visited Burns at Ellisland and was entrusted with a letter to their mutual friend the blind poet Thomas Blacklock. Apparently Heron failed to deliver the missive. Burns commemorated this inauspicious moment with bawdy tolerance in an untitled poem known as [To Dr. Blacklock]:

> The *Ill-thief* blaw the *Heron* south!
> And never drink be near his drouth!
> He tald mysel, by word o'mouth
>   He'd tak my letter;
> I lippen'd to the chiel in truth,
>   And bade nae better.
>
> But aiblins honest Master Heron
> Had at the time some dainty *Fair One,*
> To ware his theologic care on,
>   And holy study:
> And tired o'*Sauls* to waste his lear on,
>   E'en tried the *Body.*

Heron became a licentiate of the church in 1789, but Burns suggests in the poem above that he had in effect given up the idea of a church career. The obituary of Heron in the *Gentleman's Magazine* (June 1807) suggests that his prospects within the church did not answer his expectations. He arranged for his eldest brother, John, to be enrolled at Edinburgh to study for the church, perhaps as a sort of substitute for himself; but John died in 1790. Robert Heron's first acknowledged publication dates from 1789, and from then on he turned toward literature: his edition (1789) of James Thomson's *Seasons,* with a methodical and dogged "Criticism on his Poetry," was his first work in a long association with the Perth booksellers R. Morison and Son. Heron attempted to mount a series of lectures on "Law: Natural and Positive" for nonprofessional students but failed to rouse sufficient interest; his *Abstract of a Course of Lectures on Law, Natural and Positive* was published in 1797. He wrote various articles for the new edition of *Encyclopaedia Britannica,* and Sir John Sinclair employed him in an editorial capacity on the *Statistical Account of Scotland* (1791–1799). This latter job may have encouraged his work on Scottish topography as well as his sporadic political pamphleteering.

Heron's varied abilities are more apparent in his voluminous translations from the French: moral tales, political memoirs, Arabian adventures, and geographic and scientific compilations. These works seem to indicate an increasing reputation, but he had been requesting more money in letters to Colin Macfarquhar, his employer on the *Encyclopaedia Britannica,* since 1791, and the fact that Heron was imprisoned in 1792 soon afterward suggests that his literary output was the result of desperation. He apparently squandered substantial earnings through imprudence and vanity. R. Morison and Son provided his escape route from jail: he was to write *A New General History of Scotland* for them at the rate of three guineas a sheet, paying his creditors fifteen shillings on the pound (some two-thirds of his copyright fee). Heron explains in his preface that the first volume (1794) was mostly written in jail, and the five-volume work was not completed until 1799.

The year 1793 had seen the publication of other important works: his *Observations made in a Journey through the Western Counties of Scotland,* from his autumn 1792 tour of the West Highlands, the best of many such essays; and an expanded edition of Thomson's *Seasons,* this time with Heron's "Original Life" of Thomson. This handsome quarto volume, dedicated to Blair, illustrated with plates, and adorned with notes, was Heron's first experiment in biography. His materials were mostly already public: he used Samuel Johnson's biography from *Prefaces, Biographical and Critical, to the Works of the English Poets* (1779–1781); standard biographical dictionaries; Thomson's letters as recently published by the earl of Buchan; information from "a friend"; and a lot of guesswork. The text is full of phrases such as "I know not," "I believe," "I have heard or read an anecdote," and so on. Dismissed by modern biographers of Thomson, the fifty-page sketch follows a chronological course through the main works of Thomson's career – each of which receives some critical estimate – and it concludes with a neat summary of what Heron "should suppose" Thomson's character to have been "by what I have learned of the circumstances of [his] life, and by the complexion of his writings."

The luxury of this production sorts oddly with Heron's imprisonment for debt, though it shows something of his aspirations. But even here his publishers curtailed his freedom, his critique of Thomson being only part of what he wanted to write, which was, he says, too long for the press. Meanwhile his bread-and-butter work continued: systems of geography and chemistry, lives of Moroccan emperors, political memoirs – all at the behest of booksellers rather than from personal inclination. In 1797, however, there was a work which stands out from these run-of-the-mill compilations: *A Memoir of the Life of the late Robert Burns.*

There is little record of contact between Heron and Burns after the Ellisland visit of 1789, though in his *Observations made in a Journey* Heron offers some appreciative critical notice of the poet.

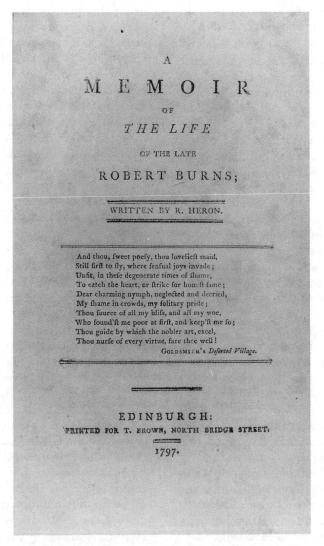

*Title page for the biography in which Heron provoked controversy
with his frank discussion of Burns's alcoholism*

Heron was the first off the mark after Burns's death in 1796 (apart from Maria Riddell's "Memoir Concerning Burns," which appeared in the *Dumfries Journal* in August 1796). Heron's biography of Burns first appeared (in briefer form) in the *Monthly Magazine, and British Register* (January–June 1797) and was soon available in the enlarged book form. It includes no documents and only a little "private" information, mostly from William Creech, a bookseller with whom Heron had already had dealings. Much of the book is generalization masquerading as detail. But it is still a powerful work, even if the nature of that power is somewhat controversial. Heron begins by rejecting annalistic and pedantic detail in favor of psychobiography, an "exposition of the nicer laws of the formation and progress of human character." In the first paragraph Heron boldly capitalizes his aim: "TO TRACE THE GRADUAL DEVELOPMENT OF THE CHARACTER AND TALENTS OF HIS HERO, WITH ALL THE CHANGES WHICH THESE UNDERGO FROM THE INFLUENCE OF EXTERNAL CIRCUMSTANCES, BETWEEN THE CRADLE AND THE GRAVE. . . ." Thus Heron seeks early influences in Burns's schooling (which led to Burns's enlightened attitude toward nature), in the devotional piety which caused peasant families to sing psalms, and in the popularity of ballads. Burns is pictured growing intellectually away from his roots and habits and waiting until his intelligence was mature before beginning to write observational poems about local life.

Heron also observes him being attracted into the convivial company of looser spirits, resisted in his early life but harbingers of disasters to come.

Heron recalls the time when he obtained a copy of Burns's "Kilmarnock" poems: "I was at that time resident in *Galloway,* contiguous to *Ayrshire;* and I can well remember, how that even plough-boys and maid-servants would have gladly bestowed the wages which they had earned the most hardly, and which they wanted to purchase necessary clothing, if they might but procure the works of BURNS. A copy happened to be presented from a gentleman in Ayrshire to a friend in my neighbourhood. He put it into my hands, as a work containing some effusions of the most extraordinary genius. I took it, rather that I might not disoblige the lender, than from any ardour of curiosity or expectation. 'An unlettered ploughman, a poet!' said I, with contemptuous incredulity. It was on a Saturday evening. I opened the volume, by accident, while I was undressing, to go to bed. I closed it not, till a late hour on the rising Sunday morn, after I had read over every syllable it contained." Heron accounts for the popularity of the book by noting Burns's passion and sensibility but also by pointing out the variety and appeal to different tastes in the poems. Heron, in his account of the lionization of Burns by Edinburgh society, aims, however, to examine the psychological effects on Burns himself, uprooted from his class. Burns was caught between his brilliant conversational ability and his social and passional origins; again he "resists such solicitations and allurements to excess in convivial enjoyment, as scarcely any other person could have withstood." But this time, Heron sorrowfully reveals, Burns eventually allowed himself to be drawn into "the tavern ... the brothel ... the lap of the woman of pleasure."

Heron criticizes Burns's patrons for failing to understand how his situation had altered, how he became intellectually unsuited to his old employments without being in a position to embark on any new profession. The farm at Ellisland (which Heron visited) is seen as a bad bargain suggested by advisers who failed to examine the full details. Nonetheless Heron sympathetically envisages Burns's momentary "felicity" on his marriage and arrival on the farm before inevitable difficulties and disillusionments set in. After the move to Dumfries, Burns's downfall was rapid: despondency led to increased drinking. Intellectually unimpaired, Burns was disastrously led astray by a pack of fools: "But, with all these failings, he was still that exalted mind which had raised itself above the depression of its

original condition, with all the energy of *the lion, pawing to set free his hinder limbs from the yet incumbering earth:* He still appeared *not less than archangel ruined!* " Heron depicts Burns's final days as a stormy contest between dissoluteness and remorse: "At last, crippled, emaciated, having the very power of animation wasted by disease, quite broken-hearted by the sense of his errors, and of the hopeless miseries in which he saw himself and his family depressed; with his soul still tremblingly alive to the sense of shame, and to the love of virtue; yet even in the last feebleness, and amid the last agonies of expiring life, yielding readily to any temptation that offered the semblance of intemperate enjoyment; he died."

It is this conclusion that has most offended modern biographers of Burns. Heron's memoir was reprinted as "Life" in early editions of Burns's works, as published in Belfast (1800 and 1803), Dublin (1803), and Cork (1804), and Robert Chambers also reprinted it in the first edition of his *Biographical Dictionary of Eminent Scotsmen* (1832–1835). Though it was soon superseded by James Currie's much fuller "authorised" biography in the four-volume *Works of Robert Burns* of 1800, this latter text came to much the same conclusion about Burns's alcoholism. Heron was quoted as an authority on the matter in John Gibson Lockhart's *Life of Robert Burns* (1828) and Principal Shairp's *Robert Burns* (1902). By 1932, according to Franklyn Bliss Snyder's biography of Burns, Heron was "a poor authority to quote in any connection" but was nonetheless quoted. In 1936 Hans Hecht, while reprinting Heron's *A Memoir of the Life of the late Robert Burns* (with variant readings), denigrated his credibility further. Scholars now think Burns's fondness for the bottle was much overestimated and are certain that he did not die because of drinking. Heron's memoir is still used: it was reprinted by Maurice Lindsay in *The Burns Encyclopaedia* (second edition, 1970) as "a fairly shrewd tribute to Burns's achievement." Donald A. Low, who printed selections from the memoir in *Robert Burns: The Critical Heritage* (1974), thinks it prurient but critically quite able. A balanced view now seems current. Certainly one should stress that the memoir is as much about genius as drunkenness.

In the final fifth of the biography Heron attempts a general estimate of Burns "as a poet and as a man," and there is no doubt that Heron thought of Burns as at least on a par with John Milton, Alexander Pope, and Thomas Gray. Burns's poetry is analyzed by Heron in terms of emotive force, and for Heron that force is not only strong but precise.

He distinguishes several main characteristics in Burns: "*comprehension of mind*," "*strength, ardour,* and delicacy of *feelings,* passions, and affections"; acute moral "discernment"; and a "*lofty-minded* CONSCIOUSNESS *of his own* TALENTS and MERITS." Burns was clearly a hero of his time, "an honest, proud, warm-hearted man; of high passions, a sound understanding, a vigorous and excursive imagination," whose effect on his nation of readers was enormous. Apart from the insistence upon alcoholism (and even that is always blamed on Heron's recurrent villains, the tavern crew), the memoir is an unexpectedly generous book – generous, too, toward Thomas Blacklock and Henry Mackenzie. Even Burns's irreligious satire wins a kind of respect. Indeed, there seems to be such fundamental sympathy that one may wonder if Heron is not sometimes writing about himself, not so much with the hypocritical austerity which Hecht imputes to him but actually with some commiseration. The happy days at the parish school, the rise from laborer to writer, the money problems, and most of all the temptations to intemperance – these situations mirror Heron's life. "For a while," Heron writes, "the native rectitude of his [Burns's] understanding, and the excellent principles in which his infancy had been educated, withstood every temptation to intemperance or impiety. Alas! it was not always so."

Heron has in fact left one direct example of self-presentation. He had not lost his attachment to the church, becoming representative elder for New Galloway and serving as a member of the General Assembly of the Church of Scotland. He is said to have been a frequent and eloquent speaker in favor of the propagation of the gospel "among the Heathen." More important, the religious habit of self-scrutiny caused him to compile "Journal of my Conduct" (1789–1798). Apart from noting his occasional preaching duties and social engagements (many of them with Blacklock), the journal is mostly an introspective but not self-flagellatory examination of failure: it details broken promises, lies, and guilt over the death of his brother. An early entry is typical: "Prayed carelessly and hastily. At breakfast read my chapter, carelessly too, although it related the trial and last sufferings of my Saviour" (19 September 1789). The journal is a candid and laconically self-knowing document, and critic Catherine Carswell calls it "one of the frankest and most touching personal revelations of his time." It also shows a deep moral tension between the precarious life of an author and the demands of Calvinism.

In 1798 *St. Kilda in Edinburgh,* Heron's attempt at writing a comic afterpiece, was a hopeless failure,

interrupted and laughed off the stage for the wrong reasons, and his publication of the play, with an angry and boastful preface denouncing the stupidity and hypocrisy of the audience, did little for his reputation. He failed to finish his only recorded poem ("The Schoolmistress"). He was heavily in debt, and none of his appeals to the lord advocate had produced any result. In the Abbey Sanctuary at Holyrood he lived dodging creditors and working at full pitch. His family situation was deteriorating too. Heron had promised to settle and educate his three sisters, Grace, Betty, and Mary, and had brought Mary, his favorite, to live with him in Edinburgh. She is said to have been mortified by Heron's intemperance and financial embarrassments, and her death at Heron's lodgings in 1798 seems to have provoked in him inconsolable guilt and despair, compounded by the death of his mother in the same year. Chambers describes him wandering hopelessly around Edinburgh, avoiding everyone, "a miserable victim of want and care."

The last entry in Heron's journal records that he had finished his *A New General History of Scotland* and intended to leave for London. With the family hold broken and his literary career faltering, Heron decided to abandon his Edinburgh connections and follow the well-worn route south. He wrote to his father on arrival in London: "My whole income, earned by full sixteen hours a-day of close application to reading, writing, observation, and study, is but very little more than three hundred pounds a-year. But this is sufficient to my wants, and is earned in a manner which I know to be the most useful and honourable – that is, by teaching beneficial truths, and discountenancing vice and folly more effectually and more extensively than I could in any other way. This I am here always sure to earn, while I can give the necessary application; and if I were able to execute more literary labour I might readily obtain more money."

Heron continued to produce new compilations on chemistry and on Scotland; he edited *The Letters of Junius* (1802), with some useful historical notes; he authored projects to prevent scarcity; and he defended the slave trade. But the newspaper was to be his mainstay. He worked as a parliamentary reporter for the *Oracle,* the *Porcupine,* and the *Morning Post* as well as editing (apparently at ministerial request) a newspaper to be circulated among French Royalists. According to an anonymous witness in *Fraser's Magazine* (1839), his brief and disastrous editorships of the *Globe* and *British Press* were obtained by deception and financial fraud. He was also connected with *Lloyd's Evening Post* and *British Neptune,* and he contributed brief articles to the *Public Characters* and *Annual Necrology* series, and the *Agricultural Magazine, Universal Magazine, Anti-Jacobin Review,* and *London Review.* He was a member of the "Wittinagemot" [*sic*], a sort of literary publisher's club which met in the Chapter Coffee-House, Paternoster Row. But he was becoming unreliable; tending to promise too much; writing only when absolutely pressed to it and then at intense speed; and getting immured in his lodgings. He usually dressed only in a shirt and morning gown and had a green veil to shield his eyes. He was freely spending money he did not have on a gentlemanly lifestyle which was beyond him. In 1806 he attempted to found a newspaper called *Fame,* which failed badly, and Heron once more found himself in prison.

His last work strikes a bizarrely upbeat note: *The Comforts of Human Life* (1807), by "Charles Chearful," is a reply to the *Miseries of Human Life,* by the Reverend James Beresford (1806). *The Comforts of Human Life* was quickly into a second printing, but Heron could take little comfort from this success. From Newgate he wrote a letter, dated 2 February 1807, to the Literary Fund to appeal for assistance. Historian Isaac Disraeli calls this final self-presentation "pathetic from its simplicity, and valuable for its genuineness." In it Heron listed every literary act he could remember, including many of which there is now no trace. He had written, he said, "a great multiplicity of articles in almost every branch of science and literature," and his "anonymous pieces have been distinguished with very high praise" (a claim not easily tested). If nothing else his output was voluminous: he had written "a greater variety of light fugitive pieces than I know to have been written by any one other person." His had been a life in the service of moral and educational literature: "I can prove the general tenor of my writings to have been candid, and ever adapted to exhibit the most favourable views of the abilities, dispositions and exertions of others," he wrote, acknowledging the essentially parasitic nature of most of his writings. *A Memoir of the Life of the late Robert Burns* is alleged to have "suggested and promoted the subscription for his family . . . and formed the basis of Dr. Currie's life of him, as I learned by a letter from the Doctor to one of his friends." Now Heron needed charity himself: "For the last ten months I have been brought to the very extremity of bodily and pecuniary distress." His appeal concluded, "I shudder at the thoughts of perishing in a gaol." But it was already too late. His health destroyed by overwork and malnutrition, he contracted what was called gaol fever and (perhaps at the intercession of the Literary Fund) was removed to the Fever Hospital in Gray's Inn Lane, Saint Pancras, where he died a week later, on 13 April 1807.

His death was noted in the *Gentleman's Magazine* that June, in an obituary which paid tribute to Heron's "promising abilities" as a young man, his "multifarious erudition," and his "several reputable works" but concluded with a moralistic judgment: "his fate adds one more to the examples of the melancholy consequences of want of prudence; a defect unhappily too common among men of literature." This obituary set the tone for subsequent accounts: most Victorian biographical dictionaries include some brief cautionary account of Heron's disastrous career. There is much vague talk of his intemperance and profligacy but little detail. His best biographer is Thomas Murray, in *The Literary History of Galloway* (1832); he reports that Heron's "figure was rather above the middle size; his gait was very erect, and impressed strangers with the idea of dignity and self-importance: his countenance was pale and care-worn, the colour of his eyes, which were, from study and confinement, generally inflamed, was blue; his nose was long; but, altogether, his countenance had a pleasing expression." Murray's estimate of Heron's abilities stresses his activity and versatility, his memory and knowledge, and his extreme assiduity; his style could be pompous and declamatory but also "chaste" and "elegant." This verdict is repeated in Chambers's derivative but overwritten account in *A Biographical Dictionary of Eminent Scotsmen,* where the note of moral admonition is rather louder: "the brief memoir of this accomplished scholar affords another striking instance of the impossibility of shielding genius from poverty and disgrace when blinded by passion, or perverted by eccentricity." An anonymous correspondent in *Fraser's Magazine* (July–December 1839) was far less sympathetic, decrying Heron's "learning" as so much empty display and dazzling talk, and calling him "a biblical cobbler, or compounder, or patcher-up of books, in which he was not over-scrupulous in arrogating to himself the labours of others." Only Disraeli suggests that Heron was worth helping and that his fate, "the fate of hundreds of authors," was somehow the fault of society at large rather than Heron's own personal deficiencies.

In the twentieth century Heron has received mixed biographical attention: to Carswell he was a victim of a repressive moral system; to Hecht he was pure humbug, his writings ("sanctimonious rubbish and smug moral admonition") contrasting with his "malodorous life" and character: "unreliable, lazy, cruel, unbridled . . . utterly false both to himself and others . . . the whole blend was utterly venomous." Such a statement is too strong to be accurate about anyone and was most probably motivated by revenge against Heron for his negative remarks about Burns. It is also against the drift of most other witnesses, and modern scholars are less judgmental, preferring to concentrate on the usefulness of Heron's biography of Burns.

Bibliography:

James Sinton, "Robert Heron and His Writings, With a Bibliography," *Publications of the Edinburgh Bibliographical Society,* 15 (October 1932): 17–33.

Biographies:

Thomas Murray, *The Literary History of Galloway* (Edinburgh: Waugh & Innes, 1822), pp. 254–281;

Robert Chambers, *A Biographical Dictionary of Eminent Scotsmen,* revised by Thomas Thomson, 3 volumes (London: Blackie & Son, 1875), II: 258–260.

References:

Anonymous, Obituary of Robert Heron, *Gentleman's Magazine,* 77 (June 1807): 595;

Catherine Carswell, "Robert Heron: A Study in Failure," *Scots Magazine,* 18 (October 1932): 37–48;

Isaac Disraeli, *Calamities and Quarrels of Authors,* new edition edited by the Earl of Beaconsfield (London: Frederick Warne, 1881), pp. 80–83;

Hans Hecht, *Robert Burns: The Man and His Work,* translated by Jane Lymburn (London: Hodge, 1936), pp. 315–354;

"How To Make A Newspaper, Without Credit Or Cash," *Fraser's Magazine For Town and Country,* 20 (July–December 1839): 746–752;

Maurice Lindsay, *The Burns Encyclopaedia,* second edition (London: Hutchinson, 1970), pp. 165–182;

Robert Donald Spector, "The American Publication of Heron's Edition of the 'Letters of Junius,'" *Notes & Queries,* 197 (June 1952): 275–276.

Papers:

The Laing Collection at the University of Edinburgh Library holds Heron's "Journal of My Conduct" as well as a few letters to the lord advocate on Heron's behalf. A manuscript of *St. Kilda in Edinburgh* is in the Larpent Collection in the Huntington Library.

Samuel Johnson

(18 September 1709 – 13 December 1784)

Gordon Turnbull
Yale University

See also the entries on Johnson in *DLB 39: British Novelists, 1660–1800; DLB 95: Eighteenth-Century Poets, First Series;* and *DLB 104: British Novelists, 1660–1800, Second Series.*

BOOKS: *A Voyage to Abyssinia by Father Jerome Lobo . . . and Fifteen Dissertations . . . by Mr. Le Grand. From the French* (London: Printed for A. Bettesworth & C. Hitch, 1735);

London: A Poem, in Imitation of the Third Satire of Juvenal (London: Printed for R. Dodsley, 1738);

Marmor Norfolciense: or an Essay on an Ancient Prophetical Inscription, In Monkish Rhyme, Lately Discover'd near Lynn in Norfolk. By Probus Britanicus (London: Printed for J. Brett, 1739);

A Compleat Vindication of the Licensers of the Stage, from the Malicious and Scandalous Aspersions of Mr. Brooke, Author of Gustavus Vasa . . . By an Impartial Hand (London: Printed for C. Corbett, 1739);

A Commentary on Mr. Pope's Principles of Morality, or Essay on Man. By Mons. Crousaz (London: Printed for A. Dodd, 1739);

An Account of the Life of Mr. Richard Savage, Son of the Earl Rivers (London: Printed for J. Roberts, 1744);

Miscellaneous Observations on the Tragedy of Macbeth: with Remarks on Sir T. H.'s Edition of Shakespear. To which is affix'd, Proposals for a New Edition of Shakeshear [sic] (London: Printed for E. Cave & sold by J. Roberts, 1745);

A Sermon Preached at the Cathedral Church of St. Paul, before the Sone of the Clergy, on Thursday the Second of May, 1745. by the Honourable and Reverend Henry Hervey Aston (London: Printed for J. Brindley & sold by M. Cooper, 1745);

Prologue and Epilogue, Spoken at the Opening of the Theatre in Drury-Lane 1747 (London: Printed by E. Cave, sold by M. Cooper & R. Dodsley, 1747);

The Plan of a Dictionary of the English Language; Addressed to the Right Honourable Philip Dormer, Earl of Chesterfield (London: Printed for J. & P. Knapton, T. Longman & T. Shewell, C. Hitch, A. Millar and R. Dodsley, 1747);

The Vanity of Human Wishes. The Tenth Satire of Juvenal, Imitated (London: Printed for R. Dodsley & sold by M. Cooper, 1749);

Irene: A Tragedy. As it is Acted at the Theatre Royal in Drury-Lane (London: Printed for R. Dodsley & sold by M. Cooper, 1749);

The Rambler, nos. 1–208 (London: Printed for J. Payne & L. Bouquet, 20 March 1750–14 March 1752); republished in 2 volumes (London: Printed for J. Payne, 1753);

A New Prologue Spoken by Mr. Garrick, Thursday, April 5, 1750. At the Representation of Comus, for the Benefit of Mrs Elizabeth Foster, Milton's Grand-Daughter, and only surviving Descendant (London: Printed for J. Payne & J. Bouquet, 1750);

A Dictionary of the English Language, 2 volumes (London: Printed by W. Strahan for J. & P. Knapton, T & T. Longman, C. Hitch & L. Hawes, A. Millar, and R. & J. Dodsley, 1755);

An Account of an Attempt to Ascertain the Longitude at Sea. . . . By Zachariah Williams (London: Printed for R. Dodsley & J. Jeffries & sold by J. Bouquet, 1755);

Proposals for Printing, by Subscription, the Dramatick Works of William Shakespeare (London, 1756);

The Prince of Abissinia. A Tale, 2 volumes (London: Printed for R. & J. Dodsley and W. Johnston, 1759); republished as *The History of Rasselas, Prince of Abissinia,* 1 volume (Philadelphia: Printed by Robert Bell, 1768);

The Idler, collected edition, 2 volumes (London: Printed for J. Newbery, 1761) – first pub-

*Samuel Johnson in 1783 (portrait by John Opie, National Portrait Galleries
of Scotland)*

lished in the *Universal Chronicle, or Weekly Gazette* (15 April 1758 – 5 April 1760);

*The Plays of William Shakespeare, in Eight Volumes,
with the Corrections and Illustrations of Various
Commentators; to which are added Notes by Sam.
Johnson* (London: Printed for J. & R. Tonson
and ten others, 1765); revised by Johnson and
George Steevens (London, 1773);

The False Alarm (London: Printed for T. Cadell,
1770);

*Thoughts on the Late Transactions Respecting Falkland's
Islands* (London: Printed for T. Cadell, 1771);

The Patriot. Addressed to the Electors of Great Britain
(London: Printed for T. Cadell, 1774);

A Journey to the Western Islands of Scotland (London:
Printed for W. Strahan & T. Cadell, 1775);

*Taxation No Tyranny; an Answer to the Resolutions and
Address of the American Congress* (London:
Printed for T. Cadell, 1775);

*Prefaces, Biographical and Critical, to the Works of the En-
glish Poets*, 10 volumes (London: Printed by J.
Nichols for C. Bathurst and thirty-five others,
1779 [volumes 1–4], 1781 [volumes 5–10]).

Editions: *Prayers and Meditations, composed by Samuel
Johnson*, edited by George Strahan (London:
Printed for T. Cadell, 1785);

The Works of Samuel Johnson, LL.D., volumes 1–11,
edited by Sir John Hawkins (London: Printed
for J. Buckland and forty others, 1787); volumes 12 and 13, *Debates in Parliament* (London:
Printed for John Buckland, 1787); volume 14
(London: Printed for John Stockdale and
G. G. J. & J. Robinson, 1788); volume 15
(London: Printed for Elliot & Kay and C. Elliot, 1789);

*The Lives of the English Poets [Prefaces, Biographical and
Critical to the Works of the English Poets]*, 3 volumes, edited by G. B. Hill (Oxford: Clarendon Press, 1905);

The History of Rasselas, Prince of Abissinia, edited by R. W. Chapman (Oxford: Clarendon Press, 1927);

Samuel Johnson's Prefaces and Dedications, edited by Allen T. Hazen (New Haven: Yale University Press, 1937);

The Life of Mr. Richard Savage, edited by Clarence Tracy (Oxford: Clarendon Press, 1971);

Samuel Johnson, edited by Donald Greene, Oxford English Authors (Oxford & New York: Oxford University Press, 1984).

The Yale Edition of the Works of Samuel Johnson (13 volumes to date):

Volume 1: *Diaries, Prayer, and Annals,* edited by E. L. McAdam, Jr., with Donald and Mary Hyde (New Haven: Yale University Press / London: Oxford University Press, 1958);

Volume 2: *The Idler and The Adventurer,* edited by W. J. Bate, John M. Bullitt, and L. F. Powell (New Haven & London: Yale University Press, 1963);

Volumes 3–5: *The Rambler,* edited by Bate and Albrecht B. Strauss (New Haven & London: Yale University Press, 1969);

Volume 6: *Poems,* edited by McAdam and George Milne (New Haven & London: Yale University Press, 1964);

Volumes 7 & 8: *Johnson on Shakespeare,* edited by Arthur Sherbo (New Haven & London: Yale University Press, 1968);

Volume 9: *A Journey to the Western Islands of Scotland,* edited by Mary Lascelles (New Haven & London: Yale University Press, 1971);

Volume 10: *Political Writings,* edited by Donald J. Greene (New Haven & London: Yale University Press, 1977);

Volume 14: *Sermons,* edited by Jean H. Hagstrum and James Gray (New Haven & London: Yale University Press, 1978);

Volume 15: *A Voyage to Abyssinia,* edited by Joel J. Gold (New Haven & London: Yale University Press, 1985);

Volume 16: *Rasselas and Other Tales,* edited by Gwin J. Kolb (New Haven & London: Yale University Press, 1990).

OTHER: *A Miscellany of Poems by Several Hands. Publish'd by J. Husbands,* includes Johnson's Latin verse translation of Alexander Pope's *Messiah* (Oxford: Printed by Leon. Lichfield, 1731);

Catalogus Bibliothecae Harleianae, 5 volumes, catalogue of the Harleian libarary, includes contri-

butions by Johnson (London: Apud Thomas Osborne, 1743-1745);

Robert James, M.D., *A Medicinal Dictionary,* 3 volumes, written with the assistance of Johnson (London: Printed for T. Osborne & J. Roberts, 1743-1745);

The Harleian Miscellany, or a Collection of . . . Pamphlets and Tracts, 8 volumes, includes an introduction and annotations by Johnson (London: Printed for T. Osborne, 1744-1746);

Preface and "The Vision of Theodore, the Hermit of Teneriffe," in *The Preceptor: Containing a Course of General Education* (London: Printed for R. Dodsley, 1748);

William Lauder, *An Essay on Milton's Use and Imitation of the Moderns in His Paradise Lost,* includes a preface and a postscript by Johnson (London: Printed for J. Payne & J. Bouquet, 1750);

Charlotte Lennox, *The Female Quixote; or, the Adventures of Arabella,* includes a dedication by Johnson (London: Printed for A. Millar, 1752);

Adventurer (London: Printed for J. Payne, nos. 1–140, 7 November 1752-9 March 1754) – includes twenty-one essays by Johnson;

Lennox, *Shakespear Illustrated: or the Novels and Histories on Which the Plays of Shakespear Are Founded,* includes a dedication by Johnson (London: Printed for A. Millar, 1753);

Sir Thomas Browne, *Christian Morals. . . . The Second Edition. With a Life of the Author by Samuel Johnson,* edited, with biography and annotations, by Johnson (London: Printed by Richard Hett for J. Payne, 1756);

Richard Rolt, *A New Dictionary of Trade and Commerce,* includes a preface by Johnson (London: Printed for T. Osborne & J. Shipton and four others, 1756);

The Greek Theatre of Father [Pierre] Brumoy. Translated by Mrs. Charlotte Lennox, includes a dedication and translations by Johnson of two essays (London: Printed for Mess. Millar, Vaillant, and six others, 1759);

Introduction on the history of early Portuguese exploration, in *The World Displayed; or a Curious Collection of Voyages and Travels,* 20 volumes (London: Printed for J. Newbery, 1759-1761), I: iii–xxxii;

Proceedings of the Committee Appointed to Manage the Contributions begun at London Dec. xviii, MDCCLVIIII, for Cloathing French Prisoners of War, includes an introduction by Johnson (London: Printed by Order of the Committee, 1760);

The marketplace at Lichfield in 1785 (engraving after a drawing by Stringer). Johnson was born in the building on the far right, which housed his father's bookshop on the ground floor.

John Gwynne, *Thoughts on the Coronation of His Present Majesty King George the Third, or, Reasons offered against confining the procession to the usual track, and pointing out others more commodious and proper,* much of the text written by Johnson (London: Printed for the Proprietor, and sold by F. Noble and three others, 1761);

"Author's Life" and dedication, in *The English Works of Roger Ascham . . . With Notes and Observations, and the Author's Life. By James Bennet,* edited in large part by Johnson (London: Printed for R. & J. Dodsley and J. Newbery, 1761);

Thomas Percy, ed., *Reliques of Ancient English Poetry,* includes a dedication by Johnson, who also provided general assistance (London: Printed for J. Dodsley, 1765);

Anna Williams, *Miscellanies in Prose and Verse* (London: Printed for T. Davies, 1766) – Johnson contributed the advertisement, a short poem, "The Ant," possibly revisions to Miss Williams's poems, and "The Fountains: A Fairy Tale";

The Convict's Address to His Unhappy Brethren. Delivered in the Chapel of Newgate, on Friday, June 6, 1777.
By William Dodd, largely written by Johnson (London: Printed for G. Kearsley, 1777);

Poems and Miscellaneous Pieces, with a Free Translation of the Oedipus Tyrannus of Sophocles. By the Rev. Thomas Maurice, includes a preface and possibly a dedication by Johnson (London: Printed for the Author and sold by J. Dodsley and three others, 1779);

Dedication to the King, in *An Account of the Musical Performances in Westminster-Abbey and the Pantheon . . . in Commemoration of Handel. By Charles Burney* (London: Printed for the Benefit of the Musical Fund and sold by T. Payne & Son and G. Robinson, 1785);

Sir Robert Chambers, *A Course of Lectures on the English Law Delivered at the University of Oxford 1767–1773 by Sir Robert Chambers and Composed in Association with Samuel Johnson,* edited by Thomas M. Curley (Madison: University of Wisconsin Press, 1986; Oxford: Clarendon Press, 1986).

The life of Alexander Pope, the longest, most carefully labored, and last to be written of Samuel Johnson's fifty-two "Lives of the Poets" (*Prefaces,*

Biographical and Critical, to the Works of the English Poets, 1779, 1781), discloses much at the heart of his pioneering and influential work as a literary biographer and biographical literary critic. At a crucial moment in his account of Pope, written with a highly characteristic balance of admiration and censure, Johnson sharply rejects Pope's "favourite theory," the "Ruling Passion," a force acting on human identity "antecedent to reason and observation." Johnson valued above all else reason and observation: in his "Lives of the Poets" observation – experienced, historically informed – ranges "with extensive view" just as it does in the opening line of Johnson's signature poem, *The Vanity of Human Wishes* (1749), and the duty of criticism is to hold poetry up to what his *Rambler* essays call the "light of reason." Response to literature, though deeply felt, is a region in which – no less than in the political order – passion should not rule, for that would risk returns to the tumultuous origins of the century of poetry Johnson surveys – the English civil war. Biography, while never shirking the duty of forceful moral assessment, must rise above the exaggerated emotions and enthusiasms of merely factional partisanship.

It is not merely that Pope has "formed his theory with . . . little skill." Johnson everywhere in his writings and recorded conversation shows himself an enemy to anything that suggests deterministic forces on human moral agency, and he rejects whatever is outside the scope of reason and observation. The doctrine of the ruling passion "is itself pernicious as well as false; its tendency is to produce the belief of a kind of moral predestination or overruling principle which cannot be resisted; he that admits it is prepared to comply with every desire that caprice or opportunity shall excite, and to flatter himself that he submits only to the lawful dominion of nature." The two most important of the early poets Johnson treats, Abraham Cowley and John Milton, wrote in the turbulent context of the English civil war (in fact, on opposite sides of it) and its political aftermath. Dangerous passions indeed ruled then, and the consequence was, for Johnson, a savage usurpation and a colossal internecine violence. Oliver Cromwell's victory came from no force of nature, from no intrinsic or natural right to dominion. For Johnson as moral thinker neither nature nor anything else exercises ultimate "dominion" over the human moral will, and for Johnson the judge of literature any author who suggests otherwise has failed to uphold writing's moral purposes and has thus violated writing's most basic and important function – to instruct by pleasing. For John-

son an author's oeuvre must not be seen as solely the issue of an authorial "nature" or a more romantically understood "personality": an author's character and works take their place in complex historical, economic, cultural, social, and generic contexts, all of which exert their pressures on literary performance and must themselves be accounted for. Cowley, representative of the poets whom Johnson's highly influential account groups as the Metaphysical school, served in the Royalist cause: the dangerous career that saw him ciphering and deciphering the letters that passed between the king and queen finds expression in his elaborately encoded metaphysical poetics, in "the discovery of occult resemblances in things apparently unlike." In the "acrimonious and surly republican" Milton of Johnson's notorious, admiring, but brilliantly caustic account, the poet's ideological allegiance with Cromwell expresses itself in a poetics that seeks in *Paradise Lost* (1667) to harass and indeed "master" its reader. In Pope the craft, cunning, and manipulativeness with which the poet managed his career become the properties of the complex effectiveness of Pope's couplets themselves.

Johnson's prefatory accounts of fifty-two English poets and dramatists were the result of an opportunistic request by a group of London publishers eager to lend the weight of Johnson's name to an ambitious, large-scale collection of poetry they were planning. But, issued separately, Johnson's prefaces quickly transcended their original occasion, and they amount to what a modern commentator, Lawrence Lipking, justly terms the *ponere totum* of eighteenth-century criticism. They flow from a lifetime's engagement in many literary modes with aesthetic theory and from a long earlier career in writing biographies. Though he composed all but a few of the prefaces hastily and unsystematically, relying largely on already-published biographical materials, and though the publishers themselves, not Johnson (with a sprinkling of exceptions), chose the poets, the prefaces stand as a landmark in the development of literary biography and biographical literary criticism. Johnson sought an integration of informed knowledge of the historical, cultural, generic, and linguistic contexts in which an author's life, character, and works took their place, evaluative assessments of what makes certain works of literature endure or survive beyond their own times and have lasting appeal and value for "the common reader." In this ambition, far from successfully deployed by Johnson, one finds a pioneering advocacy of a historically contextualist critical method, the life-and-works biography, one that has entered the later practice of literary life writing as standard procedure.

In the life of John Dryden, Johnson writes succinctly that to "judge rightly of an author we must transport ourselves to his time and examine what were the wants of contemporaries and what were his means of supplying them." To account for human moral choice by recourse to something like a fixed or static ruling passion distorts the nature of moral choice, upon which many forces are exerted, some of them random and contingent: "men are directed," says Johnson in the life of Pope, to some "particular species of excellence . . . not by an ascendant planet or predominating humour, but by the first book which they read, some early conversation which they heard, or some accident which excited ardour and emulation." In that sentence, which discloses incidentally some recurrent concerns of Johnson as a practical biographer – the effects of early reading, the importance of conversation, and the value of emulating those worthy of ardor – Johnson stands clearly forward as a pioneering advocate of a contextualist biographical critical method. Authors cannot be assessed without a knowledge of their heroes, their models, their reading, their readers' expectations, and prevailing literary and political conditions. He develops his rejection of the ruling passion, indeed, into an open assertion of cultural contingency in human character: "No man . . . can be born, in the strict acceptation, a lover of money, for he may be born where money does not exist; nor can he be born, in a moral sense, a lover of his country, for society, politically regulated, is a state contradistinguished from a state of nature, and any attention to that coalition of interests which makes the happiness of a country is possible only to those whom enquiry and reflection have enabled to comprehend it." It remains true, of course, that Johnson in the "Lives of the Poets" recurrently invokes certain static and apparently universal, panhistorical concepts as tests of any given poem's merit – nature, life, truth, and reason, against which any poem must be measured – and much can be found in his writings to echo the sage Imlac's assertion in *The History of Rasselas* (originally titled *The Prince of Abissinia,* 1759) that "the province of poetry is to describe Nature and Passion, which are always the same." Johnson also invokes a "common reader," a universally recognized idea of shared "pleasure" and singular "genius." But against such moments others such as this one in the life of Pope must be set: Johnson can declare outright that human "characters are by no means constant; men change by change of place, of fortune, of acquaintance."

Johnson's ahistorical assumptions – of consistently recurrent life, nature, truth, and reason – and his broadly Christian-humanist belief in a universal humanity have among more recent generations of critics come under challenge, and his local dispensations (often deliberately provocative) of praise and blame have produced vigorous disagreement. But his contextualist theory and practice have entered the very conduct of modern literary biography and biographical criticism. Earlier in his career, in his *Proposals for Printing, by Subscription* (1756) for an edition of the works of William Shakespeare, Johnson had declared his conviction that "in order to make a true estimate of the abilities and merit of a writer, it is always necessary to examine the genius of his age, and the opinions of his contemporaries." Johnson advocates a contextualist biography and criticism in his prefatory "Lives," although he did not precisely inaugurate it, and both his impatient compositional habits and the required brevity of the prefatory format did not allow a full or systematic prosecution. He provided the most sustained and authoritative advance in the practice of the integrated life-and-works mode of critical biography now standard in both scholarly and commercial life-writing.

Samuel Johnson was the first of two children, both sons, of Michael Johnson, bookseller and stationer in Lichfield, Staffordshire, and Sarah Ford Johnson. He was born on 18 September 1709, when his father was fifty-two and his mother forty. The family, despite some early prosperity, was generally poor. Michael Johnson had considerable local eminence, though, as a magistrate and an important local seller of books, but from what Samuel Johnson has recorded and others have reported of his early life, it seems that the marriage was unhappy and family life unhappy too. Yet the origins of his intense engagement with literature appear in the voracious reading he was able to do among the books in his father's shop. From childhood into later life Johnson suffered from serious physical ailments, and although he grew into a robust adulthood, his own authorial career, like some of those discussed in his prefaces (such as those of Milton and Pope), is a story of courage and stamina in the face of frequent physical infirmity. In 1712, the year in which his brother, Nathanael (who would die at the age of twenty-five), was born, Samuel was taken, according to the well-known story, to London to be touched by Queen Anne for scrofula. As an adult, his body shook with tics and starts, of which the most plausible modern diagnosis is Tourette's syn-

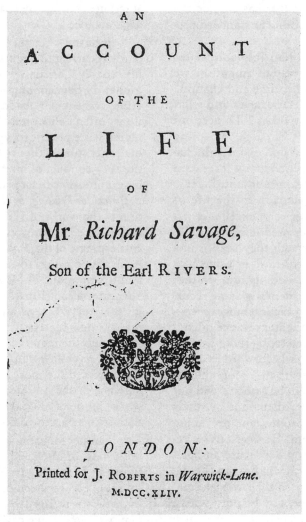

Title page for Johnson's biography of the poet who claimed to be the illegitimate son of Anne, Countess Macclesfield, and Richard Savage, Earl Rivers.

drome. He was nearsighted, almost without sight in his left eye, and deaf in his left ear, but from an early age he showed signs of superior intellectual gifts.

He entered Lichfield Grammar School in 1717. In 1726 he visited his cousin the Reverend Cornelius Ford at Stourbridge in Worcestershire, a visit which broadened his cultural and literary horizons, and for a time he attended school there. Back at his father's home and shop in Lichfield, he spent two years in avid if unsystematic reading, chiefly in the classics. His father entered him as a commoner at Pembroke College, Oxford, in October 1728, but because of the family's poverty he left in December 1729 without taking a degree, thereby debarring himself from careers that might otherwise have

claimed him, in the church and the law. In his young adulthood he suffered from acute melancholy, which at times he thought threatened his sanity. His intense psychological turmoil, and fears of its recurrences, produced in him a stoically doleful sense of the human lot that informs almost all his writings and recorded conversations. "The only end of writing is to enable the readers better to enjoy life, or better to endure it," he would later write. No major critic, in any language, is more considerate than the Johnson of the prefaces of the reader's right to pleasure, nor is any critic severer on writers who contribute to, rather than alleviate, readerly tedium, boredom, and fatigue.

Michael Johnson died in December 1731. In the next year Samuel Johnson was teaching school, unhappily, at Market Bosworth in Leicestershire, and a year later, while living in Birmingham as the guest of his old school friend Edmund Hector, he wrote journalism, projected various literary and historical works, then began his first book, *A Voyage to Abyssinia* (1735), a condensed English translation of Joachim Le Grand's French version of the manuscript account of the travels in Abyssinia by the seventeenth-century Portuguese Jesuit missionary Father Jeronimo Lobo. The work shows concerns and beliefs that would persist and recur throughout Johnson's authorial career, some of special relevance to his thinking about biography. Johnson stresses in this early work a need for eyewitness accounts, reliable reports, for firsthand knowledge wherever possible. Johnson admires the courage and endurance of the missionary in his dangerous travels and the honesty of his reporting, and he particularly values the deflation of reputed wonders. It is a work upon which he would draw for his wry antinovel *Rasselas* many years later.

On 9 July 1735 Johnson married Elizabeth Jervis Porter, widow of a Birmingham woolen draper. Johnson was twenty-five; his wife was forty-five and the mother of three children by her first husband. With her marriage settlement Johnson opened a boarding school at Edial, near Lichfield, in 1736, but he still harbored larger literary ambitions and about this time began work on his tragedy, *Irene* (1749). After the failure of his school, which attracted only a handful of pupils, he set off on 2 March 1737 for London, in the company of the young man who would become his school's best-known alumnus, David Garrick, the great actor, manager, and playwright, the dominant figure in mid-eighteenth-century London theater. Johnson settled in London and is closely identified with life in the metropolis, but between 1754 and 1784 (evidence for the early years remains scanty) he traveled frequently and made about sixty visits to Oxford, Birmingham, Lichfield, and Ashbourne.

Johnson supported himself and his wife precariously (though claims about extreme poverty seem exaggerated) with miscellaneous commercial writing, magazine journalism, and, prominently, popular short biographies. These writings, undertaken to earn a living, were certainly incidental to larger and more serious literary ambitions. In 1738 he began his long association with the *Gentleman's Magazine* and its founding proprietor, Edward Cave. Working for Cave, he assumed several editorial duties, wrote reviews, and, perhaps most important for the history of journalistic coverage of politics, pioneered modern parliamentary reporting. Yet his mind was on more enduring literary projects: translations, editions, histories, and his own original compositions. In 1738 he published his vigorously satiric poem *London,* an attack on the injustices of the Walpole era, modeled on the third satire of Juvenal. The poem, printed by Cave and published by Robert Dodsley, sheds light on Johnson's biographical practice in the "Lives of the Poets." In the poem's narrative, the aggrieved author Thales has suffered from the neglect of his poetical talents in the corrupt, capricious, venal, and dangerous world of London, and he plans to retreat to rural Wales. "Slow rises worth, by poverty depressed" – one of the most resonant lines – epitomizes a recurring Johnsonian concern: the place of literary worth in the commercial and political conditions of the literary marketplace, a concern with what will endure and what will prove ephemeral. The poem berates the undervaluing of authorship in the Age of Trade, the mercantile world of Sir Robert Walpole's Whig administration. Writing is contaminated by a general prostitution of talent – in which "looks are merchandise, and smiles are sold" – inseparable from party-faction fighting: the writers rewarded are "a laureate tribe" who peddle "servile verse." Yet while Thales flees to rural Wales, the speaker himself stayed behind in London. Nowhere would Johnson endorse an ethic of retreat or seclusion or detachment (part of the reason for his sustained attack in the *Prefaces* on modern forms of pastoral poetry); he always valued the challenge of writerly engagement. The poet of *London* remains in the city that simultaneously outrages and energizes him, to pen "angry numbers" and "in virtue's cause . . . exert his rage." Johnson in his later "Lives," like the speaker of this early poem who bids farewell to the aggrieved Thales, does not shirk the debate. He remains always a practical and engaged man of letters. In the end, while sympathetic to Thales' indignation, the sympathy – like that shown for Richard Savage later – is complex and qualified. The poem's conclusion endorses vigorous engagement over Thales' wish for pastoral retreat.

Routine periodical journalism constitutes most of Johnson's writing from this period. But he shows a consistent concern with biography and most important with biography's moral purposes and uses, a concern with appears in the form of his quasi-choric moments of interpolated commentary in writings almost entirely derived from earlier published materials. He published a life of Father Paolo Sarpi (*Gentleman's Magazine,* November 1778), historian of the Council of Trent, and began but did not complete a translation of Sarpi's *Istoria del concilio*

Tridentio (History of the Council of Trent, 1619). Johnson derived the account of Sarpi from Pierre François Le Courayer's *Vie Abrege de Fra Paolo,* which forms the preface to Sarpi's *History.* More antigovernment pamphlets followed in 1739. In the same year he published a life of the learned Dutch physician Herman Boerhaave and a translation of Jean Pierre de Crousaz's *Commentary* (1737) on Pope's *Essay on Man* (1733–1734). Johnson defends Pope against the religious strictures of the Swiss clergyman and critic Crousaz but rejects, as he would do later at length in the life of Pope, the theory of the ruling passion. Boerhaave died in 1738, and Johnson's account of him, taken mainly from a commemorative eulogy in Latin by Albert Schultens, ran in the *Gentleman's Magazine* in four parts (January–April 1739). It was later abbreviated and added, along with several other brief lives of important medical figures, to Dr. Robert James's *Medicinal Dictionary* (1743–1745). It shows what would remain an interest of Johnson's in science and medicine, especially its rational and empirical processes. Johnson admires Boerhaave's combination of scientific empiricism and sincere Christian piety, and he would later bring to bear some of those same empirical procedures to his own editorial and lexicographical projects.

His *Prefaces* advocates criticism on the basis of at least quasi-rationalistic principles, to rescue it from the operations of mere "taste" and distinguish it from the ephemeral operations of popularity and reputation. In the *Rambler* number 92 (2 February 1751) Johnson writes that the task of criticism is "to establish principles; to improve opinion into knowledge; and to distinguish those means of pleasing which depend on known causes and rational deduction, from the nameless and inexplicable elegancies which appeal wholly to the fancy, from which we feel delight, but know not how they produce it, and which may well be termed the enchantress of the soul. Criticism reduces those regions of literature under the dominion of science . . . " In the *Rambler* number 93 (5 February 1751), he says that the "duty of criticism is neither to depreciate, nor dignify by partial representations, but to hold out the light of reason, whatever it may discover." Much that appears in the *Prefaces* indeed eludes rational principle and the light of reason – in such matters as genius, sublimity, and creative fire – but early and late in Johnson's career readers see his alignments, though his Christian piety holds firm, with the ideals of the European Enlightenment and empirical inquiry.

Johnson next wrote a life of Adm. Robert Blake, Cromwell's victorious admiral and general

of the sea, derived mainly from Thomas Birch's entry on Blake in volume three of the *General Dictionary Historical and Critical* (1735) and some other sources. *The General Dictionary* (1734–1741), was a ten-volume translation of the Frenchman Pierre Bayle's *Dictionnaire historique et critique* (1695–1697), augmented by Birch and others under Birch's direction. Johnson knew Birch and admired his abilities as a life writer. The life of Blake was published in the *Gentleman's Magazine* for June 1740 and again in the same year as an octavo pamphlet. It was first published with an introductory paragraph indicating its aim – like the next life he undertook, of Sir Francis Drake – to recall the Elizabethan successes against Spain. To recall these glories once more during the Seven Years' War (1756–1763), it was printed again in the *London Chronicle* (13–20 August 1757). This life of Blake was included in the first collected edition of Johnson's works, published in 1787.

The life of Drake, based largely on a collection of four seventeenth-century pamphlets recounting Drake's voyages, first appeared in six monthly parts in the *Gentleman's Magazine* from August 1740 until January 1741. In 1767 it was added with the life of Blake to the third edition of *An Account of the Life of Mr. Richard Savage* (first published in 1744), and this collection was reprinted in 1777. The biography of Drake also recalled Elizabethan triumphs over Spain, in the context of the sea skirmishes then being fought between England and Spain during the War of Jenkins's Ear (1739–1741), so called because when an English shipmaster, Robert Jenkins, told the House of Commons how his Spanish captors had cut off his ear, Walpole was urged to declare war. These hostilities led to the War of the Austrian Succession (1740–1748). In *The Early Career of Samuel Johnson* (1987) Thomas Kaminski finds the life of Drake "perhaps the most interesting of Johnson's early lives." Johnson follows his sources factually but breaks through to his own characteristic voice when his source (in his words) "reflects on human nature in its savage condition." Johnson launches into a tirade – characteristic of his later writing – "against those who equate savagery with innocence and civilization with corruption." Whatever affinities Johnson's belief in empirical process and rational inquiry had with the ideals of the European Enlightenment, he resolutely rejected Rousseauesque ideas of noble savagery or the idea of pure native humanity "corrupted" by civilization.

Other popular derivative biographies by Johnson followed. The *Gentleman's Magazine* for July 1741 ran his translation of Bernard le Bovier de

Letter from Johnson to Goldsmith, asking him to accept Boswell as a member of The Club (Dr. Johnson's House, Gough Square)

Fontonelle's *Eloge* (1731) on Dr. Louis Morin, the French botanist and physician. The translation follows Fontonelle closely, but a Johnsonian voice can be heard in a footnote to Fontonelle's praise for Morin's *Index of Hippocrates*: "This is an Instance of the Disposition generally found in Writers of Lives, to exalt every common Occurence and Action into Wonders. Are not Indexes daily written by Men who neither receive nor expect very loud Applauses for their Labours?" In the *Gentleman's Magazine* for April 1742 Johnson contributed a life of the Dutch classical scholar Pieter Burman, who died in 1714. In July 1742 the *Gentleman's Magazine* carried a review of Jean Baptiste Du Halde's *Description de la Chine* (Description of China, 1735); the review in-cludes a biographical account of Confucius which twentieth-century scholarship has plausibly attrib-uted to Johnson. James's *Medicinal Dictionary* began appearing in 1743, and Johnson contributed about a dozen brief biographies. Johnson's life of the youth-ful prodigy Johann Philip Baratier, who had trans-lated the *Voyages of Rabbi Benjamin* from the Hebrew, was based largely on fond letters written by Baratier's father. It appeared in the *Gentleman's Mag-azine* for December 1740 and February 1741 and, with additional matter based on more detailed bio-graphical materials sent by Baratier's father to Eliza-beth Carter, in the *Gentleman's Magazine* for Decem-ber 1742. Johnson assembled these three pieces on Baratier as an octavo pamphlet published in 1742.

The December 1740 issue of the *Gentleman's Magazine* also carried what Kaminksi justly terms Johnson's first "fully developed critical essay," the "Essay on Epitaphs." On display even in this brief early essay are some central Johnsonian beliefs, especially in the moral efficacy of biography: in recording the lives of the departed, truth is paramount, vice must not be commemorated, and private virtue – worthy of emulation – must wherever possible be stressed.

A life of the seventeenth-century physician Thomas Sydenham by Johnson was prefixed to Dr. John Swan's edition of the medical works of Sydenham of 1742 and reprinted in the *Gentleman's Magazine* for December 1742. It was revised for a second edition in 1749. With no previously published biography on which to draw, Johnson turns this life into a polemic on the benefits of study and formal education. Johnson's aim again is to rescue from oblivion the private virtues of one of the many worthy men of science whose lot it has been "to be known only by their writings, and to have left behind them no remembrance of their domestic life, or private transactions."

Johnson emerges most forcefully in his own voice in the remarkable *Life of Mr. Richard Savage*. The man who called himself Richard Savage, still something of a mystery to modern biography, was a notorious, irresponsible, but apparently charismatic figure in the London literary and social world and a man with whom Johnson in younger years had been friendly. Savage died in debtor's prison in Bristol in 1743. In the account of Savage's sensational, reckless life Johnson moves away from routine journalism and more fully into a psychobiographical study. Savage's story – that he was the brutally neglected illegitimate son of Anne, Countess of Macclesfield by Richard Savage, fourth Earl Rivers, the details of which Johnson took from a earlier published accounts – seems to modern scholarship a complete fabrication. Whether or not Savage believed his own story, or whether he was a deliberate impostor, will probably never be known, although a modern biographer, Clarence Tracy, concludes that whatever the truth may have been, Savage himself believed what he said. Johnson's account is thus factually unreliable, and one recent study (*Dr Johnson and Mr Savage,* by Richard Holmes, 1993) accuses Johnson of consciously suppressing incriminating facts and changing certain dates to improve a portrait of a man he has plainly found, against his best moral instincts, attractive. Savage, with a flair for self-promotion and a knack for attracting the attentions of many worthy people, did indeed seem magnetic for Johnson, about a dozen years his junior, and

Johnson's account has been read as implying a good deal about murkier reaches of the young Johnson's own character – neurotic, sexually tortured, and attracted to the darkly glamorous world of a hard-drinking, bold, violent impostor. Such readings would explain in part the older Johnson's tolerance for such wayward younger friends as James Boswell, or his sympathy for a convicted forger such as Dr. William Dodd whom Johnson worked to save from the scaffold in 1777.

Savage's career of brazen solicitation of help and goodwill, then its rejection, and then a turning on the friendly source fueled an almost deliberate need to feel rejected. Writing, unusually, of a writer he had known personally, Johnson breaks through to a compelling study of psychopathological irresponsibility. He was sensitive to the inner tumult that made Savage's writing possible, and he was subtly aware of the unstable political conditions of the Walpole era that compelled the need to construct a social identity in writing. Savage's case illustrates in one intensive form the need in the wake of the English civil war and the early-eighteenth-century Whig ascendancy to build a social rank in writing without an identity anchored to aristocracy. *The Life of Mr. Richard Savage* is an antiromance: the hero was not secretly an aristocrat but rather believed himself to have been an aristocrat in the beginning, denied his birthright. Savage (suffering, Johnson says, from "vanity, the most innocent species of pride") was actuated by a sense of his intrinsic worth, which he felt it was society's duty to match with reward. By turns gracious and charming and then violently indignant and quarrelsome, Savage moved in depressingly recurrent rhythms of neglect and rescue by friends, temporary restitution, and a downward spiral. He showed "obstinate adherence to his own resolutions, however absurd." Johnson is simultaneously fascinated and repelled by Savage's sensationally lurid, poverty-stricken life, including a conviction for murder, then, after the interposition of friends, a reprieve; recurrent hunger; a willful homelessness; prosecution for obscenity; and chronic indignation against those who sought to help him. Savage spent nights sometimes "in cellars among the riot and filth of the meanest and most profligate of the rabble." "Having no profession," Johnson says starkly, Savage "became by necessity an author."

The lapse of the Licensing Act in 1695 had made for an explosion in the printing trade. Looking back on the eighteenth century from the nineteenth, Thomas Carlyle called it the "Age of Paper." Writing of all kinds proliferated, and reading markets expanded rapidly: the commercial presses participated in a reciprocal traffic with the spread of education and literacy, opened the way for vigorous publishing entrepreneurs, and created the newly emergent figure of the professional writer. The most central of the literary battles of the early eighteenth century involved, especially for the Pope–Jonathan Swift–Henry St. John, Viscount Bolingbroke circle, an attempt to hold on to the high cultural ground of literature against the onslaught of Grub Street hordes. Yet Johnson, throughout his career, had an insider's understanding of the commercial pressures on authorship. In his life of Pope, Johnson lavishes praise on Pope's Homeric translations yet stresses at the same time that they must be understood as a commercial coup. Debarred from civic office and other lucrative career avenues by his Roman Catholicism, Pope had to make money as a writer, while seeming to himself to occupy the moral high ground against the commercially minded hacks of Grub Street. Johnson's emphases in the *Prefaces* on commercial careers constitute less indictments of mercenary motivation than acknowledgments of sheer necessity. (The prefaces themselves issued from a commercial publishing venture.) Pope, no less than the angrily reckless Savage, wrote out of complex impulses: a proud, vexed relationship to the worlds of commercial publishing and aristocratic patronage. Both, socially disenfranchised, needed to make money to live. Both, without the older social anchors of aristocratic birth, had a need to assert the ego or impress it on both contemporary society and posterity through authorial fame.

The portrait of Savage provides English biography's first version of the figure of writer as heroically isolated, alienated, and existentially adrift. But more subtly, in allegory or outline, Johnson's life of him implies the struggle of the English character to remake or redocument itself in writing after the profound social changes of the seventeenth-century civil war. In the larger narrative Johnson invokes a time – the Walpole era – of political instability and a man, without the markers of birth to define him, seeking to fashion a social identity in writing. Like that of Johnson's poem *London,* it is a time of irrational or corrupt dispensations of favor. Without the class anchors of earlier periods of English history, the distinctive self is alienated and unrecognized, adrift in a cultural void. A product of history, of cultural contingency, Savage could only achieve secure social recognition through an entry into the world of authorship, at this point poised awkwardly between domination by aristocratic patrons and the needs of the commercial press.

Johnson's moral recoil from Savage is real, but so is the sympathy that emerges for this social outcast proudly bent on avoiding a need for dependence on erratic, vain aristocrats. Johnson's later major lives are delicately poised between moral censure and tolerance. Johnson, on occasion a stern moral preceptor in his life and writings, could also be benign, flexible, and forgiving with a capacious sense of human weakness and frailty.

Savage's writings are rambling but not without their powerful moments. He published *The Convocation* (1717) and *The Bastard* (1728), an attack on Lady Macclesfield, with a celebration of his illegitimacy and a passage that ends with the often-quoted lines:

Blest be the Bastard's birth!
No sickly fruit of faint compliance he;
He! stampt in nature's mint of extasy!
He lives to build, not boast, a gen'rous race:
No tenth transmitter of a foolish face.

His *The Wanderer,* in five cantos, was published in 1729. He wrote two plays, *Love in a Veil* (produced 1718; published 1719) and *The Tragedy of Sir Thomas Overbury* (produced 1723; published 1724), and other odes and satires including "The Progress of a Divine" (1735). He was for a time awarded a pension by Queen Caroline for providing her with an annual birthday ode. Most likely his work would now be little read had he not been a youthful companion of Johnson and the subject of this life. The first edition of *The Life of Mr. Richard Savage* was published in February 1744, a revised second edition in 1748, and a third edition (with the lives of Drake and Blake) in 1767. Johnson used it again in his *Prefaces,* in a slight revision of the first version. A twentieth-century biographer of Johnson, W. Jackson Bate, notes the critical role of this life in the development of Johnson's own career as a life writer and, as a consequence, much subsequent practice in literary biography: by "engrafting into the story of Savage's life a discussion of his writings – in order both to understand his inner life and to do justice to what was, after all, Savage's principal effort – Johnson invented 'critical biography'. . . . Here, in this anonymous rapidly written Life, Johnson created the prototype of his own Lives of the Poets, written at the end of his own career, which in turn have served as the prototype of [subsequent] 'critical biography.' "

Johnson's work in other modes continued. For the bookseller Thomas Osborne he helped prepare a catalogue of the great Harleian Library (five volumes, 1743–1745) and contributed to *The Harleian Miscellany* (1744). The mid 1740s saw the first stirrings of the great lexicographical and edi-

A meeting of The Club at Joshua Reynolds's house, showing (left to right) Boswell, Johnson, Reynolds, David Garrick, Edmund Burke, Pasquale Paoli, Charles Burney, Thomas Warton, and Oliver Goldsmith (engraving by William Walker after a painting by James Doyle)

torial undertakings that would propel Johnson to extraordinary eminence and authority as a man of letters. In 1745 proposals (not successful) for an edition of Shakespeare's plays were made, and Johnson published his *Miscellaneous Observations on the Tragedy of Macbeth*. In June of the next year he signed the contract for his *A Dictionary of the English Language* (1755), and in 1747 he published *The Plan of a Dictionary of the English Language*. The plan was dedicated to Philip Dormer, Earl of Chesterfield, who notoriously neglected Johnson while he labored then belatedly sought to attach his name and support when the project neared completion. Johnson's later indignant riposte (in his letter of 7 February 1755) shows him at his trenchant best and stands as a landmark (although Johnson continued to produce prefatory dedications to patrons) in the eighteenth-century move away from aristocratic patronage to fully professional authorship, with literary work making its own way in the literary marketplace.

The dictionary and the edition of Shakespeare occupied Johnson for about twenty years. Yet other writings, biography again prominent among them, flowed plentifully from his pen all the while. In 1747, at Garrick's request, he wrote a prologue for the opening of the season at Drury Lane Theatre; the prologue is a compact, sixty-two line summary of the course of English theater from Shakespeare and Ben Jonson, through the racy Restoration wits, through neoclassical tragedy, to the early-eighteenth-century delight in stage spectacle. The poem moves to some characteristic Johnsonian thoughts on fashion and ephemeral appeal: "Hard is his lot that here by fortune place / Must watch the wild vicissitudes of taste, / With every meteor of caprice must play, / And chase the new-blown bubbles of the day." In the end he adroitly notes the reciprocal relation between theatrical vogue and audience preference: "The stage but echoes back the public voice," he says, and he places moral responsibility for the conduct of the theater in the audience's hands. In later prefaces to plays Johnson returns to the question of the ephemeral appeal of most theater, and he indicts authors who rest their hopes for fame in the "claps of multitudes." Fashions, vogues, and fleeting appeal are dependent on the vagaries of social, cultural, and ideological context: as governments and factions strive for supremacy, theater can only mirror and echo the temperament of the times.

In 1748 Johnson published a life of Wentworth Dillon, Earl of Roscommon, in the May *Gentleman's Magazine* – an account which he rewrote substantially for the later *Prefaces*. In 1749 he published the resonant *Vanity of Human Wishes,* modeled on the tenth Satire of Juvenal – the first of Johnson's published works to bear his name. The poem offers a solemnly turned meditation on topics which would occupy him throughout his biographical work: change and permanence, the meaning of individual accomplishment in the scale of mortality, and the ways in which literature might or might not endure in the face of the ephemeral and local effects of military and political history. Johnson soberly indicts both the "weekly scribbler" (the hired hack writer) and the ambitious scholar, whose veins burn with the "fever of renown": "Unnumber'd Suppliants croud Preferment's Gate," but "Delusive Fortune hears th'incessant Call, / They mount, they shine, evaporate and fall." The Johnsonian vantage point is established in the opening couplet: "Let observation with extensive view, / Survey mankind, from China to Peru" – presaging the comprehensive, knowledgeable, abstracting, almost Olympian perspective of the biographical critic of the *Prefaces*. But the poem, like the "Lives of the Poets," depends on a generalizing detachment informed at all points by a complex engagement with particulars: in thunderous closed couplets Johnson summarizes the rise and fall of named statesmen, famous beauties, conquerors, and learned men. The *Prefaces* offers extended prose elaborations, even demonstrations, of this poem's central theme – in accounts of writers, usually the ones Johnson regards as minor, impelled by self-delusion, vanity, and folly, led on by the pursuit of delusive hope. Before ending with an appeal – out of a sense that "Life protracted is protracted Woe" – to a stoically Christian hope in the next world, the poem makes a subtle but potent claim for durability: after chronicling the ignominious fall of the once-great Charles XII of Sweden, Johnson notes sardonically that the monarch has left a name only "to point a Moral, or adorn a Tale." The satiric poet, with a totalizing and abstracting vision, can find moral meaning in the sorry trajectory of the human ambition to fame. The same sentiment informs the generally antipanegyrical strain of many of his prefatory lives, illustrating that whatever writerly ambitions originally impelled the seekers of literary immortality, their careers are all at last subsumed in a mordant narrative to point a moral and adorn a tale.

Johnson's only stage play, *Irene,* a tragedy in blank verse with a Turkish setting, was acted in 1749. Although not usually regarded as a theatrical success, the play, produced by Garrick, ran for a more-than-respectable nine nights and brought the author the considerable sum of three hundred pounds. In 1750 he began his extraordinary series of essays in the *Rambler,* in which can be found, among meditations on a wide array of social, moral, and aesthetic topics, some of his most considered pronouncements on literature. His 1751 "Life of Cheynel" (Dr. Francis Cheynel, a Puritan parliamentary divine) was included in *The Student, or the Oxford and Cambridge Monthly Miscellany*. It was reprinted in the *Gentleman's Magazine* for March and April 1775. In this piece Johnson frankly discloses his hostility to his subject and opens his account with some thoughts on his own role as biographer in preserving the memory of one not very worthy of such treatment. Johnson characteristically disdains Cheynel's parliamentary sympathies in the English civil war and sees them as the issue of "a turbulent, obstinate and petulant" temperament. There are intimations here of Johnson's complex position in the later and greater life of Milton, the single most controversial in the *Prefaces,* in which the "acrimonious and surly" republicanism of the poet and Milton's domineering domestic character are both severely indicted yet seen as inseparable from the poetic abilities responsible for the greatness of *Paradise Lost.*

The death of Cave in January 1754 led to Johnson's second biography of a figure he knew well and personally. Johnson's affectionate but coolly measured "Life of Cave" appeared in the *Gentleman's Magazine* for February 1754, and a revised version appeared in the second edition of the *Biographia Britannica* in 1784.

In 1756 Johnson published an edition of Sir Thomas Browne's *Christian Morals* (written in the 1650s and first published in 1716) with a substantial prefatory life. Browne was much admired by Johnson, who had mined his works frequently for illustrative quotations in *A Dictionary of the English Language*. Browne was an anti-Puritan and convinced Royalist, knighted by Charles II, and much of his thinking Johnson found congenial, especially his religious and ethical meditations. Johnson's edition and prefatory life contributed to a renewal of interest in Browne's work among eighteenth-century readers. A life of Frederick the Great of Prussia appeared in three monthly issues of the *Literary Magazine* (November and December 1756, January

Page from Johnson's notes, left (British Library) for "Preface to Pope" and a page from the manuscript, right (MA 205, Pierpont Morgan Library), for the same work

108

Of genius, that power which constitutes a poet, that quality without which judgement is cold, and knowledge is inert, that energy which collects, combines, amplifies, and animates, the superiority must, with some hesitation, be allowed to Dryden. It is not to be inferred that of this poetical vigour Pope had only a little, because Dryden had more, for every other writer since Milton, must give place to Pope, and even of Dryden it must be said that he has brighter paragraphs, but not better poems. Dryden's performances were always hasty, either elicited by some external occasion, or extorted by domestick necessity. he composed with little consideration, and published with little correction. When his mind could supply at call, or gather in one excursion was all that he sought, and all that he gave. The dilatory caution of Pope enabled him to condense his sentiments, to multiply his images, and to accumulate whatever study might produce, or chance might supply. The flights of Dryden therefore are higher, but Pope continues longer on the wing. Of Dryden's fire the blaze is brighter, of Pope's the heat is regular and constant. Dryden often surpasses expectation, and Pope never falls below it. Dryden is read with frequent astonishment, and Pope with perpetual delight.

1757). In the year of the emperor's death, 1786 (two years after Johnson's own), Johnson's account was republished, with a continuation by William Mavor. Johnson contributed anonymously a life of Roger Ascham to James Bennet's *English Works of Roger Ascham* (1761). The poet William Collins, with whom Johnson was acquainted, died in 1759. Johnson wrote a memoir of him for *The Poetical Calendar* (1763); the memoir was reprinted in the *Gentleman's Magazine* for January 1764. Johnson augmented and revised it slightly for inclusion among the prefaces. It is, with the life of Thomas Gray, an important index of Johnson's deep unease at the emergence in his own time of a poetry of sensibility, with its emotional and imaginative challenges to the tradition of Dryden and Pope for which the Johnson of the prefaces shows a conservative nostalgia.

These lives, memoirs, and prefatory accounts, although bearing some of the hallmarks of Johnson's maturer criticism and biography, were again on the whole incidental to his other, more serious pursuits. Between 1750 and 1752 the *Rambler* essays appeared – sturdy, lucid, solemnly witty prose sermons in a line of descent from the *Tatler* and *Spectator* essays of Joseph Addison and Sir Richard Steele in the earlier part of the century. Usually written at the rate of two a week, the essays contained, among much other social and moral commentary, in scattered and less than systematic ways many expressions of the biographical and especially critical beliefs and assumptions that would inform the *Prefaces*. Johnson's well-known and often-quoted *Rambler* number 60 essay (13 October 1750) amounts almost to a biographical manifesto, or at least the cleverest expression of Johnson's belief in the moral efficacy of biographical literature: "All joy or sorrow for the happiness or calamities of others is produced by an act of the imagination, that realizes the event however fictitious, or approximates it however remote, by placing us, for a time, in the condition of him whose fortune we contemplate; so that we feel, while the deception lasts, whatever motions would be excited by the same good or evil happening to ourselves." The whole essay, much discussed, excerpted, and anthologized, should of course be read and savored, but Johnson's central point emerges in the third paragraph: "Those parallel circumstances, and kindred images, to which we readily conform our minds, are, above all other writings, to be found in narratives of the lives of particular persons; and therefore no species of writing seems more worthy of cultivation than biography, since none can be more delightful or more useful, none can more certainly enchain the heart by ir-

resistible interest, or more widely diffuse instruction to every diversity of condition." Johnson's claims here summarize not just his attraction to a morally efficacious biographical literature but suggest also the terms of his assessment of poetry itself: it must instruct by pleasing, and the sources of that pleasure lie in an empathetic transaction between reader and text. Johnson's thoughts on biography, and his judgments of poetry that appear in his *Prefaces,* involve an affective empathy. His assessments turn outward from work to reader, to whom a writer owes pleasurable recognitions in familiar thoughts made new and new thoughts made familiar. In the success of such a transaction a poem's merit is to be located, not in any writer's own (usually deluded) sense of merit or success.

The year 1752 saw the end of the *Rambler* series. It saw, too, the death of Johnson's wife, Tetty, unfortunately a rather shadowy figure about whom only a few anecdotes survive. Johnson's fondness for her was deep and real, judging from the prayers and meditations he wrote in memory of her during the rest of his life. In 1753 he contributed about thirty miscellaneous pieces, like the *Rambler* essays, to another literary magazine, the *Adventurer,* edited by his friend John Hawkesworth, and was at work on the second volume of his dictionary. In 1755 he was awarded an honorary M.A. degree by Oxford University, and his dictionary was at last published on 15 April, in two folio volumes.

Literary journalism drew him in again soon enough, and in 1756 he began editing the short-lived *Literary Magazine,* in which he published a valuable critical assessment of Joseph Warton's important *Essay on the Genius and Writings of Pope* (1756) and a fierce review, in three parts, of the deistic *Free Inquiry into the Nature and Origin of Evil* (1757), by Soame Jenyns. Amid his customary flurry of introductions, prefatory essays, and dedications for others' editions, plays, poems, and novels, he returned to his long-held ambition for an edition of Shakespeare's plays. The *Proposals for Printing* for his edition of Shakespeare to be published by subscription appeared in June 1756. Another essay series, written as "The Idler" for the *Universal Chronicle,* occupied him from 1758 to 1760. These pieces, on the whole lighter and briefer than the *Rambler* essays, remain highly readable and critically important. *Idler* number 85 (24 November 1759) summarizes some of Johnson's most considered thoughts on the relative value of biography and autobiography: "He that writes the life of another is either his friend or his enemy, and wishes either to exalt his praise or aggravate his infamy." Johnson's characteristic procedure in his *Prefaces,* except where he draws on his own acquaintanceships and considerable firsthand knowledge of writers and books, involves soundly differing from, or exposing the apparent hyperbole in, the claims of early biographers of his subjects. A central ambition of his biographies remains the drive for authoritative modes of assessment that transcend local, ephemeral partisanship or enmity.

In January 1759 Johnson's mother died at the age of ninety in Lichfield, and Johnson, according to his own report, to pay for the funeral expenses, wrote in the evenings of one week his ironic, solemnly comic, philosophical fable *The History of Rasselas.* In 1762, in recognition of his extraordinary career as a man of letters, Johnson was awarded his annual pension of three hundred pounds by the Crown, and he at last had a measure of financial security and stability. In May 1763 the young Scotsman Boswell first made Johnson's acquaintance and began noting in his diaries his memories of Johnson's conversation that would form the basis for the artfully re-created conversational vignettes in his *Life of Samuel Johnson* (1791). In 1764 the well-known Club (later the Literary Club) had its beginnings, at the suggestion of Johnson's close friend the painter Sir Joshua Reynolds. Other early members included Oliver Goldsmith, Edmund Burke, and the antiquarian Bishop Thomas Percy. In later years the number would grow to include many of the period's most illustrious figures in literary and social circles. In July 1765 Johnson received his honorary LL.D. from Trinity College, Dublin. In October 1765, after many delays, the edition of Shakespeare's works was published, and in the same year his long friendship with the Thrales began. The pace of his writing slowed somewhat as his health deteriorated and bouts of intense depression followed – glimpses of which are in the records kept by Hester Lynch Thrale (later Mrs. Piozzi) as the relationship between them, and Johnson's dependence on the Thrale household, grew and deepened.

Starting in 1766 in Oxford, Johnson helped Robert Chambers compose his massive Vinerian lectures on English law. In the same year he helped bring into print some poems by the blind Anna Williams, who had been befriended by Johnson's wife and, bequeathed to his care, now lived as a member of his household. The slight collection, *Miscellanies in Prose and Verse,* was fleshed out with contributions from Johnson and other friends, including Johnson's curious, almost sardonic, fairy tale "The Fountains," treating in the guise of a children's story some of the themes of *Rasselas* and *The Vanity of Human Wishes.* An obituary on the Reverend Zachariah Mudge, whom Johnson had met during a visit to Plymouth with Reynolds in 1762, was written for the *London Chronicle* (April–May 1769). Vigorous political writing reappeared in *The False Alarm* (1770), *Thoughts on the Late Transactions Respecting Falkland's Islands* (1771), *The Patriot* (1774), and his anti-American *Taxation No Tyranny* (1775). In 1773 revised editions of the *Dictionary* and his Shakespeare edition appeared, and he made his tour of Scotland and its Highlands and Western Isles (the Hebrides) with Boswell. Boswell's vivid account of the tour, both a memoir of Johnson and a complex vision of Scotish/English relations from the perspective of the postunion Scot, was published in 1785, a year after Johnson's death. In 1774 Johnson visited Wales, where Hester Thrale was born, with the Thrales and went with them to Paris in 1775. (His diaries of these visits were published in 1816.) Also in 1775 he published his *Journey to the Western Islands of Scotland,* in which his career-long concerns with change, flux, and permanence and the evanescence of human culture are expressed on a national scale as he ponders the vanished Highland ways of life in postunion Scotland, effectively destroyed as an independent polity after the failed Jacobite uprising of 1745 and since ruled from Westminster. More public and offical recognition of his eminence followed: he was awarded an honorary D.C.L. by Oxford University.

In 1777 Johnson agreed with the consortium of London publishers to write prefaces for an edition of works of a century of English poets. These prefaces, the great achievement of Johnson's later career, have become popularly known as "The Lives of the Poets." The first four volumes of these prefaces appeared in 1779 and the final six in 1781. The prefaces offer grand surveys of the careers of several major poets, dramatists, and critics whose careers had been decisive and formative in the mainstream eighteenth-century poetic tradition, including the lives of Cowley (with its highly influential account of the "Metaphysical School,") Milton, Dryden, Addison, and Pope. A second tier treats John Denham; Samuel Butler; John Wilmot; Earl of Rochester; Edmund Waller; Thomas Parnell; Elizabeth Singer Rowe; Matthew Prior; William Congreve; John Gay; Swift; James Thomson; and Edward Young, to all of whom Johnson is willing to attribute some work of lasting distinction. Even among his accounts of versifiers Johnson considers barely worthy of notice, quotable nuggets are to be found: from the life of John Hughes comes the splendid definition of Italian opera as "an exotick and irrational entertainment, which has always been combated and always has prevailed." Poets of sensibility – Collins, Mark Akenside, and Gray – are treated on the whole frostily, though Johnson shows a moving sympathy for the disordered Collins, and his shining praise for Gray's well-known *Elegy on a Country Churchyard* (1751) offers a valuable sense of Johnson's notion of "the common reader." In all, the collection offers – in a highly distinctive combination of derivative lives, assessments of character, and illustrative critical readings – fifty-two poets' lives, arranged chronologically by date of death; their deaths came in the years between the mid seventeenth century and the decade in which the edition was conceived. The source materials are supplemented in some cases with Johnson's own firsthand knowledge and in almost all cases with Johnson's characteristic, skeptical, choric commentaries on and challenges to his source authors. The voice that speaks in these prefaces is that of a confident, successful, public man of letters, free to speak autobiographically, both to summarize judiciously received positions by invoking terms familiar in midcentury aesthetics and boldly to declare his own preferences and prejudices. Johnson's judgments on poets and poetry are frequently severe and just as frequently forgiving – embodying the values of balance and proportion he prized in poetry itself – and his tone ranges from caustic censure to mordant playfulness. These prefaces constitute in some ways the summary issue of his own intense lifelong engagement with the world of letters at every level, theoretical and practical, as he sensed his own life and career nearing a close. Many friends had by this time died – among them Goldsmith in 1774 and Garrick in 1779 – and Johnson finds moments to pay fond tribute to them in his *Prefaces*. He also finds ways to mention fondly his father and a friend of his youth, Gilbert Walmsley, and other friends and associates.

Henry Thrale died in 1781, and the death of one of Johnson's housemates in 1782 led to his elegy "On the Death of Dr Robert Levet." Johnson's last years were spent amid much illness and depression. It came as a severe blow to him when the widowed Mrs. Thrale, whom he deeply loved, chose to marry the Italian musician Gabriel Piozzi; the occasion led to Johnson's well-known anguished letter to her of 8 July 1784. In 1783 he suffered a stroke. He died on 13 December 1784 at his house in Bolt Court and was buried on 20 December in Westminster Abbey.

During his final illness Johnson burned a great mass of his private papers. His *Prayers and Medita-*

tions were published the next year, and his work and life soon became the center of a busy literary and biographical industry. In *Samuel Johnson, Biographer* (1978) Robert Folkenflik summarizes Johnson's own saturation in the world of biography and remarks on how Johnson in turn became a figure of intense biographical scrutiny: "if we limit our inquiry to the members of the Johnson circle and those just outside its circumference, we will not find before or after as impressive a group of biographers." In conversation and private letters as well as in his public essays, Johnson urged his friends to biographical activity, not only in the recording of public figures but for the purpose of preserving the kinds of private virtue worthy of emulation which otherwise would sink quietly. Johnson himself had projected or contemplated many more lives than the ones he wrote, and several accounts of Johnson's character and writings, of highly variable reliability, had already appeared during his lifetime. Boswell's Hebridean journal, revised with the help of the scholar Edmond Malone into a memoir of Johnson, appeared in 1785; Piozzi's *Anecdotes* in March 1786 and her *Letters* in 1788; and Sir John Hawkins, one of Johnson's literary executors, published the first book-length *Life of Samuel Johnson* as the first volume of the first collected edition of Johnson's works in 1787. Several useful memoirs by various hands appeared through the late 1780s, and the first edition of Boswell's life was published in May 1791.

Even in this necessarily brief and selective summary of Johnson's authorial career, biography emerges as a consistent concern, and the moral, literary, and aesthetic issues that preoccupied him in his copious and disparate oeuvre find their way back to life writing more often than not. It seems deeply appropriate that Johnson's first significant critical essay was an "Essay on Epitaphs" and what seems to have been his last published piece of writing was a brief obituary account of Styan Thirlby, a theologian and man of letters, some of whose Shakespearian emendations Johnson had used in his edition of 1765. The obituary appeared as part of a longer account of Thirlby in the *Gentleman's Magazine* for April and December 1784. Peter Conrad writes of Johnson's affinity with the "ancestral conscience" of art, "for conserving and remembering," and relates the "Lives of the Poets" to Johnson's sense, expressed in his other writings, on the importance of the human need to mourn and to remember.

In his early work for the periodical press Johnson wrote for a general readership which had an al-

*Mezzotint of Johnson by James Watson after a portrait by Sir
Joshua Reynolds*

most insatiable appetite for short biographies, literary ancestors of the modern journalistic profile. The period that produced the rise of the novel and the emergence of a poetry of sensibility, both largely Anglo-French developments, saw a general deepening of literate society's fascination with its own workings and a deepened exploration of the workings of individual human consciousness expressed in literary form. The same period thus saw an increasingly sophisticated historiography, the rise of the personal letter (and the establishment of the Post Office), a fictional literature of psychological introspection (in England most notably associated with the novels of Samuel Richardson, with whom Johnson was friendly and whom he finds a moment to praise in his life of Congreve), medical and psychological self-help books, and a huge ex-

pansion in the general magazine market, as literate society came more and more to want to see itself represented.

Johnson, suspicious on the whole of fiction and especially of what he saw as the dangerously corrosive powers of the unfettered imagination, wrote more often than not solidly within documentary, factual modes. His early biographies are efficient popularizations with important flashes of the distinctive Johnson in them. The early lives tend to show affinities with romance narrative and with the generally eulogistic and panegyric quality of the sources on which he drew. The distinctive Johnsonian voice emerges in moments of challenge to the credulity of the authors of his source materials. Kaminski observes that Johnson's commentaries in the early lives issue from his "insights into human motivation and his staunch determination to see mere men where others might see heroes provided the basis for his commentaries." As Kaminski shows, Johnson's talents appear in analysis rather than investigation, in "questioning the assumptions or attacking the credulity of the original writers." The same talents and limitations are on display in the *Prefaces*. The *Prefaces* develops not from the derivative traces of eulogy and panegyric but precisely from those moments of sober, deflationary commentary. Isobel Grundy suggests in *Samuel Johnson and the Scale of Greatness* (1986) that Johnson's earliest biographies, written for the *Gentleman's Magazine* between 1738 and 1742, "deal with two groups whom he loved to compare as contenders for fame: thinkers and men of action." She argues that Johnson's attitudes shift significantly in his later lives: the early biographies "invest the thinkers with the same glamour that surrounds the soldiers and explorers, an aura of heroism unmatched in Johnson's later works," and "exalt greatness into heroism as Johnson never does again." The *Prefaces* shows "changes in Johnson's underlying assumptions since the years of his earlier biographies. . . . The *Gentleman's Magazine* pieces show their heroes winning their way, as the young Johnson had once hoped to do, through sheer force of native ability; the 'Lives of the Poets' show greatness as much more hazardous."

Johnson's "Lives of the Poets," broadly conforming to a tripartite structure – a biographical account, a description of character, and an assessment of the works – seeks to establish the contexts in which poetry must be assessed and understood. The contexts and their integrated quality often appear implicitly rather than explicitly, again because the lives were written to meet the needs of a specific publication and do not comprise anything like a systematic treatise. Yet certain emphases remain consistent. The passage on Pope's ill-formed, morally and politically suspect theory of the ruling passion appears in the last of the prefaces to be written, but the principle it addresses appears in the first of the fifty-two, the life of Cowley, the one which, in the act of composition, decisively settled Johnson's conception of the whole project. The life of Cowley, in its still critically valuable account of the Metaphysical school, put into critical circulation the concept of poetic school and generic grouping. Johnson thoroughly disliked that particular school – a "Pindarick madness," he thinks, had possession of the poets of that time – as it violated Johnson's late-Augustan preferences for metrical (and by implication conceptual and political) smoothness, elegance, balance, and harmony. It featured coldly, intellectually playful wit that sought to dazzle without moving the reader's emotions to experiences of the sublime or the pathetic. Yet Johnson seeks to do justice to Cowley's oeuvre by accounting for the contemporary canons of taste, specifically for the "wit" of the metaphysical conceit, created by the wider group of poets (of whom the most widely read today remains John Donne) with which Cowley associated himself.

That principle remains at the core of later advanced critical practices, other than strictly formalist ones: however much human nature and passion might remain (as in Imlac's much-debated assertion) ahistorically the same, any authorial production is distorted if it stands in isolation, assessed in contexts inappropriate to its period and circumstances of its composition. Prevailing political climates, the vagaries of publication markets, readerly expectation, and economic circumstances change with time. Even the psychology of authorship (in which Johnson was deeply interested, especially in its anxious vanity expressed as a drive for fame) discloses itself differently in different social contexts. Milton's vain, acrimonious independence expressed itself politically as a fiery republicanism and poetically in an epic that sought to dominate its readers; Addison, similarly vain and conscious of superior powers, but in the milder post-Restoration atmosphere, wanted to introduce advanced aesthetic theory to a general readership in the form of the urbane essay. Poetry must be assessed in the contexts of genre, of period taste and style, of social expectations, and of vogues for expression (in which Johnson as philologist and lexicographer was again deeply interested). In one notably Lockean moment Johnson declares that "words being arbitrary must owe their power to association" and "have the influence, and that only, which custom has given them." In the larger scheme the productions of any poet, similarly, belong to a biographical context (sometimes in the lives inseparable from a commercial career, and that context belongs to a larger political one.)

Johnson's earlier work on Shakespeare espoused the principle of historical method in textual scholarship and expressed it in the first important attempt at a variorum textual presentation. Similarly, his dictionary, however flawed, marked an advance in historical etymology, acknowledging that words change meaning over time and that, in the words of the preface (like his preface to the 1765 edition of Shakespeare, a resonant meditation on flux, change, and evanescence in both language and the procedures of intellectual scholarship), one cannot enchain syllables and lash the wind. The aim of the edition of Shakespeare, though its preface conceded the task's ultimate impossibility, was to fix the text of the plays and rescue them forever from textual impreciseness. In his *Dictionary of the English Language* Johnson sought, though acknowledging again the tasks's impossibility, to stabilize the English language. In the lives, even while seeking to contribute to a national poetic canon by applying certain critical precepts and principles and to rescue the assessment of poetry from the disorder of a wayward, untutored "taste" (such as Dick Minim's, the figure parodied in the *Rambler* essays), Johnson remains too self-aware to imagine that he confers permanent merit or that his own local judgments will stand inscribed forever. In fact, despite many forthrightly phrased local, personal statements of preference and disapproval, he departs in no fundamental ways from the thought of his most admired precursors in the Restoration and Queen Anne periods (Dryden, Addison, and Pope). Importantly, the lives do not fix; they preface: they summarize thought that has gone before, and, while Johnson by no means shirked what he characteristically saw as the moral responsibility of firm position taking, he knew that he followed in the trail of a conversation with ancient origins and preceded a future debate. "Prefaces" they remain, designed in their original conception to precede a readerly engagement with the poems themselves and to lift that engagement to sophisticated critical levels. Even the terms in which, say, Pope's translations of Homer are praised suggest as much: Pope's *Iliad* (1715–1720), "a performance which no age or nation can pretend to equal," is in the end "a treasure of poetical elegances to posterity." The business of a poet, again according to Imlac (in a formulation drawn on later by Percy Bysshe Shelley), is to write "as the interpreter of nature, and the legislator of mankind . . . presiding over the thoughts and manners of future generations." Johnson is thus engaged in what Lipking calls a "perpetual commentary." No dogmatist, Johnson essays various quasi-definitional summaries of poetry, pleasure, diction, genius, and sublimity, but he knows, as he puts it in *Rambler* number 125, that it "is one of the maxims of the civil law, that 'definitions are hazardous.' "

Johnson wrote his prefaces when he was well advanced in years, confident and secure in his eminence as a man of letters after a long and frequently arduous career. The tone of these late pieces has been well caught by Paul Fussell, who calls them both elegiac and satiric; he notes astutely that the shadow of the Roman biographer Suetonius falls over Johnson's practice – trenchant, mordant, and dolefully ironic. Johnson deeply understood writerly self-delusion and wrote of it with an irony that Fussell terms either "overtly or covertly comical" but "softened by an elegiac twilight." Preface after preface chronicles the bad luck, botched aspirations, vagaries in the marketplace, changes in political fashion, erratic patrons, and promises half-made and unkept that dog the candidates for literary fame. Writer after writer overestimates his own powers, makes errors of judgment, has hopes blasted, and is impelled by venality, vanity, and opportunism masquerading as principle. Yet, within his generally antipanegyric framework and within a generally Augustan scale of values that invokes orthodox eighteenth-century aesthetic terms and principles, Johnson emerges as surprisingly flexible, even forgiving: balanced, generous, benign, and occasionally downright jaunty. His sense of the importance of contexts, of the pressures – psychological, economic, and political – on writing, had been earned by his own lifelong engagement with the world of letters at every level, of which world he writes as a richly informed, knowing insider. When authorial vanity does break through to a work of enduring greatness, Johnson pays thunderous tribute.

The prefaces were tailored for an intelligent and nonspecialist readership and were written in clear, accessible prose. Although he does invoke the critical commonplaces and conceptions of eighteenth-century aesthetics, he says he is "not writing only to poets and philosophers." His attempts to account for wit, genius, and the pleasures of poetry are not essays in original definition but attempts to clarify aesthetic concepts – derived from Lockean psychology and their popularization in the essays of Addison – for a general readership. Johnson was a scholar, but also, for important and formative parts of his career, a journalist and a teacher, and his aims here were many. In his criticism he sought to use, but move beyond, an aridly local analysis of "beauties" and "faults," residue of neoclassical critical methods, and to secure evaluative assessments of poetry in ways that escape the limits of immediate enthusiams. He aimed to locate the value of poetry in the morally efficacious transaction between poet and reader, involving the pleasurable recognitions of familiar truths. He sought to situate poets in valuable connections with earlier traditions but simultaneously to assess originality. He sought to situate poets and poetry in larger groupings, or schools, to understand historically contingent uses of language. Whatever agreements and disagreements his local judgments arouse, his reasons for them are made thoroughly clear. Implicitly, the prefaces mount a rearguard defense of the tradition of Dryden and Pope against the rise of a poetry of sensibility, associated with the newer poets such as Mark Akenside, Collins, and Gray. One can trace, in outline over the course of Johnson's unsystematic survey of a century of poetry, poetry's arduous arrival at a season of calm, in the world of late-Hanoverian Britain threatened with more tumults. Johnson wrote in the decade that saw the American Revolution and the stirrings of discontent against absolutism in France, and he sensed in the imaginative energies let loose by a poetry of sensibility hints of the catastrophic internecine strife of the English civil war, with which his survey begins, in the time of Cowley and Milton.

Before the complex accomplishment of the lives is discussed, some context should be provided for the genesis of the project — itself a fascinating and revealing episode in the history of the eighteenth-century book trade. On Easter Eve in 1777 a group deputed by a meeting of thirty-six of London's leading booksellers called on the eminent essayist, biographer, poet, playwright, lexicographer, critic, and editor Johnson. The group, made up of Johnson's old friends William Strahan, Thomas Cadell, and Thomas Davies (in whose bookshop in 1763 Boswell memorably first made Johnson's acquaintance), came to solicit his interest in a large-scale publishing venture, a comprehensive edition of English poetry covering works from Chaucer to their own time. (The project, as time went on, inevitably was trimmed back to cover roughly the hundred years between the Restoration and the mid eighteenth century.) The booksellers hoped to boost sales as well as lend the weight and authority of Johnson's name to the venture by having him contribute concise prefatory biographical accounts of each poet.

The immediate cause of the publishers' decision to produce a vast collection of the works of the English poets was a perceived threat from the north, an echo of continuing postunion tensions between Scotland and England, particularly as they appeared in the matter of literary copyright and access to the lucrative London and regional book-buying markets. In Edinburgh the Martin brothers, who ran the Apollo Press, had embarked on a large collected edition in small volumes, *The Poets of Great Britain: Complete From Chaucer to Churchill,* which began serial publication in 1777 and ran to 109 octodecimo (small pocket-size) volumes when finished

in June 1783. The Martins' London agent, the enterprising, young, and — in London publishing circles — widely resented John Bell, spearheaded the venture. Bell himself may have been responding to an earlier Scottish edition, *The British Poets,* published by Alexander Kincaid, William Creech, and John Balfour in 44 volumes in Edinburgh between 1773 and 1776, and was no stranger to battles with the established London booksellers: Bell's *British Theatre,* a comprehensive collection of dramatic works in 20 volumes (1776–1778), had sold well and prompted a group of twenty-seven London booksellers to respond with a rival *New English Theatre.*

The Apollo Press project triggered a lively publicity war, in which London booksellers sought to cast doubt on the quality of the Scottish venture, and Bell spiritedly defended himself. The publisher Edward Dilly declared the Apollo Press edition (in a letter now widely known from Boswell's *Life of Samuel Johnson*) an "invasion of what we call our Literary Property" and referred scornfully to Bell's "little trifling edition," accusing it of being shoddily produced with an inconveniently small typeface and many inaccuracies. Dilly spoke, of course, from the point of view of the London consortium, and recent scholarship has shown that Dilly's letter, through the authoritative prominence it achieved via publication by Boswell, is seriously misleading. Thomas F. Bonnell points out that Bell's edition was in fact considerable — typographically well-produced, priced accessibly to bring poetry to an expanding middle-income readership, and handsomely illustrated with engraved portraits of the poets and vignettes from the works commissioned especially for the edition. Boswell himself, writing to Johnson in June 1777, in perhaps a flash of his Scottish pride, spoke well of the Martins' work: "I have seen a specimen of an edition of *The Poets* at the Apollo press, at Edinburgh, which, for excellence in printing and engraving, highly deserves a liberal encouragement."

Bell was, moreover, ambitious to bring to the poems a clarity and uniformity of presentation — associated more usually at this time with editions of the Latin classics — and by implication to confer a stability on English vernacular work. His edition has, thus, considerable significance in literary as well as publishing history. Bell grouped the poems in generic categories (epistles, tales, ballads, odes, and epigrams), excluded translations (to impart a canonical solidity to poetry conceived and written in the vernacular tongue), reprinted significant critical essays (such as Addison's on *Paradise Lost*), and, importantly, prefaced each poet's work with what he termed "a biographical and critical account" to

Saint John's Gate, where the office of Gentleman's Magazine *was located*

gratify the readerly desire "to know something of the man who entertains and edifies us." Bell aimed at "a connected system of biography." These advertising boasts, however, were not fulfilled. His prefatory material was neither connected nor systematic. Ranging from a few paragraphs to more than two hundred pages long, Bell's prefaces were compiled entirely from published sources, chiefly earlier published lives in biographical collections and prefatory accounts of individual authors and general biographical dictionaries, especially the *Biographia Britannica* (1747–1766). But in Bonnell's summary Bell was the first in British publishing history to recognize the need for comprehensive, integrated life-and-works collections. He certainly helped create the market for them. His compilations of lives and works issued from and sought to gratify two concurrent readerly appetites that grew over the course of the eighteenth century: a high cultural aim to establish a secure national repository of writing of lasting value and a desire to know the details of private lives of authors. Authors themselves had become intriguing personalities and objects of a press-fed fascination.

In quick and concerted response the London booksellers decided, in Dilly's words, on an "elegant and accurate edition of all the English Poets of reputation from Chaucer to the present time." Thus "a select number of the most respectable booksellers" met. (Dilly says the number was about forty; thirty-six names appear in the published edition.) They agreed "that all the proprietors of copy-right in the various Poets should be summoned together; and when their opinions were given, to proceed immediately on the business." The idea for the edition, then, was far from original. It fell well short of its original ambitions, did not match Bell's collection in scale and scope, and in the end collected the work of poets, with certain important exceptions, now little read except by scholars specializing in this period. But for the history of literature and literary theory, specifically of literary and biographical criticism, one of the booksellers' decisions turned out to be a masterstroke: to lend the weight of Johnson's name to the edition. "The edition . . . now printing," boasts Dilly in the letter Boswell printed in *The Life of Samuel Johnson,* "will do honour to the English press; and a concise account of the life of each authour, by Dr. Johnson, will be a very valuable addition, and stamp the reputation of this edition superiour to anything that is gone before."

The booksellers themselves, not Johnson, mostly made the choices for inclusion, to cover about a hundred years of poetry from the mid seventeenth to the mid eighteenth century, excluding poets then still living. The original number of poets chosen totaled forty-seven (it rose to fifty-two when Johnson made five suggestions for inclusion), and Johnson was to be asked to contribute short prefatory biographies. Johnson readily agreed with his friends' request and, asked to name his own price, named a startlingly modest two hundred guineas. The booksellers themselves later added another hundred guineas and, at a later stage of publication, a further hundred. In a footnote to Boswell's *Life*, Malone remarks that had "he asked one thousand, or even fifteen hundred guineas, the booksellers, who knew the value of his name, would doubtless have readily given it." Johnson, at sixty-eight years old, now had a measure of financial security, and he probably saw a chance to repay the booksellers who had been his own sources of support in an arduous life of commercial and scholarly writing and of whom he regularly spoke well.

In his diary entry for 29 March 1777 Johnson wrote: "I treated with the booksellers on a bargain, but the time was not long." Boswell believed, and the modern editors of his diary agree, that Johnson was reflecting some scruples about conducting business during the solemn Easter period. But Johnson's ready agreement suggests also that the request accorded with an idea that had been in his thoughts for some time, for a literary history of Britain. He soon set about the task but worked at it only in bursts. To Richard Farmer of Cambridge he wrote in July 1777: "The Booksellers of London have undertaken a kind of Body of English Poetry, excluding generally the dramas, and I have undertaken to put before the each authors [*sic*] work a sketch of his life, and a character of his writings." July saw him working on the project in the Bodleian Library at Oxford. That was followed by recreational visits to Lichfield and Ashbourne: in a 6 September letter he confessed to Hester Thrale that he had "loitered." Steady work followed those visits, but in his letters he complained of ill health, restless nights, poor sleep, and fatigued days. Given average eighteenth-century life expectancies, Johnson had taken on this task at a remarkably advanced age, and his life remained full and active in other ways. June 1777 had been devoted to efforts to win a reprieve for the clergyman/forger Dr. Dodd, condemned to die,

and, when these failed, to comforting the doomed clergyman. (Johnson joined a great wave of public sympathy, but the judicial process remained firm.) In July he wrote to solicit information on the life of the hymn writer Isaac Watts, whom Johnson wished to include as a reward for a career of sincere piety: "I wish to distinguish Watts; a man who never wrote but for a good purpose." His 3 November letter to Hester Thrale suggests a characteristic tension between conscientiousness and dilatoriness: "It will be proper for me to work pretty diligently now for some time. I hope to get through, though so many weeks have passed. Little lives and little criticisms may serve." Several weary and dejected diary entries and letters suggest the strain of the undertaking over the next three years. At last, in his diary entry for Good Friday, 13 April 1781, he wrote: "Some time in March I finished the lives of the Poets, which I wrote in my usual way, dilatorily and hastily, unwilling to work, and working with vigour and haste."

Johnson's own summary, while seeming to diminish the actual scale of labor and accomplishment, seems not inaccurate as a succinct account of his work habits. At times in his diary and correspondence he complains of slow progress; at other periods he is seen working at extraordinary speed. Frances Burney has left a splendid vignette of life at the Thrale residence at Streatham, where Johnson produced some of the lives triumphantly in proof. Of Johnson's rapid compositional style she remarks: "Dr. Johnson composed with so ready an accuracy, that he sent his copy [she refers specifically to the life of Pope] to the press unread; reserving all his corrections for the proof sheets." Of Johnson's compositional habits Percy wrote that he "never composed what we call a foul draft on paper of anything he published, but used to revolve the subject in his mind, and turn and form every period, till he had brought the whole to the highest correctness, and the most perfect arrangement." The manuscript of the life of Pope, written in 1780, remains the longest extant manuscript of Johnson's prose works — 184 pages of which only 20 (transcriptions by Thrale and George Steevens of Pope's works and letters) are not in Johnson's hand. It bears out those descriptions. Although two sets of jotted notes for the life of Pope have survived, a stellar and still-influential section, and one of the most richly considered, seems not to have been written from notes at all. The remarkable passage which compares Dryden and Pope and produces Johnson's most considered thoughts on the nature of genius appears as what William Rees-Mogg calls a "tidy manuscript" which, "judging by the handwriting and even the density of the ink, appears to have been written in one breath." As Burney noted and as John Middendorf's study of the proofs confirms, Johnson made careful revisions at proof stage, frequently in mechanics and style aimed usually at more lexicographical exactness but sometimes, too, in substance and content.

Johnson had sent presentation sets to the king by early March 1779 and to Hester Thrale by early April. The proprietors had planned originally to publish the works of each poet, with a prefatory life by Johnson. (The printer was John Nichols, himself an assiduous and astute collector of ana and anecdotes of literary personages and the man who had succeeded Cave as proprietor of the *Gentleman's Magazine*.) But the pressures of the market obliged them to publish the poetry separately, filling fifty-six small volumes, as *The Works of the English Poets* (1779). They published at the same time four volumes of Johnson's *Prefaces, Biographical and Critical, to the Works of the English Poets,* containing twenty-two of the fifty-two prefaces commissioned. In the same year Dublin booksellers, unauthorized, published in one volume the contents of the first four volumes of the *Prefaces* under the title *The Lives of the English Poets; and a Criticism on their Works.* In 1781 the London booksellers responded with *The Lives of the most eminent English Poets; with Critical Observations on their Works.* The first four volumes (March 1779) had covered twenty-two poets, from Cowley to John Hughes, and in May 1781 the next six treated thirty poets, from Addison to Gray and his contemporaries. An octavo edition of all the prefaces, in four volumes, was published on 16 June 1781. Another, with numerous revisions by Johnson in style and sometimes content, appeared in February 1783.

Boswell, when he had first seen the edition advertised as in process, wrote to Johnson (on 24 April 1777): "Pray tell me about this edition of 'The English Poets, with a Preface, biographical and critical, to each Author, by Samuel Johnson, LL.D.' which I see advertised." Johnson replied: "I am engaged to write little Lives, and little Prefaces, to a little edition of The English Poets" (3 May 1777). The word *little* refers perhaps to the size of the volumes (small octavo) or to the conciseness of the proposed prefaces. That may have been the original thinking of Davies, Strahan, Cadell, Dilly, and the rest and even of Johnson himself, but as Johnson worked, the size of his contributions swelled. As he set to work on the life of Cowley, his critical powers moved more expansively than even he at first expected. Boswell's journal records a remark of Thomas Tyers (son of Jonathan Tyers, founder of the pleasure gardens at Vauxhall), who in

1785 would publish "A Biographical Sketch" of Johnson: "He goes on with his Lives farther than he intended. Like a chariot wheel, [he] catches fire as he runs" (9 April 1779).

Most of the prefaces are indeed brief, derivative, and rapidly written, and in some cases Johnson takes no pains to conceal his low opinion of writers chosen for inclusion. The following paragraph, for example, ends his account of Charles Montague, Earl of Halifax, a versifier and statesman in the reigns of Queen Anne and King George I: "Many a blandishment was practised upon Halifax which he would never have known, had he no other attractions than those of his poetry, of which a short time has withered the beauties. It would now be esteemed no honour, by a contributor to the monthly bundles of verses, to be told that, in strains either familiar or solemn, he sings like Montague." Of John Philips, Johnson declares: "He imitates Milton's numbers indeed, but imitates them very injudiciously. Deformity is easily copied; and whatever there is in Milton which the reader wishes away, all that is obsolete, peculiar, or licentious is accumulated with great care by Philips." Even the major figures are tossed and gored despite moments of resonant tribute, and the notoriously hostile account of Milton has continually aroused controversy. The pieces, it should be stressed, were conceived initially as prefatory accounts – designed in their self-conciously contentious way to provoke thought, to offer touchstones for debate, and to stimulate the reader's engagement at an advanced level. They are, before they are biographies, landmarks in the history of prefaces, moving the idea of a preface away from mere puff or panegyric into active critical engagement.

The factual parts of Johnson's prefaces are little more than compilations, from time to time fleshed out with personal knowledge and the skeptical moral tone of his commentaries. His voice intervenes when, as he puts it in the life of Milton, "incredulity is ready to make a stand." But Johnson retrieved many informative and frequently revealing details that otherwise might have vanished from the record; he corrected in some places some traditionally believed mistakes; and he often supplemented his printed sources from his own capacious memory and firsthand acquaintance with the eighteenth-century world of letters, from high art to avowedly commercial authorship. The selections are by no means indications of his considered preferences. Indeed, when he saw "Johnson's Poets" written on the backs of some of the sets when printed, he fired off an angry note: "It is great impudence to put

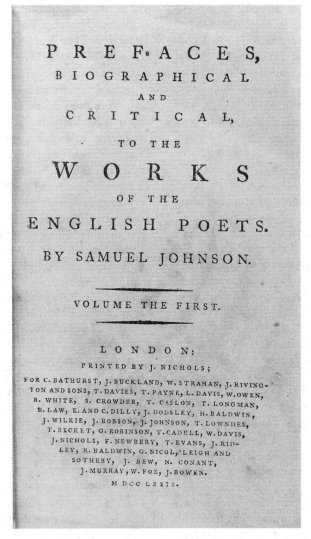

Title page for the first volume of essays that Johnson wrote as prefaces to a multivolume anthology of the works of fifty-two English poets. Because of delays in printing the anthology, Johnson's prefaces were first published separately.

Johnson's Poets on the backs of books which Johnson neither recommended nor revised. . . . This is indecent." Boswell records an amusingly revealing conversation on this topic in the *Life of Samuel Johnson, LL.D.* (1791). Confessing himself disappointed to learn that the project was not to be directed by Johnson, "but that he was to furnish a Preface and Life to any poet the booksellers pleased," Boswell says he "asked him if he would do this to any dunce's works, if they should ask him. JOHNSON. 'Yes, Sir, and say he was a dunce.' " Johnson himself added Watts, Richard Blackmore, Thomas Yalden, John Pomfret, and James Thomson. The booksellers' omission of the popular, influential, and Scottish-born Thomson is notable, perhaps a snub – part of their argument with the Martin

Brother's Apollo Press edition. Although, at least since midcentury, poetry by women enjoyed wide circulation and esteem and although Johnson frequently helped and admired intellectual women, all of the poets chosen are men. The Shiels-Cibber *Lives of the Poets* (1753) treats several women writers (and even defends Aphra Behn against a stricture of Johnson's in the "Drury Lane Prologue"). Pope's spiteful anticanon, *The Dunciad,* had been published in the final version in 1743 and was the ironic enthronement of mediocrity, an attack on the betrayal of the higher purposes of literature by hackwork. Boswell's use of the word *dunce* in his exchange with Johnson hints at one important affinity between Johnson's project and that of Pope's *Dunciad:* although Johnson is far from the furious, threatened

Pope of the *Dunciad,* dismissal of writing thought to be mediocre is as important a mode as solidifying a canon of merit. A separate essay would be needed to try to account for the choices the booksellers made, though some of the minor writers, such as William Shenstone and George, Lord Lyttelton, were probably included because of their presence in Dodsley's highly popular and influential *Collection of Poems, by Several Hands:* it was first published in three duodecimo volumes in 1748, and by 1758 it had grown to six volumes; by 1782 it had been reprinted eleven times. Goldsmith remains an odd omission. The booksellers' choices for their edition remain historically valuable, as they suggest considerable community consensus about what a generally educated and literate middle-income readership of the 1780s would want on its shelves as representative of the past century of poetry.

The derivative lives are frequently factually unreliable and must be consulted in editions with corrective scholarly annotation (usually the edition of G. B. Hill, which will eventually be supplanted by the lives in the Yale edition now in process). The prefaces were at no point conceived of as systematic critical treatises or formal biographies. But collectively the major pieces, on Cowley, Milton, Dryden, Addison, Savage, Swift, and Pope, and several of the shorter ones – Butler, Waller (with its long meditation on religious poetry), Prior, Rowe, Congreve, Thomson, Watts, Collins, Young, and Gray – stand as a major survey of a century of poetry, contain local assessments and remarks that remain touchstones for critical debate, and summarize many of Johnson's most considered critical positions.

This collection occupied Johnson at various levels of intensity from his sixty-eighth to his seventy-third year, and for periods at this time, as his diaries and letters show, he was seriously ill, often unable to sleep because of acute congestion in his lungs. Johnson himself had written in his preface to *A Dictionary of the English Language* that it "was written with little assistance of the learned, and without any patronage of the great; not in the soft obscurities of retirement, or under the shelter of academick bowers, but amidst inconvenience and distraction, in sickness and sorrow." The description applies as much to the *Prefaces* and makes Johnson sympathetic to authorial distresses. The modesty of the payment and of the terms in which Johnson's own remarks in his letters address the undertaking show no hint of the labor that would eventually be involved or the scale of Johnson's achievement and its range of influence. Johnson speaks regularly in di-

minutives ("little lives") but thus discloses complex psychological positions and needs: his vexed relation to his own writing and a desire for accomplishment contending with a fear of accomplishment – attempting great things, but in small compass. In Bate's summary the "short lives on which he was embarking now – as contrasted, for example, with the edition of Shakespeare – were not conceived as a major work in which he had to fulfill unusually high expectations." The prefaces indeed contain some of Johnson's richest meditations but resist the seductions of totalizing or all-encompassing theory. They imply a fairly continuous historical narrative yet acknowledge what is discontinuous, scattered, and fractured in the progress of a national poetry, and avoid any grand, overarching national political or historical teleology.

But just as a certain English nationalism undergirded the proprietors' enterprise, it can also be sensed in Johnson's prefatory contributions, in which he speaks regularly of a "we" and "us" – providing a sense of a collective British national self-conception, implying a nation that has shaken off the civil discord of the seventeenth century, and come to terms with the compromise of the Hanoverian succession. George III (who came to the throne in 1760) spoke English, the first of the Georges (of the German family of Hannover) to do so, and declared that he gloried in being "born a Briton." Late-Hanoverian Britain, highly historically self-conscious, felt itself more polished, stable, and secure after the turbulence of the seventeenth century and the faction-ridden party politics of the reigns of William and Mary, Queen Anne, and the controversial first two Georges. It was a time, for men of letters such as Johnson, for solidification and reappraisal, especially now that poetry itself was in the midst of important changes. The lives, moving at both a general and particular level, imply a literary biography of a nation and an age, one the monarch himself had in effect requested. In Johnson's interview in February 1767 with King George III, according to Boswell, the king "expressed a desire to have the literary biography of this country ably executed, and proposed to Dr. Johnson to undertake it. Johnson signified his readiness to comply with his Majesty's wishes." One of the younger Johnson's earlier projected schemes had been a "History of Criticism." Johnson would write neither his history of criticism nor a literary biography of the nation, yet the two ambitions coalesce, if unsystematically, in the *Prefaces.* As Leopold Damrosch remarks, Johnson's efforts needed to be "provoked rather than volunteered," and Johnson's habits of composition – described by himself as dilatory – had left him without the patience for systematic scholarly analytic survey or treatise.

Hanoverian Britain's great historical self-consciousness reflected itself, among other ways, in the copious production of histories and biographies. Bell's collections of drama and poetry, like the collection of Kincaid, Creech, and Balfour, share the impulse of the Scottish Enlightenment to encyclopedic comprehensiveness. Edinburgh, having diminished in importance as a political capital after the Union of Scotland and England, sought to reestablish itself intellectually and culturally in the post Union conditions. In both nations deepening antiquarian interests in the history of manners, in biography, and in autobiography fed an impulse to build representative collections embodying past greatness as repositories of national accomplishment. The British identity, Johnson's prefaces imply, had been arduously remaking itself since the suicidal chaos of the English civil war, in a process with which the rise of professional authorship had been intricately connected, contributing to a shared national repository of vernacular literature.

Numerous biographical and critical collections dealing with English poetry had been compiled earlier in the century, so that Johnson was far from without models. Prefatory biographies before authors' works began appearing in the late seventeenth century, as the nation began the process of healing itself after the civil war, and by the century's end these began to be collected into early versions of specialized biographical dictionaries. Edward Phillips, Milton's nephew, published *Theatrum Poetarum* in 1675. William Winstanley produced a slender *Lives of the Most Famous English Poets* in 1687. Gerard Langbaine's *Account of the English Dramatick Poets* (1691) was revised by Charles Gildon as *Lives and Characters of the English Drama* (1698). Addison had written "An Account of the Greatest English Poets" in 1694. Elizabeth Cooper collected and published *The Muses' Library* (1737) – a large anthology of poems by English writers from Edward the Confessor to Edmund Spenser and Samuel Daniel, Shakespeare's contemporaries. Cooper, who had some assistance from the antiquarian William Oldys, says in her preface that she sought to preserve worthy but neglected authors, and, in terms that clearly anticipate Johnson's lexicographical thinking (both in *A Dictionary of the English Language* and in *Prefaces*) to chart the progress of the English language from its early "Gothique rudeness." The most ambitious in scope was the Shiels-Cibber collection of 1753, covering 202 lives from Geoffrey

Chaucer to John Banks (who died in 1751). That volume drew on earlier general compilations such as the *General Dictionary,* Cooper's *The Muses' Library,* the *Biographica Britannica,* and many published individual biographies. Several of Johnson's prefaces in turn draw on this 1753 compilation. In his life of Hammond, Johnson acknowledges his indebtedness to the work and is careful to attribute the work to Robert Shiels, whose manuscript Johnson says is in his possession. (Shiels had been employed by Johnson as one of his amanuenses on *A Dictionary of the English Language*). Boswell's *Life of Samuel Johnson* reports the common belief that Johnson had in fact himself contributed in important ways to the Shiels-Cibber collection. Shiels certainly drew also on Johnson's "Life of Roscommon" (*Gentleman's Magazine,* 1748), and Shiels's life of Savage is an abridgment of Johnson's.

Individual prefatory biographical essays had also appeared before, among them Thomas Newton's edition of Milton (1749), John Hughes's edition of Spenser, John Urry's edition of Chaucer, and Birch's edition of Milton's prose works (1718). Those essays, primarily biographical with some scattered critical observations, made no real efforts at integration. What constituted Johnson's advance is well caught in Damrosch's summary: "The biographer of the poets was obliged to combine, if he could, critical evaluation with objective narrative. To rise above mere antiquarianism, he must constantly pass judgment. The 'Lives of the Poets' have analogues in the work of a number of Johnson's contemporaries, and surpass them all. They draw upon antiquarian or annalistic biography, but transcend it; they combine literary history and the analysis of specific authors in a way not hitherto accomplished." Shiels used but significantly adapted the method of Bayle: a brief text with extended notes. Shiels indented the notes into the text for a smoother, more finished piece of prose. Johnson's more integrated introductions mark a further advance over both Shiels and Bell. His three-part structure and his reference to French miscellanies in his introduction have led scholars properly to Fontonelle. But as Martine Watson Brownley shows, the basic form was not uncommon on both sides of the channel, and Johnson's own life of Sir Thomas Browne (1756), one of the early lives he composed himself rather than derived or compiled from other printed sources, adheres broadly to this structure. Johnson greatly expanded the character sketches and paved the way for the kinds of candid biography now familiar. Throughout the seventeenth century the traditional form of character

Samuel Johnson, 1756 (portrait by Sir Joshua Reynolds; National Portrait Gallery, London)

sketch was attached, as almost a natural extension, to collections of literary works. Johnson's prefaces raised more searching questions: Does a writer's life reflect his character? Is what an author writes the issue of what he intrinsically is? Of what is the author's character a product? In the longer prefaces Johnson offers surveys of career and, where available, details of everyday life, as illustrations of character – the character behind the poems – and as illustrations of the contexts in which the character was formed. The *Prefaces* are from start to finish suspect in their factual details, but Johnson regularly urges the need for systematic, exhaustive investigation. He repetitively laments the absence of accurate information on authors' early lives, childhood, and first exposures to education, as he understood – well ahead of the post-Freudian assumptions of twentieth-century biography – the formative importance of the earliest experiences of life. He deploys whenever he can the tellingly illustrative anecdote.

In more-important local contexts for Johnson's prefaces, Joseph Warton's groundbreaking essay of 1756 had challenged the preeminence of Pope, and as a consequence the Augustan school, and had tried to distinguish between the poets of the "sublime and pathetic" – including Shakespeare, Spenser, and Milton – and the "men of wit and sense," to which (second and lower) category Pope belonged. Warton argued that "wit and satire are transitory and perishable, but nature and passion are eternal." On some fundamental points Johnson and his friend Warton agreed; the idea of "nature and passion" as eternal anticipates the sage Imlac's pronouncements in *The History of Rasselas*. But Johnson's lives constitute in part, as suggested, a reassertion of the aesthetic tradition of Dryden, Addison, and Pope. For the poets of sensibility Johnson has little regard. The Warton family, Gray, Collins, and Akenside, writing a poetry of sensibility, saw a vigorous creative potential in imagination, valuing it, not fearing it as a species of vanity, solipsism, a threat to sanity, or a hunger that preys incessantly upon life. That poetry is the work of the eighteenth century upon which the Romantics would most draw as the nineteenth century approached.

The period saw also the growth of one of the particular subsets of biographical writing: collected conversations and anecdotes, specifically of writers. Increasing historical self-consciousness led to a new curiosity about the writer as not just author but as character, a public figure with a private life. The London consortium of booksellers aimed in securing Johnson to boost sales. But they sought also to add the weight of the moral authority of his name, to lift stories of writers' lives above the level of Grub Street anecdotes, to deepen them into moral matter and materials for critical pronouncement.

Though the prefaces offer little or no original research and most are reliant on printed sources, some firsthand knowledge is put to good use; some details were provided by friends (Boswell, for example, is thanked in the life of Thomson). Isaac Reed and Steevens were associates who provided some factual researches. Some shortcuts presented themselves, and Johnson took them. For the life of Parnell he used an abstract of a life written by Goldsmith. His life of Roscommon is a substantially rewritten version of a life he wrote for the *Gentleman's Magazine* in 1748. He reprinted his own *Life of Savage,* only slightly changed from its first publication thirty-five years earlier. Sir Herbert Croft contributed a life of his uncle, the enormously popular Edward Young, author of *Night Thoughts* (1742–1745). The life of Gray incorporates a memoir of him by Boswell's lifelong friend the Reverend William Johnson Temple. The project may have blocked, or may have been stimulated by, an intention to publish the collected works of Hawkesworth, in association with Hawkesworth's widow and his brother-in-law John Ryland. The prolific Hawkesworth, a frequent contributor to the *Gentleman's Magazine* in many modes and genres, had published in 1755 an edition of Swift's works, with a prefatory "Life of Swift." Johnson assisted Hawkesworth in that life and used it as a source for his own life of Swift.

He draws on published sources with whose authors he frequently parts company in emphasis, as he did in his early translations and redactions for the *Gentleman's Magazine*. In that regard, the opening move of the life of Cowley sets the tone for the whole: Johnson's first paragraph announces his intention to challenge the account of Cowley by Dr. Thomas Sprat. Sprat's "pregnancy of imagination and eloquence, has produced a funeral oration rather than a history," and "all is shown confused

and enlarged through the mist of panegyric." In *Idler* number 85 Johnson had written: "He that writes the life of another is either his friend or his enemy, and wishes either to exalt his praise or aggravate his infamy: many temptations to falsehood will occur in the disguise of passions, too specious to fear much resistance. Love of virtue will animate panegyric, and hatred of wickedness embitter censure. The zeal of gratitude, the ardour of patriotism, fondness for an opinion, or fidelity to a party, may easily overpower the vigilance of a mind habitually well disposed, and prevail over unassisted and unfriended veracity." There Johnson summarizes ahead of time his own aspiration as the writer of the *Prefaces*.

That aspiration, or complex interlocking set of aspirations, implicitly undergirds the whole collection of lives. More than merely particular affinities or aversions require historical and critical scrutiny. Time, too, is alternately the friend and the enemy of a poet's reputation. Cowley is one of those poets who have been "at one time too much praised and too much neglected at another." The search for a balanced antithesis – so much a feature of the Augustan couplet itself – or the aim to steer a middle course of "sense" between apparent extremes, informs Johnson's practice at every level. It appears in individual portraits (Pope's cunning and manipulativeness and his great capacity for loyalty, Swift's parsimony but extraordinary social generosity); in Johnson's paired analyses of beauties and faults in the poems themselves; and in his roughly equal dispensations of praise and blame in his moral appraisals of poets' lives. Johnson aims to speak in and as the voice of late Hanoverian Britain – a nation more solid and less faction torn than in the past. It was a time for review and reappraisal of the past. And in speaking as biographical critic he speaks, too, as cultural historian, custodian, and arbiter in a voice, he hopes, of "unassisted and unfriended veracity," sifting through the literary record for the contexts that propelled writers to various kinds of fame or notoriety, and seeking to denominate the reasons for what will survive and what has survived.

His vision from the start, then, though antipanegyric, is equally generous, inclusive, and tolerant, a secular equivalent of late-eighteenth-century Anglican flexibility and toleration. The "fever of renown" produces often enough a risible authorial vanity yet fuels also the greatest accomplishments. Of Pope's threats (after attacks by critics) to write no more, Johnson says: "The man who threatens the world is always ridiculous; for the world can easily go on without him, and in a short time will cease to miss him. . . . Pope had been flattered till he thought himself one of the moving powers in the system of life. When he talked of laying down his pen, those who sat round him intreated and implored, and self-love did not suffer him to suspect that they went away and laughed." But, for all that, Pope's mind was "active, ambitious, and adventurous, always investigating, always aspiring; in its widest searches still longing to go forward, in its highest flights, still wishing to be higher; always imagining something greater than it knows, always endeavouring more than it can do." Writers such as Milton, Addison, and Pope, well acquainted with their own genius, who receive censure by Johnson for their culpable vanity, receive at the same time glowing tributes. And as much as Johnson feels a need to "mourn and remember" and pay tribute to past genius, he acknowledges the reasons for forgetting. He writes in *Rambler* number 106: "No place affords a more striking conviction of the vanity of human hopes, than a publick library. . . . Of the innumerable authors whose performances are . . . treasured up in magnificent obscurity, most are forgotten, because they never deserved to be remembered, and owed the honours which they once obtained, not to judgment or to genius, to labour or to art, but to the prejudice of faction, the stratagem of intrigue, or the servility of adulation." Every period of time, Johnson continues, has produced "bubbles of artificial fame, which are kept up for a while by the breath of fashion, and then break at once and are annihilated. The learned often bewail the loss of ancient writers whose characters have survived their works; but, perhaps, if we could now retrieve them, we should find them only the Granvilles, Montagues, Stepneys, and Sheffields of their time, and wonder by what infatuation or caprice they could be raised to notice." Johnson, as ever on the side of the reader, acknowledges that the reader has the time, tolerance, and patience for only so much. Johnson wrote that *Rambler* essay in March 1751, some thirty years before his lives were completed, a testimony again to the remarkable consistency of Johnson's vision over the course of his prolific career: the prefaces include brief and at best lukewarm accounts of Granville, Montague (Lord Halifax), Stepney, and Sheffield. But the *Rambler* essay and the lives testify, at the same time, to a certain ambivalence: he remembers even as he would have them forgotten. Even as he seeks enduring merit over artificial and ephemeral bubbles of fame, he is fascinated precisely by faction and intrigue, the operations of fancy and caprice. These, too, are wor-

thy of record. A knowledge of poetry is not possible without them.

In essence Johnson valued tradition, but he disdained the merely feebly imitative. In the *Prefaces* he scorns claims to radical and disruptive innovation, but he values originality – understood as an original relationship to established tradition; he has a horror of the unfettered private vision, as both opening the mind to the hunger of imagination that preys incessantly upon life, and letting loose an egotistic will to mastery. He values rather the poet whose images trigger an affective transfer, in heightened sensibility, of recognitions of unchanging human truths. Most crucially, for Johnson and for subsequent biographical and critical practice, poetry and poetic careers valued in the lives are not separable from their contextual frames. Johnson wrote the lives at a time that for all its settled sense of harmony, proportion, and order, was (in ways not fully explicit in Johnson's own conscious project) palpably anxious. Newer revolutionary energies were making themselves heard in the North American colonies and in France, where opposition to absolutism was building. In the sequence of poets studied, from the English civil war to his own contemporaries, readers may sense in Johnson an anxiety that the poets of sensibility of the most recent generations threaten a return to the political turbulences that marked the internecine chaos of the English civil war, Cromwell's regicide, and the severe rule of the Puritan interregnum.

The writing of the life of Cowley changed, expanded, and decisively formed his conception of the project, and it remained, Boswell reports, the one Johnson considered his best "on account of the dissertation which it contains on the Metaphysical Poets." It expresses much that is characteristic of the whole endeavor in the *Prefaces*.

"About the beginning of the seventeenth century," says Johnson after a survey of Cowley's career, "appeared a race of writers that may be termed the metaphysical poets, of whom in a criticism on the works of Cowley it is not improper to give some account." (Johnson apparently builds on a disparaging remark by Dryden, that "Donne affects the metaphysics." Similar terms had been used by Pope and William Drummond of Hawthornden. In many ways misleading and inappropriate, the label has, through Johnson's authority, proved durable.) "The metaphysical poets," he says, "were men of learning, and to shew their learning was their whole endeavour; but, unluckily, resolving to shew it in rhyme, instead of writing poetry they only wrote verses. . . . " Johnson traces the origins of the style (now more commonly designated "baroque") to the Italian Giambattista Marini (whose followers became known as the Marinists) and notes that it drew powerful recommendations from Donne – "a man of very extensive and various knowledge" – and Jonson. To describe metaphysical wit, Johnson begins by parting company with Pope's widely quoted couplet in *An Essay on Man:* "True wit is nature to advantage dress'd / What oft was thought, but ne'er so well express'd." Pope's account reduces wit "from strength of thought" to mere "happiness of language," Johnson reaches for a "more noble and more adequate conception" of wit, as that "which is at once natural and new, that which though not obvious is, upon its first production, acknowledged to be just; if it be that, which he that never found it, wonders how he missed." To wit of that kind "the metaphysical poets have seldom risen. Their thoughts are often new, but seldom natural; they are not obvious, but neither are they just; and the reader, far from wondering that he missed them, wonders by what perverseness of industry they were ever found." Wit, suggests Johnson, "abstracted from it effects upon the hearer, may be more rigorously and philosophically considered as a kind of *discordia concors* [harmonious discord]; a combination of dissimilar images, or discovery of occult resemblances in things apparently unlike. Of wit, thus defined, they [the Metaphysical poets] have more than enough. The most heterogeneous ideas are yoked by violence together. . . ".

Johnson greatly dislikes the "wit" of Cowley and the poets with whom he associated his work. He admires the "copiousness and acuteness" of Cowley and Donne in "scholastick speculation" but finds them "unnecessarily and unpoetically subtle" on "common subjects." But criticism has produced no pithier summary of the distinctive paradoxical metaphors favored by the poets of this period than those in Johnson's much quoted remarks here. Furthermore, however misleading the term *metaphysical* and however much Johnson's faith in the affective quality of poetry has been challenged by later critical movements, his contribution to all subsequent literary historical practice has been enormous. Johnson provided the first major critical discussion of the so-called Metaphysical school as a group and, in the process, marked a major formative moment in the development of the very idea of *school,* or poetic grouping, and historical criticism as the attempt to distill into subtly nuanced summary the distinctive characteristics of any such group. It is wrong, Johnson suggests, to account for Cowley's poetics

through a later, inappropriate definition of wit such as Pope's. A judgment of Cowley can only be made properly through knowledge of the trajectory of the idea of wit from Marini through Donne and Johnson. This method has become by now a thoroughly familiar feature of the practice of literary history, to situate any given poet within the larger subset of poets to which the work historically belongs, and of literary biography, to place the author under discussion in appropriate genres, conventions, and authorial groupings.

The poets writing in the wake of Donne and Ben Jonson, says Johnson, working with an idea of the conceit taken from Italian poetry, understood wit to mean something different from its later eighteenth-century applications – a display of intellectual prowess, in language striving for novelty, in far-fetched or ingenious analogies and comparisons. Having established its context, Johnson sets out to account for his dislike, invoking the values that will inform his assessments of all the poets and poetry in his survey – an affective power in poetry to move the emotions, through sublimity or pathos, for the morally efficacious pleasurable engagement of the reader. The Metaphysical poets "were not successful in representing or moving the affections . . . they had no regard to that uniformity of sentiment, which enables us to conceive and to excite the pains and the pleasure of other minds." This complaint amounts to more than merely a question of difference in taste. The poetry lacks a capacity for morally efficacious transfer between minds. Metaphysical wit operates at a level of clinical detachment that seems to Johnson wholly heartless because abstracted from its effects on the hearer. These poets wrote "as beholders rather than partakers of human nature," as "Epicurean deities . . . without interest and without emotion. . . . Their attempts were always analytick: they broke every image into fragments, and could no more represent by their slender conceits and laboured particularities the prospects of nature or the scenes of life, than he who dissects a sun-beam with a prism can exhibit the wide effulgence of a summer noon." They produced no sublimity, merely hyperbole. Their poetry was void of sentiment and was a coldly, clinically, intellectual or analytic pursuit; while such wit must be understood in its own context, there yet remains for Johnson a permanent, true sense of wit – "at once natural and new," with a novelty that serves only to establish what was already in nature, in fresh recognitions. Johnsonian biography itself, as summarized in *Rambler* number 60, constitutes precisely a sympathetic inhabitation of another's mode of being

ANNALS.

1. 1709-10.

SEPT. 7*, 1709, I was born at Lichfield. My mother had a very difficult and dangerous labour, and was assisted by George Hector, a man-midwife of great reputation. I was born almost dead, and could not cry for some time. When he had me in his arms, he said, "Here is a brave boy †."

* 18 of the present stile. *Orig.*
† This was written in January, 1765. *Edit.*

Page one of An Account of the Life of Dr. Samuel Johnson, from his Birth to his Eleventh Year, Written by Himself, *edited by Richard Wright*

and self-articulation, with an awareness of the full complexity of the contexts.

Johnson's procedure moves in several stages. He establishes an historical context in which a poet's ouevre should be assessed: the historically contextualist critic assesses different canons of wit. He sets up the idea of school, or grouping. He shows his dislike for the school by invoking certain principles and values. He strives to show why those values are worthwhile – the endeavour, both explicit and implicit, of the whole collection. The life of Cowley, in these ways, serves as a prototype for much subsequent biographical procedure. So, too, does the life of Milton, and Johnson's influential practices emerge forcefully when the life of Milton and the life of Cowley are read as a pair.

In the English civil war – on which Cowley, a Royalist agent, and Milton, Cromwell's Latin secretary, took opposite sides – heterogenous ideas were, indeed, yoked by violence together. The turbulence of their poetry issues from the troubled age, one of which Johnson spoke and wrote regularly with scorn. For him the republican triumph was a "manifest usurpation" and Cromwell a violent regicide and tyrant. *Paradise Lost* is a great poem, "a poem which, considered with respect to design, may claim the first place, and with respect to performance the second, among the productions of the human mind." But it cannot be separated from what Johnson sees as its republican (Puritan) ideology. Milton is, in Johnson's well-known, trenchant formulation, an "acrimonious and surly republican." But no crudely unmeditated political prejudice compels Johnson's hostility: in the case of Addison, so formative an influence on Johnson's own essayistic practice, Johnson sets aside his resolute antipathy to

Whiggism. Addison, a career politician who rose to high office in Whig administrations, is much admired. Johnson's notorious attack on *Lycidas* (1637) stems from his belief in Milton's heartlessness: "It is not to be considered as the effusion of real passion; for passion runs not after remote allusions and obscure opinions. . . ." The poem resembles the play of Metaphysical wit analyzed in the poems of Cowley, despite other clear differences between the poets. It lacks sincerity: "Where there is leisure for art there can be little grief."

For Johnson the men who drove England into civil war were not men of feeling. He finds emotional coldness and even severity in the details of Milton's private life as much as in the poetry. In a terse, ironic sentence about the death of Milton's second wife, Catherine Woodcock, Johnson remarks dryly that "her husband has honoured her memory with a poor sonnet." The same heartlessness that Johnson sees in *Lycidas,* in which Milton used the accidental drowning of his friend Edward King as an occasion for poetic self-display, Johnson finds in the mistreatment of the women of Milton's family: "Milton's republicanism was, I am afraid, founded in an envious hatred of greatness, and a sullen desire of independence; in petulance impatient of controul, and pride disdainful of superiority. He hated monarchs in the state and prelates in the church; for he hated all whom he was required to obey. It is to be suspected that his predominant desire was to destroy rather than to establish, and that he felt not so much the love of liberty as repugnance to authority." Johnson finds a radical hypocrisy in the Puritan temperament: "It has been observed that they who most loudly clamour for liberty do not most liberally grant it. What we know of Milton's character in domestick relations is, that he was severe and arbitrary. His family consisted of women; and there appears in his books something like a Turkish contempt of females, as subordinate and inferior beings. That his own daughters might not break the ranks, he suffered them to be depressed by a mean and penurious education. He thought woman made only for obedience, and man only for rebellion."

A man who clamored for liberty while denying it to the female members of his family, the supporter of usurpation and regicide, Milton would not lightly be awarded the capacities for sympathetic moral transfer of pleasurable recognitions Johnson values in later poets. Even in *Paradise Lost,* despite the otherwise high praise, "the reader finds no transaction in which he can be engaged, beholds no condition in which he can by any effort of imagina-

tion place himself. . . . *Paradise Lost* is one of the books which the reader admires and lays down, and forgets to take up again. None ever wished it longer than it is. Its perusal is a duty rather than a pleasure. We read Milton for instruction, retire harassed and overburdened, and look elsewhere for recreation; we desert our master, and seek for companions." Out of Milton's Puritan temperament come both the greatness and the difficulty of *Paradise Lost.* Its author for Johnson was a misogynistic domestic tyrant and the truculent writer of scathing polemical prose: Milton seemed "well acquainted with his own genius" and spared no one in his own writings: "of 'evil tongues' for Milton to complain required impudence at least equal to his other powers – Milton, whose warmest advocates must allow that he never spared any asperity of reproach or brutality of insolence." The Puritan will to dominate, enacted politically for Johnson in Cromwell's violent seizure of power, enacts itself in Milton's poetics (which as ever for Johnson resides in poetry's relation to the reader): Milton seeks (as did the zealot Puritan energies that propelled Cromwell to regicidal violence and a seizure of power) to harass, to overburden, and to master. In his poems he seeks a relationship of domination, not a companionate imaginative transfer. Harassed, overburdened, and mastered, Johnson would seek out companions.

Johnson's typical disdain for the Puritan temperament comes from his sense that, as Bate says, it disguises "under a high and exacting moralism that will brook no compromise" what is in fact "an idolatory of self-will." From the brief life of Cheynel to a sustained attack on the Cromwellian insurrection in the life of Samuel Butler, Johnson wrote with consistent severity of Cromwell's ideology. Of Butler's topical burlesque *Hudibras* (1663), Johnson writes: "Much . . . of that humour which transported the last century to merriment is lost to us, who do not know the sour solemnity, the sullen superstition, the gloomy moroseness, and the stubborn scruples of the ancient Puritans. . . . It is scarcely possible, in the regularity and composure of the present time, to image the tumult of absurdity and clamour of contradiction which perplexed doctrine, disordered practice, and disturbed both publick and private quiet in that age, when subordination was broken and awe was hissed away; when any unsettled innovator who could hatch a half-formed notion produced it to the public. . . . The wisdom of the nation is very reasonably supposed to reside in the parliament. What can be concluded of the lower classes of the people when in one of the parliaments summoned by Cromwell it was seriously proposed that all the records in the Tower should be burnt, that all memory of things past should be effaced, and that the whole system of life should commence anew?" Johnson, aware of poetry's classical ancestries and a believer in innovative uses of tradition, urging in his *Prefaces* the need for accurate biography – for acts of commemoration – cherished and valued the memory of things past. Only a disordered arrogance in the unfettered political ego imagines that it obliterates what has gone before and starts creation all over again. Invention, innovation, imagination, and originality were concepts of high value for Johnson, but each of them stood only in engagement with the familiar, with what can be and has been already accessible to reason and observation. Outrageous or perverse novelty (such as Metaphysical wit) in poetry stands cognate with the disruptive forces that drove the English state to suicidal self-division and allowed the rise to power of the Cromwellian Puritan will to domination. Those are the dangers in the work of the unsettled innovator, haughtily disdaining the memory of things past – an expression with both biblical and Shakespearian resonances.

The caustic treatment of Milton, however balanced by thunderous praise, aroused bitter controversy, as Johnson knew it would. But Johnson seeks to assess the works in the context of the life, and, as Lipking summarizes Johnson's position: "the very independence, impatience, and ardor for fame which make a man impossible to live with or like may help make a poet great." But whatever particular disagreements it provokes, in its methodological principle – as an attempt at an integrated reading of an author's political psyche and his works – the life of Milton stands as a formative methodological moment in the development of literary biography.

The collisions that animated the English nation in the civil war appear, then, in literary form in the opposed poetics of Cowley and Milton. Out of the clash emerges, eventually, the Restoration, with smoother tempers and a smoother poetry. Before Cowley and Milton came Sir John Denham, whose topographical poem *Cooper's Hill* (1642) helped establish a later vogue for poetry in that mode. Denham learned from the "metrical harmony" of Edmund Waller and "gained ground gradually upon the ruggedness of his age" (as Johnson says in the life of Waller). Denham contributed to the "improvement of our numbers." His "rhymes are such as seem found without difficulty by following the sense." He "is one of the writers that improved our taste and advanced our language." All the terms here have importance: Johnson believed in a trajec-

tory of "improvement," with both the civilized political order and language moving out of an earlier barbarity into "taste," toward the high Georgian order of the later eighteenth century. These developments are correlative, and poetry is central to them, as the changes in the political order work in and through and perhaps because of "improvement" in language. The use of *our* conveys Johnson's feeling of national identity as consensus and compromise settling in after the internecine violence of the civil war. In Denham – like Cowley a committed Royalist and for Johnson a contributor to harmony and order (at the Restoration his Royalist loyalties were rewarded when he was appointed surveyor-general of works) – the dissonances of Metaphysical *discordia concors* yield to a concord of form and sense: sense both as meaning and, in a resonance highly valued by the Augustans, as concentrated intelligence and wisdom. Dryden and Pope both openly acknowledged their admiration for and indebtedness to Denham.

Neither the "Metaphysical" Cowley nor the epically ambitious Milton achieved genuine pathos, occupying extreme positions consequent on a condition of war, antithetical to Johnson's values of tolerance, compromise, balance, and harmony. The English civil war had changed the nature of the British state forever. The poetry of Milton and the Metaphysical school, chiefly Cowley's, came in a period of upheaval and experimentation – which, in Johnson's estimation, led to excesses which from the standpoint of a later age's assessment seem suspect. From the Metaphysical school's rough, harsh, inelegant diction and heterogeneous ideas yoked together by violence – literary correlative of the strife-torn political climate of the English civil war and its aftermath – Johnson moves to the polished verse on which Pope would most draw (Denham, Waller, and Dryden), placing a premium on regular versification and more precise diction, diction more suited to sentiments. Denham's now-little-read contribution to "the smootheness of our numbers" makes him for Johnson "one of the fathers of English poetry."

Dryden's essays in criticism (which Johnson acknowledges had the most formative influence on his own) "improved the public judgment" and make him a "father" of English criticism. Dryden's controversial career (which seemed to his enemies a calculated and venal set of shifting allegiances with the succession of parties in power) – his inconsistent, sometimes self-contradictory pronouncements and practice in his own works – produce in Johnson not disapproval but a sense of necessary compromise.

Dryden's career involved a complex set of adjustments to prevailing vogues and prevailing powers: similarly his style in both prose and poetry turns on subtle adjustments: "his occasional and particular positions were sometimes interested, sometimes negligent, and sometimes capricious." For Johnson these adjustments find expression in the nature of Dryden's poetry, couplets distinguished by complex modulations – subtle sets of interior adjustments to meet outer, readerly needs.

Dryden's poetry marked a further advance in "harmony" over "forced thoughts and rugged diction" – an expression as much applicable to the savage political rhetoric Johnson disliked in the civil war and the Commonwealth as to the poetry the war and its aftermath produced. Dryden established a "new versification" so that poetry would not again "relapse into former savageness." Just as Dryden as a poet regularized English verse into harmony, as a critic he introduced fixed, regular principles into criticism – principles which leave room for necessary flexibility: "Dryden may be properly considered as the father of English criticism, as the writer who first taught us to determine upon principles the merit of composition."

A resurgent roughness in poetry reappeared in the "part-poems," as Johnson terms them in the life of Tickell, that issued from the struggles for power during and after the reign of Queen Anne (the end of the Stuart monarchies) and from correlative struggles for social and literary domination, reflected in the pitched battles between the Pope-Swift circle and critics such as John Dennis and Thomas Rymer. Johnson admires Addison, who sought in his essayistic writings to create an educated, nonspecialist audience for the intelligent and polite discussion of advanced intellectual, social, and aesthetic questions. Addison admired Locke, did much to popularize his ideas, and moved criticism away from its formalistic grounds and arid classifications to the realm of sensational psychology, asking such questions as why and how poetry gives its readers pleasure and how it moves the reader's emotions and affects the passions. Addison's key concepts – among them imagination, taste, originality and original genius, beauty, sublimity, pathos, nature – recur, as almost-standard terms, in Johnson's *Prefaces.* Johnson values what he sees as Addison's depoliticization of social and critical discourse. Although a career Whig politician who rose to high office (undersecretary of state), Addison, for Johnson, subsumed politically rancorous competitive energies in new norms of politeness and civility. The reign of Queen Anne and the struggles for party as-

cendancy produced, says Johnson, a "storm of faction," above which Addison was able to rise – although Johnson is severe on Addison's vanity and capacity for resentment.

The qualities of "calmness and equability," which Johnson attributes to Addison's attempts at poetry, come at a cost. Addison's poetry "has not often those felicities of diction which give lustre to sentiments, or that vigour of sentiment that animates diction: there is little of ardour, vehemence, or transport; there is very rarely the awfulness of grandeur, and not very often the splendour of elegance. He thinks justly, but he thinks faintly. . . . Yet, if he seldom reaches supreme excellence, he rarely sinks into dulness, and is still more rarely entangled in absurdity. . . . There is in most of his compositions a calmness and equability, deliberate and cautious, sometimes with little that delights, but seldom with any thing that offends." Johnson's praise remains, as ever, qualified. The milder morality of the reign of Charles II meant, of course, deviations into culpable social and literary licentiousness, which Johnson consistently censures. Whatever the cost – and Johnson willingly concedes a lack of creative fire in Addison's poems and in much of the remorselessly smooth and elegant derivative midcentury poetry – Johnson values stability, regularity, harmony, and proportion as much in poetry as in the English political order.

He values "ardour," "vehemence," "transport," "felicities of diction," and "vigour of sentiment," but as his accounts of the earlier generations of poets make equally plain, those emotions are not without their dangers. Johnson explicitly links the development of the periodicals, such as Addison and Steele's *Spectator,* to the need to calm things down after the civil war: "This mode of conveying cheap and easy knowledge began among us in the Civil War, when it was much the interest of either party to raise and fix the prejudices of the people." But the purpose of the *Tatler* and *Spectator* of Addison and Steele was not to inflame but to calm: "they were published at a time when two parties, loud, restless, and violent, each with plausible declarations, and each perhaps without any distinct termination of its views, were agitating the nation: to minds heated with political contest they supplied cooler and more inoffensive reflections." Johnson's own essayistic practice, and his entire project in the prefaces, has a line of descent from the work of Addison, and he establishes Addison's desire to calm tempers and civilize energies let loose in earlier polemics.

The work of Congreve, now mainly remembered for his witty, complex comedy of manners

The Way of the World (1700), draws mixed though at moments revealingly high praise from Johnson, in ways that summarize much of Johnson's thought and point ahead to the terms of value recurrent in the later prefaces. As a dramatist "Congreve has merit of the highest kind: he is an original writer, who borrowed neither the models of his plot nor the manner of his dialogue." As a poet, though, he lacked the "fire requisite for the higher species of lyrick poetry"; to Congreve "we are indebted for the correction of a national error, and for the cure of our Pindarick madness." Congreve first "taught the English writers that Pindar's odes were regular" (in his *Discourse on the Pindaric Ode,* prefixed to a "Pindaric Ode" written in regular meter and versification). The claims here for Congreve strike modern readers as exaggerated, but they hint at the depth of Johnson's concern. The preeminence of Cowley and his use of the vigorous, abrupt, metrically complex odes of Pindar had had for too long a pernicious grip on English poetic practice. When Prior wrote his poetry, says Johnson, "we had not recovered from our Pindarick infatuations." In the life of Cowley, Johnson had sought to suggest the menacing political underpinnings of a poetics of abruptness and disorder. Pindaric odes become palatable for Johnson when rendered in Congreve's "regular" way. Congreve showed that "enthusiasm has its rules, and that in mere confusion there is neither grace nor greatness." By this point in Johnson's sequence of prefaces it has become apparent that enthusiasm in poetic practice carries serious implications for the political order.

The originality, then, prized by Johnson in Congreve stands far from the Metaphysical taste for perverse or outrageous novelty and, worse, the Puritan will to destroy what has gone before or imagine that it starts the world anew. For Johnson little in the world can genuinely shock or startle. As he declares in the life of Yalden, "All wonder is the effect of novelty upon ignorance." And writing of Cowley he says: "Those writers who lay on the watch for novelty could have little hope of greatness; for great things cannot have escaped former observation." Nonetheless, as he says succinctly in the life of Milton, "The highest praise of genius is original invention," and in the life of Waller, "the essence of poetry is invention; such invention as, by producing something unexpected, surprises and delights." Pope, in *The Rape of the Lock* (1714), had "with elegance of description and justness of precepts . . . exhibited boundless fertility of invention." For Johnson literary originality constitutes an en-

gagement with the past, with tradition, and consists in an ability to heighten the reader's sensibility to new knowledge, or re-cognitions, of what has long been known. Johnson does not know a "more poetical paragraph" in "the whole mass of the English poetry" than an exchange in Congreve's tragedy *The Mourning Bride*. In a resonant passage that catches the essence of much of Johnson's aesthetic theory, he writes: "He who reads those lines enjoys for a moment the powers of a poet: he feels what he remembers to have felt before, but he feels it with great increase of sensibility; he recognises a familiar image, but meets it again amplified and expanded, embellished with beauty, and enlarged with majesty."

Poets indeed have a transporting and elevating power, yet it incites at its best a reapprehension of the deepest already-familiar human intuitions. Of Thomson, included explicitly at Johnson's request, he writes, "As a writer he is entitled to one praise of the highest kind: his mode of thinking and of expressing his thoughts is original. . . . He thinks in a peculiar train, and he thinks always as a man of genius; he looks round on Nature and on Life with the eye which Nature bestows only on a poet, the eye that distinguishes in every thing presented to its view whatever there is on which imagination can delight to be detained, and with a mind that at once comprehends the vast, and attends to the minute. The reader of *The Seasons* (1726–1730) wonders that he never saw before what Thomson shews him, and that he never yet has felt what Thomson impresses. . . . In this work are exhibited in a very high degree the two most engaging powers of an author: new things are made familiar, and familiar things are made new." Imagination, invention, pleasure, and originality recur as Johnson's terms of value. Far from an enemy of imagination *tout court,* he resists only what Imlac in *The History of Rasselas* terms that hunger of imagination that preys incessantly upon life – imagination as a species of retreat into the dangerous regions of solipsism and the exaggerated egoism of private vision. Imagination must have a self-consciousness of its own processes, not operate as a delusive force that has human sensibility in its grip. Literature, indeed, must help rescue imagination from its own potentiality for corrosive solipsism, or the culpable delusions of vanity.

Johnson works in the epistemological tradition of Locke, who argues essentially that activities of mind proceed from actual sensory experience. Images are for Johnson an almost-material stock, which poets in their careers are seen gathering then deploying to efficacious effect in their works. On

Milton's composition of *Paradise Lost* he writes: "The thoughts which are occasionally called forth in the progress are such as could be produced only by an imagination in the highest degree fervid and active, to which materials were supplied by incessant and unlimited curiosity." Materials, the world of matter, transmuted by imagination and then transferred to a reader, inform Johnson's praise for Milton: "Whatever be his subject he never fails to fill the imagination." Imagination is not, as it would be for the English Romantic poets, a powerful creative faculty in its own right. In Jean H. Hagstrum's useful distinction, for "Johnson all mental action, whether rational or imaginative, is always secondary to the direct experience of reality and is, apart from reality, seriously suspect; for [Samuel Taylor] Coleridge all mental action, whether rational or imaginative, is primary; it does not depend upon experience, but constitutes experience." Thus Johnson, not surprisingly, is least drawn to the eighteenth-century poets to whom the Romantic poets owe most, the poets of sensibility. Imagination must serve, in the end, the cause of reason. In the life of Milton he says: "Poetry is the art of uniting pleasure with truth, by calling imagination to the help of reason."

Johnson favored imitation, but in a poetic "imitation" of nature (the communication of human truths) and emphatically not in a slavish duplication of available forms and modes. He had written in *Rambler* number 154, in a vivid image: "The reputation which arises from the . . . transposition of borrowed sentiment may spread for a while like ivy on the rind of antiquity; but will be torn away by accident or contempt, and suffered to rot unheeded on the ground." As the brief prefaces continue through the century of poets, some of Johnson's most consistent scorn is poured on feeble references to, or invocations for no purpose of, classical or other mythological figures and material. Hammond's "elegies have neither passion, nature, nor manners. Where there is fiction, there is no passion. He that courts his mistress with Roman imagery deserves to lose her; for she may with good reason suspect his sincerity. Hammond has few sentiments drawn from nature, and few images drawn from modern life. He produces nothing but frigid pedantry." Tickell, who "cannot be refused a high place among the minor poets," in his *Kensington Gardens* (1722) produces "fiction unskilfully compounded of Grecian Deities and Gothick Fairies. Neither species of those exploded beings could have done much; and when they are brought together they only make each other contemptible." Of Granville, Johnson says,

"his works do not shew him to have had much comprehension from nature, or illumination from learning." He "is forever amusing himself with the puerilities of mythology: his King is Jupiter, who, if the Queen brings no children, has a barren Juno. The Queen is compounded of Juno, Venus, and Minerva. His poem on the dutchess of Grafton's law-suit, after having rattled a while with Juno and Pallas, Mars and Alcides, Cassiope, Niobe, and the Propetides, Hercules, Minos, and Rhadamanthus, at last concludes its folly with profaneness." Writing of William Somerville, Johnson says: "familiar images in laboured language have nothing to recommend them but absurd novelty which, wanting the attractions of Nature, cannot please long."

Johnson places poems in their genres and poets in their groupings. He values historically informed critical knowledge. Yet connection with a traditional genre or repository of reference never stands as any guarantee of merit. Modern pastoral poetry, in particular, commits two cardinal errors: it both draws on exhausted commonplaces and seems to promote an ethic of withdrawal and retreat – breeding grounds for the unfettered imagination. Like the poet in *London,* who bids the aggrieved Thales farewell, Johnson values literary engagement – the pleasures and social safety valves of community. Johnson regularly assails a life of withdrawal and poetry drawn only from books, and he regularly praises the life of engaged commitment. Addison "not only stood long in the highest rank of wit and literature, but filled one of the most important offices of state." He "had read with critical eyes the important volume of human life, and knew the heart of man from the depth of stratagem to the surface of affectation."

But while singular genius can and does intervene decisively in tradition, its inventions and innovations are nothing without a reciprocal loop connecting prior human knowledge and subsequent endorsement and recognition. In *Rambler* number 125 Johnson signaled clearly his thoughts in these areas: "There is . . . scarcely any species of writing of which we can tell what is the essence or what are its constituents; every new genius produces some innovation which, when invented and approved, subverts the rules which the practice of foregoing authors had established." Whatever genius invents must pass the test of readerly endorsement. The inventions of genius must be "approved." The finest poetry constitutes a cultural conversation, drawing on and contributing to community and tradition, which it improves by providing a repository of reference for posterity: "Pope searched the pages of

Dryden for happy combinations of heroick diction, but it will not be denied that he added much to what he found. He cultivated our language with so much diligence and art that he has left in his *Homer* a treasure of poetical elegances to posterity."

In his *Prefaces* Johnson remains resolutely attuned to the roles, needs, and rights of readership. Although temporary popularity does not guarantee or equal merit, sustained popularity warrants full respect. "Since the end of poetry is pleasure," he writes in the life of Milton, "that cannot be unpoetical with which all are pleased." He dismisses some contemporary strictures against Pope's *Rape of the Lock* with the observation that "the opinion of the publick was already settled, and it was no longer at the mercy of criticism." Writers themselves are frequently the least reliable guides to their own performances, and the prefaces treat with scorn writers who feel grievances against the marketplace. As he puts it starkly in the life of Thomson, an "author and his reader are not always of a mind." The work is a public property and must be left to fight its own way in the commercial battlefields. Johnson provides a severe account of Pope's "counterfeited" dispositions of contempt for the world: "How could he despise those whom he lived by pleasing, and on whose approbation his esteem of himself was superstructed? Why should he hate those to whose favour he owed his honour and his ease?" With finality Johnson announces: "Of things that terminate in human life the world is the proper judge: to despise its sentence, if it were possible, is not just; and if it were just is not possible."

Poets above all owe their readers pleasure and instruction. In the life of Milton, Johnson writes: "Poetry is the art of uniting pleasure with truth, by calling imagination to the help of reason." And in the life of Butler he says that the "great source of pleasure is variety. Uniformity must tire at last, though it be uniformity of excellence. We love to expect; and, when expectation is disappointed or gratified, we want to be again expecting." Johnson's aperçu is rooted in the complex psychology of readerly desire as much as in the Enlightenment spirit of inquiry, and such beliefs lead Johnson to his figure of the "common reader." In his praise of Gray's *Elegy Wrote in a Country Church Yard* Johnson rejoices to "concur with the common reader," for "by the common sense of readers uncorrupted with literary prejudices, after all the refinements of subtilty and the dogmatism of learning, must be finally decided all claim to poetical honours." Johnson resolutely dislikes most of Gray's poetry, which makes his final resonant tribute the more striking. Johnson

himself, the culturally and historically informed critic, is not the common reader, whose cause he champions, whose decisions he respects; but he concurs in this important life of a near contemporary with that reader for reasons arduously established over the course of the *Prefaces*. (Only the brief sketch of Lyttleton follows Gray in the sequence, and Lyttleton's poems "have nothing to be despised, and little to be admired.") Gray's elegy bodies forth in an almost summary statement the essential Johnsonian criteria. The poem "abounds with images which find a mirror in every mind, and with sentiments to which every bosom returns an echo. The four stanzas beginning 'Yet even these bones' are to me original: I have never seen the notions in any other place; yet he that reads them here persuades himself that he has always felt them."

Johnson treats the elegy as exceptional, of course, in Gray's oeuvre. The terms in which Johnson assails Gray for his other works also have been arduously established throughout the prefaces, for the "regularity and composure" of late-Hanoverian Britain (as he terms it in the life of Butler) are under stress. In his own late years Johnson finds his literary values imperiled again by the challenges to Augustan norms in the new wave of poets of sensibility (a later term for them, not Johnson's), such as Collins, Akenside, and Gray, with whom Johnson, despite some admirations, has little affinity. These poets work in the wake of Warton's groundbreaking essay of 1756, quoted above, which challenges Pope's eminence and values poetry of the "sublime and pathetick" over the "men of wit and sense." In general Johnson dislikes his contemporaries among the booksellers' choices. In these poets the "Dangerous Prevalence of Imagination" shows itself again, allied by implication to a political restlessness. Johnson praises Akenside's *The Pleasures of Imagination* (1744) in by now familiar terms: the collection showed "a young mind stored with images, and much exercised in combining and comparing them." And he disparages Akenside's odes in terms equally familiar: "the sentiments commonly want force, nature, or novelty; the diction is sometimes harsh and uncouth, the stanzas ill-constructed and unpleasant, and the rhymes dissonant or unskilfully disposed."

But it is in his accounts of Collins and Gray that Johnson's unease breaks through most openly. In a revealing description of Collins's life, Johnson implies that his tastes in reading, and as a consequence his poetic aesthetics, had in fact contributed to the sad unraveling of his reason: "He had employed his mind chiefly upon works of fiction and subjects of fancy, and by indulging some peculiar habits of thought, was eminently delighted with those flights of imagination which pass the bounds of nature, and to which the mind is reconciled only by a passive acquiescence in popular traditions. He loved fairies, genii, giants and monsters: he delighted to rove through the meanders of enchantment, to gaze on the magnificence of golden palaces, to repose by the waterfalls of Elysian gardens." The description suggests a Don Quixote, the disordered hero of Miguel de Cervantes's influential novel, highly praised by Johnson in the life of Butler: "Cervantes shows a man who, having by the incessant perusal of incredible tales subjected his understanding to his imagination, and familiarised his mind by pertinacious meditation to trains of incredible events and scenes of impossible existence." Aligned with the artificial and dangerous isolation of academic bowers and the stilted and heartless world of derivative pastoral, a literature of the fantastic has proved the feeding ground for that hunger of imagination that preys incessantly upon life, and Collins's understanding has been subjected to his imagination.

The immensely sociable Johnson believed in the sociability of literature. Literature at its best is a companionable transaction, antithetical to the dangerous isolations of Collins. Collins, whom Johnson knew and liked personally, died in 1759; Johnson first wrote this character sketch of him in 1763. *The History of Rasselas* had been published in 1759, and in it Johnson sets out to deflate the apparently exotic wonders in oriental tales then much in vogue. Collins's mind, Johnson continues, was "somewhat obstructed in its progress by deviation in quest of mistaken beauties." His poetry similarly is obstructed, composed of lines commonly of "slow motion, clogged and impeded." Collins's mind is itself lost to insanity, and Johnson indirectly implies a link between Collins's extravagant poetics and his sad last years, when he languished under "that depression of mind which enchains the faculties without destroying them, and leaves reason the knowledge of right without the power of pursuing it."

Gray is treated on the whole in terms that resemble, in new contexts, Johnson's objections to the Metaphysical school: Gray's odes "are marked by glittering accumulations of ungraceful ornaments: they strike rather than please; the images are magnified by affectation, the language is laboured into harshness." What Johnson sees as the fastidious, overly labored poetry of Gray is for him again a poetry without feeling and thus without ethical purpose or effect. "I do not see," says Johnson, "that 'The Bard' promotes any truth, moral or political."

An implied full circle has been turned: as in the literature of the civil war, Johnson sees signs of an outrageous quest for novelty which unhinges human reason, unfetters the imagination, and offers madness and suicidal violence as apparent values.

Such poetry threatens the usurpation of understanding by imagination — at the individual level (as in the case of Collins) — and threatens again the release of the kinds of internecine revolutionary energies that led to usurpation on a national scale in the civil war. Johnson wrote his *Prefaces* in the decade of Lord North's administration and the American Revolution, a decade that also saw his vigorous political pamphlets *The False Alarm* (written against John Wilkes and mob rule) and *Taxation No Tyranny,* both of which show a hostility to insurgency. Johnson, of course, did not live to see the French Revolution, but the English Romantic poets sympathetic to it drew their poetics from precisely the eighteenth-century poets with whom Johnson was least at ease. Johnson's profound worries on these matters appear with remarkable consistency. In his second *Rambler* essay (24 March 1750) he had warned his readers against "suffering the imagination to riot." And in *Rambler* number 66 (3 November 1750) he states that it is his business to separate the actual "affairs of life" from "the foam of a boiling imagination." In his assessments of the newest poets, who challenge the tradition of Dryden, Addison, and Pope, one hears the same critic who urgently rejects Pope's ill-formed notion of the ruling passion. In the English civil war, when passions ruled, chaos and mass slaughter resulted. Unfettered human emotions and energies usurped the place of reasoned discourse, and the result was a triumph for forces Johnson calls usurpation.

In the individual mind of Collins, imagination has usurped reason. Gray's "The Bard" ends, of course, with the Bard's suicide. "The Ode might have been concluded with an action of better example," says Johnson (who disapproves of Pope's "Elegy on the Memory of an Unfortunate Lady" on similar moral grounds), "but suicide is always to be had without expense of thought." In the Bard's suicidally triumphant defiance, which the later Romantic poets found poetically thrilling, Johnson seems to detect only resurgent hints of the self-destructive "madness" with which his immethodical survey of a century of poets and poetry began. The two earliest of the major poets to be treated, Cowley and Milton, wrote in the aftermath of terrific turbulence and from opposed political perspectives, of which their poetics stand as correlatives. Now, in the more stable reign of George III, the time had come for reappraisal and calm review, a time to let an Olympian "observation with an extensive view" take its survey, assess and solidify merit in a way detached, Johnson hopes, from factional (religious, sectarian, and even authorial) contention and strife. The "regularity and composure of the present time" described in the life of Butler is imperiled. Smoothness, balance, order, harmony, calm, and judicious appraisal come at a cost. Johnson knows what it is, conceding a loss of "creative fire" in Addison and his tradition. But fire is destructive as well as creative. The price is one that Johnson is willing to pay, rejecting, as he brings his survey to an end, what he rejected in his most carefully written preface the life of Pope: any force on the human moral will "antecedent to Reason and Observation" – the two central forces he believes himself most centrally to be exercising in his "Lives of the Poets."

Like the poetry of Thomson, Johnsonian biography aspires to be the product of "a mind that at once comprehends the vast, and attends to the minute." Both prizing and enacting connection and continuity, not rupture, Johnson's biographical sensibility resolutely denies the vain and self-loving self. Antipanegyric, such biography will not take authorial vanity at its own estimate, for it is but a short step to the politically dangerous myth of self-invention and another short step to the Puritan will to mastery. So complex and forcefully expressed and so strongly judgmental an assembly of prefaces produced, as might be expected, extremes of response. Later critical generations would move strikingly away from Johnson's emphases, and in many ways Johnson's assessments amount to a conservative nostalgia for a tradition of poetry of which he himself was the last major exemplar. But even as later poets and critics sought to establish their difference from Johnson, his terms have been co-opted. As Robert J. Griffin remarks, "G. B. Hill's footnotes, which are themselves a course in literary history, recurrently cite opinions by Cowper, Coleridge, Wordsworth, Southey, and Tennyson among others, which either agree substantially with Johnson, or in disagreeing with him confirm nonetheless his authority to set the terms, and cite the passages for debate."

Whatever the fate of Johnson's assessments and the claims for obsolescence in his stances, Johnson was a pioneering literary biographer and biographical literary critic: Johnson's influence persists, his basic methods being adopted, adapted, and pursued with more sophistication and consistency than the proprietors' collection allowed him. Johnsonian literary biography above all attempts complex integrations, explicit and implicit. It acknowledges that writers' lives are acts of community. It mourns and commemorates yet exercises judgments on behalf of stated values and seeks to make the grounds of its valuations available. The *Prefaces* do retain some traces of an older idea of biography as moral fable: near the end of the life of Savage the morality of writing lives is still on Johnson's mind: Savage's "actions, which were generally precipitate, were often blameable; but his writings, being the productions of study, uniformly tended to the exaltation of the mind, and the propagation of morality and piety. . . . These writings may improve mankind when his failings shall be forgotten. . . . Nor can his personal example do any hurt, since, whoever hears of his faults, will hear of the miseries which they brought upon him. . . ." But this life first appeared much earlier in Johnson's career, and on this score it is slightly out of place in this reprinting. Johnson is already tending to find historic and domestic detail legitimate sources of fascination in their own right. Indeed, Boswell, in his own controversial *Life of Samuel Johnson,* would bring to its first full expression the idea of the candid biography, assembled from masses of personal recollection and quotidian detail.

Johnson flatly rejects a naive life-*in*-the-works mode of biography: "The biographer of Thomson has remarked that an author's life is best read in his works: his observation was not well-timed. Savage, who lived much with Thomson, once told me how he heard a lady remarking that she could gather from his works three parts of his character, that he was 'a great lover, a great swimmer, and rigorously abstinent': but, said Savage, he knows not any love but that of the sex; he was perhaps never in cold water in his life; and he indulges himself in all the luxury that comes within his reach." Creative writing, to Johnson and all advanced post-Johnsonian biographers, constitutes complex registrations of the political psyche, not literal autobiography. The contextualist biographical critic searches out authorial schools and groupings, assesses contemporary pressures, and charts the ways literature constitutes the residue of these things independent, often, of the author's own sense of merit. But biographical endorsements are not themselves enduring monuments: the common reader has been there before biography, and the biographer owes that reader's judgments deference. Civilization, though it must as a matter of the utmost importance commemorate and mourn its dead, is vital – kept alive by conversation and richly understood as a constant, morally motivated, informed, educated, and educative exchange. Whatever tendencies Johnson's prose has to the timelessly lapidary, Johnson remains tensely aware that he participates — however confidently, magisterially, quotably, and unevasively — only in what Lipking terms a "perpetual commentary." Johnson values reason but knows what escapes the light of reason, that literary judgment is but writers assessing other writers, and the battle is to rise above the local, the personal, and the grinding ax. Regarding a severe remark about Nicholas Rowe said by Pope to have been made by Addison, Johnson writes, "perhaps the best advice to authors would be that they should keep out of the way of one another."

The history of the century of poetry Johnson treats is complex, and one may now read his contribution as both a record of it and a moment in it. Those static, panhistorical or ahistorical concepts — nature, life, truth, and reason — are the issue of a Christian-humanist sensibility inflected by Enlightenment intellectual methods. They were for Johnson the touchstone of authorial merit, that to which an appeal must be made for permanent worth in any authorial output — so often, in Johnson's frequently severe, frequently forgiving life stories, the product of folly, delusion, vanity, spleen, anxiety, rivalry, and sheer economic necessity. Poetry must not be taken at the author's estimate, nor at the estimate of any poet's critical and ideological partisans — usually an excessive praise or damnation. After the excitement of production and initial reception has subsided, some sort of community consensus must form. That consensus offers a basis for taste, that of the common reader, which for Johnson is sometimes but not necessarily identical with merit. More sophisticated, informed assessments flow from a contextually informed scholarship. The post-Romantic nineteenth century rejected Johnson's refusal to accord the authorial temperament hierophantic or transcendent authority. In the mid twentieth century a dominant formalist aesthetic sought to detach poetry from historical context. The last decades of the century, with appeals to multicultural, multiconstituent diversity, still find Johnson's appeal to those universal human values troublesome but have in fact rediscovered the sophisticated contextualist method Johnson helped pioneer. Any attempt to assess poetry, to appraise merit, to separate the ephemeral from the enduring, to forge a national (or any cultural group or subgroup) repository of "representative" literature will inevitably appeal, implicitly or explicitly, to standards such as those Johnson assumed. It is the business of the poet, according to Imlac, to write "as

the interpreter of nature, and the legislator of mankind . . . presiding over the thoughts and manners of future generations." Johnson believed utterly in the moral experience of reading, yet remained deeply anxious about literature's capacity to teach ethically, and its corollary capacity to undermine moral precepts. His own authorial practice was grounded in the real; his aesthetic speculations were attached to the contexts of the poetry on which they were based, contexts with which poets and poems are engaged in a complex, mutually formative, reciprocal loop.

The proprietors' collection offered, then, a time for Johnson to reassert his affinities. Local challenges to various wisdoms and orthodoxies emerge, but no fundamental departures from Dryden, Pope, and Addison. Johnson brings his hallmark Christian-humanist stoicism (the voice of the end of *The Vanity of Human Wishes*) to bear on his surveys of poetic careers. He shares certain Enlightenment impulses — to rational inquiry, systematic procedure, and devotion to principle and precept. Readers find in his lives beliefs in the poetic properties the Romantic poets would make central in their own aesthetics — inspiration, creative fire, originality, invention, and genius — matters that escape precept, principle, or even rational inquiry. But where romanticism sought to locate poetic creativity in the transcendent, hierophantic isolation of solitary genius, celebrating (in the words of William Wordsworth's *Prelude,* 1850) "imagination lifting up itself," Johnson remains resolutely contextual. The last decades of the twentieth century have seen challenges to Enlightenment assumptions of a universally definable "Man," Christian-humanist assumptions of biblical universality, and a timeless and unchanging "human nature." These have yielded to a new valuation of pluralist perspectives, the rights of disjunct and separate constituencies; the Addisonian ideal of civility and politeness is seen as the suppression of an enriching diversity in the cause of coercively normative values. But while many of Johnson's assumptions and values waned with romanticism, and with mid-twentieth-century formalist textual criticism, the last decade of the twentieth century has found its way, in the very act of mounting those challenges, back to a contextually and historically informed criticism. Johnson as a life-writer was a contextualist critic *avant la lettre*.

Letters:

The Letters of Samuel Johnson, with Mrs. Thrale's Genuine Letters to Him, 3 volumes, edited by R. W. Chapman (Oxford: Clarendon Press, 1952);

The Letters of Samuel Johnson, 5 volumes, edited by Bruce Redford (Princeton: Princeton University Press, 1992–1994).

Bibliographies:

William P. Courtney and D. Nichol Smith, *A Bibliography of Samuel Johnson* (Oxford: Clarendon Press, 1915);

R. W. Chapman and Allen T. Hazen, "Johnsonian Bibliography: A Supplement to Courtney," *Proceedings of the Oxford Bibliographical Society,* 5 (1939), pp. 119–166;

Donald Greene, "The Development of the Johnson Canon," in *Restoration and Eighteenth-Century Literature,* edited by Carroll Camden (Chicago: University of Chicago Press, 1963), pp. 407–427;

James L. Clifford and Donald J. Greene, *Samuel Johnson: A Survey and Bibliography of Critical Studies* (Minneapolis: University of Minnesota Press, 1970);

Donald Greene and John A. Vance, *A Bibliography of Johnsonian Studies, 1970–1985,* University of Victoria English Literary Studies, no. 39 (Victoria, B.C.: 1987).

Biographies:

Hester Lynch Piozzi (Mrs. Thrale), *Anecdotes of the Late Samuel Johnson, LL.D. During the Last Twenty Years of His Life* (London: Printed for T. Cadell, 1786); republished, and edited by Arthur Sherbo, in William Shaw, *Memoirs of the Life and Writings of the Late Dr. Samuel Johnson,* Oxford English Memoirs and Travels (Oxford: Oxford University Press, 1974);

Sir John Hawkins, *The Life of Samuel Johnson, LL.D.,* volume 1 of *The Works of Samuel Johnson, LL.D.* (London: Printed for J. Buckland and forty others, 1787); republished (slightly abridged), edited by Bertram H. Davis (New York: Macmillan, 1961);

James Boswell, *The Life of Samuel Johnson, LL.D.,* 2 volumes (London: Printed by Henry Baldwin for Charles Dilly, 1791); republished in *Boswell's Life of Johnson, Together with Boswell's Journal of a Tour to the Hebrides and Johnson's Diary of a Journey into North Wales,* 6 volumes, edited by G. B. Hill, revised and enlarged by L. F. Powell (Oxford: Clarendon Press, 1934–1964);

G. B. Hill, ed., *Johnsonian Miscellanies,* 2 volumes (Oxford: Clarendon Press, 1897);

Aleyn Lyell Reade, *Johnsonian Gleanings,* 11 volumes (London: Privately printed for the author, 1909–1952);

Joseph Wood Krutch, *Samuel Johnson* (New York: Holt, 1944);

John Wain, *Samuel Johnson* (London: Macmillan, 1944; New York: Viking, 1975);

James L. Clifford, *Young Sam Johnson* (New York: McGraw-Hill, 1965);

The Early Biographies of Samuel Johnson, edited by O M Brack, Jr., and Robert E. Kelley (Iowa City: University of Iowa Press, 1974);

W. Jackson Bate, *Samuel Johnson* (New York: Harcourt Brace Jovanovich, 1977; London: Chatto & Windus, 1978);

James L. Clifford, *Dictionary Johnson: Samuel Johnson's Middle Years* (New York: McGraw-Hill, 1979; London: Heinemann, 1979).

References:

The Age of Johnson [annual], edited by Paul J. Korshin (New York: AMS Press, 1987–);

Paul K. Alkon, *Samuel Johnson and Moral Discipline* (Evanston, Ill.: Northwestern University Press, 1967);

Harold Bloom, ed., *Dr. Samuel Johnson and James Boswell* (New York: Chelsea House, 1986);

Fredric V. Bogel, *The Dream of My Brother: An Essay on Johnson's Authority* (Victoria, B.C.: University of Victoria, 1990);

Thomas F. Bonnell, "John Bell's *Poets of Great Britain:* the 'Little Trifling Edition' Revisited," *MP* 85 (1987): 128–152;

Bertrand H. Bronson, "The Double Tradition of Dr. Johnson," *ELH: A Journal of English Literary History,* 18 (June 1951): 90–106;

Bronson, "Johnson Agonistes," in his *Johnson and Boswell: Three Essays* (Berkeley & Los Angeles: University of California Press, 1944);

Joseph Epes Brown, *The Critical Opinions of Samuel Johnson* (Princeton: Princeton University Press, 1925);

Morris R. Brownell, *Samuel Johnson's Attitude to the Arts* (Oxford: Clarendon Press, 1989);

John J. Burke, Jr., and Donald Kay, eds., *The Unknown Samuel Johnson* (Madison: University of Wisconsin Press, 1983);

Annette Wheeler Cafarelli, *Prose in the Age of Poets: Romanticism and Biographical Narrative from Johnson to De Quincey* (Philadelphia: University of Pennsylvania Press, 1990);

Chester F. Chapin, *The Religious Thought of Samuel Johnson* (Ann Arbor: University of Michigan Press, 1968);

Greg Clingham, ed., *New Light on Boswell: Critical and Historical Essays on the Occasion of the Bicentenary of "The Life of Johnson"* (Cambridge: Cambridge University Press, 1991);

Leopold Damrosch, *Fictions of Reality in the Age of Hume and Johnson* (Madison: University of Wisconsin Press, 1989);

Philip Davis, *In Mind of Johnson* (Athens: University of Georgia Press, 1989);

T. S. Eliot, Introduction to Johnson *London and the Vanity of Human Wishes* (London: Etchells & Macdonald, 1930);

James Engell, ed., *Johnson and His Age* (Cambridge, Mass.: Harvard University Press, 1984);

J. D. Fleeman, ed., *The Sale Catalogue of Samuel Johnson's Library: A Facsimile Edition,* University of Victoria English Literary Studies, no. 2 (Victoria, B.C., 1975);

Robert Folkenflik, *Samuel Johnson, Biographer* (Ithaca, N.Y.: Cornell University Press, 1978);

James Gray, *Johnson's Sermons: A Study* (Oxford: Clarendon Press, 1972);

Donald Greene, *The Politics of Samuel Johnson* (New Haven: Yale University Press, 1960; revised edition, Athens: University of Georgia Press, 1990);

Greene, *Samuel Johnson* (New York: Twayne, 1970; revised edition, Boston: Twayne, 1989);

Greene, *Samuel Johnson's Library: An Annotated Guide,* University of Victoria English Literary Studies, no. 1 (Victoria, B.C., 1975);

Greene, ed., *Samuel Johnson: A Collection of Critical Essays* (Englewood Cliffs, N.J.: Prentice-Hall, 1965);

Isobel Grundy, *Samuel Johnson and the Scale of Greatness* (Athens: University of Georgia Press, 1986);

Grundy, ed., *Samuel Johnson: New Critical Essays* (London: Vision, 1984);

Jean H. Hagstrum, *Samuel Johnson's Literary Criticism* (Minneapolis: University of Minnesota Press, 1952);

F. W. Hilles, ed., *The Age of Johnson: Essays Presented To C. B. Tinker* (New Haven: Yale University Press, 1949);

Hilles, ed., *New Light on Dr. Johnson* (New Haven: Yale University Press, 1959);

Charles H. Hinnant, *Samuel Johnson* (New York: St. Martin's Press, 1988);

Richard Holmes, *Dr. Johnson and Mr. Savage* (London: Hodder and Stoughton, 1993);

Benjamin B. Hoover, *Samuel Johnson's Parliamentary Reporting* (Berkeley & Los Angeles: University of California Press, 1953);

Nicholas Hudson, *Samuel Johnson and Eighteenth-Century Thought* (Oxford: Clarendon Press, 1988);

George Irwin, *Samuel Johnson: A Personality in Conflict* (Auckland, N.Z., Auckland University Press / New York: Oxford University Press, 1971);

Johnsonian News Letter [quarterly] (New York: Department of English, Columbia University, 1940–);

Thomas Kaminski, *The Early Career of Samuel Johnson* (New York: Oxford University Press, 1987);

Paul J. Korshin, ed., *Johnson After Two Hundred Years* (Philadelphia: University of Pennsylvania Press, 1986);

Lyle Larson, *Dr. Johnson's Household* (Hamden, Conn.: Archon, 1985);

Mary Lascelles, James L. Clifford, and others, eds., *Johnson, Boswell, and Their Circle: Essays Presented to L. F. Powell* (Oxford: Clarendon Press, 1965);

Steven Lynn, *Samuel Johnson after Deconstruction* (Carbondale: Southern Illinois University Press, 1992);

Martin Maner, *The Philosophical Biographer: Doubt and Dialectic in Johnson's "Lives of the Poets"* (Athens: University of Georgia Press, 1988);

E. L. McAdam, Jr., *Dr. Johnson and the English Law* (Syracuse, N.Y.: Syracuse University Press, 1951);

Prem Nath, ed., *Fresh Reflections on Samuel Johnson* (Troy, N.Y.: Whitston, 1987);

Norman Page, ed., *Dr. Johnson: Interviews and Recollections* (Totowa, N.J.: Barnes & Noble, 1986);

Richard B. Schwartz, *Daily Life in Johnson's London* (Madison: University of Wisconsin Press, 1983);

Schwartz, *Samuel Johnson and the New Science* (Madison: University of Wisconsin Press, 1971);

Schwartz, *Samuel Johnson and the Problem of Evil* (Madison: University of Wisconsin Press, 1975);

Arthur Sherbo, *Samuel Johnson, Editor of Shakespeare, with an Essay on The Adventurer* (Urbana: University of Illinois Press, 1956);

James H. Sledd and Gwin J. Kolb, *Dr. Johnson's Dictionary: Essays in the Biography of a Book* (Chicago: University of Chicago Press, 1955);

Mark J. Temmer, *Samuel Johnson and Three Infidels: Rousseau, Voltaire, Diderot* (Athens: University of Georgia Press, 1988);

Edward Tomarken, *Johnson, Rasselas, and the Choice of Criticism* (Lexington: University Press of Kentucky, 1989);

Tomarken, *Samuel Johnson on Shakespeare* (Athens: University of Georgia Press, 1991);

John A. Vance, *Samuel Johnson and the Sense of History* (Athens: University of Georgia Press, 1984);

Robert Voitle, *Samuel Johnson the Moralist* (Cambridge, Mass.: Harvard University Press, 1961);

T. F. Wharton, *Samuel Johnson and the Theme of Hope* (New York: St. Martin's Press, 1984);

David Wheeler, ed., *Domestick Privacies: Samuel Johnson and the Art of Biography* (Lexington: University Press of Kentucky, 1987);

W. K. Wimsatt, Jr., *Philosophic Words: A Study of Style and Meaning in the Rambler and Dictionary of Samuel Johnson* (New Haven: Yale University Press, 1948);

Wimsatt, *The Prose Style of Samuel Johnson* (New Haven: Yale University Press, 1941).

Papers:
Although Johnson's output of writing was enormous, only a relatively small amount of manuscript material has survived. The largest holding is in the Hyde Collection, Four Oaks Farm, Somerville, New Jersey, which incorporates the collection of R. B. Adam, described in four volumes (*The R. B. Adam Library Relating to Dr. Samuel Johnson and His Era,* 1929–1930); important holdings are in other private collections. The Yale University Library, the British Library, the Bodleian Library, the library of Pembroke College, Oxford, and the Johnson Birthplace Museum, Lichfield, have important manuscripts. A useful guide is J. D. Fleeman, *A Preliminary Handlist of Documents and Manuscripts of Samuel Johnson* (Oxford Bibliographical Society Occasional Publications, no. 7, 1967). This does not include the locations of manuscripts of Johnson's letters, which are listed in Bruce Redford's edition of the letters (1992–1994).

Edmond Malone
(4 October 1741 – 25 April 1812)

Martin Beller
C. W. Post Campus, Long Island University

BOOKS: *An Inquiry into the Authenticity of Certain Miscellaneous Papers and Legal Instruments, Published Dec. 24, M DCC XCV, and Attributed to Shakspeare [sic], Queen Elizabeth, and Henry, Earl of Southampton* (London: Printed by H. Baldwin for T. Cadell, jun. & W. Davies, 1796);

A Biographical Memoir of the late Right Honourable William Windham (London: Printed by John Nichols & Son, 1810).

OTHER: "Ode on the royal nuptials," in *Gratulationes Juventutis Academia Dubliniensis in Sereniss. Regis et Regina Nuptias* (Dublin: Printed by William Watson, 1761);

Poems and Plays. By Oliver Goldsmith, M.B. To which is prefixed, the Life of the Author, 2 volumes, edited, with a preface, by Malone (Dublin: Printed for Messrs. Price, Sleater, W. Watson [and others], 1777); republished as *The Poetical and Dramatic Works of Oliver Goldsmith, M.B. Now first collected. With an Account of the Life and Writings of the Author* (London: Printed by H. Goldney, for Messieurs Rivington, T. Carnan & F. Newbery; T. Lowndes & G. Kearsley; T. Cadell & T. Evans, 1780);

"An Attempt to Ascertain the Order in Which the Plays Attributed to Shakespeare Were Written," in volume 1 of *The Works of William Shakespeare,* 9 volumes, edited by George Steevens (London, 1778);

Matteo Bandello, *The Tragicall Hystory of Romeus and Juliet,* translated and adapted by Arthur Brooke, edited by Malone (London, 1780);

The Plays and Poems of William Shakespeare, 10 volumes, edited by Malone (London: Printed by H. Baldwin for J. Rivington & Sons, 1790);

Francis Godolphin Waldron, *The Biographical Mirrour,* 3 volumes, includes contributions by Malone (London: Published by E. & S. Harding, 1795–1810);

The Works of Sir Joshua Reynolds, Knt., 2 volumes, includes a memoir by Malone (London: Printed for T. Cadell, Jun. & W. Davies, 1797);

The Critical and Miscellaneous Prose Works of John Dryden, 3 volumes, edited, with a memoir, by Malone (London: Printed by H. Baldwin & Son, for T. Cadell, Jun. & W. Davies, 1800);

William Gerard Hamilton, *Parliamentary Logick,* edited, with a memoir, by Malone (London: Printed by C. & R. Baldwin for Thomas Payne, 1808);

Joseph Spence, *Observations, Anecdotes, and Characters, of Books and Men; Arranged with notes by the late Edmond Malone, Esq.* (London: J. Murray, 1820);

The Plays and Poems of William Shakespeare, With the Corrections and Illustrations of Various Commentators: Comprehending a Life of the Poet, and an Enlarged History of the Stage, by the late Edmond Malone, 21 volumes, edited by James Boswell, Jr. (London: F. C. & J. Rivington, 1821).

Edmond Malone's relentless pursuit and scrupulous examination of documents; his refusal to accept any assertion, no matter how sanctified by tradition, not supported by physical evidence; his insistence on following the ascertainable facts wherever they led; and even his reluctance to publish – so unwilling was he to commit himself to print while there was a chance that further discoveries might shed new light on his subject – all help define the spirit of modern literary scholarship. His gifts were widely recognized during his life, and, after a century of neglect, twentieth-century critics have restored him to the honors he once claimed.

Edmond Malone was born on 4 October 1741 to Edmond and Catherine Collier Malone. The Malones had been distinguished in Irish civil and ecclesiastical life since the twelfth century, as evident in Mervyn Archdall's *Peerage of Ireland* (1789). They were substantial landowners and in 1741 were

Edmond Malone

among the wealthiest and most powerful Irish families. The young Edmond's grandfather Richard Malone had served King William; his uncle Anthony Malone became chancellor of the Irish Exchequer in 1757; and his uncles Richard and John Malone were barristers, Richard an M.P. His father had been called to both the English and Irish bars, had served as M.P. for Granard from 1760 to 1766, and, from 1766, was judge of the Court of Common Pleas. Edmond's brother Richard was raised to the Irish peerage as Lord Sunderlin in 1785.

Malone attended Dr. Ford's highly respected private school in Molesworth Street, Dublin, where his schoolfellows included the future first marquis of Lansdowne and first Lord Sheffield as well as Robert Jephson, well known in later life as a poet and playwright, with whom Malone developed an enduring friendship. At Dr. Ford's school Malone also received his first taste of the stage, participating in the school's acclaimed theatricals. At Trinity College, Dublin, which he entered in 1757, he compiled a notable record of academic achievement. He had developed early the logical rigor and passion for ac-

curate information that would distinguish his later work as a scholar. He is characterized by his first biographer, James Boswell, Jr., as having already "laid down to himself those rules of study to which he afterwards steadily adhered. . . . When sitting down to the perusal of any work, either antient [*sic*] or modern, his attention was drawn to its chronology, the history and character of its author, the feelings and prejudices of the times in which he lived; and any other collateral information which might tend to illustrate his writings, or acquaint us with his probable views and cast of thinking."

Malone first visited England in the summer of 1759, while accompanying his mother to Bath, where she lived until her death in 1765. In 1763 he undertook law studies at the Inner Temple, London. These studies no doubt accentuated habits of mind that were already well developed in him and that were to be typical of his approach to literary scholarship: a prosecutorial rigor in exposing error, carelessness, and outright fraud; an insistence on verifiable facts; an analytic approach to any problem susceptible to analysis; and a frame and method of argumentation modeled on the legal brief.

After his mother's death he visited the south of France (1766) and Paris (1767). Returning to Dublin in 1767, he was called to the Irish bar, where, typically for a young aspirant, his practice was desultory. He had, nonetheless, shown promise of brilliance and might have been headed for a successful career in the profession in which so many of his forebears had distinguished themselves when, in 1774, his father's death brought him an inheritance that provided a modest but secure income of eight hundred pounds per year. Freed from the necessity of earning an income, he soon entered politics. It is difficult to imagine as intellectually fastidious a person as Malone enjoying the rough-and-tumble Dublin political and legal life. He seems to have been deficient in the thrusting self-assertiveness required for electoral success. His native diffidence, passion for truth, and independent spirit may have hampered him, and the death of his uncle Anthony Malone in 1776 left him without a strong patron to guide his political and legal career. In any event, his political ambitions were decisively dashed when, having announced his intention to stand for election to Parliament as member for Trinity College, he was passed over in favor of another candidate. This defeat may have solidified in his mind a resolution that had been forming for several years: to devote himself entirely to literary studies and to quit Dublin for London, the most auspicious place to undertake such studies. Accordingly on 1 May 1777 he left Ireland to settle in London and pursue a literary career. From this point on he returned to Ireland only for brief, infrequent visits, during which his letters to London friends expressed an unfeigned longing to return to his work. Though his family was disappointed in his choice of a path in life and continually asked him to reconsider, they never pressed so insistently as to threaten a breach, nor was there ever a hint of alienation. Malone seems to have inspired a rare degree of affection in all whom he admitted to intimacy, and this was particularly true of his near relations. Indeed it was gifts from his brother, who enjoyed an income of six thousand pounds, that enabled Malone to amass his unparalleled collections of Shakespeare materials.

At some time around 1769 Malone and a young woman named Susanna Spencer had developed an attachment, but they were prevented from marrying by the disparity in their social rank, Spencer being poor and from an undistinguished family. Though incapable of a happy resolution, the attachment could not be overcome, and matters might have remained in a state of unsatisfactory suspension forever had not Spencer's already marked men-tal instability blossomed, in 1782, into full-fledged insanity. Malone's anguished letters from this period are painful to read.

A contemporary diarist, Joseph Farington, referring to Malone's unfailing courtesy and habitual cheerfulness, was moved to note, "Contrary to what His appearance bespoke He had lived a life of much anxiety from being disappointed in hopes and wishes which related to domestic union (marriage) that must now no longer be looked for." To his friend Lord Charlemont, Malone wrote in January 1782 of "a most unfortunate attachment, which never could have contributed much to my honour, and has ended most unhappily . . . ; there is little chance of getting over an attachment that has continued with unabated force for thirteen years; nor at my time of life, is the heart very easily captured by a new object. . . . I am a very domestic kind of animal, and not at all adapted for solitude."

Despite these protestations, Malone was to press his romantic attentions on at least two other women, both of whom appear to have been reluctant. Less than a year after Spencer's breakdown, Malone was paying court to young Sarah Loveday, who seems to have spurned him: his letters speak of her "aversion" to him. And in 1793 Farington reports that Malone, then fifty-two, "has been to Cheshire to see Miss Bover and has offered himself to her, but is not accepted." From the same source, readers learn of James Boswell's revealing remark: "tho Malone is obliging in his manners, He has never been a favorite of the Ladies, He is too soft in his manners." Whatever his efforts in other quarters, his devotion to Spencer remained lifelong. Shortly after she became incapacitated, he gave her an annuity of £100 to provide for her maintenance, and in his will he left her £100 outright, together with an annuity of £150.

Even before he settled in London permanently Malone was preparing himself, both in Dublin and during his visits to London, for his emerging vocation as literary scholar. At some point the leading Shakespeare scholar, George Steevens, had lent Malone his copy of Gerard Langbaine's *Account of the English Dramatic Poets* (1691), crammed with Steevens's own annotations as well as those of the antiquary William Oldys. Malone decided to transcribe the text and annotations and to make notes, not only with corrections and amplifications, but also with dated diary entries documenting his activities as a scholar of the early drama. A jotting dated 24 September 1776, for example, says that he accompanied Steevens on that date to see "Shakespeare's *original* Will."

Malone's first work of scholarship was an edition of his countryman Oliver Goldsmith's *Poems and Plays* with a memoir of his life, published in Dublin in 1777 and in London in 1780. This work must have occupied Malone for some time before his relocation. His biography of Goldsmith is a relaxed and affectionate performance, relying on personal memory and anonymously supplied anecdotes. While it displays some of the preoccupations that also mark Malone's mature work – in particular a concern to authenticate traditional anecdotes – it gives little promise of the distinction to come. It does offer a harrowing account of Goldsmith's death throes.

As readers of Boswell's *Life of Samuel Johnson* (1791) know, Malone was quickly admitted to the most distinguished literary circles and was particularly treasured for the brilliance and hospitality of his own dinner parties. He had met Johnson during his earlier sojourn in London in 1763, while studying at the Inner Temple, and was elected a member of the "Literary Club," of which Johnson himself was the chief ornament, not long after settling permanently in London. "The Club" (at various times called "Dr. Johnson's Club" or "The Literary Club") rose out of informal meetings held at Sir Joshua Reynolds's home. Modeled after the Ivy Lane Club, which Johnson had established in 1750, "The Club" was founded in 1764 and met at the Turks Head in Greek Street for nearly twenty years. Malone was admitted as a member in February 1782 and was entrusted with arranging the erection of Johnson's monument in Westminster Abbey after Johnson's death in 1784. Malone was particularly intimate with Reynolds and was a close friend of Boswell and of the antiquarian Thomas Percy. After 1782 this last relationship was conducted mostly through correspondence; in that year Percy was appointed bishop of Dromore and relocated to Ireland. Among other luminaries with whom Malone was on familiar terms were Horace Walpole, Edmund Burke, and the wealthy bibliophile Lord Charlemont, for whom Malone was active in acquiring rare books; their correspondence provides a fascinating glimpse of the conditions of book collecting in the late eighteenth century.

From the beginning of his permanent London residence, Malone devoted himself to Shakespeare studies. Since he was the first to understand how any responsible aesthetic criticism of the works of William Shakespeare depended on an understanding of the chronological relationships of the plays, he undertook "An Attempt to Ascertain the Order in Which the Plays Attributed to Shakespeare Were Written" (1778), the conclusions of which have been much modified but rarely overturned by over two hundred years of further research. Malone's emphasis on chronology underlies much eighteenth-century Shakespeare criticism, anticipating the evolutionary approach culminating in one of the nineteenth century's most influential formulations, Edward Dowden's organization of Shakespeare's life and his creative output into four periods: "In the Workshop" (early comedies), "In the World" (histories and mature comedies), "Out of the Depths" (problem comedies and major tragedies), and "On the Heights" (romances). Samuel Schoenbaum's appreciation of Malone's achievement is just: "Whether right or wrong, Malone sets forth in every instance the data on which he has based his conclusion.... The reader ... is in a position to form his own conclusion. Malone never claims infallibility.... The enduringly admirable characteristics of Malone's scholarship thus appear in his first Shakespearean venture: his candor; his rejection of impressionism in favor of method, which he has clearly expounded; his wide reading; his refusal to push the interpretation of evidence beyond legitimate bounds.... Because he had refrained from dogmatism at the outset, he was able afterwards to reconsider and revise his conclusions without embarrassment" (*Shakespeare's Lives,* 1970). Oddly, when Malone came to produce his own edition of Shakespeare's works, in 1790, he did not arrange the plays chronologically. The 1821 variorum, properly regarded as Malone's posthumous edition, is the first to present the plays according to his chronology.

To Steevens's 1778 edition of Johnson's works of Shakespeare, Malone contributed "Supplemental Observations" on the history of the staging and printing of Elizabethan plays, considered by David Nichol Smith as "our first authoritative treatise on the early drama"; a reprint of Arthur Brooke's *Romeus and Juliet*; editions of Shakespeare's poems (then not normally printed with the plays); and several apocryphal plays, including *Pericles,* now considered canonical. In 1783 Malone added "A Second Appendix to Mr. Malone's Supplement to the last edition of the Plays of Shakespeare," consisting mainly of suggested emendations of the text.

Around 1785 Malone's friendly relations with Steevens underwent a breach. Isaac Reed had taken responsibility for the 1785 edition of Shakespeare – like those of 1773 and 1778 a revision of Johnson's seminal edition of 1765 – and had admitted some notes by Malone in which the latter disagreed with Steevens. Steevens demanded that these notes be

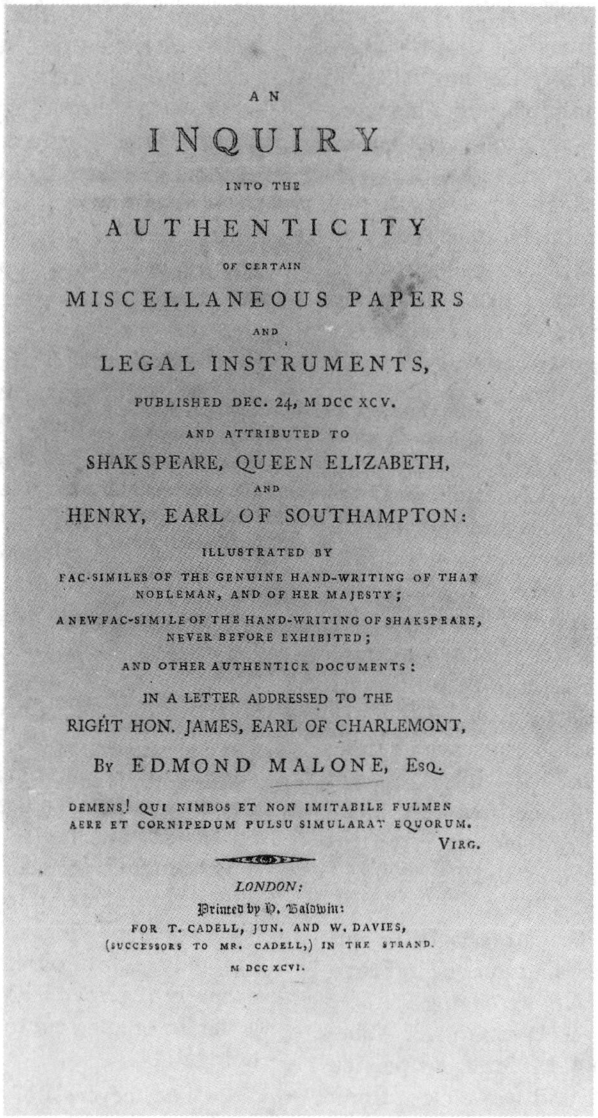

AN

INQUIRY

INTO THE

AUTHENTICITY

OF CERTAIN

MISCELLANEOUS PAPERS

AND

LEGAL INSTRUMENTS,

PUBLISHED DEC. 24, M DCC XCV.

AND ATTRIBUTED TO

SHAKSPEARE, QUEEN ELIZABETH,

AND

HENRY, EARL OF SOUTHAMPTON:

ILLUSTRATED BY

FAC-SIMILES OF THE GENUINE HAND-WRITING OF THAT
NOBLEMAN, AND OF HER MAJESTY;

A NEW FAC-SIMILE OF THE HAND-WRITING OF SHAKSPEARE,
NEVER BEFORE EXHIBITED;

AND OTHER AUTHENTICK DOCUMENTS:

IN A LETTER ADDRESSED TO THE

RIGHT HON. JAMES, EARL OF CHARLEMONT,

By EDMOND MALONE, ESQ.

DEMENS! QUI NIMBOS ET NON IMITABILE FULMEN
AERE ET CORNIPEDUM PULSU SIMULARAT EQUORUM.
VIRG.

LONDON:
Printed by H. Baldwin:
FOR T. CADELL, JUN. AND W. DAVIES,
(SUCCESSORS TO MR. CADELL,) IN THE STRAND.
M DCC XCVI.

*Title page for Malone's masterful refutation of the authenticity
of documents supposedly written by Shakespeare*

transferred unaltered to the edition Malone was then known to be preparing. The idea, presumably, was that Steevens would be able to ready his own rejoinders to these notes so they might be published the instant Malone's edition appeared.

Malone refused this demand, insisting that in the cooperative spirit of Shakespeare studies inaugurated by Johnson's edition, any note that had been, or could be, successfully refuted should be allowed to be withdrawn. Of Steevens it was said that there were only three men among his wide acquaintance with whom he had not quarreled, and two of them were the imperturbably affable Richard Farmer and the almost pathologically diffident Reed; the third was Steevens himself. Though the

disaffection between Steevens and Malone was never healed, they remained on cordial terms until Steevens's withdrawal into retirement in Hampstead, after the appearance of his 1793 edition of Shakespeare's plays.

Malone's *Dissertation on Henry VI* (which had first been published in 1787 as a second supplement to the 1785 edition of Steevens and Reed) attempts to prove that parts 2 and 3 of *Henry VI* are revisions of two earlier plays by other hands and that part 1 of *Henry VI* is an unrevised play by another dramatist. Malone's essay was described by the great classicist Richard Porson as one of the most convincing pieces of criticism that he had ever read (quoted in Boswell's "Memoirs" of Malone). Malone's thesis was not overturned until Peter Alexander's 1929 monograph – an astonishing tenure for a work of scholarship in so volatile an area – and as late as the 1950s it still retained enough vitality to attract the support of J. Dover Wilson in his preface to *Henry VI,* part 2.

From 1783 to 1790 Malone embarked on an extremely fruitful search for documents relating to Shakespeare's life and works. Malone was the first systematically to examine many of the major biographical and theatrical documents now known, including Henslowe's diary, the office book of Sir Henry Herbert (chief censor of Shakespeare's theater), the parish registers of Stratford-upon-Avon, the Stationer's Register, and other rich sources.

Malone arrived on the scene after almost seventy-five years of Shakespeare study and in the midst of a virtual explosion of knowledge. Yet, as a result of his exhaustive research, his 1790 edition was the first to offer a systematic account of the chronology of Shakespeare's plays; to separate facts from legends in the biography of Shakespeare; to present a coherent account of the authorship of such disputed plays as the *Henry VI* trilogy; to attempt to fix the Shakespearean canon; to include the sonnets according to the 1609 text or to accord them the full panoply of scholarly apparatus and notes; and to offer a systematic analysis of the First Folio's superiority to the second. Malone's analysis offers an exemplary instance of the state of eighteenth-century scholarship. He was trying to show that the First Folio was the only authoritative one and that to select readings from later folios was no different from choosing emendations by, say, Lewis Theobald or Johnson. But since Malone's demonstration was buttressed by innumerable instances of the Second Folio's bad guesses, he was criticized for not bringing forward some of its better ones. It is barely an exaggeration to say that all subsequent Shakespearean scholarship represents an effort either to reevaluate the documentary record Malone assembled or to explore more minutely the research paths he marked out.

Malone's 1790 Shakespeare edition has always been the chief pillar on which his reputation has rested. Indeed he is the first person of whom this statement can truly be made: all the earlier editors had distinguished themselves in other fields prior to editing Shakespeare. In its time Malone's edition was generally seen as having put the editing of Shakespeare on a new, more rigorous and professional basis. But this chorus of approval was accompanied by a ground bass of grumbling over the question of whether all the annotation was neces-

sary. Did not some of the commentary reflect more credit on the scholar's sagacity, wit, and erudition than it threw light on Shakespeare's work? For nineteenth-century scholars Malone's edition, as included in the 1821 variorum – which contained the bulk of eighteenth-century commentary – epitomized the earlier century's excesses, dullness, and self-indulgence, its failure to get Shakespeare right. Malone, as the last and most notable of the earlier scholars, and as the most unapologetically focused on matters of fact rather than on those of judgment, came to stand for the entire direction of Shakespeare scholarship from 1709 to 1821, and he was condemned for all its perceived failings.

The bibliographical movement of the late nineteenth to mid twentieth centuries restored to Malone credit for his achievements, elevating him to a position at or near the top of the editorial tradition. In still more recent years Malone's edition has come to be seen, as it had been on publication, not as the culmination of eighteenth-century Shakespeare scholarship but as inaugurating a new era. Gary Taylor, for example, credits (actually castigates) Malone for being "instrumental in transforming Shakespeare from the public dramatic poet of the Restoration and eighteenth century into a private lyric poet who could be embraced, celebrated, and appropriated by the Romantics" (*Reinventing Shakespeare*). And Margreta De Grazia, after reviewing the leading innovations of Malone's approach to editing Shakespeare, contends: "While it is always possible to locate adumbrations of these interests in earlier treatments, it is in this edition that they are first clearly articulated. . . . However unexceptionable they may seem now, it must be emphasized that none of these contributions had been made in previous editions. Until 1790 Shakespeare was published and read without materials and criteria that are now deemed basic to serious bibliographical and critical approaches."

Malone accepted neither remuneration nor royalties for his efforts, in keeping with his wealthy, landed family's ideal of disinterested public service, and in a further effort to ensure that his edition would be available at a modest price, he insisted it be printed in small type on cheap paper, a decision seen by his friends as blemishing the whole labor, and one which likely hastened the deterioration of his own eyesight. As Boaden reports, "His sight had never been very good; and unfortunately to keep the works of Shakespeare within any reasonable limits, he had . . . done the greatest possible injury to his eyes by selecting types both for text and notes for his edition painful and distressing to the great majority of readers." Despite this fact, and the savage critiques of the eccentric antiquary Joseph Ritson and others who objected to the depth and patience of Malone's scholarship, the edition sold briskly and was generally accounted a highly satisfactory performance. Malone was indisputably established as "Shakespearianissimus" and even anticipated remedying the physical defects of the edition with "a splendid edition of the plays and poems of our great dramatic poet . . . to be printed in fifteen volumes royal quarto." Although his Shakespearean labor occupied him until his death over twenty years later, this edition, the first two volumes of which he expected to produce by 1791, was left unfinished by Malone and only appeared, in a form far different from the one he would have chosen, in the 1821 variorum.

The Shakespeare editions by Alexander Pope (1725), Theobald (1733), Sir Thomas Hanmer (1744), William Warburton (1747), Johnson, and Steevens had all merely reprinted the first biography of Shakespeare, Nicholas Rowe's 1709 "Account," which prefaced Rowe's edition of the plays. Although Malone did not immediately undertake a complete new biography of Shakespeare, he subjected Rowe's life to a rigorous scrutiny, and his printing of the "Account" bristles with contentious footnotes, adding masses of information from the documentary records Malone had been the first to peruse, and exposing, through relentless cross-examination, the inconsistencies, secret purposes, implausibilities, and downright fabrications of supposed eyewitnesses. In Malone's work, for the first time, are brought under review the greater part of those sources of information on which knowledge of the life of Shakespeare is based. In Malone's treatment of Rowe's account of Shakespeare's life, as in his *History of the Stage* (in the 1821 variorum), are to be found, in the words of Prof. C. J. Sisson, "the foundations of modern documented study."

Malone's excursions into the exposure of fraud and forgery bear directly on his most salient qualities as a scholar: his unrelenting integrity and dogged pursuit of documentary truth. In 1781 he had been one of the first to challenge the authenticity of poems said to have been written by the fifteenth-century monk Thomas Rowley but which were actually written by Thomas Chatterton, who had committed suicide in 1770. Better known is Malone's *Inquiry into the Authenticity of Certain Miscellaneous Papers and Legal Instruments* (1796). There had been doubters of the genuineness of the astonishing horde of Shakespeare documents supposedly found by young William Henry Ireland. But all London

reserved opinion on their authenticity until Malone had spoken. Malone's *Inquiry,* offered in the form of a letter to his friend Lord Charlemont, was painstaking and patient (one might even say plodding), and it conclusively demonstrated that the Ireland documents could not be genuine. Drawing on his unparalleled familiarity with Elizabethan theater practice, law, orthography, and social history, Malone was able to demolish every scrap of the improvised structure Ireland had erected about the forgeries: the story of how the documents had come into existence, the tale the documents told, the documents themselves and their provenance, and the story of how the documents had come into Ireland's hands. Though a handful of defenders remained in the field (most notably Ireland's father, Samuel, in his *Investigation of Mr. Malone's Claim to the Character of Scholar and Critic,* and George Chalmers in his 1797 *Apology* and 1799 *Supplemental Apology for the Believers*), the blow Malone struck had been mortal.

Though Malone's attentions to Shakespeare during these years were assiduous, they were not unremitting. In 1785, the year following Johnson's death, Malone entered into a friendship with Boswell that endured without interruption until the latter's death in 1795. Malone had been known to Boswell at least since February 1782, the date of Malone's election to the Literary Club, but they seem not to have been on intimate terms until the spring of 1785. Earlier that year Malone had been the first person to declare publicly that Boswell — at that time an obscure lawyer and failed politician whose *Account of Corsica* (1768) had earned him modest fame — was the fittest person to write the life of Johnson.

By the end of May 1785 Malone had become so vital to Boswell's work on *A Tour to the Hebrides* (1785) that, as Boswell's journals attest, virtually nothing was accomplished on its preparation for publication except when the two were together. Boswell fittingly dedicated the book to Malone, "as it gives me an opportunity of letting the world know that I enjoy the honour and happiness of your friendship." He continued to rely on Malone's assistance as he wrote his *Life of Samuel Johnson.* A bicentennial tribute to Malone in the *Times Literary Supplement* (4 October 1941) lists Boswell's *Life of Samuel Johnson* (along with Malone's editions of Shakespeare and John Dryden) among *Malone's* "magna opera": "he was not, indeed, the author; but without him the book could never have been what it is."

Malone's help on *The Life of Samuel Johnson* was generously honored by Boswell (in his preface): "I cannot sufficiently acknowledge my obligations to my friend, Mr. Malone, who was so good as to allow me to read to him almost the whole of my manuscript, and made such remarks as were greatly to the advantage of the work." Malone helped Boswell with the second edition and edited and supplied additional notes to the (posthumous) third through sixth editions (1799–1811); Malone was at work on the sixth edition when he died. The same years when he was involved with the long and difficult gestation of Boswell's *Life* were the years he was producing his epochal Shakespeare edition. According to critic John L. McCollum, Jr., "Boswell's journals and letters . . . reveal a friendship which has few parallels in literary consequence; . . . while Boswell possessed extraordinary intellectual powers, they nevertheless required the restraining and directing force of a self-sacrificing guide. That he found in Malone."

The beneficial influence was not, however, all one way. Whether or not Boswell's easy ways and frank embrace of life had a special appeal to the prim and straitlaced Malone, the latter learned while working with Boswell a great deal about the effort required to reduce great masses of disconnected documents, facts, and anecdotes to a readable narrative. However, when his biographies are compared to Boswell's, Malone's weaknesses as a biographer appear only too clearly. There is no better illustration of these than in Malone's edition of *The Critical and Miscellaneous Prose Works of John Dryden* (1800), the volume-length biographical portion of which constitutes Malone's chief work in the field of biography. The memoir (volume one of three) represented a nearly unprecedented effort to gather and evaluate every available shred of information about a person: only Oldys's *Life of Raleigh* (1736) had ever made such an attempt, and, according to James M. Osborn in *Dryden* (1940), "since Oldys approached Raleigh as a historical rather than a literary figure, we can credit Malone with the first great literary biography." Since at least 1793 Malone had been collecting and editing Dryden's prose.

With characteristic gusto and success Malone applied himself to the task of unearthing every letter, reminiscence, anecdote, or other scrap of information about Dryden. Most of what is known about Dryden today was first brought to light by Malone's search. As was his habit, he insisted on admitting to the record only such items as could survive his rigorous scrutiny. Because earlier biographies of Dryden (of which Johnson's was the best known) had been based on little more than traditional stories, polished in the retelling, one of the incidental pleasures of reading Malone's biography is to watch

him demolish one after another of these apocryphal anecdotes:

> The marvelous is always so much more captivating than simple truth. . . .
> This anecdote . . . [has] a very fair genealogy: but after it has been carefully examined, we shall find, that, like many traditional tales, it is not to be implicitly relied on. . . .
> An examination of dates is generally fatal to tales of this kind. . . .

A further characteristic of Malone's approach to biography – one which brings out some of both his best and his worst qualities – was his understanding that the biographical subject must be seen as a figure whose shape and dimension can be fully understood only against the ground of his period and society. In this aspect he followed Joseph Warton, who, in writing about Edmund Spenser, had laid down the principle that any scholar of earlier authors needed "not only a competent knowledge of all antient [sic] classical learning . . . but also an acquaintance with those books, which, though now forgotten and lost, were yet in repute about the time in which each author respectively wrote, and which it is most likely he had red [sic]."

As had been the case with his biography of Shakespeare, Malone was subjected to ridicule as one who gathered together a heap of (scholarly, documentary) rubble and called it a palace of wisdom, but Sir Walter Scott, Dryden's next editor and biographer, valued Malone correctly in confessing his own inability to "produce facts which had escaped the accuracy of Malone, whose industry has removed the clouds which so long hung over the events of Dryden's life."

In Malone's biography of Dryden one can see clearly Malone's characteristic inability to distinguish between what belongs in a biographical narrative and what belongs in a footnote, and between what can be displayed in a footnote and what would be more appropriately relegated to an appendix. The two most notable instances of this failing in the Dryden biography are a long history of the Poets Laureate of England and a dissertation on Saint Cecilia's Day odes, this last occupying fully a tenth of the volume. To make matters worse, the book runs without section breaks, chapter headings, or any other typographical signposts to provide relief or guidance, and it lacks an index. Nor does Malone's prose sparkle. It is a solid, workmanlike, late-eighteenth-century prose, seldom enlivened by an unexpected word or phrase and animated only by his evident pleasure in presenting such a bonanza of facts.

As Malone's life of Shakespeare had inspired Joseph Ritson's *Cursory Criticisms* (1792), his biography of Dryden was answered by George Hardinge's *The Essence of Malone: or the 'Beauties' of that Fascinating Writer, Extracted from his Immortal Works, in Five Hundred, Sixty-nine Pages, and a Quarter, Just Published and (with his Accustomed Felicity) Entitled "Some Account of the Life and Writings of John Dryden"!!* (1800). Perhaps not surprisingly Hardinge got the title wrong: it is not "Some Account" but "*An* Account" — but the correct title would not help Hardinge's lumbering sarcasm. He begins by complaining that Malone tells the number of Dryden's house. Hardinge complains with greater validity of the amount of space Malone devotes to the Poets Laureate and the Saint Cecilia odes. The balance of Hardinge's book adopts the format of Thomas Edwards's immensely popular *Canons of Criticism* (1748), which had ridiculed many of the blunders and extravagances of Warburton's 1747 edition of Shakespeare by purporting to base a set of rules for critics on them. Representative of Hardinge's procedure is the rule which states, "The life of A should be the lives of B, C, D, &c. to the end of the alphabet; for which the reader is to pay in the additional size of the volume." Hardinge is here objecting to Malone's giving a detailed provenance for anecdotes and to his confutation of popular and traditional stories. Another of Hardinge's "rules" — which states, "A Biographer should refute *errors,* and especially if they are *trivial*" — licenses Hardinge to ridicule Malone for his detailed comparison of the drafts of *MacFlecknoe*. Even Malone's tact is held against him: his efforts to excuse some of Johnson's more flagrant errors draw from Hardinge the comment, "I give Malone ample credit as the most gentleman-like executioner I ever knew. His conquest over his predecessor is a perfect specimen of urbanity."

Hardinge's attack on Malone is so unrelenting, his jests so heavy-handed, and his sarcastic exclamations so complacent that after a few pages one merely feels increased respect for Malone. Hardinge himself may have come to feel he had gone too far. In his 1818 essay "On Shakespeare's Accentuation," written after Malone's death, he explains that his "fooleries upon Malone" were written "for no object whatever but for my own amusement. Shewing it one day accidentally to a very particular friend, and a person of taste, I found him partial to it, and was exhorted by him to publish it as a banter. . . . I should much lament if it gave him [Malone] serious pain. . . . I should wish never to laugh again if I could by laughing displease or offend a good scholar and a very ingenious man, though I cannot

admire his judgment or his taste." Hardinge neatly managed to excuse himself from the imputation of malice without withdrawing or abating any part of his criticism.

For all its faults, Malone's life of Dryden is a true landmark of literary scholarship: Osborn (in *Dryden*) calls it "the first great literary biography"; Schoenbaum claims, "The life of Dryden is the greatest triumph of his scholarly method as applied to the problems of biography"; and Nichol Smith calls Malone "more than our greatest Elizabethan scholar. He is still our greatest authority on the life of Dryden. . . . [We] find in Malone's volume the great bulk of what we know about him for certain. . . . Biographical work on Dryden, today, is largely concerned with checking what Malone collected or deduced." Osborn's searching critique of the Dryden biography gives readers what is in many ways the fullest account of Malone's qualities as a scholar. Among the notable qualities Osborn identifies are Malone's "highly developed sense of historical perspective" and his ability to apply "the new scientific method of his age." Osborn sees Malone as "the first biographer to react consciously against the transmission of error and to emphasize his reaction by force of example."

Also belonging to this period is Malone's life of Reynolds (1797). This work and his early biography of Goldsmith were, as Osborn aptly terms them (in *Dryden*), "acts of homage to countryman and friend, rather than serious biographies." The life of Reynolds has about it the feeling of a person sorting through papers and diaries. In *James Boswell, The Later Years 1769–1795* (1984) Frank Brady calls Malone's work on Reynolds "a piece of clear, colourless scholarly prose, adequate but uninspired, and pulled out of shape by a footnote running under the text for eight pages, which labours a comparison between Reynolds and Laelius, a model of the cultivated Roman."

The work that would have been the crown of Malone's career, his biography of Shakespeare, was never completed. In an act of intergenerational piety James Boswell, Jr., mauled Malone's drafts and notes into a continuous prose structure — which can hardly be called a narrative — and published it as part of the 1821 variorum edition. Considered as a finished work, it is a bizarre product, fully 40 percent of which (112 of its 287 pages) is devoted to a discussion of two Spenser poems which, it was thought by some at the time, might include oblique and cryptic references to Shakespeare. Nonetheless, Schoenbaum, who has examined the tradition of Shakespeare biography more closely than anyone

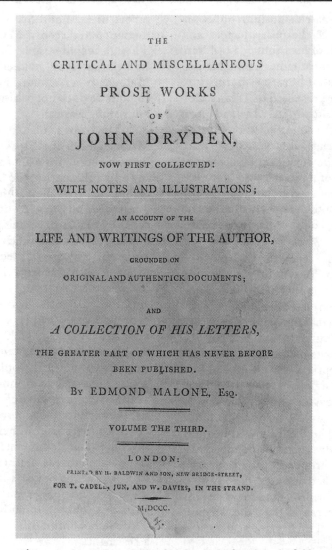

THE

CRITICAL AND MISCELLANEOUS

PROSE WORKS

OF

JOHN DRYDEN,

NOW FIRST COLLECTED:

WITH NOTES AND ILLUSTRATIONS;

AN ACCOUNT OF THE

LIFE AND WRITINGS OF THE AUTHOR,

GROUNDED ON

ORIGINAL AND AUTHENTICK DOCUMENTS;

AND

A COLLECTION OF HIS LETTERS,

THE GREATER PART OF WHICH HAS NEVER BEFORE
BEEN PUBLISHED.

BY EDMOND MALONE, ESQ.

VOLUME THE THIRD.

LONDON:

PRINTED BY H. BALDWIN AND SON, NEW BRIDGE-STREET,
FOR T. CADELL, JUN. AND W. DAVIES, IN THE STRAND.

M,DCCC.

*Title page for the first edition of Malone's chief work in the field
of biography*

else, is able to excuse the faults of Malone's work and appreciate its virtues: "Despite its fragmentary character and eccentricity of proportion, Malone's life of Shakespeare is a major achievement. One need only compare it with Rowe's life a century earlier to be made aware of the dramatic leap forward in Shakespeare studies – a leap for which Malone is largely responsible. He had limitations and made mistakes; but he found out more about Shakespeare and his theatrical milieu than anyone before or since, and, recognizing his fallibility, corrected himself in the light of new information which his own sleuthing had unearthed. He is the greatest of Elizabethan scholars."

Malone died on 25 April 1812, when, according to James Boswell, Jr., "he was just on the point of going to the press with his new edition of Shake-

speare," an edition which would not appear until nearly ten more years had elapsed. As Farington reports, "Boswell told me that . . . our friend, had been declining in health for Six months before He died. His physicians, Sir H. Halford, and Dr. Blaine recommended to Him to try country air, and He went to Lady Thomond's at Taplow for three weeks, but returned in no better state. He then fancied He had taken too much exercise at Taplow, but Dr. Blaine, speaking of Him, said it was of no consequence what He did as it was a breaking up of the constitution. He had no local complaint, it was general weakness and gradual decay." Malone's estate, while not enormous, was substantial, and he was able to bequeath three thousand pounds to each of his sisters, five hundred pounds to Jephson, Jr., and two hundred pounds to young Boswell in addition to smaller gifts. The ultimate disposition of his unparalleled collection of Shakespeare papers and books he left in the hands of his brother, Lord Sunderlin, suggesting that it might either be maintained intact as part of an ancestral library at Baronston, Lord Sunderlin's seat, or presented to Trinity College, Dublin, Malone's alma mater. Instead Lord Sunderlin arranged that the collection should be offered as a gift to the Bodleian Library, Oxford, once Boswell had published the variorum Shakespeare and no longer had need of it. So full was Malone's Shakespeare collection that, without further additions, it was unmatched until the opening of the Folger Shakespeare Library, and it remains one of the most important.

A sad footnote to the dispersal of Malone's effects is reported by James Prior, author of the only full-length biography of Malone: "After the publication of [Boswell's 1821 variorum] Shakespeare, an agreeable evening spent by the younger Boswell with the Malone family induced the ladies . . . to propose his acceptance of some memorial of their late brother. The most appropriate was deemed to be a box of papers, letters, and notes upon books, men, or miscellaneous subjects which his pursuits might turn to useful public account. A note to that effect was sent him next day. The box followed in a day or two more. No acknowledgment being made, the ladies, upon inquiry, ascertained to their surprise and regret, that his death had occurred the day after its reception. Unluckily, he proved to be in pecuniary difficulties; the creditors reckoned these papers among his property; and they became scattered at the sale of his effects in 1825."

Of Malone the man, Prior writes: "Steady, rather than shining powers, formed his characteristic feature. He had determined to accomplish anything he took in hand." The elder Boswell, too, found Malone "respectable and gentleman-like rather than shining," according to Farington. John Taylor reports, "Mr. Malone was quite a gentleman in his manners, and rather of a mild disposition, except when he had to support the truth, and then there was such firmness and spirit in what he said as could hardly be expected from one so meek and courteous; but he never departed from politeness and respect." Yet these reservations about his "powers" suffer from the same defect as the judgment that Malone's biography of Dryden is unreadable. The biography is certainly not to be perused for pleasure. But when compared with Dryden biographies which may be so read – those of Johnson and Scott – its virtues are clear, for Johnson's biography is riddled with unfounded conjectures and outright

errors of fact, and Scott's is based solidly on the documentary record Malone himself established. Though incomparably finer than Malone at structuring a narrative, neither of the others could touch Malone as a scholar. For this reason, Malone, though he does not "shine," continues to radiate a nourishing warmth.

De Grazia, in assessing the achievement of Malone's 1790 Shakespeare edition, makes a crucial discrimination. Instead of seeing Malone as embodying and culminating the highest standards of eighteenth-century scholarship, she insists that he inaugurated wholly new standards: "Malone's work is typically cast as developing earlier interests when in crucial respects it definitively broke with them. The authentic text pre-empted the received text; actual usage in Shakespeare's time superseded standards of correctness contemporary with the editor; factual accounts discredited traditional anecdotes; the order in which the plays were written replaced generic groupings; the 1609 quarto *Sonnets* supplanted the adulterated 1640 octavo; interpretations of Shakespeare's content overtook evaluations of his style. These innovations do not extend earlier interests, as the use of a graduated chronological scale implies; they render them obsolete." "Malone's edition," De Grazia says later in her book, "based on authentic copies and documents, posited a demonstrable standard that was neither self-evident nor dependent on . . . the editor's authority. . . . The editor, therefore, no longer needed the credentials of a Pope or a Johnson to authorize his procedures."

Nichol Smith offers a moderate but respectful assessment:

> Great work had been done before the time of Malone, and even without him the end of the eighteenth century would have been a great age of English Scholarship. It was the age of Johnson, Tyrwhitt, Farmer, Percy, Steevens, Capell, the Wartons, Reed, Ritson, and many more. . . . The claim cannot be made for Malone that he altered the direction or the methods of English studies. I should not like to say that he had a notably original mind. . . . Thomas Tyrwhitt was a man of more acute intellect. . . . George Steevens was quicker and was his superior in mere cleverness . . . and Thomas Warton surpassed him in ordered narrative. . . . [But] he is representative of the main movement in English scholarship. . . . His edition of Shakespeare may be described as the summing up of the work of a century – a summing up in which everything is submitted to the test of his own investigations and controlled by a remarkable amount of new evidence. . . . He has won his place among the greatest English scholars, not so much by any remarkable intellectual qualities (though I should be sorry to appear to underestimate his gifts) as by a happy and rare combination of simple moral qualities – by his

obstinate persistence in research, by his scrupulous care in weighing evidence, by his honesty. . . . Malone is persistent from first to last. He is never off his guard; he never takes anything on trust; he never covers up his traces. When he is wrong, he presents us with evidence which may help us to prove him wrong. He admits his errors. Always the servant of his subject, he has no personal vanities.

Malone's place is secure and has long been so. His superiority to his predecessor editors of Shakespeare is many faceted and constantly manifest, but the common judgment of the twentieth century has been that Malone's outstanding qualities were diligence and honesty. One may also wish to add sanity – a cheerful mental balance, a straightforwardness and freedom from idiosyncrasy characteristic of none of his colleagues.

This sanity appears in his conception of what a work of scholarship should be. One of Malone's greatest contributions to Shakespeare studies was his systematization of the scholarship which had been produced up to his time – much of it done by him in the first place. In his notes Malone's sanity makes itself felt in the qualities that most serve to distinguish the true scholar from the crank and the eccentric: a sense of proportion and a keen instinct for the relevant. These qualities are apparent – despite one's distaste for some of Malone's long notes – when his work is compared with that of his contemporaries. Malone virtually never (as they frequently did) used a long note as an opportunity to parade his familiarity with arcane reading: he used notes instead to discuss matters that simply require long notes. In both his extended "dissertations" and his isolated comments, Malone shuns picturesqueness for sobriety, sentimentality for realism, and rancor for dignity.

The credo of the modern literary historian is founded on six primary scholarly attributes: the reverence for truth even if it fails to support or flatly contradicts one's thesis, insistence on documentary evidence, exhaustive research, a keen sense of relevance and structure, a "historical" attitude or freedom from complacency about the barbarousness of former times, and specialization. Malone is hardly a pioneer in any of these areas. The injunction that biography must be more than just "collecting mere useless pieces of learning," for example, goes back to Plutarch: "As for other matters not generally known, which are found scattered in historians, or in ancient inscriptions and decrees, we shall collect them with care; not to gratify an useless curiosity, but by drawing from them the true lines of this general's character, to serve the

purposes of real instruction." The sense of relevance and structure was a weakness throughout Malone's career. But he is outstanding in all the other five and is the first scholar to combine all of them in his work. Schoenbaum points out (in *Internal Evidence and Elizabethan Dramatic Authorship*, 1966) that Malone "anticipates the modern approach by his application of knowledge and reason – rather than mere impressionism – to set forth the evidence on which his conclusions rest. . . . Reliance upon taste as final arbiter of authenticity was foreign to Malone's *modus operandi* as a scholar. He stands as a great bulwark against all casual, uninformed, or prejudiced speculation on authorship."

Though in his long digressions he retains something of the antiquary, he must be freed from that imputation, for whereas the antiquarian attitude tends to gather the "relics" of past cultures into an inventory of isolated curiosities, Malone was groping toward canons of relevance that might provide a basis for judging whether a bit belonged or did not. "Such was the life of a scholar," writes his biographer Prior:

Careless of the bustle of human existence, he was active only to read, hear, and note the progress of its letters. He loved them for their own sake; for the inquiries induced – the thought and knowledge evolved – the enlargement of mind acquired by the successful cultivator – the innocence as well as amusement of the occupation. His topics promised well for the quietude he loved. While others lost their temper or good manners toward each other in critical pursuits, nothing of that description escaped from him. . . . None of his predecessors had attempted what he accomplished. Few of his successors have, on most points, added materially to our knowledge. . . . He was studious, and selected an object of popular study; inquiring, and left nothing unexplored likely to afford information; reflective, and therefore usually accurate in drawing conclusions where positive testimony was at fault. . . . He who could throw light upon the career of Shakespeare and Dryden – give us the first and best history of the Stage – and leave, for our study and guidance, volumes at Oxford which no other spot supplies, must be considered no small benefactor to letters.

Letters:

Original Letters from Malone . . . to John Jordan, the Poet, edited by James O. Halliwell [-Phillipps] (N.p.: Privately printed, 1864);

The Correspondence of Malone with J. Davenport, Vicar of Stratford-on-Avon, edited by Halliwell [-Phillipps] (N.p.: Privately printed, 1864);

The Correspondence of Thomas Percy & Edmond Malone [Volume I of *The Percy Letters*], edited by Arthur Tillotson (Baton Rouge: Louisiana State University Press, 1944);

The Correspondence and Other Papers of James Boswell Relating to the Making of the Life of Johnson, edited by Marshall Waingrow (New York: McGraw-Hill, 1968);

The Correspondence of James Boswell with David Garrick, Edmund Burke, and Edmond Malone, edited by James Osborn, Peter S. Baker, and others (New York: McGraw-Hill, 1987).

Biographies:

James Boswell, Jr., "Memoirs and Character of Edmond Malone Esq.," *Gentleman's Magazine* (June 1813);

James Prior, *Life of Edmond Malone, Editor of Shakespeare* (London: Smith, Elder, 1860).

References:

Arthur Brown, *Edmond Malone and English Scholarship* (London: H. K. Lewis, 1963);

Thomas Caldecott, *An Investigation of Mr Malone's Claim to the Character of a Scholar, or Critic* (London, 1798);

George Carver, "Malone and the 'Dryden,'" in his *Alms for Oblivion: Books, Men and Biography* (Milwaukee: Bruce, 1946), pp. 170–180;

J. Caulfield, *An Enquiry into the Conduct of Edmond Malone Concerning the Manuscript Papers of John Aubrey* (London: Printed for I. Caulfield, 1797);

George Chalmers, *Another Account of the Incidents [from which] The Tempest [was] Derived* (London: R. and A. Taylor, 1815);

Chalmers, *An Apology for the Believers in [Ireland's Shakespeare Forgeries]* (London: T. Egerton, 1797);

Chalmers, *A Supplemental Apology for the Believers in the Shakespeare Papers which were Exhibited in Norfolk Street* (London: T. Egerton, 1799);

R. W. Chapman, "Cancels in Malone's Dryden," *Library,* 23 (1942): 131;

Margreta De Grazia, *Shakespeare Verbatim: the Reproduction of Authenticity and the 1790 Apparatus* (Oxford: Clarendon Press, 1991);

W. W. Greg, "Editors at Work and Play: a Glimpse of the Eighteenth Century," *Review of English Studies,* 2 (1926): 173–177;

James Grieg, ed., *The Farington Diaries* (London: Hutchinson, 1922–1928);

James Orchard Halliwell[-Phillipps], *A Hand-List of the Early English Literature Preserved in the Malone Collection at the Bodleian Library* (London, 1860);

George Hardinge, *Another Essence of Malone . . . Second Part* (London: Printed for T. Becket, 1801);

Hardinge, *The Essence of Malone: or the 'Beauties' of that Fascinating Writer . . .* (London: Printed for T. Becket by J. Smeeton, 1800);

Hardinge, "On Shakespeare's Accentuation," in his *The Miscellaneous Works in Prose and Verse* (London: J. Nichols, son, & Bentley, 1818), III: 84–86;

J. J. Hogan, "The Bicentenary of Malone," *Studies,* 30 (1941): 597–600;

C. J. Horne, "Malone and Steevens in Relation to Boswell's Life," *Notes & Queries,* 195 (1950): 56;

James Hurdis, *Cursory Remarks Upon the Arrangement of the Plays of Shakespeare* (London: Johnson, 1792);

Grace Ioppolo, " 'Old' and 'New' Revisionists: Shakespeare's Eighteenth-Century Editors," *Huntington Library Quarterly,* 52 (1989): 347–361;

Samuel Ireland, *Mr. Ireland's Vindication of His Conduct . . . : a Reply to . . . Malone* (London: Faulder & Robson, and others, 1796);

Anne Lancashire, "Warburton's List and Edmond Malone: a Non-Existent Relationship," *Studies in Bibliography,* 27 (1974): 240–248;

Hilton Landry, "Malone as Editor of Shakespeare's Sonnets," *Bulletin of the New York Public Library,* 67 (1963): 435–442;

Wilmarth Sheldon Lewis, "Edmond Malone, Horace Walpole, and Shakespeare," in *Evidence in Literary Scholarship: Essays in Memory of James Marshall Osborn,* edited by Rene Wellek and Alvaro Ribeiro (Oxford: Clarendon Press, 1979), pp. 353–362;

"Malone: Scholar and Antiquary," *Times Literary Supplement,* 4 October 1941;

J. Monck Mason, *Comments on the Several Editions of Shakespeare's Plays* (Dublin: Graisberry & Campbell, 1807);

John L. McCollum, Jr., "The Indebtedness of James Boswell to Edmond Malone," *New Rambler* (June 1966): 29–45;

John Bowyer Nichols, *Illustrations of the Literary History of the Eighteenth Century* (New York: Kraus Reprint, 1966);

Allardyce Nicoll, "Shakespeare's Editors from the First Folio to Malone," in *Studies in Honour of the Tercentenary of the First Folio, 1623–1923* (London: Shakespeare Association, 1924), pp. 157–178;

"Ode Addressed to Edmond Malone Esq.," *Gentleman's Magazine* (August 1782);

James M. Osborn, "Edmond Malone," in his *Dryden: Some Biographical Facts and Problems* (New York, 1940), pp. 39–71;

Osborn, "Edmond Malone and Dr. Johnson," in *Boswell, Johnson and Their Circle: Essays Presented to Lawrence Fitzroy Powell in Honour of his Eighty-Fourth Birthday,* edited by Mary Lascelles (Oxford: Clarendon Press, 1965), pp. 1–20;

Osborn, "Edmond Malone and the Dryden Almanac Story," *Philological Quarterly,* 17 (1938): 84–86;

Osborn, "Malone and Baratariana," *Notes & Queries,* 188 (1945): 35;

Osborn, "Malone: Scholar-Collector," *Library,* 5, no. 19 (1964): 11–37;

Joseph Ritson, *Cursory Criticisms on the Edition of Shakespeare* [published by Malone] (London, 1792);

Samuel Schoenbaum, *Internal Evidence and Elizabethan Dramatic Authorship* (Evanston: Northwestern University Press, 1966);

Schoenbaum, *Shakespeare's Lives* (Oxford: Clarendon Press, 1970);

Sailendra Kumar Sen, *Capell, Malone and Modern Critical Bibliography* (Calcutta, 1960);

Sen, "Malone and his Boswell," *Notes & Queries,* 32 (1985): 246–250;

Sen, "Malone's Two Shakespeare Editions," *Library,* 31 (1976): 390–391;

Sen, "The Noblest Roman of Them All," in *Shakespeare Commemoration Volume,* edited by Taraknath Sen (Calcutta, 1966);

Sen, "When Malone Nods," *Shakespeare Quarterly,* 34 (1983): 212–214;

Arthur Sherbo, *The Birth of Shakespeare Studies, 1709–1821* (Lansing, Mich.: Colleagues Press, 1982);

David Nichol Smith, "Malone," *Huntington Library Quarterly,* 3 (1939–1940): 23–36;

Arthur Tillotson, "Bishop Percy and Malone," *Notes & Queries,* 176 (1939): 172;

Ernest Walder, *Shakespearian Criticism: Textual and Literary, From Dryden to the End of the Eighteenth Century* (Bradford, U.K., 1895);

J. K. Walton, "Edmund Malone: an Irish Scholar," *Hermathena,* 99 (1964): 5–26;

Earl Reeves Wasserman, "Elizabethan Poetry 'Improved,' " *Modern Philology,* 37 (1940): 357–369;

Wasserman, "The Scholarly Origins of the Elizabethan Revival," 4 (1937): 213–243;

Rene Wellek, *The Rise of English Literary History* (Chapel Hill: University of North Carolina Press, 1941);

R. L. Widmann, "Edmond Malone's Notes on Pope and Gray," *Notes & Queries,* new series 20 (1973): 415–417;

John Dover Wilson, "Malone and the Upstart Crow," *Shakespeare Survey,* 4 (1951): 59–66.

William Mason

(12 February 1725 – 7 April 1797)

Paul Haeffner

BOOKS: *Musaeus: A Monody to the Memory of Mr. Pope, in Imitation of Milton's Lycidas,* anonymous (London: Printed for R. Dodsley & sold by M. Cooper, 1747);

Isis. An Elegy (London: Printed for R. Dodsley & sold by M. Cooper, 1749);

Ode Performed in the Senate-House at Cambridge July 1, 1749. At the Installation of His Grace Thomas Holles, Duke of Newcastle, Chancellor of the University (Cambridge: Printed by J. Bentham, 1749);

Elfrida, a Dramatic Poem (London: Printed for J. & P. Knapton, 1752);

Odes (Cambridge: Printed by J. Bentham and sold by William Thurlbourn and R. & J. Dodsley, London, 1756);

Caractatus, a Dramatic Poem (London: Printed for J. Knapton and R. & J. Dodsley, 1759);

Elegies (London: Printed for Robert Horsfield and sold by R. & J. Dodsley [and others], 1763);

Poems (London: Printed for R. Horsfield and sold by R. & J. Dodsley [and others], 1764);

The English Garden: A Poem, 4 volumes (volume 1, London: Printed & sold by R. Horsfield [and others], 1772; volume 2, York: Printed by A. Ward and sold by J. Dodsley [and others], London, and by J. Todd, York, 1777; volume 3, London: Printed by H. Goldney for J. Dodsley & T. Cadell, and sold by J. Todd, York, 1779; volume 4, York: Printed by A. Ward and sold by J. Dodsley [and others], London, and J. Todd, in York, 1781);

An Heroic Epistle to Sir William Chambers, Knight, Comptroller General of His Majesty's Works, and Author of a Late Dissertation on Oriental Gardening, anonymous (London: Printed for J. Almon, 1773);

An Heroic Postscript to the Public, Occasioned by Their Favourable Reception of a Late Heroic Epistle to Sir William Chambers, Knt., anonymous (London: Printed for J. Almon, 1774);

Mirth, A Poem in Answer to Warton's Pleasure of Melancholy (Cambridge: Sold by E. Johnson, 1774);

Ode to Mr. Pinchbeck, Upon His Newly Invented Patent Candle-Snuffers, as Malcolm MacGreggor (London: Printed for J. Almon, 1776);

An Epistle to Dr. Shebbeare; to Which is Added an Ode to Sir Fletcher Norton, in Imitation of Horace, Ode VIII, Book IV, as Malcolm MacGreggor (London: Printed for J. Almon, 1777);

Ode to the Naval Officers of Great Britain. Written, immediately after the trial of Admiral Keppel, February the eleventh, 1779 (London: Printed for T. Cadell, 1779);

Ode on Wisdom (Privately printed, 1779);

An Archaeological Epistle to the Reverend and Worshipful Jeremiah Milles, D.D., Dean of Exeter, President of the Society of Antiquaries, and Editor of a Superb Edition of the Poems of Thomas Rowley, Priest, anonymous (London: Printed for J. Nichols [and others], 1782);

The Dean and the 'Squire: A Political Ecloque, as MacGreggor (London: Printed for J. Debrett, 1782);

King Stephen's Watch. A Tale, Founded on Fact, anonymous (London: Printed for T. Longman, 1782);

Ode to the Honourable William Pitt (London: Printed for J. Dodsley, 1782);

An Occasional Discourse, Preached in the Cathedral of St. Peter in York, January 27, 1788, on the Subject of the African Slave-trade (York: Printed by A. Ward for the author and sold by J. Robson & W. Clarke, James Phillips, London, and J. Todd, and the rest of the booksellers in York, 1788);

Animadversions on the Present Government of the York Lunatic Asylum; in Which the Case of Parish Paupers is Distinctly Considered (York: Printed by W. Blanchard and sold by J. Todd, and the rest of the booksellers, and by J. Robson, London, 1788);

Essays, Historical and Critical, on English Church Music (York: Printed by W. Blanchard and sold by J. Robson, London, and J. Todd, York, 1795);

The Poetical Works of the Author of the Heroic Epistle to Sir William Chambers (London: R. Phillips, 1805);

The Works of William Mason, 4 volumes (London: T. Cadell & W. Davies, 1811);

William Mason (portrait at Nuneham Park)

*Satirical Poems Published Anonymously by William Mason,
with notes by Horace Walpole,* edited by Paget
Toynbee (Oxford: Clarendon Press, 1926).

OTHER: Thomas Gray, *The Poems of Mr. Gray. To
Which Are Prefixed Memoirs of His Life and Writ-
ings by W. Mason, M.A.* (York: Printed by A.
Ward and sold by J. Dodsley, London, and J.
Todd, York, 1775);

*A Copious Collection of Those Portions of the Psalms of
David, Bible, and Liturgy, Which Have Been Set to
Music, and Sung as Anthems,* edited, with an
"Essay on Cathedral Music," by Mason
(York: Printed by A. Ward, 1782);

Charles Alphonse Du Fresnoy, *The Art of Painting,*
translated into English verse by Mason (York:
Printed by A. Ward and sold by J. Dodsley, T.
Cadell, R. Faulder, London, and J. Todd,
York, 1783);

Poems by William Whitehead, esq. . . . Vol. III, includes
memoirs by Mason (York: Printed by A.

Ward and sold by J. Robson & W. Clarke,
London, and J. Todd, York, 1788);

The Complete Works of Sir Joshua Reynolds, 3 volumes,
includes anecdotes by Mason (London: T.
M'Lean, 1824);

John Bunyan, *The Pilgrim's Progress: From This World
to That Which Is to Come,* includes explanatory
notes by Mason (London & New York: T. Nelson & Sons, 1862);

Gray, *Ode on the Pleasure Arising from Vicissitude,* com-
pleted by Mason (San Francisco: Printed for
William Andrews Clark, Jr., by John Henry
Nash, 1933).

James Boswell admitted in his *Life of Samuel
Johnson* (1791) that he was indebted to William
Mason's memoirs of Thomas Gray (1775) for the
form his masterpiece took. Mason also published a
second biography – of William Whitehead (1788) –
generally disregarded, or at least seen as overshadowed by his work on Gray, a landmark in biographical writing because of the half-epistolary form

Facsimile of a 1761 letter from Thomas Gray to Mason inviting him to Cambridge

which so impressed Boswell and others at the time of its publication. Mason's declared aim had been to keep himself in the background, to allow his subject to speak for himself whenever possible through his correspondence. Future biographers, after Boswell and Arthur Murphy, would reject this plan, but the principle of representing lives rather than blowing life into them to inflate them still holds. Through this one work, therefore, Mason earned his place in the development of the genre. But his choice of subject – almost an inevitable outcome of a long, close, and mainly literary friendship – also played its part; for the author of one of the most celebrated and best-loved poems in the language not only merited a good biography based on personal acquaintance; he also proved to have an exceptional talent for writing letters, thus inviting a biographer to quote extensively from them in preference to merely reporting or describing.

Born to Philip and Dorothy Mason, William Mason was descended from a line of churchmen and civic dignitaries of northern England. He was born in Hull on 12 February 1725 and was the son of a vicar, grandson of a collector of customs, and great-grandson of the sheriff of Hull; his family connections apparently gave him the right to bear arms. Among his relatives were Lord Holdernesse; Archbishop Hutton; and Erasmus Darwin, who was a cousin. An august genealogy, it brought with it a strong Whig legacy of benevolence and reformist sentiment. But far from an oppressive childhood in the shadow of influential men, Mason's was happier than most and certainly more enriching. Even the death of his mother in the first year of his life seems not to have left him scarred, and it did not prevent his forming affectionate bonds with his stepmothers – for his father married two more times. William Mason's early education, strongly colored by his father's abilities and liberal culture, was likewise free from undue stress, and after attending the grammar school (where Andrew Marvell had been a century before) and making a start in classical literature as well as modern languages, he became in 1742 a pensioner at Saint John's College, Cambridge. Even if domestic, institutional, and academic life left much to be desired there, he found congenial company and the chance to live a little adventurously, at least by his standards. His reading and interests were wide, and he soon began to write seriously and to get into print. After graduation he took ecclesiastic orders, having by then been befriended by Horace Walpole and by Gray, and he had been made a fellow of Pembroke Hall (1747). He was offered his first living at Aston in Yorkshire, and three years later he became chaplain in ordinary to George II. Other appointments of consequence followed: the precentorship of York in 1762; the chaplaincy to George III; and a second rectorship in 1777, by which time he had published his edition of Gray with his memoirs.

Mason's career, apart from his literary achievements, was, if not meteoric, at least very successful. His poetry, drama, correspondence, and sermons, collected in four volumes in 1811, represent a respectable output, though his reputation has since dwindled to, for example, only one extract from his long poem *The English Garden* (1772–1781) being included in *The New Oxford Book of Eighteenth Century Verse* (1984) — a reputation far exceeded by Whitehead's. Mason made his mark early in the small world of his day and kept steadily in the public eye, though ambition was not conspicuously in his character, as it was even less in Gray's, and by the time he died he was largely forgotten. The impression of the man is one of high principles, integrity, and general kindness; he carried out his professional duties well and strived as a writer to be disciplined and purposeful. Music also held an important place in his activities, and his contribution to its national history is evidenced by Charles Burney's praise and by an entry of considerable interest in George Grove's *Dictionary of Music and Musicians* (1879–1889). In the true spirit of amateurism so dear to the period, he wrote about art, preached human rights, and invented a sort of pinhole camera and a musical instrument called a "celestinett." His omission from Johnson's *Prefaces, Biographical and Critical, to the Works of the English Poets* (1779–1781) may have been due to a lawsuit in which he aimed to protect English playwrights from piracy by Scottish booksellers.

Mason's association with Gray did not start until Mason had been at Cambridge for some years, when he was twenty-two and Gray was thirty-one. It was to continue, mainly through their correspondence — since Mason lived and worked some two hundred miles north of London throughout most of his career — for twenty-four years, until Gray's death in 1771. Their letters show a mutual respect and warmth, even if the older man enjoyed a kind of flippancy — calling his young friend "Scroodles" — a trait more persistent in his letters to Walpole; Gray could also be quite harsh with Mason. But from the first introduction, when Gray had been shown Mason's earliest serious composition, *Musaeus* (1747), an elegy on the death of Alexander Pope, to Gray's last years, when he saw in Mason someone to be trusted as an executor of his estate and with the selective preservation of his papers, he seems to have taken to Mason and even made, on occasion, what was then a far-from-easy journey north to visit him. Therefore, when *The Poems of Mr. Gray,* with Mason's memoirs, was announced in the *London Chronicle* of 28–30 March 1775, there were many who were eager to see it. "I long to be at Gray's Memoirs," David Garrick wrote to George Colman, the Elder, adding: "you have made me smack my lips — Mr. Mason is certainly peevish, but I think there is poetry in him." Walpole had offered to print the edition on his private press, but Mason, with an eye to good sales, turned down the offer. He knew there was a waiting public and had given up his chaplaincy to the king to devote his energies to the book.

Mason's memoirs of Gray show something of a sense of mission; Mason was concerned with the actualities of the friend whose affairs had been entrusted to him, no doubt with him in mind as biographer. That sense of mission included going to the trouble of touring the Lake District in the footsteps of Gray, in order to check on the journal Gray wrote on the occasion of his own visit. True to his declared aim, Mason, letting his subject speak for himself and maintaining his role in the background, proves generally helpful, discriminating, and objective. The memoirs have a firmness of appeal, albeit limited for the general reader by the very virtues of form which commend them, for they depend on an excessive use of the footnote, often too dense or lengthy for the average reader's patience. Many notes are of sufficient interest in themselves to warrant their inclusion, but by no means is such always the case. What lends the text undoubted vitality is the selection and grouping of the letters, as well as Gray's naturalness as a correspondent. An academic poet and scholar of distinction he surely was; in his letters he was able to express a personality peculiar to these roles. Even as they stand, the letters as edited were "purified," their colloquialisms and eighteenth-century crudenesses ironed out, and

THE

WORKS

OF

THOMAS GRAY

WITH

MEMOIRS OF HIS LIFE AND WRITINGS

BY WILLIAM MASON

TO WHICH ARE SUBJOINED

EXTRACTS

PHILOLOGICAL POETICAL AND CRITICAL

FROM THE AUTHOR'S ORIGINAL MANUSCRIPTS

SELECTED AND ARRANGED

BY THOMAS JAMES MATHIAS

ΣΟΦΙΑΝ ΕΝ ΜΥΧΟΙΣΙ ΠΙΕΡΙΔΩΝ.
PINDAR. P. 6.

IN TWO VOLUMES

VOL. I.

LONDON

PRINTED BY WILLIAM BULMER AND CO.

Shakspeare Press

FOR JOHN PORTER IN PALL-MALL BOOKSELLER TO

HER ROYAL HIGHNESS THE PRINCESS CHARLOTTE

1814

*Title page for Mason's edition of Thomas Gray's works that includes a
biography of Gray notable for its half-epistolary form*

some new passages were inserted. Modern attitudes to this kind of editing are often overly critical; the memoirs nevertheless convey a fairly complete account of Gray as man and poet.

There are five sections and an appendix with Gray's correspondence with Walpole and Charles-Victor Bonstetten. The greatest part of the other correspondence is with Richard West, Dr. Thomas Wharton, Mason himself, and a few other friends and academic acquaintances, such as James Beattie, professor of philosophy at Aberdeen. An introductory account of Gray's birth and parentage, schooling at Eton, and friendships with Walpole and West leads into a group of eighteen letters to and from both these men. Mason, emphasizing that the life he is to lay before the public was an uneventful one, promises to concern himself with Gray as scholar and poet by using papers, notebooks (including Gray's commonplace book in three volumes), and other records, since in these is revealed the man, his

"head and heart" and his "fertility of fancy." Gray was born in Cornhill, London, in 1716, and Mason supplies one small anecdote of infancy concerning a narrow escape from suffocation, when the child's mother saved his life by opening a vein – an action which impressed the biographer. At Eton an uncle kept an eye on the boy and, being a fellow of Saint Peter's College, Cambridge, saw him admitted as a pensioner there. Information follows about West – son of a lord chancellor of Ireland – who, although less gifted than Gray, showed great promise until his leaving Oxford to study law in London when his health was already deteriorating. (He died of consumption in 1742.) It was an unsatisfactory friendship in some ways, West complaining constantly of his health while Gray was enjoying life; but the tragedy of a considerable talent meeting with serious illness moved Gray to write in a sympathetic vein and to do what he could to help. Mason concludes the section by saying that he will print a selection of their letters and juvenilia, and by this means, throughout the memoirs, he allows Gray to be his own biographer, with the help of "a few notes." Mason intervenes briefly before the fourth letter to note that Gray's views on academic education, held all his life, brought him enemies, especially in the climate of Jacobitism and hard drinking fashionable those days in Cambridge. After the closing letter the reader is informed of West's movements on leaving Oxford, and Gray's on leaving Cambridge when he was invited to accompany Walpole on a foreign tour. Reasons for omitting their correspondence in this connection are rather mysteriously excused with an appeal to "those of taste and candour." In this way Mason shows his hand early in the selection of material.

The section covering the European tour consists of thirty letters to West and Gray's parents, and it is introduced by Mason again stressing his function as editor and praising the elegant style of the letters and Gray's "exquisitely finished" exercises in Latin verse. Praise is nevertheless tempered with disappointment at the absence of descriptions of Venice, due to Gray and his volatile companion falling out and parting company. Mason is at his most confident and convincing when writing about literature and related subjects, and when he is able to contribute items from his own memories and experience. In the remaining sections 3 and 4 his passages of commentary between the letters take up questions of critical, aesthetic, and academic interest where these have direct bearing on Gray's work. The milestones and minor events of Gray's life are briefly treated with basic information – his return to Cambridge to study law being a move to placate his mother and aunt, who were devoted to him and worked at their own business to compensate for his father's neglect of *his* business as a scrivener; the difficult time Gray went through trying to help his dying friend West; and the relationship of that event to the composition of the *Odes* (1757) and the *Elegy Written in a Country Church-Yard* (1751). Gray's attempt at writing "Agrippina," a tragedy inspired by Racine, leads Mason to air his views on drama and the acting of Shakespeare: "Actors," he says, "must be able to *speak,* as well as study Greek authors intensively." The same concern with standards of spoken English recur in Mason's next biography.

Having come to a halfway point in his memoirs of Gray, and having covered Gray's youth and early adulthood, Mason notes that at this point the poet had not yet written verse in English ("Shall we attribute this to his having been educated at Eton?"), and he commends Gray's later mature judgment, correct taste, and extensive learning, demonstrated in the letters penned during his settled years at Cambridge as professor of modern history. There he had informed Mason that reading was much more agreeable to him than writing: never far from books and libraries, Gray had lodged for three years close to the British Museum to study the Harleian and other manuscripts. He still did not neglect his friendships, and Mason recalls the part Gray had played in his nomination to a fellowship at Pembroke Hall, an appointment the master of the college succeeded in blocking for two years for internal political reasons. An occasion for another anecdote is afforded in the context of the private circulation of Gray's *Elegy*. Walpole, to whom it was first sent, showed it to a fashionable lady. Her admiration for it and desire to meet the poet in person resulted in a lengthy versification of the social visits involved, which Gray called "A Long Story." Farcical and somewhat spun out, the tale lacked, thought Mason, a "pure sense of humor"; so he embarks on a further digression about humor, with a passing sneer at Laurence Sterne, whom it can be assumed he had at least met, if not come to know, in York.

The death of Gray's mother in March 1753 emphasized a reluctance Gray felt to give expression to deeper emotions. A man of his time, he could sympathize movingly with the bereavements of others, as he did in a well-written letter, often quoted, when Mason experienced the last illness and death of his wife.

The "Exordium" to one of Gray's best poems, "The Bard," prompts an editorial explanation that changes were hardly ever made to the first drafts of poems, nor were they roughed out. The compositional approach was slow, a striving for perfection of finish; larger, more ambitious projects were rarely carried through, and Mason does not print many fragments in the memoirs. Gray's complete poems amount to only thirty-three.

In the final section of the memoirs the question of Gray's lack of interest in making money from his work or seeking fame is discussed and attributed to a form of pride, which does not find much sympathy from a writer of memoirs out to portray a great man of letters. Mason moves on to outline Gray's range of interests, wide like his own, and says that, among the papers bequeathed to him, some were devoted to the study of geography and Linnaean natural history, with copious learned notes, as well as some on Gothic architecture and vocal music. A harpsichord player, Gray said his favorite composer was Giovanni Pergolesi; Gray enjoyed music and contemplated it as an adjunct of poetry. He had acquired competence in most branches of learning, and in some a "consummate mastery." Glancing at the duties of a university professor, Mason, after a few thoughts about the discipline of history, bears witness to Gray's achievements and reports that Gray insisted he would resign if he felt he could not be of real service in his profession. His last years are summarized, with emphasis on his poor health, despite temperate habits. Severe gout and a terminal abdominal illness led to Gray's death, the details as given having been drawn from a letter written by one of the doctors in attendance. The news arrived too late for Mason to make the journey for the funeral. Several years later he joined with two other admirers to erect a monument in Westminster Abbey, and he composed the epitaph. The biography closes – rather unexpectedly – with an anonymous "character" of Gray extracted from the *London Magazine*.

Mason's prolific footnotes contribute much to one's grasp of events, issues, and people in Gray's life. Frequently they are intrusive, naive, or sentimental when the correspondence should be left to speak for itself – as indeed Mason intended it should. Even for contemporaries there must surely have been irritation in having to take in such remarks as these: "Persons of very high rank, and withal very good sense, will only feel the pathos of this exclamation"; and "some readers will think this paragraph very trifling; yet many, I hope, will take it, as I give it, for a pleasing example of the amiableness of his (Gray's) domestic character." Other notes are better phrased and stay in the mind: "To be his friend it was always either necessary that a man should have something better than an improved understanding, or at least that Mr. Gray should believe he had." Occasionally footnotes take up and argue points made in the letters, one of some length being an attempt to refute criticisms of Mason's method of writing verse, and another countering Gray's opinion of Mason's play, *Elfrida* (1752); a third differs over the authenticity of Erse fragments, and a fourth over Jean-Jacques Rousseau's *Nouvelle Heloise* (1761), which Gray disliked. Readers may have the feeling that Mason was anxious to prove himself an intellectual equal; on the other hand, many of Mason's notes provide essential information, such as the explanation of how Dr. Wharton, a sufferer from asthma, came to be one of Gray's main correspondents, having met Gray at Cambridge when a fellow of Pembroke; and the fact that Mason had been commissioned to offer the laureateship – unsuccessfully – to Gray in 1757.

An enthusiasm for antiquities provided Mason the scope for other interesting footnotes, and readers learn that Gray had commissioned the artist Paul Sandby on one occasion to make a drawing of a Gothic chapel at York. The reader's concentration becomes strained, however, when an entire paper in note form, written by Gray in Italy on "several subjects proper to painting," is duly reproduced. Perhaps the main weakness of the memoirs lies in this discontinuity of narrative, where inadequacy in the main text is compensated for by another kind of inadequacy inherent in some footnotes, and there is little or no story. Boswell was able to bring his subject to life through well-recorded and remembered conversations and Johnson's larger-than-life personality. Gray, like another self-effacing Cambridge poet/professor much later in time, A. E. Housman, took his academic duties seriously, was no great conversationalist, and wrote very little, but he left English poetry immeasurably richer.

As well as with Walpole, Mason was in close touch with Edward Bedingfield, who knew Gray well, over publication of the memoirs, which Mason had planned soon after Gray's death. His handling of the correspondence, and the resulting questionableness of dates and sequence, has met with inevitable disapproval from later editors. Two editors of Gray's correspondence, Paget Toynbee and Leonard Whibley, found that thirty letters were recomposed by Mason from parts taken from seventy, and words such as *brag* and *oaf* were changed for politer ones. Mason in fact had fundamental scruples about keeping private letters at all, and he was by no means alone in that.

Mason aimed to write up the memoirs of William Whitehead "as a duty incumbent on friendship." Without the benefits of a legacy of personal documents, Mason was too restricted and at the same time too free to intrude; where this work falls short is in its failure to breathe life into the man. In the dozen or so years between the two biographies, Mason had been busy in his church career and his writing, but he had published little more of consequence and was beginning to fade from public esteem. His relations with Walpole were souring, and while it is true he came to know Johnson and to help found the Blue-Stocking Club, a lack of sympathy between the two stemming from Johnson's dislike of most of Gray's poetry and his treatment of the poet in the *Prefaces* meant that, for Mason, little came out of the association. He had also been closely associated with Sir Joshua Reynolds, who painted his portrait – an engraving of which appears in Mason's collected *Works* in four volumes –

Silhouette of William Mason by Francis Mapletoft (Pembroke College)

and he knew George Romney, as well as theater celebrities such as Mrs. Siddons, the author of a lively portrait of him. His readiness to help those in need extended to organizing a fund in aid of the poet Christopher Smart, who was stricken with insanity, poverty, and debt, leading to his early death. Mason published over a period of nine years the four books of his long poem *The English Garden* and published an *Ode to the Honourable William Pitt* in 1782. But the good years were almost over for him, and the "Memoirs of the Life and Writings of William Whitehead, Poet Laureate," occupying most of volume three of that poet's works, suggest a certain tiredness and even disenchantment with people.

The essay, like the one on Gray, is in five sections and starts with the main events of a childhood in Cambridge, where Whitehead was born in 1715 (a year before Gray) as the son of a baker – a humble background which, Mason suggests, should not be concealed but boasted of. After the early death of his father, Whitehead was brought up by his mother and must have shown precocious ability; he

attended Winchester School and, although rejected for Oxford, was admitted as a scholar at Clare Hall, Cambridge. Mason was able to use an informative account of the Winchester period provided by a canon of the cathedral who recalled that Whitehead had great promise in the writing of verse and acting in plays, as well as in the forming of prestigious friendships. Readers are told of a visit to the school by Alexander Pope, who awarded a prize to the young boy-poet and (Mason thinks) became too strong a literary influence when Edmund Spenser and John Milton might have better brought out Whitehead's expressive powers. A curious footnote claims that boys were maturing intellectually sooner at this time, due to "an improved mode of education." Whitehead continued his successes at Cambridge, and Mason took the opportunity to pay his respects to the memory of his own tutor – also Whitehead's – Dr. William Samuel Powell. At the age of twenty-seven Whitehead earned a fellowship at Clare Hall and then had to face the death of his mother. A juvenile poem to her is quoted, with the admission that some of the wording had been changed by Mason where it was "boyish" or "inappropriate."

Whitehead's achievements, social and literary, made him a natural choice for the post of tutor to two sons of the aristocracy, which would in due course see him on a grand tour with them. As a virtual member of Lord Jersey's family, Whitehead found time to write for the theater, and with surprising success. A tragedy, compared favorably to Pierre Corneille's best, provoked Mason to comment on the tragic style and to attack Garrick for his "despotic" method of selecting plays that offered him roles he could play to his own advantage. Garrick, Mason almost snarls, "disliked to perform any part whatsoever, where expression of countenance was not more necessary than recitation of sentiment."

Whitehead's tour abroad is cursorily treated. As Mason explains, he had already published Gray's letters often penned from the same places. Mason reports the conversation Whitehead had with Gray about the composition of Gray's *Elegy*, though this conversation is in the form of a footnote. Whitehead, whose muse was "now in her fullest vigour," and who was at last free of his noble pupils, was attempting elegies too, which, it seemed to Mason, could only puzzle the public with obscurities. After the death of Colley Cibber, Whitehead was offered the laureateship, with Mason acting as mediator once more. He further reveals that he himself had been suggested for the honor but, being in holy orders, was deemed ineligible. Gray had apparently been offered the honor as "a mere sinecure," and Mason wonders why such was not the case with Whitehead, "as the late King would readily have dispensed with hearing music, for which he had no ear, and poetry for which he had no taste."

The same tinge of maliciousness returns in connection with advice Mason gave to Whitehead to subcontract needy poets to write the obligatory odes, tailoring the verse to his demands, "as the subalterns whom Handel employed did with great obsequiousness, whenever the Oratorio exigencies of their musical General required them to new-array the rank and file of their metres." Mason's sarcasm bites deeper when a comparison is made between the highly placed and their poetic preferences and Johnson's views on art and taste, "of which he [Whitehead] had no comprehension – like the blind man's comparison of scarlet to the sound of a trumpet." Whitehead's appointment as laureate drew such jealously spiteful comments, notably from the poet Charles Churchill, and Mason's reporting makes enjoyable reading. But his subject quickly becomes little more than a cipher: the thirty years remaining of a seventy-year life contain, Mason protests, so few incidents that "they might be comprized in almost a single page." Whitehead, having brought more vilification on his head for his "Charge to the Poets," resulting in Garrick's refusal to stage more of his plays, devoted himself over a great many years to the ailing earl and countess of Jersey out of gratitude for their kindness to him, and he wrote little apart from the twice-yearly odes expected from him. After the death of the countess he appears to have split his time between the country estates of Middleton and Newnham while preparing his poems for publication. Yet he did anonymously write a successful farce for Garrick to perform. Mason did not see it in production, though he was pleased with the script. Whitehead's powers as a playwright were, according to Mason, considerable, and Whitehead continued all his life to study acting and dramatic speech; he was an excellent reciter with an abhorrence of rant.

Mason reports Whitehead's 1785 death, by merely stating that the end – after a bad cold – was "sudden and without a groan." The burial took place at Audley Street Chapel, and Mason pays tribute to a poet whose remarkable memory was "a living library." The later poems moved Mason to write: "Had Whitehead possest the powers of Bunbury's pencil, he might have reached his public through the *rolling*, rather than the printing press."

The essay on Whitehead is unlikely to have many readers today, partly because of the relative obscurity of the subject but also because of a crucial absence in it of commitment. It is not a life to peruse on its own and separate from the main body of Whitehead's writings, except insofar as it has value to the literary or theater historian. As a sample of the craft of biography it largely fails to arouse any deep curiosity about an almost-forgotten laureate.

William Mason lived on in Yorkshire for another nine years after this publication. His politics were those of old Liberal ideals tempered with the prevailing fear of radicalism and revolution. He died in 1797 "from a mortification occasioned by breaking his shin in stepping from his carriage," as his biographer John W. Drapper reports. Mason was buried at Aston, where he had been appointed rector forty-two years before. A tablet to his memory was placed in Westminster Abbey near Gray's memorial, an honor Mason could hardly have hoped for.

With only two contributions to the genre, so unequal in merit, Mason figures less as a notable biographer than as a typical product of the age and its busy, exploring temperament. Typical, too, was his talent for friendships, and as friendships so often found fullest expression in letters, material for the writer of lives or memoirs was usually abundant. It was Mason's good fortune to be the executor of Gray's will and the recipient of his papers. Although too often coupled with William Collins, Gray has remained a poet of distinction and quintessential Englishness, and Mason's memoirs of him are assured of continuing respect, serving Gray's reputation well. *Respect* seems the appropriate word to use for a work that bears the hallmarks of sound modern biography (being fully committed) but so little of the pleasure and warmth that makes a life possible to read and reread with affection.

Letters:

The Correspondence of Thomas Gray and William Mason (London: R. Bentley, 1858);

The Letters of Thomas Gray, including the Correspondence of Gray and Mason, 3 volumes, edited by Duncan C. Tovey (London: G. Bell & Sons, 1900–1912);

The Correspondence of Richard Hurd and William Mason, edited by Leonard Whibley (Cambridge: Cambridge University Press, 1932);

Horace Walpole's Correspondence with William Mason, 2 volumes, edited by W. S. Lewis, Grover Cronin, Jr., and Charles H. Bennett (New Haven: Yale University Press, 1955).

Biography:

John W. Drapper, *William Mason: A Study in Eighteenth-Century Culture* (New York: New York University Press, 1924).

References:

Matthew Arnold, *Essays in Criticism: Second Series* (London & New York: Macmillan, 1888);

Thomas Gray, *The Correspondence of Thomas Gray,* 3 volumes, edited by Paget Toynbee and Leonard Whibley (Oxford: Clarendon Press, 1971).

Papers:

The Albert and Henry Berg Collection at the New York Public Library holds the manuscript of *The Correspondence of Thomas Gray and William Mason.* Harvard University holds Horace Walpole's copy of Mason's edition of *The Poems of Thomas Gray.* Mason's commonplace book is in the York Minister Library. Pembroke College, Cambridge, holds Mason's transcriptions of Gray's journal for 1754 and his diaries for 1755.

Arthur Murphy

(27 December 1727 – 18 June 1805)

Paul Haeffner

See also the Murphy entry in *DLB 89: Restoration and Eighteenth-Century Dramatists, Third Series*.

BOOKS: *Gray's Inn Journal. By Charles Ranger, Esq.*, 52 nos. (London: Printed for W. Faden & J. Bouquet, 29 September 1753–21 September 1754); revised and republished in 2 volumes, with nos. 1–49 from *Craftsman* (21 October 1752–22 September 1753) and three new numbers (London: Printed by W. Faden for P. Vaillant, 1756);

The Apprentice, a Farce in Two Acts. As it is Performed at the Theatre-Royal in Drury-Lane (London: Printed for P. Vaillant, 1756);

The Spouter: or, the Triple Revenge. A Comic Farce in Two Acts. As it was Intended to be Perform'd. With the Original Prologue. Written by the author; and intended to be spoken by Mr. Garrick, dress'd in black, attributed to Murphy (London: Printed & sold by W. Reeve, 1756);

The Test, nos. 1–35 (London: S. Hooper, 6 November 1756–9 July 1757);

The Upholsterer, or What News? A Farce, in Two Acts. As it is Performed at the Theatre-Royal, in Drury-Lane. By the Author of the Apprentice (London: Printed for P. Vaillant, 1758);

The Orphan of China, a Tragedy, as it is Perform'd at the Theatre-Royal, in Drury-Lane (London: Printed for P. Vaillant, 1759);

The Desert Island, a Dramatic Poem, in Three Acts. As it is Acted at the Theatre-Royal in Drury-Lane (London: Printed for Paul Vaillant, 1760);

A Poetical Epistle to Mr. Samuel Johnson, A.M. By Arthur Murphy (London: Printed for Paul Vaillant, 1760);

The Way to Keep Him, a Comedy in Three Acts: as it is Perform'd at the Theatre-Royal in Drury-Lane (London: Printed for P. Vaillant, 1760); expanded as *The Way to Keep Him, a Comedy in Five Acts, As it is performed at the Theatre-Royal in Drury-Lane. By Mr. Murphy. The Fourth Edition* (London: Printed for P. Vaillant, 1761);

All in the Wrong. A comedy. As it is Acted at the Theatre-Royal in Drury-Lane. By Mr. Murphy (London: Printed for P. Vaillant, 1761);

The Examiner. A Satire. By Arthur Murphy, Esq. (London: Printed for J. Coote, 1761);

An Ode to the Naiads of Fleet-Ditch: By Arthur Murphy, Esq. (London: Printed for M. Cooper, 1761);

The Old Maid. A Comedy in Two Acts, as it is Performed at the Theatre-Royal in Drury-Lane. By Mr. Murphy (London: Printed for P. Vaillant, 1761);

The Auditor (London, 1762–1763 [lost]); also published in *The Political Controversy: or, Weekly Magazine of Ministerial and Anti-Ministerial Essays, Consisting of the Monitor, Briton, North Briton, Auditor, and Patriot, Entire; (with Select Pieces from the News-Papers) . . . By the Editor, John Caesar Wilkes, Esq.* (London: Printed for S. Williams, 1762–1763);

The Citizen. A farce. As it is Performed at the Theatre-Royal in Covent-Garden. By Arthur Murphy, Esq. (London: Printed for G. Kearsley, 1763);

No One's Enemy but His Own. A Comedy in Three Acts, as it is Performed at the Theatre-Royal in Covent-Garden (London: Printed for P. Vaillant, 1764);

What We Must All Come To. A Comedy in two Acts, as it Was Intended to be Acted at the Theatre-Royal in Covent-Garden (London: Printed for P. Vaillant, 1764); republished as *Three Weeks after Marriage; A Comedy, In Two Acts: as performed at the Theatre-Royal in Covent-Garden* (London: Printed for G. Kearsley, 1776);

The School for Guardians. A Comedy. As it is Performing at the Theatre-Royal in Covent-Garden (London: Printed for P. Vaillant, 1767);

Zenobia: a Tragedy. As it is Performed at the Theatre-Royal in Drury-Lane. By the Author of The Orphan of China (London: Printed for W. Griffin, 1768);

The Grecian Daughter; a Tragedy: as it is Acted at the Theatre-Royal in Drury-Lane (London: Printed for W. Griffin, 1772);

Arthur Murphy

Alzuma, a Tragedy. As Performed at the Theatre-Royal in Covent-Garden (London: Printed for T. Lowndes, 1773);

Know Your Own Mind: a Comedy, Performed at the Theatre-Royal, in Covent-Garden (London: Printed for T. Becket, 1778);

Seventeen Hundred and Ninety-One; a Poem, in Imitation of the Thirteenth Satire of Juvenal. By Arthur Murphy Esq. (London: Printed for G. G. J. & J. Robinson, 1791);

An Essay on the Life and Genius of Samuel Johnson, LL.D. By Arthur Murphy, . . . (London: Printed for T. Longman, B. White & Son, B. Law, J. Dodsley, H. Baldwin [and 32 others], 1792);

The Rival Sisters. A tragedy. Adapted for Theatrical Representation, as Performed at the Theatre-Royal, Drury-Lane. Regulated from the Prompt-Book, . . . (London: Printed by John Bell, 1793);

Arminius; a Tragedy. By Arthur Murphy, Esq. (London: Printed for J. Wright, 1798);

The Life of David Garrick, Esq. By Arthur Murphy, Esq., 2 volumes (London: Printed for J. Wright, 1801);

New Essays/By Arthur Murphy, edited by Arthur Sherbo (East Lansing: Michigan State University Press, 1963);

The Englishman from Paris (Los Angeles: William Andrews Clark Memorial Library, University of California, 1969).

Collections: *The Works of Arthur Murphy, Esq. In Seven Volumes* (London: Printed for T. Cadell, 1786);

The Way to Keep Him, and Five Other Plays, edited by John Pike Emery (New York: New York University Press, 1956);

The Plays of Arthur Murphy, edited by Richard B. Schwartz (New York: Garland, 1979).

OTHER: "An Essay on the Life and Genius of Henry Fielding," in *The Works of Henry Fielding,* 4 volumes, edited by Murphy (London: A. Millar, 1762);

Belisarius. By M. Marmontel. A New Edition, by Jean-François Marmontel, translated by Murphy (London: Printed for P. Vaillant, 1768);

The Works of Cornelius Tacitus; with an Essay on His Life and Genius, 4 volumes, translated, with an essay, by Murphy (London: For the author, 1793);

The History of Cataline's Conspiracy, with the four Orations of Cicero; to which are added notes and illustrations, translated by Murphy as G[eorge] F[rederic] Sydney (London: Printed for T. N. Longman and Hookham & Carpenter, 1795); republished as *The Works of Sallust. Translated into English By The Late Arthur Murphy, Esq.* (London: Printed for James Carpenter and J. Cuthell and P. Martin, 1807);

Jacques Vanière, *The Bees. A Poem. From the Fourteenth Book of Vanière's Praedium Rusticum. By Arthur Murphy,* translated by Murphy (London: Printed for F. & C. Rivington, 1799).

Arthur Murphy's claim to critical notice now rests, as it did with his contemporaries, on his success as a playwright rather than on his biographical writing, journalism, or verse translations. Having been an actor of note, he saw his own plays produced and acted in by David Garrick, and by the end of the eighteenth century he was second only to Richard Brinsley Sheridan in public esteem. Murphy's career in the theater gave him the drive and material to write biographies. In all three of his biographical works a strong theatrical element persists, often to the detriment of the narrative and the handling of fact. These works may be little known today except by reference in other works, yet their value is far from merely academic, if for no other reason than that they vividly transmit the personality of Murphy himself as a late-eighteenth-century figure popular with Charles Burney, Hester Lynch [Thrale] Piozzi, and Samuel Johnson's literary club. Overambitious he may have been, but, like his subjects, he worked with great energy and style. What commends him in a survey of biographical literature is perhaps not the actual merits of his major works, nor even a sense of direct encounter with the figures they portray, but his striving to contain the subjects and their huge achievements within the requirements of the genre, with its ever-growing public readership and scholarly interest.

Murphy's early life – up to the time he made a conscious choice to earn a living with his pen – was, if not exactly novelistic, rich enough in experience of the world to imbue him with an interest in character and a love of society that led him to write biographies. The younger of two sons, he was born in Roscommon, Ireland, to Richard and Jany French Murphy on 27 December 1727. When his father died at sea in 1729, his uncle, Arthur French, took responsibility for the family. Following a move to London, Murphy was sent abroad to live with an aunt in Boulogne, France, and subsequently, under the name Arthur French, he attended for six years the Jesuit College of Saint Omer. Completing his schooling in Greek, Latin, and the humanities, he returned to London and to the care of another uncle, Jeffrey French, who planned for him a career in commerce. But his education had given him no relevant skills for this pursuit, and he was obliged to remedy the deficiencies (which included arithmetic) at Webster's Academy so he could take an apprenticeship in Cork with the merchant Edmund Harrold. Back in Ireland, although he appears to have found the society congenial (and no doubt fruitful for his writing for the theater), he made a decision that was to change the course of his life. His uncle's ambition was to dispatch Murphy to Jamaica; his own was clearly to become well known in the world of letters. In 1747 he returned to London to work in the banking house of Ironside and Belchier. After two years as a writer he began to frequent theaters and coffeehouses and cultivate friendships with the actor Samuel Foote and with Henry Fielding, some twenty years his senior and a public figure of great repute and notoriety. Murphy had edited his own publication, the *Gray's Inn Journal* (29 September 1753–21 September 1754), and had also written essays for the *Craftsman,* a major outlet for Fielding's writings when Murphy came to know him.

At the age of thirty-four, after Fielding's death in Lisbon on 8 October 1754, Murphy took on the editorship of Fielding's works and wrote an introductory essay on his life. Murphy had known his subject personally for about two years. They had met as literary men, having in common a convivial and extroverted temperament, and Murphy was about to enter the legal profession to which Fielding had made an important contribution as a London magistrate and reformer. In no way were the two writers comparable in intellect or creative genius, nor were they on the kind of easy, intimate terms Murphy seems to have enjoyed with Johnson. The association must nevertheless have been cordial enough, as Fielding's bookseller-publisher Andrew Millar employed Murphy as editor. Fielding's closest friend, James Harris of Salisbury, with the novelist's sister, Sarah, had already planned a memorial publication. Harris's "Essay of the Life and Genius of Henry Fielding Esqr.," never published, though extant, bore almost the same title as

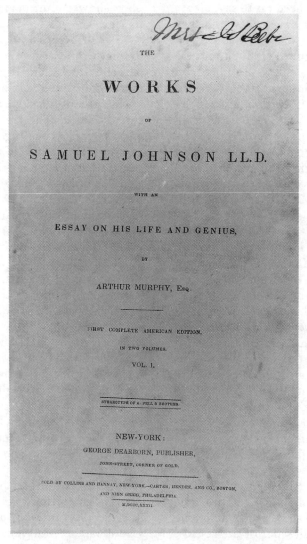

THE

WORKS

OF

SAMUEL JOHNSON LL.D.

WITH AN

ESSAY ON HIS LIFE AND GENIUS,

BY

ARTHUR MURPHY, Esq.

FIRST COMPLETE AMERICAN EDITION,

IN TWO VOLUMES.

VOL. I.

STEREOTYPE OF A. PELL & BROTHER.

NEW-YORK:

GEORGE DEARBORN, PUBLISHER,

JOHN-STREET, CORNER OF GOLD.

SOLD BY COLLINS AND HANNAY, NEW-YORK.—CARTER, HENDEE, AND CO., BOSTON,
AND JOHN GRIGG, PHILADELPHIA.
M.DCCC.XXXII.

*Title page for the first American edition of the complete works of
Samuel Johnson, which includes Murphy's biography of
Johnson, first published in England in 1792*

Murphy's. Murphy likely had seen the manuscript and did not go out of his way to research his material independently.

Fielding's last request to Millar had been "to take all Care" when he should hear of Fielding's death, "to prevent his Life from being undertaken by any of the Grubstreet Writers, who are so ready & officious on such Occasions." Murphy did not fall into the "Grubstreet" category at that level or with those attitudes, but his "An Essay on the Life and Genius of Henry Fielding" (1762) has been roundly condemned by later biographers. Fielding's son, in fact, had replied to one enquirer: "You ask whether an authentic account of my father has been published, to which the answer is — 'certainly not.' All that is to be found relative to him in print, is con-

tained in the Life written by Arthur Murphy . . . [who] knew nothing of my father; but patched that history up, from the accounts given to him by Millar, & a variety of *good jokes* that were handed about concerning him, & which would perhaps have lost much of their *merit* if they had been confined within the bounds of truth." Murphy's stock of stories about his fellow writers and actors must have been plentiful. What most incensed Sarah Fielding, however, when she was shown "An Essay on Henry Fielding" prior to publication, was the denigration of her brother's character, making of him "a shocking Creature" by highlighting his notorious and much-satirized early dissipation. Some of this information she convinced Millar to cut from the final version, which, she told Harris, would "only be tedious and dull." There was, needless to say, plenty to relate which could not have pleased Henry Fielding's family.

The essay, now difficult to read without exasperation, labors under a prose style padded with clichéd locutions hindering the flow of straight narrative, and it is further marred by learned digressions and sententiousness. Admittedly it was to be a memoir only: "it never was intended, in this little tract, to observe the rules of strict biography." Such "strict" biographical writing, if it could be said to have existed at that time, was not followed even in Murphy's last and full-scale biography, which was of Garrick. In "An Essay on Henry Fielding," after disingenuously assuring the reader that Fielding's reputation would not be allowed to suffer at his hands, Murphy enters on his account of one of the richest personalities and most versatile and productive authors in the literature of the time. An almost-routine sketch of Fielding's early life describes his studentship at Leiden in Holland and his return to London, where a vigorous constitution was "still unshaken by excesses of pleasure and unconquered by midnight watchings." Gout, however, was soon to take its course and is presented as a tragic nemesis for the "melancholy repentant" and his youthful indulgences. Moralizing of this sort leads to a man-of-the-world perspective on Fielding's good humor and ready mirth. Arriving at Fielding's years in the theater world, Murphy finds securer ground; displaying a direct acquaintance with events, issues, and people, he shows an awareness of both sides of the censorship issue as raised by the Licensing Act passed in 1737, which he deems to be a direct reaction on the part of ministers to the staging at Drury Lane of Fielding's *Historical Register* (1737), and he warns of "entailing slavery on the muses"; yet he declares himself on the side of authority, never being one to take risks with it: "his Majesty's servants should not be made ridiculous. . . . let licentiousness be banished from the theatres." Far from doing justice to the dramatist he both praises and censures, he in fact sees Fielding as a failure with no prospect of long-lasting fame as a playwright. It may be argued that the judgment was a fair one: of Fielding's eight full-length comedies and eighteen other pieces only *Tom Thumb* (1730) is well known today. But Fielding the dramatist enjoyed immense success at the time with works of fierce political and social satire. Fielding, Murphy asserts, left off writing for the stage when he ought to have begun, although every one of his

plays shows "some degree of merit very striking in its kind."

Well before Murphy has fully covered the drama in his survey of Fielding's works, he launches into a long digression on genius and the talents of his subject, which, by way of John Locke's association-of-ideas theory and Alexander Pope, carries him back to the ancient customs of Egypt and Greece. Repenting his digression, he tries to forestall criticism: "It may be observed by the reader, that in pursuing the foregoing train of reflections, sight has been lost of Henry Fielding." Murphy also makes the gross understatement that Fielding "was not inattentive to the calls of his duty" during his arduous work as a magistrate and makes a brief reference to Fielding's marriage to "Miss [Charlotte] Craddock, a beauty from Salisbury." When the Licensing Act, penury, and the squandering of her fortune led to Fielding's taking up law, Murphy reports what he has heard about these legal studies: Fielding's thirst for knowledge "amidst all his dissipations" and the delight in reading learned authors from whom he made abstracts and abridgments. The death of Charlotte Fielding, "whom he tenderly loved," precedes a summary of the progress of the novelist's talents. Couched in high-flown imagery, the summary likens that progress to the sun in the morning, afternoon, and evening. *Joseph Andrews* (1742) is summarized with praise for its "fabulous narration," and the masterpiece to follow (*Tom Jones,* 1749) is lauded for its "complete performance," establishing its author as the English Miguel de Cervantes, superior to Pierre Carlet de Chamblain de Marivaux – a comparison argued at some length. *Tom Jones* was penned during the "severe exercises of his understanding, and all the laborious duties of his office." His creativity unable to lie still, "he found leisure to amuse himself, and afterwards the world, with the History of *Tom Jones.*" *Amelia* (1751) represents the sun in its decline, "abating from his ardor, but still gilding the western hemisphere." Murphy, perhaps unhappy with the harsh social comment in *Amelia,* as well as the unromantic heroine with a blemished nose, deals briefly with it. After treating *The Journal of a Voyage to Lisbon* (1754), where "the last gleams of his wit and humour faintly sparkled," the biographer hastens to the end: Fielding's last days, his illness, and his family's plight. Of Fielding's second marriage, to his wife's servant – a minor scandal at the time – Murphy gives a very brief, discreet mention. The huge stature of Fielding is referred to, along with his admirable character and his satiric yet humane writings, in simpler, more direct prose: "Thus was closed a course of disappointment, distress, vexation, infirmity, and study." William Hogarth's drawing "at the head of this work" is, readers are told, taken from a profile cut by a lady with a pair of scissors, and it "recalls to all, who have seen the original, a corresponding image of the man."

Murphy's essay, well enough received at the time despite family disapproval, remained the only biography in use for well over a century; however, this fact had less to do with its intrinsic merits than changing taste, puritanism, and a rapid development of the novel as an art form. In Wilbur L. Cross's three-volume edition of Fielding's works, published in 1918, a chapter is headed "The Shadow of Arthur Murphy." "At the very outset," says Cross, "Fielding was most unfortunate in having Arthur Murphy as his first editor." According to Cross accuracy did not concern Murphy, and he put fiction in the place of it. Later biographers seem more tolerant. The biography by Martin C. and Ruthe R. Battestin, *Henry Fielding* (1989), resumes the criticisms of Murphy while freely citing and quoting from him. Incompetence and negligence do not appear to have entirely disqualified his work. "According to Arthur Murphy" remains a repeatedly used phrase in Fielding criticism.

At the time of Fielding's death Murphy, having made his mark as an essayist, was establishing himself as an actor and playwright. Because his friendship with Johnson was just beginning, it has been suggested that he seized his chance to impress the literary establishment by accepting the editorship of Fielding's works. In the thirty years that were to follow before his second biographical venture, *An Essay on the Life and Genius of Samuel Johnson, LL.D.* (1792), he widened his knowledge of people, furthered his writing ability, and became altogether a more mature personality, while his success as a playwright continued until after Johnson's death in 1784. In James Boswell's *Life of Samuel Johnson* (1791) Murphy's name appears frequently, and an account is given of his first meeting with Johnson related by Murphy himself – an amusing and touching story concerning the younger writer's inadvertent retranslation into English of one of the tales from the *Rambler,* a tale which had been translated and published in a French magazine. When Murphy came in person to explain the error, his talents and "gentleman-like manners" won Johnson's lasting affection.

Boswell's *Life of Samuel Johnson* was published a year before Murphy's; a biography of Johnson by Sir John Hawkins appeared in 1787, and Piozzi's *Anecdotes of the Late Samuel Johnson, LL.D.* (1786) was published the year before that. Material was available and plentiful: many had known Johnson well enough to recall his conversations and convey his thoughts and feelings to an eager public. Most important, high standards had been set so that the danger of hurrying over inadequately prepared subject matter was much less than it had been in 1762. Biographer (Murphy) and subject (Johnson) shared a mutual affection and a puritanical outlook on life. Boswell confirms that his master "very much loved" Murphy but was unreasonably prejudiced against the author of *Tom Jones.* As to Johnson's writings Murphy was less than objective and considered the great man "a model of piety, virtue, perseverance and creativity." In the course of Murphy's *An Essay on Samuel Johnson* attacks are repeatedly made on Hawkins's more astringent biography, and angry repudiation is made regarding Hawkins's "malevolent" motives. He is finally dismissed in this lofty sentence: "But Sir John is no more: our business is with Johnson." The respect between Johnson and Murphy, though, was not entirely mutual. Piozzi confides that, when she once praised Murphy as a conversationalist, Johnson's reply was: "tis certain . . . that Man by some happy Skill displays more knowledge than he really has."

The essay on Johnson, warmer in tone than that on Fielding, opens with a claim to thirty years' acquaintance with the subject and with an assertion that Murphy has nothing new to say, "no secret anecdotes," "no private conversation" – "everything has been gleaned." In the ensuing account of Johnson's early years mention is made of the child's visit to the royal court to be touched by the queen for his scrofula; of his marriage at age twenty-five to the widow Elizabeth Porter, twenty years his senior ("another mode of advancing himself"); of the "early symptoms of the wandering disposition of mind"; and of a memory of which "wonders are told." Readers are reminded of Johnson's legendary association with the young Garrick and their move to London, where, the actor making his own way, "Johnson was left to toil in the humble walks of literature." His early mature writings receive due attention – after a sustained discussion of his first literary exercise, an abridged translation of Father Jerome Lobo's *Voyage to Abyssinia* (1735). The play *Irene* (1749), staged by Garrick many years later; the much-anthologized poem *London* (1738); and the distinguished *Life of Mr. Richard Savage* (1744), resulting from a moving friendship with the ill-fated poet, are all discussed at length, with Murphy – as throughout the essay – specifying rates of payment. These were hard years for Johnson, and his poignant line "Slow rises worth by poverty depress'd" leads Murphy to reflect that "It is mortifying to pursue a man of merit through all his diffulties." When Murphy comes to Johnson's period of employment in the earl of Oxford's library, however, he enjoys relating the story about the hapless bookseller being felled with a heavy folio by the massively built Johnson. As Murphy covers these stages of Johnson's life and works, he suspects he is boring his readers: "There may, perhaps, be a degree of sameness in this regular way of tracing an author . . . but in the life of Johnson there are no other landmarks." Johnson's success and fame with the *Dictionary* (1755) and the *Rambler* (1750–1752) are recounted, and a protracted account is given of his involvement in an attempt to charge John Milton with plagiarism, providing Murphy further opportunity for his running skirmishes with Hawkins's *Life*.

According to Murphy, Elizabeth Johnson's death in 1752 emphasized her husband's deeply religious temperament, and Johnson was then befriended by Samuel Richardson, who was "endanger'd" by his own indolence and still relatively poor. After Johnson's application to the author of *Clarissa* (1747–1748) for a loan of five pounds, Richardson's response was a gift of six guineas. Murphy discloses his own part in the procurement from the king of a pension for Johnson of three hundred pounds.

"We have now," writes Murphy, "travelled through that part of Dr. Johnson's life which was a perpetual struggle with difficulties." Discussion of the well-known "Club," revived with Edmund Burke, Joshua Reynolds, Oliver Goldsmith, and Hawkins as members, leads Murphy to his proud introduction of Johnson, then a sought-after celebrity, to the Thrales and their Streatham home and circle – an event also recorded by Piozzi herself, along with other reminiscences involving Murphy, Johnson, and Garrick. First meetings indeed had their magic, and Johnson's meeting with Boswell had to be set down, too, for Murphy was there, but both he and Boswell footnote the fact that their respective accounts differ. *Prefaces, Biographical and Critical, to the Works of the English Poets* (1779–1781), later titled *The Lives of the Poets*, "the last of his [Johnson's] literary labours," offers Murphy a cue to declare his special interest in biography and to indulge his weakness for orotundity, as he laments the fates of the well-known whose lives have suffered neglect: "Was there no friend to pay the tribute of a tear? No just observer of life to record the virtues of the deceased? Was even envy silent?" He proposes an academy to make good the neglect.

What has still to be said about Johnson "may soon be despatched": the last days at Bolt Court, with only Johnson's black servant Frank for company; Johnson's generosity and bequest of the residue of his estate to Frank; Johnson's death "without a groan"; and his burial in Westminster Abbey close to Garrick's tomb. About a quarter of the whole essay remains, though, and it is devoted to a summary of the life and works, so divided. Johnson's piety; his superstition; his benevolence "tinctured with particular prejudices"; and his attitude toward the passions, especially regarding Garrick's acting, which he viewed with near contempt ("Punch has no feelings!"), are all effectively conveyed. Among the writings the *Dictionary* stands out as the "Mount Atlas of English Literature," but it falls outside the scope of Murphy's critique and gives way to *The Lives of the Poets*, "the most brilliant, and certainly the most popular" of the works. Some lives are discussed: Thomas Gray, Murphy notes, is harshly treated; in the case of Pope, Murphy repeats a Swiss professor's criticism and submits that "This is not the place for controversy about the Leibnitzian system." He concludes with the "Life of Milton," on which criticism was severe enough to warrant a lengthy argument but is dismissed at last with the words: "But why all this rage against Dr. Johnson?" Johnson's writings offer "a perpetual source of pleasure and instruction."

Millar paid three hundred pounds for this essay of forty thousand words. There was a demand for a concise and authoritative memoir, and it earned the publisher five thousand guineas. Murphy, having left the theater for the law, enjoyed his reputation as an author. The year before his *An Essay on Samuel Johnson* appeared, he had published an imitation of Juvenal and, two years after the essay, an edition in translation of the works of Cornelius Tacitus. Of Johnson's personal troubles and his struggles with poverty, ill health, and drudgery, Murphy could speak as a close acquaintance, but the work suffers from a defective structure: there is again too much moralizing and digressing. On the other hand, a neat turn of aphorism lends freshness where it is needed. *An Essay on Samuel Johnson* has been described as "a distinguished example of late Augustan critical biography," and it certainly merits wider availability. In studies of Johnson the acknowledgment "according to Murphy" sounds like a refrain, in spite of a general distrust of his reliability in matters of fact. Perhaps the best quality of the essay is the recurring warmth of tone, which, bordering on adulation if not hero worship, communicates the desire of the devoted biographer to do justice to his subject at all levels.

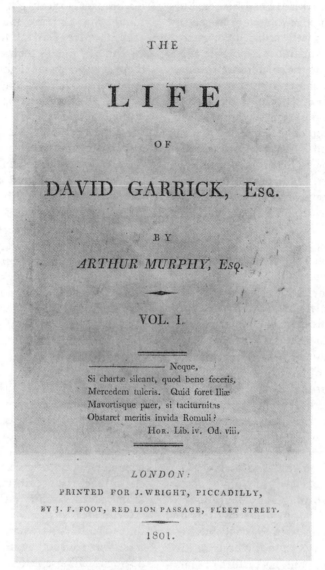

THE

LIFE

OF

DAVID GARRICK, Esq.

BY

ARTHUR MURPHY, Esq.

VOL. I.

———————— Neque,
Si chartæ sileant, quod bene feceris,
Mercedem tuleris. Quid foret Iliæ
Mavortisque puer, si taciturnitas
Obstaret meritis invida Romuli?
Hor. Lib. iv. Od. viii.

LONDON:
PRINTED FOR J. WRIGHT, PICCADILLY,
BY J. F. FOOT, RED LION PASSAGE, FLEET STREET.

1801.

*Title page for volume 1 of Murphy's biography of David
Garrick, his colleague on the stage for more than twenty years*

Murphy's third and final biographical work, *The Life of David Garrick* (1801), was published four years before his death and gave him the opportunity to write a full-scale life of the man with whom he had been most closely associated professionally. Thomas Davies's *Life of Garrick* had run through four printings since its appearance in 1780. Both biographers were, along with Garrick himself, members of the Johnson-Boswell circle, so knowledge of the man would have been a shared resource. Murphy had written successful plays produced and acted by Garrick at Drury Lane, however, and Murphy's vigorous personality and articulacy had engaged with Garrick's as a colleague over some twenty years behind the scenes – a relationship which, to quote the editors of Garrick's correspondence, had been "a lifelong dispute, punctuated by brief but never lasting intervals of friendliness." Thus of the thirty-five or so surviving letters to Murphy, one, at the start of their association, is couched in magisterially tart language; the last, dated the year before Garrick's retirement, reads: "Dear Murphy, I have a noble turtle to-morrow. . . . if you have no objection to drinking his [the donor's] health, and meeting some of your friends, be to-morrow at my house at four, and you will oblige."

As readers of Boswell's *Life of Samuel Johnson* become aware, the best-known actor-manager played almost as big a part in society as on stage, prompting Johnson to remark: "He had friends, but no friend." As a theatrical legend memorialized in Johnson's remark that his death "eclipsed the gaiety of nations," Garrick was an almost-inevitable subject for Murphy. Regarding the man himself, Murphy could draw on ample material then in print to bolster his own memories and store of anecdotes: the life of the actor-manager seemed wholly at his disposal. But they had been colleagues, and just as his affectionate closeness to Johnson tended to prejudice his literary judgment, so his professional dealings with Garrick blurred his focus on the man. Once again the overriding problem was one of organizing the mass of material, both public and private, and creating out of it an objective and balanced whole. A story in circulation quoted Murphy as saying that "Off-stage he [Garrick] was a little sneaking rascal, but on stage, Oh My God!" Murphy had contempt for the managerial and play-selection procedures from which he had himself suffered as a playwright, so his by-now-familiar vein of lionizing rings especially false in this work.

Published in two volumes, with a fine engraving of Reynolds's portrait of Garrick as frontispiece, it runs to fifty-two chapters and no less than twenty appendices, including a medical report of the last illness, the will, and the Charles Macklin correspondence referred to in the text. A short introduction stresses Murphy's aim as a biographer: to trace "the man into his closest retirement" and to lay "the whole character open to our view." Murphy repeats his reproach that English biography (except for Johnson's *Lives of the Poets*) has neglected writers of genius. His own friendship with Garrick having been one of "great intimacy . . . to the hour of his death," he feels qualified to paint his picture of Garrick "with a firm, and impartial hand." He deals lightly with the early years, according to his general practice, up to Garrick's unlikely start on law studies, and then begins a production-by-production coverage of Garrick's career at Drury Lane – Garrick by then being "Undoubted master of the *Sock and Buskin*." Murphy intersperses theatrical events, reminiscences, and anecdotes about the great man and other stage personalities; disputes; extended quotations of prologues and the like; along with authorial opinions and criticisms. Here and there Murphy ventures a little self-advertisement, as when he reminds his readers of his essay on Fielding's life in connection with that author's play *The Wedding Day* (1743), produced unsuccessfully at Drury Lane. Virtually contradicting his earlier statement of intent, he writes that his work is "the history of Garrick in his profession." The private

man in fact is rarely glimpsed, though it is only fair to add that Garrick had been a very public figure and that Mrs. Garrick lived on as guardian of the two homes and all their contents until 1823. Of her there is a somewhat slighting mention: "the fair Violetti . . . who [chose] to grace herself with an Italian name." She had been La Violette, a leading dancer at the Haymarket, and was Viennese by birth. But speaking firsthand, Murphy does bring his narrative to life on a more intimate level. Garrick's marriage came soon after his affair with Peg Woffington, the widely adored actress, whom "this writer has heard declare at different times, that he went so far as to try the wedding-ring on her finger."

The biography certainly does justice to Garrick's powers on the stage, which could leave "the whole audience electrified," and Murphy remembers particularly Garrick's acting of King Lear as a "tour de force," depicting madness with "total alienation of mind from every idea, but that of his unkind daughters." Murphy also recalls other players quite as memorably, such as Mrs. Cibber, whose voice in *King John* was "harmony in an uproar." Garrick's theater managership receives a well-balanced analysis, with quarrels, crises, and mistakes set against the most triumphant period, when, as patentee of Drury Lane, Garrick launched the new season with a prologue written by Johnson. "We enter now," writes Murphy with infectious excitement, "upon a new aera in the history of the English stage; the greatest and most splendid that the drama of this country has ever known." Rioting and intertheater warfare are vividly recorded, if sometimes crudely, as when "the spirit of the inferior class was roused" against "a gang of Frenchmen" during a Chinese festival. When he feels obliged to explain a disagreement (the only one, he falsely claims, he and Garrick ever had), events are recounted to his own advantage, ending in a characteristically fulsome apology for "too much prolixity about things chiefly relating to himself." More telling, he details his disapproval of Garrick's version of *Hamlet* and of Garrick's "rage for re-touching, and, as it was said, correcting and improving our best authors." A further charge is directed at Garrick over his uncritical selection of new plays for staging, a charge which carries a degree of resentful bitterness on Murphy's part: this selection process had been a cause of their falling out. He considers that Garrick's practice of reading the manuscripts to his cast in the greenroom "was not a serious exercise."

Consistent with primarily writing about his subject's professional life, Murphy does not follow the Garricks on their Continental tour in 1763, when troubles in the theater had soured the great actor and his enemies seemed to have triumphed. These events bring the biography to the end of volume one and are the cue for Murphy's introduction of a favorite extended metaphor: the audiences have been left "to cast a mournful look at the setting of the theatrical sun." After his return Garrick staged one of the most important – though notoriously not one of the most successful – events of his life, the Shakespeare Jubilee at Stratford-upon-Avon in 1769. It is rather flatly reported, but Murphy is ready with the kind of anecdote that makes him so worth reading. The actor Foote, bored with the proceedings and the rain, had dragged Murphy away, saying, "Murphy, let us take a turn on the banks of the Avon, to try if we can catch some inspiration." The Jubilee is then described in its transfer to Drury Lane, and there is praise, albeit brief, for a farce by Garrick. The final chapters concern the last season and Garrick's inner struggle, in the face of ill health, to keep going or retire: he "who had lived in the sunshine of public admiration" fluttered and hesitated. When he delivered his farewell speech at Drury Lane, the audience is reported to have been overcome with emotion: "The people saw the theatrical sun, which had shone with translucent lustre, go down beneath the horizon, to rise no more." After such fame and great material fortune it was a sad ending, and during that farewell speech "Every face in the theatre was clouded with grief," all concurring "in one demonstration of sorrow."

The Life of David Garrick was sold to the bookseller John Wright for three hundred guineas in 1801. Together with the Davies biography it was popular for thirty years, as the Garrick legend flourished and persisted throughout the century. Murphy as playwright was not to the taste of Romantics such as Charles Lamb and William Hazlitt, who compared him unfavorably with Sheridan. But *The Life of David Garrick* continued to have a place in theatrical tradition and, as with his biographies of Fielding and Johnson, to be quoted and used. Modern biographers complain of the style and lack of discipline, but at the same time they repeat many of the quotable remarks and stories. For all the faults of rhetoric, imbalance, and bias, the biography has many enjoyable and instructive moments. It is a mine of theatrical interest, and though it would be too much to claim for it even the merit of a readable work, with the laborious coverage of productions, the stature and the phenomenon of Garrick in Murphy's best chapters and passages are transmitted with some energy and force.

Murphy was still writing plays and translations into the late 1790s, although little more of his work got into print. Having left the bar and sold his Lincoln's Inn chamber, he continued as commissioner of bankrupts until the year of his death. Despite generous legacies, he was never out of financial straits, for, in addition to living beyond his means and enjoying the social life he had always courted – including being in the entourage of the Prince of Wales – he had paid out heavily to publish his translations. He moved twice and, his health failing rapidly, died in Knightsbridge on 18 June 1805, two years after being granted a pension by the king. As he had wished, he was buried in Saint Paul's, Hammersmith. Jesse Foot, who wrote Murphy's biography (1811), provided an epitaph. The biography draws on a commonplace book, an autobiographical sketch, and other personal documents. Few, in any case, would have remembered Murphy as he was in the heyday of Garrick's Drury Lane. His portrait had been painted by Reynolds (now lost) and by Nathaniel Dance, the latter's used for an engraving printed in Murphy's collected works, published in 1786 in seven volumes. The face is rather ponderous but has a certain arresting quality, the kind of authority he would have wished to be associated with his three biographies.

Murphy's biographies were written during a time in which the genre developed rapidly. He left it if not the better for his contribution at least the richer. He had recorded innumerable passages of conversation and anecdotes from his own memory of personal friendships with his subjects. But these subjects were the giants of the time, each prolific in achievement and generous in their friendships. A two-edged advantage, this fact offered an abundance of material while guaranteeing public interest, especially among the cultural elite of the day. It also challenged the biographer to interpret and make sense of a vast amount of material in order to present a coherent and convincing picture. Murphy was often convincing but too often disorganized. His failings lay partly in his vanity and self-indulgence as a stylist; although able to tell a good story well, he floundered in the volume of facts and gossip at his disposal. He also betrayed a weakness in personal insight, except on occasions in his essay on Johnson, with whom he seems to have felt most in harmony, and that biography remains the most readable and most valued today of Murphy's works. Being a man of the theater, a successful writer, and sought-after companion and raconteur, he had the confidence to attempt biographies about three major celebrities, but in the end overconfidence flawed much of his work as a biographer.

Biography:
Jesse Foot, *The Life of Arthur Murphy, esq.* (London: J. Faulder, 1811) — includes correspondence.

References:
Roy E. Aycock, "Shakespearian Criticism in the *Gray's-Inn Journal* and the *Craftsman:* Some Publication Mysteries," *PBSA,* 67 (1973): 68–72;

Joseph M. Beatty, Jr., "The Battle of the Players and Poets, 1761–1766," *Modern Language Notes,* 34 (December 1919): 449–462;

Tuvia Bloch, "The Antecedents of Sheridan's Faulkland," *Philological Quarterly,* 49 (April 1970): 266–268;

Harold L. Bruce, "Voltaire on the English Stage," *University of California Publications in Modern Philology,* 8 (June 1918);

J. Homer Caskey, "Arthur Murphy and the War on Sentimental Comedy," *Journal of English and Germanic Philology,* 30 (October 1931): 563–577;

Caskey, "Arthur Murphy's Commonplace-Book," *Studies in Philology,* 37 (October 1940): 598–609;

Caskey, "The First Edition of Arthur Murphy's *Sallust,*" *Philological Quarterly,* 13 (October 1934): 404–408;

H. MacL. Currie, "Arthur Murphy, Actor and Author," *New Rambler,* 14 (1973): 9–13;

Howard Hunter Dunbar, *The Dramatic Career of Arthur Murphy* (New York: Modern Language Association, 1956);

John P. Emery, *Arthur Murphy: An Eminent English Dramatist of the Eighteenth Century* (Philadelphia: University of Pennsylvania Press, 1946);

Emery, "Murphy's Criticisms in the *London Chronicle,*" *PMLA,* 54 (December 1939): 1099–1104;

Martin Lehnert, "Arthur Murphy's *Hamlet*-Parodie (1772) aut David Garrick," *Shakespeare-Jahrbuch* (1966): 97–167;

Henry Knight Miller, "Internal Evidence: Professor Sherbo and the Case of Arthur Murphy," *Bulletin of the New York Public Library,* 69 (1965): 459–470;

Susan M. Passler, "Coleridge, Fielding and Arthur Murphy," *Wordsworth Circle,* 5 (Winter 1974): 55–58;

Robert Donald Spector, *Arthur Murphy* (Boston: Twayne, 1979);

Spector, "Arthur Murphy: Embattled Dramatist," *Notes & Queries,* 26 (February 1979): 40–41;

Simon Trefman, "Arthur Murphy's Long Lost *Englishman from Paris:* A Manuscript Discovered," *Theatre Notebook,* 20 (Summer 1966): 137–141.

Papers:
Manuscripts of many of Murphy's plays are housed in the Larpent Collection of Huntington Library, San Marino, California. Manuscript letters are housed in the John Rylands Library, Manchester (Eng. Mss. 548, 891), and the Rush Rhees Library, University of Rochester.

Hester Lynch [Thrale] Piozzi

(27 January 1741 – 2 May 1821)

Michael Mandelkern
Graduate Center of the City University of New York

See also the Piozzi entry in *DLB 104: British Prose Writers, 1660–1800, Second Series.*

BOOKS: *Anecdotes of the Late Samuel Johnson, LL.D., During the Last Twenty Years of His Life* (London: Printed for T. Cadell, 1786);

Letters to and from the Late Samuel Johnson, LL.D., to which are added some Poems never before Printed, 2 volumes, letters by Johnson and Piozzi, edited by Piozzi (London: Printed for A. Strahan & T. Cadell, 1788);

Observations and Reflections Made in the Course of a Journey through France, Italy, and Germany, 2 volumes (London: Printed for A. Strahan & T. Cadell, 1789);

British Synonymy; or, an Attempt at Regulating the Choice of Words in Familiar Conversation, 2 volumes (London: Printed for G. G. & J. Robinson, 1794);

Three Warnings to John Bull before He Dies (London: Printed for R. Faulder, 1798);

Retrospection: or a Review of the Most Striking and Important Events, Characters, Situations, and Their Consequences, which the Last Eighteen Hundred Years Have Presented to the View of Mankind, 2 volumes (London: John Stockdale, 1801);

Autobiography, Letters, and Literary Remains of Mrs. Piozzi (Thrale), 2 volumes, edited by Abraham Hayward, second edition (London: Longman, Green, Longman & Roberts, 1861; Boston: Ticknor & Fields, 1861);

The French Journals of Mrs. Thrale and Dr. Johnson, edited by Moses Tyson and Henry Guppy (Manchester: Manchester University Press, 1932);

Thraliana: The Diary of Mrs. Hester Lynch Thrale (Later Mrs. Piozzi), 1776–1809, 2 volumes, edited by Katharine C. Balderson (Oxford: Clarendon Press, in cooperation with the Huntington Library, 1942; second edition, revised, 1951);

The Thrales of Streatham Park [Family Book], edited by Mary Hyde (Cambridge, Mass. & London: Harvard University Press, 1977).

Editions: *The Letters of Samuel Johnson, with Mrs. Thrale's Genuine Letters to Him,* 3 volumes, edited by R. W. Chapman (Oxford: Clarendon Press, 1952);

Observations and Reflections Made in the Course of a Journey through France, Italy, and Germany, edited by Herbert Barrows (Ann Arbor: University of Michigan Press, 1967);

Anecdotes of the Late Samuel Johnson, LL.D., during the Last Twenty Years of His Life, edited by Arthur Sherbo (London: Oxford University Press, 1974).

OTHER: "The Three Warnings" and "Epistle of Boileau to his Gardener," in Anna Williams, *Miscellanies in Prose and Verse* (London: Printed for T. Davies, 1766); "The Three Warnings" republished in *A Collection of Poems in Four Volumes. By Several Hands,* edited by George Pearch (London: Printed for G. Pearch, 1770);

"Journal of the Welsh Tour" (1744), in *Dr. Johnson and Mrs. Thrale,* edited by A. M. Broadley (London: John Lane, 1910), pp. 155–219.

Although she was a prolific and versatile writer, Hester Lynch [Thrale] Piozzi is remembered primarily for being a friend of Samuel Johnson and for the scathing portrayal of her which James Boswell wrote in his *Life of Samuel Johnson* (1791). To a certain extent she defies categorization as a person and as a literary figure. In terms of the former, her character is elusive, "a bundle of contradictions," as James L. Clifford, one of her biographers, calls her; in terms of the latter, she was a poet, diarist, and letter writer, but she was also the author of works on English grammar and European history. She was one of the first women to attempt these genres, wherein part of her significance lies. Furthermore, she was one of Johnson's earliest biographers, although the work that she wrote, the *Anecdotes of the Late Samuel Johnson, LL.D., During the Last Twenty Years of His Life* (1786), has been dwarfed by Boswell's *The Life of Samuel Johnson,* much as her

Hester Lynch [Thrale] Piozzi

own life was dwarfed by Johnson's. Fueled partially by the interest in feminist criticism, which seeks to rediscover an author who may have been overlooked because of her gender, her oeuvre has, in the twentieth century, undergone a reevaluation – or, one might say, a *first* evaluation, in that some of her works have only been published recently – a reevaluation which has led to an emerging sense of her importance as a major woman writer before Jane Austen.

Piozzi was born Hester Lynch Salusbury in Wales on 27 January 1741. Her parents, John and Hester Maria Cotton Salusbury, were cousins who were plagued by financial troubles throughout their lives. In an attempt to improve his fortunes, her father made several trips to Nova Scotia under the auspices of Lord Halifax, none of which led him to prosperity. His forced reliance upon his younger brother, Sir Thomas Salusbury, was no doubt humiliating. John Salusbury and his wife were hoping that Thomas, a childless widower, would select their daughter for his heir. They were greatly fond

of Hester – their only child – whom they spoiled considerably. John Salusbury was afraid that his precarious financial position would lead his wife to force his daughter into a loveless marriage, a fear which materialized when Mrs. Salusbury began to consider Henry Thrale, the son of a wealthy brewer, as a suitable match for Hester. Knowing the dangers of an imprudent marriage all too well (her husband was improvident, although loved by his family) and fearing the interest of her daughter's tutor, Arthur Collier, Mrs. Salusbury sought, first and foremost, to provide her daughter with a husband who was reliable, and she felt that she had found one in Thrale. The situation came to a head upon the news that Sir Thomas Salusbury was going to remarry, which lessened the chances that Hester would inherit his estate. This remarriage possibly precipitated John Salusbury's death in December 1762. Hester married Thrale on 11 October 1763.

Hester and her husband were very different from each other. She was romantic and wrote po-

*First Card from the Thrale Family
30 Septr. 1769.*

*Mr and Mrs Thrale present their best
Compliments to Mr Boswell, and should
think themselves highly favour'd in his
Company to Dinner at Stretham any day
he shall think fit to appoint.*

30: Sep:

Note from Mrs. Thrale to James Boswell inviting him to Streatham Park for dinner. After Johnson's death in 1784, the two were rivals in writing biographies of him.

etry, while he was stolid and prosaic. Yet their marriage was not unhappy, according to the era's precepts. There may have been no pretense of love, and Hester expected her uncle, in spite of his remarriage, to provide for her, but she and her husband got on reasonably well together. For seventeen years, until Henry Thrale's death in 1781, they divided their time between their famed country home at Streatham and their second home at Southwark, where his brewery was located. For Hester these years were greatly filled with childbearing and despondency. She had twelve children, eight of whom died in infancy. Two of these were male, the deaths of whom were particularly disheartening in that she had failed to provide Thrale with something he sought from a wife: an heir.

In January 1765, at a dinner party arranged by the playwright Arthur Murphy, Hester met Johnson. In spite of the difference in their ages (Johnson was fifty-seven, Hester twenty-four), she had a good deal in common with him – more, certainly, than she had with her husband. She could discuss poetry and the classics, in which she had been educated by her tutor, Collier. Upon Johnson's suggestion he

and Hester undertook a translation of works by Boethius. Originally he came to see her once a week, attending dinner parties to which he brought some of his extraordinary acquaintances, including Sir Joshua Reynolds, Oliver Goldsmith, and Edmund Burke. In 1766 Johnson underwent a series of emotional collapses, however, leading Hester to suggest that he move to Streatham, where, for the next sixteen years, he was a constant guest. There is no doubt that she proved a salutary influence on him during these years; she helped him overcome his fits of depression, which were brought on by his fears of insanity. She was the only person in whom he confided then – an indication of the strength of their attachment.

Johnson's influence on Hester was not confined to Boethius, and at his suggestion she began to keep a diary. Originally titled "The Children's Book," the *Family Book* (17 September 1766–31 December 1778; published in 1977) was intended as a record of her children, of whom Hester was exceedingly proud and whose merits she wanted to see recorded. As time went on, however, she began to shift the emphasis unconsciously to herself, which indicates her burgeoning sense of self-esteem and importance. She was encouraged by Johnson to publish her poetry, and one of her poems, "The Three Warnings," was included in *Miscellanies in Prose and Verse* (1766) by Anna Williams, Johnson's blind houseguest, with whom he lived when he was not at Streatham. The poem later became popular through republication in other volumes. When it appeared in *Poems by Several Hands* (1770), Hester acknowledged herself as its author for the first time in print. An amusing poem, it is written in octameter couplets and consists of exchanges between a farmer and Death, who comes for him.

As a dedicated wife, Hester Thrale helped her husband win a Parliament seat in 1772, the same year she helped revive his struggling business. Perhaps the greatest testimony to her fidelity, however, is her handling of the rumors which were swirling around him in the newspapers, accusing him of infidelity, rumors which appear to have been true. Supposedly Hester had the dubious honor of welcoming an illegitimate son of his at her own dinner table. In 1773 Hester's mother died, an event which Johnson commemorated by writing her epitaph. Shortly afterward one of Hester's children, Lucy, died; Hester appears to have been closer in temperament to Lucy than she was to her other daughters. The antagonistic relationship she had with her daughters has been noticed by critics, one of whom, Margaret Anne Doody, writes in her introduction to the second edition of *Hester Lynch Piozzi (Mrs. Thrale)* (1941) by James L. Clifford: "the real mystery about Hester lies not in her relation to Henry Thrale or to Samuel Johnson but in that to her children. Why were the daughters so cold – even harsh – to such a warm-hearted woman who was proud of them?" Clifford maintains that in emotions they resembled their father, who was never overly affectionate or effusive.

In 1774 and 1775 Hester and Henry Thrale traveled with Johnson and their eldest daughter, Queeney, to Wales and to Paris. In the former place Hester was disappointed when Johnson and her husband failed to respond as ardently as she had hoped. They made little effort to conceal their dissatisfaction from her. Johnson had not expected to enjoy Wales – much as he had not expected to enjoy his journey to the Hebrides with Boswell – but, in the latter instance, his experience belied his preconception, which unfortunately did not happen in Wales.

Hester's quarrel with Boswell began almost with their first meeting, both of them realizing that they would be rivals. Hester had another bitter quarrel: with Joseph Baretti, whom she employed to teach Queeney Italian. Hester and Baretti disagreed as to the proper method of raising the Thrale daughters: Hester was strict, while Baretti was indulgent. Baretti regarded her behavior toward her children as abject cruelty. A bachelor, he pardoned their misbehavior, excusing it with forbearance.

On 15 September 1776, again with encouragement from Johnson, Hester began writing *Thraliana* (published in 1942), its title suggested by her husband. *Thraliana* is difficult to describe: it is ostensibly a diary, but the entries fall into a bewildering range of categories, "family troubles, gossip, scandal, political events, amusing tales, and serious reflections," in the words of Charles Hughes (quoted by Clifford). The book is valuable not only for the picture which emerges of Hester as a lively and perspicacious observer but as a record of the age in which she lived. It is not without flaws, however, one of them being the disregard she showed for dates. So extreme is this problem that Clifford remarks, "In the early volumes there is no semblance of chronology." Undoubtedly this flaw resulted from the undisciplined nature of her mind. Clifford describes her mind as "erratic," a quality he ascribes to her education, which was often neglected or interrupted. The diary format suited her, in spite of this problem. Her talent lay in brief flourishes, for which the book is memorable. Her description of her first son's death is moving, for example; the passage is not easily forgotten.

Hester had met the noted musicologist Dr. Charles Burney sometime before 1776, but in December of that year she employed him as Queeney's music teacher. He became a familiar figure in the Streatham circle. Hester had also met his daughter Fanny, diarist and author of *Evelina* (1778), sometime earlier, but, owing to her father's employment with the Thrales, she, too, became familiar. Two other important meetings Hester had during this time were with Elizabeth Montagu, known as the "Queen of the Blue-Stockings" – a group of women with literary pretensions – and Gabriel Piozzi, the Italian singer, whom Hester would later marry.

Henry Thrale suffered a stroke on 8 June 1779, from which he never recovered. Characteristically for him his stroke occurred soon after he learned from his brother-in-law's will that his financial state was worse than he thought. He was thrown into a depression and could not stop overeating, which hastened his death on 4 April 1781. His death gave rise to rumors that Hester would marry Johnson, a testament not only to the exploitative instincts of the newspapers but to the genu-

Engraving of Streatham Park

ineness of the friends' feelings for one another. Clifford writes, "Many people have believed that Johnson was in love with Mrs. Thrale, and it must be admitted that there is much evidence to support such a belief. Yet if he was, Johnson himself would have refused to admit it, in fact would probably have not even allowed himself to consider such a notion." Clifford adds, however, that if Johnson was unwilling to marry her – or even to admit that he was in love with her – he was unwilling to accord the same rights to anyone else.

After Thrale's death, Hester – acting with Johnson who, for some time, had taken a lively interest in Thrale's business affairs – sold the brewery at Southwark. She also considered marrying Piozzi, an idea of which fashionable London society, Johnson, and her daughters disapproved. Piozzi was not only a foreigner, he was not of noble birth. He was dependent on a profession, and however genteel that profession might have been, it was not enough to overcome prejudices. Furthermore Hester was perceived as the aggressor; it was not as if she had succumbed to Piozzi's advances. She desisted, not wanting to offend her daughters, with whom her relationship was precarious. The struggle

she went through over Piozzi indicates one of the contradictions in her character: fiercely individualistic, she was nevertheless afraid of incurring public censure. It is also one of the aspects of her life which endears her the most to modern readers: having married once for practical considerations, she sought marriage for a second time to please herself. During this time a further strain on her was the fact that Johnson, whose health had been deteriorating, became difficult to live with. A sensible view of the situation, which Clifford puts forth, is that Johnson was having trouble adapting to the changes in the world around him. He wanted to go back to the early years of the Thrales' marriage when he could be a live-in guest at their home at Streatham and monopolize the attention of Hester. On the other hand, she wanted to go forward. She was only forty-one when Thrale died; Johnson was in his seventies.

Following the break with Piozzi, Hester became sick, or hypochondriacal. As a result, her daughters decided to "allow" the marriage, a precondition of which seems to have been her renunciation of them. The marriage took place on 23 July 1784. It was a marriage for which she was never forgiven by Johnson; according to some of his friends, including Boswell, it hastened Johnson's death on 13 December 1784. After her marriage she and her husband traveled to Italy, where she was involved with the publication of the *Florence Miscellany* (1785), a collection of poems by English travelers and native Italians, to which she contributed ten poems herself. The work is politically pro-Italian and draws upon Italian meter and rhyme schemes. Also in 1785 Hester and Boswell had an open conflict when the latter wrote in his *Journal of a Tour to the Hebrides* (1785) that neither she nor Johnson had been able to finish reading Elizabeth Montagu's *Essay on Shakespeare*. As a result of Boswell's disclosure Hester saw herself separated from a woman whose friendship she had cultivated and whose approval she had sought.

Johnson's death had led to a scramble on the part of publishers who sought to capitalize on the public's fascination with him. Anxious to use her position as Johnson's friend to establish her own literary reputation, Hester Piozzi wrote the *Anecdotes of the Late Samuel Johnson, LL.D., During the Last Twenty Years of His Life* hurriedly and without the benefit of her notes from England. Published on 25 March 1786, the *Anecdotes* preceded Sir John Hawkins's biography of Johnson by two years and Boswell's by four years. Clifford writes that she began the book "with a divided purpose: to justify her treatment of Johnson, and to achieve fame as one of his biographers." She had a vested interest in proving that he had been difficult to live with, and she wrote the book partially to vindicate herself.

The *Anecdotes of the Late Samuel Johnson* sold well; the first printing sold out in a day, and it ran to four others within six weeks of publication. Critical reaction, on the other hand, was mixed. Reviewers in the *Gentleman's Magazine* and the *English Review* praised the work; others, however, excoriated it for its negative portrayal of Johnson. The negative criticism seemed to take one particular form. Clifford writes, "Horace Walpole ... expressed the chief objection which many people felt to the publication. While protesting openly and constantly her veneration for Dr. Johnson, Mrs. Piozzi yet repeated anecdote after anecdote which did not redound to his credit." Her presentation method thus seems an outgrowth of the "divided purpose" of which Clifford spoke. Generally Piozzi either makes a statement about Johnson's character and uses an anecdote to illustrate it, or she provides an anecdote and draws a conclusion from it. The problem is that the anecdote and the general statement do not always bear each other out. For example, Piozzi relates an anecdote concerning Johnson's

love of Oxford, which he attended. She begins by describing his veneration for that university; then she describes his behavior to two of her friends who went to Cambridge: Johnson was less than cordial. The anecdote begins as if it is going to be about Johnson's love for his school, but it ends as an illustration of his irascibility.

Another factor which may have disconcerted original readers is the uncertain structure of the book. It begins as if it is going to be a conventional biography, with a description of Johnson's childhood. Piozzi soon lost interest in this approach, however, and the work merely becomes what the title has indicated it would be: a series of anecdotes. Boswell's biography, which is itself heavily anecdotal, follows some semblance of structure, or chronology, until the end. Piozzi's work was again marred by her lack of concern with following a coherent approach.

Others who disliked the book included Hannah More, a bluestocking, who objected to the portrayal of her friend David Garrick; and Dr. Charles Burney, who agreed with Walpole that the presentation of Johnson was one-sided. Boswell, of course, objected to it, although Piozzi's sins in regard to him seem to have been of omission rather than of commission. He must have been upset to find his name so visibly absent from a biography of his well-known friend, and he wrote the venomous portrait of Piozzi in his *Life of Samuel Johnson* at least partially in response. Possibly her disregard rankled him for another reason: it reminded him of the seeming casualness with which she had discarded Johnson. Perhaps this acrimony is why, in avenging himself upon Piozzi in his *Life of Samuel Johnson,* Boswell chose, as one approach, to ignore her: there are surprisingly few references to her in the work, leading to the perception that she was unimportant to Johnson – an impression which has survived in some quarters. Coupled with the generally denunciatory remarks Boswell makes about her, the impression left of Piozzi was generally negative, where she is discussed at all. Indeed, so vitriolic was Boswell's portrait – and so skillfully executed – that, as Virginia Woolf observed, it was nearly impossible to undo.

Boswell's attacks on Piozzi took one particular form: he continually refers to her as "inaccurate." The accusation was easy to make in that she had never been especially careful about dating her material; nor was she scrupulous about recording her conversations with Johnson at the time of their occurrence – unlike Boswell, whose journals reveal that he usually wrote them down immediately after-

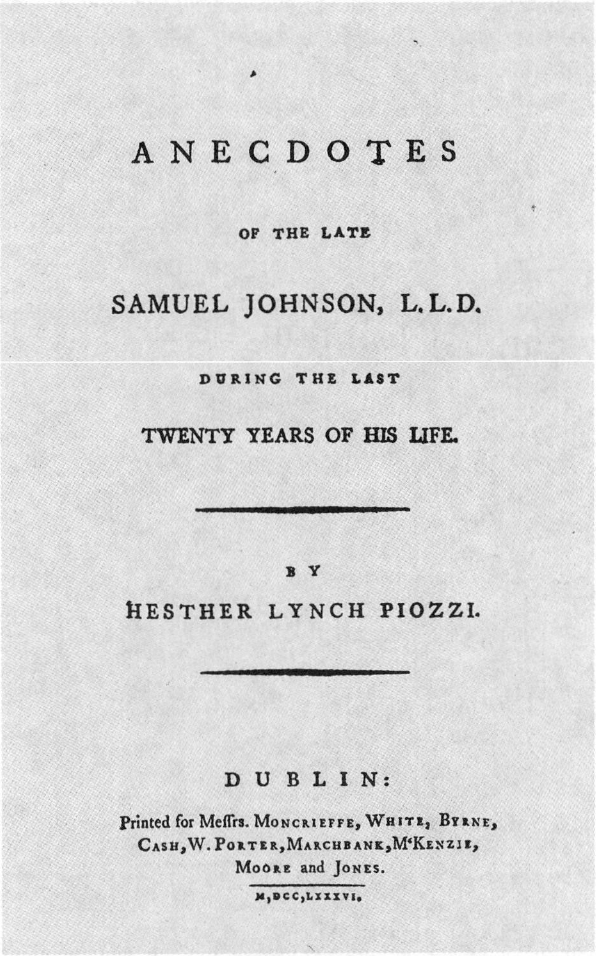

ANECDOTES

OF THE LATE

SAMUEL JOHNSON, L.L.D.

DURING THE LAST

TWENTY YEARS OF HIS LIFE.

BY

HESTHER LYNCH PIOZZI.

DUBLIN:

Printed for Meſſrs. Moncrieffe, White, Byrne,
Cash, W. Porter, Marchbank, M'Kenzie,
Moore and Jones.
M,DCC,LXXXVI.

*Title page for the Irish edition of Piozzi's book of recollections,
many of them unflattering, concerning Johnson*

ward. The charge was also one of which it was not easy to divest herself. According to Clifford, "Boswell reiterated [it] so often that to this day it is the adjective most often applied to her as a writer." After undertaking an extensive inquiry into the veracity of the anecdotes, Clifford writes, "Suffice it to say that Mrs. Piozzi was not essentially untruthful or inaccurate." He admits, however, that "in matters of age she was apt to be vague" and that she was handicapped by the alacrity with which she wrote the work, as well as by the fact that her notes pertaining to Johnson were not at hand.

Ironically, given Boswell's distaste, *Anecdotes of the Late Samuel Johnson* is not as far from his *Life of Samuel Johnson* as he seemed to think. Clifford claims that Piozzi "attempted the same type of biographical method as Boswell, and was greeted with similar criticism." Aside from the heavy reliance of both on the anecdote – a technique the use of which in biography dates back to Plutarch – Johnson is

shown with "shading": he is not presented as all good or all bad but rather as a mixture of both. The negative side of Johnson typically involves his propensity to be curt, especially with strangers. Boswell, however, admired Johnson's brusque manner; Piozzi found it tiresome, no doubt because she was more often its object – abundant examples of which are given in the *Anecdotes of the Late Samuel Johnson*.

A further similarity between the two works is their modernity. Clifford says, "the outcry occasioned by her portrayal of the rougher side of Johnson's nature is difficult for us to understand; the twentieth-century biography demands that the bitter be mingled with the sweet." Piozzi's account may also seem modern because of its feminism. William McCarthy, in *Hester Thrale Piozzi: Portrait of a Literary Woman* (1985), referring to an instance in the *Anecdotes of the Late Samuel Johnson* in which Piozzi stood up to Johnson, writes: "This explosion, and other asperities in the *Anecdotes,* erupt out of the fem-

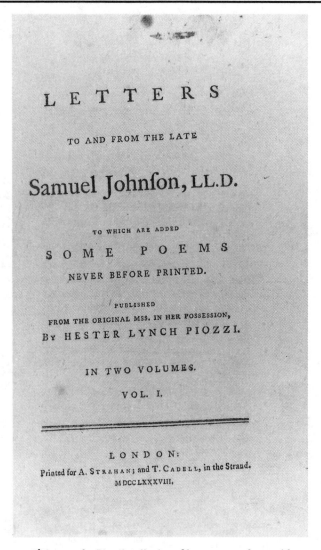

Title page for Piozzi's collection of her correspondence with Samuel Johnson. Some of her letters were rewritten for publication.

inist in Piozzi, who is here allowing herself to feel tired to death of what it has meant to her to be a woman. It has meant being an object of emotional importunity, being badgered, being always on call." The feminist strains in her writings are one of the aspects of her life which make her appealing to modern readers, along with the circumstances of her scandalous second marriage, which – in her rebellion against the norms of her time – indicates some of those same tendencies.

Anecdotes of the Late Samuel Johnson is important in spite of its flaws. As Clifford says, "the little volume has value for Johnsonian scholars. It has been our chief authority for many of Johnson's minor poems; it provides evidence of many facets in the great man's character altogether ignored by Bos-

well," including Johnson's fondness for the Thrale children. Clifford writes, "Johnson's love for young people was an element in his character which Boswell almost completely ignored." McCarthy, too, concurs on the importance of the work, saying that it "quickly became a canonical text about Johnson."

Upon her return to England in 1781 Piozzi began to prepare a volume of Johnson's letters, which she had originally intended to publish with *Anecdotes of the Late Samuel Johnson*. Evidence suggests that she rewrote some of her letters for the volume, which was published as *Letters to and from the Late Samuel Johnson* (1788). The book excited the ire of Boswell and Baretti – never her warmest admirers – among others. Both were irate at seeing their names mentioned in print in terms less than flattering. Living in London, Piozzi published a record of the tour she had made after her second marriage: *Observations and Reflections Made in the Course of a Journey through France, Italy, and Germany* (1789). Its reception was varied: some praised the work; others criticized the style for being colloquial. Piozzi believed that language in literature should not differ from that in everyday speech. In believing this she was acting in contradiction to the prevailing wisdom of the time, which held that it should be elevated. In this way she anticipated many of the principles William Wordsworth was later to expound in his preface to *Lyrical Ballads* (1800).

Piozzi's next publication was *British Synonymy; or, an Attempt at Regulating the Choice of Words in Familiar Conversation* (1794), a dictionary of English usage. Recognizing the difficulty which English posed for foreigners such as her husband, she sought to produce a work which would distinguish among nuances in meaning. For scholars the work has always been of interest for the references to Johnson, further proof that Piozzi was never afraid to return to memories of him. Frequently in illustrating the meaning of a word, Piozzi provides a Johnsonian anecdote. The technique is particularly appropriate, one could argue, in that Johnson himself was a distinguished lexicographer.

In 1795 she and her husband moved to Brynbella, a house they had built in Wales. Unlike her first husband, her second approved of her native land enough to make it his own. The transition may have been easier for him to make in that it resembled his native Lombardy. In any case he adapted to it with great elasticity and, as Clifford writes, in his final years became a "typical English squire." Having no male heir to whom she might leave her estate, in 1798 Piozzi adopted her husband's nephew, John Salusbury Piozzi. He had been named after her father to cultivate her favor. She succumbed to the flattery, although her nephew, like her daughters, did not endear himself to her. He did, in fact, rather resemble them in temperament, and as a result, he may have found her character difficult to understand.

Her next publication was *Retrospection: or a Review of the Most Striking and Important Events, Characters, Situations, and Their Consequences, which the Last Eighteen Hundred Years Have Presented to the View of Mankind* (1801). Never a success, it is regarded as dull even by her fans. Clifford notes that the work was difficult to write because of the paucity of historical works being written for a mass audience; there were few precedents on which she

could draw. It is also flawed by the lack of care which she took in citing sources.

One of the ways in which her second husband was a "typical English squire" was in suffering from gout. His anguish over it, described vividly in *Thraliana*, dominated Piozzi's life in the early 1800s. Just as she had done with Johnson many years earlier, she organized her life around caring for an invalid. Her second husband's death finally came on 30 March 1809. Afterward she divided her time among Brynbella, Bath, and London. Although she was regarded at Bath as a relic of a bygone era, her wit and vivacity were enough to win her new admirers, one of whom was Sir James Fellowes, with whom she became intimate in 1815.

Around this time she tried making a scholar out of John Salusbury Piozzi and failed, thereby showing her characteristic bad judgment. As Clifford writes, "There seemed to be an ironic fatality which thwarted all of Mrs. Piozzi's schemes for her children. She had no sense of fitness, no innate ability to judge the capabilities of those around her. She had attempted to make intellectual prodigies out of the daughters of a stolid Southwark businessman . . . now she tried to make an English scholar out of a lazy, indifferent, Italian *emigre*." She gave him Brynbella upon his marriage, however, and her generosity to him did not end there. In 1819 she purchased him a baronetcy, recognizing all the while that he cared for her money, not for her. His response was less than grateful: he fought to suppress her papers, fearing that they would be compromising to him. His goal was to preserve his social position which was now well established, owing to her influence. On 10 March 1821 Hester Piozzi fell while getting onto a couch, an accident which affected her physically if not mentally. She died on 2 May 1821 and was buried next to her second husband.

According to Clifford, "we shall probably never be able to discover the mainspring of her character . . . and it is just this human unaccountability which is her most engaging quality." He adds, "It is not as a biographer, or as a historian, or as a philologist that she will be remembered . . . it is as a diarist and correspondent." While hardly propitious for *Anecdotes of the Late Samuel Johnson*, this assessment is by no means a final verdict. The work will garner more attention as Piozzi emerges from Johnson's shadow — a process well under way — and as her biography of him emerges from the shadow of Boswell's.

Letters:

Autobiography, Letters, and Literary Remains of Mrs. Piozzi (Thrale), 2 volumes, edited by Abraham Hayward, second edition (London: Longman, Green, Longman & Roberts, 1861; Boston: Ticknor & Fields, 1861);

The Intimate Letters of Hester Piozzi and Penelope Pennington, 1788-1821, edited by Oswald G. Knapp (London: John Lane, 1914);

Letters of Mrs. Thrale, edited by R. Brimsley Johnson (London: John Lane, 1926; New York: L. MacVeagh, Dial, 1926);

The Queeney Letters, edited by Henry William Edmund Petty FitzMaurice, Marquis of Lansdowne (London: Cassell, 1934);

The Letters of Samuel Johnson, with Mrs. Thrale's Genuine Letters to Him, 3 volumes, edited by R. W. Chapman (Oxford: Clarendon Press, 1952);

The Piozzi Letters: Correspondence of Hester Lynch Piozzi, 1784-1821 (formerly Mrs. Thrale), 2 volumes, edited by Edward A. Bloom and Lillian D. Bloom (Newark: University of Delaware Press, 1989; London & Toronto: Associated University Presses, 1989).

Biography:

James L. Clifford, *Hester Lynch Piozzi (Mrs. Thrale),* second edition, revised (Oxford: Clarendon Press, 1968).

References:

Edward A. and Lillian D. Bloom and Joan Klingel, "Portrait of a Georgian Lady: The Letters of Hester Lynch (Thrale) Piozzi, 1784-1821," *Bulletin of the John Rylands Library,* 60 (Spring 1978): 303-338;

Morris R. Brownell, "Hester Lynch Piozzi's Marginalia," *Eighteenth-Century Life,* 3 (1977): 97-100;

Martine Watson Brownley, "Samuel Johnson and the Printing Career of Hester Lynch Piozzi," *Bulletin of the John Rylands Library,* 67 (Spring 1985): 623-640;

Brownley, "'Under the Dominion of *Some* Woman': The Friendship of Samuel Johnson and Hester Thrale," in *Mothering the Mind,* edited by Ruth Perry (New York & London: Holmes & Meier, 1984), pp. 64-79;

James L. Clifford, "Mrs. Piozzi's Letters," in *Essays on the Eighteenth Century Presented to David Nichol Smith,* edited by James Sutherland and F. P. Wilson (Oxford: Clarendon Press, 1945), pp. 155-167;

Mary Hyde, *The Impossible Friendship: Boswell and Mrs. Thrale* (Cambridge, Mass.: Harvard University Press, 1972);

William McCarthy, *Hester Thrale Piozzi: Portrait of a Literary Woman* (Chapel Hill & London: University of North Carolina Press, 1985);

John C. Riely, "Johnson's Last Years with Mrs. Thrale: Facts and Problems," *Bulletin of the John Rylands Library,* 57 (Autumn 1974): 196-212;

Patricia Meyer Spacks, "Scrapbook of a Self: Mrs. Piozzi's Late Journals," *Harvard Library Bulletin,* 18 (July 1970): 221-247.

Papers:

The John Rylands University Library of Manchester has a large collection of Piozzi manuscripts, including letters, journals, miscellaneous prose, poetry, and translations, and drafts of *Observations and Reflections.* A five-volume account of herself and her poetry that she composed from 1810 to 1814, along with "Minced Meat for Pyes," a collection of miscellaneous extracts and quotations (1796-1820), is in the Houghton Library, Harvard University. The Princeton University Library has Piozzi's letters to Penelope Pennington and Edward Mangin and the autobiography she composed in 1815 for Sir James Fellowes. The six volumes of *Thraliana* are at the Henry E. Huntington Library.

William Roberts

(1767 – 21 May 1849)

Thomas L. Blanton
Central Washington University

BOOKS: *Essay on Refinement* (Oxford, 1788);

The Looker-On: A Periodical Paper. By the Rev. Simon Olive-Branch, A.M. (London: Printed for J. Evans, 1794);

A Treatise on the Construction of the Statutes ... Relating to Voluntary and Fraudulent Conveyances and on the Nature and Force of Different Considerations to Support Deeds and Other Legal Instruments, in the Courts of Law and Equity (London: Printed by A. Strahan, for J. Butterworth, 1800; Philadelphia: William P. Farrand, 1807);

A Treatise on the Statute of Frauds, as it Regards Declarations in Trust, Contracts, Surrenders, Conveyances, and the Execution and Proof of Wills and Codicils (London: J. Butterworth, 1805; New York: Brisban & Brannan, 1807);

A Treatise Upon Wills and Codicils, With an Appendix of the Statutes, and a Copious Collection of Useful Precedents, With Notes, Practical and Explanatory (London: J. Butterworth, 1809); enlarged as *A Treatise on the Law of Wills and Codicils,* 2 volumes (Exeter, N.H.: G. Lamson, 1823);

The Portraiture of a Christian Gentleman. By a Barrister [anonymous] (London: J. A. Hessey, 1829); republished under Roberts's name (London: John Hatchard & Son, 1831; New York: T. & J. Swords, 1831);

Letters on Parliamentary and Ecclesiastical Reform (London: Saunders & Benning, and J. Hatchard & Son, 1831);

Memoirs of the Life and Correspondence of Mrs. Hannah More, 4 volumes (London: R. B. Seeley & W. Burnside, 1834; revised, 1834; revised again, 1835); 2 volumes (London: R. B. Seeley & W. Burnside, 1835; New York: Harper, 1835);

History of Letter-Writing, From the Earliest Period to the Fifth Century (London: W. Pickering, 1843).

William Roberts, a barrister by profession, wrote weighty legal treatises and was the editor of the *Looker-On,* an early-nineteenth-century London quarterly journal of evangelical sympathies. As a lit-

erary biographer he is remembered as the author of *Memoirs of the Life and Correspondence of Mrs. Hannah More* (1834), a work that has not fared well in the view of critics and historians of biography. Shortly after the publication of *Memoirs,* the influential critic and editor of the *Quarterly Review,* John Gibson Lockhart, wrote of the work that "had it been possible for any literator, with Mrs. Hannah More's correspondence at his hand, to produce an uninteresting work ... we are obliged to confess our belief that the task must have been accomplished by Mr. Roberts." Lockhart admits that "the regard with which Mrs. More honored ... him [Roberts] would of itself be a sufficient pledge of the purity of his intentions.... But the selection of him for this undertaking appears, on the whole, to have been about as unfortunate as any that could have been thought of." Critics have consistently echoed this view of More's first biographer and the work he produced. Richard D. Altick, a historian of literary biography, wrote in 1965 that More was, in Roberts's *Memoirs,* "the heroine of one of the worst biographies ever written." While not all critics and historians have been so tersely dismissive of Roberts, the failings of the work clearly attract more attention than whatever might be claimed for it – and perhaps for good reason, given the fate of More's reputation as a writer and historical figure over the past century and a half.

Today More may be the most misunderstood and neglected woman writer in English literature of the late eighteenth and early nineteenth centuries, a neglect which seems to have resulted from the persistent, negative portrayal of her during her middle years and later as a "bishop in petticoats," and the equally insistent characterization of her, following her death and especially today (albeit for different reasons), as a pious, evangelical writer to be remembered primarily for her religious tracts and didactic works of religious and moral improvement – a view Roberts's *Memoirs* has fostered. Roberts saw More as a paradigm (which she might very well

*Hannah More, a British evangelical novelist and reform writer, the
subject of William Roberts's best-known book (portrait by John
Opie; from M. G. James,* Hannah More, *1952)*

have been), a "glorious pattern of Christian worth."
Unfortunately his religious enthusiasm as a Tory
and Church of England member got the best of him.
Lockhart concludes his review by expressing his
"respect, nay, veneration for the memory of Mrs.
More, who perhaps did as much real good in her
generation as any woman that ever held the pen," a
respect and veneration which has made "us lenient
critics of his [Roberts's] part in the work." In the
same spirit Lockhart is willing to respect Roberts
"for his motives and intentions," yet regret for the
biographer's "narrowness of mind and feeling"
prompts Lockhart to hope that "the valuable letters in
these volumes may be printed by themselves." His is a
wish likely shared by readers today whose interest in
More has led them to Roberts's *Memoirs of the Life
and Correspondence of Mrs. Hannah More.* Two hundred
years after More established herself as a major letter
writer in a great age of letter writing, her collected letters have yet to be published. Roberts's *Memoirs,* on
the other hand, has been followed and superseded by
other More biographies, yet because of the letters his
work as a literary biographer has survived, ironically,
for each new generation of readers who have wished
to read of the life of More.

The Reverend Arthur Roberts, rector of Wood-
rising, Norfolk, and son of William Roberts, wrote
The Life, Letters, and Opinions of William Roberts, Esq.
(1850), a labor of love and the source of nearly all
that is known about his father. For Arthur Roberts
his father was nothing less than "a pattern and exemplar of a Christian gentleman." The biography is
a testimony to his father's influence as a writer of biography in that it is essentially the same kind of eulogistic memoir his father wrote about More, and in
its narrative, interspersed between letters and documents, it duplicates the form of his father's work.
Arthur Roberts is also to be remembered as the editor of *Letters of Hannah More to Zacharay Macaulay*
(1860) and for his edition of Martha More's journal,
*Mendip Annals: or A Narrative of the Charitable Labours
of Hannah and Martha More in Their Neighborhood*
(1859).

William Roberts was born at Newington Butts,
Surrey, in 1767 to parents of modest means who, in
time, sent him to both Eton and Saint Paul's
schools, an "inversion of the usual order," Arthur
Roberts notes, "but the petty tyranny of the fagging
system, then carried on at Eton to a great extent,
was so intolerable to his sensitive mind as to lead

his parents to remove him." At fifteen, because of his proficiency as a student of classical languages, he obtained a scholarship at Corpus Christi College, Oxford. Judged by the standards of the day, he had a brilliant career at Oxford. The president of Corpus Christi later remembered him as "the splendid ornament of his college." In 1788, after receiving his B.A., he won the English essay prize on the subject of refinement. In 1791 he received his M.A. and then toured the Continent, including Paris, where he witnessed the effects of the French Revolution. On his return he was employed for a while as a tutor and then founded and wrote articles for a periodical paper, as Arthur Roberts explains, "on the plan of the 'Spectator' which he gave the name 'The Looker-on.' " Writing under the pseudonym of the Reverend Simon Olive-Branch, he published eighty-six biweekly numbers before ending the venture in 1793. His entry into law ended his Oxford connection, since he could not qualify for a college fellowship unless he was ordained. His marriage in 1796 to Elizabeth Anne Sidebottom, daughter of a Middle Temple barrister, produced ten children. As a barrister Roberts, according to his son, was "never well reconciled to his profession," but he wrote legal treatises and served as a bankruptcy commissioner and as a member of government commissions, including an inquiry to examine the condition of prisons.

In 1811 Roberts met William Weyland, an evangelical minister, who was in the process of founding a periodical, the *British Review and London Critical Journal,* to counter the influence of the *Edinburgh Review* and the *Quarterly Review,* the leading journals of criticism and opinion at the time. Roberts assumed the editorship shortly after the first issue of March 1811 and remained in control until 1822, when the publication effectively came to an end, although it published its last number in 1825. During the period of his editorship Roberts wrote nearly all the leading articles and often most of the rest of the articles and reviews in a given number. Hannah More's comments about the *British Review* in 1815, after it resumed publication following a temporary suspension, expresses succinctly what Roberts believed to be the purpose of the review: " 'The British Review' is now revived, and I flatter myself will hold out a wholesome counteraction to the other two [the *Edinburgh* and the *Quarterly*]. It is not merely the review of religious works in which its utility consists, but that it reviews secular works in a Christian spirit." That spirit, however, led Roberts to an ongoing crusade against the works of Lord Byron, culminating in 1819 in Byron's outra-

geous claim in Canto I of *Don Juan* that he had bribed the editor of what he describes as "my grandmother's review – the British." Unfortunately Roberts took the bait and responded self-righteously, much to the amusement of Byron and other readers at the time. Roberts continued to edit and write, but he never recovered from the indignity and the humiliation of his exchange with Byron.

After leaving the *British Review,* Roberts continued his legal career, served for several years on a government commission investigating the abuses of charitable foundations, and became an honorary member, in 1823, of the Royal Society of Literature. In 1827 he engaged in a battle in print with the *Quarterly Review* as defender of the British and Foreign Bible Society, a dispute he later claimed as probable cause for Lockhart's negative review of his More memoirs. In 1829 he published *The Portraiture of a Christian Gentleman,* a lengthy "Theophrastan" character study joined, rather incongruously, to a devotional treatise. He dedicated the work to More, whose *The Spirit of Prayer* (1825) had suggested the subject for his book. In chapters under the title "The Force of High Example" he considers the character and the careers of eminent men during the reigns of George II and George III. His portrayals include John Wilkes, "Junius," the two Georges, Horace Walpole, William Pitt, and William Burke. His treatment is far less than systematic, and his "brief lives" are generalized portraits of vice and virtue, success or failure, measured against his ideal of the Christian gentleman.

The Scripture Garden Walk (1832), by Roberts's sisters but containing prose and verse by him, offered, as his son explains, a "botanical exposition, and natural history of every plant . . . in the Sacred Scriptures." In 1834 he published in four volumes his *Memoirs of the Life and Correspondence of Mrs. Hannah More.* In 1837 he wrote an essay which tied for the prize in a national competition for the best essay on "the character, qualifications and conduct requisite in the ministers of religion . . . throughout the land." A reviewer in the *Christian Observer* praised Roberts for his essay and commented on his long career as a writer:

Mr. Roberts has been a keen observer of men and manners for, at least, half a century; his professional works as a barrister earned him a reputation in his own profession; his lighter effusions of elegant literature, and his able and edifying moral, political, and miscellaneous papers in the "British Review," extended his celebrity to a wider circle, and, in later years, his "Portrait of a Christian Gentleman," his invaluable biography of Hannah

More, and now the essay before us have exhibited him still more prominently as an instructor of his countrymen upon subjects of the most serious import.

In his later years Roberts retired first to rural Surrey and then to Saint Albans in Hertfordshire, spending his life, as Arthur Roberts writes, "in quiet and retirement, chiefly dividing his time between his study, his garden, and the cottages of the poor." He continued to write verse, some light and some serious, as he had done throughout his life. He concerned himself with the plight of the Irish in the late 1840s. And he wrote a final book, the *History of Letter-Writing, From the Earliest Period to the Fifth Century* (1843), a pleasant, academic labor for a man who would have preferred to have been an Oxford don. Sadly for Roberts, the book was a money loser to the extent of two hundred pounds.

Hannah More died on 7 September 1833 in Clifton, now Bristol, not far from Stapleton, where she was born over eighty-eight years earlier. She had spent much of her life in the area, first in Bristol, then a short time in nearby Bath, then in rural Somerset at Cowslip Green, and finally near Wrington at Barley Wood, the house she and her four sisters built, where for more than twenty-five years a steady stream of visitors came for the friendship and counsel of this much admired woman. Two of her closest friends in her old age were Mary and Margaret Roberts, sisters of William Roberts, who are always referred to in More's correspondence collectively as the "Misses Roberts." Sometime before 1825 More made the Roberts sisters her executrixes, entrusting them with her letters and papers. In a letter to Sir W. W. Pepys in 1825 More explains that her sister Martha (known as "Patty") had, without her knowledge, "committed to them [the Misses Roberts] my posthumous reputation. I should be happy to think that nothing would be said of me when I was for ever out of hearing; but I believe it was the only way to stop less qualified persons. I will always remain entirely ignorant of all that has been done even by them."

No evidence suggests clearly when William Roberts became the designated biographer of More, but his letter to Mary Roberts of 26 August 1824, written when More was seriously ill and thought to be near death, may suggest that his role had been defined by then: "It appears as if she was born to edify mankind by her life, by her death, and by her memory. Whatever I may have to do with this last part of her, will be done with a care for her honour, and the influence of her sweet example, worthy of the greatness of the charge." *Memoirs* contains no correspondence between More and Roberts, and the few letters in Arthur Roberts's life, while they suggest mutual respect and regard, do not place Roberts along with his sisters in More's primary circle of friends and associates. That he depended on his sisters for the little intimate detail there is in the work is clear, just as it is evident that for him the letters of More and her correspondents detail a life he had earlier seen only in broad outline and from afar. Indeed his work is lacking for the same reason More, in 1804, found a biography she was reading "not impressively written": it "does not enter into those domestic details so interesting in the lives of good men." Roberts unconsciously calls attention to this deficiency in his work in recording, in *Memoirs,* an anecdote about Samuel Johnson in a conversation of 1824 between More and "a friend" (likely one of his sisters): "She [More] remembered that when Johnson was intending to write the Life of [Mark] Akenside, he asked her, as a friend of Sir James Stonehouse, his contemporary at Northhampton, if she could supply him with any information concerning him [Akenside]; upon which she made an effort to recollect some sayings she had reported of his, when he [Johnson] interrupted her with impatience – 'Incident, child! incident is what a biographer wants – did he break his leg?' "

The first edition of two thousand copies of *Memoirs* was sold in three weeks; the second edition, also two thousand copies, was sold within three months. These editions in four volumes were followed in 1835 by a third edition in the same format and a fourth edition with the same text reduced to two volumes. According to a note in Roberts's papers, four printings of the latter, each of two thousand copies, were published in 1835. A two-volume New York edition published in 1835 was reprinted eleven times by 1885. The original four-volume edition and its two-volume successor contained over five hundred letters, nearly three hundred of which were written by More, with the rest from her correspondents.

In his preface to the first edition of *Memoirs* Roberts makes it clear that the biography was authorized by More, who "could not but foresee that an account of her life, in this age of biography, must inevitably, with or without authority, come before the public after her death." Consequently "it was natural for her to be desirous that the care of her memory should be committed to those whose intimate knowledge of her opinions, principles, and connections, would secure her character from misrepresentation and mistake." It is noteworthy that he emphasizes protection rather than presentation.

Roberts refers also to the "mass of letters and papers" – entrusted to the surviving executrix (Margaret Roberts, although he does not name her) – which he was required to reduce "within the present compass," as well as to the need to avoid "offending the feelings or delicacy of any of those whose names occur in the course of the ensuing correspondence." Again the emphasis is on editing to protect individuals. He disclaims any pecuniary benefit from the publication by informing his readers that the proceeds from the sale of the copyright will go to "charitable purposes."

A lengthier preface to the second edition includes what appears to be a response to his portrayal of young Hannah as a woman lacking seriousness, particularly of a Christian sort. He explains (referring to himself in the third person) that "it never was his intention by means of selections and suppressions, to carve out of Mrs. More's correspondence and intercourse, a perfect model of Christian excellence. His purpose has been to make an honest exhibition of character – to bring before the world this distinguished woman as she really was when she mixed with it, when she sympathized with it, and when she overcame it." For him More's story is one of transformation, a story for those "who delight to dwell on every token of grace and providence, a case wherein by a mysterious agency a fellow mortal more than ordinarily endowed, has been carried through great temptations and trials to an exemplary eminence in the attainments of practical religion." When this view of More was challenged, along with his competence as editor and biographer, by Lockhart, Roberts answered the criticism in the preface to the third edition. He chose there, however, to ignore all but what he represents as Lockhart's attack on his religion and that of More. Few would share Arthur Roberts's view that his father's retort to Lockhart was "a specimen of literary castigation no less effective than well-merited."

Most of the more than nine hundred pages of the two-volume edition are devoted to the texts of the letters with interspersed notes and commentaries by Roberts, some no more than a sentence or a brief paragraph. His most developed biographical writing is at the beginning, in a sketch of More's childhood and her early years before going to London when she was just under thirty years of age, and at the end of the final volume, where he sums up her life and writing. His greater interest in her middle years and onward is reflected in the longer passages of introduction and commentary in the latter half of the work.

When Arthur Roberts refers to his father as a "judicious editor" of More's correspondence and as the author of "biographical sketches interspersed throughout the volume," he is praising both Roberts and *Memoirs*. Yet it is precisely Roberts's "judicious . . . sketches" which have irritated and frustrated critics and readers since Lockhart's review in 1834. For example, Mary Alden Hopkins, author of *Hannah More and Her Circle* (1947), writes that "Any life of Hannah More must be based on William Roberts's . . . book [*Memoirs*]." The work is valuable, she writes, for the hundreds of letters Roberts had access to through his sister Margaret, yet his portrayal of More suffers from a slanted presentation: "Being himself an intensely religious man, his interest centered on her work and personality in the latter part of her life, leading him to neglect her earlier, gayer years, and to present her later years in a somewhat dreary light. . . . Nevertheless one must draw lavishly from his rich storehouse of information and I acknowledge my indebtedness, even while I regret his preoccupation with only one side of her nature." Mary Gwladys Jones is less forgiving in her 1952 biography of More, where she writes of Roberts that "few persons could have been less well equipped to write Miss More's memoirs or edit her letters. He possessed neither literary grace nor constructive gifts. He was not always informed, and as comparison of some of the published letters with their originals shows, he corrected Miss More's letters and diary when in his judgement they required emendation." He even went so far, she concludes, to omit material to "safeguard her reputation, but which, instead, impugned Hannah More's most striking characteristic, her honesty."

Hopkins also takes Roberts to task for editing "with abandon, eliminating and altering sections of the letters, and even changing dates to achieve unity of subject and time." These defects did not escape the notice of Marianne Thornton (daughter of Henry Thornton, More's friend from the "Clapham Sect"), who became a young friend and correspondent during More's last years. In her "Recollections" (published in E. M. Forster's biography of her) Thornton wrote of Roberts's revision of More's prose: "She [More] calls Sir Thomas Acland in one of her notes to me 'the recreant knight of Devonshire' which Roberts thinking uncivil I suppose, has altered into 'the excellent and estimable Sir T. Acland' – two words that playful woman never used in her life. Somewhere else she began to me 'When I think of you I am gladerer and gladerer and gladerer,' which he, thinking bad English has done into 'I am very glad.' Now if such an oaf as that will write a book at least he should be honest." Whether or not he was an oaf, and even granting him, as Lockhart does, the best of intentions, Roberts as editor and interpreter tampered with texts and seriously oversimplified More's life to prove his thesis that she was a "glorious pattern of Christian worth."

As Hopkins, Jones, and other scholars have reported, hundreds of unpublished More letters – whole volumes of correspondence – exist outside the Roberts collection. The More story has yet to be told in full – and it may never be told. Yet even a reading of Roberts's flawed book conveys, often in spite of the "biographical sketches," a picture of a woman of deep convictions not only about religion but also about education (especially for the poor and for women), about slavery, about politics and economics, and about books and the life of the mind. She loved people and was generous to a fault with her time and her hospitality. She corresponded with an extraordinary variety of people, including the nonbeliever Horace Walpole for twenty years until his death – an embarrassing fact Roberts cannot cover up – as well as with such important evangelicals and reformers as William Wilberforce and John Newton. She corresponded with her bluestocking friends in London long after her "retirement" to Somerset. In fact she maintained her London contacts from her first lengthy stay there in 1773 and 1774 through the next thirty-five years in her annual visit to the city, where she stayed with her lifelong friend the widow of David Garrick, who himself had produced her *Percy* at Covent-Garden-Theatre-Royale on 10 December 1777. None of this varied, interesting, and perhaps contradictory life is adequately explored or explained in Roberts's "biographical sketches." For him, she spent her early years consciously and unconsciously preparing for the later and significant portion of her life. In his view:

> She had been brought up in two schools – the school of the world, and the school that calls us out of it. In the early part of her course, the world's vanities and flatteries had got the start of her better counsels and somewhat engrossed her for a time; but her principles remained sound, and concentrating themselves in the recesses of her bosom, waited there for the quickening influences of those truths which come with a mysterious vocation to the hearts of some, showing them to themselves as the heirs of corruption and the pupils of grace, – beset with numberless perils, and having one only way of escape. The learning of the latter school, long before age or infirmity had imposed their interdicts, had brought this eminent lady entirely under its discipline, and armed her for those frequent conflicts in which she became a

conqueror through Him who, by the trials and exercises of affliction, fulfills his purposes of preparation and reward.

Not only does this quotation illustrate Roberts's style but it reveals his habit of generalization without regard for "domestic detail" or "incident." The letters of More, however, in juxtaposition to Roberts's prose, offer details and incidents as well as the clear and energetic prose of a woman who wrote with her eye on the object. Occasionally Roberts does cite – especially in his summary of her life at the end of *Memoirs* – the particulars of character and action which suggest her many-sided life, yet he is unable to make anything of them and returns to his reductive thesis, as he does in describing two of her most important works on manners and morals, *Thoughts on the Importance of the Manners of the Great* (1788) and *An Estimate of the Religion of the Fashionable World* (1791):

> They were produced at a time in which, to decide between God and the flattering world by which she was surrounded must have caused her something of that agony of resolution which on less solid grounds those of her sex probably experience in passing from life and its endearments into the seclusion of the cloister; a separation certainly more violent and rending, and more threatening as a spectacle of self-conquest; but when it is considered how easily the mind that has surrendered itself to impulses is thrown from one extreme to another, and transported beyond its natural temperament, we shall see perhaps less real effort in the change and transition wrought under their influence, than in that quiet renunciation of habits, associations, and friendships, and that discriminative choice between what God and what the world approves, which are the results of an humble and teachable wisdom, bowing implicitly to the will of Heaven, as authentically communicated by the word of inspiration. It is indeed uphill labour, and a strong struggle against the stream, to turn the hopes, affections, and delights of the soul from their habitual tendencies, into a sober, spiritual, and self-denying course; but it is a labour and a struggle for eternal life.

One only wishes Roberts could have written more often as he did in this sentence: "She was a person to live with, to converse with, and to pray with." But since he did not, he stands judged by Lockhart as a writer who "writes with the facility of a practiced turner of periods, but with the confusion and verbosity of one whose brain has been less exercised than his hand." With reference to Roberts's "biographical sketches," Lockhart observed, "We are not aware that Mr. Roberts's connecting narrative has given us any one fact that is not stated in the text of the correspondence, either following or preceding the page where he has chosen to make it the subject of his circumlocutory prose."

If the attraction of literary biography, as Altick writes, "is essentially that of the psychological novel and the confessional lyric" and its aim is to reveal to the reader "the mystery of the artistic process," Roberts did not write literary biography. In his zeal to portray More as one who "mixed with the world" then "sympathized with it" only to overcome it, he reveals little or nothing about what led More to write plays for the London stage and later in life to write her didactic works for England's upper classes, or what made her "retire" to Cowslip Green and Barley Wood, where she devoted her energies to educating poor children in rural Somerset while teaching their parents and ordinary English people everywhere about the dangers of revolution, or what made her write against slavery or take up other humanitarian causes. In all these instances, and especially in treating serious periods as, for example, when her efforts as a founder of schools for the poor were bitterly challenged during the Blagdon Controversy (1800–1804) – a time when she suffered slander and abuse in print – Roberts gives scant notice to the details of the outer story and treats the inner story as if it were self-evidently a story of transformation. Furthermore, he does not appear to make use of source material apart from the letters – most notably Martha More's journal, *Mendip Annals* – for information about the More sisters' humanitarian work among the rural poor.

Rather than a literary biography, Roberts's *Memoirs* is a saint's life, "a case wherein by a mysterious agency" a gifted woman passed through temptation to triumph. Readers, he observes in the preface to the second edition, will find "that in the latter period of the life of Mrs. More, expressions, quotations, and allusions continued to escape from her pen, which bore the marks of her early associations." These facts, he reassures those who will be made uncomfortable by them, will be understood by recollecting "that religion, even its more advanced state, will often in outward circumstances, and habitual characteristics, reflect something of the thoughts and sentiments which had an antecedent existence in the mind in its early days of susceptibility and inexperience." He makes a claim for objectivity, intended for "those who know the true uses of biography" and who "will thank the Editor, if they thank him for nothing else, for his open and integral display of the correspondence and intercourse of the interesting subject of his memoir. If he errs in his judgment, he trusts he does not mistake

or mis-state his own principles, when he declares himself incapable of presenting Mrs. Hannah More to the world either better or worse than she has shewn herself to be by her letters, her life, and her labours." His claim for objectivity, however, should not be mistaken for evidence of impartiality.

His saint's life (or legend) of More, like others in the genre, seeks, as Altick writes, "to inspire mortals to emulate the saintly spirit and selfless deeds of other mortals whom the Church had canonized." In the typical saint's life a pattern for living rather than a strong portrayal of human individuality is required. In a saint's life, Altick continues, "no matter under what auspices it was written, ecclesiastical or secular, biography should be an instrument of inspiration and instruction." Such a work is not meant to entertain or delight with the particulars of personal life: "Haloes and homely details . . . [do] not go well together, nor . . . [do] crowns and crotchets."

In two ways, both conventional in biography, Roberts seeks to support with details his view of More's life, and in each instance he allows the words of his subject to make his point for him. First, as he suggests vaguely in the preface to the second edition, "Mrs. More . . . has shown by her secret self-abasing confessions, preserved in these volumes, in what light she regarded her own merits." Roberts alludes to extracts from More's diary found throughout *Memoirs,* especially in the latter half of the work. He attempts, with these diary entries, to get beyond the surface of daily living, as expressed in her letters, to her private, spiritual life. Yet instead of employing the diary to help reveal the private alongside the public dimensions of a complex life, Roberts allows the diary to be the essential, whole truth. In the other instance, Roberts records in uncharacteristic detail the "deathbed" dramas during three of More's serious illnesses in her later life, including her final illness and death. The deathbed scene was commonplace, even obligatory, in nineteenth-century biography and was frequently employed, as Altick observes, "as a means of religious and ethical inspiration." More had three "final illnesses," and Roberts's lengthy transcripts of her final words and oracles, so excessive in light of the absence of any comparable detailed treatment of her living moments and her speech in times of health, further emphasize his bias and become simply more tedious moralizing. Furthermore, in the intervening portions of the work, between deathbed scenes, when More has revived to go on to write books, continue her correspondence, receive guests, and even write light verse, there is no accounting, in Roberts's commentary, for the way this extraordinary woman continued to live her life with energy and commitment between her encounters with the beyond. Here and elsewhere the conflict between Roberts's sober monody and the vital polyphony of More's life, as it is revealed by her pen, leaves the reader with the task of fashioning a life of More in spite of the ponderous and tireless efforts of her "editor" to canonize her.

Arthur Roberts convincingly portrays his father as a good man, devoted to his family, devout in his religion, and ready to employ his pen in the cause of truth as he saw it. As a writer and editor he was public spirited and motivated by a genuine desire to aid in the moral and social betterment of people. Contemporary critics, including Lockhart, who called attention to Roberts's "circumlocutory prose," were obviously right. He should have deleted many lines. But he also had his defenders in his own day. Had it been a better book he might be remembered today for his *Portraiture of a Christian Gentleman,* which allowed him to follow his natural bent in developing a generalized portrait rather than narrating the life of an illustrious contemporary. Unfortunately for him, he is remembered today for Byron's joke and ironi-cally, given his regard for the subject, for his failure as Hannah More's first biographer.

Biography:

Arthur Roberts, *The Life, Letters, and Opinions of William Roberts, Esq.* (London: Seeleys, 1850).

References:

Richard D. Altick, *Lives and Letters: A History of Literary Biography in England and America* (New York: Knopf, 1965);

Anonymous [John Gibson Lockhart], "Memoirs of the Life and Correspondence of Mrs. Hannah More," *Quarterly Review,* 52 (August–November 1834): 416–441;

Mary Alden Hopkins, *Hannah More and Her Circle* (New York: Longmans, Green, 1947);

M. G. [Mary Gwladys] Jones, *Hannah More* (Cambridge: Cambridge University Press, 1952);

Elizabeth Kowaleski-Wallace, "Hannah and Her Sister: Women and Evangelicalism," in *Their Fathers' Daughters, Hannah More, Maria Edgeworth, and Patriarchal Complicity* (New York: Oxford University Press, 1991), pp. 56–93.

Robert Southey

(12 August 1774 – 21 March 1843)

Lisa Heiserman Perkins

See also the Southey entry in *DLB 93: British Romantic Poets, 1789–1832, First Series.*

BOOKS: *The Fall of Robespierre. An Historic Drama,* act 1 by Samuel Taylor Coleridge, acts 2 and 3 by Southey (Cambridge: Printed by Benjamin Flower for W. H. Lunn and J. & J. Merrill, sold by J. March, Norwich, 1794);

Poems: Containing The Retrospect, Odes, Elegies, Sonnets, etc., by Southey and Robert Lovell (Bath: Printed by R. Cruttwell, 1795);

Joan of Arc, an Epic Poem (1 volume, Bristol: Printed by Bulgin & Rosser for Joseph Cottle, Bristol, and Cadell & Davies and G. G. & J. Robinson, London, 1796; revised edition, 2 volumes, Bristol: Printed by N. Biggs for T. N. Longman and J. Cottle, 1798; Boston: Printed by Manning & Loring for J. Nancrede, 1798);

Letters Written During a Short Residence in Spain and Portugal. With some Account of Spanish and Portugueze Poetry (Bristol: Printed by Bulgin & Rosser for J. Cottle, 1797); third edition revised as *Letters Written during a Journey in Spain, and a Short Residence in Portugal,* 2 volumes (London: Printed for Longman, Hurst, Rees & Orme, 1808);

Poems, 2 volumes (Bristol: Printed by N. Biggs for Joseph Cottle and G. G. & J. Robinson, London, 1797, 1799; volume 1, Boston: Printed by Manning & Loring for Joseph Nancrede, 1799);

The Annual Anthology, 2 volumes, by Southey and others (Bristol: Printed for T. N. Longman & O. Rees, London, 1799, 1800);

Thalaba the Destroyer, 2 volumes (London: Printed for T. N. Longman & O. Rees by Biggs & Cottle, Bristol, 1801; Boston: Published by T. B. Wait & Charles Williams, 1812);

Madoc, 2 volumes (London: Longman, Hurst, Rees & Orme, 1805; Boston: Printed by Munroe & Francis, 1806);

Metrical Tales, and Other Poems (London: Longman, Hurst, Rees & Orme, 1805; Boston: C. Williams, 1811);

Letters from England: By Don Manuel Alvarez Espriella. Translated from the Spanish (3 volumes, London: Printed for Longman, Hurst, Rees & Orme, 1807; 1 volume, Boston: Printed by Munroe, Francis & Parker, 1808; New York: Ezra Sargent, 1808);

The Curse of Kehama (London: Printed for Longman, Hurst, Rees, Orme & Brown by J. Ballantyne, 1810; New York: Published by David Longworth, 1811);

History of Brazil, 3 volumes (London: Longman, Hurst, Rees, Orme & Brown, 1810, 1817, 1819; volume 1 revised, 1822);

Omniana, or Horae Otiosiores, 2 volumes (London: Longman, Hurst, Rees, Orme & Brown, 1812) – also includes contributions by Coleridge;

The Origin, Nature, and Object of the New System of Education (London: Printed for J. Murray, 1812);

The Life of Nelson, 2 volumes (London: Printed for John Murray, 1813; New York: Eastburn, Kirk / Boston: W. Wells, 1813);

Roderick, the Last of the Goths (London: Printed for Longman, Hurst, Rees, Orme & Brown by James Ballantyne, Edinburgh, 1814; Philadelphia: E. Earle / New York: Eastburn, Kirk, printed by W. Fry, 1815);

Odes to His Royal Highness The Prince Regent, His Imperial Majesty The Emperor of Russia, and His Majesty the King of Prussia (London: Longman, Hurst, Rees, Orme & Brown, 1814); republished as *Carmen Triumphale, for the Commencement of the Year 1814. Carmina Aulica. Written in 1814 on the Arrival of the Allied Sovereigns in England* (London: Printed for Longman, Hurst, Rees, Orme & Brown, 1821);

The Minor Poems of Robert Southey, 3 volumes (London: Printed for Longman, Hurst, Rees, Orme & Brown, 1815);

The Poet's Pilgrimage to Waterloo (London: Longman, Hurst, Rees, Orme & Brown, 1816; New York: W. B. Gilley and Van Winkle & Wiley, printed by T. & W. Mercein, 1816; Boston: Published by Wells & Lilly, 1816);

Robert Southey (portrait attributed to Edward Nash; from Jack Simmons,
Southey, *1945)*

The Lay of the Laureate. Carmen Nuptiale (London: Printed for Longman, Hurst, Rees, Orme & Brown, 1816);

Wat Tyler. A Dramatic Poem (London: Printed for Sherwood, Neely & Jones, 1817; Boston: J. P. Mendum, 1850);

A Letter to William Smith, Esq., M.P. (London: J. Murray, 1817);

The Life of Wesley; and the Rise of Progress of Methodism, 2 volumes (London: Printed for Longman, Hurst, Rees, Orme & Brown, 1820; New York: Published by Evert Duyckinck & George Long, printed by Clayton & Kingsland, 1820; New York: Wm. B. Gilley, 1820);

A Vision of Judgement (London: Longman, Hurst, Rees, Orme & Brown, 1821); republished in *The Two Visions; or, Byron v. Southey* (London: W. Dugdale, 1822; New York: W. Borradaile, 1823);

The Expedition of Orsua; and the Crimes of Aguirre (London: Longman, Hurst, Rees, Orme & Brown, 1821; Philadelphia: Hickman & Hazard, 1821);

History of the Peninsular War, 3 volumes (London: J. Murray, 1823, 1827, 1832);

The Book of the Church, 2 volumes (London: J. Murray, 1824; Boston: Wells & Lilly, 1825);

A Tale of Paraguay (London: Longman, Hurst, Rees, Orme, Brown & Green, 1825; Boston: S. G. Goodrich, 1827);

Vindiciæ Ecclesiæ Anglicanæ (London: J. Murray, 1826);

All for Love; and the Pilgrim to Compostella (London: J. Murray, 1829);

Sir Thomas More: or, Colloquies on the Progress and Prospects of Society, 2 volumes (London: J. Murray, 1829);

The Devil's Walk; A Poem. By Professor Porson [pseud.]. *Edited with a biographical memoir and notes by H. W. Montagu* [pseud.], by Southey and Coleridge (London: Marsh & Miller / Edinburgh: Constable, 1830);

Essays, Moral and Political, 2 volumes (London: J. Murray, 1832);

Lives of the British Admirals, with an Introductory View of the Naval History of England, 5 volumes, volume 5 by Robert Bell (London: Longman, Rees, Orme, Brown, Green & Longmans, 1833, 1834, 1837, 1840);

The Doctor, &c., 7 volumes, volumes 6 and 7 edited by J. W. Warter (London: Longman, Rees, Orme, Brown, Green & Longmans, 1834–1847; volumes 1–3 republished in 1 volume, New York: Harper, 1836);

The Poetical Works (10 volumes, London: Printed by Longman, Orme, Brown, Green & Longmans, 1837, 1838; 1 volume, New York: D. Appleton, 1839);

The Life of the Rev. Andrew Bell. . . . Comprising the History of the Rise and Progress of the System of Mutual Tuition, volume 1 (London: Murray / Edinburgh: Blackwood, 1844 [volumes 2 and 3 by Charles Cuthbert Southey]);

Oliver Newman: A New-England Tale (Unfinished): With Other Poetical Remains, edited by Herbert Hill (London: Longman, Brown, Green & Longmans, 1845);

Robin Hood: A Fragment. By the Late Robert Southey and Caroline Southey. With Other Fragments and Poems by R. S. & C. S. (Edinburgh & London: Blackwood, 1847);

Southey's Common-Place Book, edited by John Wood Warter, 4 series (London: Longman, Brown, Green & Longmans, 1849–1851);

English Seamen, edited by David Hannay (London: Methuen, 1895);

Journal of a Tour in the Netherlands in the Autumn of 1815, edited by W. Robertson Nicoll (Boston & New York: Houghton, Mifflin, 1902; London: Heinemann, 1903);

Journal of a Tour in Scotland in 1819, edited by C. H. Herford (London: Murray, 1929);

Journal of a Residence in Portugal 1800–1801 and a Visit to France in 1838, edited by Adolfo Cabral (Oxford: Clarendon Press, 1960);

The Contributions of Robert Southey to the Morning Post, edited by Kenneth Curry (University: University of Alabama Press, 1984).

OTHER: *On the French Revolution, by Mr. Necker,* 2 volumes, volume 2 translated by Southey (London: Printed for T. Cadell & T. Davies, Jun., 1797);

The Works of Thomas Chatterton, 3 volumes, edited by Southey and Joseph Cottle (London: T. N. Longman & O. Rees, 1803);

Vasco Lobeira, *Amadis of Gaul,* 4 volumes, translated by Southey (London: Printed by N. Biggs for T. N. Longman & O. Rees, 1803);

Francisco de Moraes, *Palmerin of England,* 4 volumes, translated by Southey (London: Printed for Longman, Hurst, Rees & Orme, 1807);

Specimens of the Later English Poets, 3 volumes, edited, with notes, by Southey and Grosvenor Bedford (London: Longman, Hurst, Rees & Orme, 1807);

The Remains of Henry Kirke White, of Nottingham, late of St. John's College, Cambridge; With an Account of His Life, 3 volumes, edited, with a biography, by Southey, volumes 1 and 2 (London: Printed by W. Wilson for Vernor, Hood & Sharp; Longman, Hurst, Rees & Orme; J. Dighton, T. Barret & J. Nicholson, Cambridge; W. Dunn & S. Tupman, Nottingham, 1807; Philadelphia: Printed & sold by J. & A. Y. Humphreys, 1811); volume 3 (London: Printed for Longman, Hurst, Rees, Orme & Brown, 1822; Boston: Wells & Lilly, 1822);

Chronicle of the Cid, translated by Southey (London: Longman, Hurst, Rees & Orme, 1808; Lowell, Mass.: Bixby, 1846);

The Byrth, Lyf, and Actes of King Arthur, 2 volumes, edited by Southey (London: Printed for Longman, Hurst, Rees, Orme & Brown by T. Davison, 1817);

John Bunyan, *The Pilgrim's Progress. With a Life of John Bunyan,* edited, with a biography, by Southey (London: John Murray and John Major, 1830; Boston: Crocker & Brewster / New York: Jonathan Leavitt, 1832);

Select Works of the British Poets, from Chaucer to Jonson, edited, with biographical sketches, by Southey (London: Longman, Rees, Orme, Brown & Green, 1831);

Attempts in Verse, by John Jones, an Old Servant; with Some Account of the Writer, Written by Himself: and an Introductory Essay on the Lives and Works of the Uneducated Poets, introduction by Southey (London: J. Murray, 1831); republished as *Lives of the Uneducated Poets, to Which Are Added Attempts in Verse by John Jones, an Old Servant* (London: H. G. Bohn, 1836);

Isaac Watts, *Horae Lyricae. Poems, Chiefly of the Lyric Kind, in Three Books,* edited, with a memoir, by Southey (London: J. Hatchard & Son, 1834);

Greta Hall, Keswick, where Southey lived from 1805 until his death in 1843

The Works of William Cowper, Esq., Comprising His Poems, Correspondence, and Translations. With a Life of the Author, 15 volumes, edited, with a biography, by Southey (London: Baldwin & Craddock, 1835–1837).

SELECTED PERIODICAL PUBLICATIONS –
UNCOLLECTED: Review of *Lyrical Ballads,* anonymous, *Critical Review,* second series 24 (October 1798): 197–204;

Review of *Gebir,* by Walter Savage Landor, *Critical Review,* second series 27 (September 1799): 29–39;

"Malthus's Essay on the Principles of Population," *Annual Review,* 2 (1804): 292–301;

"Ritsons Ancient English Romances," *Annual Review,* 2 (1804): 515–533;

"Thomas Clarkson's History of the Abolition of the African Slave Trade," *Annual Review,* 7 (1809): 127–148;

"The State of Public Affairs," by Southey and R. Grant, *Quarterly Review,* 22 (January 1820): 492–560;

"The Life of Cromwell," *Quarterly Review,* 25 (July 1821): 279–347;

"Superstition and Knowledge," by Southey and F. Cohen, *Quarterly Review,* 29 (July 1823): 440–475;

"Dr. [Frank] Sayers's Work," *Quarterly Review,* 35 (January 1827): 175–220;

"History of the Dominion of the Arabs and Moors in Spain," *Foreign Quarterly Review,* 1 (July 1827): 1–60;

"On the Corn-Laws," *Quarterly Review,* 51 (March 1834): 228–283.

Robert Southey, today the least known of the Romantic "Lake Poets," was originally the most prominent. He was also among the most prolific figures of his generation. Having written five major epics and hundreds of shorter poems – ballads, historical pieces, and lyrics on domestic pleasures – he was made poet laureate during the Tory administration in 1813. The position had lost much of its cachet but still indicated significant renown. Even George Gordon, Lord Byron, whose mockery of Southey's political apostasy is now better known than Southey's poetry, admired it immensely, as did Percy Bysshe Shelley, who, despite their political differences, respected him as "an advocate of liberty and equality. . . . a great Man." Indeed Southey's deep concern for the industrial poor helped to initiate the tradition of English progressive thought. He contributed well over one hundred articles to the conservative *Quarterly Review* between 1809 and 1839, and although he regarded journalism as "task-work" undertaken to support his large family, in time he became politically influential. He also developed a lucid, elegant prose style and wrote approximately forty-five books, which include extensive historical writing, as well as three full-length biographies: *The Life of Nelson* (1813); *The Life of Wesley* (1820); and the long biography of the eighteenth-century poet William Cowper, prefixed to Southey's edition of *The Works of William Cowper, Esq.* (1835–1837). As early as 1803 he had added a biographical essay to his edition of *The Works of Thomas Chatterton,* and he continued to write biography in one form or another throughout his career. For example, his four volumes of *Lives of the British Admirals, with an Introductory View of the Naval History of England* were published between 1833 and 1840.

The massive quantity of prose Southey produced resulted in part from his lifelong effort to cope with an excessive emotional excitability that he developed as a child. Southey included recollections of his childhood in a series of autobiographical letters which he wrote at age forty-six (collected in volume one of *The Life and Correspondence of Robert Southey,* 1849). He was born into a family of farmers and tradespeople in Bristol on 12 August 1774. His father, Robert Southey, was an unsuccessful linen draper; his mother, Margaret Hill Southey, the loving and gracious but uneducated daughter of a gentleman. Neither were important figures for him. From age two until age thirteen he lived mostly with his mother's half sister, Elizabeth Tyler of Bath, an imperious, socially pretentious, and neurotic beauty who utterly intimidated Southey's mother. She was tempestuous, an emotional recluse, and a compulsive eccentric who was at once overprotective and neglectful. Southey was lonely, troubled by nightmares, and preoccupied with death (five of his siblings died in childhood). Although life with Tyler was in many ways damaging, she also took him to the theater and stimulated his love of books.

He went to the Westminster School from 1788 until 1792, when he was expelled for attacking flogging in an essay published by the school paper. Immediate experiences of injustice, both at home and school, developed into a lifelong, passionate hatred of tyranny. They also perhaps increased the ambitions that he shared with other young men inclined to literature in that era of revolutionary zeal: grandiose visions of personal heroism to be realized via stupendous careers either in the military or as poets. At the age of nine, having read William Shakespeare's history plays and concluding that England was again on the brink of civil war, Southey dreamed of playing the part of a war hero. Later, attempting to realize his ambitions as the poet who would complete the Edmund Spenser's *The Faerie Queene* (1590, 1596), he actually produced three cantos. Throughout his life he retained a Spenserian interest in fashioning the ideal gentleman and worked to create, both in himself and in his biographical subjects, men of surpassing virtue.

In 1793 Southey attended Balliol College, Oxford, for two terms, where his self-fashioning was extraordinarily self-conscious and deliberate. In 1806 he wrote: "Twelve years ago [while at Oxford] I carried [the Stoic philosopher] Epictetus in my pocket till my very heart was ingrained with it.... And the longer I live, and the more I learn, the more I am convinced that Stoicism, properly understood, is the best and noblest of systems." Self-regulation was the Stoic principle by which Southey lived most relentlessly. He studied for the clergy at the suggestion of his uncle, the Reverend Herbert Hill, who was both friend and father to Southey after the death of Robert Southey, Sr., in 1792. But the modern science, history, and literature he had absorbed before being expelled from the Westminster School, together with his perception of inequities within the church, made this choice uncongenial. Instead he planned to travel – first to America and then, as a writer, into the lives of the dead.

When Samuel Taylor Coleridge visited Oxford in 1794, he and Southey formed a scheme to immigrate to the wilds of Pennsylvania and build a simple yet cultured egalitarian society, a pantisocracy. As biographer Edward Dowden explains, "Each young man should take to himself a mild and lovely woman for his wife; it would be her part to prepare their innocent food, and tend their hardy and beautiful race." In anticipation of this venture, each planned to marry one of the Fricker sisters; Southey would marry Edith, for whom he had already developed an attachment; and Coleridge, Sarah. At the prospect of their happiness, Dowden says, "all the faculties of his [Southey's] mind dilated." For financial reasons, however, their dream never materialized; instead they lived in Bristol, lecturing and writing propagandist pieces for the radical cause.

Southey's sympathy with the French Revolution at this time inspired him to produce the work that initiated his rise to fame. His first success, *Joan of Arc, An Epic Poem* (1796), featured a historical emblem of revolutionary ardor. During the summer of 1793, while still at Oxford and while his "young brain" was "a-seethe with revolution and romanticism," Southey had written the first draft in a mere six weeks; two years later he spent six months revising it. This first epic, promoting democracy and pacifism, was designed to outrage complacent readers: in the story Henry V is consigned to hell. Joseph Cottle, who had published William Wordsworth's *Lyrical Ballads* (1798), published *Joan of Arc* in a handsome edition. Southey had also written overtly political shorter lyrics which, in simple, dignified meters adapted from the classics, featured a shocking assortment of antiheroes: convicts, beggars, and squalling babies. Despite the scoffing reactions that he succeeded in provoking in the press, *Joan of Arc* won him a considerable reputation.

His fame was then firmly established by the popularity of the four epics that followed. Pursuing the prodigious ambition to devote an epic poem to each major religion, he wrote *Thabala the Destroyer* (1801), *Madoc* (1805), *The Curse of Kehama* (1810), and *Roderick, the Last of the Goths* (1814). Coleridge admired the "pastoral charms and streaming lights" of *Thabala the Destroyer;* Sir Walter Scott read *Madoc* three times with increasing enjoyment; Byron thought that *Roderick, the Last of the Goths* was "as near perfection as poetry can be." Yet these long poems have fallen out of the canon. Southey's poetry in general is now rarely enjoyed and almost never taught. It is often said to lack magic and music. Wordsworth accounts for its blandness: "He never inquires on what idea his poem is to be wrought, what feeling or passion is to be excited; but he determines on a subject, and then reads a great deal and combines and connects industriously, but he does not give anything which impresses the mind strongly and is recollected in solitude." Southey was, in fact, a man of such strong passions that he feared and curbed them; composing verse excited him to a distressing degree, and he turned for relief to prose. His biographies are still read today because his prose is at times charged with the deep love of virtue that is Southey's most distinctive characteristic.

E. R. H. Harvey has discerned beneath the "inventive fancy" of all of Southey's epics "the author's admiration for everything that is elevated in human nature." The focus on individual figures in Southey's early work shows that from the beginning he was inclined toward the kind of intellectual venturing that would lead him to the genre in which it is now felt he did his best work: biography. Southey's task as historian and epic poet was to record the manners, habits, and religions of foreign cultures; as biographer, as chronicler and custodian of British culture, he extended his historical research into his own. His vocation, once he discovered what it would be, entailed the maintenance of British heroes.

While discovering his vocation, Southey spent eight years casting about. The day after he secretly married Edith Fricker, 14 November 1795, he sailed for Lisbon with Hill, under contract with Cottle to write a volume on his travels. *Letters Written During a Short Residence in Spain and Portugal* (1797) – a medley of anecdote, description, social comment, translation, original verse, historical information, and curious learning – sold well and went through three printings. Southey was dismayed by the squalor he witnessed, inspired by the nationalistic pride among the peasants, and attracted to the chivalric literature of Spain. He translated Vasco Lobeira's *Amadis of Gaul* (1803), Francisco de Moraes's *Palmerin of England* (1807), and *Chronicle of the Cid* (1808). Since boyhood he had been roused by tales of chivalry and fascinated by the power of castles and cathedrals. *Joan of Arc* had been full of stained glass and burning lamps, full of the spirit of chivalry that Edmund Burke associated with conservative sensibility, which Southey later embraced.

With this first trip Southey began his restless wanderings in Portugal, Bristol, London, and Dublin (among other places). When he returned as a twenty-two-year-old married man without means, he entered his name at Gray's Inn and began, without enthusiasm, to study law. His energy was instead spent composing the meditative works for which he is best known as a poet, an activity which brought on a nervous fever. He went back to Portugal, this time with Edith, to recover; there he finished his second epic, *Thabala the Destroyer,* and began research for a "History of Portugal," a project he never completed. Home again in London, he served briefly as secretary to the Irish chancellor of the exchequer before joining Coleridge at Greta Hall, a move precipitated by the death of his one-year-old daughter, Margaret, in 1803. He remained there for forty years.

Between his arrival at Greta Hall and 1813, the year he was made poet laureate and published *The Life of Nelson,* Southey's reputation as a man of letters rose steadily. In 1807 he published *Letters from England: By Don Manuel Alvarez Espriella,* a combination of travelogue, satire, and familiar essays by a fictitious Spanish traveler, designed, as Southey says, to set forth in an amusing way "all I know and much of what I think respecting this country and these times." The book gives an excellent account of life in early-nineteenth-century England. Research and documentation were popular during the

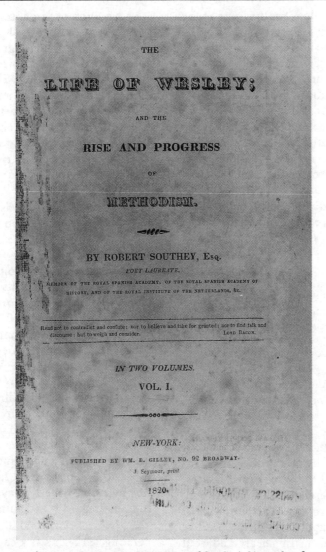

THE

LIFE OF WESLEY;

AND THE

RISE AND PROGRESS

OF

METHODISM.

~~~~

BY ROBERT SOUTHEY, Esq.

POET LAUREATE,

MEMBER OF THE ROYAL SPANISH ACADEMY, OF THE ROYAL SPANISH ACADEMY OF
HISTORY, AND OF THE ROYAL INSTITUTE OF THE NETHERLANDS, &c.

Read not to contradict and confute; nor to believe and take for granted; nor to find talk and
discourse : but to weigh and consider.   LORD BACON.

IN TWO VOLUMES.

VOL. I.

NEW-YORK:

PUBLISHED BY WM. B. GILLEY, NO. 92 BROADWAY.

J. Seymour, print

1820.

Title page for the American edition of Southey's biography of
John Wesley, the eighteenth-century Methodist leader.
The book is more a history of Methodism than
strictly a biography.

Romantic period, and Southey was on his way to becoming the leading English authority on Portuguese and Spanish history. His massive *History of Brazil* (1810, 1817, 1819), begun in 1807 and published in three volumes, the first ever written, is still a good resource and has recently been translated into Portuguese. Like his *History of the Peninsular War* (1823, 1827, 1832), it suffers from Southey's tendency toward excessive inclusiveness but is thought to be a remarkable feat of research. In 1807 he published his first successful biographical piece, *The Remains of Henry Kirke White,* about a butcher's boy and protégé of Southey's whose poems, collected in *Clifton Grove* (1803), had been harshly reviewed and who, like Thomas Chatterton, had died young.

Southey's biography of White ran through ten printings.

Before he arrived at Greta Hall, Southey's political sympathies had shifted. He had reacted not only against the Reign of Terror and what he saw as the ambition of Napoleon to rule Europe under a military dictatorship, but also against the depredations of industrialization at home. These were rapidly squelching the chivalric virtue of disinterestedness. Southey's apostasy has been more notorious than that of Wordsworth and Coleridge, in part because *Wat Tyler. A Dramatic Poem* (1817), which he had dashed off while a young man, was pirated by his political enemies. Seeking to humiliate the laureate by exposing evidence of his early radicalism, they published it in 1817, when Southey was at the height of his fame. The play eulogizes a leader of the Peasant Revolt in 1381 who had come to signify the spirit of reform. (Ironically, Southey claimed to be an heir of Tyler via his elitist aunt Elizabeth Tyler.) Like Joan of Arc, Wat Tyler exhibited in his chivalric martyrdom virtues similar to those that inspired Southey to chronicle other lives: the independence and courage that make a hero. Southey's *A Letter to William Smith, Esq. M.P.* (1817) is his rebuttal to his detractors in the *Wat Tyler* affair and a cogent statement of his detestation of tyranny in any form.

Byron's relentless ridicule, however, ensured that Southey would survive as a stock figure of the despicable turncoat. Byron's well-known dedication to *Don Juan* (1818) begins:

> Bob Southey! You're a poet – Poet-laureate,
>   And representative of all the race;
> Although 'tis true that you turned out a Tory at
>   Last, yours has lately been a common case;
> And now, my Epic Renegade! what are ye at?
>   With all the Lakers in and out of place?

Yet Southey never became the rigid Tory that Byron made him out to be. Although essentially conservative, his political sympathies were always oddly mixed: for example, he favored the liberal James Charles Fox over the conservative William Pitt. By the time Southey moved to the Lake District in 1803, he supported the war against France; by 1805 his hatred of the French was in full bloom. In 1808 he wrote, "I believe that this country must continue the war while Napoleon is at the head of France.... I, therefore, from my heart and soul execrate and abominate the peace-mongers. I am an enemy to any further concessions to the Catholics; I am a friend of the Church Establishment. I wish for reform, because I cannot but see that all things are tending towards revolution, and nothing but reform can by any possibility prevent it."

During his conservative years, as a regular and vital contributor to the *Quarterly Review,* Southey protested energetically against the dehumanizing commercial spirit regretted by all parties. The spectacle of brutality toward the workers – especially children – in the modern factories horrified Southey, who predicted an equally brutal workers' revolution. Indeed, in 1810 revolution seemed to be in the offing. The memory of his own radicalism made Southey take the threat of immediate danger more seriously than some of his conservative friends did, and he undertook a campaign of reform that would contain or remove the pressures leading to a revolution. He initiated what was to become a long tradition of promoting literature as a humanizing antidote to the moral poisons of the new laissez-faire economy. His biographies were part of an effort to keep moral culture and material culture in pace with one another. He celebrated the lives of men that, in one way or another, might have a disciplinary effect on increasing moral bankruptcy by exemplifying the ideal chivalric virtues. The Southeyan hero was presented to inspire the courage, energy, dutifulness, patriotism, sincerity, and selflessness desperately needed by a self-interested society.

The Life of Nelson was a tremendous success, in part because Southey so passionately revered his hero. After the Battle of Trafalgar, in a letter to Grosvenor Bedford he wrote, "What a death is Nelson's! ... It seems to me one of the characteristics of the sublime that its whole force is never perceived at once. The more it is contemplated, the deeper its effect." In 1810 William Gifford, editor of the *Quarterly Review,* commissioned Southey to review the four biographies of Horatio Nelson that had already appeared. When Southey, who regarded them all as "slovenly performances," produced a forty-page distillation of the hero's career, the publisher John Murray commissioned a full-length biography. *The Life of Nelson* has remained immensely popular (a new edition appearing as recently as 1990) and is more widely read than the more accurate, technical history of Nelson's sea battles by Adm. Albert Thayer Mahan that succeeded it. Some regard it as Southey's masterpiece.

Ignorant of naval life, Southey said he walked "among sea terms as a cat does in a china pantry." Although he regarded his job as being merely to arrange coherently materials "in themselves, so full of character, so picturesque, and so sublime," Southey's admiration for Nelson and his own patriotic zeal suffuse his prose with warm emotion. In response to Murray's request, referring to the biographies he hoped to supersede, he wrote, "there is nothing like a clear lucid narrative in any of them. I could make a good book and a useful one, and it would give me an opportunity of saying some things which I think are worth saying, and want a place for." Southey "usefully" created the quintessential naval hero, British to the core, who might compete in stature with Napoleon and become an enduring object of emulation for British seamen of every rank. Printed on fine paper for officers and on coarse paper for all others, *The Life of Nelson* was distributed throughout the naval world.

Thus every cabin boy would read the series of anecdotes from Nelson's boyhood that manifest fantastic fearlessness and honor. These flash by like snapshots. The critical consensus is that no biography of Nelson has succeeded so well in offering a portrait of his character. Throughout the book one can see that character under construction. Readers see Nelson himself determining to play a role; his "character" is less that of an individual than of a model hero. Southey explains that his methodology was merely "to account for the actions of men by their own principles and represent them as the persons represent them to themselves." Nelson the hero was designed first by Nelson himself and then by Southey to stand as a sort of allegorical figure of patriotism. Southey could both treat his documents scrupulously and produce a sublime portrait.

Passages such as the following, in which one can see Nelson and Southey working hand in hand to create "the great little warrior," appear like a refrain. During a risky attempt to blockade the French from trading with Genoa, Nelson manifests another essential ingredient of heroism – the delicate balance between independence and a desire to win personal glory via dutiful service:

> "I am acting," said Nelson, "not only without the orders of my commander-in-chief, but, in some measure, contrary to him. However, I have . . . a consciousness that I am doing what is right and proper for the service of our king and country. Political courage, in an officer abroad, is as highly necessary as military courage."
>
> This quality, which is as much rarer than military courage as it is more valuable, and without which the soldier's bravery is often of little avail, Nelson possessed in an eminent degree. . . . Admiral Hotham commended him for what he had done; and the attention of government was awakened. . . . "What changes in my life of activity!" said this indefatigable man. . . . "I do not write less than from ten to twenty letters every day; which, with my . . . own little squadron, fully employ my time. This I like; – active service, or none." It was Nelson's mind which supported his body through these exertions. He was at this time almost blind, and wrote with very great pain.

As in the following excerpts, however, there are more realistic glimpses of Nelson's experiences that prevent the portrait from becoming too ideal and present him as a charming, as well as an awesome, figure. Having lost the American colonies, in the hope of building a yet more splendid empire (a hope Southey most ardently shared), the British fought the Spanish in Nicaragua and Honduras:

> On the 9th of April they [Nelson and his men] reached an island in the river . . . which the Spaniards had fortified, as an outpost, with a small, semi-circular battery. . . . It commanded the river in a rapid and difficult part of the

navigation. Nelson, at the head of a few of his seamen, leaped upon the beach. The ground upon which he sprung was so muddy, that he had some difficulty in extricating himself, and lost his shoes: bare-footed, however, he advanced, and, in his own phrase, *boarded the battery*.

In the following passage readers again see a merely life-size, though delightful, man:

> Nelson took up his abode at the [his father's] parsonage, and amused himself with the sports and occupations of the country. Sometimes he busied himself with farming the glebe; sometimes he spent the greater part of the day in the garden, where he would dig as if for the mere pleasure of wearying himself. Sometimes he went a birdsnesting, like a boy: and in these expeditions Mrs. Nelson always, by his express desire, accompanied him. Coursing was his favorite amusement. Shooting, as he practiced it, was far too dangerous for his companions: for he carried his gun upon the full cock, as if he were going to board an enemy; and the moment a bird rose, he let fly, without ever putting the fowling-piece to his shoulder. It is not, therefore, extraordinary, that his having once shot a partridge should be remembered by his family among the remarkable events of his life.

It took Southey over three years to write the biography; he thought it would take him only one. The delay can be partly explained by this confession to his brother: "I am such a sad lubber that I feel half ashamed of myself for being persuaded ever even to review the *Life of Nelson,* much more to write one." Nelson's violent loathing for the French, which Southey increasingly shared, may have inspired him to take on a writing project that was in other ways uncongenial.

Southey's strong feelings make for rousing prose, but, despite his ambition to write the "clear lucid narrative" that the previous biographers had failed to supply, his book is at times confusing. As he documents Nelson's rise to world fame, Southey gives most of the space to reports of military action and, for the major battles, includes the size and name of every ship in the squadron, usually those on both sides, as well as the names of the important officers, often with a few words on their characters. Southey himself complained that it was difficult for him to envision the battles; especially if the reader is also a "lubber," Southey's attempts to present coherent battle scenes are only partially, occasionally successful.

Long descriptions of the rapid maneuvers, noise, and smoke of battle are broken up, however, by passages from Nelson's dispatches and letters home. These express again and again his willingness to die for his country and his hope that he will

Page from the manuscript for Southey's biography of William Cowper, published in volume one of Southey's edition of Cowper's works (1835–1837; MA 412 Pierpont Morgan Library) be remembered. There are also brief scenes between Nelson and his fellow officers, which are almost invariably opportunities for Southey to relate not Nelson's brilliant war tactics but behavior that reveals his noble, selfless character.

Nelson's patriotism was an obsession that drove him to defeat the detested French with honor, glory, and fame for himself on behalf of his nation. Yet there are two blots on Nelson's character that Southey makes no attempt either to conceal or excuse: his affair with Lady Hamilton and his unjust trial and merciless execution of Prince Caracciolo, a distinguished, elderly Neapolitan nobleman believed to be a rebel. Southey had doubts about the prince's guilt, and, a bit like Nelson himself, in what must have been a strenuous moment, Southey performs his duty. He reports the facts. However, he refrains from analysis or speculation.

Southey not only admired but shared Nelson's devotion to duty. Patriotism was also the salient feature of the other war heroes Southey celebrated. In his "Life of Wellington" (1815) and "Life of Marlborough" (1820), review essays for the *Quarterly Review,* he presented men who would inspire loyalty to Britain's religious and political institutions. He strove to develop the traits commonly found in the subjects of his biographies during his forty years at Greta Hall, where he enjoyed a regular, simple life surrounded by children – seven of his own and three of Coleridge's – and though he loved them deeply and took the time to teach them, he was usually in his library, which eventually contained fourteen thousand books. His life was interrupted by occasional trips to the Continent and to other parts of England and by visits from a large acquaintanceship, including Scott, Walter Savage Landor, and Wordsworth, Southey's neighbor. Southey's relationship with his singularly irregular brother-in-law, Coleridge, was strenuous, despite their genuine, if intermittent, mutual affection and respect. Coleridge proved to be an unhappy husband and a negligent father. Southey failed to persuade him to join his family on several occasions; Coleridge left permanently in 1809. Uncomplainingly Southey supported his sisters-in-law Sarah and the widowed Mary (Mrs. Robert Lovell), as well as nieces and nephews. As Wordsworth put it, he had "a little world dependent on his industry." Poetry would not generate enough income. Even at the end of Southey's career, the last of his major biographical writings, *Lives of the British Admirals,* was, as he put it, undertaken "for lucre, not love." Southey's regular, industrious habits yielded prose that did more than simply sustain his family; as Wordsworth says,

"His style is eminently clear, lively and unencumbered, and his information unbounded; there is a moral ardour about his compositions which nobly distinguishes them. . . . "

"Moral ardour," Southey's most distinctive characteristic, also enlivens his polemical religious, political, and socioeconomic opinions in *The Book of the Church* (1824), *Vindiciæ Ecclesiæ Anglicanæ* (1826), and *Sir Thomas More: or, Colloquies on the Progress and Prospects of Society* (1829). However, his moral ardor was in fact so strong that it also often irritated those around him. Coleridge, for one, complained that Southey had "too high a state of health" in moral matters; Thomas Carlyle, more sympathetically, saw that Southey had developed his "methodic virtue" in a futile attempt to conceal and suppress what Southey referred to as his "mimosa sensibility." He coped with the distressing "continuous excitement" produced by deep engagement with his writing by working on several projects simultaneously. Between journalism, histories, and the preoccupation of the *Wat Tyler* affair, he began *The Life of Wesley* in 1817. Like *The Life of Nelson,* it took three years to finish.

Southey's prefatory remarks indicate that, since the publication of *The Life of Nelson,* his hatred of revolutionary France had, if possible, intensified. He introduces the man whose massive influence as the founder of Methodism helped to avert a proletariat revolution in England by comparing John Wesley to Voltaire:

> While the one was scattering, with pestilent activity, the seeds of immorality and unbelief, the other, with equally unwearied zeal, laboured in the cause of religious enthusiasm. . . . The principles of the arch-infidel were more rapid in their operation: . . . in his latter days he trembled at the consequences which he then foresaw; and indeed, his remains had scarcely mouldered in the grave before those consequences brought down the whole fabric of government in France, overturned her altars, subverted her throne, carried guilt, devastation and misery into every part of his own country, and shook the rest of Europe like an earthquake. [John] Wesley's doctrines, meanwhile, were slowly and gradually winning their way; . . . and their effect must ultimately be more extensive, more powerful, and more permanent, for he has set mightier principles at work.

Although Southey admits that "the one was not all darkness, neither was the other all light," the Burkean eloquence with which he contrasts Voltaire and Wesley indicates that Southey venerated the religious leader largely for saving England from the catastrophe that he had dreaded since his childhood.

Southey did not sympathize with the Methodists. The book appeared at a time when their leader's personal influence was still felt, and Southey undertook it in part to promote Wesley's wish to see Methodism retained within the framework of the Church of England. Nor did he worship Wesley. The biography, however, is both charitable and judicious and, according to Simmons, has the quality of "cold clear daylight which makes its portrayal of Wesley so convincing." Like *The Life of Nelson, The Life of Wesley* remains preferred to the fuller and more accurate three-volume *Life and Times,* published later by Luke Tyerman in 1870 and 1871 — perhaps because, in Dowden's words, Southey's prose has "a lucidity and a perfect exposition . . . such as we rarely find outside a French memoir." As has been frequently observed, however, *The Life of Wesley* is more a history of the Methodist movement than a biography of its founder. It suffers from the unfortunate inclusiveness that characterizes Southey's historical writing. Southey himself seems to have been aware of this: he referred to it as "this great tesselated tablet." Yet the detailed stories of George Whitefield, the popular evangelical preacher, and of the Moravians, a Protestant sect, do not read like digressions but are fused into a continuous and captivating narrative. Indeed, Southey also regarded his "mosaic" as skillfully rendered: "In parts I think some of my best writing will be found."

Southey begins with a hair-raising account of a fire in the parsonage of the Reverend Samuel Wesley from which John Wesley, age five and the youngest of a large family, was saved at the last minute. John's salvation seemed an act of providence to his parents, who therefore bestowed special attention on him that was thought to account for his prodigious strength of character. Like Nelson's, Wesley's salient virtues were courage, energy, and, above all, passionate devotion.

At Oxford Wesley refined his expertise in logical discriminations and applied them to theological argument in a fashion Southey admired. Familiar with ecclesiastical history and with the writers who had most affected religious thought in England, Southey brought a deep intellectual background to his task. He tells how just before Wesley's ordination, in reaction to Jeremy Taylor, whose writings he debated with his eminently rational mother, Wesley articulated the religious principles he was to develop later: the duty of absolute (as opposed to comparative) humility, the belief that one knows if one is in a state of salvation, and abhorrence of the Calvinist doctrine of predestination. Wesley, his

older brother Charles, and their circle at Oxford were seized with religious enthusiasm so intense that they lived astonishingly arduous and austere lives; one of them actually died of his self-denials. Southey reports on these years with consistently cool neutrality interrupted periodically by brief, strong personal reactions to their eccentricities. After describing the rigorous schedule followed by the fledgling Methodists — of studying, fasting, visiting the sick and imprisoned, praying, and self-examination — he comments that such "simplicity" produces "the worst of artificial characters," "for where it [makes] one out of a thousand a saint, it [makes] the rest inevitably formalist and hypocrites. Religion is defined in this scheme to be *a recovery of the image of God*. It cannot be doubted that they who framed it were filled with devotion the most fervent, and charity the most unbounded, however injudicious in many respects the means were whereby they thought to promote and strengthen such dispositions in themselves. But Wesley, when he had advanced in his career, looked back upon himself as having been in a state of great spiritual ignorance."

Southey indulges an attitude toward the "injudicious zeal" shared by the young Wesley brothers that is at once awed and disapproving, tinged from time to time with barely perceptible humor. After their time at Oxford, John and Charles made a disastrous expedition to Georgia to administer to the Indians and colonists. Southey presents scenes of this adventure that resemble works by Henry Fielding:

Charles Wesley attempted the doubly difficult task of reforming some of the lady colonists, and reconciling their petty jealousies and hatred of each other; in which he succeeded no farther than just to make them cordially agree in hating him, and caballing to get rid of him in any way. He had not been six days at Fredrica before he was involved in so many disputes and disagreeable circumstances, that he declared he would not spend six days more in the same manner for all Georgia. . . . As he was at prayers in a myrtle grove, a gun was fired from the other side of the bushes, and the ball passed close by him: he believed it was aimed at him; yet if there had really been a design against his life, they who make the attempt would not so easily have given up their purpose. [Gov. James Edward] Oglethorpe was at this time gone inland with the Indians, to see the limits which they claimed. During his absence the [town] doctor chose to shoot during service-time on the Sunday, in the midst of the sermon, and so near the church, that the constable thought it his duty to go out and deliver him to the commanding-officer, who put him under arrest in the guard room. This was of course imputed to the chaplain [Wesley]; the doctor's wife poured out a torrent of execrations against him [Wesley] in the street;

*Southey in his study at Greta Hall, 1804 (portrait by Henry Elridge;
National Portrait Gallery, London)*

and to heighten the indignation which was excited, the doctor himself refused to go out to any patient, though his services were wanted by a woman at the time. When Oglethorpe returned, he found Fredrica in an uproar . . . and that Charles Wesley was the prime mover of the mischief.

Ultimately Southey had enormous respect for the preacher who many believe was the greatest single influence for good in the eighteenth century. Southey's design was to display the conditions of that century which fostered the religious revival and to provide another place to address issues about which he felt passionately: Wesley, too, had been zealously interested in the education and welfare of the illiterate industrial poor. In chapter 9, "State of Religion in England," Southey supports Wesley's position that literacy alone is useless; education must be moral and religious as well. Coleridge, too, was interested in the issues raised in this book and left his passionate responses to *The Life of Wesley* in the blank leaf of the first volume of his copy for Southey to read (after Coleridge's death).

For Coleridge it was "The favorite of my library among many favorites, the book I can read for the twentieth time when I can read nothing else at all."

Southey also shared with Coleridge and Wordsworth a nationalistic ambition to establish a distinctively British canon of poetry. His biographies can be seen as part of that effort: to memorialize the virtues of distinctively British heroes. Southey wrote of great warriors, religious leaders, and poets who exhibit the gentlemanly virtues of patriotism, honor, courage, and sincerity that he wished to see thriving in every British heart. Believing that these spectacles of virtue would have a morally medicinal effect, he aimed to arouse a passion of emulation with both the spectacle of ideal character and the spectacle of his own admiration of that character.

In the biography that prefaces *The Works of William Cowper,* for the most part Cowper is allowed to tell his own story. Southey merely supplies a connective framework of exhaustively detailed, basic information that chronologically holds together long passages from letters and memoirs. As always, his prose seems effortlessly clear, is pleasingly paced, and is particularly suited to this task because it blends so unobtrusively with Cowper's, which has the same qualities. Southey only begins to restrict his commentary, however, after having established Cowper's virtue and sincerity in the early chapters.

In these chapters Southey frequently has a simultaneous double focus: Cowper and the state of the nation. The interest in national moral discipline in *The Life of Nelson* is also palpable here. Southey's description of Cowper's painful school days, for example, gives rise alternately to comments on the deplorable failings of education in Cowper's time and to the dire consequences of its current failings. Cowper had been tyrannized by a boy of fifteen. The specific nature of the "cruel acts" remains vague, although when they were discovered, the boy was expelled. Southey takes this opportunity to recommend "restraint upon brutal dispositions, at that age when they are subject to control, [for it] would be one of the surest means of national reformation."

The importance of education in reforming the national character was a frequent subject for Southey. In his *Quarterly Review* articles he liberally deplores social injustice but typically does so in an authoritative and paternalistic manner. Similarly, his introductory remarks on Cowper's family name epitomize the ubiquitous overlaps and interpenetrations of opposing political sensibilities that characterize the period in general and Southey's views in particular: "Free as he [Cowper] was, as every Christian ought to be, from the leaven of ancestral pride, it cannot be supposed that he was insensible to the value of a good name – in the hereditary sense of that word." The clash between Southey's republican and traditionalist views on hereditary privilege is almost amusingly evident in this moralistic excuse for admiring Cowper's bloodlines.

In his analysis of Cowper's character Southey adduces long passages from his letters but at every turn seems eager to prevent Cowper from making a bad impression. He constantly interrupts to explain away the weakness, error, and vice that Cowper confesses with becoming frankness and self-irony. When Cowper says that as a boy he became "adept in the infernal art of lying," Southey insists that he "imposed upon himself"; when Cowper says that he lived for two years with a doctor in whose family religion "was neither known or practiced," Southey insists that "Here, too, he seems to have looked back through the same distorting medium. His

words can only mean that family prayers were not performed in that house. . . . of their private devotions it was impossible that he could know anything"; after quoting passages from Cowper's memoir that describe mental suffering, Southey writes, "But the accuracy with which such cases are described may be sometimes questioned, even when, as in this instance, the sincerity of the individual is unquestionable. Present feeling gives a coloring to the past." Throughout the first chapters Southey repeatedly reminds the reader to receive Cowper's statements about himself as interpretive, as fictive; he, however, remains oblivious to his own inevitable coloring.

In the third and fourth chapters Cowper almost drops out of sight entirely while Southey inserts biographical accounts of his literary contemporaries and friends: Bonnell Thornton, George Colman, Robert Lloyd, and Charles Churchill. (Many of Cowper's letters were in possession of a rival biographer, and Southey simply needed to fill up the space.) The fifth chapter is mostly a long, unabridged excerpt from the portion of Cowper's memoir where he describes the onslaught of his first devastating bout of melancholy madness. Confident that he has by this time in the narrative presented the man he wants his reader to know – having instructed the reader to be wary of taking Cowper's self-representations at face value, having taught the reader to appreciate a wiser, kinder, happier, and (ironically) more honest man than Cowper makes himself out to be – Southey leaves readers to enjoy the alternately ardent and ironic voice audible in Cowper's concise prose. Southey's prose becomes so utterly plain that his presence becomes imperceptible.

Recent critics of Southey's prose have agreed with his contemporaries that it was exemplary. His great talent is for delivering lots of information in a small space. Aiming, in his own words, to keep his prose plain as a Doric column, Southey made most eighteenth-century prose sound labored – an impractical medium for scholarly debate. His prose was praised by Coleridge for being a model of transparency. But his poetry often lacks color, imagery, and wit. Thus Byron could both praise his unsurpassed classical elegance as being "perfect" and joke about his "blank verse and blanker prose."

Southey's less important biographical writings include his "Life of John Bunyan" in his edition of *The Pilgrim's Progress* (1830). Partly because publishers speculated that his name on the title page would ensure sales, he was also invited to edit *Select Works of the British Poets, from Chaucer to Jonson* (1831), which includes his brief biographical introductions. In the same year he published *Attempts in Verse, by John Jones, an Old Servant; with . . . an Introductory Essay on the Lives and Works of the Uneducated Poets*. At about this time he also agreed to write what editor David Hannay claims was to be "a volume of Naval History in biographical form for the *Cabinet Cyclopedia*"; by 1840 he was well into the fifth volume, which was completed by Robert Bell when Southey's intellect began to fail. Hannay, who culled *English Seamen* (1895) from the gigantic fragment originally published as *Lives of the British Admirals,* accounts for why the project grew to become a "colossal enterprise." Southey quoted from his original authorities with "unerring tact" everything that was worth quoting. "But this fine quality of seeing, which in his case was accompanied by an extraordinary dexterity in extracting and weaving together, has also its shadow from which the possessor cannot jump. He who can see what is worth quoting is sorely tempted to quote every worthy thing he sees." Furthermore, as he wrote, Southey found it difficult to resist including anything picturesque or pathetic of which he may have been reminded. Although his brevity is everywhere applauded, he could not limit the number of stories he wished to tell. This "defect" may have prevented his *Lives of the British Admirals* from being a naval history, strictly speaking, but it constitutes the charm of what Hannay calls "the finest portrait gallery of Elizabethan sea heroes in the English language."

Another asset of the book is the "styleless" style Southey felt he had by this time perfected. He explains how his prose is "written without any other immediate object than that of expressing what it is to be said in the readiest, and most perspicuous manner. But . . . in the proof sheet, every sentence is then weighed upon the ear, euphony becomes a second object, and ambiguities are removed. But of what is now called style not a thought enters my head at any time." Furthermore, the general knowledge of character and conduct that Southey brought to his mature work has never been equaled in studies of the Elizabethan seamen. Because he knew Spanish and Portuguese history in minute detail, Southey was also able to supply a vivid picture of the men against whom the Elizabethan heroes fought. The heroes themselves, although not represented as mere slavers and pirates, are essentially like the "evil" conquistadores: lovers of adventure and gold. Sir John Hawkins, for example, according to Southey, had no scruples about "how he obtained his negroes, or what papers he exhibited, or what story he told, and he was determined that . . .

if he could not obtain his price by fair means, he would extort it from his customers by fear." Sir Walter Ralegh is portrayed as a self-seeking intriguer. Yet, like so many of Southey's other subjects, these men are also brave, patriotic, and ready to risk all for a cause.

Virtues such as these are found in the subjects of Southey's minor late biographical writings, including the October 1825 *Quarterly Review* article about Pierre Terrail, Seigneur de Bayard, the *Chevalier sans peur et sans reproche*. Other *Quarterly Review* pieces celebrate what might be regarded as de Bayard's British equivalents: the duke of Marlborough (May 1820), who "in all his relations, public and private, almost as nearly as human frailty will allow, is the model of a great patriot, a true statesman, and a consummate general." John Evelyn (April 1818), a perfect English gentleman, was another.

Southey never relinquished his ideal of flawless moral virtue, and he wished to leave for posterity a portrait of the perfect English man of letters. According to Jack Simmons, Southey described himself as "a lean, lank, greyhound-like creature," but by all other accounts he looked suave and dignified. After meeting him, Byron confessed, "To have that poet's head and shoulders, I would almost have written his Sapphics." Thomas De Quincey described Southey's equally impressive mannerisms: "he has a remarkable habit of looking up into the air, as if looking at abstractions. The expression of his face is that of a very acute and aspiring man. So far, it was even noble, as it conveyed a feeling of serene and gentle pride, habitually familiar with elevating subjects of contemplation. . . . chastened by the most unaffected modesty." De Quincey also recalled the nuances of Southey's verbal mannerisms: "His heart is continually reverting to his wife, viz. his library; and, that he may waste as little effort as possible upon his conversational exercises – that the little he wishes to say may appear pregnant with much meaning – he finds it advantageous, and, moreover, the style of his mind much prompts him, to adopt a trenchant, pungent, aculeated form of terse, glittering, stenographic sentences – saying which have the air of laying down the law without any . . . privilege of appeal, but are not meant to do so."

Southey's tranquil and productive years at Keswick were rarely disturbed. In 1816 his son Herbert died at the age of ten; he had been a brilliant child so deeply loved by his parents that they never entirely recovered. Four of Southey's eight children died in childhood. Greta Hall then became an increasingly quiet and sad place as the others grew up

*Cousins Sara Coleridge, daughter of Samuel Taylor Coleridge,
and Edith May Southey, daughter of Robert Southey,
1820 (portrait by Edward Nash; National Portrait
Gallery, London)*

and moved away. In 1834 Southey's wife, Edith, suddenly lost her senses and died the following year. Southey married Caroline Bowles, a friend of twenty years standing, in 1839, but his own mind began to fail shortly after, and he died on 21 March 1843.

Southey had developed what he called his "cold and courteous" demeanor in an effort to conceal the "mimosa sensibility" that he so regretted. Some people, he said, "make me draw into myself like a tortoise, or roll myself up in prickles, like a hedgehog; and sometimes . . . I bristle like a porcupine at an odious presence." Since childhood he had been profoundly troubled not only by death but by the diabolic. Like the Boiling Well near Bristol, he said, he seethed beneath a smooth surface. As these expressions indicate, however, Southey also had wit and charm that is most evident in his Rabelaisian, Shandean autobiographical novel, *The Doctor, &c.* published in seven volumes from 1834 to 1847. Although he usually trained himself to repress his feelings stoically, he was less successful at rendering them invisible than he supposed. "How has this man contrived," Thomas Carlyle exclaimed, "with such a nervous system, to keep alive, for nearly sixty years? Now blushing under his grey hairs, rosy like a maiden of fifteen; now slatey almost, like a rattlesnake, or fiery serpent? How has he not been torn to pieces long since, under such furious pulling this way and that?" The effort to stay in one piece resulted in moral rigor that sometimes irritated those less committed to leading lives of perfect virtue. Wordsworth found Southey's elegant habits "finical"; Southey in turn complained, "To introduce Wordsworth into one's library is like letting a bear into a tulip-garden."

Wordsworth, who nevertheless had much in common with Southey, thought Southey's brief, autobiographical lyric "My Days Among the Dead Are Past," written when he was forty-four, was a touching expression of Southey's character. The poem ends thus:

> My thoughts are with the dead, with them
>   I live in long-past years,
> Their virtues love, their faults condemn,

Partake their hopes and fears,
And from their lessons seek and find
    Instruction with a humble mind.

My hopes are with the dead, anon
    My place with them will be,
And I with them shall travel on
    Through all futurity;
Yet leaving here a name, I trust,
    That will not perish with the dust.

Musing on the afterlife, Southey also seems to sur-
mise that he will "travel on" with the subjects of his
major biographies – Nelson, Wesley, and Cowper – because having imbibed and then shared
what he learned from them, he, too, had become
worthy of lasting fame. Furthermore, these lines
quietly describe the "moral ardour" that made his
prose, in Coleridge's words, "quick and buoyant"
and his biographies therefore memorable.

In spite of relentless attacks in the liberal
press, Southey succeeded in his desire to promote
virtue well into the nineteenth century. Indeed, he
may be regarded as a prototype of the Victorian pa-
triarch. Critical attention to Southey earlier in the
twentieth century has been relatively scant and
stems neither from his ability to elevate his readers
morally nor from his vast learning, knowledge of
character, "perfect" prose, or poetic beauties and innovations. Historicist critics such as Marilyn Butler,
however, remind readers that Southey's now-more-
famous contemporaries were frequently responding
directly to his then-more-famous poems. Butler argues that Southey is a sophisticated narratologist
worthy of critical interest. For David Eastwood his
importance lies in what his ouevre can reveal about
such topics as the struggle between radicals and
conservatives of the revolutionary era over the language of patriotism – a struggle in which Southey,
as a biographer of great patriots, held a pivotal position. Southey's contribution to the genre of biography has not yet received the sustained critical attention it deserves.

Letters:

*A Memoir of the Life and Writings of the Late William
    Taylor, of Norwich . . . (Containing his Correspon-
    dence with Robert Southey . . . and Other Eminent
    Literary Men)*, 2 volumes, edited by J. W.
    Robberds (London: Murray, 1843);
Joseph Cottle, *Reminiscences of Samuel Taylor Coleridge
    and Robert Southey* (London: Houlston & Stone-
    man, 1848);
The Life and Correspondence of Robert Southey, 6 vol-
    umes, edited by Charles Cuthbert Southey

(London: Longman, Brown, Green & Long-
    mans, 1849–1850);
Selections from the Letters of Robert Southey, 4 volumes,
    edited by John Wood Warter (London: Long-
    man, Brown, Green & Longmans, 1856);
*The Correspondence of Robert Southey with Caroline
    Bowles*, edited by Edward Dowden (Dublin:
    Hodges, Figgis / London: Longman, 1881);
Letters of Robert Southey: A Selection, edited by Mau-
    rice H. Fitzgerald (London, New York & To-
    ronto: Oxford University Press, 1912);
New Letters of Robert Southey, 2 volumes, edited by
    Kenneth Curry (New York & London: Colum-
    bia University Press, 1965);
The Letters of Robert Southey to John May, 1797–1838,
    edited by Charles Ramos (Austin: Jenkins,
    1976).

Bibliographies:

Ernest Bernbaum, *Guide through the Romantic Move-
    ment*, revised and enlarged edition (New York:
    Ronald Press, 1949);
Kenneth Curry, "Southey," in *The English Romantic
    Poets & Essayists: A Review of Research and Criti-
    cism*, edited by Carolyn Washburn Houtchens
    and Lawrence Huston Houtchens (New York:
    Published for the Modern Language Associa-
    tion by New York University Press, 1966), pp.
    155–182;
Curry and Robert Dedmon, "Southey's Contribu-
    tions to the *Quarterly Review*," *Wordsworth Circle*,
    6 (Autumn 1975): 261–272;
Curry, *Robert Southey: A Reference Guide* (Boston:
    Hall, 1977);
Mary Ellen Priestley, "The Southey Collection in
    the Fitz Park Museum, Keswick, Cumbria,"
    Wordsworth Circle, 11 (Winter 1980): 43–64.

Biographies:

Edward Dowden, *Robert Southey* (London: Macmil-
    lan, 1879);
William Haller, *The Early Life of Robert Southey* (New
    York: Columbia University Press, 1917);
Jack Simmons, *Southey* (London: Collins, 1945);
Malcolm Elwin, *The First Romantics* (New York:
    Longmans, Green, 1948).

References:

Ernest Bernhardt-Kabisch, *Robert Southey* (Boston:
    Twayne, 1977);
Jane Britton, *Catalogue of the Bertram R. Davis "Robert
    Southey" Collection* (Waterloo, Ont.: University
    of Waterloo Library, 1990);

Marilyn Butler, "Plotting the Revolution: The Political Narratives of Romantic Poetry and Criticism," in *Romantic Revolutions: Criticism and Theory,* edited by Kenneth R. Johnston and others (Bloomington & Indianapolis: Indiana University Press, 1990), pp. 103–157;

Butler, "Revising the Canon," *Times Literary Supplement,* 4–10 December 1987, pp. 1349, 1359–1360;

Adolfo Cabral, *Southey e Portugal: 1774–1801* (Lisbon: Fernandez, 1959);

Geoffrey Carnall, *Robert Southey* (London & New York: Longmans, Green, 1964);

Carnall, *Robert Southey and His Age: The Development of a Conservative Mind* (Oxford: Clarendon Press, 1960);

Alfred Cobban, *Edmund Burke and the Revolt Against the Eighteenth Century: A Study of the Political and Social Thinking of Burke, Wordsworth, Coleridge, and Southey* (New York: Macmillan, 1929);

Kenneth Curry, *Southey* (London & Boston: Routledge & Kegan Paul, 1975);

Maria O. Da Silva Dias, *O Fardo Do Homem Branco: Southey, historiador do Brazil* (São Paulo, Brazil: Companhia Editora Nacional, 1974);

David Eastwood, "Robert Southey and the Intellectual Origins of Romantic Conservatism," *English Historical Review,* 104 (April 1989): 308–331;

Eastwood, "Robert Southey and the Meanings of Patriotism," *Journal of British Studies,* 31 (July 1992): 265–287;

E. R. H. Harvey, Introduction to Southey's *The Life of Nelson,* edited by Harvey (London: Macdonald, 1953);

Richard Hoffpauir, "The Thematic Structure of Southey's Epic Poetry," *Wordsworth Circle,* 6 (Autumn 1975): 240–249; 7 (Spring 1976): 109–116;

Kenneth Hopkins, *The Poets Laureate* (London: Bodley Head, 1954);

Mary Jacobus, "Southey's Debt to *Lyrical Ballads,*" *Review of English Studies,* 22 (February 1971): 20–36;

Lionel Madden, ed., *Robert Southey: The Critical Heritage* (Boston: Routledge & Kegan Paul, 1972);

Edward W. Meachen, "From a Historical Religion to a Religion of History: Robert Southey and the Heroic in History," *Clio,* 9 (Winter 1980): 229–252;

Meachen, "History and Transcendence: Robert Southey's Epic Poems," *Studies in English Literature,* 19 (Autumn 1979): 589–608;

Warren U. Ober, "Lake Poet and Laureate: Southey's Significance to His Own Generation," Ph.D. dissertation, Indiana University, 1959;

Ludwig Pfandl, "Southey und Spanien," *Revue Hispanique,* 28 (March 1913): 1–315;

Jean Raimond, *Robert Southey: L'homme et son temps; L'œuvre; Le rôle* (Paris: Didier, 1968);

Brian Wilkie, *Romantic Poets and Epic Tradition* (Madison: University of Wisconsin Press, 1965);

Herbert G. Wright, "Three Aspects of Southey," *Review of English Studies,* 9 (January 1933): 37–46.

Papers:

Major public collections of Southey's letters (of which some two thousand remain unpublished) and manuscripts are in the Berg Collection of the New York Public Library, the Bodleian Library, the British Library, the Fitz Park Museum in Keswick, the Huntington Library, the University of Rochester Library, the National Library of Wales, and the Victoria and Albert Museum.

Biographia Britannica

Donald W. Nichol
Memorial University of Newfoundland

Biographia Britannica was the most ambitious attempt in the latter half of the eighteenth century to document the lives of notable British men and women. The first edition of *Biographia Britannica,* under the general editorship of William Oldys, was published between 1747 and 1766 (six volumes in seven). The incomplete second edition, under Andrew Kippis, was published between 1778 and 1793 (five volumes). The purpose is set out in the preface to the first edition: "to collect into one Body, without any restriction of time or place, profession or condition, the memoirs of such of our countrymen as have been eminent, and by their performances of any kind deserve to be remembered." Not all readers agreed that the project or the way it was organized was sound: "There is a miserable & enormous heap of stuff, called *Biographia Brit.* for the composition of which, the undertaking Booksellers called from the way side the lame & the blind &c. yet it suited the People & preserved some little credit with others by means of Mr. Cambel [*sic*] a man of sense & industry who has written much for the Booksellers and composed some few lives in this Collection." This was William Warburton's impression of *Biographia Britannica* in a letter dated 28 March 1764 to Sir David Dalrymple, Lord Hailes. Warburton had reason to slight this biographical dictionary; one of its contributors apparently attempted to blackmail him. But respectable contributors such as the three chief compilers Oldys, Thomas Broughton, and John Campbell, who had previously compiled the four-volume *Lives of the Admirals* (1742–1744), made the venture worthwhile. As with the later *Dictionary of National Biography, Biographia Britannica* was produced by many scholars of varying talents. In concept and contents the project changed considerably from the completed first edition to the curtailed second.

The full title of the first volume of the first edition is *Biographia Britannica: or, the Lives of the Most eminent Persons Who have flourished in Great Britain and Ireland, From the earliest Ages, down to the present Times: Collected from the best Authorities, both Printed and Manuscript, and digested in the Manner of Mr Bayle's Historical and Critical Dictionary*. It was published in 1747 in London, "Printed for W. Innys, W. Meadows, J. Walthoe, T. Cox, A. Ward, J. and P. Knapton, T. Osborne, S. Birt, D. Browne, T. Longman and T. Shewell, H. Whitridge, R. Hett, C. Hitch, T. Astley, S. Austen, C. Davis, R. Manby and H. S. Cox, C. Bathurst, J. and R. Tonson and S. Draper, J. Robinson, J. Hinton, J. and J. Rivington, and M. Cooper." Given the highly expensive nature of the project, *Biographia Britannica* had to be undertaken by a considerable network of booksellers, some of whom – John and Paul Knapton, Jacob and Richard Tonson, and Thomas Longman – were also then engaged in other literary landmarks such as Samuel Johnson's *Dictionary,* Alexander Pope's *Works,* and various editions of the works of William Shakespeare.

The main editor of and principal contributor to the first edition, Oldys, was the illegitimate son of the chancellor of Lincoln and was librarian to the earl of Oxford, whose substantial collection of books and manuscripts he catalogued. Oldys's biography of Sir Walter Ralegh prefaced the 1736 edition of Ralegh's *History of the World*. In addition, he worked extensively on compiling *The British Librarian* (1737) and *The Harleian Miscellany* (1753). His predilection for fine detail is revealed in his life of Ralegh: "a great discovery of genius may be made through a small and sudden repartee." James Boswell, in his *Life of Samuel Johnson, LL.D.* (1791), describes Oldys as "a man of eager curiosity and indefatigable diligence."

The volumes of the first edition were published in the following order: volume one (1747): preface; Aaron, martyr, to Benignus, archbishop of Armagh; volume two (1748): Henry Bénnet (or Benet), earl of Arlington, to Henry Compton, bishop of London; volume three (1750): John Conant, divine, to Francis Gastrell, bishop of Chester; volume four (1757): Thomas Gatacre (or Gataker), scholar and divine, to John Knox, reformer of the Scottish church; volume five (1760): Hugh Latimer, martyred bishop of Worcester, to Sir Henry Savile, scholar; volume six, part 1 (1763): John Scott, divine, to James Ussher, archbishop of Armagh; volume six, part 2 (1766): William Wake, archbishop of Canterbury, to Richard Zouche, Regius Professor of Law at Oxford. This volume includes a supplement; an appendix to the supplement; and the index and chronological index by subject (with no pagination). Each large folio volume runs to approximately seven hundred pages.

The main influences on *Biographia Britannica* are acknowledged in the preface to the first edition. The preface traces the origins of biographical study through Nicholas Lloyd's *Dictionarium Historicum, Geographicum, Poeticum* (1670; revised, 1686); Conrad Gesner's *Bibliotheca Universalis* (1545), which gave a synoptic view of all books written in Greek, Latin, and Hebrew to date; and Robert and Charles Stephens's *Dictionary* (1596). Louis Moreri, the French ecclesiast, compiled the *Grand dictionnaire* (1674) before the age of thirty; eighteen printings were sold throughout Europe between 1674 and 1740. It was translated ("but indifferently") into English in 1694. As acknowledged on the title page of *Biographia Britannica*, Pierre Bayle's *Dictionnaire historique et critique* (1695–1697), whose skeptical inquiries inspired the French philosophes and led to the *Encyclopédie* (1751–1772), proved the greatest recent model for British biographical writing. Bayle's *Dictionnaire* was translated into English by Pierre Des Maizeaux as *The Dictionary Historical and Critical* (1734–1738). While knowledgeable about Continental sources, the compilers of *Biographia Britannica* naturally looked to native sources for antiquarian material, including Benedictine monk John Boston's manuscript catalogue of all abbey libraries in the reign of Henry IV and John Leland's *Commentarii de Scriptoribus Britannicis (Commentaries of British Writers)*, which he compiled as Henry VIII's antiquary (edited by Antonius Hall in 1709). The contributors to *Biographia Britannica* read over such standard collected and individual British biographies as William Roper's 1626 life of Sir Thomas More, Izaak Walton's series of lives beginning with that of John Donne in 1640, Thomas Fuller's *History of the Worthies of England* (1662), and Thomas Sprat's *Life of Cowley* (1668).

One of the crucial problems facing eighteenth-century biographers was the scarcity of reliable source material. The sixteenth-century Protestant bishop and antiquary John Bale had an invaluable collection, but he became violently anti-Papist. According to the preface, "He had in his own possession a large treasure of MSS. relating to our History, and it must be owned, there are many things in his book that are not to be found elsewhere; but

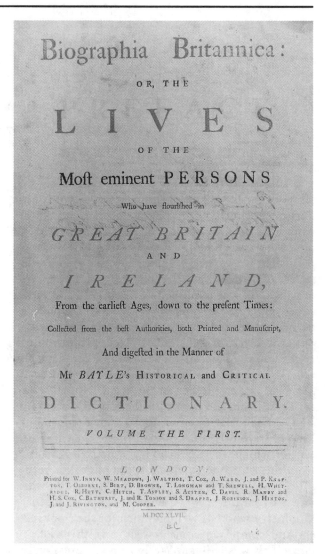

Title page for the first volume of the most ambitious attempt in the eighteenth century to document the lives of noble British men and women

then he is hardly to be relied on, especially where there is the least room to suspect he might be prejudiced, for there, as we shall in many instances shew, he had little or no command of himself, but allowed more to his temper than authorities; for he very seldom produces any voucher for what he says, though sometimes he could hardly expect to be believed without it." The religious and political dispositions of the biographer and biographee can make for entries that are far from objective.

The first entry, "AARON and JULIUS (*Saints*)," exemplifies the arrangement and idiosyncrasies of *Biographia Britannica*. The single-column entry is flanked on both margins by brief notes linked to the main text by lower-case letters in italics and parentheses. At the end of this entry are three longer footnotes identified by italicized capital letters in square brackets. The brief main text concludes by way of an explanatory note on methodology: "They [Aaron and Julius] are here joined together in one article, because, like Saul and Jonathan, *in their death they were not divided.*" However laudable such a scripturally inspired rationale may be, it does not help that Julius is not cross-referenced, although the reader is directed to the entry on Saint Alban. The entry states that these two early British saints were martyred in the year 303 A.D. during the rule of Diocletian and that churches were erected in their memory.

The footnotes typically outweigh the main text of the entry: in "AARON and JULIUS" the first note acknowledges the Venerable Bede; the second raises the question of protomartyrdom – Aaron and Julius died in the same year as Saint Alban, "the first who impurpled Britain with his blood" (had their martyrdom preceded Saint Alban's, they might have been better known); and the third note refers to Giraldus Cambrensis, who mentions where they were buried. The footnotes themselves are annotated in the margins, using numbers in parentheses. Finally, the article is signed "T.," for Thomas Broughton, although a list of contributors is not apparent in the first edition. The key to the contributors of the first edition is given by Kippis in his prefaces to the first and second volumes of the second edition:

C	= Philip Morant
D	= William Harris
E and X	= John Campbell
G (for Gray's Inn) and R	= Oldys
H	= Henry Brougham
I	= anonymous
P	= Philip Nichols
R	= Mr. Hinton
T	= Thomas Broughton
Z	= anonymous

Brougham also contributed entries to the second edition, according to the preface to the second volume.

While contributors' researches (aided by the founding of the British Museum in 1753) were far-reaching, the accuracy of entries is occasionally questionable. The biography of Pope in volume five, signed by "P" (for Philip Nichols), for example, errs in giving 1715 as the date the poet moved to Twickenham: according to Maynard Mack in his 1985 biography, Pope moved into his celebrated villa along with his mother and nurse (significantly, after the publication of his collected *Works* and the death of his father, both in 1717) "in the early months of 1719." Overall, entries are given in alphabetical order, but in the case of identical surnames, entries are arranged chronologically, so that, for example, the entry on Thomas Pope (1507–1559) precedes that of Alexander Pope (1688–1744).

The publication of the first edition of *Biographia Britannica* was not without controversy. One of the contributors, Nichols, sent news of a forthcoming entry on Joseph Smith of Queen's College, Oxford, to Warburton, bishop of Gloucester. The entry included a potentially embarrassing letter concerning the alleged plagiarism of notes on Shakespeare. The letter, from Sir Thomas Hanmer to Smith, dated 24 October 1742, maintained that Warburton paid Hanmer a "sly, designing visit" in order to plunder his work on Shakespeare. Upon reading the entry, Warburton wrote a letter dated 29 January 1761, presumably to one of the booksellers of *Biographia Britannica,* claiming that Hanmer's letter was "one continued falshood from beginning to end." When the offending leaf from the entry (sheet 41 Q, pages 3743 and 3744) was removed, Nichols published it separately as *The Castrated Sheet of Sir Thomas Hanmer* (also entitled *The Castrated Letter*) in 1763 in the same format, with a damaging preface and a dedication: "To my Fellow-Proprietors of Biographia Britannica." The letter was followed by "An Account of the Extraordinary Means that were used to Suppress Sir Thomas Hanmer's Letter": "The detriment done to the Biographia Britannica by the castration of Sir Thomas Hanmer's letter, discovering the first rise and occasion of the quarrel betwixt Him and Mr. Warburton, is universally acknowledged by all who have seen it; and several complaints having been made to me of the Proprietors of the work, for submitting to such an injury, in which imputation I found myself involved, I have thought it necessary, in my own vindication, as well as in justice to the rest of the proprietors, to lay before the public a full and true account of the matter." Such adverse publicity likely tarnished the reputation of *Biographia Britannica.*

Subjoining the lengthy, extraneous, yet colorful biographical entry on Joseph Smith is a footnote on Sir Orlando Bridgeman, who squandered his inheritance of four thousand pounds per annum and then disappeared. Shortly thereafter a body was recovered from the Thames and positively identified as Bridgeman's by Sir Francis Dashwood (of Hellfire Club fame). However, Bridgeman was subsequently discovered disguised as a laborer in an inn on the road to Bath (his quick identification of the crests on passing coaches having given him away). He was thrown into Gloucester Jail "until death, that general jail deliverer, released him from all the troubles of this world in the year 1746."

Oldys did not live to see the completion of the first edition; he died in 1761, five years before the publication of the second part of volume six. The chronological index shows the eccentricities of the project as well as the primary concerns of the contributors, ranging from antiquities, architecture, and astronomy to physics, poetry, and wit. Here biography was broken down into its encyclopedic parts.

The second edition of *Biographia Britannica*, undertaken by Kippis, turned into one of the great unfulfilled projects of the eighteenth century. Born in 1725 in Nottingham and educated at Philip Doddridge's well-known dissenting academy in Northampton, Kippis was a nonconformist divine who became the pastor of a Presbyterian congregation in Westminster for forty-three years. According to his obituary in the *Gentleman's Magazine* in 1795, he was a voracious reader who claimed to have read sixteen hours a day for three years; he absorbed the ten-volume *General Dictionary* at an early age. He was awarded the degree of Doctor of Divinity by the University of Edinburgh through the influence of William Robertson, the historian and principal of the university.

Like Oldys, Kippis relied on a network of helpers to supply biographical information, the most important of whom was Joseph Towers. Towers was well acquainted with researching the lives of the great, having compiled seven volumes of *British Biography; or, an accurate and impartial account of the lives and writings of eminent persons, in Great Britain and Ireland; from Wickliff . . . to the present time* (1766–1772), which was modeled after the first edition of the *Biographia Britannica*.

The ink had barely dried on the final leaf of the first *Biographia Britannica* when the booksellers cast about for someone to edit the second edition. One of the most obvious choices of the time was Johnson, whose *Life of Mr. Richard Savage* (1744) was widely admired. Johnson's capacity for large projects was remarkable, but, perhaps fortunately, his biographical writings were diverted to his *Prefaces, Biographal and Critical, to the Works of the English Poets* (1779–1781). In his *Life of Samuel Johnson*, Boswell wrote in his entry for 19 September 1777 that Johnson had told him: "he had been asked to undertake the new edition of the *Biographia Britannica*, but had declined it; which he afterwards said to me he regretted. In this regret many will join, because it

would have procured us more of Johnson's most delightful species of writing; and though my friend Dr. Kippis has hitherto discharged the task judiciously, distinctly, and with more impartiality than might have been expected from a Separatist, it were to have been wished that the superintendence of this Literary Temple of Fame had been assigned to 'a friend to the constitution in Church and State.' We should not then have had it too much crowded with obscure dissenting teachers, doubtless men of merit and worth, but not quite to be numbered amongst 'the most eminent persons who have flourished in Great-Britain and Ireland.' " Boswell footnoted this observation with a disclaimer: "In this censure which has been carelessly uttered, I carelessly joined. But in justice to Dr. Kippis, who with that manly candid good temper which marks his character, set me right, I now with pleasure retract it." Others also raised some concern over Kippis's selection of entries.

The effort proved too onerous for Kippis, and, after the first volume, Towers's assistance was noted on the title page. Kippis's and Towers's new or revised entries are initialled "K" and "T" respectively. The second edition was launched a dozen years after the completion of the first. The title page of the second edition declared it was "with corrections, enlargements, and the addition of new lives: by Andrew Kippis, D.D. and F.S.A. with the assistance of other gentlemen." The first volume of this new edition of *Biographia Britannica* was printed in London by "W. & A. Strahan; for C. Bathurst, W. Strahan, J. Rivington & Sons, L. Davis, G. Keith, T. Longman, B. Law, E. & C. Dilly, T. Cadell, G. Robinson, J. Robson, T. Evans, S. Fox, J. Nichols, Whieldon & Waller, H. Gardner, and W. Otridge." The volumes of the second edition were published in the following order: volume one (1778): prefaces; Aaron, martyr, to Ralph Bathurst, poet; volume two (1780): preface; table; corrigenda and addenda; Allen Bathurst, statesman, to George Bull, bishop of Saint David's; volume three (1784): preface; corrigenda and addenda; table; William Bulleyn, physician and botanist, to Sir Edward Coke, Lord Chief Justice; volume four (1789): preface; corrigenda and addenda; table; Henry Cole, divine, to John Davies, critic; volume five (1793): preface; corrigenda and addenda; table; John Davis, explorer, to John Fastolff, knight.

Progress on the second edition was slow in comparison to the first: Oldys had reached the Gatrell entry within three years; Kippis halted at Fastolff after fifteen years. Kippis allowed his passion for comprehensiveness to get out of hand, which put considerable strain on the coffers of some of London's most prominent printers and booksellers. Even such a powerful gathering of publishers and patrons could not sustain the exponential growth of the project. At the rate Kippis was going – adding updated information to earlier entries with each successive volume – he threatened to fill a folio volume for every letter of the alphabet.

One of the changes brought about by Kippis lay in the area of patronage. Unlike the first edition, which had no dedication pages, the second edition proclaimed its most influential supporters. Kippis found a patron for each volume over the fifteen years of the project: volume one was dedicated to the Right Honourable Philip, earl of Hardwicke (dated 1 May 1778); volume two to the earl of Shelburne (1 January 1780); volume three to the duke of Richmond (12 May 1784); volume four to Sir Joseph Banks, president of the Royal Society (15 August 1789); and volume five to Sir David Dalrymple (22 October 1793).

In his preface to the first volume, Kippis singles out Oldys's article on John Atherton, bishop of Waterford and Lismore, for omission because "The story . . . is shocking and indelicate, and told in a manner extremely disagreeable." Yet Atherton's scandal-ridden story had been told many times before Oldys recounted it as "a very remarkable warning-piece in history, to future ages." Kippis evidently removed the entry on the basis of the bishop's bisexuality. Atherton was said to have been "defiled or corrupted in his youth, by one of his own sex"; he then went on to commit incest with his sister-in-law and eventually was sentenced to death on charges Oldys was unable to ascertain. The account of Atherton in the *Dictionary of National Biography* merely states that he was "accused of unnatural crime," that is, homosexuality. Modern readers will infer from this that Oldys was more permissive than Kippis and was inclined to include the more sensational aspects of biography, as a novelist such as Henry Fielding would have been.

Kippis maintained his objective method of selection by claiming to Boswell: "I am not conscious . . . of any partiality in conducting the work. I would not willingly insert a Dissenting Minister that does not justly deserve to be noticed, or omit an established Clergyman that does. At the same time, I shall not be deterred from introducing Dissenters into the *Biographia,* when I am satisfied that they are entitled to that distinction, from their writings, learning and merit." To back up his point, Kippis listed the new entries of dissenting ministers, which included John Abernethy, Thomas Amory,

George Benson, Hugh Broughton, Simon Browne, Joseph Boyse, Thomas Cartwright, and Samuel Chandler, and he then compared that to a new list of twenty-one ministers from the Church of England.

Kippis retained many entries from the first edition. One of his better innovations was to introduce tables of contents after the first volume. He identified new biographies with three asterisks and those with "some Additions" by a dagger. The first volume offers 18 new biographies and 82 revised entries out of a total of 199 subjects. Kippis's revisions often take the form of appended information on interim publications and newly discovered letters. For example, the main text of the entry on Oliver Cromwell is only slightly modified from the original, although Kippis expanded the notes considerably with passages from Tobias Smollett's *Complete History of England* (1757–1758), as continued by David Hume. The Cromwell entry thus swelled from forty-two to fifty-four pages. Kippis's religious convictions are apparent in entries on fellow Dissenters. His former teacher Doddridge, the nonconformist minister who published six volumes of *The Family Expositor* between 1739 and 1756, is accorded forty-eight pages. The eighteen-page entry on Hugh Farmer (condensed to two pages in the *Dictionary of National Biography*) concludes: "It is scarcely necessary to say of Mr. Farmer that he was free from religious bigotry. His temper was too liberal, his understanding too enlarged, and his acquaintance with the world too extensive, to permit him to be the slave of so base a principle."

Entries on the more recent biographees in the volume tend toward sensationalism. Kippis acknowledged the contribution by John Wilkes to his entry of Charles Churchill. The question about the breakdown of Churchill's early marriage grows distinctly turgid, yet the issue of who was the more injured party remains inconclusive:

He plunged into various irregularities, and no longer lived with his wife; though whether his quitting her was at this particular juncture we are not able to determine. "Some people, observes a certain writer, have been unkind enough to say, that Mrs. Churchill gave the first just cause of separation. But nothing can be more false than this rumor; and we can assure the public, that her conduct in private life, and among her acquaintances, was irreproachable" (*Annual Register,* part ii, page 61). We have our doubts about what is here asserted, notwithstanding the positivity with which it is delivered. It was always understood in Westminster, that Mrs. Churchill's imprudence kept too near a place with that of her husband. However, we do not hence mean in the least to justify his disorderly and licentious manner of living.

Thomas Edwards, the barrister, critic, and F.S.A., is mainly remembered for having crossed swords with Warburton. Edwards's satiric attack, *A Supplement to Mr. Warburton's Edition of Shakespear* (1747), earned him a place in the 1749 edition of Pope's *Dunciad*. Later under the title *The Canons of Criticism* Edwards's attack was enlarged and proved popular, with a seventh printing in 1765. Kippis includes Edwards's twenty-five satiric canons as well as a sampling of his sonnets, one mocking Warburton, another sadly reflecting on being the sole survivor of a large family.

As one would expect in an eighteenth-century national biography, accounts of men far outnumber those of women. Colley Cibber receives ample treatment in a dozen pages, but his illustrious daughter-in-law, Susannah (née Arne), is confined to a few passing references. In five volumes Kippis includes twelve new biographies of women, occupying 33 out of 3,481 pages. Separate entries appear for Mary Astell, the writer; Mary Beale, the painter; Juliana Berners, "Learned Lady in the Fifteenth Century"; Margaret Cavendish, Duchess of Newcastle; Susanna Centlivre, the playwright; Catharine Cockburn, the writer; Lady Mildred Burleigh, Lady Anna Bacon, Lady Elizabeth Russel, and Lady Katherine Killigrew (the four daughters of Sir Anthony Cooke, all born between 1526 and 1530); Mary Delany, the writer; and Elizabeth Elstob, the antiquary. Three entries are revised: Margaret Beaufort, Aphra Behn, and Lady Mary Chudleigh. There are three unrevised survivors from the first edition: Arlotta, mother of William the Conqueror; Elizabeth Barton, the impostor; and Joan Beaufort, Queen of Scotland. Some women are included under family entries. Finally, ten short biographies of women are listed as given in the notes.

The entry on Behn, originally written by Broughton, then revised by Kippis, ranges from the commonplace to the caustic. The date of her birth is not given by either biographer. Noting that she was "descended from a good family in the city of Canterbury," the original entry briefly sums up her background, travels, and literary pursuits. It starts with her early misfortune when her father died en route to Suriname as the lieutenant general. There she met Oroonoko, who later became the subject of her novel of that name. She eventually married a London merchant of Dutch extraction. She came to the attention of Charles II, who enjoyed her account of Suriname and sent her as an agent into

Flanders during the Dutch war, although her warning that the Dutch were planning to burn English ships was disregarded and she soon gave up spying for the state. Broughton briefly sums up her later years: "The rest of her life was entirely dedicated to pleasure and poetry." His footnote elaborates: "Her novels, *Oroonoko* excepted, are chiefly translations: Her *Poetry* is none of the best; and her *comedies*, though not without wit and humour, are full of the most indecent scenes and expressions." There the entry originally ended in 1747, but Kippis in 1780 extended the attack on her morals and talents as a writer: "It is some consolation to reflect, that Mrs. Behn's works are now little regarded, her novels excepted, which, we suppose, have still many readers among that unhappily too numerous a class of people who devour the trash of circulating libraries."

Kippis retells a feeble anecdote by an anonymous gentleman who likened her inclusion in *Biographia Britannica* to her burial in Westminster Abbey as an honor far above her station. Kippis then turns his footnote into a defense of commemorating morally suspect figures:

> But it may be answered, that Mrs. Behn's genius, adventures, and writings, gave her, whether justly or unjustly, such a celebrity in her time, that she could not be omitted in a work of this kind. Strictly virtuous characters we shall always treat of with singular pleasure, and shall select them as our favourite articles. But other persons must be recorded, whose abilities, productions, and actions rendered them famous in their day, though they are very deficient in moral qualities. Nor can the Biographia be confined, in the rigid sense of the terms, to wits and heroes: for, in that case, what would become of the many sound Divines, faithful Historians, learned Antiquaries, and judicious Lawyers? It may be added, that Mrs. Behn was undoubtedly a Wit, though, to her indelible disgrace, her talents were prostituted to licentious purposes.

Such is the disdainful rationale of the morally righteous biographer. Cockburn is remembered for her spirited defense of John Locke against Winch Holdsworth. Although her marriage and familial duties curtailed her studies, she eventually overcame domestic circumstances to produce a substantial body of works, which were published by subscription in 1749, the year of her death. While the representation of women biographees is minimal in both editions, Kippis did at least include more than Oldys, although quantity does not necessarily match quality.

In 1784 one anonymous writer complained in an article titled "Biographical Anecdotes of William Oldys, Esq.," in the *Gentleman's Magazine,* that subscribers were growing irritated with the tardiness of the volumes: the second edition of *Biographia Britannica* had stalled at the Fastolff entry. Part 1 of volume six, running from Featley to Foster, was published in 1795, the year of Kippis's death. Dr. George Gregory, who contributed the preface to the volume, planned to succeed Kippis, but the printing and publication were delayed. The plates were destroyed in the February 1808 fire at John Nichols's printing shop. There the project ended.

One of the reasons for the collapse of the remainder of the project was the impossible demands the editors placed on themselves, thereby creating a considerable pressure on the booksellers, who were becoming increasingly concerned about seeing a return on their capital investments. The project grew increasingly cumbersome as entries were revised, supplemented, and resupplemented. This expansion led to an imbalance in the length and cohesiveness of individual entries. One of the causes of delays of the first few volumes was no doubt Kippis's desire to amend existing entries in the light of newly emerging information. For example, the first volume of 1778 has an entry on Joseph Addison which is slightly shorter than the entry for John Brown, a decidedly less important figure. The second volume has an addendum on the life of Addison; volume three than adds more details, taking into account the 1781 publication of Johnson's "Life of Addison"

in his *Prefaces*. Finally, volume four takes into account more information about Addison given in Sir John Hawkins's 1787 *Life of Samuel Johnson*.

According to the editors of the *Dictionary of National Biography,* the second edition of *Biographia Britannica* "hardly deserves the high praise which has been sometimes bestowed upon it," as many imperfections and errors were not corrected. They also reiterated the claim lodged (but then apparently regretted) in Boswell's *Life of Samuel Johnson* that the "prominence given to nonconformists laid the editor open to a charge of impartiality." They also felt that the work was marred by too many overly long and irrelevant footnotes. Kippis's main sins as an editor were bias, pedantry, and padding. Questioning Kippis's habit of offering the best possible interpretation of a subject's faults – his overall lack of harsh biographical criticism – Horace Walpole thought that *Biographia Britannica* ought to have been renamed *Vindicator Britannica,* "for that it was a general panegyric upon everybody." *Biographia Britannica* failed to excite an intellectual movement in the way that Denis Diderot and Jean d'Alembert's *Encyclopédie* did in France. Oldys, Kippis, and their associates are scarcely regarded today, yet *Biographia Britannica* was the most substantial biographical dictionary of its time and the forerunner of the *Dictionary of National Biography*.

The Lives of the Poets

Donald W. Nichol
Memorial University of Newfoundland

With the increasing demand placed on the publishing industry by the voracious reading habits of the expanding middle class, the eighteenth century was ripe for large publishing projects. Born of an antiquarian urge for more reference material on one's bookshelf, the modern encyclopedia, of which biography is a major component, began with the publication of John Harris's *Lexicon Technicum* in 1704. This work was surpassed by Ephraim Chambers's *Cyclopedia* in 1728, a translation of which inspired Denis Diderot and Jean Le Rond d'Alembert's massive French *Encyclopédie* (1751–1771). With the arrival of the first *Encyclopedia Britannica* in 1768 the pattern of collective biography was firmly established.

The public's desire to know about the lives of poets begins with Homer. The wish to learn more about Troy is inevitably linked with the wish to learn more about the first singer of slain heroes. Poets' lives come as a natural subject after those of royals, politicians, generals, and other worthies. The idea for collective biography goes hand in glove with the encyclopedic urges of the antiquarian. William Shakespeare was able to exploit Plutarch's *Parallel Lives* (of twenty-three paired Greeks and Romans), known to him in Sir Thomas North's translation of 1579, which was based on the 1559 French translation of Jacques Amyot. In the middle of the eighteenth century (with John Aubrey's *Lives of Eminent Men* (1813) remaining dormant in manuscript), a rough attempt was made to provide the general public with a relatively affordable, yet comprehensive, assembly of the lives of native writers. Two years before the release of another feat of compilation, Samuel Johnson's *Dictionary* (1755), the enterprising and occasionally shady publisher Ralph Griffiths launched *The Lives of the Poets*.

The full title page reads as follows: "*The Lives of the Poets of Great Britain and Ireland to the Time of Dean Swift. Compiled from Ample Materials Scattered in a Variety of Books, and especially from the MS. Notes of the Late Ingenious Mr. Coxeter and Others, Collected for this Design by Mr. Cibber. In Four Volumes*, London:

printed for R. Griffiths, at the Dunciad in St. Paul's Church-yard, 1753." In spite of the title, *The Lives of the Poets* runs to five volumes – originally published in twenty-five parts – suggesting that the project was initially expected to be shorter and that an extra volume was subsequently found to be necessary. The set, in duodecimo, sold for 10s. 6d. and likely had a large print run. Thomas Coxeter, referred to in the title, was an antiquarian friend of Johnson and was acknowledged by Lewis Theobald in his 1733 edition of Shakespeare for the loan of a collection of early quarto plays. The *Eighteenth-Century Short Title Catalogue* lists a second printing of *The Lives of the Poets,* also published in 1753.

Griffiths had founded the *Monthly Review* in 1749, and it ran for almost a century. He published works of James Boswell and Sir John Hill, as well as other works by Theophilus Cibber and Robert Shiells. Oliver Goldsmith, who was a live-in journalist for five months in 1757, found Griffiths a difficult employer. He was one of the few booksellers capable of fighting his way back from bankruptcy. Griffiths issued a proposal, dated 1 December 1752, for publishing *The Lives of the Poets* by subscription. Shortly afterward Griffiths published Cibber's *The Lives and Characters of the most Eminent Actors and Actresses of Great Britain and Ireland* (1753), which consists only of the life of Barton Booth. The failure of this project in the same year as the completion of *The Lives of the Poets* suggests Griffiths and Cibber abandoned one biographical project for another.

Born in Roxburghshire, Scotland, in the late seventeenth century, Shiells (or Shiels), who had been a journeyman printer, was one of the six amanuenses employed by Johnson on his *Dictionary*. Shiells wrote *Marriage: a Poetical Essay* (1748) as a tribute to Johnson's play *Irene* (published in 1749). He is mentioned as one of the several visitors to Gough Square after the death of Johnson's wife in 1752. The fact that Johnson (according to Boswell) "had then little for himself, but frequently sent money to Mr. Shiels when in distress" suggests that Shiells was destitute. Johnson evidently provided Shiells (who died of consumption on 27 December

294

1753) with material that formed the basis of *The Lives of the Poets*.

There is doubt surrounding the exact role played by Cibber, the son of Colley Cibber, the poet laureate from 1730 to 1757 and manager of the Theatre Royal in Drury Lane. Educated at Winchester College, Theophilus Cibber was more renowned as an actor than as a writer. His stormy marriage to Susannah Arne ended in one of the more sensational criminal conversation cases of the century. He likely had a hand in some of the entries, and his name supplanted that of Shiells, presumably because Griffiths thought the Cibber name would help sell more sets. Boswell, in his journal entry for 10 April 1776, recorded Johnson's remarks: "He told us, that the book entitled *The Lives of the Poets,* by Mr. Cibber, was entirely compiled by Mr. Shiels, a Scotchman, one of his amanuenses. 'The bookseller (said he,) gave Theophilus Cibber, who was then in prison, ten guineas, to allow *Mr. Cibber* to be put upon the title-page, as the authour [*sic*]; by this, a double imposition was intended: in the first place, that it was the work of a Cibber at all; and, in the second place, that it was the work of old Cibber.' " Griffiths challenged Johnson's version of events through a third-party account in the *Monthly Review* (May 1792); Boswell duly appended the account to the 1793 edition of his *Life of Samuel Johnson LL.D.*: "Shiels was the principal collector and digester of the materials for the work: but as he was very raw in authorship, an indifferent writer in prose, and his language full of Scotticisms. Cibber, who was a clever, lively fellow, and then soliciting employment among the booksellers, was engaged to correct the style and diction of the whole work . . . with power to alter, expunge, or add, as he liked. He was also to supply *notes*. . . . He also engaged to write several of the Lives. . . . He was farther useful in striking out the Jacobitical and Tory sentiments, which Shiels had industriously interspersed wherever he could bring them in."

The Griffiths version of the story maintains that Shiells was paid "nearly" seventy pounds, while Cibber accepted twenty-one pounds, some gift sets, and an unmerited bonus of twenty guineas. Shiells soon argued with "his Whiggish supervisor" and might have challenged Cibber to a duel had Griffiths not "fairly laughed him out of his fury." In the end Cibber made so many changes to the proofs that the printer's surcharges wiped out the bookseller's profits. Griffiths also maintained his innocence of attempting to pass the younger Cibber off as his better-known father. The unevenness of style between one entry and another suggests various

hands at work. According to critic William R. Keast, Shiells was responsible for all entries except for the lives of Mary Chandler, Aaron Hill, and Eustace Budgell; and he borrowed freely from the ten-volume *General Dictionary, Historical and Critical* (1734–1741), the first three volumes of *Biographia Britannica* (1747, 1748, 1750), and *Muse's Library* (1737), as well as Johnson's work on Samuel Boyse, Earl of Roscommon, and Richard Savage, among others. Recent works such as *Eighteenth-Century Women Poets: an Oxford Anthology,* edited by Roger Lonsdale (1989), accept Shiells as the main biographer and Cibber as the nominal latecomer.

The Lives of the Poets has nothing by way of a preface; and the index (usually stitched at the beginning of the second volume) seems to have been a hasty afterthought. The arrangement of entries is by period and is roughly chronological, the first volume running from Geoffrey Chaucer (circa 1343–1400) to Thomas Middleton (circa 1570–1627); the second from Thomas Brewer ("*fl.* 1624") to Wentworth Dillon, fourth Earl of Roscommon (1633?–1685); the third from Sir John Denham (1615–1669) to Elkanah Settle (1648–1724); the fourth, from Peter Motteux (1660–1718) to John Ozell (died 1743); and the fifth, from Budgell (1686–1737) to Chandler (1687–1745). In terms of literary output *The Lives of the Poets* spans more than 350 years, from Chaucer's earliest works to those of the most recently deceased writer, John Banks, who died in 1751. Each volume runs to between 353 and 356 pages.

Of the 210 entries 15 are biographies of women, and 195 are biographies of men. The women biographees are Aphra Behn; Susanna Centlivre; Chandler; Lady Mary Chudleigh; Catherine Cockburn; Constantia Grierson; Anne Killigrew; Delarivière Manley; Mary Monck; Margaret Cavendish, Duchess of Newcastle; Katherine Philips; Laetitia Pilkington; Elizabeth Rowe; Elizabeth Thomas; and Ann Finch, Countess of Winchilsea. Accounts of Chudleigh and Monck bear comparison with those found in George Ballard's *Memoirs of Several Ladies of Great Britain who have been Celebrated for their Writings* (1752).

The four-page entry on Grierson (née Crawley; circa 1705–1732) tells the reader that she was born in Ireland, died in 1733 at the age of twenty-seven, and was "one of the most extraordinary women that this age, or perhaps any other, ever produced." The entry gives the impression that she produced an edition of Tacitus, whereas she corrected the proofs of the three-volume edition her husband, a Scottish printer, published in Dublin in

1730 and wrote the Latin dedication to Lord Carteret. She placed little value on her poems written in English. Everything after the first paragraph of this entry is taken directly from Mary Barber, who included a selection of Grierson's works in her own *Poems on Several Occasions,* printed by Samuel Richardson in 1734. A footnote to the entry in *The Lives of the Poets* adds Hebrew to the list of languages Grierson knew and refers the reader to the first volume of Pilkington's *Memoirs* (1748). A. C. Elias's "A Manuscript Book of Constantia Grierson's" (*Swift Studies,* 2, 1987) has superseded previous accounts. Not noted in *The Lives of the Poets* is the fact that she studied midwifery under Dr. Van Lewen, the father of Pilkington, and that she, Pilkington, and Barber later came into Jonathan Swift's sphere.

The biographical entry on Pilkington (circa 1708–1750) offers one of the raciest accounts in *The Lives of the Poets.* Yet, because she found sympathy and support from Colley Cibber toward the end of her life, certain details in this account vary from those found in later biographies: the younger Cibber seems to press for her vindication. Dubbed the "unfortunate poetess," in 1725 she married Matthew Pilkington, a clergyman and poet whose collection *Poems on Several Occasions* (1730) was proofread by Swift. Matthew Pilkington eventually became excessively jealous of his wife's talents and tried to stop her from writing poetry altogether. Swift secured an appointment for him in London as the lord mayor's chaplain, a move which brought complaints from Alexander Pope and Henry St. John, Viscount Bolingbroke. She eventually followed him to London, where he was having an affair with an actress. The account reports how, at one point in their estrangement, he employed a dozen men to break down the door to her bedroom in the middle of the night; she was found in the company of a gentleman. Denying that she was caught in flagrante delicto, she maintained that "Lovers of Learning will, I am sure, pardon me, as I solemnly declare, it was the attractive Charms of a new Book, which the Gentleman would not lend me, but consented to stay till I read it through, that was the sole Motive of my detaining him." Even the biographer seems doubtful of her account as he writes soon after, "When Mrs. Pilkington arrived in London, her conduct was the reverse of what prudence would have dictated." Colley Cibber took pity on her, effecting her release from Marshalsea prison (where she had been jailed for debt) and encouraging her to publish her anecdotes of Swift and others; Griffiths published the London editions of her three-volume *Memoirs* (1748, 1749, 1754). This biographical entry dwells on the sensational aspects of Pilkington's life without passing judgment on her literary output. That is left for the reader to decide from the poem which ends her entry, "To the Revd Dr. Hales."

The entry on the minor playwright Charles Johnson (1679–1748) is typical of the structure of most of the *The Lives of the Poets,* answering questions of background, achievement, and habit. Johnson was "designed for the law" but set his sights on the stage, where he scored several successes with plays such as *The Gentleman Cully* (1702) and *Fortune in her Wits* (1705). He frequented Will's and Button's coffeehouses; at the latter establishment he became a part of the coterie known as Joseph Addison's "little senate," which included Sir Richard Steele, along with Eustace Budgell, Ambrose Phillips, Thomas Tickell, and other writers who would later find themselves ridiculed in Pope's *The Dunciad* (1728, 1743). While scarcely regarded today, Johnson attracted the patronage of Queen Anne and King George I. His popularity was such that box-office receipts on benefit nights were high, "by which means he lived (with œconomy) genteelly." Johnson married a young widow "with a tolerable fortune" and kept a tavern in Bow Street, although his wife's name and the dates of his marriage and proprietorship are not given. His plays apparently died with him as "His parts were not very brilliant." Pope satirized him as "fat Johnson" in his 1715 poem "A Farewell to London" and as a plagiarist in *The Dunciad.* Johnson's plays also include *The Sultaness* (1717), *Medea* (1731), and some fifteen others.

The vagueness surrounding many dates throughout *The Lives of the Poets* would vex a modern reader and suggests that the biographers, possibly under pressure from the bookseller to produce copy for a deadline, preferred to guess rather than look up specific details. Much information seems to have been drawn from memory or hearsay rather than extant documents. Cavendish, for example, is said to have been born "about the latter end of the reign of James I." Such lack of detail is not reassuring, although, in this case, the biographer availed himself of an abundance of other material: born in Saint John's near Colchester, Essex, she was the youngest daughter of Sir Charles Lucas, who died when she was very young. Her mother took great care over her education, though "some of her Biographers have lamented her not being acquainted with the learned languages." In 1643 she went to Oxford as a maid of honor to Henrietta Maria, Royal Consort of Charles I, and she escaped with her to France. During Cavendish's period of exile she became the second wife of William Cavendish, Marquis (later Duke) of Newcastle, in 1645. They returned to England after the Restoration in 1660. In order to devote herself as fully as possible to her writing, the duchess "kept a great many young ladies about her person, who occasionally wrote what she dictated. Some of them slept in a room, contiguous to that in which her grace lay, and were ready, at the call of her bell, to rise any hour of the night, to write down her conceptions, lest they should escape her memory." In the course of outlining such demanding habits, the biography makes a tactless connection between the duchess's literary output and the absence of progeny: "the young ladies, no doubt, often dreaded her Grace's conceptions, which were frequent, but all of the poetical or philosophical kind, for though she was very beautiful, she died without issue." She is described as being "very reserved and peevish" perhaps because "of having never been honoured with the name of mother."

As a member of the Restoration nobility Cavendish was amply remembered. She set the vogue for female autobiography with *Natures pictures drawn by Fancies Pencil* (1656). The entry cites several sources of information: Gerard Langbaine's *An Account of the English Dramatick Poets* (1691) and Giles Jacob's two-volume *Poetical Register, or the Lives and Characters of the English Dramatic Poets* (1719, 1720) as well as the Fulman manuscript collection in the archives of Corpus Christi College at Oxford. According to Jacob, "she was the most voluminous writer of all the female poets," and Langbaine adds that her plays were original as regards language and plot, which "will very well atone for some faults." She was buried in Westminster Abbey on 7 January 1674. The entry in *The Lives of the Poets* lists ten volumes of prose and poetry as well as nineteen plays which were unperformed and collected in *Plays* (1662) and *Plays Never Before Printed* (1668). *The Blazing World* (1666) is now her best-known work in prose. The specimen of her versification emphasizes the originality of her plots: "But noble readers, do not think my plays / Are such as have been writ in former days." This sample ends on a note of bathos: "From Plutarch's story, I ne'er took a plot, / Nor from romances, nor from Don Quixote."

Chandler was born in Malmesbury, Wiltshire, in 1687 and was the eldest daughter of Henry Chandler, who later became a Dissenting minister in Bath. She went through an early period of religious crisis, after which "Her religion was rational and prevalent." The entry in *The Lives of the Poets* cites a letter to a friend about her regard for Horace: "O could I read his fine sentiments cloathed in his own dress." The reader gains a sense of her voice and personality: "his [Horace's] precepts are plain, and morals intelligible, though not always so perfect as one would have wished. But as to this, I consider when and where he lived." For readers who might want to sample her verse, the entry includes "Sweet solitude, the Muses dear delight." This ten-page entry was evidently written by her brother Samuel Chandler.

The overall balance of entries seems reasonable for the time: Chaucer warrants seventeen pages; Shakespeare, twenty-one; and Spenser, fifteen; Behn's account runs to fifteen pages, Chandler's is ten, and Finch's fourteen. By comparison, Sir Thomas Wyatt, or "Wyat" as the surname is spelled in *The Lives of the Poets,* is dispensed with in three pages. Wyatt's extensive travels throughout Europe are summed up in a phrase. His relationship with King Henry VIII is inadequately dealt with: "The affair of Anne Bullen came on, when he made some opposition to the King's passion for her, that was likely to prove fatal to him; but by his prudent behavior, and retracting what he had formerly advanced, he was restored again to his royal patronage." There is some debate over what mission Wyatt was engaged in at the time of his death, and the writer of the entry cagily offers the location as "a little country-town in England, greatly lamented by all lovers of learning and politeness," which is to say, Sherborne, Dorset. Wyatt is ranked as a poor second in poetic reputation to Henry Howard, Earl of Surrey. The entry is dismissive of Wyatt's literary output – "in his poetical capacity, he does not appear to have much imagination" – and leaves unchallenged a claim "by which it will be seen how much he falls short of his noble cotemporary [sic], lord Surrey." There is not a single mention of Wyatt's greatest gift to English poetry: the importation of the Petrarchan sonnet form.

The entry on Shakespeare bears some evidence of Cibber's editing of Shiells's work. It gets off to a bombastic start, reminiscent of Cibber's dramatic style:

There have been some ages in which providence seemed pleased in a most remarkable manner to display it self, in giving to the world the finest genius's [sic] to illuminate a people formerly barbarous. After a long night of Gothic ignorance, after many ages of priestcraft and superstition, learning and genius visited our Island in the days of the renowned Queen Elizabeth. It was then that liberty began to dawn, and the people having shook off the restraints of priestly austerity, presumed to think for themselves. At an Aera so remarkable as this, so famous in his story [sic], it seems no wonder that the nation should be blessed with those immortal ornaments of wit and learning, who all conspired at once to make it famous. — This astonishing genius, seemed to be commissioned from above, to deliver us not only from the ignorance under which we laboured as to poetry, but to carry poetry almost to its perfection.

As if to satirize itself, the passage concludes, "But to write a panegyric on Shakespear appears as unnecessary, as the attempt would be vain." If there is any truth to Johnson's supposition that Cibber was brought in to tone down Shiells's pro-Catholic sentiments, this anticlerical proclamation seems to err on the side of excessive Protestantism. Yet later in the entry the following statement appears: "Mr. Warburton has strongly contended for Shakespear's learning, and has produced many imitations and parallel passages with ancient authors, in which I am inclined to think him right." It is unlikely that Cibber would have written this, as he was not inclined to agree with anything William Warburton wrote. The bathetic irony of the introduction is compounded by legendary assumptions and basic errors: John Shakespeare is described as a dealer in wool and the father of ten children (only eight are now known); Anne Hathaway's name is given as "Hatchway"; and, perhaps confusing Shakespeare with Lear, the Bard is said to have had three daughters.

The entry shows the transmission path of an oral tradition of information having been passed down from Sir William Davenant to Thomas Betterton to Nicholas Rowe to Pope to Thomas Newton, who eventually passed it on to Cibber and Shiells. The Shakespeare family is described as being "of good figure and fashion," although William was taken out of school early to help support the family. The entry becomes highly digressive, giving little biographical information as it turns into an inquiry into Shakespeare's learning as divined from his plays. This dubious hypothesizing finally comes to a conclusion after six pages with a simple phrase: "But to return to the incident of his life." As to the explanation behind his move from Stratford-upon-Avon to London, Shakespeare "was obliged to quit the place of his nativity, and take shelter in London, which luckily proved to occasion of displaying one of the greatest genius's that ever was known in dramatic poetry. He had the misfortune to fall into ill company."

The biography favors the tale of his flight from prosecution for having poached deer belonging to Sir Thomas Lucy (later satirized as Justice Shallow in *Henry IV,* part 2, 1598) in Charlecote, which occasioned Shakespeare's first poem, a bitter ballad now lost. Shakespeare is cast in *The Lives of the Poets* as an unemployed balladeer who fell into taking care of patron's horses while their owners went to the theater. Then his talents attracted the attention of the players, who took him on as a writer and fellow actor.

The biographer is not averse to making blanket judgments such as this one: "Nothing is more certain than that Shakespear has failed in The Merry Wives of Windsor" for rendering Falstaff too weakly. The earl of Southampton's gift of one thousand pounds — "a bounty at that time very considerable, as money then was valued" — is compared to contemporary standards: "there are few instances of such liberality in our times." The biographer also offers some extraordinary comments on genre distinction: "Our author's plays are to be distinguished only into Comedies and Tragedies. Those which are called Histories, and even some of his Comedies, are really Tragedies, with a mixture of Comedy amongst them. That way of Tragi-comedy was the common mistake of that age." The entry concludes that Shakespeare's strongest influence on the Restoration is apparent in the plays of John Dryden. Mention is made of the campaign organized by the earl of Burlington, Pope, Dr. Richard Mead, and others to raise a monument in Westminister Abbey from proceeds of *Julius Caesar* performed at the Theatre Royal in Drury Lane on 28 April 1738. If the writer is Cibber, he also makes sure to mention his own successful 1748 production of *Romeo and Juliet.*

The biography attributes forty-three plays to Shakespeare, although only forty-two are listed. Those outside the accepted canon (some of which are in the later quarto editions) include *The London Prodigal* (a comedy of unknown authorship published in 1605); *The Life and Death of Thomas Lord Cromwell, The History of Sir John Oldcastle, The Puritan* (a comedy published in 1607 now thought to be by John Marston), *A Yorkshire Tragedy* (now thought to be by Thomas Middleton), and *The Lamentable Tragedie of Locrine* (published in 1595 and now attributed to George Peele).

The long entry on Pope in *The Lives of the Poets* might well have been an occasion for character assassination, especially given his long-standing feud with Colley Cibber. Pope condemned Cibber to occupy the throne in his final version of *The Dunciad* and had implicated his son: "Ye Gods! shall *Cibber's* Son, without rebuke / Swear like a Lord? or *Rich* out-whore a Duke?" In January 1744, five months before Pope's death, *Another Occasional Letter from Mr. Cibber to Mr. Pope* accused the poet of having venereal disease. When Theophilus Cibber slighted Warburton's Shakespeare edition in *A Serio-Comic Apology*, which was appended to his revamping of *Romeo and Juliet* in 1748, Warburton attacked Cibber in the footnotes to his 1751 edition of Pope's *Works*. In 1753 (the same year of *The Lives of the Poets*) Griffiths also published Cibber's attack on Warburton's edition of Pope, *A Familiar Epistle to Mr. Warburton*, which was prefixed to *The Lives and Characters of the Most Eminent Actors and Actresses of Great Britain and Ireland*. Yet the account of Pope in *The Lives of the Poets* is discreet, even favorable, which suggests that Shiells was mainly responsible for writing it.

The event of Pope's writing his first extant poem before age twelve – his "Ode on Solitude" – gives rise to a discussion on early signs of poetic genius. The entry compares Pope and Dryden as child prodigies. Christ's miracle of transforming water into wine was paraphrased by Dryden in a school exercise as: "the conscious water saw its God, blush'd." According to the entry, "This was the only instance of an early appearance of genius in this great man, for he was turn'd of thirty before he acquired any reputation; an age in which Mr. Pope's career was in its full distinction." Two pages are devoted to a somewhat sensationalistic interpretation of Pope's "Elegy to the Memory of an Unfortunate Lady" (1717), which was "built on a true story" of a lady "possessed of an opulent fortune," whose uncle prevented her from seeing her "young gentleman." She was sent to the Continent, was closely guarded by her uncle's "spies," and eventually "bribed a maid-servant to procure her a sword"; she was subsequently found "weltering in her blood." Yet the source for this story, the controversial bookseller Edmund Curll, was far from reliable.

Pope's *Essay on Criticism* (1711) is praised, and the entry notes Addison's initial promotion of it in the *Spectator* number 253 (1711) and his subsequent attempt to tarnish its reputation. The entry refers the reader to the lives of Addison and Tickell, in which "we have thrown out some general hints concerning the quarrel." In reference to Pope's unflattering portrait of Addison in *An Epistle From Mr. Pope To Dr. Arbuthnot* (1735), the entry stands favorably disposed toward Pope: "some readers may think these lines severe, but the treatment he received from Mr. Addison was more than sufficient to justify them." The account touches on attempts "to proselyte [*sic*] him from the Popish faith."

Pope's financial success is noted: "he was never subjected to necessity, and therefore was not

to be imposed upon by the art or fraud of publishers." Yet he was unable to make his mark in one significant area: "It has been the opinion of some critics, that Mr. Pope's talents were not adopted for the drama, otherwise we cannot well account for his neglecting the most gainful way of writing which poetry affords." The collaboration of John Arbuthnot, John Gay, and Pope on *Three Hours after Marriage* (1717) is held up as a failure. Still, his artistic and popular successes are proclaimed: "Of our poet's writings none were read with more general approbation than his Ethic Epistles, or multiplied into more editions."

Avenues of potential controversy are approached only to be avoided. Pope's relationship with Martha Blount, "with whom he lived in the strictest friendship," is treated discreetly. Regarding the *Patriot King* scandal, which erupted in 1749 over Pope's having surreptitiously printed Bolingbroke's treatise, "the reader, no doubt, will find it amply discussed in that account of the life of this great author, which Mr. Warburton has promised the public." Warburton abandoned his proposed biography and turned his material over to Owen Ruffhead, who published *The Life of Alexander Pope* in 1769.

The entry concludes by measuring Pope's literary reputation. Only Shakespeare, John Milton, and Dryden, the entry maintains, are superior to Pope. *The Dunciad* is mentioned in relation to Dryden's *Mac Flecknoe* (1682) as the better poem: "in superior writing the Palm must justly be yielded to him [Pope]." Yet the main reason for putting Dryden above Pope in the literary pantheon is Dryden's plays, "though not the most excellent of his writings." The Dryden-Pope comparison is expanded to the point of breaking: "Perhaps it may be true that Pope's works are read with more appetite, as there is a greater eveness [*sic*] and correctness in them; but in pursuing the works of Dryden the mind will take a wider range, and be more fraught with political ideas: We admire Dryden as the greater genius, and Pope as the most pleasing versifier." There is scant mention of *The Dunciad* and no reference to the Cibbers. As harshly critical as it might have been of Pope's life, the account overflows with praise: "His works, which are in the hands of every person of true taste, and will last as long as our language will be understood, render unnecessary all further comments on his writings."

As Keast argues, there is a considerable overlap between the Cibber-Shiells *Lives of the Poets* and some of the fifty-two entries in Johnson's *Lives of the English Poets* (originally entitled *Prefaces, Biographical and Critical, to the Works of the English Poets*, 1779–

1781), particularly in the lives of Hammond, Rowe, Fenton, Smith, Pitt, Philips, and Thomson. As Paul Fussell observes in *Samuel Johnson and the Life of Writing* (1971), "The irony is that much of what he [Johnson] is taking he is rather repossessing than pilfering, for it was Johnson who, much earlier, had given Shiells the materials for the Lives of these authors."

While *The Lives of the Poets* makes for lively reading and stands as an interesting model of what mid-eighteenth-century readers expected in the way of biography, it should be used with caution. Neither of its known editors was renowned for scholarship, and the errors limit its use as a source. Overshadowed by the more reliable information in *Biographia Britannica* (1747–1766; second edition [incomplete], 1778–1793) and Johnson's *Prefaces, The Lives of the Poets* nonetheless was the only compara-

tively inexpensive and comprehensive source of its kind in the mid eighteenth century. For some minor writers *The Lives of the Poets* offered the first account of their lives and works in print.

References:

William R. Keast, "Johnson and 'Cibber's' *The Lives of the Poets,* 1753," in *Restoration and Eighteenth-Century Literature: Essays in Honour of Alan Dugald McKillop,* edited by C. Camden (Chicago: University of Chicago Press, 1963), pp. 89–101;

Mark Longaker, *English Biography in the Eighteenth Century* (Philadelphia: University of Pennsylvania Press, 1931);

Donald A. Stauffer, *The Art of Biography in Eighteenth-Century England* (New York: Russell & Russell, 1941).

Checklist of Further Readings

Aaron, Daniel, ed. *Studies in Biography*. Cambridge, Mass.: Harvard University Press, 1978.

Alter, Robert. *Motives for Fiction*. Cambridge, Mass.: Harvard University Press, 1984.

Altick, Richard Daniel. *The Art of Literary Research*. New York: Norton, 1963.

Altick. *Lives and Letters: A History of Literary Biography in England and America*. New York: Knopf, 1965.

Altick. *The Scholar Adventurers*. New York: Macmillan, 1950.

Anderson, James William. "The Methodology of Psychological Biography," *Journal of Interdisciplinary History*, 11 (Winter 1981): 455–475.

Atlas, James. "Literary Biography," *American Scholar*, 45 (Summer 1976): 448–460.

Barzun, Jacques. "Biography and Criticism – a Misalliance Disputed," *Critical Inquiry*, 1 (March 1975): 479–496.

Bell, Susan Groag, and Marilyn Yalom, eds. *Revealing Lives: Autobiography, Biography, and Gender*. Albany: State University of New York Press, 1990.

Berry, Thomas Elliott, ed. *The Biographer's Craft*. New York: Odyssey Press, 1967.

Birkets, Sven. *An Artificial Wilderness: Essays on 20th-Century Literature*. New York: Morrow, 1987.

Bloom, Harold, ed. *Dr. Samuel Johnson and James Boswell*. New York: Chelsea House, 1986.

Bloom, ed. *James Boswell's Life of Johnson*. New York: Chelsea House, 1986.

Bowen, Catherine Drinker. *Adventures of a Biographer*. Boston: Little, Brown, 1959.

Bowen. *Biography: The Craft and the Calling*. Boston: Little, Brown, 1969.

Brady, Frank, John Palmer, and Martin Price, eds. *Literary Theory and Structure: Essays in Honor of William K. Wimsatt*. New Haven: Yale University Press, 1973.

Britt, Albert. *The Great Biographers*. New York: McGraw-Hill, 1936; London: Whittlesey House, 1936.

Bromwich, David. *Choice of Inheritance: Self and Community from Edmund Burke to Robert Frost*. Cambridge, Mass.: Harvard University Press, 1989.

Browning, J. D., ed. *Biography in the 18th Century*. New York & London: Garland, 1980.

Cafarelli, Annette. *Prose in the Age of Poets: Romanticism and Biographical Narrative from Johnson to De Quincey*. Philadelphia: University of Pennsylvania Press, 1990.

Clifford, James Lowry. *From Puzzles to Portraits: Problems of a Literary Biographer*. Chapel Hill: University of North Carolina Press, 1970.

Clifford, ed. *Biography as an Art: Selected Criticism, 1560–1960*. New York: Oxford University Press, 1962.

Clingham, Greg. *James Boswell: The Life of Johnson*. New York & Cambridge: Cambridge University Press, 1992.

Clingham, ed. *New Light on Boswell: Critical and Historical Essays on the Occasion of the Bicentenary of* The Life of Johnson. New York & Cambridge: Cambridge University Press, 1991.

Cockshut, A. O. J. *Truth to Life: The Art of Biography in the Nineteenth Century*. London: Collins, 1974; New York: Harcourt Brace Jovanovich, 1974.

Connely, Willard. *Adventures in Biography: A Chronicle of Encounters and Findings*. London: W. Laurie, 1956; New York: Horizon, 1960.

Daghlian, Philip B., ed. *Essays in Eighteenth-Century Biography*. Bloomington: Indiana University Press, 1968.

Daiches, David. *Critical Approaches to Literature*. Englewood Cliffs, N.J.: Prentice-Hall, 1956.

Davenport, William H., and Ben Siegel, eds. *Biography Past and Present*. New York: Scribners, 1965.

Denzin, Norman K. *Interpretive Biography*. Newbury Park, Cal.: Sage, 1989.

Dowling, William C. *Language and Logos in Boswell's Life of Johnson*. Princeton: Princeton University Press, 1981.

Dunn, Waldo H. *English Biography*. London: Dent, 1916; New York: Dutton, 1916.

Durling, Dwight, and William Watt, eds. *Biography: Varieties and Parallels*. New York: Dryden, 1941.

Edel, Leon. *Literary Biography*. Toronto: University of Toronto Press, 1957; London: Hart-Davis, 1957; revised edition, Garden City, N.Y.: Doubleday, 1959; revised again, Bloomington: Indiana University Press, 1973; revised and enlarged as *Writing Lives: Principia Biographica*. New York & London: Norton, 1984.

Edel. *Stuff of Sleep and Dreams: Experiments in Literary Psychology*. New York: Harper & Row, 1982.

Ellmann, Richard. *Golden Codgers: Biographical Speculations*. New York & London: Oxford University Press, 1973.

Ellmann. *Literary Biography: An Inaugural Lecture Delivered Before the University of Oxford on 4 May 1971*. Oxford: Clarendon Press, 1971.

Epstein, William H., ed. *Contesting the Subject: Essays in the Postmodern Theory and Practice of Biography and Biographical Criticism*. West Lafayette, Ind.: Purdue University Press, 1991.

Epstein, *Recognizing Biography*. Philadelphia: University of Pennsylvania Press, 1987.

Flanagan, Thomas. "Problems of Psychobiography," *Queen's Quarterly*, 89 (Autumn 1982): 596–610.

Folkenflik, Robert. *Samuel Johnson, Biographer*. Ithaca, N.Y.: Cornell University Press, 1978.

Fowler, Alastair. *Kinds of Literature: An Introduction to the Theory of Genres and Modes.* Cambridge, Mass.: Harvard University Press, 1982.

Frank, Katherine. "Writing Lives: Theory and Practice of Literary Biography," *Genre,* 13 (Winter 1980): 499–516.

Friedson, Anthony M., ed. *New Directions in Biography: Essays.* Honolulu: Published for the Biographical Research Center by the University of Hawaii Press, 1981.

Fromm, Gloria G., ed. *Essaying Biography: A Celebration for Leon Edel.* Honolulu: Published for the Biographical Research Center by the University of Hawaii Press, 1986.

Frye, Northrop. *Anatomy of Criticism: Four Essays.* Princeton: Princeton University Press, 1957.

Frye. *The Well-Tempered Critic.* Bloomington: Indiana University Press, 1963.

Gardner, Helen Louise, Dame. *In Defence of the Imagination.* Cambridge, Mass.: Harvard University Press, 1982.

Garraty, John Arthur *The Nature of Biography.* New York: Knopf, 1957.

Gittings, Robert. *The Nature of Biography.* London: Heinemann, 1978; Seattle: University of Washington Press, 1978.

Greene, Donald. " 'Tis a Pretty Book, Mr. Boswell, But – , " *Georgia Review,* 32 (Spring 1978): 17–43.

Hamilton, Ian. *Keepers of the Flame: The Making and Unmaking of Literary Reputations from John Donne to Sylvia Plath.* New York: Paragon House, 1993.

Hampshire, Stuart N. *Modern Writers and Other Essays.* London: Chatto & Windus, 1969; New York: Knopf, 1970.

Havlice, Patricia Pate. *Index to Literary Biography,* 2 volumes. Metuchen, N.J.: Scarecrow Press, 1975.

Heilbrun, Carolyn G. *Hamlet's Mother and Other Women.* New York: Columbia University Press, 1990.

Heilbrun. *Writing a Woman's Life.* New York: Norton, 1988.

Hoberman, Ruth. *Modernizing Lives: Experiments in English Biography, 1918–1939.* Carbondale: Southern Illinois University Press, 1987.

Holland, Norman Norwood. *The Dynamics of Literary Response.* New York: Oxford University Press, 1968.

Holland. *Poems in Persons: An Introduction to the Psychoanalysis of Literature.* New York: Norton, 1973.

Holmes, Richard. *Footsteps: Adventures of a Romantic Biographer.* New York: Viking, 1985.

Homberger, Eric, and John Charmley, eds. *The Troubled Face of Biography.* New York: St. Martin's Press, 1988.

Honan, Park. *Authors' Lives: On Literary Biography and the Arts of Language.* New York: St. Martin's Press, 1990.

Honan. "The Theory of Biography," *Novel,* 13 (Fall 1979): 109–120.

Horden, Peregrine, ed. *Freud and the Humanities*. New York: St. Martin's Press, 1985; London: Duckworth, 1985.

Hough, Graham. *Style and Stylistics*. London: Routledge & Kegan Paul, 1969; New York: Humanities, 1969.

Hyde, Marietta Adelaide, ed. *Modern Biography*. New York: Harcourt, Brace, 1926.

Johnson, Edgar. *One Mighty Torrent: The Drama of Biography*. New York: Stackpole, 1937.

Johnson, ed. *A Treasury of Biography*. New York: Howell, Soskin, 1941.

Kaplan, Justin. "In Pursuit of the Ultimate Fiction," *New York Times Book Review*. 19 April 1987, pp. 1, 24–25.

Kazin, Alfred. *The Inmost Leaf: A Selection of Essays*. New York: Harcourt Brace, 1955.

Kendall, Paul Murray. *The Art of Biography*. New York: Norton, 1965.

Kenner, Hugh. *Historical Fictions: Essays*. San Francisco: North Point, 1990.

Kermode, Frank. *The Art of Telling: Essays on Fiction*. Cambridge, Mass.: Harvard University Press, 1983.

Kermode. *The Genesis of Secrecy. On the Interpretation of Narrative*. Cambridge, Mass.: Harvard University Press, 1979.

Kermode. *The Sense of an Ending: Studies in the Theory of Fiction*. New York: Oxford University Press, 1967.

Krupnick, Mark L. "The Sanctuary of Imagination," *Nation*, 209 (14 July 1969): 55–56.

Levin, David. *In Defense of Historical Literature: Essays on American History, Autobiography, Drama, and Fiction*. New York: Hill & Wang, 1967.

Levin, Harry. *Contexts of Criticism*. Cambridge, Mass.: Harvard University Press, 1957.

Lomask, Milton. *The Biographer's Craft*. New York: Harper & Row, 1986.

Longaker, Mark. *English Biography in the Eighteenth Century*. Philadelphia: University of Pennsylvania Press, 1931.

Mandell, Gail Porter. *Life into Art: Conversations with Seven Contemporary Biographers*. Fayetteville: University of Arkansas Press, 1991.

Maner, Martin. *The Philosophical Biographer: Doubt and Dialectic in Johnson's Lives of the Poets*. Athens: University of Georgia Press, 1988.

Mariani, Paul L. *A Usable Past: Essays on Modern and Contemporary Poetry*. Amherst: University of Massachusetts Press, 1984.

Marquess, William Henry. *Lives of the Poet: The First Century of Keats Biography*. University Park: Pennsylvania State University Press, 1985.

Maurois, Andre. *Aspects of Biography*. New York: D. Appleton, 1929.

Meyers, Jeffrey. *The Spirit of Biography*. Ann Arbor, Mich.: UMI Research Press, 1989.

Meyers, ed. *The Biographer's Art: New Essays*. New York: New Amsterdam, 1989.

Meyers, ed. *The Craft of Literary Biography*. New York: Schocken, 1985.

Mintz, Samuel T., Alica Chandler, and Christopher Mulvey, eds. *From Smollett to James: Studies in the Novel and Other Essays Presented to Edgar Johnson*. Charlottesville: University Press of Virginia, 1981.

Nadel, Ira Bruce. *Biography: Fiction, Fact and Form*. New York: St. Martin's Press, 1984.

Nagourney, Peter. "The Basic Assumptions of Literary Biography," *Biography*, 1 (Spring 1978): 86–104.

Nicolson, Harold George, Sir. *The Development of English Biography*. London: Hogarth, 1928; New York: Harcourt, Brace, 1928.

Noland, Richard. "Psychohistory, Theory and Practice," *Massachusetts Review*, 18 (Summer 1977): 295–322.

Novarr, David. *The Lines of Life: Theories of Biography, 1880–1970*. West Lafayette, Ind.: Purdue University Press, 1986.

Oates, Stephen B., ed. *Biography as High Adventure: Life-Writers Speak on Their Art*. Amherst: University of Massachusetts Press, 1986.

Pachter, Marc, ed. *Telling Lives, The Biographer's Art*. Washington, D.C.: New Republic Books, 1979.

Pascal, Roy. *Design and Truth in Autobiography*. Cambridge, Mass.: Harvard University Press, 1960.

Passler, David L. *Time, Form, and Style in Boswell's Life of Johnson*. New Haven: Yale University Press, 1971.

Pearson, Hesketh. *Ventilations: Being Biographical Asides*. Philadelphia & London: Lippincott, 1930.

Plagens, Peter. "Biography," *Art in America*, 68 (October 1980): 13–15.

Powers, Lyall H., ed. *Leon Edel and Literary Art*. Ann Arbor, Mich.: UMI Research Press, 1987.

Quilligan, Maureen. "Rewriting History: The Difference of Feminist Biography," *Yale Review*, 77 (Winter 1988): 259–286.

Reed, Joseph W. *English Biography in the Early Nineteenth Century, 1801–1838*. New Haven: Yale University Press, 1966.

Reid, B. L. *Necessary Lives: Biographical Reflections*. Columbia: University of Missouri Press, 1990.

Rose, Phyllis. *Writing of Women: Essays in a Renaissance*. Middletown, Conn.: Wesleyan University Press, 1985.

Runyan, William McKinley. *Life Histories and Psychobiography: Explorations in Theory and Method*. New York: Oxford University Press, 1982.

Said, Edward W. *Beginnings: Intention and Method*. New York: Basic Books, 1975.

Schaber, Ina. "Fictional Biography, Factual Biography and Their Contaminations," *Biography*, 5 (Winter 1982): 1–16.

Scholes, Robert E. *Structuralism in Literature: An Introduction*. New Haven: Yale University Press, 1974.

Shelston, Alan. *Biography*. London: Methuen, 1977.

Siebenschuh, William R. *Fictional Techniques and Factual Works*. Athens: University of Georgia Press, 1983.

Smith, Barbara Herrnstein. *On the Margins of Discourses: The Relation of Literature to Language*. Chicago: University of Chicago Press, 1978.

Sontag, Susan. "On Style," *Partisan Review*, 32 (Fall 1965): 543–560.

Spence, Donald Pond. *Narrative Truth and Historical Truth: Meaning and Interpretation in Psychoanalysis*. New York: Norton, 1982.

Stauffer, Donald A. *The Art of Biography in Eighteenth-Century England*. Princeton: Princeton University Press, 1941; London: H. Milford, Oxford University Press, 1941.

Stauffer. *English Biography before 1700*. Cambridge, Mass.: Harvard University Press, 1930.

Thayer, William Roscoe. *The Art of Biography*. New York: Scribners, 1920.

Vance, John A., ed. *Boswell's Life of Johnson: New Questions, New Answers*. Athens: University of Georgia Press, 1985.

Veninga, James F., ed. *The Biographer's Gift: Life Histories and Humanism*. College Station: Published for the Texas Committee for the Humanities by Texas A&M University Press, 1983.

Vernoff, Edward, and Rima Shore. *The International Dictionary of 20th Century Biography*. London: Sidgwick & Jackson, 1987; New York: New American Library, 1987.

Weintraub, Stanley, ed. *Biography and Truth*. Indianapolis: Bobbs-Merrill, 1967.

Wendorf, Richard. *The Elements of Life: Biography and Portrait-Painting in Stuart and Georgian England*. Oxford: Clarendon Press, 1990; New York: Oxford University Press, 1990.

Wheeler, David, ed. *Domestick Privacies: Samuel Johnson and the Art of Biography*. Lexington: University Press of Kentucky, 1987.

Whittemore, Reed. *Pure Lives: The Early Biographers*. Baltimore: Johns Hopkins University Press, 1988.

Whittemore. *Whole Lives: Shapers of Modern Biography*. Baltimore: Johns Hopkins University Press, 1989.

Winslow, Donald J. *Life-Writing: A Glossary of Terms in Biography, Autobiography, and Related Forms*. Honolulu: Published for the Biographical Research Center by the University of Hawaii Press, 1980.

Woolf, Virginia. *Collected Essays*. London: Hogarth, 1967; New York: Harcourt, Brace & World, 1967.

Contributors

Paul Baines ....*University of Liverpool*
Martin Beller ....*C. W. Post Campus, Long Island University*
Lance Bertelsen...*University of Texas at Austin*
Thomas L. Blanton ....*Central Washington University*
Leith Davis ....*Simon Fraser University*
Paul Haeffner ....*Oxford, England*
Gary Harrison...*University of New Mexico*
Susan Kubica Howard...*Duquesne University*
Mark Loveridge ....*University of Swansea*
Michael Mandelkern ....*Graduate Center of the City University of New York*
Donald W. Nichol..*Memorial University of Newfoundland*
William Over ....*Saint John's University*
Lisa Heiserman Perkins ....*Watertown, Massachusetts*
Glyn Pursglove ....*University College of Swansea*
John H. Rogers ....*Vincennes University*
Gordon Turnbull...*Yale University*
Eleanor Ty...*Wilfrid Laurier University*
John A. Vance ....*University of Georgia*
Karina Williamson ....*University of Edinburgh*

Cumulative Index

Dictionary of Literary Biography, Volumes 1-142
Dictionary of Literary Biography Yearbook, 1980-1993
Dictionary of Literary Biography Documentary Series, Volumes 1-11

Cumulative Index

DLB before number: *Dictionary of Literary Biography,* Volumes 1-142
Y before number: *Dictionary of Literary Biography Yearbook,* 1980-1993
DS before number: *Dictionary of Literary Biography Documentary Series,* Volumes 1-11

M

Peake, Mervyn 1911-1968 ....DLB-15

Pear Tree Press DLB-112

Pearson, H. B. [publishing house] DLB-49

Peck, George W. 1840-1916......DLB-23, 42

Peck, H. C., and Theo. Bliss
  [publishing house] DLB-49

Peck, Harry Thurston
  1856-1914 ....DLB-71, 91

Peele, George 1556-1596 ....DLB-62

Pellegrini and Cudahy DLB-46

Pelletier, Aimé (see Vac, Bertrand)

Pemberton, Sir Max 1863-1950 ......DLB-70

Penguin Books [U.S.] DLB-46

Penguin Books [U.K.] DLB-112

Penn Publishing Company DLB-49

Penn, William 1644-1718 ....DLB-24

Penna, Sandro 1906-1977 ....DLB-114

Penner, Jonathan 1940- Y-83

Pennington, Lee 1939- Y-82

Pepys, Samuel 1633-1703 ....DLB-101

Percy, Thomas 1729-1811 ....DLB-104

Percy, Walker 1916-1990 ... DLB-2; Y-80, 90

Perec, Georges 1936-1982 ....DLB-83

Perelman, S. J. 1904-1979 ....DLB-11, 44

Perez, Raymundo "Tigre"
  1946- DLB-122

Periodicals of the Beat Generation ...DLB-16

Perkins, Eugene 1932- DLB-41

Perkoff, Stuart Z. 1930-1974 ....DLB-16

Perley, Moses Henry 1804-1862 .....DLB-99

Permabooks DLB-46

Perry, Bliss 1860-1954 ....DLB-71

Perry, Eleanor 1915-1981 ....DLB-44

"Personal Style" (1890), by John Addington
  Symonds DLB-57

Perutz, Leo 1882-1957 ....DLB-81

Pesetsky, Bette 1932- DLB-130

Pestalozzi, Johann Heinrich
  1746-1827 ....DLB-94

Peter, Laurence J. 1919-1990 ....DLB-53

Peter of Spain circa 1205-1277......DLB-115

Peterkin, Julia 1880-1961 ....DLB-9

Peters, Lenrie 1932- DLB-117

Peters, Robert 1924- DLB-105

Peters, Robert, Foreword to
  Ludwig of Bavaria DLB-105

Petersham, Maud 1889-1971 and
  Petersham, Miska 1888-1960 .... DLB-22

Peterson, Charles Jacobs
  1819-1887 ....DLB-79

Peterson, Len 1917- DLB-88

Peterson, Louis 1922- DLB-76

Peterson, T. B., and Brothers DLB-49

Petitclair, Pierre 1813-1860 ....DLB-99

Petry, Ann 1908- DLB-76

Pettie, George circa 1548-1589 .....DLB-136

Pforzheimer, Carl H. 1879-1957 ...DLB-140

Phaidon Press Limited DLB-112

Pharr, Robert Deane 1916-1992 .....DLB-33

Phelps, Elizabeth Stuart
  1844-1911 ....DLB-74

Philippe, Charles-Louis
  1874-1909 ....DLB-65

Philips, John 1676-1708 ....DLB-95

Philips, Katherine 1632-1664 ......DLB-131

Phillips, David Graham
  1867-1911 ....DLB-9, 12

Phillips, Jayne Anne 1952- Y-80

Phillips, Robert 1938- DLB-105

Phillips, Robert, Finding, Losing,
  Reclaiming: A Note on My
  Poems DLB-105

Phillips, Stephen 1864-1915 ....DLB-10

Phillips, Ulrich B. 1877-1934 ....DLB-17

Phillips, Willard 1784-1873 ....DLB-59

Phillips, William 1907- DLB-137

Phillips, Sampson and Company DLB-49

Phillpotts, Eden
  1862-1960 ....DLB-10, 70, 135

Philosophical Library DLB-46

"The Philosophy of Style" (1852), by
  Herbert Spencer DLB-57

Phinney, Elihu [publishing house] ... DLB-49

Phoenix, John (see Derby, George Horatio)

PHYLON (Fourth Quarter, 1950),
  The Negro in Literature:
  The Current Scene DLB-76

Piccolo, Lucio 1903-1969 ....DLB-114

Pickard, Tom 1946- DLB-40

Pickering, William
  [publishing house] DLB-106

Pickthall, Marjorie 1883-1922 ....DLB-92

Pictorial Printing Company DLB-49

Piel, Gerard 1915- DLB-137

Piercy, Marge 1936- DLB-120

Pierro, Albino 1916- DLB-128

Pignotti, Lamberto 1926- DLB-128

Pike, Albert 1809-1891 ....DLB-74

Pilon, Jean-Guy 1930- DLB-60

Pinckney, Josephine 1895-1957 ....DLB-6

Pindar, Peter (see Wolcot, John)

Pinero, Arthur Wing 1855-1934 .....DLB-10

Pinget, Robert 1919- DLB-83

Pinnacle Books DLB-46

Pinsky, Robert 1940- Y-82

Pinter, Harold 1930- DLB-13

Piontek, Heinz 1925- DLB-75

Piozzi, Hester Lynch [Thrale]
  1741-1821 ....DLB-104, 142

Piper, H. Beam 1904-1964 ....DLB-8

Piper, Watty DLB-22

Pisar, Samuel 1929- Y-83

Pitkin, Timothy 1766-1847 ....DLB-30

The Pitt Poetry Series: Poetry Publishing
  Today Y-85

Pitter, Ruth 1897- DLB-20

Pix, Mary 1666-1709 ....DLB-80

Plaatje, Sol T. 1876-1932 ....DLB-125

The Place of Realism in Fiction (1895), by
  George Gissing DLB-18

Plante, David 1940- Y-83

Platen, August von 1796-1835 ....DLB-90

Plath, Sylvia 1932-1963 ....DLB-5, 6

Platt and Munk Company DLB-46

Playboy Press DLB-46

Plays, Playwrights, and Playgoers ...DLB-84

Playwrights and Professors, by
  Tom Stoppard DLB-13

Playwrights on the Theater DLB-80

Der Pleier flourished circa 1250 ....DLB-138

Plenzdorf, Ulrich 1934- DLB-75

Plessen, Elizabeth 1944- DLB-75

Plievier, Theodor 1892-1955 ....DLB-69

Plomer, William 1903-1973 ....DLB-20

Plumly, Stanley 1939- DLB-5

Plumpp, Sterling D. 1940- DLB-41

Plunkett, James 1920- DLB-14

Plymell, Charles 1935- DLB-16

Pocket Books DLB-46

Poe, Edgar Allan
  1809-1849 .... DLB-3, 59, 73, 74

ISBN 0-8103-5556-6

90000

9 780810 355569

(Continued from front endsheets)

Documentary Series

Yearbooks